THE INTERNATIONAL CRITICAL COMMENTARY

A CRITICAL AND EXEGETICAL COMMENTARY

ON THE

GOSPEL ACCORDING TO ST. JOHN

BY

ARCHBISHOP J. H. BERNARD

VOLUME I

A CRITICAL AND EXEGETICAL COMMENTARY

ON THE

GOSPEL ACCORDING TO ST. JOHN

BY THE

Most Rev. and Right Hon. J. H. BERNARD, D.D.

EDITED BY THE

Rev. A. H. McNeile, D.D.

(IN TWO VOLUMES)

VOL. I

EDINBURGH

T. & T. CLARK, 38 GEORGE STREET

PRINTED IN GREAT BRITAIN BY
MORRISON AND GIBB LIMITED

FOR

T. & T. CLARK, EDINBURGH
NEW YORK: CHARLES SCRIBNER'S SONS

FIRST IMPRESSION . . . 1928
SEVENTH IMPRESSION . . . 1969

PREFACE

DR. BERNARD'S many friends will be glad at last to have his Commentary. Fortunately he had completed the manuscript of both volumes before his visible presence was taken from us in August 1927, so that I have been responsible only for seeing it through the Press. Dr. L. C. Purser saw the proofs as far as Chapter XIX., but I have been through the whole, trying to gather up the fragments that remained. The Indices have been prepared by the Rev. R. M. Boyd, Rector of Shinrone I would thank him gratefully for his help, but he needs no thanks.

A. H. McNEILE.

DUBLIN, *October* 1928.

CONTENTS

ABBREVIATIONS

THE evangelist has been designated throughout as Jn., to distinguish him from John the son of Zebedee as well as from John the Baptist. This abbreviation is not intended to imply that he must be identified with John the presbyter, although the editor regards this as highly probable; [1] but it is convenient to have a brief designation which stands for the writer of the Gospel, without prejudging his personality. A few other abbreviations that have been adopted are the following:

D.B.	Hastings' *Dictionary of the Bible*, 5 vols. (1898–1904).
D.B.[2]	Smith's *Dictionary of the Bible*, 3 vols., 2nd ed. (1893).
D.C.G.	Hastings' *Dictionary of Christ and the Gospels*, 2 vols. (1906).
Diat.	E. A. Abbott's *Diatessarica*, including his *Johannine Vocabulary* and *Johannine Grammar*, Parts I.–X. (1900–1915).
E.B.	Cheyne's *Encyclopædia Biblica*, 4 vols. (1899–1903).
E.R.E.	Hastings' *Encyclopædia of Religion and Ethics*, 12 vols. (1908–1921).
J.T.S.	*Journal of Theological Studies* (1900–1926).
Moulton-Milligan .	*Vocabulary of the Greek Testament*, illustrated from the papyri, by J. H. Moulton and G. Milligan (1914–). This is being completed by Dr. Milligan; it is indispensable.

[1] See p. lxviii.

INTRODUCTION

CHAPTER I

THE TEXT

(i) Authorities for the Text.
(ii) Dislocations of the Text.
(iii) The Structure of the Gospel.

(I) AUTHORITIES FOR THE TEXT

FULL accounts of the manuscript material available for the text will be found in Gregory's *Prolegomena* (1894), in his *Textkritik* (1902, 1909), and in von Soden's *Die Schriften des neuen Testaments* (1902). During the last twenty-five years several additional manuscripts and versions of first-rate value have come to light. Only a few of the more important authorities for the Gospel, in whole or in part, are named here, von Soden's notation being placed in brackets, and the century to which each MS. is ascribed being given in Roman numerals. No attempt has been made in these volumes to print an *apparatus criticus*. Tischendorf's (1872) is still the most useful, von Soden's (1913) being constructed on the basis of a new classification of textual authorities, which has not commanded general acceptance. Westcott and Hort's *Notes on Select Readings* (1884) are indispensable, although their doctrine of the inferiority of the " Western Text " is now regarded as too strongly stated. A. Souter's brief critical apparatus is valuable, and his table of MS. authorities admirably clear (*Nov. Test. Græce*, Oxford).

Papyri

The earliest extant remains of Gospel manuscripts in Greek were written in Egypt on papyrus. Of these some of the most interesting were found at Oxyrhynchus, and have been published by Drs. Grenfell and Hunt. A few contain fragments of the Fourth Gospel.   They are generally in the form of a book or codex, and not in the form of rolls of papyrus.   Most of those mentioned here present a text similar to that of B:

Pap. Oxyrh. 208 (von Soden, ε 02) and 1781 form fragments of the same MS., the oldest extant text of Jn. (sæc. iii), and are at the British Museum.   They give in a mutilated form Jn. 1^{23-41} 16^{14-30} 20^{11-25}.   This MS. was a codex, made up of a single quire of some twenty-five sheets. See p. xxix.

Pap. Oxyrh. 1228, Glasgow, iii.   This has a good text of Jn. 15^{25}–16^{31}

Pap. Oxyrh. 847, British Museum, iv, contains Jn. 2^{11-22}.

Pap. Oxyrh. 1780, British Museum, iv, contains Jn. 8^{14-21}.

Pap. Oxyrh. 1596, British Museum, iv, contains Jn. $6^{8-12. \ 17-22}$.

There are many other papyrus fragments, some of early date; the above are mentioned as specimens of the available material.

Uncials

Information as to most of these will be found in the text-books.   We give brief references for those which have been recently brought to light:

B . *Vaticanus* (δ 1).   Rome.   Cent. iv.

א . *Sinaiticus* (δ 2).   Leningrad.   iv.

A . *Alexandrinus* (δ 4).   British Museum.   **v.**   Cc. 6^{50}–8^{52} are missing.

C . *Ephræmi* (δ 3).   Paris.   v.   Palimpsest.   Contains considerable fragments of Jn.

D . *Bezæ* (δ 5).   Cambridge.   v–vi.   Græco-Latin.   Cc. 18^{14}–20^{13} are missing in the Greek text, and the gap has been filled by a ninth-century scribe (D^{supp}).

T . *Borgianus* (ε 5).   Rome.   v.   Græco-Sahidic.   Contains cc. 6^{28-67} 7^6–8^{31}.

T^{b} . *Muralt* (ε 31).   Leningrad.   vi.   Contains cc. 1^{25-42} 2^9–4^{14} 4^{34-50}.

T^{w} . (ε 35).   British Museum.   vi.   Græco-Sahidic.   Contains cc. 3^5–4^{49} with a few gaps.   For a collation by Crum and Kenyon, cf. *J.T.S.* April 1900, p. 415 f. See on 3^{18} 4^6.

W . *Freer* (ε 014).   Washington.   iv–vi.   Discovered in Egypt in 1906.   The Gospels are in the order Mt., Jn., Lk., Mk.   Collation in *The Washington MS. of the Four Gospels*, by H. A. Sanders (1912).

N . *Purpureus Petropolitanus* (ε 19). Dispersed through the libraries of Leningrad, Patmos, Rome, Vienna, and British Museum. vi. Some pages are missing. Edited by H. S. Cronin in Cambridge *Texts and Studies* (1899).

L . *Regius* (ε 56). Paris. viii. Cc. $15^{2\text{-}20}$ $21^{15\text{-}25}$ are missing.

Θ . *Koridethi* (ε 050). Tiflis. viii–ix. Discovered at Koridethi, in Russian territory, and edited by Beermann & Gregory (Leipzig, 1913). The text is akin to that of *fam*. 13, *fam*. 1, and the cursives 28, 565, 700. See Lake and Blake in *Harvard Theol. Review* (July 1923) and Streeter, *The Four Gospels*. Cf. also *J.T.S.* Oct. 1915, April and July 1925.

Γ . (ε 70) Oxford and Leningrad. ix–x. Contains cc. $1^1\text{-}6^{13}$ $8^3\text{-}15^{24}$ 19^6 to end.

Δ . *Sangallensis* (ε 76). St. Gall. ix–x. Græco-Latin.

Secondary uncials are not specified here; nor has reference been made to two fragmentary palimpsest uncials of the fifth century, at Leningrad and the British Museum respectively (von Soden's ε 1 and ε 3).

Cursives

Of the vast mass of minuscules, only a few need be mentioned.

The following are notable: 33 (δ 48), Paris, ix–x, perhaps the best of all the cursives, akin to BDL at many points; 28 (ε 168), Paris, xi; 157 (ε 207), Rome, xii; 565 (ε 93), Leningrad, ix–x; 700 (ε 133), London, xi, ed. Hoskier (under the numeration 604).

The twelve cursives numbered 13, 69, 124, 230, 346, 543, 788, 826, 828, 983, 1689, 1709, are descended from a lost common ancestor. Salmon directed Ferrar's attention to 13, 69, 124, 346; and Ferrar began a collation, which was completed and published by T. K. Abbott in 1877.[1] The group may be cited as *fam*. 13. See above on Θ, and for the position of $7^{52}\text{-}8^{11}$ in this group, see note on the Pericope.

Nos. 1, 118, 131, 209 are also akin to each other and to Θ, and may be cited as *fam*. 1 (see K. Lake, *Cod. 1 and its Allies*, 1902).

Ancient Versions

The Old Latin MSS. are cited under the letters *a, b, e, f, ff*₂, etc., Jerome's Vulgate being *vg*. The relative value of the

---

[1] Cf. also Rendel Harris, *The Ferrar Group* (1900).

African and European texts of the O.L. is too intricate for discussion here.

The Old Syriac version probably goes back to Tatian's *Diatessaron*, and in any case to sæc. iii *sub init.* We have it in two MSS.; *Syr. sin.* of sæc. iv, discovered at Mt. Sinai in 1892, and *Syr. cur.* of sæc. v, edited by Cureton in 1858, both being accessible in Burkitt's indispensable *Evangelion da Mepharreshê* (1904).[1] The Peshitta or Syriac vulgate is of sæc. v.

The Coptic vss. have been fully edited in the Sahidic and Bohairic texts by G. Horner (1901–1924). The Sahidic generally follows אB, but has a Western element.

The oldest MS. of Jn. in this version (sæc. iv) was discovered in 1913 and edited by Sir H. Thompson in 1924. By him it is called Q, and it is now in the Bible Society's House in London. It is in codex form, made up of twenty-five sheets of papyrus, folded together so as to make a single quire (cf. p. xiv above). It has a good text like אB, and omits the *Pericope de adultera*.

The text printed in this volume is similar to that followed by Westcott and Hort, and by Bernhard Weiss, although not identical with either. It is convenient to indicate here the more important instances in which the reading that has been adopted after due consideration of the evidence (of the manuscripts and of the context alike) differs from that accepted by most recent critics. At 1^{41} 19^{29} 20^{17} readings have been suggested or adopted which have very little manuscript authority (if any), but which must be judged on their own merits as emendations. Other weakly attested readings are accepted at 10^{29} 11^{42} 12^9 17^{11} 18^1. And at 9^4 $14^{4.\ 14}$ 16^{22} reasons have been given for following the *textus receptus* rather than its modern rivals. In each case, the variants have been examined in the notes *in loc*.

(II) DISLOCATIONS OF THE TEXT

There are some passages in the Fourth Gospel which present difficulties in their traditional context; and critical opinion has, during the last half-century, been favourable, on the whole, to the conclusion that, whether by accidental transposition of pages of the original, or by perverse editorial revision, they have been removed from their proper position.

---

[1] For harmonistic rearrangements of the text in *Syr. sin.*, cf. p. xxvi.

A

Of such instances of dislocation of the text, perhaps the strongest case can be made for the transposition of cc. 5 and 6. The first modern critic to urge that the order of these chapters should be interchanged was Canon J. P. Norris,[1] and his suggestion has been accepted by many scholars.

The words of 6[1], "After these things (μετὰ ταῦτα) Jesus went away to the other side of the sea of Galilee," are oddly chosen if a journey from Jerusalem is in the author's mind, which must be the case if the events of c. 6 are consecutive to those of c. 5. To know which is the " other " side of the lake, we must know the point of departure. In 6[22] πέραν τῆς θαλάσσης means the *eastern* side, in 6[25] the *western* side; just as in Mk. 5[1] the same phrase means the eastern side, and in 5[21] the western side. No doubt, for one who followed the ordinary road from Jerusalem northward, the " other " side would be either the northern or the eastern coast. But a journey from Jerusalem through Samaria and Lower Galilee, which extended either round the northern end of, or across, the lake to the neighbourhood of Bethsaida Julias, would be described very elliptically by the sentence, " He went away to the other side of the sea." On the other hand, the phrase is quite natural if we suppose Him to start from Capernaum, *i.e.* if we treat c. 6 as following immediately on c. 4. Then all is clear. The nobleman's son at Capernaum has been healed by Jesus (4[54]), who is in the neighbourhood, that is, near the western shore of the lake; and the next thing recorded is that " after these things Jesus went away to the other side " (*i.e.* the north-eastern shore) of the lake, where, it is added, " a great multitude followed Him because they beheld the signs which He did on them that were sick." Among the more noteworthy of these was the " second sign " in Galilee, *i.e.* the healing of the nobleman's son.

Again, the opening words of c. 7, " After these things Jesus walked in Galilee, for He would not walk in Judæa, because the Jews sought to kill Him," do not follow naturally upon c. 6. The whole of c. 6 is occupied with Galilæan discourse and miracle; why, then, should the fact that " He walked in Galilee " be emphasised at 7[1]? And no hint has been given in c. 6 that " the Jews " were so indignant at His words that they sought to kill Him.. On the other hand, the words of 7[1] come naturally in succession to the narrative of c. 5 (but see below,

---

[1] In the *Journal of Philology*, 1871, p. 107. Norris added later that the suggestion had been made by a fourteenth-century writer, Ludolphus de Saxonia.

p. xix), which contains the controversy of the Jews consequent on the healing of the impotent man on the Sabbath, after which it is expressly said that the Jews sought to kill Jesus (5^{18}). A retirement from Jerusalem to Galilee was quite natural *then*; but it was only for a short time, and He went back to Jerusalem to resume His ministry there at the Feast of Tabernacles (7^{10}). That no very long interval of time elapsed between the controversies of c. 7 and those of c. 5 is shown by the allusion in 7^{21} to the healing of 5^5. We cannot interpolate between these two points a long ministry in Galilee.

The narrative proceeds smoothly if we adopt the order, c. 4 (Samaria and Galilee), c. 6 (Galilee), c. 5 (Jerusalem, a period to which we must assign, as we shall see, 7^{15-24}; see p. xix), c. 7^{1-9} (a retirement to Galilee), $7^{10-14. \ 25-52}$ (another visit to Jerusalem).

It should be added that, if the traditional order of cc. 4–7 be followed, there is a difficulty in identifying the Feast mentioned at 5^1; the Passover, Pentecost, Dedication, Tabernacles, Purim, being advocated in turn by various expositors. But if we place c. 5 after c. 6, the identification is obvious. It is the Feast of the Passover, which has been mentioned at 6^4 as " at hand."

Of independent evidence for this transposition of cc. 5 and 6, there is none that can be relied on.

Irenæus, *e.g.*, a very early commentator on the Fourth Gospel, regards the feast of 5^1 as the Passover, and does not mention the feast of 6^4. But, nevertheless, he takes cc. 5 and 6 in their traditional order, and places the Feeding of the Five Thousand after the Healing of the Man at Bethesda (*Hær.* II. xxii. 3).

Origen, too, has a phrase which, if it stood by itself, would favour the view that cc. 5 and 7 are consecutive. When commenting on c. 4, he says (p. 250) that the feast of 5^1 was not likely to be the Passover, because " shortly afterwards it is stated " ($\mu\epsilon\tau$' ὀλίγα ἐπιφέρεται) ὅτι ἦν ἐγγὺς ἡ ἑορτὴ τῶν Ἰουδαίων, ἡ σκηνοπηγία (7^2). In other words, he says that 7^2 comes " shortly after " 5^1, a quite reasonable statement if c. 6 precedes c. 5, but hardly defensible if c. 6, with its seventy-one verses, separates c. 5 from c. 7. However, in the same commentary (pp. 268, 280), he clearly takes c. 5 as following on c. 4 in the traditional order.

Tatian's distribution of Johannine material in his *Diatessaron* is remarkable. He does not scruple to disturb the Johannine order of incidents, as we have them in the traditional text; and, in particular, he adopts the order cc. 6 4^{4-45} 5, 7. He was probably led to this by internal evidence;

but it is possible (although not likely) that he may be following the authority of texts or documents no longer accessible to us. In any case, the evidence of the *Diatessaron* provides a corroboration, *ualeat quantum*, of the conclusion that cc. 5 and 6 are not now in their right order.

B

A second case of " dislocation " of the original text of Jn. has already been mentioned (p. xviii). If we remove the section 7^{15-24} from its traditional position, and append it to c. 5, we shall find not only that its language is more appropriate as the conclusion of c. 5, but that $7^{25f.}$ follows most naturally upon 7^{14}.

The allusion to the γράμματα of Moses (5^{47}) provokes the question " How does this one know γράμματα " (7^{15}); *i.e.* the writings of the Law with their interpretation. But there is nothing in 7^{14} which suggests any such query, for nothing has been said in 7^{14} as to the *learned* nature of the teaching which Jesus is giving. The more natural sequel to 7^{14} is 7^{25}, where the citizens of Jerusalem express surprise that such a teacher should be an object of suspicion to the rulers.

Again in 7^{19} the question, " Why seek ye to kill me ? " is very abrupt, and is hardly consistent at this point with the favourable reception from the people of which 7^{12} tells. But it is quite in place if the section 7^{15-24} is a continuation of the controversy of c. 5; one of the consequences was that the Jews *had* sought to kill Jesus (5^{18}). Indeed, the themes of 7^{15-24} are throughout the same as in c. 5; and at $7^{16.\ 17}$ Jesus defends Himself, exactly as at 5^{30}, by explaining that His doctrine was not His own, but given Him by the Father, whose will He came to do.

Again at 7^{18} He reverts to what has been said at $5^{41.\ 44}$, about the untrustworthiness of those who seek only their own glory. At 7^{22} He turns against themselves their appeal to Moses as the exponent of the Law, as He had done at 5^{46}.

And at 7^{23} He makes a direct reference to the cure of the impotent man at Bethesda (5^9), which, because it was wrought on a Sabbath day, was the beginning of their quarrel with Him. It is very difficult to interpret 7^{23} if we suppose it to refer to something which had happened months before; it is evidently present to the minds of His interlocutors, whose feelings as aroused by it He describes in the present tense, θαυμάζετε . . . χολᾶτε ($7^{21.\ 23}$). And, finally, the mention of " just judgment " at 7^{24} brings us back to 5^{30}.

It is possible that the transference of the section 7^{15-24} from its true position was due to the mistake of a copyist, who took the words " Is not this He whom they seek to kill ? " in 7^{25} as requiring 7^{19} in the immediate context, forgetting that 5^{18} 7^1 are both equally apposite.

But, however that may be, that a dislocation of the text is here apparent has been accepted by Wendt,[1] Bacon,[2] Moffatt,[3] Paul,[4] and many other critics.

C

We proceed next to consider the difficulties presented by the traditional order of cc. 13, 14, 15, 16, 17; and some reasons will be given for the conclusion that the order adopted in this commentary, viz. $13^{1\text{-}30}$ 15, 16, $13^{31\text{-}38}$ 14, 17, more nearly represents the intention of the original writer.

It is plain that " Arise, let us go hence," at the end of c. 14 is awkward in this position, if the teachings of cc. 15, 16 follow immediately. This suggests that cc. 15, 16 should precede c. 14; and then 14^{31} would be the last word of the discourse delivered in the upper room, c. 17 (the high-priestly prayer) being offered as the Lord with the Eleven stood up before they left the house for Gethsemane. Again, " I will no longer talk much with you " (14^{30}) is followed by two chapters of further discourse, in the traditional order of the text, whereas it would be a natural phrase, if the discourse were reaching its end, and $14^{25\text{-}31}$ were the final paragraph of farewell.

There are several sayings in c. 16 which suggest that it should come before c. 14. Thus Jesus says (16^5), " None of you ask where I am going." But Peter asked this very question (13^{36}), and Thomas implied that he would like to know the answer (14^5). These queries more naturally come *after* 16^5 than *before* it.

Another point emerges on comparison of 16^{32} with Mk. 14^{27}. Both of these passages tell how Jesus warned the Eleven that they would shortly be put to a severe test of faithfulness, in which they would fail. " All ye shall be made to stumble : for it is written, I will smite the shepherd, and the sheep shall be scattered abroad " (Mk. 14^{27}). " The hour is come when ye shall be scattered, every man to his own, and shall leave me alone " (Jn. 16^{32}). Now Mk. places the confident assurance of Peter, and the sad prediction of his denial, immediately after this. We should expect the same sequence in Jn.; and we find it very nearly, if $13^{31\text{-}38}$ is placed after 16^{33}, for the incident of Peter's boast and rebuke is narrated in $13^{35\text{-}38}$.

[1] *Gospel according to St. John*, p. 85.   [2] *The Fourth Gospel*, p. 499.
[3] *Introd. to N.T.*, p. 554.   [4] *Hibbert Journal*, April 1909

Again, 14^{19} seems to come more naturally *after* $16^{16f.}$ than before these verses in which the disciples express bewilderment at the enigmatic saying, " A little while and ye behold me not," etc. The language of 16^{17} suggests that this saying was new to the hearers, whereas it occurs with an explanation in 14^{19} (cf. 13^{33}). See also on 14^{19} for the priority of the verse 16^{10}.

We now turn to c. 15. The allegory of the Vine in the traditional text begins abruptly, nor is there any sequence with what precedes in the last verses of c. 14. But, as we have shown elsewhere,[1] if we place c. 15 immediately after 13^{30}, the point in the narrative at which the Eucharist was instituted, we find a complete explanation of the sacramental thoughts which appear in 15^{1-8}. And there are other clues which point to the sequence of $15^{1f.}$ with 13^{30}.

Thus the unfruitful branch of 15^2 has an obvious allusion to Judas, who has just gone away to his act of treachery, if c. 15 follows 13^{30} directly. The words ὑμεῖς καθαροί ἐστε of 15^3 become more forcible the nearer they are brought to ὑμεῖς καθαροί ἐστε, ἀλλ' οὐχὶ πάντες of $13^{10.\ 11}$ (where see note). So also the nearer that $15^{16.\ 20}$ can be brought to $13^{18.\ 16}$, being the verses to which they respectively carry an allusion, the easier are they to explain. Again, in our arrangement of the text, $15^{12.\ 17}$ give the first statement of the duty of Christians to love each other (which has been adumbrated 13^{12-15}), but it is not described as a New Commandment (13^{34}) until it has been thoroughly explained what love implies.[2]

Similarly, the teaching about prayer of 14^{14} shows an advance on the teaching of 15^{16} 16^{23}, in that at 14^{14} it is Jesus, not the Father, who is described as the answerer of prayer. See the note on 14^{14}.

It is not suggested here that we are to look for exact logical sequence, such as would be appropriate in a philosophical treatise, in the Last Discourses of Jesus as reported many years after they were spoken. On the contrary, cc. 14–16 of the Fourth Gospel abound in repetitions of the same thoughts and phrases, held in the memory of an aged disciple, but not necessarily put together in the order in which they were originally delivered. Yet, where sequence can be detected, it is worthy of notice.

The teaching about the Paraclete seems to fall into shape more readily if we place cc. 15, 16 before c. 14. In 15^{26} 16^7 we have the παράκλητος described as the Advocate of Christ, confuting the hostility of the world and confounding its judgments. This is the primary meaning of παράκλητος (see on 15^{26}); and so far, the idea of the παράκλητος as the Helper or

---

[1] See on 15^1; and cf. p. clxxiii. f. [2] See, further, note on 15^{10}.

Guide of Christian disciples has not appeared.   Then, at 16¹³,
we pass to a new thought: the παράκλητος is to guide the
apostles into all truth about Christ, and is to reveal future
things to them.   He is now the Paraclete of the *Church*, not
of *Christ*.   Then, at 14¹⁶, it is promised that He will abide
with the Church until the end of time, so that Christian disciples
may not be left ὀρφανοί, or without a Friend.   Finally, at 14²⁶,
we return to the idea that He will lead them to the truth, which
is now described as " teaching " them, and will always keep
in their memory the words of Jesus Himself.   At this point,
for the first time, He is explicitly identified with the " Holy
Spirit " of God.

The only phrase [1] which would be favoured by the traditional order of chapters rather than by the order cc. 15, 16, 14
is, " He shall give you *another* Paraclete," at 14¹⁶.   This, it
may be thought, is more naturally said at the *first* mention of
the Paraclete than at a point in the discourse after He has
already been named three or four times.   But (see note *in loc.*)
this phrase is apposite here, and here only, because Jesus has
just been speaking of His own office as the Advocate with God
who secures an answer to the prayers of the faithful, although
He has not explicitly claimed the title παράκλητος for Himself.

It may be added, in conclusion, that the consolations of
14¹·² seem to come more appropriately towards the end, than
at the beginning, of the Farewell Discourse.   The disciples
have been assured that the world will one day be proved to
have been wrong in its rejection of Jesus (15²⁶ 16⁸ᶠ·); they are
told, moreover, that they, themselves, will again " see " Jesus
after His departure (16¹⁹), which will turn their grief into joy
(16²²); they think that they understand this, although it is not
so (16²⁹), and are warned that they will fail in the impending
hour of trial (16³²).   This hurts them, and Peter asks why
they cannot follow Jesus to death even now (13³⁷); but he is
again warned that he will fail at the pinch (13³⁸).   Then, and
not until then, is explained to them the great assurance of life
after death in the heavenly places which Jesus will prepare
(14²).   This is a consolatory promise of a quite different kind
from any of those given in cc. 15, 16, for it leads the thoughts
of the disciples beyond this earthly life.

On grounds such as these, I follow Spitta [2] and Moffatt [3] in

---

[1] Westcott (*Introd.* cxxxi) finds, indeed, a " progress " in the
teaching about the Paraclete, taking the chapters in the usual order ;
but he takes no account of the difference between the Paraclete of
Christ in 15²⁶ 16⁷ and the Paraclete of the *Church* in 16¹³ 14¹⁶·²⁶.

[2] See also Bacon, *Fourth Gospel*, p. 500.

[3] See, for the various hypotheses as to the place of cc. 15, 16,
Moffatt, *Introd. to Lit. of N.T.*, p. 556.

supposing a dislocation of the text at 13³⁰. Wendt [1] and Paul [2] find the break at 13³⁵, but vv. 33 and 36 f. seem to be in complete sequence.

D

The position of the verses, 3³¹⁻³⁶, provides another example of difficulties of interpretation, probably due to a disturbance of the textual order.

As the verses 3³¹⁻³⁶ stand in the traditional text, it would seem at first sight that they were intended to be a continuation of the Baptist's " witness " to our Lord, contained in vv. 27–30; and many of the older commentators (*e.g.* Meyer, Alford) held this to be the case. But most modern exegetes recognise that in this section, as in 3¹⁶⁻²¹, we have an evangelistic commentary on what has preceded. The style of 3³¹⁻³⁶ is unmistakably that of Jn., when writing in his own person. However, it does not bear any clear relation to what *immediately* precedes in the traditional text. Abbott (*Diat.* 2501 f.) endeavours, indeed, to interpret 3³³ of John Baptist; it is the Baptist, he holds, that is said to have *sealed* his attestation that God is true. But, if so, the words in v. 32, τὴν μαρτυρίαν αὐτοῦ οὐδεὶς λαμβάνει, must also be interpreted as Jn.'s paraphrase of the Baptist's account of the ill success of Jesus' mission. This is entirely inconsistent with the report of the Baptist's disciples about Jesus, πάντες ἔρχονται πρὸς αὐτόν (v. 26), which drew from their master a confident and joyful assurance that Jesus was, indeed, the Coming One, the Christ Himself (vv. 27–30).

An examination of the section 3³¹⁻³⁶ shows, on the contrary, that it is a continuation of Jn.'s commentary (vv. 16–21) upon the pronouncement of Jesus in vv. 11–15. Thus v. 32, in both its clauses, reproduces almost verbatim the words ascribed to Jesus in v. 11; and v. 31 goes back to v. 12. V. 36ª, " He that believeth on the Son hath eternal life," has been said already at v. 16; and the sombre warning to the unbeliever or disobedient at v. 36ᵇ has been given before, although less explicitly, at v. 18. " He whom God hath sent " (v. 34) recalls v. 17. There is no saying in vv. 31–36 which naturally arises out of the section vv. 22–30, but everything in vv. 31–36, on the other hand, goes back to vv. 11–21.

Hence, it suggests itself that vv. 22–30 are out of place; and this conclusion has been reached by several scholars. Lewis proposed to transfer 3²²⁻³⁰ to a position immediately

[1] *Gospel according to St. John*, p. 104.
[2] *Hibbert Journal*, April 1909.

following 2^{12}, and this has been approved by Moffatt,[1] Lewis,[2] J. M. Thompson,[3] Garvie,[4] etc. That 3^{25} speaks of καθαρισμός is thought to recall 2^6, and the bridegroom of 2^{10} to suggest the image of 3^{28}. But the sequence of μετὰ τοῦτο in 2^{12}, followed by μετὰ ταῦτα in 3^{22}, would be strange and not like the style of Jn. Nor can it be said that there would be any special appositeness in such a position of 3^{22-30}. To place these verses *before* the Cleansing of the Temple and the subsequent " signs " at Jerusalem (2^{23}) makes it difficult to explain the crowds who flocked to the ministry of Jesus (3^{26}). For, according to this arrangement of the text, Jesus has not been in Jerusalem at all, and the miracle at Cana of Galilee is the only " sign " that has attracted attention.

A simpler explanation is that 3^{22-30} originally *followed*, instead of *preceding*, 3^{31-36}.[5] Everything then falls into place. The evangelist's commentary or paraphrase, $3^{16-21.\ 31-36}$, is continuous; and a new section (3^{22-30}) of the narrative beginning with μετὰ ταῦτα, as usual in Jn., deals with the second witness of the Baptist, and connects itself directly in the opening verses of c. 4 with the journey to Samaria. It may be added that the sequence between 3^{22-30} and $4^{1.\ 2}$ is as natural as that between 3^{36} and $4^{1.\ 2}$ is unreal.

E

Another example of " dislocation " may be found, if we mistake not, in c. 10, the traditional order of verses being difficult to interpret, and the order vv. 19–29, vv. 1–18, vv. 30 ff. suggesting itself as preferable.[6]

First, as is pointed out in the note on 10^1, the introductory " Verily, verily " is employed to begin a new discourse on a new topic in a manner without parallel in the rest of the Gospel. There is no connexion between the end of c. 9 and the beginning of c. 10, which opens (as we have it) with the allegory of the shepherd and the sheep. This has nothing to do with the controversy about the healing of the blind man, which occupies the whole of c. 9. On the other hand, it is plain that 10^{19-21} comes naturally after 9^{41}. The end of the long and tedious argument about this miraculous cure was that the Pharisees who were inquiring into the matter were not unanimous in the conclusion they reached. Some said that Jesus was mad; others that He really had restored the man's sight, and that

---

[1] *Introd. to N.T.*, p. 553 n.   [2] *Disarrangements, etc.*, pp. 25–31.
[3] *Expositor*, VIII. ix. 422.   [4] *The Beloved Disciple*, pp. 20, 84.
[5] For this transposition, see Cadoux, *J.T.S.*, July 1919, p. 317.
[6] Moffatt has adopted this order in his *New Translation of the N.T.*

this could not be explained away by saying that He was a madman. There is no connexion apparent between 10^{18} and 10^{19-21}. The traditional text represents the allegory of the shepherd and the sheep following (after an undefined interval) the condemnation of the Pharisees for refusing to recognise in the cure of the blind man a confirmation of Jesus' claims; and then, abruptly, at vv. 19–21, we turn back to the Pharisees still in controversy about this very matter. The end of the story of the blind man is in vv. 19–21, and this naturally follows on 9^{41}.

This controversy had gone on for some weeks, and by the time that we have reached the end of it, a couple of months have elapsed since the Feast of Tabernacles, and so a new paragraph begins by telling us that the Feast of Dedication (see on 10^{22}) had now arrived. The hostile Jews are determined to get a plain answer to the question " Art thou the Christ ? " (10^{24}), and Jesus tells them that their unbelief is due to their not being of His flock, assigning a moral cause for their want of faith as He had done before (see on 10^{26}). If they were His sheep, they would hear His voice and follow Him, and so would be safe in His keeping (10^{27-29}). Then follows, quite naturally, the allegory of the shepherd and the sheep, introduced by ἀμὴν ἀμήν inasmuch as it takes up and enlarges the theme already suggested by vv. 27–29.

We believe, then, that vv. 1–18 are out of their true position, which was lost owing to some accident. The scribe who placed them immediately after 9^{41} noticed no doubt that the sequence of vv. 29, 30 was intelligible, and it satisfied him. In v. 28 Jesus had said that His sheep were safe in His hand, and in v. 29 (even more strongly) that they were safe in the Father's hand. " I and my Father are One " is a declaration which would be quite in place here. But it is in even a more appropriate place if it follows (as we have argued it should follow) v. 18: " I have authority to lay it down, and authority to take it again. This commandment did I receive from my Father. I and my Father are One." It is this unity which explains the seeming inconsistency of the assertion, " I lay it down of Myself," with the former statement, " the Son can do nothing of Himself " (5^{19} and see on 10^{18})—an inconsistency which, as the text stands, is not relieved by the assertion of unity with the Father, which is essential to the argument.

F

A sixth example of " dislocation " appears at 12^{44-50}, a section which comes in more naturally after 12^{36a}, the verses 12^{36b-43} following 12^{50}.

At v. 36[b] it is said that Jesus went away and "was hidden," the evangelist noting the incredulity of His hearers, in which he finds a fulfilment of prophecy (vv. 39–41), and adding that nevertheless many of the rulers were secretly believers, although they were afraid to confess it (vv. 42, 43). But then at v. 44, the public and authoritative teaching of Jesus begins again, the word ἔκραξε being inconsistent with ἐκρύβη of v. 36[b]. And, moreover, the topics of vv. 35, 36 are continued in vv. 44 ff. Thus the contrast between the believer who walks in the light and the unbeliever whom darkness overtakes is carried on from v. 35 to v. 46. But in vv. 35, 36 it has not yet been explained what the Light is to which reference is made; to go back to 8[12] is easy for a modern reader, but it would not be suggested by anything in vv. 35, 36. We get the explanation in v. 46, "*I* am come as a Light into the world," etc., an explanation which is not only natural, but necessary, if vv. 35, 36 are to be intelligible in their original context. And then Jesus reverts to the theme, frequent throughout the Gospel, that His claim for attention is not "of Himself," but because He is God's messenger.

There is no change of scene between v. 36[a] and v. 44. Vv. 35–36[a] and vv. 44–50 form a continuous discourse, the effect of which is summarised vv. 36 –43.[1]

To this argument, the evidence of Tatian's *Diatessaron* gives corroboration. For, whatever his reason may have been, Tatian rearranges the text of Jn. 12. His order is, Jn. 12[19-36a], then verses from Mt., Lk., Jn. 12[42-50], verses from Lk., Jn. 12[36-41]. He differs from the conclusion which we have reached as to vv. 42, 43; but either he noticed that 12[36b-41] could not stand in the text in the position in which we find them, or (less probably) he was following manuscripts which placed these verses in the order that we have adopted as the true one.[2]

G

Mention must be made here of a rearrangement of the text in c. 18 which has been adopted by many good critics, but which is not followed in the present commentary.

In 1893 F. Spitta,[3] taking the view that ὁ ἀρχιερεύς of 18[19] must mean Caiaphas, and noticing the repetition of the phrase Πέτρος ἑστὼς καὶ θερμαινόμενος in vv. 18, 25[a], suggested that, perhaps owing to the displacement of a leaf of papyrus,

---

[1] Cf. Wendt, *l.c.* p. 96, and Moffatt, *l.c.* p. 556.

[2] Cf. Bacon, *The Fourth Gospel*, p. 509, and Moffatt, *Introd. to the N.T.*, p. 556.

[3] *Gesch. und Lit. d. Urchristenthums*, 1893, p. 158.

the text of vv. 13–27 was in disorder, and that the original sequence was vv. 13, 19–24, 14–18, 25ᵇ–28, 25ᵃ being a copyist's addition. This conjectural restoration of the text was thought to be confirmed shortly afterwards by the discovery of the Sinai Syriac codex, in which the verses are found in the order 13, 24, 14, 15, 19–23, 16–18, 25ᵇ–28. F. Blass accepted this as the true text,[1] stating that the traditional order of verses was only a narrative " of blundering scribes." Later, G. G. Findlay and Moffatt adopted the order vv. 13, 14, 19–24, 15–18, 25ᵇ–28, which only differs from Spitta's in the place assigned to v. 14, an unimportant variation.

It will be observed that while Spitta's proposal and that of Moffatt involve only a transposition of sections of nearly equal length—in Spitta's case vv. 14–18 and 19–24, and in Moffatt's case vv. 15–18 and 19–24—the Sinai Syriac, besides transposing the sections vv. 16–18 and 19–23, also divorces v. 24 from its traditional place and inserts it after v. 13. It is in the highest degree improbable that this *double* divergence of the normal text from the Sinai Syriac can be the result of accident; something more, therefore, is involved in the traditional order than the mere displacement of a leaf of the exemplar.[2] In other words, there is a presumption that the text of Syr. sin. has been rearranged from harmonistic motives just as those of Spitta and Moffatt have been.[3] See also on 4⁸.

The advantage claimed for these rearrangements is that they present a more coherent story. In the case of Syr. sin. the removal of v. 24 to a place after v. 13 enables us to get rid of Annas altogether, except for a short halt at his house. As in Mt., everything is done by Caiaphas, who conducts the preliminary examination of Jesus (26⁵⁷⁻⁶⁷), as well as presiding at the formal meeting of the Sanhedrim (27¹). Again, the title ἀρχιερεύς is thus strictly reserved for Caiaphas, who was the recognised high priest at the time, Annas having been deposed from office previously. And the bringing together of the sections vv. 15–18 and 25–27 is thought to be helpful in regard to an understanding of the story of Peter's denials.

In the text as reconstructed by Spitta and Moffatt, Jesus remains in the house of Annas for the preliminary cross-examination, after which (v. 24) He is sent to Caiaphas. But

---

[1] *Philology of the Gospels*, 1898, p. 59.

[2] C. H. Turner (*J.T.S.*, Oct. 1900, p. 141) suggested that the O.L. codex *e*, from which the leaf between 18¹² and 18²⁵ᵇ has been cut, might have supported Syr. sin. ; but cf. Burkitt in *Ev. da Mepharr.*, II. 316 *contra*.

[3] Cf. Wendt, *Fourth Gospel*, p. 164, and see also Schmiedel (*E.B.* 4580), who takes the view adopted in this commentary that no re-adjustment of the text is necessary.

this does not bring the narrative into harmony with Mt., unless we suppose that Caiaphas (although in the house of Annas) conducts the inquiry of vv. 19–23; and in that case v. 24 is extraordinarily clumsy after v. 23.

It is argued in the notes on this chapter (see on 18¹³ for a brief summary of the sequence of events) that two erroneous assumptions underlie these rearrangements of text. First, ἀρχιερεύς, as a title, was not confined to the high priest at the moment in office, but was used of ex high priests, such as Annas, as well (see on 7³² 11⁴⁹ 18¹⁹). In 18¹⁵⁻²³ Annas is the ἀρχιερεύς, but Caiaphas was the ἀρχιερεὺς τοῦ ἐνιαυτοῦ ἐκείνου. And, secondly, we cannot get rid of 25ᵃ, as is done by Syr. sin., as well as by Moffatt, without removing a characteristic note of Johannine style (see note *in loc.*). Further, the separation of the later denials of Peter from his first brings out the interval of time (occupied by the cross-examination of Jesus) which elapsed since Peter began to wait in the courtyard (see on 18¹⁸. ²⁵).

These considerations, which are given more fully in the notes, show, I believe, that the traditional order of verses in 18¹³⁻²⁶ is more probably original than those which have been proposed in substitution for it. It may be added that the traditional order is followed by Tatian, who did not scruple to transpose verses where the sense seemed to demand it.

H

That a document may contain genuine, but misplaced, passages is, as Moffatt has shown, a legitimate hypothesis; and profane, as well as sacred, literature supplies illustrations.[1] But where manuscript evidence is wholly lacking, and internal evidence alone is available, hypotheses as to transposition of sections are necessarily precarious, and ought to be accepted only when the internal evidence is very strong. A method, however, of obtaining objective corroboration of such hypotheses has been adopted during recent years by several scholars,[2] which must not be ignored.

If we knew the number of lines of writing, or of letters, in a single leaf (*recto* and *verso*) of a manuscript in codex form, we should know the length of a section that would be involved by the accidental displacement of a leaf. Let us count the letters in the various sections in which we have found traces of

[1] See Moffatt, *Introd. to N.T.*, p. 39.
[2] See especially F. J. Paul (*Hibbert Journal*, April 1909), A. C. Clark (*Primitive Text of the Gospels and Acts*, 1914), and J. M. Thompson (*Expositor*, VIII. ix. 421 f., 1915).

displacement. It is not possible to be certain as to the exact numbers in the original, because we cannot be sure what contractions were used. But the following figures, derived from our printed text, will give at any rate the *comparative* lengths of the sections:

$$\text{I. c. } 5 = 3630 \text{ letters.}[1]$$
$$\text{II. } 7^{15\text{-}24} = 763 \text{ letters.}$$
$$\text{III. } 13^{31}\text{--}14^{31} = 3120 \text{ letters.}$$
$$\text{IV. } 3^{22\text{-}30} = 730 \text{ letters.}$$
$$\text{V. } 10^{1\text{-}18} = 1495 \text{ letters.}$$
$$\text{VI. } 12^{36b\text{-}43} = 598 \text{ letters.}$$

Let us suppose that each leaf of two pages (*recto* and *verso*) of our manuscript contained about 750 letters. This would not be abnormal, and might happen in a variety of ways; *e.g.* a page of 34 lines, each of 11 letters,[2] would have 374 letters, and thus the leaf would have 748 letters. The same result would be reached if the writing were in double columns, and each column were of 17 lines. Or, as Thompson suggested, we might have an arrangement of 25 lines of 15 letters each to a page, which would give us 750 letters to the leaf.[3]

A leaf might carry from 700 to 1500 letters of our printed text. Thus the oldest extant Greek MS. of Jn. is the Oxyrhynchus Papyrus numbered 208 and 1781 (see p. xiv), which goes back to the end of the third century. This MS. was in book form, consisting of a single quire of some 25 sheets, and it is demonstrable[4] from the fragments which remain that each page contained about 710 letters, and each leaf 1420. On the other hand, the papyrus codex 1780 (see p. xiv) carried only about 700 letters a leaf. Both of these provide examples of early Gospel manuscripts written on papyrus, the leaves being fastened together so as to make a codex. Scribes are conservative people, and it is probable that the normal Gospel book was similar to this pattern in the first century, whatever its size.

We take, then, 750 letters for each leaf, and make no other hypothesis, leaving as an open question the disposition of the lines of the manuscript of Jn. under consideration. It appears at once that §§ II. and IV. occupy approximately one leaf each; § V. occupies almost exactly two leaves; § I.

---

[1] If v. 4 were included, we should have 3795 letters.

[2] Codex ‭א‬ is probably derived from a MS. having 11 letters to the line (H. S. Cronin, *J.T.S.*, 1912, p. 563) ; and the same may be true of B (Clark, *Primitive Text, etc.*, p. 33).

[3] Thompson also finds traces of a unit of 208 letters ; Clark, on the other hand, attaches special significance to a unit of 160 to 167 letters.

[4] See *Oxyrhynchus Papyri*, vol. ii. (1899), and vol. xv. (1922).

occupies nearly five leaves ($750 \times 5 = 3750$, which is slightly in excess of 3630, or only 45 letters less than 3795, the number if the verse 5^4 is included); § III. has 3120 letters, which is only 120 letters in excess of four regular leaves ($750 \times 4 = 3000$); § VI. would not quite fill a leaf, having only 598 letters, but the quotation marks in this section would take up space that would normally be occupied by text, and moreover on the hypothesis of dislocation, § VI. would conclude Part II. of the Gospel, after which a blank space would naturally be left before entering on Part III.

These figures are remarkable. If the leaves on which the Gospel was written became disarranged from any cause, a faulty rearrangement of them would produce in §§ II., IV., V., almost exactly the displacements of text to which internal evidence has pointed; and in §§ I., III., VI., the figures would be close to what we should expect.[1]

The argument drawn out above stands quite apart from, and is independent of, the arguments based on internal evidence; and even if it fail to win acceptance, the conclusions as to the dislocations of the text in Jn. must be considered on their own merits.

(iii) The Structure of the Gospel

The Gospel falls into three parts, preceded by a Prologue and followed by an Appendix.

Part I. (cc. 1^{19}–4^{54} with c. 6) begins at Bethany beyond Jordan, goes on to Galilee, thence to Jerusalem, and back to Samaria and Galilee. It deals with the ministry of a little more than one year.

Part II. (cc. 5, 7, 8–12) has to do with the Jerusalem ministry of Jesus, and extends over a second year.

Part III. (cc. 13–20) is wholly concerned with the Passion and Resurrection.

More at length, the structure may be exhibited as follows:

THE PROLOGUE [2]

This (1^{1-18}) is primarily a Hymn on the Logos, interspersed with explanatory comments by the evangelist.

---

[1] The unit of about 750 letters appears again in Jn.'s account of the Cleansing of the Temple, viz. $2^{14-22} = 764$ letters. Reasons have been given (on 2^{13}) for the opinion that this section is also out of place, but we cannot be sure that Jn. did not deliberately place the Cleansing of the Temple at the beginning of Jesus' ministry, and it has accordingly been left in its traditional position. It would remove some difficulties to place 2^{14-22} after 12^{19}, but new difficulties would arise. E.g., the Jews' question τί σημεῖον δεικνύεις ἡμῖν; (2^{18}) would not be suitable after the Raising of Lazarus.

[2] See p. cxxxviii.

PART I

PART II

The concluding sentences in each of these sections are noteworthy, as indicating the careful planning of the narrative.

The last words of the Prologue are a summary of the theme of the Gospel, viz. the Manifestation of the Father through His Son (1[18]).

Part I. is mainly occupied with the Ministry of the first year, which was largely in Galilee. Its happy progress is recorded, but this ends with the defection of many disciples (6[66]). Here is the first suggestion of failure.

Part II. tells of the Ministry at Jerusalem, the success of which would be fundamental, and of the fierce opposition which it provoked. Its climax is the final rejection of Jesus by the Jews, upon which the evangelist comments in a few sombre words (12[36b-43]).

Part III. narrates the Passion, which seemed the end, and the Resurrection, which was really the victorious beginning. The final words explain the purpose of the writing of the Gospel which is now concluded (20[30, 31]).

The authentication at the end of the Appendix (21[24, 25]) has its own special significance. For the Appendix, see on 21[1f.].

NON-JOHANNINE GLOSSES

It is generally recognised that the story of the adulterous woman (7[53]–8[11]) is not Johannine, and that it was interpolated by scribes at an early date. This is discussed in the note on the Pericope. There are three or four other passages which suggest a hand other than that of Jn., and are probably due to editorial revision, being added after the Gospel was finished, perhaps before it was issued to the Church. Thus 4[1, 2] is a passage which has been rewritten for the sake of clearness, but the style is not that of Jn. So 6[23] is an explanatory non-Johannine gloss. The verse 5[4] is rejected by modern editors from the text as insufficiently attested, but linguistic evidence alone would mark it as non-Johannine. 11[2] is undoubtedly an explanatory or parenthetical comment, but it is possible that it is added by Jn., although there are non-Johannine touches of style: cf. 11[5]. There is also some doubt about the comment at 12[16], which reads as if it was not due to the original evangelist, but to some one who had the Synoptic, rather than the Johannine, story in his mind at this point.

EVANGELISTIC COMMENTS

These non-Johannine glosses must not be confused with the comments which Jn. makes, as he proceeds, on his narra-

c

tive, and on the words which he records. These appear not only in the body of the Gospel, but in the Prologue (cf. p. cxlv; see on $1^{6f.\ 12.\ 15}$) and in the Appendix (21^{19}). At $2^{21}\ 7^{39}\ 12^{33}\ 17^3$ Jn. offers an explanation of words of Jesus which he thinks may be misunderstood, and at $6^{61.\ 64}$ he calls attention to a point that may be missed. He points out a misunderstanding on the part of the Jews ($7^{22}\ 8^{27}$) and of the disciples (11^{13}). He notes that certain words of the Jews correspond with what Jesus had said about His death (18^{32}; cf. 4^{44}). He ascribes motives to Judas (12^6) and to the rulers (12^{43}). He gives brief elucidations, such as could be needed only by those to whom the details would be new ($4^9\ 6^{71}$; cf. $2^{24}\ 7^5$). He pauses to note the irony of Caiaphas' unconscious prophecy (11^{51}). His general habit, however, is to pass over without comment (see on 1^{45}) any obvious mistake or misapprehension as to the Person of Christ. These mistakes his readers will correct for themselves, while they need help in regard to obscure sayings.

The special interest of the concluding paragraph of Part II. has already been noticed (p. xxxiii). Here the evangelist ends the narrative of the ministry of Jesus at Jerusalem and His rejection there, by quoting, as part of his own comment, several verses from the O.T. which show how Jewish unbelief had been foreordained in prophecy (12^{36b-43}).

CHAPTER II

THE APOSTLE JOHN AND THE FOURTH GOSPEL

(i) John the Apostle was the Beloved Disciple.
(ii) John the Apostle did not suffer Death by Martyrdom.
(iii) John the Apostle and John the Presbyter.
(iv) The Muratorian Fragment and the Latin Prefaces on the Authorship of the Gospel.
(v) The Gospel and the Johannine Epistles were written by John the Presbyter.
(vi) The Apocalypse is not by John the Presbyter, but probably by John the Apostle.
(vii) Summary of Argument as to Authorship.
(viii) Early Citations of the Fourth Gospel.

(i) JOHN THE APOSTLE WAS THE BELOVED DISCIPLE

THE notices of John by name are infrequent in the N.T. He was, apparently, the younger of the two sons of Zebedee, the proprietor of a fishing-boat on the Lake of Galilee and a man of sufficient substance to employ servants (Mk. 1[19. 20]). His mother, Salome, was a sister of the Virgin Mary (see on 19[35] 2[12]), so that John was a maternal cousin of Jesus. With his brother James, he obeyed the call of Jesus to follow Him as a disciple (Mk. 1[20]); and it is probable that he had been attracted to His company at an even earlier period (see on Jn. 1[40]). In the earliest list of the Twelve (Mk. 3[17]) James and John [1] are given the next place after Peter, but that is only due to the order in which they appear in Peter's reminiscences. Peter, James, and John are specially associated with Jesus three times in the Synoptic narrative (Mk. 5[37] 9[2] 14[33]), these incidents disclosing their intimacy with Him. In the last week of His ministry they are found, with Andrew, questioning Him privately (Mk. 13[3]).

John was rebuked for his uncompromising temper of exclusiveness (Mk. 9[38], Lk. 9[49]), a story which agrees with the report of Irenæus that John would not stay under the same roof as the heretic Cerinthus (*Hær.* iii. 3. 4). Lk. (9[54]) adds another illustration of his intolerance, James and John being desirous of invoking the Divine vengeance on those who would not receive their Master hospitably. Finally, the two brothers aroused the indignation of the other apostles by asking that when Messiah's kingdom was established they should be given the two principal places of honour as His viziers (Mk. 10[35]; cf. Mt. 20[20], where it is their mother Salome that makes the request). It is clear that they regarded themselves as in no way inferior to Peter; nor is he represented as specially aggrieved by their claim; nor, again, does Jesus in His reply suggest that they were *not* entitled to the chief place among the Twelve (cf. note on 13[23]). But He declares that earthly precedence is reversed in His Kingdom, only asking of James and John if they are able to drink His cup and be baptized with His baptism. They assure Him that they can, and He tells them that so it shall be (Mk. 10[39]).

James is generally mentioned before John, but in Lk. 8[51] 9[28], Acts 1[13], the order is Peter, John, James. Lk. specially associates Peter with John. He notes (Lk. 22[8]) that it was Peter and John who were entrusted with the preparation for the Last Supper. In Acts 3[1. 11] 4[13], Peter and John together bear the brunt of Jewish hostility; and, again, these two are selected by the apostles as delegates to confirm the Samaritans (Acts 8[14]). As early as the year 55, Paul mentions Peter and

---

[1] Mk. (3[17]) adds that Jesus gave them the title βοανηργές, which he interprets " sons of thunder." But no Aramaic word has been suggested, corresponding to βοανηργές, which could mean υἱοὶ βροντῆς, and the title remains obscure (cf. *D.C.G.* i. 216).

John, with James the Lord's brother, as the pillars of the Church at Jerusalem (Gal. 2⁹). Peter is always represented as the spokesman, but John shares with him the responsibilities which leadership brings.

John is represented in Acts 4¹³ as being, like Peter, ἀγράμματος καὶ ἰδιώτης. That is, he was not learned in the lore of Rabbinical schools. To call him " illiterate and ignorant " would be to exaggerate, but the words employed do not suggest that he was a man of learning or of literary gifts.

John the son of Zebedee is not mentioned by name in the Fourth Gospel, and " the sons of Zebedee " collectively appear only in the Appendix (21²). Having regard to the important position given to John by the Synoptists, it would be strange if he were ignored by the Fourth Evangelist. As has been said above, he may be indicated at 1³⁵ (where see note); and we now inquire if any disciple is mentioned by Jn., without being named, who is specially associated with Peter, as John is by Luke.

An unnamed disciple is mentioned (18¹⁵) as having, in company with Peter, followed Jesus after His arrest; being known to the high priest, he was admitted to the inner court, while Peter had to stay outside. This *might* have been John the son of Zebedee, but there is no real evidence that it was one of the Twelve (see note on 18¹⁵).

In three passages, however, an unnamed friend of Peter is described as " the disciple whom Jesus loved." First, the Beloved Disciple has a place next Jesus at the Last Supper, and Peter beckons to him to discover the name of the traitor. This must have been one of the Twelve [1] (see on 13²³), and so his identification with John the son of Zebedee is suggested.

Secondly, Peter and " the other disciple whom Jesus loved," run together to the sepulchre which Mary Magdalene had reported to be empty (20²ᶠ·). The Beloved Disciple's eagerness to be first at the tomb, his hesitation to enter it when it was reached, and his " belief " when he saw that it was empty, are graphically described.

Thirdly, the two disciples whose fates are contrasted in 21¹⁵⁻²³ are, again, Peter and ὁ μαθητὴς ὃν ἠγάπα ὁ Ἰησοῦς ; and the latter is, apparently, a fisherman, as we know John the son of Zebedee to have been. The narrative of the Appendix helps the identification in another way. The " Beloved Disciple " must be one of the seven persons indicated in 21², and among these the sons of Zebedee are expressly included. James is excluded, for the tradition of v. 23 could not have

[1] Cf. *contra*, Sanday (*Criticism of Fourth Gospel*, p. 98), and Swete (*J.T.S.*, July 1916, p. 374).

arisen in regard to him (Acts 12²), so that if the Beloved Disciple were not John the apostle, he must be either Thomas, Nathanael, or one of the two *innominati* (see on 21² for the possibilities).

Now the constant tradition of the early Church was that the *name* of the Beloved Disciple was John. Irenæus (*Hær.* III. i. 1) and Polycrates (see p. 1. below) are explicit about this. So are the second-century *Acts of John* (ἀνακείμενον ἐμὲ ἐπὶ τὰ ἴδια στήθη ἐδέχετο, § 89). So is Origen (cf. Eusebius, *H.E.* vi. 25). This is a point on which tradition could not have gone astray, and there is no other tradition. There can be no reasonable doubt that the name of the Beloved Disciple was John, and therefore Thomas and Nathanael are excluded.[1] If there was another John among the two *innominati*, we might claim *him* as the Beloved Disciple, but for this there is no evidence.

The only other mention of the Beloved Disciple in Jn. is at 19²⁶, where he is standing near the Cross in company with the Virgin Mother, whom he received εἰς τὰ ἴδια " to his lodging." This (see on 19²⁷) is not inconsistent with his being the " witness " to whom appeal is made in 19³⁵, for ample time had elapsed to permit of his return to the Cross. And when we find at 21²⁴ that it is the Beloved Disciple who is designated as " the disciple who bears witness of these things," it is difficult to avoid the conclusion that the " witness " of 19³⁵ is the same person (cf. p. lxix below).[2]

(ii) JOHN THE APOSTLE DID NOT SUFFER DEATH BY MARTYRDOM

Accepting the identification of the Beloved Disciple with the apostle John, the tradition of the early Church that John lived to extreme old age, which is suggested in 21²³ (see note *in loc.* and cf. p. xlvii f.), is consistent at every point.

This tradition has, however, been challenged; and some critics have put forward the theory that John the apostle, the son of Zebedee, died as a martyr early in his apostolic career,[3]

---

[1] So also is Lazarus, of whom it is said three times that Jesus loved him (Jn. 11³· ⁵· ³⁶). He was suggested as possibly the beloved disciple by W. K. Fleming, *Guardian*, 19th Dec. 1906, but he must be ruled out.

[2] The theory that the Beloved Disciple is an ideal figure, and not a man of flesh and blood, has been put forward by a few critics, *e.g.* Réville : " Il apparait comme un être irréel . . . le disciple idéal qui est sur le sein du Christ, comme le Christ est sur le sein de Dieu," quoted by Latimer-Jackson, *The Problem of the Fourth Gospel*, p. 155. But to dismiss the vivid notices of the Beloved Disciple in this way is a desperate expedient of exegesis.

[3] This view is favoured by Schwartz, Wellhausen, Schmiedel (*E.B.* 2509), Moffatt (*Introd.* p. 602), Bacon (*Fourth Gospel*, p. 132),

while a different person, viz. John the Beloved Disciple, lived to be an old man, and died peacefully at Ephesus. In a seventh- or eighth-century Epitome of the History of Philip of Side (fl. *circa* 450) the statement is found that " Papias in the second book says that John the Divine and James his brother were killed by the Jews." A ninth-century writer, George the Sinner, reproduces part of this, and claims the fact that both of the sons of Zebedee met a violent death as a fulfilment of the Lord's prediction, Mk. 10³⁹. For this story there is, however, no other authority than the epitomiser of Philip of Side, while, since the second century, the Christian Church has always accepted the statement of Irenæus that John died a natural death.

The problem as to the death of John the apostle is so important in view of the inferences which have been drawn from it, that the method adopted by the epitomiser of Philip of Side, and also his trustworthiness, must be examined in detail, however tedious.

A

The series of extracts from ecclesiastical histories,[1] one of which is here in question, are headed by the rubric: " A collection of different narratives, from the birth of our Lord according to the flesh, beginning from the first book (λόγου) of the ecclesiastical history of Eusebius." The collection falls into seven sections, all of which borrow matter from Eusebius, but in one or two instances make use of tradition not found in that author's extant works. The sixth of these sections is concerned with Papias, and is printed in full in Lightfoot's *Apostolic Fathers*, p. 518. Much of the collection is in Eusebius; and it must be borne in mind that the Epitomiser does not profess to quote Papias at first hand. He only gives a summary (like a series of notes) of what he found in Philip of Side, who may or may not have had direct access to the writings of Papias. We shall describe him throughout as the Epitomiser, leaving it an open question (as we must) whether he correctly represents Philip of Side or not.

Burkitt (*Gospel History and Transmission*, p. 252), Charles (*Revelation*, i. p. xlv), and others. It is rejected by Lightfoot (*Essays on Supernatural Religion*, p. 212), Drummond (*Character and Authorship, etc.*, p. 228), Zahn (*Forsch.* vi. 147), Chapman (*John the Presbyter*, p. 95), Harnack (*Chronol.* i. 665 f.), Loofs, Clemen, Armitage Robinson (*Historical Character of St. John's Gospel*, p. 64). I have discussed the problem at some length in *Studia Sacra*, p. 260 f.

[1] Printed from the Oxford *Cod. Barocc.* 142 by De Boor in *Texte und Untersuchungen*, v. 2 (1888).

(*a*) The Epitomiser begins: " Papias, bishop of Hierapolis, who was a hearer of John the Divine and a companion of Polycarp, wrote five books (λόγους) of Oracles of the Lord." [1] The description of Papias as ἀκουστὴς Ἰωάννου, Πολυκάρπου δὲ ἑταῖρος is in Eusebius (iii. 39. 1), who is avowedly quoting from Irenæus (v. 33. 4). The context in Irenæus (v. 30. 3) is explicit as to John, whose hearer Papias was, being the author of the Apocalypse. The title ὁ θεολόγος cannot have been in Papias, as it does not appear before the fourth century.

The *Epitome* proceeds: " Wherein [*i.e.* in Papias' work], when giving a list of the apostles, after Peter and John, Philip and Thomas and Matthew, he included among the disciples of the Lord, Aristion and another John (Ἰωάννην ἕτερον), whom also he called πρεσβύτερος." This [2] again is abbreviated from Eusebius (iii. 39. 4), Andrew and James being omitted.

The next sentence, beginning ὥς τινας οἴεσθαι, probably does not reproduce statements of Papias, but is a comment of the Epitomiser, although Lightfoot takes it differently. " So that some think that [this] John is the author of the two short and catholic epistles, which are published in the name of John; because the ἀρχαῖοι [*i.e.* the early Church leaders] only accept the first epistle. Some, too, have wrongly thought the Apocalypse also to be his [*i.e.* John the presbyter's]." [3] Papias himself would never have spoken of the ἀρχαῖοι as authorities who passed judgment on the Johannine writings. The comment evidently comes from a later age, when questions of authorship and canonicity had arisen. It may be found in substance in Eusebius (iii. 25. 3). The Epitomiser deprecates the idea that the Apocalypse was not written by John the apostle.

(*b*) The *Epitome* proceeds: " Papias also goes wrong about the Millennium, and from him Irenæus also." This also comes from Eusebius (iii. 39. 12), who says in connexion with it that Papias was a man of limited intelligence. The reference to Irenæus is to v. 33. 4, as before.

(*c*) We pass by the next sentence, viz. about the martyrdom of John and James, until the rest of the *Epitome* has been examined.

(*d*) " The aforesaid Papias stated on the authority of the daughters of Philip, that Barsabbas, who is also called Justus, when challenged by the unbelievers, drank viper's poison in the name of Christ, and was preserved scathless." This is reproduced from Eusebius (iii. 39. 9). Eusebius does not

---

[1] The Papias memoranda in the *Epitome* have been analysed also by Dom Chapman, *John the Presbyter*, p. 95 with whose general conclusion, that they are mainly derived from Eusebius, I agree.

[2] See p. lii for this passage.   [3] Cf. p. liv.

mention the nature of the poison (cf. [Mk.] 16¹⁸), and he cites
Philip's daughters not as the authority for this story, but for
something similar to the next.

(*e*) " He relates also other wonderful things, and particularly the story about the mother of Manaimus, who was raised
from the dead." Eusebius (iii. 39. 9) notes that Papias had a
story about a resurrection from the dead, and it is no doubt
this to which the Epitomiser refers, giving, however, the
additional detail of the name of the resuscitated person.

(*f*) The last note is: " about those raised from the dead by
Christ, that they lived until the time of Hadrian." The
Epitomiser does not say expressly that this comes from Papias,
although it is among the Papias memoranda.   It may have
been added only because of its similarity to (*e*).   In any case,
it was told by Quadratus in his Apology addressed to Hadrian
(Eusebius, iv. 3. 2) that some of those raised by Christ " survived
to our own times."   It is hardly doubtful that the Epitomiser
is here again borrowing from Eusebius.

We observe, then, that the paragraphs *a*, *b*, *d*, *e*, *f* give no
information about Papias or his writings that is not in Eusebius,
except in regard to the name Manaimus, which may be a detail
of independent tradition.   If these memoranda were directly
taken from Papias' writings, it is hardly credible that Philip
of Side should have chosen exactly those points as notable
which had already been selected by Eusebius.   In short, it is
doubtful that Philip of Side knew anything about Papias
except what he found in Eusebius.¹

We now go back to the fragment of importance : (*c*) Παπίας
ἐν τῷ δευτέρῳ λόγῳ λέγει ὅτι Ἰωάννης ὁ θεολόγος καὶ Ἰάκωβος ὁ
ἀδελφὸς αὐτοῦ ὑπὸ Ἰουδαίων ἀνῃρέθησαν.

As in (*a*) the title ὁ θεολόγος has been added by the
Epitomiser (or by Philip); it could not have been used by
Papias.   The statement then is that " John and James his
brother were killed by Jews."   Now James the son of Zebedee
was not killed by Jews, but by Herod (Acts 12²), and Christian
historians have never laid the guilt of his death upon the Jews.
It is impossible to believe that Papias had any different tradition on the subject.   Again, if Papias said that John the son of
Zebedee was killed by Jews, we should have expected that
in the *Epitome* incredulity would have been indicated.   The

¹ Philip's contemporary, Socrates, says of him that he was a
laborious student who had amassed many books, but that his history
was useless, being both loose and inexact, especially in regard to
chronology (Socrates, *Eccl. Hist.*, vii. 27).   This agrees well with the
mistakes and omissions that are to be observed in the fragments of
the *Epitome* (including those about Papias) which have been printed
by De Boor.   Either Philip or his epitomiser was a blunderer.

Epitomiser believed (see p. xxxix above) that John wrote the Apocalypse, but this would have been impossible had John suffered martyrdom at the hands of the Jews. Nevertheless, the Epitomiser adds no adverse comment upon the belief with which he seems to credit Papias here, as he does in paragraph (*b*). This statement, then, both in regard to John and to James, provokes the suspicion that it is a misrepresentation or corruption of what Papias said.

I have shown elsewhere [1] that the clue to the corruption is found in Jerome's version of the *Chronicle* of Eusebius; " Jacobus, frater domini quem omnes Justum appellabant a Judaeis lapidibus opprimitur." If we compare this with the Armenian version and also with the Greek history of Syncellus which is based on Eusebius, we find that the Greek text of the *Chronicle* at this point was : ὁ ἀδελφὸς τοῦ κυρίου Ἰάκωβος ὁ ὀνομασθεὶς ὑπὸ παντῶν δίκαιος λίθοις ὑπὸ Ἰουδαίων ἀναιρεῖται.[2] Now the story of the martyrdom of James the Just is reproduced in Eusebius' History in full from Hegesippus, Josephus also being cited (ii. 23. 18, 20), both writers specially emphasising the fact that he was killed by Jews. When Eusebius comes to record this in his *Chronicle* he uses the very words ascribed in our *Epitome* to Papias ὑπὸ Ἰουδαίων ἀναιρεῖται. The Epitomiser has used of the martyrdom of James the Great a phrase which really belonged to the martyrdom of James the Just.

It is true that the Epitomiser expressly assigns his statement to Papias, and appears to specify (for the only time in his record) the actual *book* of the Ἐξηγήσεις from which his memorandum is derived. It is in the second λόγος, this term being used by him, as in paragraph (*a*), for a volume or section of Papias' work. But these sections were called βιβλία, not λόγοι, by Irenæus (v. 33. 4), as well as by Maximus Confessor [3] (seventh cent.), who shows direct acquaintance with the Ἐξηγήσεις. No doubt λόγος may be only a slip on the part of the Epitomiser for the more accurate βιβλίον.[4] But it is suspicious [5] that λόγος is the very term used by Eusebius (not by Papias) for the divisions of his History, and the Epitomiser knew this (see p. xxxviii). Is it not then probable that when the Epitomiser gives ἐν τῷ δευτέρῳ λόγῳ as his reference, he is quoting from the

---

[1] *Studia Sacra*, p. 271 f.
[2] So it is restored in Migne's text ; cf. also Schoene's edition of the *Chronicle*, ii. p. 154.
[3] Cf. Lightfoot, *Apostolic Fathers*, pp. 522, 523.
[4] Eusebius describes the Five Books of Papias as συγγράμματα (iii. 39. 1).
[5] This was first pointed out by W. Lockton (*Theology*, Aug. 1922, p. 81).

second λόγος of Eusebius (whose third book he has been using freely) rather than from the second βιβλίον of Papias, which there is no good evidence that he had ever seen?[1] In other words, the Epitomiser is going back to the story of the martyrdom of James the Just, told in Eus. ii. 23, as well as briefly in Eus. *Chron.* s.a. 61 in the words ὑπὸ Ἰουδαίων ἀναιρεῖται.

It may be that Papias said something about the martyrdom of James the Just by the Jews, as Hegesippus did; but it is doubtful that the Epitomiser has any more ultimate authority than Eusebius. Ἰάκωβος ὁ ἀδελφὸς αὐτοῦ is in some way corrupted from Ἰάκωβος ὁ ἀδελφὸς τοῦ κυρίου. Ἰωάννης ὁ θεολόγος is not an expression that Papias could have used. It is not possible to discover with certainty how this double blunder in the *Epitome* arose. Lightfoot [2] suggested that a whole line had dropped out, the fates of John and James his brother being contrasted in the original sentence. I made a different suggestion in 1908,[3] viz. that the sentence in Eusebius' *Chronicle*, ὁ ἀδελφὸς τοῦ κυρίου Ἰάκωβος, had been corrupted by scribes into ὁ ἀδελφὸς αὐτοῦ καὶ Ἰάκωβος, a bad Greek sentence, but one which would suggest that both the sons of Zebedee were intended. All that can, however, be said with confidence is that the sentence as found in the *Epitome* is corrupt, and that no historical inference can be drawn from a corrupt sentence in a late epitome of the work of a careless and blundering historian. To base upon De Boor's fragment an argument for the martyrdom of John the son of Zebedee is, as Harnack has said, " an uncritical caprice." [4]

B

Another argument in support of the idea that John died a martyr's death has been based on the evidence of ecclesiastical calendars.

In a Syriac Martyrology (before 411 A.D.) [5] we find the entries:

Dec. 26. Stephen, chief martyr, etc.
Dec. 27. John and James, the apostles, at Jerusalem.
Dec. 28. At Rome, Paul and Peter, the chief of the Lord's apostles.

[1] ἐν τῷ δευτέρῳ λόγῳ is also the phrase used by George the Sinner (p. xxxviii), but he is merely copying the *Epitome* of Philip of Side.
[2] *Supernatural Religion*, p. 212. He is referring to the passage in George the Sinner, but the suggestion is applicable also to De Boor's fragment.
[3] Cf. *Studia Sacra*, p. 273.   [4] *Theol. Literaturzeitung*, 1909, nr. 1.
[5] Printed by Wright in the *Journal of Sacred Literature* for 1866. Cf. *Studia Sacra*, p. 278.

Also in the Calendar of Carthage (505 A.D.) we find :

Dec. 26. S. Stephani primi martyris.
Dec. 27. S. Iohannis Baptistae et Jacobi apostoli quem
Herodes occidit.
Dec. 28. Sanctorum Infantum quos Herodes occidit.

It is argued that, as John Baptist is commemorated in the
same Calendar on June 24, the entry *S. Iohannis Baptistae*
here must be a mere mistake for *S. Iohannis Evangelistae*,
whose day is Dec. 27 in later Calendars of the West. And
the conclusion is drawn that, in the Syriac Martyrology and
in the Carthage Calendar alike, John is commemorated *as a
martyr*.

This argument misconceives the principle on which the
early Calendars were constructed. The Syriac Martyrology
may be compared with a passage in Aphrahat (†344): "After
Christ was the faithful martyr Stephen whom the Jews stoned.
Simon also and Paul were perfect martyrs. And James and
John walked in the footsteps of their Master Christ." [1] It
will be noticed that it is not said explicitly here that James and
John suffered a martyr's death. Now the selection of Stephen,
Peter, James, John, Paul, as the great leaders whose memory
was celebrated after Christmas, is specially mentioned by
Gregory of Nyssa (*circa* 385) as customary. He explains [2]
that they were commemorated as "leaders of the apostolic
chorus" (τῆς ἀποστολικῆς ἁρμονίας ἔξαρχοι); and adds that
they endured the combat with different kinds of martyrdom
(διαφόροις δὲ τοῦ μαρτυρίου τρόποις ἐναθλήσαντες), Peter
being crucified, James beheaded, and John's witness being
fulfilled, first in his trial when flung into the cauldron of boiling
oil, and secondly in his continual willingness to die for Christ.
The praise of the proto-martyr is followed, Gregory says, by a
commemoration of apostles, "for neither are martyrs without
apostles, nor are apostles separated from them." The insertion of names in the Church Calendars did not depend on
their title of μάρτυς in the restricted meaning of one who
suffered death for his Christian witness. And the same
principle is enunciated by Gregory of Nazianzus about the same
time in his panegyric on St. Basil the Great.[3] He compares
Basil to the great men of the O.T. and N.T., mentioning in
order John the Baptist, "the zeal of Peter, the intensity of
Paul . . . the lofty utterance (μεγαλόφωνον) of the sons of

[1] *De Persecutione*, 23 (cf. *Nicene and Post-Nicene Fathers*, vol. xiii.
p. 401).
[2] See Migne, *Patr. Gr.*, xlvi. cols. 789, 725, 729.
[3] Cf. *Nicene and Post-Nicene Fathers*, vol. vii. p. 149.

Zebedee, the frugality and simplicity of all the disciples," adding that he did not suffer Stephen's fate, although willing to face it.   Like Aphrahat, he mentions the five great leaders, making it plain that the pre-eminence of Peter, Paul, James, and John, which made them worthy of special commemoration, did *not* rest on their martyrdom, for this is only mentioned in the case of Stephen.

Thus the evidence for John's death by martyrdom, which is derived from the evidence of Church Calendars, must be dismissed, for Calendars included the names of great leaders, whether they were " red " martyrs or no.[1]

C

A third, and minor, plea in support of the theory that John the apostle died a martyr's death is based on a statement quoted by Clement of Alexandria (*Strom.* iv. 9) from the commentary of Heracleon on Lk. 12⁸ᶠ·. Schmiedel observes that Heracleon, while expressly mentioning Matthew, Philip, Thomas, and Levi among many who did not suffer death by martyrdom, does not mention John the apostle, who would have been entitled to the first place had Heracleon known of his peaceful end.[2]   But this is to misunderstand Heracleon, who is combating the extravagant claims sometimes made on behalf of " confessors."   We must distinguish, he says, those who have been called to make public confession of their faith before a magistrate from those who have only made their Christian confession in peaceful ways of life.   For instance, we must place Matthew, Philip, Thomas, etc., in the latter category.   Heracleon does not claim these apostles as " confessors with the voice."   And he does not put John the apostle among them, because he inherited the general Christian tradition that John *had* made confession and had been exiled to Patmos διὰ τὴν μαρτυρίαν Ἰησοῦ (Rev. 1⁹).   Whether Heracleon were right or wrong as to the fortunes of the apostles whom he names is not to the point.   But, on his view, it is certain that he could not have excluded John from those who bore *public* witness to their faith.   The example of John would not have served his purpose on any view of the apostle's end.   I submit that Schmiedel's argument based on Heracleon must be set aside.

[1] For a fuller discussion, I may refer to *Studia Sacra*, pp. 275 ff. The argument has been accepted by Harnack (*Theol. Literaturzeitung*, 1909, p. 11), by J. A. Robinson (*Hist. Character of St. John's Gospel*, p. 69 f.), and others.

[2] *E.B.* 2511.

D

Lastly, the idea that Mk. 10[39, 40] contains a prediction of John's death by violence rests upon a forgetfulness of the context and a misunderstanding of the words employed. (1) None of the apostles believed at the time that Jesus was going to die, and the affirmation of James and John that they could drink His cup and be baptized with His baptism did not contemplate death for themselves any more than for Him. He knew this, and knew, too, that a prediction of violent death for them both was a prediction which they could not have understood. (2) The present tenses πίνω, βαπτίζομαι, do not point to what was still in the future for Jesus, but to that ministry of sorrow which had already begun for Him. (3) To " drink the cup " is a familiar O.T. metaphor, often descriptive of accepting tribulation appointed by God (Ps. 11[6] 75[8], Isa. 51[17], Jer. 25[15]). It always involves pain, but not necessarily a violent death. (4) βαπτίζεσθαι means here " to be overwhelmed " as it were with a flood of calamity, the verb being used thus Isa. 21[4] (LXX), Ps. 69[2] (Symmachus), and Ps. 9[15].[1] For the image of an afflicted saint being overwhelmed with tides of misfortune (which do not always end in death), cf. Ps. 32[6] 42[7] 69[14] 88[7]. (5) βάπτισμα βαπτίζομαι is a literal Greek rendering of an Aramaic expression meaning " I am being overwhelmed," i.e. by the deep waters of God's appointment (cf. Lk. 12[50]). (6) To suppose that βάπτισμα βαπτίζομαι carries allusion to a " baptism of blood " is an anachronism suggested by the patristic notion that death by martyrdom was like baptism, in that it too brought remission of sins. This idea is found nowhere in the N.T. (7) Origen, even while struggling to relate Mk. 10[39, 40] to a " baptism of blood," regards John's banishment to Patmos and James' exccution by Herod as equally fulfilments of Christ's saying that they would drink His cup and be baptized with His baptism.[2] (8) The plain meaning of Mk. 10[39, 40] is that they should both endure tribulation and pain even as He was enduring it; and so it came to pass.[3]

(III) JOHN THE APOSTLE AND JOHN THE PRESBYTER

In the preceding section (II) of this chapter we have reached the conclusion that the evidence alleged in favour of the martyrdom of John the apostle by Jews is worthless. We continue to follow the tradition of the second century, that he died in

---

[1] See Field, Hexapla, in loc.   [2] Comm. in Matt. tom. xvi. 6.
[3] I have treated Mk. 10[39, 40] more fully in J.T.S., Apr. 1927.

extreme old age at Ephesus, where he was buried. The first allusion to his long life is found in the Appendix to the Fourth Gospel (Jn. 21$^{21-24}$), a passage which is harmonious with the earliest tradition.

There is no doubt as to the belief of the second century, which was followed by all Christendom, that John the apostle was the *author* of the Fourth Gospel, at any rate in the sense that his apostolic witness was behind it. Papias, Irenæus, Clement of Alexandria, Origen, Hippolytus, Tertullian, and others are clear as to this, as we shall see; and most of them ascribed to John the apostle the authorship of the Apocalypse and of the Johannine Epistles as well. We shall examine in detail the evidence of Irenæus, Polycrates, and Papias, as much depends on the precise words which they use. We shall find ourselves compelled by Papias to recognise the existence of two Johns, both of whom lived at Ephesus at the end of the first century; although the literature of the second century, outside Papias, betrays no knowledge of that.

The evidence of second-century writers cannot be interpreted until we have apprehended the meanings which they attach to the words *apostle, presbyter, disciple.* Most of our evidence as to this terminology must come from Irenæus, as little is extant of the writings of Papias and Polycrates, while Justin has not much to tell about John.

A. IRENÆUS

The term " apostles " stands primarily for the Twelve, Paul also being an apostle (cf. Justin, *Dial.* 81, Irenæus, *Hær.* iii. 13. 1, iv. 21. 1). As in Acts 1^{22}, 1 Cor. 9^1, the essential condition is that an " apostle " has " seen the Lord," and can therefore give his testimony at first hand. Clement of Alexandria speaks of Barnabas as an ἀπόστολος (*Strom.* ii. 6), while in another place (*Strom.* ii. 20) he calls him ἀποστολικός, as a companion of apostles. Tertullian distinguishes *apostolici* from *apostoli* in the same way (*de Præscr.* 32, *adv. Marc.* iv. 2).

As in Acts 15$^{4. 22}$, the distinction between ἀπόστολοι and πρεσβύτεροι is clearly marked, the *apostles* being the original leaders, while the *presbyters* were those who carried on their work. Irenæus uses the term πρεσβύτεροι to designate those who, whether officially or unofficially, had succeeded to the position of leadership which the apostles held. Thus " quapropter eis qui in ecclesia sunt, presbyteris obaudire oportet, his qui successionem habent ab apostolis " (iv. 26. 2); οἱ πρεσβύτεροι τῶν ἀποστόλων μαθηταί (v. 5. 1); " presbyteri qui Ioannem discipulum domini uiderunt " (v. 33. 3); " dicunt

presbyteri apostolorum discipuli," etc. (v. 36. 2; cf. *Demonstr.*
§ 3). Again, the term πρεσβύτερος is sometimes used by
Irenæus of men of the *third* Christian generation: " quemad-
modum audiui a quodam presbytero, qui audierat ab his qui
apostolos uiderant et ab his qui didicerant " (iv. 27. 1). That
is to say, presbyters are either disciples of apostles, or disciples
of *their* disciples; they are the leaders of the Church in the
second and third generations. There is no example, in the
literature of the second century, of the equation πρεσβύτεροι =
ἀπόστολοι.

The term " the Lord's disciples " is used sometimes, as it
is still, in the widest sense. Those who leave all and follow
Jesus are thus described by Irenæus (iv. 8. 3), while the phrase
discipuli Christi is used more generally still (v. 22. 1). But
the term is also applied in a stricter sense to those who were
among the *first* disciples, a circle including, but wider than,
that of the Twelve. Thus Irenæus in one place distinguishes
the " apostles " from the " disciples of the Lord." Commenting on Acts 4²⁴ᶠ· he says, αὗται φωναὶ τῆς ἐκκλησίας . . .
αὗται φωναὶ τῶν ἀποστόλων, αὗται φωναὶ τῶν μαθητῶν τοῦ
κυρίου (iii. 12. 5). Among the company present on that
occasion were others besides the Twelve, and " the disciples of
the Lord " would have included those who were μαθηταί
although not of the inner circle. Some of these early disciples,
including some who had actually seen and heard Jesus in the
flesh, may well have outlived the original apostles; and
" Aristion and the presbyter John " are described by Papias
as οἱ τοῦ κυρίου μαθηταί, some of the apostles being described
by him in the same way. To this passage from Papias we
shall return presently (p. lii).

We must collect now what Irenæus says about John (as
distinct from John the Baptist). The title " the disciple of
the Lord " in the singular is applied by Irenæus to *no* one but
John; and he speaks a dozen times of " John the disciple of the
Lord." *E.g.* this is the designation of the author of the Prologue to the Gospel (i. 8. 5, ii. 2. 5, iii. 11. 1. 3), as of the author
of the Gospel itself (ii. 22. 3, iii. 16. 5), Jn. 2²³ and 20³¹ being
quoted. Irenæus is explicit about this (iii. 1. 1): Ἰωάννης ὁ
μαθητὴς τοῦ κυρίου ὁ καὶ ἐπὶ τὸ στῆθος αὐτοῦ ἀναπεσών, καὶ
αὐτὸς ἐξέδωκε τὸ εὐαγγέλιον, ἐν Ἐφέσῳ τῆς Ἀσίας διατρίβων.
In this passage " John the disciple of the Lord " is he who
" lay on His breast," and " gave out " the Gospel at Ephesus,
the verb ἐξέδωκε being used rather than ἔγραψε.[1] Irenæus
also mentions John the disciple of the Lord as the author of
Epp. I. and II. (i. 16. 3, iii. 16. 5); and as the seer of the

[1] See p. lix below.

Apocalypse, the vision being seen towards the end of Domitian's reign (iv. 30. 4, v. 26. 1, 30. 3). He cites Papias as his authority for a Chiliastic prophecy, introducing it in the words " the presbyters, who saw John the disciple of the Lord, relate that they had heard from him how the Lord used to teach concerning those times and to say," etc. (v. 33. 3); and adding at the end, ταῦτα δὲ καὶ Παπίας, Ἰωάννου μὲν ἀκουστής, Πολυκάρπου δὲ ἑταῖρος γεγονώς, ἀρχαῖος ἀνήρ, ἐγγράφως ἐπιμαρτυρεῖ κτλ. (v. 33. 4). Thus the habit of Irenæus is to describe the Beloved Disciple as " John, the disciple of the Lord," as if he were pre-eminently entitled to that designation. He explicitly names him as the author of Gospel, First and Second Epistle, and Apocalypse.

Finally, for Irenæus, John was an *apostle*. Having cited the language of the Prologue, which he ascribes to John, he notes: ὅτι δὲ οὐ περὶ τῶν συζυγιῶν αὐτῶν ὁ ἀπόστολος εἴρηκεν (i. 9. 2). Again, mentioning a tradition handed on by John the disciple of the Lord to " all the presbyters who had intercourse " with him in Asia, he adds that these presbyters had the tradition not only from John, but from other *apostles* (ii. 22. 5). So again: " the Church in Ephesus founded by Paul, John remaining with them until the times of Trajan, is a true witness of the tradition of the *apostles* " (iii. 3. 4). And, speaking of Polycarp's observance of Easter, Irenæus adds that Polycarp followed the custom of " John the disciple of our Lord, and of *other apostles* with whom he had associated " (Eusebius, *H.E.* v. 24. 16), explaining in another place that John was one of those who had seen the Lord (Eus. *H.E.* v. 20. 6).

We have already seen that *apostle* for Irenæus (as for other writers) means one of the Twelve, or some one of similar status, such as Paul. Hence to call John the disciple of the Lord an " apostle " means that he is to be identified with John the son of Zebedee. And Irenæus makes no attempt to distinguish two Johns. He mentions the early preaching of Peter and John (iii. 12. 3, " Petrus cum Iohanne "), and describes it as the teaching of *apostoli* (iii. 12. 4). " The apostles whom the Lord made witnesses of every action and every doctrine " included " Peter and James and John " who were everywhere present with Him (iii. 12. 15; cf. also iii. 21. 3).

Irenæus became bishop of Lyons about 177 A.D., and his great work on *Heresies* was written about 180. He tells in his Letter to Florinus (Eus. *H.E.* v. 20) that when a boy he had often seen Polycarp, bishop of Smyrna (born about 70 A.D., martyred in 155), who had been a disciple of John, and who used to tell what he had heard from him and other apostles

about our Lord. Irenæus was born about 130, and lived until
201 or thereabouts, having left Asia Minor for Rome and
the West not later than 155.[1] It is difficult to suppose that he
had misunderstood what Polycarp had been accustomed to
tell about John, or that Polycarp could have been mistaken
as to the career of John the apostle. Irenæus tells the story
of John's horror of Cerinthus and his doctrine (iii. 3. 4) on
Polycarp's authority, although he does not say that he got it
directly from him. He alleges in another place (iii. 11. 1) that
John's purpose in his Gospel (*per euangelii annuntiationem*),
and especially in the Prologue, was to combat the heretical
teaching of Cerinthus.

Irenæus, then, only knows of one John at Ephesus, whom
he speaks of as John the Beloved Disciple and an apostle; he
regards him as the author of the Gospel and the Apocalypse,
as well as of Epp. I. II.

B. POLYCRATES

We possess part of a letter written by Polycrates, bishop of
Ephesus, to Pope Victor, about 190 A.D., on the subject of the
observance of Easter.[2] Polycrates defends the Quartodeciman
practice,[3] not only as " in accordance with the Gospel," but
because it was the tradition of the Church in Asia Minor.
Accordingly, he begins by naming " the great lights " (μεγάλα
στοιχεῖα) of that Church, viz. Philip the apostle and his
daughters,[4] John, Polycarp, Thraseas, Sagaris, Papeirius,

---

[1] See, for details, Lipsius in *Dict. Chr. Biogr.*, iii. 253 f.

[2] Cf. Eusebius (*H.E.* iii. 31, v. 24).

[3] Apparently the Asian Quartodecimans celebrated Easter on
Nisan 14 (the day of the Jewish Passover), irrespective of the day of
the week, while the Western Church had the celebration on the Sunday,
irrespective of the day of the month. But the arguments by which
the Quartodecimans supported their practice are not very clear. If
it was because they celebrated, in particular, the Institution of the
Eucharist, and held that this was at a Passover meal, of which Jesus
partook, then they would seem to follow the Synoptic chronology
(see p. cvi). If, however, the stress was laid on Jesus being Himself
the true Paschal Lamb, they relied on the Fourth Gospel. But the
probability is that what was intended by all Christians on Easter Day
was to commemorate the Redemption of Christ generally, which
included the Last Supper, the Crucifixion, and the Resurrection alike.
No conclusive argument for or against their reliance on the Fourth
Gospel can be built on their practice as to the day of the month. See
Stanton, *The Gospels as Historical Documents*, i. pp. 173–197, for an
admirable account of the matter.

[4] Polycrates has been thought to have confused Philip the apostle
with Philip the evangelist, but of this there is neither evidence nor
probability.

d

and Melito as eminent persons whose example should command respect in the matter of Easter observance.

Philip's memory was revered at Hierapolis, where he died (cf. *Acts of Philip*, §§ 107, 139). He is not called μάρτυς, nor is there any early tradition that he died by violence (cf. Clem. Alex. *Strom.* iv. 9).

Polycarp of Smyrna, Thraseas of Eumenia, and Sagaris are briefly described in the same way, viz. ἐπίσκοπος καὶ μάρτυς, the two first being buried at Smyrna and the last-named at Laodicea. On Papeirius the Blessed and Melito of Sardis we need not delay. Melito had written a book relating to Quartodecimanism.

Polycrates, however, has something more to say of John, who is mentioned immediately after Philip: [1] Ἰωάννης ὁ ἐπὶ τὸ στῆθος τοῦ κυρίου ἀναπεσών, ὃς ἐγενήθη ἱερεὺς τὸ πέταλόν πεφορεκώς, καὶ μάρτυς καὶ διδάσκαλος· οὗτος ἐν Ἐφέσῳ κεκοίμηται. Like Irenæus (iii. 1. 1), Polycrates describes John by quoting *verbatim* Jn. 13²⁵, viz. ἀναπεσὼν ἐπὶ τὸ στῆθος [τοῦ Ἰησοῦ], thus identifying him with the Beloved Disciple. He, as bishop of Ephesus, is an even weightier authority than Irenæus, when he associates John's last years with that city.

By Polycrates John is called μάρτυς. We have already examined and set aside the idea that John the apostle came to his death by martyrdom at the hands of the Jews in early days (p. xxxviii f.). But Polycrates cannot mean that John the apostle was μάρτυς in this sense, for, if that were so, he would have had no connexion with the Church of Ephesus, and he could not have been cited as one of the great lights of the Church in Asia Minor. And if it be suggested that Polycrates has here in mind some other John, it must be rejoined that no one with that name is known to the tradition of the first or second century (or even later) as having come to a violent end at Ephesus because of his Christian profession.

Further, had Polycrates meant to describe the John to whom he refers as having ended his life by martyrdom, the fact that he was μάρτυς would have been mentioned last, *after* his career as διδάσκαλος had been noted. In the cases of Polycarp and the rest, ἐπίσκοπος καὶ μάρτυς is the description of their Christian course. They were bishops *before* they were martyrs, and to have written μάρτυς καὶ ἐπίσκοπος would have been both clumsy and ambiguous.

It is clear, then, that μάρτυς as applied to John of Ephesus by Polycrates must mean " witness " or " confessor " rather than " martyr." We have already referred to the description

[1] Not as a less important person than Philip, but because he came to Asia Minor later than Philip.

of John in later literature as a "martyr," the idea going back
to Rev. 1⁹ (see p. xliv). But the famous person to whom Polycrates refers, viz. the Beloved Disciple, is specially noted in the
Fourth Gospel for his μαρτυρία. " This is the disciple which
beareth witness (μαρτυρίαν) of these things . . . and we know
that his witness is true " (Jn. 21²⁴). It was because of the
value of his μαρτυρία that the recollections of John were regarded with such veneration, and were certified as authentic
by the Ephesian Church when the Fourth Gospel was first
published. He was the witness to whom solemn appeal is also
made at Jn. 19³⁵ (cf. 3 Jn. 12). To the Ephesian Church,
where this Gospel was first put forth, John the Beloved Disciple,
as the final authority for the facts which it records, was pre-
eminently μάρτυς after a fashion that no other Ephesian
Christian could ever be.

Polycrates also calls John of Ephesus διδάσκαλος. This
is a title which might fitly be used of any Christian teacher.[1]
But it is perhaps significant that the second-century Acts of
John have preserved this title as applied to John the apostle.[2]
In § 37 Andronicus is made to say of him, ὁπόταν ὁ διδάσκαλος
θέλῃ, τότε πορευθῶμεν (cf. also § 73). It does not appear that
any other apostle is described in the apocryphal Acta, or elsewhere, as ὁ διδάσκαλος, " the Teacher," par excellence.[3]

Like Irenæus, Polycrates does not suggest that there were
two eminent Christian leaders called John in Ephesus at the
end of the first century. Had there been a second John of
such wide reputation that his name and position were known
and respected at Rome, we should have expected the bishop of
Ephesus to include him also among the " great lights," whom
he mentions in his letter to Pope Victor. It does not follow,
however, that Polycrates had never heard of a second John.
That might be true of Irenæus, but the traditions of the see of
Ephesus could not have been unknown to its bishop. All that
can be inferred from the language of Polycrates is that, if
there were at Ephesus in the first century a John other than
John the Beloved Disciple, he was not adduced as an authority
on the Paschal controversy.

An argument based on silence is generally precarious.
In this instance, Polycrates does not mention at all the name of
Claudius Apollinaris of Hierapolis, who took an active part

---

[1] Jülicher (Introd. to N.T., p. 406) explains " Witness " and
" Teacher " as allusive respectively to the Apocalypse and the Epistles.
[2] The fifth-century Acta Joannis, ascribed to Prochorus, give the
same title : ὁ διδάσκαλος ἡμῶν (p. 164 ed. Zahn ; cf. pp. 152, 159).
[3] For the statement of Polycrates that the Beloved Disciple wore
the priestly frontlet, see Additional Note on Jn. 18¹⁵.

at Laodicea in supporting the Quartodeciman practice, about the year 165, and wrote on the subject. It could not be argued that Polycrates did not know of him, although it is not clear why he does not name him as one of the " great lights " of Asia.[1] Equally, we must not infer that he did not know of a second John, whose existence, as we shall see, Papias had mentioned (p. liii) half a century before.

So, too, Polycrates does not speak (at least in the extant fragment) of John the Beloved Disciple as the actual writer of the Fourth Gospel. It is remarkable that Polycrates does not adduce as a notable honour to Asia Minor the fact that the Fourth Gospel was produced there ; but, again, no argument built on omissions of this kind can be conclusive. To the fact, however, we shall return presently.

C. PAPIAS

Papias, who was bishop of Hierapolis in Phrygia, was born about A.D. 70, and died about 146, being thus of the generation preceding Irenæus. A fragment of his λογίων κυριακῶν ἐξηγήσεις tells of the sources from which he gathered information as to Christian origins: " I shall not hesitate to add whatever at any time I learnt well from the presbyters (παρὰ τῶν πρεσβυτέρων καλῶς ἔμαθον). . . . If I met anywhere with any one who had been a follower of the presbyters, I used to inquire [2] what the presbyters had told (τοὺς τῶν πρεσβυτέρων ἀνέκρινον λόγους); (viz.) what Andrew or Peter said (εἶπεν), or Philip or Thomas or James or John or Matthew, or any other of the Lord's disciples ; and also what Aristion and the presbyter John (ὁ πρεσβύτερος Ἰωάννης), the Lord's disciples, say (λέγουσιν). For I did not expect to gain so much from books as from a living and abiding voice " [3] (Eus. H.E. iii. 39).

(a) The opening sentence claims for Papias that he had had opportunity of learning directly from πρεσβύτεροι, i.e. from followers of the apostles. Papias was hardly of an age to begin collecting information until the year 90 or 85 at earliest. The only apostle alive at that time was John, and Papias might, indeed, as a man of twenty, have heard him speak. Irenæus calls Papias Ἰωάννου ἀκουστής (v. 33. 4), which means that Irenæus believed him to have been a hearer of John the apostle

---

[1] It is possible that Apollinaris was alive at the time of writing, and that Polycrates only cites the authority of those who had passed away.

[2] The Syriac translation (ed. Wright and M'Lean, 1898) has " Neither did I compare," which makes havoc of the sense.

[3] It was probably from traditions of this kind that the story of the adulterous woman was derived.

(see p. xlviii). But Papias does not say so, as Eusebius (*H.E.* iii. 39. 2) is careful to point out. πρεσβύτεροι in the opening sentence does not stand for ἀπόστολοι (and it never does so, see p. xlvii above), but for those who were followers of the apostles, Christians of the second generation. Such men as these Papias had naturally met and conversed with, although he was probably younger than they.

(*b*) He proceeds to say that he had also seized every opportunity of making inquiry of *their* followers (*i.e.* Christians of the third generation) as to anything they could report about the sayings of *apostles*, viz. Peter, John, and the rest. And (*c*) Papias had sought to find out what sayings were ascribed to two of the disciples of the Lord, still living at the time when he made his inquiries, viz. Aristion and the presbyter John. That is, Papias speaks of Aristion and the presbyter John as the last survivors of the presbyters who were successors of the apostles, being indeed themselves " disciples of the Lord." [1] Of the outer circle of the original μαθηταί, some of the younger people must have survived the original Twelve. Themselves in time reckoned as presbyters, and being specially respected in the next generation as those who had seen Jesus in the flesh, some who were only boys at the Crucifixion, lived on as younger contemporaries of the apostles. There would be nothing surprising if one or two of these survived until Papias had reached full manhood, and were able to tell (although Papias only learnt from hearsay what they told) of the sayings of some of the Twelve, *e.g.* of John the apostle.

Eusebius (iii. 39. 7) reports that " Papias says that he was himself a hearer of Aristion and the presbyter John." This does not appear from the passage cited, and Eusebius seems to have been uncertain about it, for he adds : " At least (γοῦν) he mentions them frequently by name, and gives their traditions in his writings " (cf. iii. 39. 7, 14). That is a different matter, and there is nothing to discredit it. Of the John who is mentioned first by Papias, along with Peter and the rest, Eusebius says that Papias clearly identified him with the evangelist ; and he adds later in the chapter (iii. 39. 17) that Papias had " used testimonies " from the first Epistle of John. [2]

Eusebius is, in our view, right in holding that Papias distinguished the apostle John from " the presbyter John."

---

[1] Bacon, *The Fourth Gospel*, p. 112, would emend οἱ τοῦ κυρίου μαθηταί here to οἱ τούτων μαθηταί. Larfeld (*Die beiden Johan. von Ephesus*) would read οἱ τοῦ Ἰωάννου μαθηταί. But the emendations are unnecessary when the general usage of the phrase " the disciples of the Lord " has been apprehended. See above, p. xlvii.

[2] See p. lxxii.

For the sayings of the first John, Papias apparently had to make inquiry at a time when John had passed away ; but for the sayings of the second John he was able to inquire while John was yet alive. In both cases his informants were the followers of the presbyters who had succeeded the apostles. It is implied that the apostle John died before the presbyter John. Probably the former lived to a great age, as Irenæus implies (cf. p. xlviii) ; but that a yet younger disciple of Jesus, who may only have been a child during his Master's public ministry, outlived the aged apostle is in no way improbable.

Another passage from the ἐξηγήσεις of Papias, quoted by Eusebius (*H.E.* iii. 39. 15) begins with the words καὶ τοῦτο ὁ πρεσβύτερος ἔλεγε κτλ. Here the context in Eusebius shows that ὁ πρεσβύτερος is none other than John the presbyter, some of whose traditions Papias had received. That is, the designation ὁ πρεσβύτερος is treated as sufficiently identifying John the presbyter, although his name is not given. To this we shall return (see p. lxiii).

We conclude that Papias knew of the presbyter John, as distinguished from his older namesake, the apostle John.[1]

D

No writer for a hundred years after Papias seems to have supported the tradition that more than one John had to be reckoned with. Dionysius of Alexandria (250 A.D.) distinguished two Johns, but he reached this conclusion on critical grounds, as a modern scholar would do. Observing that the style of the Apocalypse differs from that of the Gospel and Epistles,[2] he claimed the apostle John as the author only of the latter, while the other John (whom he does not call the πρεσβύτερος) was held by him to be the seer of the Apocalypse.[3] In confirmation of this he says that he had heard of two monuments at Ephesus, each bearing the name of John. Eusebius takes up this idea from Dionysius, and mentions it [4] as corroborating the existence of two Johns which he had noted in the work of Papias.

It will be convenient at this point to summarise what is said about John by other writers before the time of Dionysius. For none of them is there a Johannine problem.

Clement of Alexandria (fl. 190–200) does not mention a

---

[1] The distinction has often been challenged, *e.g.* by Zahn (*Einleit.*, ii. 217 f.), Salmon (*Dict. Christ. Biogr.*, iii. 401), Chapman (*John the Presbyter*, p. 28 f.), and Lawlor (*Hermathena*, 1922, p. 205 f.).

[2] Cf. p. lxv below.   [3] Eusebius, *H.E.* vii. 25

[4] *H.E.* iii. 39. 6.

second John. As to the son of Zebedee, he is unambiguous. The apostle John, " when on the tyrant's death he returned to Ephesus from the isle of Patmos, went away to the neighbouring districts to appoint bishops to set in order whole churches and to ordain " (*Quis diues saluetur*, § 42). As to the composition of the gospels, Eusebius preserves (*H.E.* vi. 14. 7) a tradition recorded by Clement : " Last of all, John, perceiving that the external facts (τὰ σωματικά) had been made plain in the gospels, being urged by his friends and inspired by the Spirit, composed a *spiritual gospel*." This he cites (*Pæd.* i. 6. 38) as the " Gospel according to John," and quotes as well the Apocalypse (*Strom.* vi. 13) and Epistle I. (*Strom.* iv. 16) as the work of John.

Origen (fl. 210–250), who was Clement's pupil, says that John the Beloved Disciple wrote both Gospel and Apocalypse (*Comm.* 438, Eus. *H.E.* vi. 25. 9), and in another place expressly ascribes the Apocalypse to John the son of Zebedee (*Comm.* 16). He notes (Eus. *l.c.*) that, while John wrote the first Epistle, it is not universally admitted that he wrote the second and third. He tells elsewhere that the emperor (probably Domitian) banished John to Patmos.[1]

The Gnostic *Acta Iohannis* (second century) in like manner speak of John as an apostle and the brother of *James* (§ 88), also as the Beloved Disciple (§ 89); these *Acta* tell of John's residence at Ephesus (§ 18), and use language which betrays knowledge of the Fourth Gospel (§§ 97, 98).

In the West, the tradition is the same. On the Chair of Hippolytus (fl. 190–230) both the Gospel and Apocalypse are ascribed to John, whom Hippolytus describes (ed. Lagarde, p. 17) as at once ἀπόστολος καὶ μαθητὴς τοῦ κυρίου.

Tertullian (c. 208) ascribes Gospel, the first Epistle, and the Apocalypse to the apostle John (*adv. Marc.* iii. 14, iv. 5, v. 16), and describes the churches of Asia (cf. Rev. 2, 3) as John's *alumnas ecclesias*.

None of these writers mentions a second John, except Papias.

(iv) The Muratorian Fragment and the Latin Prefaces on the Authorship of the Gospel

We have seen that, with the important exception of Papias, no Christian writer before 250 A.D. mentions the presbyter John as a person distinct from the apostle John; and also that the apostolic authorship of the Fourth Gospel and the Apocalypse was accepted without argument by Irenæus, Hippolytus,

---

[1] Comm. *in Matt.* tom. **xvi**. 6.

Clement of Alexandria, Tertullian, and Origen. The unanimity of these writers shows how deep-rooted was the early tradition that the Fourth Gospel and the Apocalypse alike were the work of the apostle John. In the case of the Apocalypse this was afterwards challenged on the ground of style by Dionysius of Alexandria about the year 250 (see p. liv above).

But we have now to reckon with the fact that the early traditions as to the way in which the Fourth Gospel was given to the Church do not suggest that it was written by the unassisted pen of John the apostle, although he was reckoned (and, as we hold, correctly) to be its *author* in the sense that it rests upon his authority. These traditions must be examined.

A

The famous *Muratorian Fragment* [1] on the Canon of the N.T. is part of a book produced at Rome about the year 170, perhaps written by Hippolytus. The fragment is in Latin, but Lightfoot held that probably it had originally been written in Greek.[2] It preserves a remarkable story about the composition of the Fourth Gospel. John, *ex discipulis*, wrote the Fourth Gospel. At the instigation of his fellow-disciples and bishops to write, he bade them fast with him for three days, in order that they should relate to each other afterwards whatever revelation they had received. It was revealed to the apostle Andrew that, with the revision of all (*recognoscentibus cunctis*), John should describe all things in his own name. " . . . What wonder is it that John brings forward details with so much emphasis in his epistles . . .," 1 Jn. 1[1] being then cited. " For so he professes that he was not only a spectator (*uisorem*), but also a hearer (*auditorem*), and moreover a writer (*scriptorem*) of all the wonders of the Lord in order." Later on, the Fragment mentions among the canonical epistles two of John (*superscripti Johannis duas*). The author also names the Apocalypses of John and Peter as received by him, although some were unwilling that they should be read in church.

The circumstantial story about the composition of the Fourth Gospel cannot be historically exact. That the apostle Andrew (and apparently the other apostles as well) lived up to the time when the Gospel was produced is inconsistent with all the evidence on the subject. But that others besides the

---

[1] Printed in Routh, *Reliq. Sacr.*, i. 394, in Westcott, *Canon of N.T.*, p. 523, and elsewhere.
[2] Lightfoot, *Clement*, ii. 408.

apostle John were concerned in the publication of the Gospel at Ephesus is probable, and, as we shall see, is a tradition that appears elsewhere.   The sentence, "ut recognoscentibus cunctis Iohannes suo nomine cuncta describeret," does not give the whole credit of authorship to John, whose name, never-theless, the Gospel bore from the time of its issue.   That John was not only *uisor* and *auditor*, but actually *scriptor*, might be taken to lay stress on his being the *penman*, as well as the *witness*, of what is narrated.   But, as we have urged in the note on Jn. 21^{24}, γράψας in that passage does not necessarily mean more than "dictated to a scribe."

B

Mention must next be made of the well-known Latin Preface to the Vulgate text of Jn.[1]   Here tradition again re-produces the belief that *Johannes euangelista unus ex discipulis dei* wrote the Gospel in Asia after the Apocalypse had been written in Patmos, and his death is thus described: " Hic est Johannes qui sciens superuenisse diem recessus sui, conuocatis discipulis suis in Epheso, per multa signorum experimenta promens Christum, descendens in defossum sepulturae locum facta oratione positus est ad patres suos, tam extraneus a dolore mortis quam a corruptione carnis inuenitur alienus." This goes back to the second-century *Acts of John*, where it is told at greater length (§§ 111–115). The legend that John's body did not taste corruption, but that the earth used to tremble over his grave as if he were breathing, is mentioned by Augustine (*in Jn.* 21) as held by some.

In this Preface (and the corresponding prefaces to the Synoptic Gospels) Corssen[2] has found traces of Monarch-ianism. The phrase *discipulus dei* for *discipulus domini* is significant ; and special stress is laid on the virginity of John. The Preface, as originally written, implies that St. John's Gospel came next after St. Matthew's in the accepted order of the books ; *i.e.* that the order was Mt., Jn., Lk., Mk.

Here, the expression " conuocatis discipulis suis in Epheso " is to be noted, for although this is not directly connected by the author with the composition of the Gospel, as is the similar phrase in the *Muratorianum*, both go back to some early tradition based on, or interpretative of, Jn. 21^{24}. Corssen ascribes these Monarchian Prefaces to the first quarter of the third century.

---

[1] See Wordsworth-White, *Nov. Test. Lat.*, p. 485.
[2] See his essay in *Texte und Untersuchungen*, xvi. (1896).

C

More important than the Monarchian Prefaces just mentioned, is another Latin Preface to Jn., found in a tenth-century Bible at Toledo,[1] which contains the following passage:

"The apostle John, whom the Lord Jesus loved most, last of all wrote this Gospel, at the request of the bishops of Asia, against Cerinthus and other heretics, and specially against the new dogma of the Ebionites, who say that Christ did not exist before He was born of Mary." Another reason is added for the writing of the Gospel, viz., that the evangelist wished to supply information, lacking in the Synoptic Gospels, as to the first two years of the public ministry of Jesus.

This is found in substance in Jerome's *de uirr. illustr.* § 9, but the Codex Toletanus gives the earlier form. The phrase *postulantibus Asiæ episcopis* recalls the Muratorian tradition.

But the writer goes on: "This Gospel, it is manifest, was written after the Apocalypse, and was given to the churches in Asia by John while he was yet in the body (*adhuc in corpore constituto*); as Papias, bishop of Hierapolis, a disciple of John and dear to him, related in his *Exoterica*, at the end of the five books,[2] viz., he who wrote this Gospel at John's dictation (*Johanne subdictante*)."

This paragraph is also found in a ninth-century Vatican codex.[3] It was apparently translated from the Greek; e.g. *adhuc in corpore constituto* is a rendering of ἔτι ἐν τῷ σώματι καθεστῶτος, as Lightfoot pointed out. That it goes back to an original of the third or fourth century is a reasonable inference. Burkitt holds that we have in the Toletan Preface the earliest known form of the tradition that the Fourth Gospel was dictated by the aged apostle to a disciple.[4]

The idea that Papias was the disciple who wrote the Gospel at John's dictation must be rejected, although it is found at a much later date in a Greek Catena, in the form Ἰωάννης ὑπηγόρευσε τὸ εὐαγγέλιον τῷ ἑαυτοῦ μαθητῇ Παπίᾳ.[5] Corssen suggested that there is some confusion between *Papias* and *Prochorus*, as in the fifth-century *Acta* (quite distinct from the second-century Gnostic *Acta*). Prochorus, a disciple of

---

[1] See Wordsworth-White, *l.c.* p. 490, and cf. Burkitt, *Two Lectures on the Gospels*, p. 90 f.

[2] *In Exotericis suis, id est in extremis quinque libris.* Lightfoot (*Supernat. Religion*, p. 213) proposed to read *exegeticis* and *externis*, and a similar emendation is given by Corssen (*exegeticis, extraneis*), *l.c.* p. 114.

[3] Quoted by Wordsworth-White, *l.c.* p. 491.

[4] *L.c.* p. 94.

[5] Cf. Corssen, *l.c.* p. 116, and Burkitt, *l.c.* p. 68.

John, claims that John dictated [1] the Gospel to him at Patmos not long before his death at Ephesus, adding that fair parchment had to be obtained that a faii copy might be made (εἰς καθαρογραφίαν τοῦ ἁγίου εὐαγγελίου).[2]

No one accepts this as historical, whether it applies to Papias (see p. lviii) or Prochorus. But we note once more the widely current tradition that the Gospel was not written by John's own hand, but that it was dictated to a disciple. We have already seen that the *Muratorianum* has the curious clause that the Gospel was ultimately to be produced *in the name* of John (*suo nomine*), others apparently having had some share in its production. Further, the expression of the Toletan Preface that the Gospel *datum est ecclesiis in Asia* recalls the careful phrase of Irenæus, ἐξέδωκε τὸ εὐαγγέλιον ἐν Ἐφέσῳ, to which attention has already been drawn.[3] The writer of the Preface, like Irenæus, was satisfied that the ultimate author of the Gospel was John the apostle, the Beloved Disciple; and he also, again like Irenæus, regards Papias as a hearer of John, while he exaggerates this by calling him a *carus discipulus* (if indeed the text is not corrupt). The language of Irenæus as to John's authorship of the Gospel, while it is more definite than that of Polycrates, who will only say that John was the μάρτυς behind it (p. l), suggests something less than that John wrote it with his own hand, and is entirely consistent with the view that a disciple had a share in the writing of it out. The apostle John was ultimately responsible for it, ἐξέδωκε τὸ εὐαγγέλιον: but it may have been written by another's pen.

This last conclusion is supported, so far, by direct statements of Christian tradition and by some phrases of Polycrates and Irenæus. But, as we have seen (p. li), there are traces in the Gospel itself of the writer as distinct from the person whose testimony is behind the narrative. Jn. 19[35] and 21[24] (see notes *in loc.*) clearly distinguish the writer from the witness. The language, in particular, of 19[35] is emphatic as to this. The evangelist appeals to the testimony of an eye-witness, and he does not suggest at all that he himself saw the incident which he describes. We are, then, in a position to examine the Epistles and the Apocalypse with a view to determine, first, if they are all written by the same hand; and secondly, if there is any hint of the person whom Papias calls John the presbyter having a share in the authorship of any of these books.

---

[1] A frontispiece to Jn. in Cod. i (twelfth cent.) represents John dictating to Prochorus the Deacon.

[2] Zahn, *Acta Ioannis*, p. 154 f.

[3] Cf. p. xlvii.

(v) The Gospel and the Johannine Epistles were written by John the Presbyter

A. THE FIRST EPISTLE

The Church has been accustomed to describe 1 Jn. as a " general " or " catholic " epistle, its appeal being applicable to all Christians alike. It does not mention any individuals, nor does it allude to any historical incident, except the supreme event of the Incarnation. This epistle, however, seems to have been intended in the first instance for the edification of a group of Christians or of Churches, with whom the writer was associated so intimately that he could call them " my little children." He speaks of himself as one who had been a personal witness of the life of Jesus ($1^{1. 2}$); and this, apart from his long Christian experience, gave him a claim to write with authority on the Christian life. He was one of those whom the next generation described as a μαθητὴς τοῦ κυρίου.

This Epistle is so closely allied with the Fourth Gospel, alike in its doctrine and its phraseology, that internal evidence confirms the traditional belief that it is written by the same hand that wrote the Gospel.[1]

The two works proceed from the same theological environment, and (omitting the narrative portions of the Gospel) deal with the same themes. The doctrines of Eternal Life, of the mutual indwelling of God and man, of Christian believers as the children of God, begotten with a spiritual begetting, of the Love of God and love of the brethren, of the Son of God as come in the flesh, are specially characteristic of both books. In both, Jesus is the " Saviour of the world " and the " Only begotten Son " of God.

The opening sentences of 1 Jn. form a prologue to the Epistle, similar in several respects to the prologue to the Gospel. Thus we have in 1 Jn. 1^{1-3}, ὃ ἦν ἀπ' ἀρχῆς, ὃ ἀκηκόαμεν, ὃ ἑωράκαμεν τοῖς ὀφθαλμοῖς ἡμῶν, ὃ ἐθεασάμεθα καὶ αἱ χεῖρες ἡμῶν ἐψηλάφησαν, περὶ τοῦ λόγου τῆς ζωῆς—καὶ ἡ ζωὴ ἐφανερώθη κτλ.—ἀπαγγέλλομεν καὶ ὑμῖν. ὁ λόγος τῆς ζωῆς is equivalent to " the Word who gives Life " or " the Word who has life in Himself " (see on 6^{35} for parallel phrases). This is exactly the conception of ὁ λόγος set out in Jn. 1^4

---

[1] Holtzmann and Pfleiderer do not accept this. But the unity of authorship is upheld by the majority of critics, e.g. Jülicher, Wrede, Harnack, E. A. Abbott, as well as by more conservative scholars. Dionysius of Alexandria was the first to argue the matter, and the reasons which he produced for the unity of authorship are still convincing (Eus. H.E. vii. 25).

(where see note). ἀπ' ἀρχῆς does *not* refer here to the beginning of the Incarnate Life or of the public ministry of Jesus (as at Jn. 15²⁷, where see note), but to the eternal and prehistoric origins of that life (as at Jn. 8⁴⁴ ; cf. 1 Jn. 2¹³·¹⁴ 3⁸). Here, again, we go back to ἐν ἀρχῇ ἦν ὁ λόγος (Jn. 1¹). ἐθεασάμεθα is the verb used (Jn. 1¹⁴) of actual bodily seeing, and ἐφανερώθη is the right word for the manifestation on earth of the Life of the Word (see on Jn. 1⁴). "That which was in being eternally, that which we have seen with our own eyes and touched with our own hands of the Word of Life, the Life which was made manifest in the flesh—*that* we declare to you." [1]

In this preface, the writer of the Epistle, while he does not offer any personal witness as to the historical incidents of the ministry of Jesus, claims to have seen Him in the flesh, just as the writer of the Prologue to the Gospel does: ἐθεασάμεθα τὴν δόξαν αὐτοῦ (1¹⁴, where see note). The use of the first person plur. for testimony to the broad facts of Christian experience appears both in the Gospel (1¹⁴ 3¹¹, where see note) and in the Epistle (1 Jn. 4¹⁴); while in the body of the Epistle, the personal relation of the writer to his correspondents is shown by the frequent use of " I," as contrasted with " you."

The number of verbal coincidences between the Gospel and Epistle is very large. Lists have been printed by Holtzmann, and also by R. Law,[2] and need not be reproduced here. The similarity extends to grammar as well as to choice of words and of phrases; cf., *e.g.*, the elliptic use of ἀλλ' ἵνα (Jn. 9³, 1 Jn. 2¹⁹), the emphatic use of πᾶς ὁ with a pres. part. (Jn. 3¹⁶, 1 Jn. 3⁴·⁶·¹⁰), the collective use of πᾶν ὅ (Jn. 6³⁷, 1 Jn. 5⁴). ἐκεῖνος is used sometimes of Christ as the main subject of the sentence, as it is in the Gospel (see on 1⁸). The constr. πιστεύειν εἰς (see on 1¹²), frequent in the Gospel, is found also in 1 Jn. 5¹⁰·¹³. There are, indeed, some differences, especially in the use of particles. οὖν, so frequently expressing historical transition in the Gospel (see on 1²²), does not appear in the Epistle, which is not a narrative. δέ, which is found 212 times in the Gospel, very often in dialogue, is only used 8 times in the Epistle.[3] But, on the whole, the linguistic similarities are far more striking than the divergences.

The Epistle probably is a little later in date than the Gospel, the characteristic doctrines of which reappear occasionally in a slightly modified form. In both books the spiritual presence

---

[1] For a trenchant criticism of Westcott's exegesis of 1 Jn. 1¹, see R. Law, *The Tests of Life*, pp. 43, 354.
[2] *L.c.* pp. 341 ff. See also Brooke, *The Epp. of St. John* (pp. ii ff.).
[3] Cf. Law, *l.c.* pp. 346 ff., for some divergences of style ; and see Moffatt, *Introd.*, p. 590 f.

of Christ with His people is taught, as in both Eternal Life is at once a present reality and a future hope.[1]   In both, again, judgment is a present fact, as well as a κρίσις of the future, which was its significance for Judaism (cf. Jn. 5[28. 29]).   But the Epistle (4[17]) lays more stress on the judgment of the future than the Gospel does; to the writer in his later work it seems as if Antichrist has come already (4[3]), and that " the last hour " is at hand (2[18. 22]).   In the Gospel (cf. 14[3]) as well as in the Epistle (2[28]), the Parousia or Second Coming of the Lord is contemplated; but there is a difference of emphasis.

In the Epistle, the controversies with Judaism, with which the narrative of the Gospel has much to do, have dropped out of sight; and Gnosticism, only hinted at in the earlier work, has come into full view as the most formidable opponent of the Christian religion (1 Jn. 4[2]).   The necessities of the case prompt a fuller (although not a deeper) treatment of *sin* and of the atoning and cleansing efficacy of the Passion of Christ than is found in the Gospel.   Cf. 1 Jn. 1[8]–2[2] 3[4-9] 4[10] with Jn. 1[29] 8[24] 16[8].   It is implied, but not asserted, in the Gospel (14[16]) that Jesus is the first Paraclete, the Spirit being " another " whom He will send; but Jesus is explicitly described only in 1 Jn. 2[1] as our Paraclete or Advocate with God.

The doctrine of the mutual indwelling of God and man, again, appears in a slightly different form in the Gospel and in the Epistle.   In the Gospel the disciple abides in Christ, and Christ in him (6[56] 15[4f]); but in the Epistle he who has faith in Christ abides in God and God in him (4[15. 16]).   " The Gospel is Christocentric, the Epistle Theocentric." [2]   In the former Christ's own teaching about His Person is reproduced; in the latter its practical significance for the children of God is expounded.

We have elsewhere [3] called attention to the verbal citation by Polycarp of 1 Jn. 4[2. 4] and to the statement of Eusebius that Papias " used testimonies from this Epistle." [4]   The evidence of its acceptance by Irenæus, the Epistle to Diognetus, the Epistle of the Churches of Lyons and Vienne, and Clement of Alexandria, is as clear as is that for the Gospel.

B. THE SECOND AND THIRD EPISTLES

The two short letters, 2 Jn. and 3 Jn., which might each have covered a single sheet of papyrus, are private letters of exhortation; 3 Jn. being addressed to one Gaius, and 2 Jn. either to a Christian lady of position or to a particular Church.

[1] See p. clx.   [2] Cf. Law, *l.c.* p. 355.
[3] P. lxxii.   [4] P. liii.

Origen mentions that they were not accepted by all, and Eusebius says that some placed them among the ἀντιλεγόμενα or controverted books; but their *occasional* character may well have prevented them from being ranked as Canonical Scripture, in some quarters, when the idea of a Canon of the New Testament was being anxiously examined.

That they were written by the same hand that wrote the First Epistle has been often disputed, both in ancient and modern times. But the internal evidence which the three Epistles present of a common author is strong. Thus emphasis is laid on ἀλήθεια (2 Jn.[1, 2], 3 Jn.[8, 12]) and on "walking in the truth " (2 Jn.[4], 3 Jn.[3, 4]); on ἀγάπη (2 Jn.[3], 3 Jn.[6]), which is the love of the brethren, after the "new commandment" of Christ (2 Jn.[5], 3 Jn.[5]); on "abiding" in the teaching of Christ (2 Jn.[9]; cf. Jn. 8[31]); on the joy of Christian disciples being fulfilled (2 Jn.[12]; cf. 1 Jn. 1[4]); on the value of μαρτυρία (3 Jn.[12]); on the confessing that Jesus Christ came in the flesh, as opposed to the doctrine of Antichrist (2 Jn.[7], 1 Jn. 4[2, 3]); on sin forbidding the vision of God (3 Jn.[11], 1 Jn. 3[6]). These are all doctrines and precepts characteristically Johannine.

There are also in 2 and 3 Jn. turns of phrase which recall both Gospel and First Epistle. Cf. 2 Jn.[9] Θεὸν οὐκ ἔχει with 1 Jn. 5[12] ὁ ἔχων τὸν υἱόν : 3 Jn.[12] οἶδας ὅτι ἡ μαρτυρία ἡμῶν ἀληθής ἐστι with Jn. 21[24]: 3 Jn.[12] καὶ ἡμεῖς δὲ μαρτυροῦμεν with Jn. 15[27] καὶ ὑμεῖς δὲ μαρτυρεῖτε. Charles calls attention to the use of μή with the participle, which is found in Jn. (11 times), 1 Jn. (8), 2 Jn. (2), 3 Jn. (1), although never in the Apocalypse.[1]

We hold that the cumulative evidence thus available from the style and diction of two short letters sufficiently proves that they are written by the same hand that wrote the Gospel and the First Epistle.

We next observe that the writer of 2 and 3 Jn. describes himself to his correspondents as ὁ πρεσβύτερος, as if that were a description of his personality which would identify him without question. He is *the* Presbyter, although there were, no doubt, many other presbyters in the Christian community. Now, as we have already pointed out, πρεσβύτερος is never used (for 1 Pet. 5[1] is not really an exception) of one of the Twelve.[2] And, further, 3 Jn. shows that a certain Diotrephes had actually repudiated the writer's authority. This would have been strange indeed if the writer had been recognised

---

[1] See Charles, *Revelation*, i. p. xxxiv, for other minute points of grammar which support the view that the Gospel and all three Epistles are from the same hand.

[2] See p. xlvii above.

as one of the original apostles.   But the writer has a distinctive
title; he is *The Presbyter*, ὁ πρεσβύτερος, a title which is only
found elsewhere in its use by Papias as descriptive of " John
the Presbyter, the disciple of the Lord." [1] We thus go back
for the authorship of 2 and 3 Jn. to the conclusion which Jerome
mentions [2] as held by some in his day, viz. that they were
written by John the presbyter.

C. GENERAL CONCLUSION AS TO AUTHORSHIP OF THE GOSPEL AND THE EPISTLES

The author of 2 and 3 Jn. is also the author of 1 Jn.; and
we have already observed that this longer Epistle was written
by one who claims to have been in the company of Jesus when
on earth, *i.e.* that he heard and saw and touched Him.[3] This
corroborates our identification of " the Presbyter " of 2, 3 Jn.
with John the presbyter, who was a disciple of Jesus—that is,
who belonged to the outer circles of disciples although not
one of the Twelve.[4]

Hence we conclude that, since as to style and diction and
theological standpoint, the Gospel is not to be distinguished
from the First Epistle, John the presbyter was the writer and
editor of the Fourth Gospel, although he derived his narrative
material from John the son of Zebedee.[5] John the presbyter,
in short, is the *evangelist*, as distinct from John the apostle,
who was the *witness* to whose testimony the evangelist appeals
(19[35] 21[24]). To the mind of the early Church at Ephesus, it
was the *evidence* for the words and deeds of Jesus' life and
death that was the important matter; and for this they had the
testimony of the last of the apostles. The language of Polycrates [6] and of Irenæus,[7] not to speak of the widespread tradition that the Gospel was *not* written by the apostle's own hand,
but was dictated to a disciple, is consonant with the conclusion
that has emerged from an examination of the style of the several
Johannine books.

(VI) THE APOCALYPSE IS NOT BY JOHN THE PRESBYTER, BUT PROBABLY BY JOHN THE APOSTLE

An examination of the style and diction of the Fourth
Gospel shows that it is not from the same hand that wrote the

---

[1] See p. lii above.   [2] *De uirr. ill.* 9.   [3] P. lx.   [4] P. xlvii.
[5] This is, substantially, the view of Harnack : " That in some way,
John, the son of Zebedee, is behind the Fourth Gospel must be admitted, and hence our Gospel is to be considered as a Gospel of John
the presbyter, according to John the son of Zebedee " (*Chronol.*, i. 677).
[6] P. 1   [7] P. xlvii.

Apocalypse, while it markedly resembles in these respects the Johannine Epistles, and especially the First Epistle. The vocabulary of Jn. is small. In the Johannine writings only 990 words are used altogether, and in the Gospel only 919. The Apocalyptist has an even scantier vocabulary of 866 words. Only 441 words are common to both writers; *i.e.* Jn. has 545 words not used by the Apocalyptist, while the Apocalyptist has 425 not used by Jn.

Among Jn.'s 990 words, there are 84 exclusively Johannine, *i.e.* not occurring elsewhere in the N.T.; 74 of these are found in the Gospel only, viz. :

ἀγγέλλειν, ἁλιεύειν, ἀλλαχόθεν, ἀλόη, ἀνθρακιά, ἀντλεῖν, ἄντλημα, ἀποσυνάγωγος, ἀρχιτρίκλινος, βαΐον, βιβρώσκειν, γενετή, γέρων, γλωσσόκομον, δακρύειν, διαζωννύναι, ἐγκαίνια, ἐκνεύειν, ἕλιγμα, ἐμπόριον, ἐμφυσᾶν, ἐξυπνίζειν, ἐπάρατος, ἐπενδύτης, ἐπιχρίειν, ἧλος, θεοσεβής, θήκη, θρέμμα, κειρίαι, κέρμα, κερματιστής, κηπουρός, κλῆμα, κοίμησις, κολυμβήθρα, κομψότερον, κρίθινος, λέντιον, λίτρα, λόγχη, μεσοῦν, μετρητής, μονή, νύττειν, ὄζειν, ὀνάριον, ὀψάριον, πενθερός, περιδεῖσθαι, πέτρος, πότερον, προβατική, προβάτιον, προσαίτης, προσκυνητής, προσφάγιον, πτέρνα, πτύσμα, ῥέειν, σκέλος, σκηνοπηγία, συγχρῆσθαι, συνεισέρχεσθαι, τεταρταῖος, τετράμηνος, τίτλος, ὑδρία, ὑφαντός, φανός, φραγέλλιον, χείμαρρος, χολᾶν, ψωμίον.[1]

The subject-matter of the Apocalypse naturally calls for a vocabulary distinct from that of either the Gospel or the Epistles; and reasons may be found for some obvious differences. Thus the Apocalyse treats much of sorrow and warfare, and accordingly it has πάσχειν, πόλεμος, πένθος, ὑπομονή, which Jn. does not use ; on the other hand, Jn. has ἐλπίς, χαρά, which are not mentioned in Apoc. Again, the words εἰκών, μυστήριον, νοῦς, σιγή, σοφία, which the Apoc. uses, are studiously avoided by Jn., probably because of their place in Gnostic doctrine, and the same may be said of his avoidance of the mystical numbers seven[2] and ten, both of which appear in the Apoc. Perhaps Jn. avoids πίστις (only in 1 Jn. 5⁴, four times in Apoc.) for a similar reason, while he uses πιστεύειν a hundred times (see on 1⁷). γνῶσις is used by neither author.

Other divergences, however, are not susceptible of such an explanation. The variety of use of ἀληθής, ἀληθινός, is puzzling (see on 1⁹). Jn. never uses ἀπόστολος of the Twelve (but see on 13¹⁶), while the Apoc. never uses Jn.'s favourite title μαθητής (see on 2²). So, too, Jn. avoids πρεσβύτερος (except

---

[1] The words ἀγγελία, ἀντίχριστος, ἐπιδέχεσθαι, ἱλασμός, νίκη, φιλοπρωτεύειν, φλυαρεῖν, χάρτης, χρίσμα are only found in the Johannine Epistles. ἀνθρωποκτόνος is found both in Gospel and 1 Ep., but nowhere else in the N.T.

[2] See p. lxxxix.

2 Jn.[1], 3 Jn.[1]), while the Apoc. has it a dozen times. δύναμις, θαῦμα, ἰσχύς, κράτος, used in the Apoc., do not appear in Jn., although we might have expected to find them in his report of the Gospel miracles. The Apoc. has ἀρνίον (for Christ), μνῆμα, πέτρα, φονεύς, ψευδής, while Jn. uses the synonyms ἀμνός, μνημεῖον, πέτρος, ἀνθρωποκτόνος, ψεύστης. Where the Apocalyptist writes Ἱερουσαλήμ, Jn. has Ἱεροσόλυμα (see on 1[19]).

With the use of prepositions, adverbs, and connecting particles, Jn. is more at home than is the Apocalyptist. None of the following appears in Apoc.: ὑπέρ (16 times in Jn.), ἀντί (1), σύν (3), πρό (9); ἤδη (18), νῦν (30), καθώς (45), μέν (8). ἐπί, on the contrary, is four times as frequent in Apoc. as in Jn. To these may be added ἀλλά (120 Jn., 13 Apoc.), γάρ (70 Jn., 17 Apoc.), and Jn.'s favourite οὖν (see on 1[22]; in the Apoc. it occurs only 6 times and always as illative). On the other hand, the prep. ἐνώπιον with the gen. is only used thrice by Jn.; but 34 times by the Apocalyptist, where it is probably due to Semitic influence. The instrumental use of ἐν in the Apoc. is found 33 times, although hardly at all in Jn. (see however, on 13[35]).

The proper names Ἰησοῦς and Ἰωάνης are always anarthrous in Apoc.; whereas the usage is different in Jn. (see on 1[29. 50]). The Apoc. never uses the possessive pronouns ἡμέτερος (twice in Jn.), ὑμέτερος (3), σός (6), ἴδιος (15), while ἐμός, which is used by Jn. forty times, appears only in Rev. 2[20].

More remarkable than any differences in *diction* are the differences in the *constructions* used by Jn. and the Apocalyptist. The grammar of the Apocalypse has been thoroughly studied by Charles, who brings out its Hebraic character.[1] Its Greek is unique in its solecisms, and points to a certain awkwardness in using the Greek language on the part of its author, who thinks in Hebrew or Aramaic throughout. The Greek of the Apocalypse has none of the idiomatic subtleties which meet us in the Fourth Gospel [2] (see, *e.g.*, note on 3[8]).

It was held by some critics in the nineteenth century that the Apocalypse was written in the time of Nero; and thus a period of perhaps twenty years intervened between it and the issue of the Fourth Gospel. Here, it was supposed, we may find time for a fuller mastery of Greek style being acquired by the author of the Apocalypse, before he wrote the Gospel. However, the Neronic date of the Apocalypse is now abandoned by most scholars, who have reverted to the traditional date in

---

[1] See Charles, *Revelation*, i. pp. cxvii–clix.
[2] For the argument of Dionysius of Alexandria as to difference of style, cf. Euseb. *H.E.* vii. 25, and see p. lvi.

the reign of Domitian; so that we cannot reckon on any long interval between the issue of the two books.[1] The differences between the Greek of Gospel and Revelation are so marked that we cannot account for them by the assumption that the common author altered his style so fundamentally in a short period.

Reference must here be made to Dr. Burney's theory that the Fourth Gospel was of Aramaic origin, and that its Greek is only translation-Greek, betraying its Aramaic base at every point.[2] Despite the established facts that behind the Fourth Gospel there was a Jewish mind, and that an undertone of Semitic ways of thought and speech may be discerned in its language (see further, p. lxxxi), Burney's view has not been generally accepted by scholars. Many passages that have been cited by him and others as Aramaic in form are quite defensible as Greek; see, e.g., on 3^{29} 7^{21} 8^{56} 10^{12}. See also the notes on $1^{10. 50}$ 7^{38} 10^{29} 12^{40}. Classical parallels can be produced[3] for the diction in 4^7 8^{25} $9^{21. 36}$ 14^{23} $16^{8. 27}$ 17^2 19^5 20^{19} (see notes in loc.), which show that Jn'.s Greek in these places is not the Greek of a mere translator. At 3^{34} $10^{11. 24}$ it is true that a precise Greek parallel cannot be cited, but even at these points an Aramaic origin is not suggested, nor can Jn.'s Greek be challenged. Another difficulty in the way of accepting Burney's theory is the identity of style between the Gospel and the First Epistle. The latter is, admittedly, an original Greek letter, and its author is not to be distinguished from the writer of the Fourth Gospel (see p. lxi).

To return to the Apocalypse. There are, indeed, some similarities in language as in thought with the Gospel. Both authors, e.g., quote Zech. 12^{10} with ἐξεκέντησαν, which is not the LXX rendering (see on Jn. 19^{37}). But this only proves the common use of a prevalent translation of the Masoretic text. οἵτινες ἐξεκέντησαν in Rev. 1^7 does not refer to the piercing of the Lord's side, which is mentioned only by Jn., but to those who crucified Him. The phrase τηρεῖν τὸν λόγον or τηρεῖν τὰς ἐντολάς is frequent both in Jn. and in Apoc. (cf. Rev. $3^{8. 10}$ $22^{7. 9}$ 12^7 14^{12}, and see on Jn. 8^{51} 14^{15}).

---

[1] Hort, who was a supporter of the Neronic date, acknowledged that without a considerable interval of time between the two books, identity of authorship cannot be maintained (Apocalypse of St. John, p. xl).

[2] The Aramaic Origin of the Fourth Gospel, by C. F. Burney (1922). He ascribes both Gospel and Apocalypse to John the presbyter (see pp. 149-152).

[3] Lightfoot, who urges the Aramaic flavour of the Greek, goes so far as to say that there are " no classicisms " in Jn. (Biblical Essays, p. 135).

Cf. also ὁ διψῶν ἐρχέσθω (Rev. 22¹⁷) with Jn. 7³⁷, where see note. The verb νικᾶν, " to overcome," is applied to Christ both in Jn. and in Apoc., but nowhere else in the N.T. (see on Jn. 16³³). Both writers express the same idea when they speak of Christ as ὁ ἀμνὸς τοῦ θεοῦ (Jn. 1²⁹), or τὸ ἀρνίον (Rev. 5⁶ passim). The phrase ἐγώ εἰμι introducing great utterances of Christ is also used, in both Apoc. and the Fourth Gospel, in the same way.[1]

Apart from verbal correspondences of this kind, the Christology of Apoc. has marked resemblances to that of the Fourth Gospel. That Christ is Judge (Rev. 6¹⁶), that He was pre-existent (Rev. 1¹⁷ 3¹⁴), and that He had divine knowledge of men's hearts and thoughts (Rev. 2²³) are thoughts familiar to Jn. And that the abiding of God with man is a permanent issue of Christ's work is a specially Johannine dogma (cf. Rev. 3²⁰ 21³ with Jn. 14²³). The application of the mysterious title " the Word of God " to Christ in Rev. 19¹³ prepares the reader for the more explicit Logos doctrine of the Prologue to the Gospel.[2]

These similarities[3] cannot outweigh the differences which compel us to recognise that the Gospel and the Apocalypse proceed from different hands; but they point to some contact between the two writers. The simplest explanation is that the writer of the Fourth Gospel had sat at the feet of the Apocalyptist as a disciple. If the Apocalypist was John the son of Zebedee (a view which seems to the present writer to be reasonable[4]), then from a new angle we reach the conclusion that John the son of Zebedee is the " witness " behind the Fourth Gospel, which was, however, written by a younger disciple of Christ.

(VII) SUMMARY OF ARGUMENT AS TO AUTHORSHIP

1. John the apostle was the Beloved Disciple (p. xxxvii). He did not suffer a martyr's death (p. xxxviii f.), but lived to extreme old age in Ephesus (p. xlviii).

2. The tradition that John the apostle was himself the actual writer of both Gospel and Apocalypse must be rejected

---

[1] See p. cxviii.   [2] P. cxlii.

[3] See Charles, Revelation, vol. i. p. xxxii, for other resemblances.

[4] This is too large a question to be argued here. Charles holds that John the seer is a personage distinct not only from John the presbyter but also from John the apostle, and his careful study of the authorship of the Apocalypse challenges scrutiny. But much of his argument depends on the hypothesis that John the apostle was put to death by the Jews at an early date. This I am unable to accept for the reasons set out above (pp. xxxviii–xlv).

because of the far-reaching difference of style between the two books (p. lxv).

3. The theory that John the apostle was the sole author of the Gospel is not established by its general recognition (p. lix) in the second and following centuries as "the Gospel according to St. John." That may unhesitatingly be accepted, in the sense that John was behind it, and that it represents faithfully his picture of Jesus Christ, and reproduces His teaching. It was this that the early Church deemed to be of importance, and not any literary problem as to the method by which the reminiscences of John the apostle came to be recorded. The reason why the Second Gospel was regarded as authoritative was because it reproduced the witness of Peter, and not because it was known to have been compiled by Mark. The ground of its authority was belief in its apostolic origin, as Papias tells us.[1] This it was which was claimed for the Fourth Gospel by the elders of the Church at Ephesus (21^{24}), where, as Irenæus says (p. xlvii), it was first published, and this it was which gave it authority. There could be no higher testimony than that of John the Beloved Disciple. But that he wrote it with his own hand is not asserted by the second-century Fathers; and the only traditions that remain as to the manner of its composition (pp. lvi ff.) reveal that John was *not* regarded as the sole author by those who accepted his Gospel as canonical.

4. Further, the internal evidence of the Gospel indicates that the writer was a distinct person from the "witness" to whom he appeals. The certificate of authentication in 21^{24} is written by the same person who wrote the Gospel as a whole, for the style is identical with the style of Jn. throughout. No doubt it is the certificate not of the evangelist avowedly, but of the elders of the Church; nevertheless it is written for them by *him*, and the writer is distinct from the Beloved Disciple whose witness is certified as true. And the language of 19^{35} (where see note) is even more conclusive, as distinguishing between the evangelist and his authority.

5. We shall see that the evangelist not only sometimes corrects the statements of the Synoptists (p. xcvii f.), but that he occasionally adopts the actual words used by Mk. and Lk. (p. xcvi f.). Now that he ventures to *correct* anything told in the earlier Gospels, shows that he is relying on an authority that cannot be gainsaid. Jn. depends on the Beloved Disciple, and is careful to reproduce his corrections of the current evangelical tradition. On the other hand, he is thoroughly familiar with the phrases in which Mk. and Lk. embody that

[1] See Eusebius, *H.E.* iii. 39. 15.

tradition, and he does not scruple on occasion to make them his own.   This is quite natural on the part of one who is telling a story as to the details of which he has not personal knowledge, although Jn. was, in a sense, $\mu\alpha\theta\eta\tau\dot{\eta}s$ $\tauο\hat{υ}$ $\kappa\upsilon\rhoίου$ (p. lii). He follows his authorities verbally, for such was the literary habit of the time.   But it is improbable that the aged apostle, John the son of Zebedee, would have fallen back on the words of others when he could have used words of his own.   This is specially improbable when we remember that John was not slow to correct when necessary what Mk. and Lk. had recorded. An examination of the relation to the Synoptics of the Fourth Gospel thus reveals the presence of two persons concerned in the production of the latter, viz. the apostle who was an original authority, and the evangelist who put the reminiscences of his teacher into shape.[1]

6. The actual writer (as distinct from the " witness ") of the Fourth Gospel is also the writer of the Johannine Epistles. This is not only shown by identity of style (p. lxii f.), but is confirmed by Church tradition.

7. The *name* of the writer cannot be given with as complete confidence.   But, if the writer, like the Beloved Disciple, had the name " John," a very common name among Jews, we may find here a plausible explanation for some confusion of him in later times with his greater namesake.   There is, indeed, no likelihood that Irenæus associates any John except John the apostle with the Fourth Gospel (p. xlix); or that the Christian writers of the second and third centuries had any special curiosity as to the name of the writer who compiled the Gospel on the apostle's authority (p. lxiv).   But the fact that master and disciple had the same name might readily lead to a forgetfulness of the distinct personality of the lesser man.

8. The Second and Third Epistles attributed to " John " claim to be written by one who calls himself ὁ πρεσβύτερος (p. lxiii), which at once suggests John the presbyter of whom Papias tells us (p. lii).

9. The writer of Epp. II. III. was, however, also the author of Ep. I. and of the Fourth Gospel (p. lxiii) ; and thus we reach the final inference that the Fourth Gospel was written by John the presbyter from the reminiscences and the teaching of John the apostle (p. lxiv).

No claim can be made for absolute certainty in the solution of so intricate a problem as the authorship of the " Gospel according to St. John."   There are many links in the chain of

---

[1] For a criticism of this argument, first developed by Weizsäcker, see Drummond, *Character and Authorship, etc.*, p. 398.

argument, and each must be tested separately. In this short summary an attempt has been made to bring out the main points at issue, which have been examined in detail in the preceding sections.

(VIII) EARLY CITATIONS OF THE FOURTH GOSPEL

The date of the *Epistle of Barnabas* is uncertain. Lightfoot tentatively placed it between 70 and 79 A.D. In any case it is of too early a date to make it possible for Barnabas to have quoted the Johannine writings. In the notes on 2^{19} 3^{14} 6^{51} we have suggested, however, that Barnabas may refer to sayings of Jesus which were traditionally handed down, and which were afterwards definitely ascribed to Him in the Fourth Gospel. For other phrases of Barnabas which elucidate in some slight degree passages in Jn., see on 8^{12} 16^{32} $19^{23. 28}$ $21^{18. 19}$.

Ignatius, bishop of Antioch, suffered martyrdom between the years 110 and 118. His Epistles to the churches of Asia Minor and of Rome are deeply impressed with the doctrine of Jesus Christ as having come in the flesh (as opposed to the prevalent Docetism) which is characteristic of the Fourth Gospel (and the first Epistle), and also with the Pauline conception of the redemptive efficacy of the Passion. The idea of canonical books of the N.T., as distinct from the O.T., had not been formulated or accepted by the Church at the early date when Ignatius wrote; and he never quotes directly or avowedly from the Gospels or the Apostolic Epistles.[1] He moved in the circles where the Johannine presentation of Christianity first found explicit expression; and this may account, in part, for the remarkable likeness of his thought and religious diction to the writings of Jn. It does not follow that in the Ignatian Epistles there is any conscious literary obligation to the Fourth Gospel, although this is possible. But it is in accordance with all probabilities, that Ignatius had read this famous book which had been produced with the imprimatur of the Church at Ephesus a quarter of a century before he wrote to the Christians of that place. He uses several Johannine phrases after a fashion which is difficult to explain if they are no more than reflexions of current Christian teaching. See, *e.g.*, the notes on Jn. 1^{18} 3^8 4^{13} 5^{19} $6^{27. 32. 53}$ 7^{38} 8^{29} $10^{7. 9. 30}$ $12^{3. 31}$ $13^{3. 20}$ $15^{8. 19}$ 17^{21} 20^{20}, where the Ignatian parallels are cited.[2]

In the Antiochene *Acts of Martyrdom* (end of fourth

---

[1] Cf. Lightfoot, *Ignatius*, i. 403.
[2] Cf. Burney, *Aramaic Origin*, pp. 153 ff. ; Drummond, *Fourth Gospel*, p. 259 ; and for other references, Moffatt, *Introd.*, p. 578 f.

century), Ignatius is styled ὁ τοῦ ἀποστόλου Ἰωάννου μαθητής, but there is no early evidence for this.[1] In his letter to the Ephesians, Ignatius does not mention John, although (§ 12) he bids them be Παύλου συμμύσται τοῦ μεμαρτυρημένου. But it must be borne in mind that Ignatius was on his way to Rome, to suffer martyrdom as Paul had suffered, and this gives special point to his mention of Paul. He could not have cited John in this context, for John died a peaceful death at Ephesus and was not a martyr. In another place (§ 11) he recalls the fact that the Ephesians were ever of one mind with the *apostles*, *i.e.* not only Paul the founder of their Church, but other apostles as well; and this is most simply explained as carrying an allusion to John. Indeed, that a bishop who had visited the churches of Ephesus, Magnesia, Tralles, Philadelphia, and Smyrna (as well as Polycarp himself) was not familiar with the activities of the great John of Asia, is highly improbable.

Ignatius does not name John, nor does he mention his writings; but his circumstances could not have left him ignorant of the personality of the man, while the phraseology of the Ignatian Epistles betrays acquaintance with the teaching, and probably with the text, of the Fourth Gospel.

Polycarp of Smyrna (born about 70 A.D. and died a martyr's death in 155 or 156)[2] was a disciple of John (see p. xlviii). There is no chronological difficulty in this. If, as is possible, John lived until 100 A.D., although 95 is more probable, then Polycarp would have been thirty years old at the time of his death; he may indeed have been appointed bishop by John, as Tertullian states (*de Præscr.* 32). There is no reason to doubt that he had some intercourse in his young days with the old apostle. In his *Epistle to the Philippians* (§ 7) 1 Jn. 4² ⁻ ⁴ is quoted almost *verbatim*, ὃς ἂν μὴ ὁμολογῇ Ἰησοῦν Χριστὸν ἐν σαρκὶ ἐληλυθέναι ἀντίχριστός ἐστιν. There is no certain reminiscence of the Fourth Gospel, although Lightfoot compares Jn. 15¹⁶ with § 12.

A Christian Apocalypse, called *The Rest of the Words of Baruch*, contains a clear reference to Jn. 1⁹ (see note *in loc.*). If Rendel Harris is right in dating this Apocalypse about the year 136 A.D., we have here one of the earliest of all extant citations of the Fourth Gospel.

We have already examined (p. liv) the relation of *Papias* (d. 146 A.D.) to John the presbyter and John the apostle; but it should be noted here that Eusebius tells that Papias *quoted* the First Johannine Epistle (*H.E.* III. xxxix. 17), and his recognition of this as authoritative involves also the recognition of the Gospel.

---

[1] See Lightfoot, *Ignatius*, ii. 477.

[2] See, for these dates, Lightfoot, *Ignatius*, i. pp. 647 ff.

Basilides, a Gnostic teacher of Alexandria, flourished in the reign of Hadrian (*i.e.* 117–138 A.D.; cf. Clem. Alex. *Strom.* vii. 17). In an abstract of a work by Basilides, found in Hippolytus (*Ref.* vii. 22), the words of Jn. 1⁹ are quoted verbally. "This, says he, is what is called in the Gospels ἦν τὸ φῶς τὸ ἀληθινὸν ὃ φωτίζει πάντα ἄνθρωπον ἐρχόμενον εἰς τὸν κόσμον." There is a later reference to Jn. 2⁴ (*Ref.* vii. 27). If Hippolytus is quoting here the work of Basilides himself,[1] as distinct from books written by members of his school, the citation of 1⁹ seems to prove not only Basilides' use of Jn., but his acceptance of it as among "the Gospels" generally recognised. This may be a too bold inference, but the attention paid to the Fourth Gospel by Gnostic teachers of the middle of the second century shows that at an early date, certainly before 150 A.D., it was reckoned by them to be a Christian book of special significance.

The earliest commentary upon the Fourth Gospel, of which we have any considerable remains, was that of the Gnostic *Heracleon*, who wrote towards the end of the second century.[2] His endeavour was to find support for the doctrinal system of Valentinus, as he understood it, in the Fourth Gospel, which he regarded as authoritative Scripture. In his extant fragments the name of the author of the Gospel does not expressly appear; but it is implied in the comment of Heracleon on Jn. 1¹⁸, which he says proceeds not from the Baptist but from the Disciple (οὐκ ἀπὸ τοῦ βαπτιστοῦ ἀλλ᾽ ἀπὸ τοῦ μαθητοῦ).[3] This is plainly meant to distinguish words of John the Baptist from that of the Disciple who had the same name.

Moreover, the Fourth Gospel was accepted and used by some, at least, of the Valentinian heretics against whom Irenæus directed his polemic (*Hær.* iii. 11. 7). It is even probable that Valentinus himself recognised its authority, as is indicated by Tertullian when he contrasts Valentinus with Marcion, as one who did not, like Marcion, mutilate the Gospels, but used the "entire instrument."[4] The acceptance of the Fourth Gospel by many Gnostics as well as Catholics creates a strong presumption that it had been given to the public as an authoritative work at a time before controversy had arisen between Christian heretic and Christian orthodox. And this pushes the date back to a period before the time of Basilides.

---

[1] This was held by Lightfoot (*Bibl. Essays*, p. 108) ; Westcott (*Comm.* p. lxvii); Ezra Abbot (*Fourth Gospel*, p. 82) ; Drummond regarded it as *probable* (*Fourth Gospel*, p. 331).

[2] See, for the extant *Fragments of Heracleon*, A. E. Brooke, in Cambridge *Texts and Studies* (1891).

[3] Cf. Brooke, *l.c.* p. 55.

[4] " Si Valentinus integro instrumento uti uidetur " (*de Præscr.* 38).

There is nothing, then, extraordinary in the fact that Basilides quoted the Fourth Gospel, as the simplest interpretation of the words of Hippolytus assures us that he did.

Of other Gnostic writings produced not later than 150 A.D. the fragmentary *Gospel of Peter* and the *Acts of John* disclose clear traces of the Johannine tradition.

Pseudo-Peter (§ 5) suggests 18[6] (see note); he agrees (§ 2) with Jn. as to the relation of the Crucifixion to the first day of unleavened bread (19[31]); he refers to the nails by which the hands of Jesus, the feet not being mentioned, were fastened to the Cross (§ 6; cf. 20[20]); he tells (§ 4) of the *crurifragium*, in a confused manner (cf. 19[33]); and the end of the fragment reports the departure of some disciples, after the Passover solemnities were over, to the Sea of Galilee for fishing, apparently being about to introduce the narrative of Jn. 21. These points of the apocryphal writer are not derived from the Synoptists. See also on 19[23. 28. 41].[1]

The latter part of the *Acts of John* tells of John as reclining on the Lord's breast, when at a meal (§ 89; cf. 13[23]). In these *Acts* (§ 97) the Crucifixion is on Friday at the sixth hour (cf. 19[14]), and allusion is made to the piercing of the Lord's side (§ 97 λόγχαις νύσσομαι καὶ καλάμοις, and § 101 νυγέντα; cf. 19[34] and note thereon). In the Gnostic hymn (§ 95), Christ claims to be both *Door* and *Way*: θύρα εἰμί σοι κρούοντί με. Ἀμὴν ὁδός εἰμί σοι παροδίτῃ (see on 10[9] 14[6]). The Fourth Gospel is distorted, but that it was known to the writer of these Acts is certain.

It is true that some persons in the second century rejected the Fourth Gospel as authoritative. Irenæus mentions some who would not accept the promise of the Paraclete, and so " do not admit that form [of the Spirit], which is according to John's Gospel" (*Hær*. iii. 11. 9). Epiphanius in his account of heretical systems (probably based in a confused way upon Hippolytus) mentions people to whom he gives the nickname of *Alogi*, because they rejected the Logos doctrine of John ; " they receive neither the Gospel of John nor the Apocalypse," which they ascribed to the heretic Cerinthus.[2] Whether these persons were few or many, they held (according to Epiphanius) that the Fourth Gospel was of the first century, as Cerinthus was a contemporary of John.[3] It is probable from what Epiphanius adds, that they are to be identified with the impugners of the Fourth Gospel mentioned by Irenæus. We are not, however, concerned here with the history of the N.T. Canon, but only with the time of the appearance of the

---

[1] Cf. *contra* Gardner-Smith, *J.T.S.*, April 1926, p. 256.
[2] *Hær*. li. 2, 3.   [3] See above, p. xlix.

Gospel " according to St. John " ; and this cannot be placed at a later date than the end of the first century.

Justin Martyr wrote his *Apologies* and *Dialogue with Trypho* about 145–150 A.D. He mentions John the apostle once, and then as the seer of the Apocalypse: " A certain man among us (παρ' ἡμῖν), by name John, one of the apostles of Christ, prophesied in a revelation (ἀποκαλύψει) which was made to him," etc., alluding to Rev. 20⁴⁻⁶ *(Dial.* 81; cf. *Dial.* 45). This *Dialogue*, according to Eusebius,[1] is the record of a controversy held by Justin with Trypho at Ephesus ; § 1 places Justin at Ephesus soon after the Barcochba revolt, or about the year 136. When writing then of John the apostle as παρ' ἡμῖν, he is writing of one who was at Ephesus forty years before, and of whose influence and personality he must have been fully informed.

It is noteworthy that Justin does not speak of John the apostle as the writer of the Gospel, only the Apocalypse being specially mentioned as his work. This may be taken in connexion with the carefully chosen language used by Irenæus, when speaking of the relation of John to the Fourth Gospel and its publication at Ephesus.[2] It is possible that Justin was aware of the tradition which associated another personality with that of John the apostle in the composition of the Gospel.

However that may be, Justin's doctrinal system is dependent as a whole upon the Fourth Gospel, and especially on the Prologue. He was undoubtedly familiar with its general teaching. His books being apologetic (for Roman use) and controversial (with the Jews) rather than exegetical or hortatory, we could not expect him to cite *verbatim* and as authoritative the books of the N.T., after the fashion of Irenæus in the next generation. None the less, the traces of his acquaintance with the text of the Fourth Gospel are apparent.[3]

A conclusive passage is *Apol.* 61. Justin is explaining how converts are " new made through Christ." They are brought where there is water; and " after the same fashion of regeneration (ἀναγεννήσεως) with which we ourselves were regenerated, they are regenerated," for in the name of Father, Son, and Holy Spirit, " they receive the washing of water (τὸ ἐν τῷ ὕδατι τότε λουτρὸν ποιοῦνται); for Christ said, Except ye be regenerated (ἀναγεννηθῆτε), ye shall not enter the kingdom of heaven. It is plain that it is impossible for those who were born once for all to enter into their mothers' wombs." Here we have an almost verbal reproduction of Jn. 3³⁻⁵ (see

---

[1] *H.E.* iv. 18. 6.   [2] Cf. p. xlvii.

[3] The details are discussed at length in Ezra Abbot's *The Fourth Gospel*, pp. 25–48 (ed. 1880).

note *in loc.*). Again, in *Dial.* 88, οὐκ εἰμὶ ὁ Χριστός, ἀλλὰ
φωνὴ βοῶντος comes directly from Jn. 1²³ and not from the
Synoptists ¹ (see note *in loc.*). The allusion in *Dial.*
69 to Christ's cure of those blind *from birth* (ἐκ γενετῆς), and the
lame and deaf, presupposes 9¹ (where see note). Attempts
to get rid of these allusions to the Fourth Gospel are unreasonable. See also notes on Jn. 4¹⁴ 12⁴⁹ 16¹³ 18³⁷ 19¹³. ²⁴ 20¹⁹. ²¹,
where other parallels from Justin are given. With 1 Jn. 3¹
may be compared *Dial.* 123.

Justin, then, used the Fourth Gospel a little before 150 A.D.;
and at one point (*Apol.* 61) quotes it as authoritative for a
saying of Jesus.

The " Diatessaron " of *Tatian* sufficiently shows the co-
equal authority of Jn. with that of the Synoptists, when his
Harmony was composed. Tatian was born about 110 A.D.,
and had been in intimate relationship with Justin at Rome.
His acceptance of the Fourth Gospel would, almost by itself,
suggest that Justin took the same view of its importance and
its authority.

The *Shepherd of Hermas* was written at Rome about 140
A.D., or perhaps at an earlier date.² The allegorist's allusions
to Scripture are few, as might be expected from the nature of his
book. He speaks (*Sim.* ix. 12. 5) of baptism as a condition of
entrance into the kingdom of God, a doctrine which recalls
Jn. 3⁵ (where see note). His allusion to Christ as the Gate ³
(ἡ πύλη, *Sim.* ix. 12), through which those who are to be saved
enter into the kingdom of God, is reminiscent of the teaching
of Jn. 10⁹. He speaks of the law (τὸν νόμον) which Christ
received from the Father (*Sim.* v. 6. 3); this is Johannine in its
thought (cf. 10¹⁸). The phrase ὁ κύριος ἀληθινὸς ἐν παντὶ ῥήματι
καὶ οὐδὲν παρ᾽ αὐτῷ ψεῦδος (*Mand.* iii. 1) is verbally similar to
1 Jn. 2²⁷. These are suggestions of the prevalence of Johannine teaching at Rome in the middle of the second century;
but no more definite proof is forthcoming of the acquaintance
of Hermas with the text of the Fourth Gospel.

The *Epistle to Diognetus* is dated about 150 A.D. by
Lightfoot.⁴ In x. 2, 3 he speaks of God's love for men (ὁ γὰρ
θεὸς τοὺς ἀνθρώπους ἠγάπησε), adding that to them He sent
His only begotten Son (ἀπέστειλε τὸν υἱὸν αὐτοῦ τὸν μονογενῆ),
and then suggesting that their love for Him who thus loved

---

¹ Cf. p. c.   ² See Lightfoot, *Apostolic Fathers*, p. 294.
³ The doctrine of Christ as the Gate (ἡ πύλη) appears also in Clem.
Rom. 48, a document which is contemporary with Jn., but is independent of the Johannine writings.
⁴ It breaks off in c. 10, and cc. 11, 12 are by a different, probably
a later, hand. Cf. Lightfoot, *Apostolic Fathers*, p. 488; and see on
16²⁹ 17³.

them will be the issue. Not only the thoughts but the words of Jn. 3[16], 1 Jn. 4[9, 19] are reproduced here. In vi. 3 the thought that Christians are *in* the world, but not *of* the world, and that therefore the world hates them, is an echo from Jn. 17[11, 14]. The writer of the Epistle is not writing for Christians or for Jews, but for heathen, so that he never quotes expressly from either O.T. or N.T. But that he is acquainted with the Johannine writings is hardly doubtful. See on 16[29].

A document, purporting to report conversations of the Risen Jesus with His disciples, and entitled *Epistula Apostolorum*,[1] has recently been edited from Coptic and Ethiopic versions by Schmidt, who holds that it was written in Asia Minor about 160–170 A.D. It is anti-Docetic in tone, and attaches much weight to the Fourth Gospel, John being named first when the apostles are (very confusedly) enumerated. There are several allusions to Jn.; *e.g.* the Miracle at Cana is mentioned (c. 5 [16]); at c. 11 [24] there is a curious note about the test offered to Thomas (Jn. 20[20, 27]), with which Peter and Andrew are associated; in c. 18 (29) the " new commandment " of Jn. 13[34] is mentioned; and in c. 29 (40) Jn. 20[29] is quoted precisely. For other Johannine reminiscences cf. cc. 33, 39. The Fourth Gospel was very familiar to the author of this imaginative work.

The *Didache* seems to be indebted for some of its phrases to Jn. 6[12] 11[52] 17[11] (see notes *in loc.*). This would be very important if the early date once ascribed to this interesting manual could be taken as established. But I am not prepared to make this assumption or to claim that the *Didache* was composed in its present form earlier than the third century.[2]

For the use of the Fourth Gospel, or at any rate of its characteristic phraseology, by the second-century *Odes of Solomon*, see p. cxlvi below.

The *Testaments of the Twelve Patriarchs* present some parallels to Johannine language; see on 1[9] 3[19] 4[22] 5[41] 15[26]. But Christian interpolations abound in the *Testaments*, the base of which is Jewish, and 15[26] (the most striking parallel) may be one of these. Charles would treat the language of 1[9] as dependent upon the *Testaments*; [3] but this is hardly probable (see note *in loc.*). We cannot safely assume that the *Testa-*

---

[1] *Epistula Apostolorum*, ed. C. Schmidt (*Texte und Untersuchungen*, 1919).

[2] For the problems presented by the *Didache*, see C. Bigg, *The Doctrine of the Twelve Apostles*, and J. A. Robinson, *Barnabas, Hermas, and the Didache* (especially pp. 93–95).

[3] See Charles, *Testaments of the Twelve Patriarchs*, p. lxxxv.

ments in their present form were in existence before the time of Origen.

The use made of the Fourth Gospel by Christian writers before 175 [1] enables us, therefore, to fix the time of its appearance within narrow limits. It is hardly earlier than 90 A.D., and cannot be later than 125. Probably the year 95 is the nearest approximation to its date that can be made.

CHAPTER III

CHARACTERISTICS OF THE EVANGELIST

(i) The Evangelist was a Jew.
(ii) The Literary Method of the Evangelist is not that of Allegory.
(iii) The Idea of "Witness" is prominent.
(iv) Philo and the Fourth Gospel.

(1) THE EVANGELIST WAS A JEW

REFERENCE is made elsewhere [2] to Burney's explanation of the style of the Fourth Gospel, viz. that it was translated into Greek from an Aramaic original. This explanation has not commanded the general assent of scholars; but that there is an undertone of Semitic ways of thought and speech behind the Gospel can hardly be gainsaid. The evangelist, in our view, is dependent for many of his facts upon the aged disciple, John the son of Zebedee, who was a Jew of Palestine, and whose native speech was Aramaic. It is natural that the record, however carefully edited, of such a disciple's reminiscences, should bear traces of his nationality. More than this, however, can be said. We observe the Semitic undertone, not only in the narrative, but in the evangelist's comments upon it. The style, *e.g.*, of such passages [3] as $3^{16-21. \ 31-36}$ or 12^{36b-43} is unmistakably Semitic; and, speaking generally, one cannot distinguish, by any features of internal evidence, those parts of the Gospel narrative which plainly rest upon the report of an eye-witness, and those which may be referred to the evangelist, whom we identify with the writer of the Johannine epistles.[4]

The evangelist prefers to string together independent sentences by the use of "and," rather than to use subordinate

---

[1] See p. lxxii f. for notices of Jn. in Christian books written between the time of Irenæus, whose testimony is explicit, and 250 A.D.
[2] P. lxvii.   [3] P. xxiii.   [4] P. lxx.

clauses. That is, he likes the form of writing which the grammarians call *parataxis*. This is not unknown in Greek, but one accustomed to listen to conversations in Aramaic would be more likely to employ *parataxis* than a Greek writer ignorant of Aramaic or Hebrew. This appears in the Prologue and in 3^{16-21} (to which reference has already been made), as well as in Jn.'s reports of a discourse.[1] The Oriental trick of *repetition* of what has been said before, generally in a slightly altered form, is very common in the Fourth Gospel (see on 3^{16}). It is because of these frequent repetitions of the same doctrinal statement that the style of Jn. has been described as " monotonous." A good illustration of repetitions in an Oriental report of a conversation is found at 16^{16-19}, where it will be noticed that the thrice-repeated, " A little while . . . and again a little while " adds to the vividness of the impression produced.

It has been thought by some [2] that there is a tendency in the Fourth Gospel to reproduce O.T. *testimonia* in a form recalling the Hebrew text rather than the LXX version. If the actual author were a Jew of Palestine, this is perhaps what we might expect, and at certain points Jn. seems to give a free rendering of the Hebrew; see, *e.g.*, the notes on 1^{23} 6^{45} $12^{15.\ 40}$ 13^{18}. On the other hand, the LXX (as distinct from the Hebrew) is behind the citations at 2^{17} 12^{38} 17^{17} 19^{24}. The quotation at 19^{37} is probably derived from some current version other than the LXX. No inference can be drawn from the form of the O.T. text cited 6^{31} 7^{42} 8^{17} 10^{34} $12^{13.\ 34}$ 15^{25} $19^{28.\ 36}$. The evidence, taken as a whole, hardly proves that the evangelist was more familiar with the Hebrew O.T. than he was with the LXX; although a knowledge of the Hebrew as well as of the LXX seems to be behind the Gospel quotations.[3]

The tendency of Jn. to reproduce Aramaic names of persons and places, and to interpret them for Greek readers, has often been remarked, *e.g. Messiah* (Jn. being the only evangelist who gives this Hebrew or Aramaic title, 1^{41} 4^{25}), *Kephas* (1^{42}), *Thomas* (20^{24} 21^{2}); the title *Rabbi* (1^{38}), *Rabboni* (20^{16}); *Golgotha* (19^{17}); *Gabbatha*, only at 19^{13}; *Bethesda* or *Bethzatha*, only at 5^{2}; *Siloam* (9^{7}). But too much may be made of this. Mk. (15^{22}) interprets *Golgotha*, as Jn. does, and even cites Aramaic sentences (Mk. 5^{41} 15^{34}). Mk. also uses both the titles *Rabbi* and *Rabboni* (9^{5} etc., 10^{51}). Mt. (1^{23}) interprets the

---

[1] Cf. $5^{39.\ 40}$ $17^{8.\ 10.\ 11}$.

[2] *E.g.* Lightfoot, *Biblical Essays*, p. 136 f. ; and Burney, *Aramaic Origin, etc.*, p. 114 f.

[3] It is possible that many of Jn.'s O.T. citations are taken from a volume of *Testimonia* compiled in Greek for Christian use.

Hebrew *Immanuel.* Even Lk. gives the Greek meaning of the names *Barnabas* and *Elymas* in Acts 4³⁶ 13⁸, although he does not interpret Aramaic names in his Gospel. All that we can say is that Jn. relies on Palestinian tradition, or on a Palestinian Jew (if he had not been himself in Palestine, which is quite possible) for his native names, and he finds it convenient (as Mk., Mt., and Lk. do on occasion) to interpret them for Greek readers. But we must not infer that his knowledge of Aramaic went very far, or that he was a native speaker.

Jn.'s familiarity with the topography of Jerusalem is, however, more noteworthy. The Synoptists know of Bethany, the Temple, the Prætorium of Pilate, and the place Golgotha with its sinister interpretation. Jn., however, has more intimate knowledge of the Holy City than the Synoptists display. He is aware how far from Jerusalem is the village of Bethany (11¹⁸); he knows not only the Temple, but Solomon's Porch (10²³); not only the Prætorium, but *Gabbatha* or the Pavement (19¹³); he does not mention *Gethsemane* by name, but he knows its situation " beyond the brook *Kidron*, where was a garden " (see on 18²); he alone mentions the Pool of Siloam, and knows why it was called *Siloam* (see on 9⁷); also the Pool of *Bethesda* or *Bethzatha*, of which he (quite unnecessarily) says that it had five porches and was ἐπὶ τῇ προβατικῇ (see on 5²). The Synoptists do not tell of the visits to Jerusalem at which the men were healed at Bethesda and Siloam, so that they have no necessity to use these place-names. But in his account of the Passion Jn.'s knowledge of the various localities at Jerusalem appears to be more detailed than that of Lk. or even of Mk.

Jn. gives geographical notes with equal confidence, when he has need to mention places outside Judæa. " Cana of Galilee " (2¹ 21²); " Ænon near to Salim " (3²³); " Bethany beyond Jordan " (Jn. being specially careful to distinguish it from the other Bethany, which he knows: see on 1²⁸); " the city called Ephraim," in the country near the wilderness (11⁵⁴), are obscure places, which, however, have been identified to a reasonable degree of probability. But that their situation should have been expressly indicated by Jn. shows that he is not depending upon vague general knowledge, such as an occasional pilgrim or tourist might pick up. It is interesting that his one site as to which it is not easy to speak with confidence is Sychar, which he says was near the traditional Well of Jacob (see on 4⁶). The indication of the Sea of Galilee as " of Tiberias " is probably due to an editor other than Jn. (see on 6¹ 21¹).

These topographical allusions, taken together, point to the reliance of the evangelist on evidence given him at first hand and incidentally in conversation, unless we might suppose that he himself had personal knowledge of the places to which he refers. The latter explanation is inevitable for those who hold that the evangelist was, himself, John the son of Zebedee; but the allusions in question are sufficiently explained if we take the view that John the apostle is the "witness" behind the evangelist's record,[1] but not the actual writer of the Fourth Gospel.

The frequent explanatory allusions of the evangelist to the manners and customs of "the Jews" have been supposed by some to indicate that he was not himself a Jew. "He speaks as if they and their usages belonged to another race from himself," is the comment of Matthew Arnold.[2] The "feasts of the Jews" (6^4 5^1 7^2), "the purifying of the Jews" (2^6), "the chief priests of the Jews" (19^{21}), "the custom of the Jews" (19^{40}), "the Preparation of the Jews" (19^{42}), are thus designated. But Paul did not separate himself from his own people when he wrote of "the Jews" (1 Thess. $2^{14\text{-}16}$, 2 Cor. 11^{24}); nor does the evangelist when he thus invites the attention of his Greek readers to Jewish observances unfamiliar to them. Indeed, Jn. shows an intimate knowledge of these matters. He alludes several times to the Jewish regulations about ceremonial purification (3^{25} 11^{55} 18^{28} 19^{31}), upon which the Pharisees laid much stress (Mk. 7^4). He gives details, as to spices being used at burials, not found in the Synoptists (19^{40}). His use of the word τεταρταῖος is significant (see on 11^{39}). Again, he knows the time of year at which the Jews celebrated the feast of the Dedication, which was not one of the great obligatory festivals of Judaism (10^{22}). The strongest proof, however, that a Jew is behind the Fourth Gospel, whether as "witness" or as author, is the familiarity which it displays with Jewish doctrine current in the first century, as well as with Rabbinical methods of argument.

The universal claim which the evangelist makes for the gospel of Jesus is preceded by what is for him fundamental, viz. that Jesus is the Messiah (20^{31}). This thesis is continually present, while we might antecedently have expected that it would be kept in the background by one who had reached the

[1] Cf. p. lxix.
[2] *God and the Bible*, p. 142. Lord Charnwood's comment is more penetrating: "In style and mind he is an intense Jew. His very anger with his own race is that of a Jew. No Gentile, though he might dislike Jews, would have shown it in the same way; he would have felt, *e.g.*, no interest in shifting more blame on to the Jewish Sanhedrim off the shoulders of Pilate" (*According to St. John*, p. 52).

f

more profound doctrine of Jesus as the Logos of God. Yet
that Jesus is the Christ was for Jn., as it was for Paul, the
essential germ of the fuller belief that He was the Saviour of
the world. Jn. was well acquainted with Jewish popular
beliefs as to the form of the Messianic expectation ($1^{19.\ 20}$).[1]
He knew that it was expected that Messiah would be a worker
of miracles, for the Jews expected this of any Divine messenger
($2^{18}\ 2^{23}\ 3^2\ 9^{17}$; cf. 1 Cor. 1^{22}); and that the miracles would be of
specially convincing character ($7^{31}\ 10^{25}$; cf. 6^{15}). Again, 7^{27}
alludes to the current idea that Messiah, when He appeared,
would emerge suddenly from obscurity. The note on 12^{34}
shows that the eternal reign of Messiah was not unfamiliar to
Jewish thought. The Messiah was expected to have prophetic
powers ($1^{48}\ 4^{25.\ 29}$). Little is known of the Samaritans' doctrine
as to Messiah, but Jn. is aware that they looked for Him (4^{25}).
He recalls also not only their feud with the Jews (which was
doubtless well known) but their veneration for their special
sanctuary on Mount Gerizim (4^{20}).

The evangelist moves with ease in his reports of the controversies about Sabbath observance, and the emphasis placed
upon it by the Pharisees ($5^{10}\ 9^{16}$). He knows not only that it
was much debated at Jerusalem, but also that the casuistry of
the Rabbinical schools had dealt with it (7^{23}). So, too, he is
aware of the contempt of the native Jew for the Jew of the
Dispersion (7^{35}); he knows the accepted Jewish doctrine that
no human being can ascend to heaven (3^{13}); he gives the
Jewish title " the prince of this world " to the Evil One (12^{31}
$14^{30}\ 16^{11}$); he knows of the Rabbinical superstition as to the
merit gained by searching the Scriptures for fantastic arguments (5^{39}); and he makes allusion to the visiting of the father's
sins upon his children (9^2).[2] He knows that in Rabbinical
arguments a claim to *originality* would damage the case of
him who put it forward (7^{16}); and he knows the Rabbinical
rules about evidence, and the inconsequence of bearing witness
about oneself (5^{31}, 8^{13}). Finally, the polemic described in
cc. 5, 7, 8, 9 is thoroughly characteristic of Jewish controversies
and quite unlike a Greek dispute. The argument placed in
the mouth of our Lord at 10^{34}, depending as it does on nice
verbal points, is of special interest in this connexion.[3]

[1] Cf. p. cxlviii.
[2] See Sanday, *Criticism of the Fourth Gospel*, p. 135.
[3] Many Talmudic and Rabbinical parallels to the Fourth Gospel
have been collected by Schlatter (*Die Sprache und Heimat des vierten
Evangelisten*), who specially quotes Midrashim of the second century.
" Most remarkable," wrote the Rabbinical scholar Dr. Abrahams,
" has been the cumulative strength of the arguments adduced by
Jewish writers favourable to the authenticity of the discourses in the

These considerations, it is submitted, show that not only the witness from whom the evangelist derived much of his material, but the evangelist himself, had special knowledge of Palestine during the ministry of Jesus.

(ii) The Literary Method of the Evangelist is not that of Allegory

A view of the Fourth Gospel which has many advocates is that " the book's method and form are prevailingly allegorical . . . its truth depends not on the actual accuracy of the symbolising appearances, but on the truth of the ideas and experiences thus symbolised " [1] Such a sentence raises a question of grave importance, viz. Did Jn. *intend* to write history ? This question takes precedence of any inquiry into the historical trustworthiness of his Gospel. We must come to some conclusion, in the first place, as to what he meant to do. His Gospel is a " spiritual " gospel (as Clement of Alexandria called it); no one challenges its spiritual value. He wrote to convince his readers that " Jesus is the Christ, the Son of God " (20[31]). In the endeavour to do this, did he permit himself to bring out spiritual lessons by portraying scenes which he knew were not historical ? Is not spiritual truth, for him, more important than historical truth ? And, therefore, is not the allegorical method of interpretation the key to the secrets of the Fourth Gospel ?

Before these questions can be answered, we must have a clear conception of what is meant by the " allegorical method," and we must distinguish between *allegorical* interpretation and teaching by *parable*.

A

In many literatures attempts have been made to *allegorise* the statements of a notable book, *i.e.* to find a hidden meaning in incidents which were originally set down as having actually taken place, or in conversations which were narrated as historical. Thus the Stoics allegorised Homer, in the interests of Greek religion, to vindicate the character of the gods. Sometimes, again, allegorical interpretations were placed upon sacred books, not because what was narrated was believed to be unhistorical, but because the interpreters found in a book divinely inspired a spiritual meaning underlying the literal

Fourth Gospel, especially in relation to the circumstances under which they are reported to have been spoken " (*Cambridge Biblical Essays*, p. 181).
   [1] Von Hügel in *Ency. Brit.*, xv. p. 455 (in his article on the Gospel).

narrative. To seek for the spiritual meaning of history is an exercise with special attractiveness for men who believe that history is controlled by Divine Providence.

Thus, when Paul says that the story of Abraham, Sarah, and Hagar contains an "allegory" (Gal. 4²⁴), he does not suggest that it was not a true historical record of what had happened in the olden time; he means that the history symbolised a spiritual lesson (cf. also 1 Cor. 10¹⁻¹¹). In like manner, Philo sought a spiritual meaning behind the narratives of the O.T., of many of which, however, he rejected the literal truth. He treated the O.T. as the allegorising Greeks treated Homer. Philo is, in truth, the father of the allegorical interpretation of the O.T., which occupied so large a place in patristic exegesis, and which has always appealed to those who feel the charm of poetry. The *incidents*, *names*, and even the *numbers* of the Jewish Scriptures had for him a mystical significance, in which their true value resided, and by which their divine inspiration was most readily established. Because the O.T. was divine, it was natural to seek a deeper meaning in its every phrase than was apparent to a superficial reader.

The Christian fathers inherited this Jewish tradition of the allegorical interpretation of the O.T., but it was first applied to the N.T. by the Gnostics, with whose doctrine of a secret *gnosis* it was congruous. The aged Simeon taking Jesus in his arms and giving thanks was a type of the Demiurge who on the arrival of the Saviour gave thanks.[1] That Jesus was *twelve* years old when He discoursed with the doctors in the temple was an indication of the Duodecad of the Æons.[2] And the healing of the woman afflicted with an issue of blood for twelve years in like manner typified the healing of the twelfth Æon.[3] These allegorisings of the Synoptic Gospels are denounced as blasphemous by Irenæus, and Tertullian afterwards took the same line. But in the next generation the allegorical interpretation of the N.T. was adopted by teachers of influence such as Clement of Alexandria and Origen; and it has ever since been favoured by Christian expositors of high repute, from Cyril of Alexandria and Augustine down to our own time. Most of those, however, who have found a mystical meaning in Gospel incidents or Gospel conversations have been firmly persuaded, nevertheless, that these incidents and conversations were historical. They allegorised history, but they did not challenge its literal truth.

Origen went a little further than this. He explains that, as man consists of body, soul, and spirit, so there are generally three senses in Scripture, the *corporeal*, the *moral*, and the

[1] Irenæus, *Hær.* I. viii. 4.   [2] Iren. *l.c.* I. iii. 2.   [3] Iren. *l.c.* I. iii. 3.

spiritual.[1] But occasionally, although not often, the corporeal or literal meaning is lacking, and this applies to the N.T. as well as to the O.T. "Non solum in ueteri testamento occidens litera deprehenditur : est et in nouo testamento litera quae occidat eum, qui non spiritualiter, quae dicuntur, aduerterit." [2] This applies primarily to the interpretation of precepts, *e.g.* Lk. 10[4], "salute no man by the way," but it may also be applied to incidents. Even the Gospels, Origen says, do not contain everywhere a pure history, but have things interwoven according to the literal sense, which yet did not happen.[3] He only gives one example, viz. the story of our Lord's Temptation, which (he points out) could not *literally* be true, for you could not see all the kingdoms of the earth from one mountain in Judæa. Thus Origen leaves it open to an interpreter not only to find a spiritual meaning beneath the letter of a Gospel story, but also to reject the literal meaning, if it is manifestly absurd or impossible. But it is plain that he would only have admitted this plea in rare cases,[4] such as the story of the Temptation where the language used is figurative; like all his contemporaries he would have repudiated the suggestion that the miracle stories are *only* parables of edification, although they are pregnant with spiritual truths (see on 2[10]).

B

It is now to be observed that none of the early masters of the allegorical method, whether Jewish or Christian, *invented* an incident or *constructed* a number, in order to teach a spiritual lesson. Just because they deemed the Scriptures to be divinely inspired, they were sure that they must be edifying in every phrase; and if the plain meaning of the words was *not* edifying, they sought edification beneath the surface. Indeed, the Gnostics always looked for a meaning that was not plain or obvious. But none of these allegorical interpreters *composed* fictitious narratives for the purpose of moral or spiritual instruction. That is a quite legitimate method of teaching, as it is a method of extraordinary power. The *Fables* of Æsop were, frankly, constructed to convey moral lessons. Our Lord gave to this method the sanction of His own authority, for He habitually taught by parables, "earthly stories with a heavenly meaning"; and His example has been followed by Christian teachers in every age, from the *Shepherd of Hermas* in the

---

[1] *de princ.* iv. 11.   [2] *Hom. in Levit* .vii. 5.
[3] οὐδὲ τούτων πάντη ἄκρατον τὴν ἱστορίαν τῶν προσυφασμένων κατὰ τὸ σωματικὸν ἐχόντων, μὴ γεγενημένων (*de princ.* iv. 16).
[4] Cf. *de princ.* iv. 19.

second century to the *Pilgrim's Progress* in the seventeenth. But the allegorical *interpreter* and the *author* of parables follow distinct paths, and are not to be confused, the one with the other.

It is one thing to spiritualise history; it is quite another to put forth as history a narrative which is not based on fact. Neither Philo nor any of the Alexandrines adopted the latter course; *i.e.* they never wrote books of which the literal meaning was not the intended meaning. The allegorists would have been the first to admit that a spiritual sense, underlying the literal sense, was not claimed by them for their own writings. Neither Philo, nor Clement, nor Origen, were writers of *parables*.

Nor did the Gnostics compose books in the form of parable. For them the highest knowledge of spiritual things was not for the vulgar; it was only to the elect that the true γνῶσις was accessible. Accordingly, they applied the method of allegorical interpretation to the N.T., in order to draw out the deeper meaning (as they supposed) of the Gospels. They also re-wrote some N.T. narratives in the interests of Gnostic doctrine, a notable example of this being the Gospel of Peter, which tells the story of the Passion from the Docetic point of view. Other Gnostic books are filled with alleged revelations to the Apostles, or to the Virgin Mary, these revelations, of course, supporting Gnostic tenets. But their books are not written in the form of history which requires to be spiritualised before its purport can be determined.

C

We have now seen that the phrase " allegorical method " requires careful definition. Many writers of the apostolic and sub-apostolic age were drawn to " allegorise " the narratives of the O.T., and some to apply a like operation to the N.T. But that is not to say that they themselves wrote in the form of parable, viz. that their own writings have an inner meaning which is not apparent on the surface.

Thus the Fourth Evangelist saw a Christian meaning in O.T. sayings and customs (*e.g.* 13^{18} $19^{24. 36}$); in that sense, he was an allegorist as Paul was. But it does not follow that his Gospel was intended by him to be treated as the Gnostics treated the O.T., viz. that its literal meaning should be discarded, and its spiritual teaching alone remembered. Indeed, the significance of Jn. to his contemporaries was that he was steadily opposed to Gnosticism of every type. He insists that Jesus Christ came *in the flesh* (1 Jn. 4^2); it is the very spirit of antichrist to explain this away or to spiritualise it. That *the Word became flesh* is his starting-point. He lays special stress on the true humanity of Jesus (*e.g.* 4⁶ 11³⁵ 19²⁸·³⁴). His purpose and his method alike are wholly inconsistent with the view that his narrative is a congeries of parables. So little inclination has he for the parabolic method, that he is the only evangelist who reports no parables of Christ. Whether we accept Jn.'s Gospel as historically trustworthy or no, it was written that his readers might accept as facts, and not only as symbols, the incidents which he records.[1]

D

Those who find symbol rather than fact in the Fourth Gospel have called special attention to the *numbers* which occur in the course of the narrative; and what has been said above about the allegorical method in general may fitly be illustrated by one or two examples of the way in which it has been applied to Scripture numbers, both by Jews and Christians.

Philo finds esoteric meanings in the statement (Gen. 5²³) that Enoch's age was 365 years; just as he finds in Gen. 6³, which gives the average age of patriarchal man as 120 years, " a divine and sacred number." [2] The Christian fathers take the same line. Barnabas (§ 9) finds in the number of Abraham's servants, viz. 318 (Gen. 14¹⁴ 17²³), a prophecy of the Crucifixion. So does Clement of Alexandria (*Strom.* vi. 11), who proceeds in the same passage to take over from Philo the idea that 120 in Gen. 6³ is a mystery, explaining that 1+2+3+ . . . 15 = 120, while 15 is a specially significant number, because the moon at 15 days is full.

The later fathers inherited this doctrine of the mystical value of numbers, and some of them applied it to the Fourth Gospel. The 153 fishes of Jn. 21¹¹ provide scope for much ingenious speculation. Thus Augustine (*Enarr. in Ps.*, xlix. § 9) tells us that 1+2+3+ . . . 17 = 153, while 17 is formed by adding the two sacred numbers, 10 for the Law and 7 for the Spirit. It is no more likely that Jn. intended this, than that the author of Gen. 6³ intended the like comment to be made upon his text. See, for other examples, on 1³² 2²⁰ 19²³.

Numerical coincidences such as these are supposed by their discoverers to reveal the significance of Johannine numbers, which are believed to have an esoteric meaning. It remains, however, for some one to show that books were really written in this way. Can any parallel be produced to support the theory that the numbers in Jn. (38, 46, 153, etc.) were con-

---

[1] See below, p. xc, on the value attached to " witness " by Jn.
[2] *Quæst. in Gen.* i. 83 f.

structed by him to provoke his readers, in pursuit of the true *gnosis*, to discover what he meant ?   " The idea," said Hatch, " that ancient literature consists of riddles which it is the business of modern literature to solve has passed for ever away."[1] The idea still survives, and in unexpected quarters, but it is certainly not applicable to the Fourth Gospel, in which not *gnosis* but *pistis* is the supreme aim of the writer.   The true inheritors of Gnostic methods of interpretation are the commentators who find in the " Gospel according to St. John " a hidden purpose and an esoteric meaning.   Jn. was not an allegorist; that rôle has been assumed by his critics, who teach that his Gospel is written in the form of a parable, of which the literal meaning was not meant by him to be the true meaning.

E

Something must be added about the alleged adoption by Jn. of a sevenfold arrangement in his work.

The number seven appears in religious or mystical literature in many parts of the world,[2] as well as in folk-lore.   Its significance may go back to the periods of seven days which correspond to the moon's phases, for it is thus that the choice of a week as a definite unit of time probably originated.   In the O.T., besides the use of *seven* as expressing an exact number, a use which is inevitable in all narrative, it sometimes indicates merely a round number (*e.g.* sevenfold vengeance, Gen. 4^{15} Ps. 79^{12}, or sevenfold restitution, Prov. 6^{31}), and it occasionally serves to indicate completeness (*e.g.* the seven nations of Deut. 7^1 or the seven withes of Judg. 16^7), and specially as a feature of ceremonial or ritual observance (*e.g.* seven bowings to the earth, Gen. 33^3, or the blowing of seven trumpets round the walls of Jericho, Josh. 6^4, or Balaam's seven altars, Num. 23^1, or the seven beasts of each kind for a sin-offering, 2 Chr. 29^{21}).   Seven is a number that is common in stories (*e.g.* the seven cattle of Pharaoh's dream, Gen. 41^2, or the woman who married seven husbands, Mk. 12^{20}).   It appears in Apocalyptic (*e.g.* the seven weeks of Dan. 9^{25}, or the seven mountains in the Book of Enoch), as the Hebdomad, or seven planetary powers, plays a part in Gnostic systems.   Some have thought that the sevenfold repetition of the Name of Yahweh in Ps. 92 is deliberately devised by the poet so as to make it suitable as a " Psalm for the Sabbath day."

Similar uses of the number seven are found in Christian literature, early and late, sacred and secular.   The mediæval idea of *seven* deadly sins may go back to Prov. 6^{16}, or to that of

[1] *Hibbert Lectures* for 1888, p. 84.   [2] Cf. *E.B.* 3436.

possession by seven evil spirits (Lk. 8^2 11^{26}). That there are *seven* gifts of the Spirit goes back to the LXX, which has added to the six gifts of Is. 11^2 a seventh, no doubt with the idea of seven as a mystical number. The Seven Sleepers of Ephesus illustrate Christian folk-lore.

The number of deacons was fixed at seven (Acts 6^5 21^8), and this may have been deliberate. There is not much in Lk. which calls attention to this number; but he, with Mt., reproduces from Q the command to forgive seven times (Lk. 17^4), and the parable of the seven evil spirits (Lk. 11^{24}). Both Mt. and Lk. follow Mk.'s story of the woman with seven husbands. Mt., however, shows a partiality for sevenfold grouping. He has seven parables in c. 13, and the seven woes are gathered in c. 23. This indicates deliberate arrangement, such as does not appear in Mk., Lk. Mt. follows Mk. in telling of the feeding of the four thousand with *seven* loaves (Mk. 8^5).

In the Apocalypse, the tendency of the seer to dwell on the number seven is inherited from previous apocalyptic literature, and is unmistakable, ἑπτά occurring over fifty times.

Here is a marked contrast to the Fourth Gospel, where ἑπτά does not occur at all, and ἕβδομος only once (4^{52}). It has been thought by some that Jn. avoids ἑπτά deliberately,[1] because of its abuse in Gnostic literature. That may be the case. But it has also been suggested [2] that the arrangement of the Gospel betrays a deliberate sevenfold grouping, although it is skilfully concealed. We shall examine presently (p. xci) the sevenfold witness to Jesus which may be discovered in the Gospel ; but it is not clear that these forms of μαρτυρία are meant to be, significantly, seven in number, neither more nor less. And similar difficulties beset other attempts to find an intentional sevenfold arrangement.

The sevenfold repetition, in c. 6 (see on 6^{33}) or in the Farewell Discourses, of solemn refrains (see on 15^{11}) is striking when it is discovered, but it is not clear that the number seven is intended thus to convey any special meaning, or that it was present to the writer's mind. Exegetes have often commented on the *seven* Similitudes by which Jesus describes Himself in the Fourth Gospel, beginning with ἐγώ εἰμι (6^{35} 8^{12} $10^{7. 11}$ 11^{25} 15^1 14^6). But with these must be associated ἐγώ εἰμι ὁ μαρτυρῶν περὶ ἐμαυτοῦ (8^{18}), which brings the number of these Divine Pronouncements up to eight.[3]

Or, again, the number of the "seven signs" of Jesus which are recorded in the Fourth Gospel has been sometimes

---

[1] See p. lxv.　　　　[2] Cf. Abbott, *Diat.* 2625. 6.
[3] See p. cxviii.

thought to imply deliberate arrangement. But, as we have shown on another page,[1] the wonderful works called σημεῖα by Jn. are only five in number, although a sixth might be included by way of inference. To Jn. the incident of the Storm on the Lake is not a σημεῖον at all (see on 6[17f.]).

Indeed, if Jn. attached mystical importance to the number *seven*, and dealt in allegory, as some suppose, we should have expected him to select for record the story in which the multitudes were miraculously fed with seven loaves and seven basketsful of fragments remained over, rather than that in which the loaves are but five (6[9]). Both of the miracles of feeding are recorded by Mk. (6[35f.] 8[1f.]), whose Gospel was known to, and used by, Jn.[2] If he were an allegorist, the seven loaves would have presented a mystical meaning, which the five loaves do not offer.

The conclusion seems to be that Jn. did not set any special value on the number seven; it is not prominent in Jn. as in Mt. The intentional presence of the number seven in the narrative and the structure of the Fourth Gospel is not proved. He does not deal in allegory, but in facts.

The view that is taken in this commentary on the Fourth Gospel is that, primarily, the evangelist intended to present narratives of fact, of the truth of which he himself was fully persuaded. He is not only a historian, but he is an interpreter of history, as is shown not only by his comments on his narrative as he proceeds,[3] but also by his selection and arrangement of his materials so as to persuade his readers most effectively of his main thesis (20[30]). That he is insistent upon the importance of "witness," μαρτυρία, in relation to matters of fact, must next be shown to be part of his historical method.

(iii) The Idea of "Witness" is Prominent

The narrative of the Fourth Evangelist is, to a considerable extent, a narrative of controversy. He relates more fully than the Synoptists the story of the hostility with which the claims of Jesus were greeted at Jerusalem; and he recalls the "evidences" (as a modern writer would call them) or the "witness" to which Jesus pointed as justifying and explaining His claims. "Witness" is a necessary correlative of intelligent belief.

But there is another, and a more far-reaching reason for the prevalence of the idea of μαρτυρία in Jn. It is due to the circumstances in which the Fourth Gospel was produced, and to the purpose of the evangelist in writing it.[4] The book

[1] P. clxxvii.   [2] Cf. p. xcvi.   [3] P. xxxiv.   [4] See on 1[14].

was not written in the earliest days of the Church's life, when terms of allegiance to the Church's Master were still unformu-lated, and when the disciples in the first flush of enthusiasm and devotion had hardly asked themselves what was the in-tellectual basis of the faith in which they had found strength. The clear definitions of Christian theology had not yet been elicited by the growth of error and of misunderstanding which had to be repressed. But by the end of the first century in intellectual centres such as the Greek cities of Asia Minor, it became imperative that the false *gnosis* should be expelled by the true, and that the faith in Jesus as the Christ, the Son of God, should be justified to thinking men.[1] On what evidence did this wonderful faith rest itself? So men asked, and an answer had to be given. It is natural that the Gospel which originated under such conditions should lay emphasis on the " witnesses " to which the early preachers and Jesus Himself had appealed. The author is conscious, as he writes, that the facts which he narrates will be scrutinised by keen critics, and that his interpretation of them may be challenged.

1. He begins, then, as the Synoptists did, with the witness of *John the Baptist*, upon which he lingers, however, longer than they. The Forerunner came εἰς μαρτυρίαν (1^7 3^{26} 5^{33}). He bore witness that He who was coming was the Pre-existent One (1^{15}), while he himself was only the herald ($1^{19f.}$; cf. 3^{28}). When Jesus came, John bore witness that he saw the Spirit descending upon Him (1^{32}), and that this was the ap-pointed token that He was the Son of God (1^{34}).

2. Of *other human witnesses*, who may be summoned to give their testimony, Jn. mentions:

(a) The Samaritan woman, whose witness did not go further than her own limited experience would justify, and was therefore all the more impressive—τῆς γυναικὸς μαρτυρούσης ὅτι Εἶπέν μοι πάντα ἃ ἐποίησα (4^{39}).

(b) Similar to the Samaritan woman's witness is that of the blind man whose sight was restored ($9^{15f.}$), although the *word* μαρτυρία does not occur in this story.

(c) The multitude who had seen the raising of Lazarus bore witness to the fact—ἐμαρτύρει ὁ ὄχλος (12^{17}).

(d) The Twelve, whose authority rested on the intimacy of personal companionship—ὑμεῖς δὲ μαρτυρεῖτε ὅτι ἀπ᾽ ἀρχῆς μετ᾽ ἐμοῦ ἐστέ (15^{27}); cf. also 3^{11}.

---

[1] So in the Pauline Epp. it is not until we reach the latest phase of his teaching that we come upon the assertion ἡ μαρτυρία αὕτη ἐστὶν ἀληθής (Tit. 1^{13}). Generally, in Paul, the verb μαρτυρεῖν bears the sense of painful testifying, rather than of bringing forward evidence to prove something that is in dispute.

(*e*) The eye-witness of the Passion, *i.e.* the Beloved Disciple, on whom Jn. depends for his facts—ὁ ἑωρακὼς μεμαρτύρηκεν (19³⁵, where see note); whose testimony was regarded as unimpeachable by those who published the Gospel—οἴδαμεν ὅτι ἀληθὴς αὐτοῦ ἡ μαρτυρία ἐστίν (21²⁴).

3. The witness of the *Old Testament Scriptures* to Christ is appealed to as explicit—ἐκεῖναί εἰσιν αἱ μαρτυροῦσαι περὶ ἐμοῦ (5³⁹).

4. The *works* which Jesus did are His witness—τὰ ἔργα . . . μαρτυρεῖ περὶ ἐμοῦ ὅτι ὁ πατήρ με ἀπέσταλκεν (5³⁶; cf. 10²⁵).

5. These works were " given Him by His Father " to do; and Jesus speaks of the witness of *the Father* to His claims—ὁ πέμψας με πατήρ, ἐκεῖνος μεμαρτύρηκεν περὶ ἐμοῦ (5³⁷; cf. 5³² 8¹⁸).

6. The witness of *Jesus* to Himself. Such self-witness in the case of man does not, indeed, carry conviction (5³¹); it is only when the Person giving it is conscious of His origin in the bosom of Deity that it can fitly be brought forward—κἂν ἐγὼ μαρτυρῶ περὶ ἐμαυτοῦ, ἀληθής ἐστιν ἡ μαρτυρία μου, ὅτι οἶδα πόθεν ἦλθον καὶ ποῦ ὑπάγω (8¹⁴). Such an One alone, when speaking of the secrets of the spiritual world, could say ὁ ἐκ τοῦ οὐρανοῦ ἐρχόμενος ὃ ἑώρακεν καὶ ἤκουσεν τοῦτο μαρτυρεῖ (3³²). It is for this reason also that the witness of Christ to "the Truth " (18³⁷) is of unique significance. Only He could say ἐγώ εἰμι ὁ μαρτυρῶν περὶ ἐμαυτοῦ, with the serene confidence of Divinity (8¹⁸).

7. Lastly, we have the witness of *the Spirit*. When the visible presence of the Christ has been withdrawn, so that men can no longer be drawn to Him by His own witness, by the compelling attraction of a Divine Personality incarnate in human nature, then—ὁ παράκλητος . . . τὸ πνεῦμα τῆς ἀληθείας . . . ἐκεῖνος μαρτυρήσει περὶ ἐμοῦ (15²⁶; cf. Acts 5³²).

There is, therefore, if it is profitable so to regard it, a presentation of a *sevenfold* witness in the Fourth Gospel. It would, however, be easy so to co-ordinate the various passages in which the idea of μαρτυρία emerges that the number might be reduced or enlarged; and it is precarious and may be misleading to lay stress in this connexion on the number 7.[1]

In the First Johannine Epistle the " witness " is explicitly set out as *threefold* (1 Jn. 5⁷ᶠ·), that of the Spirit, the Water, and the Blood; *i.e. primarily* (1) the Descent of the Spirit upon Jesus at His baptism (cf. Jn. 1³³), (2) His visible baptism with water, (3) His Passion and Death; and *secondarily* (1) the internal witness of the Spirit which is perpetually testifying of Jesus, (2) the baptism by which believers are incorporated in Him,[2] and (3) the Atonement of His Cross in which they find

[1] See p. lxxxix above.   [2] Cf. Jn. 3⁵.

deliverance. Thus the historical witness yields place to the moral; the " witness of God " is greater than the " witness of man " (1 Jn. 5⁹). The " witness of God " is that God gave eternal life to us in Christ (1 Jn. 5¹¹; cf. Jn. 17³), of which we are assured not on historical grounds only, but also on those of present spiritual experience—ὁ πιστεύων εἰς τὸν υἱὸν τοῦ θεοῦ ἔχει τὴν μαρτυρίαν ἐν αὐτῷ (1 Jn. 5¹⁰).

(iv) PHILO AND THE FOURTH GOSPEL

Philo of Alexandria (b. 20 B.C., d. 49 A.D.) set himself to reconcile Hebraism and Hellenism, and to that end his aim throughout his voluminous writings was to expound the spiritual and philosophical meaning latent in the O.T. literature. His influence was far-reaching among Alexandrian Jews, and the teaching at Ephesus of the learned Alexandrian Apollos (Acts 18²⁴) was probably not carried on without occasional reference to Philo and his theological speculations. In any case, we should expect to find among educated people at Ephesus some acquaintance with Philo's doctrine of the λόγος, as well as with his interpretations of Hebrew Scripture.

A comparison of the thoughts of Philo with those of the Fourth Gospel shows that in many instances Philo provides useful illustrations of Johannine doctrine, which might be expected *a priori* in so far as both writers deal with similar topics. But that there is any literary dependence of the Fourth Gospel upon the earlier writer has not been fully proved, although there is no reason to doubt that Jn. might have used the language of Philo on occasion when it suited his purpose.

Thus the doctrine that genuine worship must be of the spirit appears in Philo, as well as in Jn. 4²³ (see note). The mystical saying that the Son cannot do anything except what He sees the Father doing recalls Philo's language about the πρεσβύτατος υἱός who imitates the ways of the Father (see on 5¹⁹). Philo contrasts the ἀγαθὸς ποιμήν with a mere herd, in a fashion that is similar to 10¹¹ (where see note). So, too, Philo distinguishes the φίλοι of God from His δοῦλοι (see on 15¹⁵). Even more noteworthy is Philo's comparison of the manna to the Divine Logos, which is the heavenly, incorruptible food of the soul (see on 6³⁴·³⁵). And the doctrine of 1 Jn. 2¹⁵, " If any man love the world, the love of the Father is not in Him," is remarkably like the following: ἀμήχανον συνυπάρχειν τὴν πρὸς κόσμον ἀγάπην τῇ πρὸς τὸν θεὸν ἀγάπῃ, ὡς ἀμήχανον συνυπάρχειν ἀλλήλοις φῶς καὶ σκότος.[1]

These are close and remarkable Philonic parallels, and

---

[1] Fragm. ex Joh. Damasc., *Sacr. Parall.*, p. 370 B.

they suggest that Jn. was acquainted with Philo's works. Some will regard them as establishing a real literary dependence of the Fourth Gospel upon Philo, but this cannot be regarded as certain. A large number of illustrative passages from Philo have been cited in the notes, but they can be used only as *illustrations*, not as *sources* which the evangelist uses. See on $1^{5. 9. 16. 38. 50. 51}$ $3^{14. 19}$ $4^{10. 42}$ 5^{32} $8^{12. 32}$ 11^{51} 14^{6} $15^{2. 26}$ $19^{3. 23. 31}$.

For Philo's doctrine of the Λόγος, see below, p. cxl.

CHAPTER IV

THE FOURTH GOSPEL IN ITS RELATION TO THE SYNOPTICS

(i) The Use made by Jn. of the Synoptists.
(ii) The Chronology of Jn. and of the Synoptists.
(iii) The Words of Jesus in Jn. and in the Synoptists.

(I) THE USE MADE BY JN. OF THE SYNOPTISTS.

AT some points the Fourth Gospel reproduces a more primitive tradition of the Ministry of Jesus than is to be found in the Synoptists. Jn.'s word for the chosen followers of Jesus is μαθηταί, which doubtless goes back to the earliest period; he does not use the term apostles (see on 2^2 13^{16}). His account of the way in which disciples, both of the inner and outer circles, used to address Jesus, has every mark of historical truth (see on 1^{38} 4^1). Again, Jn.'s allusions to the Baptism of Jesus (see on 1^{32}) seem to go back to a more primitive (and probably a better authenticated) tradition than those followed in the Synoptic Gospels; and the same may be said of his narrative of the Storm on the Lake (see on $6^{16f.}$). These are illustrations of the contemporary authority behind much that is recorded in the Fourth Gospel; it is the " Gospel according to St. John," relying in many instances on the reminiscences of the Beloved Disciple.

That the Fourth Gospel was written at a time when the general Synoptic tradition was familiar to Christians does not need proof. To the evangelist, the writer of the book, the outline of the Gospel story was already well known, and he assumes previous knowledge of it on the part of his readers. " The Twelve " are mentioned without any previous indication that twelve companions had been specially chosen by Jesus (6^{67}; cf. 6^{13}). It is for him a sufficient account of Andrew to say that he was the brother of Peter (1^{40}), of whom everybody knew. Every one knew, again, of the fact that John the Baptist had been imprisoned; it is alluded to only as marking the time of his ministry near Salim, viz. before his imprisonment (3^{24}). Jn. does not attempt to tell over again the story that has already been told to Christian disciples from the beginning. He omits much that is present in the Marcan tradition, *e.g.* the Transfiguration; or that was found in that common source of Mk., Lk., Mt., now generally described as Q, *e.g.* the Temptation, the Sermon on the Mount, the Lord's Prayer. In Part I. of the Gospel, at any rate, the scene of which is largely laid in Galilee, we might expect to meet with *publicans*, *lepers*, and *demoniacs*, or to read of the preaching of *repentance* or *forgiveness*, as in the Synoptic Gospels. But Jn. introduces none of these people and neither of these topics (cf., however, 20^{23}).

Yet Jn. does not avoid the Synoptic stories altogether. He has, *e.g.*, the Cleansing of the Temple [1] ($2^{13f.}$), the Healing of the Nobleman's Son ($4^{46f.}$), the Feeding of the Five Thousand ($6^{1f.}$), the Storm on the Lake ($6^{16f.}$), while he treats these and other incidents in his own manner.

All this is self-evident. And since the time of Eusebius, at any rate, it has been recognised that Jn. knew the general story which we now have in the Synoptists. Eusebius,[2] indeed, accepts a tradition of his day that Jn. wrote his Gospel in order that he might supply what was lacking in the earlier narratives, especially in regard to the beginnings of the ministry of Jesus. This does not give us the only or main purpose of the composition of the Fourth Gospel; but that Jn. wrote with a knowledge of what had previously been written about the Life of Jesus is, *a priori*, probable.

We have now to ask, Had Jn. ever *seen* the Synoptic Gospels in their present form ? Is there any trace of his having used Mk., Lk., or Mt. ? Does he reproduce phrases which are found in any of the earlier Gospels ? Such questions may be approached quite dispassionately. The study of the Synoptic problem, which has now been continued for a century, has resulted in a general acceptance of the conclusion that both Lk. and Mt. used Mk. in addition to a source now lost, which is commonly described as Q. The words of Mk. were adopted in many instances both by Lk. and by Mt., sometimes without change and sometimes with corrections, which in the judgment of the later evangelists improved the style or made for accuracy.

---

[1] Here Jn. seems to have amplified and altered the Marcan narrative (see notes *in loc.*). Cf. also p. xxx.

[2] *H.E.* iii. 24. 7.

It is possible that Jn. (*i.e.* the evangelist, not John the Beloved Disciple) may have used the Synoptists in like manner. It would have been quite consistent with the literary habits of the time if he occasionally borrowed a sentence from his predecessors. There will, then, be nothing to surprise if we find in Jn. not only traditions which he shared with earlier evangelists, as well as with the whole Church of his day, but also traces of the actual incorporation in his text of descriptive phrases from the Synoptic Gospels, or from their sources.

It will be convenient to state briefly at this point that the conclusions which have been adopted in this commentary [1] are (*a*) that Jn. almost certainly uses Mk.; (*b*) that most probably he uses Lk., or perhaps we should say uses Q; and (*c*) that there is no good evidence that he used Mt. at all, or was aware of the Matthæan tradition as distinct from that of Mk. (see nevertheless 6^3 16^4 20^{17} for passages with some similarity to Mt.). It is, indeed, possible that the " Gospel according to St. Matthew " is in its present form the latest of the four canonical Gospels; but upon this I do not enter here.

A. COMPARISON OF JN. WITH MK.

1. The most remarkable agreements in language between Jn. and Mk. occur in the narratives of the Anointing at Bethany (Jn. 12^{1-8}, Mk. 14^{3-9}). These narratives, and also that of Lk. 7^{36-49}, have been compared and examined in the Additional Note on Jn. 12^{1-8}. Here we note only the verbal coincidences:

Jn. 12^3: μύρου νάρδου πιστικῆς πολυτίμου reproduces Mk. 14^3 μύρου νάρδου πιστικῆς πολυτελοῦς, the word πιστικῆς being both uncommon and obscure.

Jn. 12^5: διὰ τί τοῦτο τὸ μύρον οὐκ ἐπράθη τριακοσίων δηναρίων καὶ ἐδόθη πτωχοῖς; reproduces Mk. 14^5 ἠδύνατο γὰρ τοῦτο τὸ μύρον πραθῆναι ἐπάνω δηναρίων τριακοσίων καὶ δοθῆναι τοῖς πτωχοῖς.

Jn. 12^7: ἄφες αὐτήν, ἵνα εἰς τὴν ἡμέραν τοῦ ἐνταφιασμοῦ μου τηρήσῃ αὐτό recalls Mk. $14^{6.\ 8}$ ἄφετε αὐτήν· . . . προέλαβεν μυρίσαι τὸ σῶμά μου εἰς τὸν ἐνταφιασμόν.

Jn. 12^8: τοὺς πτωχοὺς γὰρ πάντοτε ἔχετε μεθ' ἑαυτῶν, ἐμὲ δὲ οὐ πάντοτε ἔχετε reproduces Mk. 14^7 πάντοτε γὰρ τοὺς πτωχοὺς ἔχετε μεθ' ἑαυτῶν . . . ἐμὲ δὲ οὐ πάντοτε ἔχετε.

These verbal coincidences are so close that they cannot

---

[1] The literature is vast. See Abbott, *E.B.* ii., *s.v.* " Gospels," and for evidence from vocabulary, *Diat.* 1665–1874 ; Bacon, *The Fourth Gospel*, p. 366 f. ; Stanton, *The Gospels as Historical Documents*, iii. p. 214 f. ; and recently Streeter's admirable study in *The Four Gospels*, ch. xiv.

reasonably be explained by reference to a common oral tradition being the source of the story in Jn. as in Mk. And the care with which Jn. has amplified and corrected in the course of his narrative certain statements of Mk. (see notes on Jn. 12¹⁻⁸) shows that where he follows Mk. verbally, he does so deliberately. See below.

2. A second example of the reproduction of Mk'.s words by Jn. appears in the story of the cure of the impotent man at Bethesda.

The command ἔγειρε ἆρον τὸν κράββατόν σου καὶ περιπάτει (Jn. 5⁸) is repeated from Mk. 2⁹ ἔγειραι καὶ ἆρον τὸν κράββατόν σου καὶ περιπάτει. So, too, the result εὐθέως ἐγένετο ὑγιὴς ὁ ἄνθρωπος, καὶ ἦρεν τὸν κράββατον αὐτοῦ καὶ περιεπάτει (Jn. 5⁹) recalls Mk. 2¹² ἠγέρθη καὶ εὐθὺς ἄρας τὸν κράββατον ἐξῆλθεν ἔμπροσθεν πάντων. No doubt the narratives describe two quite distinct incidents; although, on the other hand, it may be contended that the words urging the paralytic of Mk. and the impotent man of Jn. to make a special effort would probably be similar in both instances. Yet, as Streeter points out,[1] Jesus must be supposed to have spoken in Aramaic, and that the Greek version of what He said in one case should be so close to an independent version of what He said in the other (both including the vulgar word κράββατον, which is not used in the parallels Mt. 9, Lk. 5) is unlikely. And there is also a close *verbal* similarity (see on 5⁹) in the reports of the man going off immediately carrying his pallet. It is more likely that Jn. here avails himself of words used by Mk. in describing a somewhat similar scene than that these verbal coincidences should be accidental. This, be it observed, is not an instance of Jn.'s *correction* of Mk., but of his use of Mk.'s vocabulary.

3. The Johannine stories of the Feeding of the Five Thousand and of the Storm on the Lake (6¹⁻²¹) recall the words used in Mk. 6³⁰⁻⁵² at some points. The detail διακοσίων δηναρίων ἄρτοι, which does not appear in Mt., Lk., is verbally identical in Jn. 6⁷, Mk. 6³⁷; the verb ἀναπίπτειν, used in Jn. 6¹⁰, is also used in Mk. 6⁴⁰, but not in Mt., Lk.; the χόρτος of Jn. 6¹⁰ is reproduced from Mk. 6³⁹ (so Mt. 14¹⁹), but is not in Lk.; the pronouncement ἐγώ εἰμι, μὴ φοβεῖσθε (Jn. 6²⁰) is identical with Mk. 6⁵⁰ (followed by Mt. 14²⁷). Lk. does not tell of the Storm on the Lake. These verbal similarities between Jn. and Mk. are the more remarkable by reason of the tendency in Jn'.s narrative to *correct* Mk.'s report at other points.

Thus the *sacramental* suggestiveness of Jesus lifting up His eyes to heaven and breaking the bread in blessing (Mk. 6⁴¹,

[1] *The Four Gospels*, p. 398.

g

Mt. 14^{19}, Lk. 9^{16}) does not appear in Jn. (see on 6^{11}), and the omission is probably deliberate. So, too, Jn. avoids the word πλήρωμα (see on 6^{12}) which Mk. has at 6^{43}. And he retells the Marcan story of the Storm on the Lake in such a way that he removes any suggestion of the miraculous walking on the sea (see on 6^{16}), while he retains some of Mk.'s words.

That Jn. knew these Marcan narratives, but adopted their phraseology only after scrutiny and correction, seems to be the most probable explanation.

4. In regard to the *order* in which the incidents at the Last Supper are narrated, there is remarkable agreement between Jn. and Mk., as contrasted with the divergent order suggested by Lk. This is discussed in the note on 13^4. It does not follow that Jn. is using the text of Mk. in c. 13, but that both adopt the same order of events recommends it as most probably historical.

5. Peter's three denials of his Master are described in Jn., as in Mk., as having happened while he was waiting in the courtyard of the high priest while the preliminary examination of Jesus was proceeding; and both Jn. (18$^{18.\ 25}$) and Mk. (14$^{54.\ 67}$) mention *twice* that Peter was warming himself (θερμαινόμενος) during his parley with the slaves and the police. Perhaps Jn. here follows Mk., while he departs from the Marcan story in other particulars (see on 13^{38} 18$^{18.\ 25.\ 27}$). When the first examination of Jesus by Pilate has taken place, the question βούλεσθε οὖν ἀπολύσω ὑμῖν τὸν βασιλέα τῶν Ἰουδαίων; is recorded by Jn. (18^{39}) in words almost identical with those of Mk. 15^9, but not of Mt., Lk. There is thus a probability that Jn. 18 goes back at some points to Mk. 14, 15; but this is not certain.

6. The account of the mock coronation of Jesus by Pilate's soldiers and of His investment with a purple robe (Jn. 19^2) is similar in several phrases to the Synoptic narratives, and suggests Mt. 27$^{28.\ 29}$ and Lk. 23^{11} as well as Mk. 15^{17}. But having regard to the differences as well as the agreements it is not proved that Jn. is conscious either of Mt. or of Lk. at this point, while it is probable that he is using the text of Mk. (see for details on Jn. 19^2).

7. The passage 12$^{27f.}$ shows traces of the language of Mk., and in a less degree of Lk. (see notes *in loc.*). It would be rash to conclude that Jn. is here reproducing, consciously or unconsciously, phrases from the earlier Gospels; for he seems to be following an independent tradition as to the words which the Synoptists ascribe to Jesus at Gethsemane. But the verbal similarities are striking.

8. The verse 20^{17} (see note *in loc.*) seems to indicate the

adoption by Jn. of words ascribed to the Risen Lord in Mt. 28¹⁰, where they were probably derived from the lost conclusion of Mk. Jn. here is aware of, but corrects, the Marcan tradition.

B. COMPARISON WITH LK.

1. A comparison of Jn. 12³ (see Additional Note on the Anointing at Bethany) with Lk. 7³⁸ shows that Jn., for whatever reason, tells the story of the anointing at Bethany in terms of the Lucan narrative. The words ἐξέμαξεν ταῖς θριξὶν αὐτῆς τοὺς πόδας αὐτοῦ, which are common to both narratives, disclose not only a traditional, but a literary, relation between them. That Jn. is using words which he derived either from Lk. directly, or from Q (the source of Lk.'s narrative), is difficult to gainsay.[1]

2. The prediction by Jesus of Peter's denial and of the cock-crowing in Jn. 13³⁸ is verbally very close to Lk. 22³⁴, while it is conspicuously different from Mk. 14³⁰. But the prefatory ἀμὴν ἀμήν indicates that Jn. knew the text of Mk. here (while he corrects it) as well as the text of Lk. See on 13³⁸.

3. Jn. 19⁴¹ ἐν τῷ κήπῳ μνημεῖον καινόν, ἐν ᾧ οὐδέπω οὐδεὶς ἦν τεθειμένος recalls Lk. 23⁵³ ἐν μνήματι λαξευτῷ οὗ οὐκ ἦν οὐδεὶς οὔπω κείμενος. That the tomb had not been used before is not told by Mk., nor by Mt., who, however, adds the word καινόν to Mk.'s statement. The verbal similarity between Lk. and Jn. suggests that Jn. is here using Lk., substituting οὐδέπω for οὔπω (see on 19⁴¹ 20⁹).

4. Jn. agrees more nearly with Lk. than with Mk., Mt., in his account of the Resurrection, both evangelists recording appearances of the Risen Lord in Jerusalem (see on 20¹). The mention, e.g., of two angels at the tomb (20¹²) is another form of Lk.'s tradition (Lk. 24⁴). In two other instances (Jn. 20¹². ¹⁹. ²⁰), Jn.'s language recalls two passages in Lk.'s text (Lk. 24¹². ³⁶), which are treated by Hort as " Western non-interpolations," and as inserted by scribes in Lk. from Jn.[2] It is not certain that Hort's view can be pressed, and it may be that Jn. is here correcting and adapting Lucan texts (see on 20⁵. ¹⁹). The relation between Jn. 12⁴⁷ and the Western text of Lk. 9⁵⁵ is not easy to explain, but here, again, Jn. may be correcting Lk.

---

[1] For the relation between Jn. and Lk., see Harnack's brief study of their vocabulary (*Luke the Physician*, p. 224 f.). He holds it possible, but not certain, that Jn. used Lk. Cf. also Gaussen, *J.T.S.*, July 1908, for words and ideas common to both.

[2] The addition to the text (in אBCL) of Mt. 27⁴⁹ is undoubtedly derived from Jn. 19³⁴ (where see note).

From a survey of these passages, we conclude that, although Jn. does not use Lk. as frequently as he uses Mk., he was nevertheless acquainted with the Third Gospel as well as with the Second.

C. SAYINGS IN DIFFERENT CONTEXTS IN JN. AND IN THE SYNOPTISTS

Several sayings of Jesus recorded by the Synoptists, whether derived from the Marcan tradition or from Q, also appear in Jn. in a different context. It is probable that many of His sayings were repeated by Him more than once. See notes on 12^{25} $13^{16.\ 20}$ $15^{20.\ 21}$. In none of these cases, however, is the form of expression in Jn. identical with that in Mk., Lk., or Mt., while the matter of the precept or aphorism or warning remains the same. It is possible that ἐγείρεσθε ἄγωμεν of 14^{31} was taken from Mk. 14^{42}, where the same words appear. But Jn. places them in a somewhat different context, which may represent a more accurate tradition than that of Mk. (see on 14^{31}). In any case, that this brief command is reproduced in the same terms by both evangelists is not sufficient to establish a literary dependence of Jn. upon Mk. at this point.

D. THE BAPTIST IN JN. AND IN THE SYNOPTISTS

The Fourth Gospel, like that of Mk., begins with the preliminary ministry of John the Baptist, as ordained in the Divine counsels to prepare for the greater ministry that was to follow. Jn.'s account of the Baptist's proclamation of Jesus, which he represents as explicit and unqualified, is marked by vivid details derived apparently from a contemporary witness; while at the same time the language used reproduces phrases already familiar from the Synoptic narratives.

(a) Jn. describes the Baptist as a man " sent from God " (1^6; cf. 3^{28}). This is implied in the quotation of Mal. 3^1 in Mk. 1^2 and Q (Mt. 11^{10}, Lk. 7^{27}). Mk. 1^2 was probably present to the writer of Jn. 1^6; or we may say that Mal. 3^1 was a familiar text from its presence in Christian *testimonia*.

(b) To the Baptist is applied Is. 40^3 by Mk., Mt., Lk., but Jn. 1^{23} represents him as claiming the prophecy for one of himself.

(c) Jn.'s proclamation of the Coming One is found in similar, but not identical, terms in Jn., Mk., Mt., Lk.

Jn. $1^{15.\ 30}$: ὁ ὀπίσω μου ἐρχόμενος ἔμπροσθέν μου γέγονεν, ὅτι πρῶτός μου ἦν.

Jn. 1^{27}: ὁ ὀπίσω μου ἐρχόμενος, οὗ οὐκ εἰμὶ ἐγὼ ἄξιος ἵνα λύσω αὐτοῦ τὸν ἱμάντα τοῦ ὑποδήματος.

52019

Mk. 1⁷: ἔρχεται ὁ ἰσχυρότερός μου ὀπίσω μου, οὗ οὐκ εἰμὶ
ἱκανὸς κύψας λῦσαι τὸν ἱμάντα τῶν ὑποδημάτων αὐτοῦ.

Mt. 3¹¹: ὁ δὲ ὀπίσω μου ἐρχόμενος ἰσχυρότερός μου ἐστίν,
οὗ οὐκ εἰμὶ ἱκανὸς τὰ ὑποδήματα βαστάσαι.

Lk. 3¹⁶: ἔρχεται δὲ ὁ ἰσχυρότερός μου, οὗ οὐκ εἰμὶ ἱκανὸς λῦσαι
τὸν ἱμάντα τῶν ὑποδημάτων αὐτοῦ.

Cf. Acts 13²⁵: ἔρχεται μετ᾽ ἐμὲ οὗ οὐκ εἰμὶ ἄξιος τὸ ὑπόδημα
τῶν ποδῶν λῦσαι.

It is clear that Jn. 1¹⁵ (see note) puts into fresh words the
Synoptic phrase ὁ ἰσχυρότερός μου, which is also found in
Justin (*Tryph.* 49, 88). Jn. has ἄξιος for the Synoptic ἱκανός,
but ἄξιος is the adj. used in Acts 13²⁵ (see note on Jn. 1²⁷).
Mk. is alone in adding κύψας, *stooping down* to unloose the
thong of the sandal. Mt. has the different image of *carrying*
the sandals or shoes (see on Jn. 1²⁷), but it is remarkable that
Justin (*Tryph.* 49, 88) also has βαστάσαι for λῦσαι. Jn.
characteristically adds ἐγώ for emphasis before ἄξιος. Also
ἵνα λύσω is the constr. with ἵνα which he favours rather than
λῦσαι (see on Jn. 1⁷). He agrees with Mk., Lk. in the constr.
οὗ . . . αὐτοῦ.

When these variations are examined, it becomes doubtful
whether it can be claimed that Jn. here follows Mk. rather
than Lk. Perhaps the true inference is that Jn. and Mk. are
following Q at this point, as was suggested by Salmon.[1]

(*d*) Jn. differs from the Synoptists in some details as to
the Baptism of Jesus; *e.g.* he omits any mention of the heavens
being opened, or of the Voice from heaven (see on 12²⁸). In
particular, the sight of the dove descending on Jesus at His
baptism is, for Jn., no spiritual vision seen only by Jesus
(cf. Mk. 1¹⁰), but was perceived by the Baptist with his bodily
eyes (see on 1³²), and was acclaimed by him as a Divine sign
that Jesus was the expected Messiah. This was the beginning
and the foundation of that " witness " of the Baptist on which
stress is laid throughout the Gospel (cf. 10⁴¹).[2]

(*e*) Neither in Mk. nor Lk. is it expressly stated that the
Baptist recognised Jesus as the Messiah, when He presented
Himself for baptism, although this is indicated in Mt. 3¹⁴.
And the clearness of the Baptist's perception that Jesus was
the Coming One, as indicated by Jn. (1²⁶·²⁹·³³), has been thought
by some to be inconsistent with the Synoptic presentation of
John's ministry, and in particular with John's hesitation as to
the Messiahship of Jesus at a later stage, which was described
in Q (Mt. 11²ᶠ·, Lk. 7¹⁹). Such hesitation is, however, not
incompatible with a previous outburst of enthusiastic conviction, as every student of psychology will recognise. And,

[1] *Human Element in the Gospels*, p. 52. [2] Cf. p. xci.

apart from such considerations, the Synoptic tradition of the
discomfiture of the ecclesiastical authorities by the simple
question, "The baptism of John, was it from heaven?"
(Mk. 11[30], Lk. 20[5], Mt. 21[25]) proves decisively that the Baptist
had definitely proclaimed Jesus as the Expected One. "Why
then did ye not believe him?" There would have been no
force in this retort, if it had not been common knowledge that
the witness of the Baptist to the Divine authority of Jesus had
been express.[1] It is exactly this which Jn. 1[26f.] implies, as
also Mt. 3[14], although it is not stated explicitly in Mk. 1 or
Lk. 3. The announcement of the Baptist's conviction in the
startling words, "Behold the Lamb of God," probably marks
a later rendering of the Christian doctrine of Redemption (see
on 1[29]); but for the fact that the Baptist recognised in Jesus
the expected Christ, the Synoptists are (implicitly) witnesses
as well as Jn.

(II) The Chronology of Jn. and of the Synoptists

The Fourth Gospel seems to have been constructed on a
rough chronological plan more precise than appears in the
Synoptists. Jn. does not attempt to tell the Life of Jesus in
full; and he warns his readers about this (21[25]). He only
describes selected incidents: perhaps because they have a special
bearing on his chosen thesis (20[31]); perhaps too because of
these he is able to write with special authority, or can correct
what has been written by earlier evangelists.

There is no such thing as a chronological scheme, properly
speaking, in the Synoptic Gospels, although Lk. (1[1]) recognises
the value of orderly presentation of facts (cf. also Lk. 3[1, 2]). But
Jn. likes to tell of things in historical sequence. His report
of the opening week of the public ministry of Jesus distinguishes five distinct days at least on which something happened
(cf. 1[29, 39, 43] 2[1], and see on 1[19]). "The morrow" (6[22] 12[12]), "six
days" (12[1]), "two days" (4[43] 11[6]), "four days" (11[17]), "not
many days" (2[12]), "after eight days" (20[26]) exhibit not only
his anxiety to mark the sequence of events, but the confidence
with which he indicates their order. Jn. is especially careful
to mention the visits of Jesus to Jerusalem for the national
feasts; and his statements on this head, which are characteristic of the Fourth Gospel, must be examined both in regard to
their precision and their intrinsic probability.

1. The three great festivals of the Jews were Passover,
Pentecost, and Tabernacles. All male Jews above the age of
twelve years were under obligation to attend these at Jerusalem;

[1] See, for this, J. O. F. Murray in *Expository Times*, Dec. 1925.

and it would have been out of keeping with a reputation for piety for any one to absent himself. There was no similar obligation to be present at the Feast of the Dedication or the Feast of Purim, although even at these Jews were accustomed to assemble from all quarters. According to Jn., Jesus followed the national custom as to the attendance at feasts, of which the following are mentioned:

(1) The *Passover* of the year 27 (2^{13}). This was held at the beginning of the sacred year, about the time of the spring equinox, on 14th Nisan.

(2) The *Passover* of the year 28 (5^1), which is mentioned as near at hand in the earlier passage (6^4). (See above, p. xvii, on the transposition of cc. 5 and 6).

(3) The Feast of *Tabernacles* of the same year, *i.e.* 28 A.D. (7^2). This was the most important of all the national festivals, and began on 15 Tishri (about the month of October). Jn. takes special note of what Jesus said on the last day of this feast (7^{37}), as well as during the middle of the celebration (7^{14}).

(4) The Feast of *Dedication* of the same year, *i.e.* 25 Chislev (December, 28 A.D.). This was attended by Jesus (see 10^{22}).

(5) The *Passover* of the year 29 A.D., at the time of the Passion (11^{55} 12^1).

These records, if the order of the traditional text is trustworthy, prove that the public ministry of Jesus extended over at least two years, and there is nothing intrinsically improbable in this. But it has been thought by some that so long a period of ministry is inconsistent with the report of the Synoptists, who tell only of *one* Passover, and from whose records the *prima facie* inference would be that Jesus was crucified at the Passover season which followed His baptism. This would involve that the public ministry of Jesus lasted for one year only.

I have suggested elsewhere the possibility that the Cleansing of the Temple is misplaced in the ordinary text of Jn. (see on $2^{13.\ 23}$ 3^1). If we could take it in connexion with the *last* visit of Jesus to Jerusalem, as the Synoptists do, then the Johannine narrative does not involve a longer ministry than something more than *one* year, viz. the whole year described in Part II., and as many months as are necessary for the incidents of Part I.[1] There would, in that case, be no chronological inconsistency between the Synoptists and an original text of Jn., which placed c. $2^{13f.}$ somewhere after 12^{18}. But, taking

[1] This is the period expressly assigned to the ministry by Origen : ἐνιαυτὸν γάρ που καὶ μῆνας ὀλίγους ἐδίδαξεν (*Philocal.* i. 5).

the text of Jn. as we have printed it, the ministry of Jesus lasted
for more than two years, which is not suggested by the Synoptists, who do not mention explicitly the visits of Jesus to Jerusalem for the purpose of keeping the national feasts.

In connexion with this omission in the Synoptic narratives,
we must bear in mind their character and structure. None of
them professes to give a complete account of the public
ministry. Mk., which is the oldest of them, is a record of the
Galilæan ministry only, until the last scenes. Mt. and Lk.
are based partly on this, and partly on a collection of discourses
of Jesus, which contained also a few notable incidents. None
of them aims at telling the story in complete detail or in exact
sequence. It is unreasonable to assert that events undescribed
by them could not have happened. Positive evidence is
always more weighty than a mere *argumentum e silentio*, and
hence, unless the Synoptic accounts definitely contradict what
Jn. tells about the visits of Jesus to Jerusalem for the feasts,
the latter must be allowed to stand. No such contradiction
can be alleged.

According to Lk. (2^{41}), it was the habit of the family at
Nazareth to go up to Jerusalem " every year " for the Passover,
as all pious Jews were accustomed to do. We cannot doubt
that, during the thirty years of preparation for His work, Jesus
did the same. It is difficult to believe that, even if His public
ministry lasted but for one year, He would have abstained
from going up to Jerusalem in that year for Pentecost, or for
the Feast of Tabernacles, which was the greatest of the religious celebrations. Such an attitude would have shocked the
piety of His disciples, and would naturally have provoked
the charge of carelessness in observation of the Law. Yet
there is no hint anywhere that it was one of the counts in His
indictment by the priests, that He neglected to attend the
national festivals. His opponents were quick to point to the
freedom with which He treated the laws about the Sabbath;
it would have been an additional breach of law and tradition,
which the people would have viewed with grave suspicion,
could He have been accused of disregarding the obligation to
attend the Feast of Tabernacles. That the Synoptists make
no mention of such an accusation indicates that none such
was made—that it is probable, therefore, that it could not
have been made with truth—and hence that their narratives
are not inconsistent with visits to Jerusalem paid by Jesus
during the period of which they treat. But if one such visit be
admitted, there is nothing to prevent the acceptance of several,
such as Jn. records, and hence of the extension of the public
ministry of Jesus over a longer period than one year.

Moreover, when we remember what Jesus conceived His mission to be, even if we limit ourselves to what the Synoptists tell of Him, it is difficult to suppose that He made no effort to appeal in person to Jerusalem, the home of the national religion and the central seat of its authority, until the last week of His life on earth. Unless Jerusalem were approached, His mission as the Messiah of the Jews would be incompletely fulfilled. It is, on the other hand, entirely in agreement with what we should have expected from One who claimed to be the Fulfiller of the Law (Mt. 5¹⁷), that He should, again and again, have endeavoured to gain the allegiance of the citizens of Jerusalem, as is indicated in the report of Jn.[1]

One positive piece of evidence is supplied by the Synoptists themselves in corroboration of this conclusion. The source called Q, from which both the First and the Third Gospels have taken large part of their material, places in the mouth of Jesus a lament over the obduracy of Jerusalem, in the face of frequent appeals. " O Jerusalem, Jerusalem . . . *how often* would I have gathered thy children together . . . and ye would not " (οὐκ ἠθελήσατε, Mt. 23³⁷, Lk. 13³⁴). Mt. and Lk. do not agree as to the occasion on which these words were spoken; but, whenever spoken, they point back to previous ministries of exhortation and warning. They are not sufficiently explained by a reference to mere aspirations such as Jesus may have felt on visits to Jerusalem before His public ministry had begun; [2] they seem to imply definite appeals which were rejected by those to whom they were addressed. And of these the Johannine record provides adequate illustration, Jn. 12³⁴⁻³⁶. ⁴⁴⁻⁵⁰ corresponding to the lament preserved in Q.

Further evidence of former Jerusalem ministries may be found in such passages as Lk. 19³⁰ᶠ. 22⁸ᶠ., which show that Jesus, on the occasion of His last visit, was already known to persons dwelling in or near the capital. The owners of the ass, riding on which He made His triumphal entry, did not demur when the animal was borrowed ; ὁ κύριος αὐτοῦ χρείαν ἔχει was sufficient excuse. And the master of the house where the Last Supper was eaten received Jesus as a welcome guest. Yet, as Drummond urges,[3] these acquaintanceships or friendships may have been formed during earlier visits to Jerusalem which were not associated with any public teaching,

---

[1] The mention of the Temple in Mt. 4⁵ Lk. 4⁹ suggests an agony of Temptation occasioned by a visit to Jerusalem.

[2] This is the explanation of Drummond, *Character and Authorship of the Fourth Gospel*, p. 45.

[3] *Loc. cit.*

and it would be precarious to build an edifice of theory upon them. But the use in the passages cited (from Lk.) of the titles ὁ κύριος and ὁ διδάσκαλος suggests that these Jewish acquaintances of Jesus were accustomed to speak of Him thus, and such a designation marks the relation of a master to his disciples (see on 13¹³). They were not mere acquaintances and well-wishers; they were among those who recognised that He claimed at least to be a Rabbi and an authoritative Teacher. And this brings us round again to the conclusion that this claim had been made by Him before at Jerusalem as well as in Galilee. Thus the Johannine account of several ministerial visits to Jerusalem on the part of Jesus is corroborated by several Synoptic touches. And this confirms the view that the length of the ministry of Jesus is more accurately indicated by Jn. than by the Synoptists.

2. The discrepancy between Jn. and the Synoptists as to the actual date of the Last Supper and consequently of the Crucifixion has been the subject of much discussion. The Synoptists treat the Last Supper as the Paschal Feast. Jn., on the other hand, does not represent it as a Paschal meal, holding that the Passover was celebrated on the day after the Supper, and that Jesus died on the cross at the time that the Paschal lambs were being killed.

The account of Jn. is without ambiguity. At the Supper some present thought that Judas departed in order to buy some things for the Feast, which had therefore not yet been celebrated (13²⁹). The eating of the Passover was still to come when, on the morning after the Supper, the priests refused to enter the Prætorium lest they should contract cere-monial defilement (18²⁸). When Jesus died on the cross, the soldiers did not break His legs, the O.T. precept that the bones of the Paschal Lamb should not be broken being thus fulfilled, in the view of Jn. (19³⁶). Paul, it is to be observed, took the same view of the death of Jesus as that of the true Paschal Lamb (1 Cor. 5⁷· ⁸), this being the earliest tradition on the subject that is extant.[1] See also on 19¹⁴· ³¹· ⁴².

When we speak of the Synoptic tradition about the date, we must remember that it ultimately rests on Mk., from whom Mt. and Lk. take the framework of their narratives of the Passion. As Burkitt points out, in regard to this matter, we

---

[1] So Justin regards the Paschal Lamb as a σύμβολον of Christ (*Tryph.* 40) ; and Irenæus is explicit as to the Crucifixion being on the actual day of the Passover : " in eadem ipsa, quae ante tantum temporis a Moyse praedicata est, passus est dominus adimplens pascha" (iv. 10. 1). Earlier still, Pseudo-Peter follows the Johannine tradi-tion (*Gospel of Peter*, § 3). See above, p. xlix, on the Quartodeciman practice.

are not dealing with a consensus of three *independent* authorities.[1] There is no doubt that Lk. (22[13]) and Mt. (26[19]) follow Mk. (14[16]), when they all say of the preparations for the Last Supper, "they made ready *the Passover*." Mk. 14[12] introduces this by recording, "On the first day of unleavened bread, when they sacrificed the Passover," the disciples asked Jesus where were they to prepare for the Feast. That they came into Jerusalem from Bethany for the supper is quite consistent with a regulation that the Passover was to be eaten in the city area (cf. Deut. 12[5]); but this is no proof. Nor is the fact that they sang a hymn (Mk. 14[26]) after supper any proof that this was the Paschal *Hallel*. Indeed, there are some difficulties in the Synoptic narratives as they stand. According to Mk 14[2], the Sanhedrim had decided *not* to arrest Jesus during the Paschal Feast, and yet they actually did so (Mk. 14[43]). The carrying of arms during the Feast was, at any rate, unlawful, although perhaps the disciples would not have refrained from this in the circumstances (Lk. 22[38], Mk. 14[47]; see on Jn. 18[10]). To hold a formal trial before the high priest on the Feast day would, again, be unlawful (Mk. 14[53]). And the purchase of a linen cloth (Mk. 15[46]), and the preparation of spices and ointments (Lk. 23[56]) during such a Festival, would be strange, if not forbidden. Finally, the language of Lk. 22[15] (even though Lk. regards the Supper as the Passover Feast) implies that, although Jesus eagerly desired to celebrate one more Passover with His disciples, yet in fact He did *not* do so.

These considerations indicate that the Johannine tradition as to the occasion of the Last Supper and the day of the Crucifixion is preferable to that of the Synoptists, who are not consistent with themselves. That the Johannine reckoning seems to have been adopted in the second century by the Quartodecimans is a further consideration.[2]

The attempts which have been made to harmonise the two divergent traditions by identifying the Last Supper with the *Chagigah* or the *Kiddusch*,[3] or by amending the text of Mt. 26[17] [4] with Chwolson, are not convincing. It emerges from the discussion that Jn.'s chronology must not be treated as inferior to that of the earlier Gospels; and that as to the date of the Crucifixion he is more probably right than they. So also as to the *hour* of the Crucifixion, placed by Jn. at

---

[1] *J.T.S.*, April 1916, p. 292, a valuable article ; cf. also *J.T.S.*, July 1908, p. 569.

[2] See p. xlix above.

[3] See G. H. Box, *J.T.S.*, 1902, p. 357 ; and cf. Burkitt, *J.T.S.*, 1916, p. 294.

[4] See references in Moffatt, *Introd. to N.T.*, p. 545.

noon, which is more probable than Mk.'s ὥρα τρίτη (see on
Jn. 19¹⁴).

Reasons have been given in the notes on 2¹³. ²³ (see also
p. xxx) for preferring, on the contrary, the Marcan tradition
that the Cleansing of the Temple took place during the last
week of our Lord's ministry at Jerusalem, to accepting the early
date assigned to it in the traditional text of Jn. It may be
added that Tatian in his *Diatessaron* removes both the Cleansing
of the Temple and the Nicodemus incident from the beginning
of the ministry of Jesus. Tatian adopts the following order of
events and discourses: the Parable of the Pounds, the Cleansing
of the Temple, the Parable of the Pharisee and Publican, the
Cursing of the Fig Tree, the Conversation with Nicodemus,
the Discovery that the fig tree has withered away. He does
not place these events in the last week of the ministry of Jesus
(for he puts the Triumphal Entry a good deal later), but he
treats them as happening at Jerusalem on His last visit but one
to that city.

3. In connexion with Jn.'s notes of time, his use of the
expressions μετὰ τοῦτο and μετὰ ταῦτα should be noticed.

μετὰ τοῦτο, which is not found in the Synoptists, appears
four times in Jn. (2¹² 11⁷. ¹¹ 19²⁸), and always implies that
only a short interval of time has elapsed.

μετὰ ταῦτα is not so precise; it is used at 5¹⁴ 13⁷ 19³⁸ as
equivalent to " subsequently " or " afterwards." [1]

It is used in an even looser way in the Apocalypse (Rev. 4¹
7⁹ 15⁵ 18¹ 19¹) to introduce a new vision, and in the Fourth
Gospel to introduce a new section of the narrative (3²² 6¹ 5¹ 7¹
21¹), the idea of causal or immediate sequence not being present
at all. It would seem that in 3²² 6¹ 5¹ 7¹ μετὰ ταῦτα merely
indicates the beginning of a new set of reminiscences of the
aged " witness " behind the Gospel, which were taken down
from his dictation by the evangelist who subsequently put
the whole in shape. In these passages μετὰ ταῦτα is not
strictly chronological.

(iii) The Words of Jesus in Jn. and in the Synoptists

The contrast between the words of Jesus as found in the
Synoptists and in the Fourth Gospel respectively has been
observed even by superficial readers. Differences in the various
books might have been anticipated. Perhaps the first collection

---

[1] It is used thus in Lk. 5²⁷ 10¹ [Mk.] 16¹², Rev. 9¹², not appearing
in Mt. or Mk. ; in the LXX (as at Lk. 12⁴ 17⁸ 18⁴, Acts 13²⁰ 18¹) it
generally connotes strict sequence.

of Jesus' sayings was that included in the documentary source behind all the Gospels which critics designate as Q. This doubtless contained some stories of what Jesus did, but it was mainly concerned with what He *said*, especially with the parables, which were so characteristic of His method of teaching, and the terse, pointed epigrams which arrested the attention of all who heard Him. Then we have the Marcan Gospel, representing in the main the Galilæan tradition of the Ministry, said by Papias and Irenæus to depend on the recollections of Peter.[1] Mt. and Lk. use both of these sources, with others. Jn. was later in date than Q or Mk. or Lk., all of which sources he had probably read, but he depends mainly, for his facts, on the reminiscences of the apostle John, then in his old age. It is not the purpose of Jn. to retell the story of the Ministry, as it was told by Mk. and Lk., but to tell it from a new point of view. The story of Jesus is being misunderstood and in some ways perverted by Gnostic Christians. Jn. not only relies for his new narrative on the sole survivor of the apostles, but he selects for special record such facts and sayings as seem to him to need restatement, or which have hitherto remained unwritten. The authority for his facts is not mere vague tradition, but the " witness " of the Beloved Disciple himself. The purpose of the Fourth Gospel is not to set down all that the writer has learnt about his theme; but to tell what may persuade Christian disciples of the truth of his great thesis that Jesus is the Son of God, in whose Name they, believing, may find life (20[31]). Jn. is not only an historian : he is an interpreter of history. And, moreover, he himself was one of the first disciples, although not of the inner circle; [2] he had heard Jesus speak, and he knew how He was accustomed to speak, when in controversy with Jewish opponents, no less than in His discourse with simple people.

In books, then, which came into being under such different conditions, we should expect differences in the several reports of the discourses of Jesus. Further, we need not be surprised if there are also differences of arrangement and of style, corresponding to the temperament, education, design, and authority of the several writers. We are presented, moreover, with discourses, now expository, now argumentative; now exoteric for the public, now esoteric for the most intimate disciples of the Speaker; now addressed to Galilæan peasants, now to the Rabbis of Jerusalem. That there is a wide difference between the sayings collected in either version of the Sermon on the Mount (Mt. and Lk.) and the subtle arguments of Jn. 5, 8, 9, and again the sacred farewells of cc. 14, 15, 16, is obvious. But

---

[1] Eus. *H.E.* iii. 39. 15, v. 8. 2.   [2] Cf. p. xlvii.

if such differences were *not* apparent, we should have to conclude that some of the reports were unduly coloured.

We pass on to some comparisons in detail of the Synoptic reports and those in Jn. of the sayings of Jesus; and we find that some of the similarities are quite as striking as the differences.

1. Naturally, all accounts record the *authority* with which Jesus spoke. It astonished the people in the synagogue at Capernaum (Mk. 1^{22} 6^2), as it astonished the Sanhedrim police at Jerusalem who had been so overawed that they did not arrest Him (Jn. 7^{46}). It was the same tone as that which He used to Pilate (Jn. 18^{37}).

2. "Brief and concise," says Justin Martyr, "were His sayings, for He was no sophist." [1]   Justin is referring to those terse, short sentences of which the Synoptic Gospels are full; other examples of which have been preserved in non-canonical sayings, some cited by the early Fathers, others only discovered in papyrus collections in our own time. It should be remembered that these telling aphorisms are exactly the kind of saying that would become traditional at once, would pass from mouth to mouth, and would be incorporated in a document such as Q. Paradoxes have been called the " burrs " of literature, because they " stick "; and one of our Lord's methods was to teach by paradoxes. Mk. $2^{17.~27}$ 4^{25} 10^{25} are examples of sayings which provoke the attention and so make men think. Of such sayings Jn. mentions some which the Synoptists also have, *e.g.* Jn. 12^{25} (the most famous of all) and 13^{20}. In addition, he has preserved some which are not found elsewhere, *e.g.* " My meat is to do the will of Him that sent me " (Jn. 4^{34}); " Work not for the meat which perisheth, but for the meat which abideth unto eternal life " (6^{27}); and "Greater love hath no man than this, that a man lay down his life for his friends " (15^{13}); cf. also 12^{24}. These are all addressed to inquirers and disciples, and are of a type with which the Synoptic Gospels have made us already familiar. So, too, the beautiful illustration of the woman in travail (16^{21}) recalls the manner of the speech of Jesus in the Synoptists.

3. It is common both to the Synoptic and to the Johannine tradition that while Jesus spoke in parable or mystery to outsiders (Mk. 4^{34}, Jn. 10^6) He was accustomed to explain His meaning more fully to His disciples (Mk. 4^{34} 7^{17}, Jn. $16^{25.~29}$). Yet even they did not quite understand His words (Mk. 9^{32}, Jn. 16^{29}); always there was a certain aloofness in His bearing, and despite His tender affection for His near friends they were afraid of questioning Him too far (Mk. 9^{32} 10^{32}, Jn. 2^4). This

[1] *Apol.* i. 14.

becomes even more apparent in the post-Resurrection narratives, but it is present throughout the ministry in its early stages.

4. A feature of the discourses of Jesus in Part I. of the Fourth Gospel must now be examined, because it discloses a similarity to some of His speeches in the Synoptists which has often been overlooked. Some critics have rightly called attention to the form in which the discourses in cc. 3, 4, 6 are cast, and which has been called their "schematism." A saying of deep import is uttered by Jesus; His hearers misunderstand it, after a fashion that seems stupid; and then He repeats the saying in a slightly different form before He explains it and draws out its lesson. At least six instances of this may be noticed in Jn.:

(*a*) Jesus says, "Except a man be born from above, he cannot see the Kingdom of God" (3³); Nicodemus asks, "How can a man be born when he is old?" (3⁴); and then Jesus repeats the saying in the form: "Except a man be born of [water and] the Spirit, he cannot enter into the Kingdom of God" (3⁵), explaining it further in vv. 6, 7, 8. Nicodemus does not understand all at once (3⁹).

(*b*) Jesus tells the Woman of Samaria that if she had asked Him, He would have given her "living water" (4¹⁰). The woman is puzzled. How could He provide spring water, when there is no other well but the old well of Jacob, and He has no bucket to draw with (4¹¹·¹²)? Jesus repeats that He can give "water" which shall become in the heart of the recipient a well of water springing up unto eternal life (4¹³·¹⁴). The woman does not understand all at once (4¹⁵).

(*c*) Jesus says to His attendant disciples, "I have meat to eat that ye know not" (4³²). They think that He speaks of ordinary food (4³³). He explains that His meat is to do the Father's will (4³⁴ᶠ·).

(*d*) Jesus says to the multitudes who had been fed, "Work not for the meat which perisheth, but for the meat which abideth unto eternal life" (6²⁷). They think He is referring to manna, and they ask Him to produce it (6³¹·³⁴). Jesus tells them that He is Himself the Bread of Life (6³⁵), and explains that those who come to Him shall never hunger (vv. 36–40). The hearers are not satisfied (6⁴¹).

(*e*) Jesus says again, "I am the Bread which came down from heaven" (6⁴¹). The inquirers ask how could that be, since they know His father and mother (6⁴²). He explains again, and repeats, "I am the Bread of Life."

(*f*) Jesus utters another, even harder, saying, "The Bread which I will give is My Flesh" (6⁵¹). The puzzled questioners

ask, " How can this man give us His Flesh to eat ? " (6⁵²).
Jesus says again, " Except you eat the Flesh of the Son of
Man and drink His blood, you have no life in you " (6⁵³), and
then He expands and explains.   Upon this many would-be
disciples leave Him (6⁶⁰).

Thus the Discourses of Jesus, with Nicodemus about the
New Birth (3³⁻¹⁴), with the woman of Samaria about the Living
Water (4¹⁰⁻¹⁵), with the disciples about the spiritual nourishment which sustains Him (4³²⁻³⁴ᶠ·), together with the three
connected, but distinct, sections of the Discourse about the
Bread of Life (6²⁷⁻⁴⁰· ⁴¹⁻⁵¹ᵃ· ⁵¹ᵇ⁻⁵⁸), all follow similar paths.   But
these similarities do not by any means prove that the discourses
are constructed thus by the evangelist, without any historical
tradition behind them.[1]

It is a remarkable circumstance that discourses such as
those in cc. 3, 4, 6 do not occur anywhere in Part II. of the
Gospel.   Cc. 5, 7–12 are full of the discourses of Jesus, but
Jn. does not report them on the lines of those which have been
cited, viz. Saying of Jesus ; Misunderstanding of it ; Saying
repeated, expanded, and explained.   If the method or plan of
the discourses indicated in Part I. is entirely the invention of
the evangelist, adopted monotonously to bring out the nature
of the teaching which he ascribes to Jesus, how is it that no
trace of this method is found in Part II. ?

The fact is that the discourses in Part I. of the Fourth
Gospel are not reported as polemical arguments ; they were
addressed to sincere inquirers and well-wishers who were seeking discipleship.   We have already seen (p. xxxiii) that Part I.
is a record of the early welcome which the teaching of Jesus
received, mainly in Galilee, but also in a lesser degree in
Jerusalem.   That is, it deals with situations similar to those
described in the Synoptic Gospels, and specially in Mk.   And,
accordingly, the method which Jesus used in teaching as set
out in Part I. of Jn. is indicated also in the Synoptic narratives.
It is the method of paradox (to arrest the attention of the
hearer), followed (after the hearer has shown himself puzzled
and therefore curious) by an explanation.   In this, it resembles
the method of teaching by parables.

Thus at Mk. 7¹⁵⁻²³, Jesus puzzles the disciples by saying:
" Nothing from without the man, going into him, can defile
him; but the things which proceed out of the man are those
that can defile him."   The disciples see that this is a " parable,"

---

[1] For this view see Jülicher, *Introd.*, p. 392 ; and for an even more
extravagant inference cf. Loisy (on Jn. 3²), who says that the Nicodemus discourse was constructed at first " comme poâme didactique
sur la régéneration spirituelle que procure le Fils."

but they do not understand. Jesus then repeats the saying and explains it. Again, at Mk. 8[15-20] Jesus says to His disciples, " Beware of the leaven of the Pharisees." The disciples are dull enough to think He is speaking about some kind of bread. He explains with a rebuke what He means, and repeats His precept again (cf. Mt. 16[11]). This is similar to the method by which Nicodemus was taught.

In short, the plan on which the teaching of Jesus to inquirers and disciples was fashioned, according to the Synoptists, recalls at several points the discourses addressed to such hearers according to the Johannine report of them in Part I. of the Fourth Gospel. The parallels to Jesus' method of argument with hostile critics in the last week of His public ministry as recorded by the Synoptists are found, on the other hand, in Part II. of Jn.

5. The form of the polemic against Jewish objectors in Part II. of the Fourth Gospel has disconcerted some readers as savouring of Rabbinical subtlety,[1] rather than of what is thought to be evangelical simplicity. In particular, the Rabbinical arguments at Jn. 7[22f.] 8[17] 10[34] (where see notes) do not appeal directly to a modern mind as very convincing or on a lofty plane of thought. But if Jn. 7[22f.] be only an *argumentum ad hominem*, the same might be said of the puzzling query, " The baptism of John, was it from heaven or from men ? " (Mk. 11[30]). Neither argument did more than exhibit the inconsistency of the Pharisees, and this is not the highest type of reasoning as we understand it. Or, again, the argument in Mk. 3[23f.] which begins, " How can Satan cast out Satan ? " is rather satire than close reasoning. " It is not logically convincing, since Satan might very well sacrifice some of his subordinates for the sake of a greater victory, and it reaches a conclusion which is true from premises, those of the scribes, which are false or shaky." [2] The truth is, that the polemic which Jn. records in cc. 7, 8, 10 is not dissimilar from the kind of argument which is represented by Mk. as being used against similar opponents, viz. the scribes and Pharisees. Such opponents had to be met with their own methods of argument, and this is brought out by the Synoptists as well as by Jn., although they are so much less familiar with the story of the rejection of Jesus at Jerusalem than he is. The kind of argument against the Pharisees reproduced in Part II. of the Gospel is not recorded by Jn. with the view of convincing Greek readers. It is included by the evangelist to bring out the profundity of the thoughts of Jesus, who even while He had to dispute with the Rabbis as to the validity of His claims knew

[1] See p. lxxxii above. [2] A. Menzies, *The Earliest Gospel*, p. 101.

h

that nothing could really be set against the tremendous pronouncement, "I am He that beareth witness of Myself" (8[18]).[1] And, as has been noticed above, the faithfulness with which these controversies have been recorded[2] is illustrated by the very feature which the modern mind is apt to repudiate. It is not to be overlooked, moreover, that in these reports the commentary of the evangelist cannot always be distinguished from the sayings of Jesus which he has set down.[3]

6. The Discourses of Farewell (cc. 15, 16, 13[31-38] 14) stand alone, and are not strictly comparable with any other sayings in the Gospels. They are not like the parables or sermons to the multitudes which the Synoptists preserve; nor do they recall the arguments by which (either in the Synoptists or in Jn.) Jesus strove with those who rejected His claims. They were for his faithful and sorrowing friends, and spoke of them in particular and their future needs and duties. "I go" is behind every word (16[5. 7. 28] 13[36] 14[2]). There are precepts of life, both *practical*, "bear fruit" (15[2. 8. 16]), and *mystical*, "Abide in me" (15[4-10]), for to observe this last is to be enabled to obey the other. There are warnings (15[18-25] 16[1-3]); promises (15[26f.] 16[14] 14[26]); consolations (14[1. 27]); counsels and assurances of love (15[12. 13. 17] 13[34. 35]). These sayings are unique, because as the circumstances were unique, the Speaker is unique. And this is also true of the Last Prayer (see on 17[1]). We cannot expect to find literary parallels to utterances such as these. They are not the invention of good disciples, even though they were men of high spiritual genius. The record of these sacred words is a record of faithful memories, quickened, we need not hesitate to say, by the Divine Spirit, whose help had been promised (so the evangelist tells) for this very purpose (14[26]).

We have, indeed, no title to invoke miraculous intervention in such guidance of the evangelist's pen, if that would imply that every syllable of the Master's last words has been infallibly preserved. The evangelist sat at the feet, as he made his record, of the last survivor of the men who heard Jesus speak on the eve of His Passion. The aged apostle had been pondering these words all through his long life. Hardly did he remember *all*, but he remembered without any misunderstanding the purport, and very likely, in some instances, the actual words that had been used. The evangelist takes them down from the lips of the old saint, possibly not all at once, but on more than one occasion. Their original language was Aramaic, but they must be translated into Greek, for this is

---

[1] Cf. p. xcii.   [2] P. lxxxii.   [3] See p. cxvi.

to be a Greek gospel. And, besides, an evangelist has his own methods of literary workmanship.

The wonderful record, *e.g.*, in Mt. of the Sermon on the Mount is not quite the same as that in Lk., while it contains more. But no one supposes that what we call the " Sermon on the Mount " was a discourse that could be delivered in thirty minutes, in which time Mt. 5, 6, 7 could be read aloud, or that the vast volume of teaching in these chapters, packed with counsel, epigram, illustration, was ever included in any *one* discourse. These teachings of Mt. 5–7 are certainly authentic; no one doubts that they express, with complete lucidity, the message of Jesus to those whom He addressed as well as to succeeding generations. But we must recognise that the record has been put into shape, and that it is not the less precious because it has been arranged with such rare skill.

No doubt the record in Jn. 14, 15, 16 is not put into shape, as it were, with the same freedom as that employed in Mt. 5, 6, 7. In the " Sermon on the Mount " the author is putting materials together which he has gathered from more sources than one. For the Last Discourses the evangelist has only one authentic source of information, and that has doubtless been followed closely and reverently. At one point, indeed (16[16-20]), we seem to have an example of that method of teaching by paradox and repetition, which as we have seen (p. cxi) was a favourite method of the Master when dealing with His disciples. Again, these discourses recall those terse, illuminating, compelling phrases, which the Synoptists teach us were characteristic of the way in which Jesus spoke. Not to recall (see p. cx), 15[13] or 16[21], is there anything in literature more arresting than, " In my Father's house are many mansions " (14[2]) ? No saying about the future life is more familiar. And this brings out one of the most remarkable features of Jn. 14, 15, 16. These are among the most difficult passages of the N.T. Every phrase challenges an explanation. They contain teachings of such profundity that he who attempts to explain them must feel that he has essayed too hard a task. Yet no chapter in the Bible is more greatly beloved by simple Christian folk than Jn. 14; as no text in the Bible has brought more consolation than, " Let not your heart be troubled . . . if it were not so, I would have told you "; although, at the same time, its exact meaning is exceedingly obscure (see note on 14[1. 2]). That is, the Last Discourses of the Fourth Gospel appeal to all men, and not merely to the philosopher or the theologian. The directness and universality of their appeal are not easy to reconcile with the view that they proceed, in the last resort, from any speaker other than the Son of Man Himself.

The style of Jn. is, nevertheless, impressed on cc. 14–16, as on the other discourses in the Fourth Gospel. It is Jn.'s habit to repeat words and thoughts again and again ; and it is probable that this was the habit of Jesus Himself, which the evangelist has caught from listening to the reminiscences of the old apostle. It is not always easy to disentangle Jn.'s commentary from his report of the Lord's words; *e.g.* in 5²⁰⁻²⁹ commentary and quotation are intermingled [1] (see note *in loc.*). The most striking example of an evangelical commentary, elucidating and enforcing the teaching of Jesus, is in 3¹⁶⁻²¹·³¹⁻³⁶ (see on 3¹⁶). The verses preceding 3¹⁶ show how naturally the report of the words of Jesus slips into free paraphrase (see on 3¹¹); but nearly all exegetes recognise that from v. 16 onward the evangelist is speaking in his own person.

Now the method of teaching by iteration, by going back upon a word, by recalling a thought already expressed that it may be put in a new setting, is clearly apparent in cc. 14–16. The key-words *abide* (15⁴·⁵·⁶·⁷·⁹·¹⁰), *bear fruit* (15²·⁸·¹⁶), *love* (15¹²·¹³·¹⁷), *friends* (15¹³·¹⁴·¹⁵), *hate* (15¹⁸·¹⁹·²³⁻²⁵), recur again and again in c. 15. The solemn refrain, "These things have I spoken unto you," appears seven times in cc. 14–16 (see on 15¹¹; and cf. the refrain in 6³⁹·⁴⁰·⁴⁴·⁵⁴). There is no more reason to suppose that the use of such refrains is a literary artifice of the evangelist's (although it might be so), rather than a reminiscence of our Lord's habit of speech, than to suppose that He was not accustomed to say, "Verily, verily" (see on 1⁵¹).

The view of the Last Discourses which has been adopted in this Commentary is, accordingly, that while the evangelist has left his mark upon the report of them, by arranging the sentences, by shortening them, by bringing together counsels which may have been repeated more than once, by using the Greek phrases and constructions with which he himself is specially familiar, the Teaching is not that of a pupil, however spiritually gifted, but that of the Master Himself, whose last words had been preserved in the memory of the Beloved Disciple, the last of the apostles.

7. A special feature of the way in which Jn. reports the words of Jesus outside the Last Discourses is the use of the phrase ἐγώ εἰμι, by which Jesus in the Fourth Gospel frequently introduces His august claims. There is nothing quite similar

---

[1] Cf. 1 Cor. 15⁴⁵, where Paul combines a quotation with his own comment.

to this in the Synoptists, and the Johannine use of ἐγώ, ἐγώ εἰμι, must now be examined in detail.

(i) The frequency with which the personal pronouns ἐγώ, ἡμεῖς, σύ, ὑμεῖς occur in Jn. is a marked feature of his style. Thus ἐγώ is found 134 times in Jn., as against 29 occurrences in Mt., 17 in Mk., and 23 in Lk. In large measure this is due to the emphasis which in the Fourth Gospel Jesus lays upon His claims and His personality, although the pronoun often appears when no such reason can be assigned.[1] Thus we have ἐγὼ δὲ ἔχω τὴν μαρτυρίαν μείζω τοῦ Ἰωάνου (5³⁶); ἐγὼ ἀναστήσω αὐτὸν ἐν τῇ ἐσχάτῃ ἡμέρᾳ (6⁴⁴); ἐγὼ τίθημι τὴν ψυχήν μου, ἵνα πάλιν λάβω αὐτήν (10¹⁷); ἐγὼ φῶς εἰς τὸν κόσμον ἐλήλυθα (12⁴⁶), etc. In these and the like instances the use of ἐγώ adds dignity and impressiveness to the sentence, just as it does in the hymn on Wisdom in Ecclus. 24, where Wisdom makes her majestic claims: ἐγὼ ἀπὸ στόματος Ὑψίστου ἐξῆλθον (v. 3); ἐγὼ ἐν ὑψηλοῖς κατεσκήνωσα (v. 4); ἐγὼ ὡς τερέμινθος ἐξέτεινα κλάδους μου (v. 16); ἐγὼ ὡς ἄμπελος βλαστήσασα χάριν (v. 17).

(ii) We have next to consider the combination ἐγώ εἰμι, which is specially frequent in Jn.

ἐγώ εἰμι often appears, of course, in the Greek Bible, followed by a proper name or by a descriptive clause or word. Thus Peter says ἐγώ εἰμι ὃν ζητεῖτε (Acts 10²¹). Jesus says after His Resurrection ἴδετε τὰς χεῖρας καὶ τοὺς πόδας μου, ὅτι ἐγώ εἰμι αὐτός, "that it is I myself" (Lk. 24³⁹). ἐγώ εἰμι is often used in deliberate affirmations as to the speaker's personality. Thus we have ἐγώ εἰμι Ἰωσήφ (Gen. 45³), ἐγώ εἰμι Γαβριήλ (Lk. 1¹⁹), and ἐγώ εἰμι Ἰησοῦς ὃν σὺ διώκεις (Acts 9⁵ 22⁹ 26¹⁵).

But we have to reckon with a more distinctive use of this introductory phrase. In the O.T. ἐγώ εἰμι is often the style of Deity, and its impressiveness is unmistakable. A few instances may be cited from the LXX, in each case Yahweh being the Speaker:

ἐγώ εἰμι ὁ Θεός σου (Gen. 17¹).
ἐγὼ γάρ εἰμι Κύριος ὁ Θεός σου ὁ ἰώμενός σε (Ex. 15²⁶).
σωτηρία σου ἐγώ εἰμι (Ps. 35³).
ἐλεήμων ἐγώ εἰμι (Jer. 3¹²).
Θεὸς ἐγγίζων ἐγώ εἰμι (Jer. 23²³).
ἐγὼ γάρ εἰμι Κύριος ὁ ἀγαπῶν δικαιοσύνην (Isa. 61⁸).

---

[1] Burney held that the personal pronouns in Jn. often "represent close translation of an Aramaic original in which the pronoun was expressed with the participle" (Aramaic Origin, etc., p. 81). Cf. p. lxvii.

In all these passages ἐγώ εἰμι is the rendering of אני ;
while in the specially emphatic passages—

ἐγώ εἰμι, ἐγώ εἰμι ὁ παρακαλῶν σε (Isa. 51¹²),

ἐγώ εἰμι, ἐγώ εἰμι ὁ ἐξαλείφων τὰς ἀνομίας σου (Isa. 43²⁵),

the doubled ἐγώ εἰμι is the rendering of the doubled אנכי.[1]

We find this style in the Apocalypse, where it rests on the
O.T.[2] Thus the Divine words ἐγώ εἰμι τὸ Ἄλφα καὶ τὸ Ὠ
(Rev. 1⁸ 21⁶ 22¹³) go back to ἐγὼ Θεὸς πρῶτος, καὶ εἰς τὰ
ἐπερχόμενα ἐγώ εἰμι (Isa. 41⁴); or to ἐγώ εἰμι πρῶτος καὶ ἐγώ εἰμι
εἰς τὸν αἰῶνα (Isa. 48¹²), or some such passage. Moreover,
words like these or like Isa. 44⁶ ἐγὼ πρῶτος, καὶ ἐγὼ μετὰ ταῦτα
are placed in the mouth of the Risen Christ in Rev. 1¹⁷, viz.:

ἐγώ εἰμι ὁ πρῶτος καὶ ὁ ἔσχατος, καὶ ὁ ζῶν.

Again in Rev. 2²³ the Son of God declares that all the churches
shall know ὅτι ἐγώ εἰμι ὁ ἐραυνῶν νεφροὺς καὶ καρδίας, which goes
back to Jer. 11²⁰ 17¹⁰, where it is Yahweh who searches the
reins and the heart. And finally in Rev. 22¹⁶ Jesus says:

ἐγώ εἰμι ἡ ῥίζα καὶ τὸ γένος Δαβίδ, ὁ ἀστὴρ ὁ λαμπρός, ὁ
πρωϊνός,

which, although not a citation of any single O.T. passage,
depends on the prophetic teaching, e.g. Isa. 11¹ 60³.

It is, then, clear that the ἐγώ εἰμι of these sentences from the
Apocalypse is a reflexion of the manner of speech appropriate
to God in the O.T., and being placed in the mouth of Jesus
involves His Divinity, which the author thus claims for Him.

We now approach the Similitudes by which Jesus describes
Himself in the Fourth Gospel:

ἐγώ εἰμι ὁ ἄρτος τῆς ζωῆς (6³⁵).

ἐγώ εἰμι τὸ φῶς τοῦ κόσμου (8¹²).

ἐγώ εἰμι ἡ θύρα τῶν προβάτων (10⁷).

ἐγώ εἰμι ὁ ποιμὴν ὁ καλός (10¹¹).

ἐγώ εἰμι ἡ ἀνάστασις καὶ ἡ ζωή (11²⁵).

ἐγώ εἰμι ἡ ἄμπελος ἡ ἀληθινή (15¹).

ἐγώ εἰμι ἡ ὁδὸς καὶ ἡ ἀλήθεια καὶ ἡ ζωή (14⁶).

With these we may compare: ἐγώ εἰμι ὁ μαρτυρῶν περὶ ἐμαυτοῦ
(8¹⁸).

---

[1] The LXX translators of certain books of the O.T. render אנכי
(to distinguish it from אני) with curious pedantry by ἐγώ εἰμι, even
when a verb follows. Thus Jephthah is made to say ἐγώ εἰμι οὐκ
ἥμαρτόν σοι (Judg. 11²⁷; cf. Judg. 11³⁵· ³⁷, Ruth 4⁴, 2 Sam. 11⁵). But
this eccentricity does not concern us in the present discussion. (See
Thackeray, J.T.S., Jan. 1907, p. 272.)

[2] Cf. p. lxviii.

This is clearly the style of Deity, of which we have already had examples from the O.T. and from the Apocalypse; and it can hardly be doubted that the author of the Gospel has cast the words of Jesus into this particular form. Its force would at once be appreciated by any one familiar with the LXX version of the O.T. It is further to be observed that this style would also have been familiar to Greeks who knew the phraseology of the Egyptian mystery religions.[1] Deissmann[2] quotes a pre-Christian Isis inscription, which was graven about 200 A.D., containing these lines:

Εἶσις ἐγώ εἰμι ἡ τύραννος πάσης χόρας

. . . .

Ἐγώ εἰμι Κρόνου θυγάτηρ πρεσβυτάτη

. . . .

Ἐγώ εἰμι ἡ παρὰ γυναιξὶ θεὸς καλουμένη, κτλ.

And, in like manner, in an Egyptian magical payprus (also quoted by Deissmann) we find:

ἐγώ εἰμι Ὄσιρις ὁ καλούμενος ὕδωρ
ἐγώ εἰμι Ἴσις ἡ καλουμένη δρόσος.

More familiar is the Isis inscription, given by Plutarch:[3]

ἐγώ εἰμι πᾶν τὸ γεγονὸς καὶ ὂν καὶ ἐσόμενον
καὶ τὸν ἐμὸν πέπλον οὐδείς πω θνητὸς ἀπεκάλυψεν.

This is of the first century A.D.

In a Mithraic liturgy[4] we come on:

ἐγὼ γάρ εἰμι ὁ υἱός . . .
ἐγώ εἰμι μαχαρφν . . . and again
ἐγώ εἰμι σύμπλανος ὑμῖν ἀστήρ.

Instances of like phraseology are not infrequent in the magical literature current during the first three centuries in Egypt and Asia Minor, e.g.,

ἀκουσάτω μοι πᾶσα γλῶσσα . . . ὅτι ἐγώ εἰμι Περταω.[5]

(iii) There is yet another use of ἐγώ εἰμι. It appears sometimes without any predicate, although the predicate may be clear from the context. Thus, in answer to the question, "Art thou the Christ, the Son of the Blessed?" Jesus says ἐγώ εἰμι, according to Mk. 14⁶² (cf. Lk. 22⁷⁰), meaning, "Yes, I

---

[1] A string of sentences beginning ἐγώ εἰμι is put into the mouth of the dragon in *Acta Thomæ*, § 32.
[2] *Light from the East*, p. 134 f.   [3] *De Iside*, c. 9, p. 354 C.
[4] Dieterich, *Eine Mithrasliturgie*, pp. 6, 8.
[5] Deissmann, *Bible Studies*, p. 328 (from a Lyons papyrus).

am the Christ." So, at Jn. 4²⁶, ἐγώ εἰμι ὁ λαλῶν σοι may mean, in like manner, "I that speak to you am the Christ" (but see note *in loc.*). Or, again, the blind beggar of Jn. 9⁹ admits his identity by saying simply ἐγώ εἰμι, "I am he of whom you have been speaking." It is probable that a similar explanation is to be given of Jn. 18⁵, where Jesus says to those who are seeking Him, ἐγώ εἰμι. Yet another explanation is possible here, for the sequel, "they went backward and fell to the ground," might suggest that they recognised in the words ἐγώ εἰμι not merely an admission of identity, but a claim of mystery which inspired them with dread. See, however, note on 18⁶.

An examination of the passages in the LXX where ἐγώ εἰμι is used absolutely, shows that in general it is the rendering of אֲנִי־הוּא, which is literally "I (am) He," and that this Hebrew phrase appears to occur only when God is the Speaker.[1] Instances of this usage in the LXX are:

> Deut. 32³⁹: ἴδετε ἴδετε ὅτι ἐγώ εἰμι,
> Isa. 43¹⁰: ἵνα . . . συνῆτε ὅτι ἐγώ εἰμι,
> Isa. 46⁴: ἕως γήρως ἐγώ εἰμι,
>   καὶ ἕως ἂν καταγηράσητε ἐγώ εἰμι—

such proclamations being usually followed by the assertion of the Unity of God, viz., "And there is none other beside Me."

It has been suggested that ἐγώ εἰμι is used in this way in the narrative of the Storm on the Lake. Both the Marcan and Johannine versions make Jesus say ἐγώ εἰμι· μὴ φοβεῖσθε (Mk. 6⁵⁰, Mt. 14²⁷, Jn. 6²⁰). And it is argued that to render ἐγώ εἰμι by "It is I," and treat the words as a simple affirmation that it was Jesus the Master who had appeared, is to do violence to the Greek language. So Abbott[2] regards ἐγώ εἰμι in 6²⁰ as a rendering of the Hebrew אֲנִי־הוּא, *I (am) He*, which is the comforting assurance, several times repeated in the prophets, of a Divine Deliverer. This is possible, but does not seem necessary. We have εἰμί used for πάρειμι in Jn. 7³⁶ (see note there), and clumsy Greek as ἐγώ εἰμι for "I am present" may seem, it cannot be ruled out as certainly wrong (cf. 9⁹).

A more plausible case may be made for this mystical use of ἐγώ εἰμι in Mk. 13⁶, Lk. 21⁸. Here Jesus foretells that false Christs will arise saying ἐγώ εἰμι. The parallel place, Mt. 24⁵, has ἐγώ εἰμι ὁ Χριστός, which is obviously the meaning; but neither Mk. nor Lk. supply ὁ Χριστός. There is no predicate

---

[1] ἐγώ εἰμι translates אֲנִי (without הוּא) in Isa. 47⁸, Zeph. 2¹⁵, where the careless city says in arrogance, "I am, and there is none else beside me," which is almost an assumption of the style of Deity.

[2] *Diat.* 2220 f.

for ἐγώ εἰμι in the Marcan and Lucan passages, and it seems probable, therefore, that the original tradition was that Jesus said that the claim of the false Christs would be the claim אֲנִי־הוּא, *I* (*am*) *He.*

(iv) Such considerations prepare us for the remarkable phrase πρὶν 'Αβραὰμ γενέσθαι ἐγώ εἰμι which Jn. (8⁵⁸) places in the mouth of Christ. In c. 8 we have had ἐγώ εἰμι three times before, but twice with a predicate expressed or understood (8¹⁸·²⁸). In 8²⁴·⁵⁸, however, and again at 13¹⁹, we have ἐγώ εἰμι used absolutely; and we must conclude that, in these passages at any rate (whatever may be thought of the Synoptic passages that have been cited **above**), ἐγώ εἰμι is the rendering of the Divine proclamation אֲנִי־הוּא, which the prophets ascribe to Yahweh.

This way of speech, elliptical and mysterious, was due, perhaps, to unwillingness to repeat the Sacred Name, the Tetragrammaton, which was revealed to Moses at the Bush. In Ex. 3¹⁴ the Name of God is declared to be אֶהְיֶה אֲשֶׁר אֶהְיֶה, ἐγώ εἰμι ὁ ὤν, as the LXX has it ; that is, His Name is אֶהְיֶה or ὁ ὤν. Moses was to say to the Israelites that אֶהְיֶה had sent him : "QVI EST misit me ad uos." But the English versions would mislead, if it were supposed that ἐγώ εἰμι in the sentence ἐγώ εἰμι ὁ ὤν (Ex. 3¹⁴) explained for us the ἐγώ εἰμι of Jn. 8⁵⁸. ἐγώ εἰμι in Ex. 3¹⁴ is followed by the predicate ὁ ὤν, and is not used absolutely. To get an illustration of this absolute use, we must go to the prophetic אֲנִי הוּא, *Ego ipse* (Isa. 46⁴), which, by its studied avoidance of the Name revealed in Ex. 3¹⁴, suggests its mystery and awe. Probably that Name did not connote *self-existence* (which is a later metaphysical conception) so much as *changelessness* and so *uniqueness* of being, " He that IS."

(v) In the attribution to Jesus of the solemn introduction of His claims by the phrase ἐγώ εἰμι, which, as we have seen, is suggestive of Deity in some of its various constructions, Jn. may possibly be reproducing actual words of Jesus, comparable to those cited in Mk. 13⁶ (see p. cxx above). But it is also possible that such utterances as ἐγώ εἰμι ἡ ἀνάστασις καὶ ἡ ζωή have been cast into this special form by the evangelist, it being a form whose significance would be instantly appreciated by his readers, whether Jewish or Greek.

CHAPTER V

CHRISTOLOGY

(i) The Title " Son of Man " in the Synoptists and in Jn.
(ii) The Doctrine of Christ's Person in the Synoptists, Paul, and Jn.
(iii) The Doctrine of the Logos and the Prologue to the Fourth Gospel.

(i) THE TITLE " SON OF MAN " IN THE SYNOPTISTS AND IN JN.

A

THE title " the Son of Man " as a designation of Jesus is found in the N.T. outside the Gospels only at Acts 7^{56}.[1] It is never employed by Paul, nor was it adopted by Christian writers of the sub-apostolic age. In the Gospels it occurs about eighty times, and always (for Jn. 12^{34} is not an exception) in the words of Jesus as a designation of Himself. It is never used of Him by the evangelists, when reporting His deeds or His words.

That Jesus should have made a practice of speaking of Himself in the third person is very remarkable,[2] and it is not less remarkable that no one seems to have thought it curious.[3] But that He did so speak, describing Himself either as " the Son of Man " or less frequently as " the Son," is attested by all four Gospels, and by the several strata of narrative which modern scholarship has detected as underlying the evangelical records. A table drawn up by Dr. Armitage Robinson [4] conveniently exhibits the distribution of the title in the Synoptic Gospels, and shows that it appears (1) in Mk., (2) in the document which critics call Q, (3) in the matter peculiar to Lk., (4) in the matter peculiar to Mt. So deeply rooted is this title in the traditional report of the words of Jesus, that in two passages at least it has been inserted by the later evangelists where it is absent from their Marcan source. Thus Mk. 3^{28}, " All their sins shall be forgiven unto the sons of men," becomes " Whosoever shall speak a word against the Son of Man, it shall be forgiven him," at Mt. 12^{32}, Lk. 12^{10}, the sense of the saying being materially affected. And again the momentous question, " Who do men say that I am ? " (Mk. 8^{27}, Lk. 9^{18}), assumes at Mt. 16^{13} the form, " Who do men say that the Son of Man is ? " or (according to some MSS.), " Who do men

---

[1] Cf. Hegesippus, in Eus. *H.E.* ii. 23. 13.
[2] Cf. Abbott, *Diat.* 2998 (xix.).
[3] Cf., however, Jn. 12^{34}.
[4] *The Study of the Gospels*, p. 50 f.

say that I, the Son of Man, am ? " Such editorial alterations presuppose a fixed tradition that Jesus habitually spoke of Himself as " the Son of Man."

B

A further inference may be derived from Mt. 16[13]. The evangelist who reported the question of Jesus in the form, " Who do men say that I, the Son of Man, am ? " or the like, could not have thought that " the Son of Man " was a recognised title for " the Christ." Had he thought so, his report of the Confession of Peter and its context would be unintelligible. For it would represent Jesus as announcing that He was the Christ in the question which asked His disciples to say who He was; and also as solemnly blessing Peter for a confession which only repeated what he had been told already. According to the Matthean tradition, then, the title " the Son of Man " as used by Jesus of Himself did not necessarily convey to His hearers His claim to be the Messiah. It was not a customary or familiar designation of the Messiah in the first century.

The Synoptic narratives represent the Confession of Peter (Mk. 8[29] and parallels) as marking a critical point in the training of the Twelve. They had been accustomed to the title " the Son of Man " on the lips of Jesus before this point, but they had not understood hitherto that He who called Himself the Son of Man was the Christ. Henceforward this method of self-designation may have connoted for them the claim of Jesus to be the promised Deliverer of the Jewish race, but in the earlier days of their association with Him it could not have carried this meaning. Nor would it at any stage of His ministry have conveyed to His hearers, who were not among the chosen Twelve, that He claimed to be Messiah.

Two instances of the prevailing ignorance that the title had any Messianic significance appear in the Fourth Gospel. At Jn. 9[35] (according to the true text), Jesus asks the blind man who had been cured, " Dost thou believe on the Son of Man ? " The answer is one of complete bewilderment, viz., " Who is He that I should believe on Him ? " He had not been a listener to the teaching of Jesus, and so he was not aware that He designated Himself " the Son of Man " ; and it is also clear that he did not recognise " the Son of Man " as a Messianic title. At Jn. 12[34] we have another illustration of the same ignorance. The multitude at Jerusalem had heard Jesus saying, " The Son of Man must be lifted up "; like the blind man, they did not know that He spoke of Himself when

He spoke of " the Son of Man." He had been speaking of the judgment which was impending, and they had been wondering if He was going to assert Himself as Messiah. But, on the contrary, He began to speak of " the Son of Man." Who might this be ? This was not a Messianic title known to them (see on 12³⁴).

C

Before examining more closely the significance which Jesus Himself attached to the title " Son of Man," some further instances may be cited from the Gospels of its use by Him as a designation of Himself, where there is no suggestion of His Messiahship.

Four instances occur in the non-Marcan document (behind Mt. and Lk.) generally known as Q. Jesus, when addressing the crowds, contrasts Himself with the austerely living Baptist as " the Son of Man who came eating and drinking " (Mt. 11¹⁹, Lk. 7³⁴). Also, addressing the crowds, He said that as Jonah was a sign to the Ninevites, so shall " the Son of Man be to this generation " (Mt. 12⁴⁰, Lk. 11³⁰). Addressing a scribe, He explained that, while the birds and beasts had homes, " the Son of Man hath not where to lay His head " (Mt. 8²⁰, Lk. 9⁵⁸). And while Mt.'s report of a beatitude in the Sermon on the Mount is, " Blessed are ye when men shall reproach you . . . and say all manner of evil against you falsely, for my sake " (Mt. 5¹¹), Lk. has in the parallel place, " Blessed . . . shall cast out your name as evil for the Son of Man's sake " (Lk. 6²²). In none of these passages is there any hint of a Messianic claim. " The Son of Man " is simply His description of Himself. In the last-mentioned passage (Lk. 6²²) it may be due to an editor; but in the other three it would seem to have been actually employed by Jesus, and there is no hint that those to whom it was addressed did not understand that it was thus that He spoke of Himself.

Two further instances, in which Lk. alone has the phrase, may be due to editorial revision, but they illustrate at all events the Lucan tradition. " Betrayest thou the Son of Man with a kiss ? " (Lk. 22⁴⁸), i.e., " Do you betray me with a kiss ? " And, " The Son of Man came to seek and save the lost " (Lk. 19¹⁰) is a sentence addressed to Zacchæus which the other evangelists have not preserved.

We come next to the earliest occurrences of the phrase in the Marcan tradition. In Mk. 2²⁷. ²⁸ we find the words, " The Sabbath was made for man, and not man for the Sabbath; so that the Son of Man is lord even of the Sabbath." The principle here set forth is that man is not to be the slave of an ordinance instituted for his benefit, and the stress of the reply would seem to reside in the word *man*, even in the phrase "the Son of Man." Some have thought that "the Son of Man" in this passage is an Aramaism for man in general, and that a parallel usage may be found in Ps. 8[4] 144[3]. Jesus is vindicating against the Pharisees not His own freedom only, but the freedom of the disciples, and incidentally of every man, in regard to the Rabbinical rules as to Sabbath observance, and so He says that "man is lord of the Sabbath." If this were the only occurrence on His lips of the phrase "the Son of Man," such an explanation might suffice, although the thesis that "man" (if by that is meant "every man") is free to observe only such rules of Sabbath rest as he may frame for himself, would go beyond anything ascribed elsewhere on the subject to Jesus. And, in fact, Mt. and Lk. when reporting this incident give quite a different turn to the argument by omitting the words, "The Sabbath was made for man, and not man for the Sabbath" (cf. Mt. 12[8], Lk. 6[5]). It is because of the dignity of the "Son of Man" and His superiority to ordinary men that, according to Mt. and Lk., He—and apparently He alone— may claim to be above Sabbath regulations. "A greater than the temple is here" (Mt. 12[6]). Cf. Jn. 5[17], "My Father worketh hitherto, and I work." The argument there, as in Mt. and Lk., is not that every man is free to keep the Sabbath just as he pleases, but rather that Jesus, because of His unique relation to God, who gave the Sabbath, may be fitly regarded as its Lord. We conclude, then, that even in Mk. 2[28] the title "the Son of Man" implies something more than "man in general" or "the son of man" of the Psalter. Undoubtedly the emphasis is on the word *man*, but it rests also on the uniqueness of Him who was in such special relation to humanity that He could, and did, call Himself "*The* Son of Man." It is not to be supposed that the Pharisees who rebuked Him for allowing His disciples to break the Sabbath (Mk. 2[24]) attached any very precise significance to this title which He assumed. They must have seen that by its use He meant to designate Himself, but they did not regard it as Messianic, or they would immediately have accused Him of blasphemy.

Something similar may be said of the phrase as it appears in Mk. 2[10] (Mt. 9[6], Lk. 5[24]). Here Jesus healed the paralytic as an indication of His far-reaching power, "that ye may know that the Son of Man has power on earth to forgive sins," it being admitted by every one that God has this power. Here, again, is no affirmation of His Messiahship. But at the same time the sentence suggests a certain mysteriousness of

personality.   He did not say that man in general has the power
to forgive sins, but only that He—the Son of Man—had it.[1]

D

We must now ask, however, if there is any trace in pre-
Christian times of the use of " the Son of Man " as a title of
Messiah, and if it be possible that Jesus chose it as a self-
designation because it included the Messianic prerogatives.

In the Psalter " the son of man " is a poetical way of
designating man in general (Ps. 8[4] 144[3]; cf. Job 25[6] 35[8]);
and throughout Ezekiel the Divine Voice addresses the prophet
as " son of man."   A similar use of this pleonasm for " man "
appears at Dan. 7[13], a passage which deeply affected Jewish
speculation as to the future : " I saw in the night visions, and,
behold, there came with the clouds of heaven one like unto
a son of man (ὡς υἱὸς ἀνθρώπου), and He came even to the
Ancient of Days, . . . and there was given Him dominion . . .
and a kingdom." [2]   This passage lies behind the vision recorded in 2 Esd. 13 (about 80 A.D.), where one comes out of
the sea " as it were the likeness of a man," who " flew with
the clouds of heaven," and who is plainly regarded by the
seer as Messiah.[3]   The Messianic interpretation of Dan. 7[13] is
also found in a Rabbinical saying of the third century A.D.[4]

There is, however, no trace in the O.T. of the title " the
Son of Man " being used as descriptive of Messiah, the earliest
instance of this usage being found in the Book of Enoch, and
for the most part in that part of the book which is entitled the
Similitudes of Enoch, and which is judged by Dr. Charles to
have been composed about 80 B.C.   The first passage in
Enoch which need be cited is based on Dan. 7[13].   It runs as
follows (xlvi. 1–5) : " I saw One who had a head of days, and
His head was white like wool, and with Him was another being
whose countenance had the appearance of a man . . . and
I asked the angel concerning that son of man who He was,
etc.   And he answered, ' This is the son of man who hath

---

[1] With the Pauline phrases ὁ ἔσχατος Ἀδάμ or ὁ δεύτερος ἄνθρωπος
(1 Cor. 15[45. 47]), the title " the Son of Man " may be compared, but there
is no evidence of any literary relation between them.

[2] " One like a son of man " is probably meant *by the author* to be a
personification of Israel (see Daniel *in loc.*).

[3] See J. M. Creed, *J.T.S.*, Jan. 1925, p. 131, who holds that Dan. 7[13]
does not sufficiently account for the picture of the Son of Man in the
later Jewish Apocalypses, and suggests that the conception of the
Heavenly Man entered Judaism from without, perhaps from Persian
sources.

[4] See Driver, *Daniel*, p. 108; and Dalman, *Words of Jesus* (Eng. Tr.),
p. 245.

righteousness . . . because the Lord of spirits hath chosen Him . . . and this son of man will . . . put down the kings from their thrones,' " etc. There follows an account of this son of man (it will be noted that the phrase is not yet used as a title) executing judgment at the Great Assize. Next follows a passage at xlviii. 2: " At that hour, that son of man was named in the presence of the Lord of spirits, and His name before the head of days . . . He will be a staff to the righteous . . . all who dwell on earth will bow before Him . . . and will bless the Lord of spirits. And for this reason has He been chosen and hidden before Him before the creation of the world and for evermore." Then the days of affliction of the kings of the earth are mentioned, and it is said of them, " They have denied the Lord of spirits and His Anointed," a sentence which identifies the son of man, who has been the subject of the preceding chapters, with Messiah.

These passages do not seem to exhibit the phrase " the son of man " used as a *title*. We get nearer to such a usage in lxix. 26, 27: " There was great joy among them, and they blessed and glorified . . . because the name of the son of man " (*i.e.* the son of man who has been mentioned already) " was revealed unto them. And He sat on the throne of His glory, and the sum of judgment was committed to Him, the son of man, and He caused the sinners . . . to be destroyed from off the face of the earth." At lxix. 29 we have: " The son of man has appeared and sits on the throne of His glory, and all evil will pass away before His face, but the word of the son of man will be strong before the Lord of spirits." Here we approach, but do not actually reach, the usage of the phrase " the son of man " as a title of Messiah. It does not appear that it ever became a popular or well-established title, while it is certain that, as it is used in *Enoch*, it goes back to Dan. 7[13].

E

When, with this in our minds, we examine afresh the passages in the Gospels in which Jesus calls Himself "the Son of Man," the significant fact emerges that a majority of these passages relate to the Advent of Jesus in glory and triumph as the judge of nations and of individuals, an Advent which is to be catastrophic and unexpected. These eschatological passages occur in all the strata of the evangelical record. We begin with some which belong to the Marcan tradition:

Mk. 14[61. 62]: " The high priest asked Him, Art Thou the Christ, the Son of the Blessed ? And Jesus

said, I am; and ye shall see the Son of Man sitting
at the right hand of power, and coming in the clouds
of heaven " (Mt. 26⁶⁴, Lk. 22⁶⁹). The high priest,
who denounced this reply as blasphemous, seems to
have detected the allusion to Dan. 7¹³ (and perhaps
also to Ps. 110¹), but this is not quite certain. At
any rate, Jesus had openly claimed to be Messiah,
and had also declared that as the Son of Man He
would come again in the clouds to the confusion of
His accusers.¹

Mk. 8³⁸: "Whosoever shall be ashamed of me and of
my words . . . the Son of Man also shall be ashamed
of him, when He cometh in the glory of His Father
with the holy angels " (Lk. 9²⁶; cf. also Lk. 12⁸).
In the corresponding place Mt. has: "The Son of
Man shall come in the glory of His Father with His
angels; and then shall He render unto every man
according to his deeds. . . . There be some of them
that stand here which shall in no wise taste of death,
till they see the Son of Man coming in His Kingdom "
(Mt. 16²⁷· ²⁸).²

Mk. 13²⁶· ²⁷: "Then shall they see the Son of Man
coming in clouds with great power and glory. And
then shall He send forth the angels, and shall gather
together His elect from the four winds, from the
uttermost part of the earth to the uttermost part of
heaven " (Mt. 24³⁰, Lk. 21²⁷). This is preceded in
Mt. by the words, "Then shall appear the sign of the
Son of Man in heaven, and then shall all the tribes
of the earth mourn," the report of Mt. thus carrying
an allusion not only to Dan. 7¹³ but also to Zech. 12¹⁰
(cf. Rev. 1⁷ for a similar combination).

Some critics have thought that underlying Mt. 24 is a fragment of a lost Jewish Apocalypse, but however that may be,
there are four occurrences of the title " the Son of Man " in
the non-Marcan material (Q) common to Mt. 24 and Lk. 12 and
17, as follows:

Mt. 24²⁷, Lk. 17²⁴: "As the lightning . . . so shall be
the coming of the Son of Man."

¹ See p. cxxix below.
² No mention is made in Dan. 7¹³ of *angels* accompanying the
descent from heaven of "one like unto a son of man "; but this
additional feature of His Advent is mentioned by Justin (as well as
in the Gospels). Cf. *Tryph.* 31 : ὡς υἱὸς γὰρ ἀνθρώπου ἐπάνω νεφελῶν
ἐλεύσεται, ὡς Δανιὴλ ἐμήνυσεν, ἀγγέλων σὺν αὐτῷ ἀφικνουμένων. (Cf. also
Apol. i. 52.)

Mt. 24[37], Lk. 17[26]: "As were the days of Noah, so shall
be the coming of the Son of Man."

Mt. 24[39], Lk. 17[30]: "So shall it be in the day that the
Son of Man is revealed," with a reference to the days
of Lot in Lk. which is omitted in Mt.

Mt. 24[44], Lk. 12[40]: "In an hour that ye think not the
Son of Man cometh."

It is probable that Q is also the source of Lk. 17[22], "The
days will come when ye shall desire to see one of the days of
the Son of Man and ye shall not see it," although the saying
is not found in Mt.

Other occurrences of the title in similar contexts which
are found only in Lk. are:

Lk. 18[8]: "When the Son of Man cometh, shall He find
faith on the earth?"; and

Lk. 21[36]: "Watch . . . that ye may prevail to escape
all these things that shall come to pass, and to stand
before the Son of Man."

Occurrences of the title in similar eschatological contexts
which are found only in Mt. are:

Mt. 10[23]: "Ye shall not have gone through the cities of
Israel until the Son of Man be come."

Mt. 13[37, 41]: "He that soweth the good seed is the Son
of Man. . . . The Son of Man shall send forth His
angels, and they shall gather out of His Kingdom all
things that cause stumbling," etc.

Mt. 25[31, 32]: "When the Son of Man shall come in His
glory, and all the angels with Him, then shall He sit on
the throne of His glory (cf. Mt. 19[28]), and before
Him shall be gathered all the nations: and He shall
separate them one from another. . . ." This representation of the Son of Man *as judge* goes beyond
what is said in Dan. 7[13], but it appears in *Enoch* lxix.
26, which has been cited above.

It must now be observed that, like the Synoptists, Jn. associates the title "the Son of Man" with eschatological doctrine.
Thus at 5[27] we have, "He gave Him authority to execute
judgment, *because He* is the Son of Man." This is closely
parallel to Mt. 25[32].

Again, in 1[51] the mysterious words, "Ye shall see the heaven
opened, and the angels of God ascending and descending
upon the Son of Man," cannot be explained of any temporal

i

experience which Nathanael was to enjoy. They must refer to some vision of the Last Things [1] (see note *in loc.*).

In 3^{13}, " No man has ascended into heaven, save He who descended from heaven, viz. the Son of Man," primarily refers to the Incarnation, but it also recalls Dan. 7^{13} as well as the Book of Enoch (see note *in loc.*).

In 6^{62}, " What if ye shall see the Son of Man ascending where He was before ? " the doctrine of the pre-existence of the apocalyptic " Son of Man " is again suggested, as in *Enoch*.

In these passages of the Fourth Gospel, the title " the Son of Man " is used with that suggestion of its reference to a wonderful, heavenly Being, which we have already seen is frequent in the Synoptists.

There are two other passages in Jn. 6 where the title is used, which are not so explicit in their eschatological suggestion, but which should be noted as indicating that for Jn., as for the Synoptists, " the Son of Man " always points to the uniqueness and mystery of the personality of Jesus as One whose home is in heaven. Jn. 6^{27}, " The meat which endures unto eternal life, which the Son of Man will give you," is expressed even more powerfully at Jn. 6^{53}, " Except ye eat the flesh of the Son of Man and drink His blood, you have no life in you." The narrative here implies that the hearers of Jesus understood that by " the Son of Man " He meant Himself. " How can this one give us his flesh to eat ? " (6^{52}). No Messianic doctrine is implied or suggested in these passages. But " the Son of Man " is the solemn title which is used of One Who has descended from heaven (6^{33}) that He may give life to the world (cf. 6^{51}).

F

The passages that have been cited, while they do not suggest that " the Son of Man " was a Messianic title in common use, seem to show that Jesus used it of Himself with the implication that in Him was the fulfilment of the vision of Dan. 7^{13}.[2] He was conscious of an infinite superiority to the sons of men among whom His Kingdom was to be established. He did not call Himself the " Christ," although He did not deny, when pressed, that He *was* the Christ (Jn. 4^{26} 5^{39} 8^{28} 10^{25}). He preferred to use a greater and a more far-reaching designation of Himself. He was not only the Deliverer of the Jewish people. He was the Deliverer of humanity at large, being

---

[1] The use of the title at Acts 7^{56}, which describes the vision of the dying Stephen, is similar to this.

[2] Cf. p. cxxxiii below.

" the Son of Man," who had come down from heaven.　He took over the phrase from Jewish Apocalyptic, but He enlarged its meaning.　It is a title which, properly understood, includes all that " Christ " connotes ; but, unlike the title " the Messiah," it does not suggest Jewish particularism.　In the only place where He suggested a form of confession as a test of faith, it is not, " Dost thou believe in the Son of God ? " (for that was a recognised synonym for Messiah), but, " Dost thou believe in the Son of Man ? " (Jn. 9[35]).　Nothing short of this would satisfy Him.　And it is an irony of history, that since the first century His most familiar designation by His disciples has been *Christ*, and the religion which He founded has been called *Christianity*, rather than the religion of *Humanity*, the religion of the Son of Man.　The Gospel has been preached with a Jewish accent, ever since the disciples of Jesus were first called " Christians " at Antioch.[1]

G

While, then, the actual title " the Son of Man " may have been suggested by Jewish Apocalyptic, on the lips of Jesus it was used in an enlarged and more spiritual significance. Another feature of its use by Him must now be noted.　It is the title which He specially employed, when He was fore-telling to His disciples the Passion as the inevitable and pre-destined issue of His public ministry.　Such forecasts, it may be observed,[2] do not appear in the non-Marcan document behind Mt. and Lk. (Q); but they are found both in Mk. and Jn., with a similar employment of the title " the Son of Man."

In Mk. these forecasts do not begin until after the Confession of Peter that Jesus was the Christ, which marked a turning-point in the education of the apostles.

> Mk. 8[31]: " He began to teach them that the Son of Man must suffer many things and be rejected . . . and be killed, and after three days rise again " (Mt. 16[21], Lk. 9[22]; cf. Lk. 24[7]).
>
> Mk. 9[31]: " The Son of Man is delivered up into the hands of men, and they shall kill Him ; and when He is killed, after three days He shall rise again " (Mt. 17[22], Lk. 9[44]).

[1] The majority of patristic interpreters (*e.g.* Justin, *Tryph.* 100) found in the title " the Son of Man " an allusion to His descent on the human side ; and it may be that early theologians avoided the use of the title, because they dreaded the suggestion of human *fatherhood* in the case of Jesus.

[2] This is pointed out by J. A. Robinson, *l.c.* p. 52.

> Mk. 10³³: "The Son of Man shall be delivered unto the chief priests and the scribes, . . . and they shall kill Him, and after three days He shall rise again (Mt. 20¹⁸, Lk. 18³¹).

In these three passages the prediction of the Resurrection is associated with that of the Passion ; and it is probable that the comment of Mk. 9³², "They understood not the saying," has special reference to this (cf. Mk. 9¹⁰). The announcement of the Passion disconcerted (Mk. 8³²) and grieved (Mt. 17²³) the Twelve; but they did not believe that it was to be taken literally.[1]

Next, we have:

> Mk. 10⁴⁵: "The Son of Man came not to be ministered unto, but to minister, and to give His life a ransom for many " (Mt. 20²⁸).
> Mk. 14⁴¹: "The Son of Man is betrayed into the hands of sinners " (Mt. 26⁴⁵).
> Mt. 26²: "The Son of Man is delivered up to be crucified " (the title is not given in the parallels Mk. 14¹, Lk. 22¹).

And, finally, two Marcan passages speak of the Passion of the Son of Man as the subject of O.T. prophecy, while this is not said (in these contexts) of the Resurrection, viz.:

> Mk. 9¹²: "How is it written of the Son of Man that He should suffer many things and be set at nought ? "
> Mk. 14²¹: "The Son of Man goeth, even as it is written of Him; but woe unto that man through whom the Son of Man is betrayed " (Mt. 26²⁴, Lk. 22²²).

The title "Son of Man " is associated with predictions of the Passion in Jn., as in Mk. :

> Jn. 3¹⁴: "As Moses lifted up the serpent . . . so must the Son of Man be lifted up," *i.e.* on the Cross (see note *in loc.*).
> Jn. 8²⁸: "When ye shall have lifted up the Son of Man, then shall ye know that I am He "; cf. also 12³⁴.
> Jn. 12²³: "The hour is come that the Son of Man should be glorified " (see note *in loc.*).
> Jn. 13³¹: "Now is the Son of Man glorified, and God is glorified in Him."

In these passages Jesus speaks of Himself as the Son of Man who was destined to suffer and die. There is nothing in

[1] See p. xlv.

the vision of Dan. 7^{13} to suggest this ; but, on the other hand, there is nothing to preclude the combination [1] of the vision of One who was to come in glory with the vision of the suffering Servant of Yahweh as it is depicted in Deutero-Isaiah. And this combination seems to have been present to the mind of Jesus. In calling Himself the Son of Man, the primary thought is that of a heavenly messenger whose kingdom is set up on earth, but He foresaw that He could not achieve His full purposes except through Death. And this, as He said in passages already cited (Mk. 9^{12} 14^{21}), was "written" of Him; *i.e.* the Passion was foreshadowed in O.T. prophecy, and most conspicuously in Isa. 53. The conception, then, of the "Son of Man," as it presents itself in the Gospels, is widely different from the popular conception of Messiah.[2] It was not a recognised title of Messiah, and was not interpreted as such ; rather was it always enigmatic to those who heard it applied by Jesus to Himself. For Him it connoted all that "Messiah" meant, and more, for it did not narrow His mission to men of one race only. It represented Him as the future Judge of men, and as their present Deliverer, whose Kingdom must be established through suffering, and whose gift of life was only to become available through His Death.[3]

(ii) The Doctrine of Christ's Person in the Synoptists, Paul, and Jn.

In the Synoptic Gospels the acceptance of Jesus by His disciples as the Messiah was not the immediate consequence of discipleship. As they associated with Him, observed His deeds, and listened to His words, they gradually realised that He was a very wonderful Person, whom they could not completely understand (Mk. 4^{41} 6^2 7^{37}). Some of those whom He cured of mental disorders seem to have acclaimed Him as the Son of God, that is, as Messiah, at an early stage in His ministry (Mk. 3^{12} 5^7); but the conviction of this was not reached all at once by the chosen Twelve. The confession,

[1] See Gould in *D.C.G.* ii. 664.

[2] Cf. Dalman, *l.c.* p. 265 : "Suffering and death for the actual possessor of the Messianic dignity are, in fact, unimaginable, according to the testimony of the prophets. . . . But the 'one like unto a son of man' of Dan. 7^{13} has still to receive the sovereignty. It was *possible* that he should also be one who had undergone suffering and death."

[3] The literature on the subject of this title of Jesus is very large. See especially Dalman, *Words of Jesus* (Eng. Tr., 1902); Drummond in *J.T.S.* (April and July 1901) ; J. Armitage Robinson, *Study of the Gospels* (1902) ; and the articles by Driver in Hastings' *D.B.*, and by G. P. Gould in Hastings' *D.C.G.*, with the references there given.

Thou art the Christ (Mk. 8²⁹), marks a crisis in their training, when a new vision of the meaning of Jesus' ministry came to them. Further, the Synoptic narratives represent Jesus as dissuading the onlookers from making known His miraculous doings (Mk. 3¹² 5⁴³ 7³⁶), although they did not altogether refrain from talking about them (7³⁷). In the Q tradition, there is a hint that Jesus was not always so reticent in this matter. When John the Baptist sent anxiously to inquire whether Jesus was really the Messiah, He directed the messengers to report His wonderful works as His credentials (Lk. 7²², Mt. 11⁴), with an allusion to the Messianic forecast of Isa. 35⁵· ⁶. The meaning of this could not have been misinterpreted, so that He departed here at any rate from His practice of reticence and reserve. Cf. also Mk. 9⁴¹. At the last His claim is explicit and final (Mk. 14⁶²).

Now in the Fourth Gospel, the impression left is somewhat different. It is true that in this Gospel, as in the Synoptists, Jesus prefers to speak of Himself as the Son of Man—an unfamiliar and ill-understood title—rather than as the Christ (5²⁶ 8²⁸ 9³⁵). The Jews accuse Him of being ambiguous as to His claim to Messiahship (10²⁴), and only once does He explicitly affirm it in the early stages of His ministry (4²⁶). But Jn. does not describe the *gradual* development of the disciples' acceptance of Him as the Christ. Jn. does, indeed, relate Peter's confession as marking a turning-point in the ministry of Jesus (6⁶⁹), just as the Synoptists do. But he makes Andrew and Philip recognise Jesus as the Christ almost immediately after they came into His company (1⁴¹· ⁴⁵). He does not tell this expressly of Peter, but his story suggests it (1⁴²). Nathanael at his first introduction to Jesus greets Him as " King of Israel," that is, as Messiah in the sense of the political deliverer who was expected (1⁴⁹). John the Baptist's cry, " Behold, the Lamb of God," probably represents a form of words which are a later paraphrase of what was said (see on 1²⁹); but that the Baptist recognised Jesus as the Messiah from the moment of His baptism (although he hesitated about this later) is clear not only in Jn. (1³³), but also in Mt.[1]

The truth is that it is not the purpose of the Fourth Evangelist to describe the Training of the Twelve. For him, the important matter is to bring out the impression which was left upon them at last of His Person. Nathanael in 1⁴⁹ has not got as far as Peter in 6⁶⁹, still less as far as Thomas in 20²⁸ ; but Jn. does not dwell upon this, and he may have antedated the complete conviction of Jesus as Messiah, which he ascribes to Andrew and the rest in c. 1.[2] What is of supreme import-

---

[1] Cf. p. ci.   [2] See note on 1⁴¹.

ance for Jn. is to expound the true conclusion which the original disciples reached, and which he desires all future disciples to accept, viz. that " Jesus is the Christ, the Son of God."

This conception of the purpose of Jn. in his Gospel marks a difference of standpoint between the earlier evangelists and the last.   Jn. is anxious to prove the truth of Jesus as the Son of God to a generation which had not seen Jesus in the flesh, and at a time when He had been the Object of Christian worship for more than half a century.   Christian reflexion and Christian experience had reached a doctrine of Christ's Person which had not been clearly thought out by Christians in the first enthusiasms of devotion to their Master.   The Synoptists draw a picture of Jesus as viewed by His contemporaries; the Fourth Gospel is a profound study of that picture, bringing into full view what may not have been clearly discerned at the first.

It used to be argued in the middle of the nineteenth century that the Christology of Jn. is so markedly different from that of the Synoptists, that if we wish to get " back to Jesus " we shall do well to confine ourselves to the Marcan picture of Him, as more primitive and less sophisticated than the Johannine narrative.   A closer inspection of the narratives has failed to recommend such counsels.   The distance of time between the publication of the Marcan Gospel and that of the Johannine Gospel cannot exceed thirty years—a time all too short for the development of any fundamental change in the picture of Jesus as accepted by Christian disciples.

The claims made for Jesus in Mk. transcend any claims that could be made for a mere human being of genius and magnetic personality.   We have seen that the claim to Messiahship, made for Jesus and by Himself, in the Marcan narrative, while only gradually understood and accepted by the Twelve, reaches very far.   The Jesus of Mk. claimed the power of forgiving sins (Mk. 2¹⁰); Jn. does not mention that, while he implies it in the terms of the Commission to the apostles, of which he alone tells (Jn. 20²³).   The Jesus of Mk. claimed to be the final judge of mankind (Mk. 14⁶²); the doctrine of Christ as judge in Jn. (see 12⁴⁷ and p. clviii) hardly goes beyond this.   Indeed, the only hint of any limitation of the powers of Jesus in Mk. is in reference to His vision, when on earth, of the *time* of the Last Judgment; what such limitation involves may be asked of the exegete of Jn. 14²⁸, as justly as in the case of Mk. 13³².   Or, again, the sacramental efficacy of Jesus' Death is not more definitely stated in Jn. 6⁵³ than in Mk. 14²⁴, τὸ αἷμά μου τῆς διαθήκης τὸ ἐκχυννόμενον ὑπὲρ πολλῶν.

We do not cite the uncorroborated testimony of Mt. in this

connexion, for his Gospel in its present form may be even later than Jn.[1] But, besides Mk., there is another "source" behind Mt. and Lk., viz. the document now called Q. In this (Mt. 10[32], Lk. 12[8. 9]), the public acceptance or denial of Jesus as Master will determine the judgment of the Last Assize; Jn. 12[48] does not make a more tremendous claim. And (not to cite other passages) there is nothing in Jn. which presents a more exalted view of Jesus than the saying: "All things have been delivered unto me of my Father; and no one knoweth who the Son is, save the Father; and who the Father is, save the Son, and he to whomsoever the Son willeth to reveal Him" (Mt. 11[27], Lk. 10[22]). Now Q may be older than Mk., as it is certainly older than Mt. and Lk. Yet here it offers a Christology which is as profound as that of Jn., and which is expressed in phrases that might readily be mistaken for those of the Fourth Gospel itself.

There is a difference between the Christology of the Synoptists and of Jn.; but it is not the difference between a merely human Jesus and a Divine Christ. What is implicit in the earlier Gospels has become explicit in Jn.; the clearer statement has been evoked by the lapse of time, by the growth of false *gnosis*, and by the intellectual needs of a Greek-speaking society which sought to justify its faith.

This is not the place to examine in detail the Christology of Paul, but it is important to observe how rapidly he reached that exalted conception of our Lord which is so prominent in his letters. The Epistles to the Romans, Corinthians, and Galatians are all earlier in date than the earliest date which we can ascribe to Mk.; for they were written before the year 58 of our era, or about a quarter of a century after his conversion. That is to say, the letters in which he indicated his view of Christ are earlier than any other extant Christian document.

The primitive gospel, "Jesus is the Christ," soon reaches the formula, "Jesus is Lord," and the title "Lord" includes for Paul the Divinity of his Master. This becomes so fundamental for his conception of Jesus, that while he continues always, as a Jew, to linger on the phrase "the Christ," he uses the title "Christ" frequently as a personal name (Rom. 5[8] 6[4] 8[10], Phil. 1[10. 23], Col. 1[27. 28]). As early as 1 Cor. 1[12], he treats Χριστός as a personal name comparable to Ἀπολλώς or Κηφᾶς. This usage is never found in the Gospels, for the passages Mk. 9[41], Lk. 23[2], Mt. 26[68], where Χριστός is found without the definite article, nevertheless treat Χριστός as a title. Paul often uses the full designation Ἰησοῦς Χριστός without any suggestion of Messianic office. Jn.'s habit[2] is

to use the personal designation *Jesus*, a primitive touch which
he shares with Mk., but which is seldom found in Paul.

In the four great Epistles (Rom., 1 and 2 Cor., Gal.), Paul
has many phrases which recall Johannine teaching. Jesus is
not only " the Son " (1 Cor. 15^{28}), which is common to all the
evangelists (see on Jn. 3^{17}), but is God's "own Son," ὁ ἴδιος
υἱός (Rom. 8^{32} ; cf. Jn. 5^{18}). That God "sent His Son"
(Rom. 8^3, Gal. 4^4) is a conception common to all the Gospels,
but cf. Jn. 3^{16} in particular. For the phrase τέκνα θεοῦ (Rom.
8$^{16. 17. 21}$) cf. Jn. 1^{12}. For Paul, Christ is ἐπὶ πάντων (Rom. 9^5) ;
cf. ἐπάνω πάντων ἐστίν (Jn. 3^{31}). χάρις is a characteristic term
in Paul; it is only used in the Prologue to the Gospel by Jn.,
but Paul means particularly by " grace " what Jn. means
when he writes, " God so loved the world " (see note on 1^{14}).
The Pauline contrast between " law " and " grace " (Rom.
4^{16} 6$^{14. 15}$, Gal. 5^4) is, again, explicitly enunciated in the Prologue (see on 1^{17}). Jn. does not use Paul's word πίστις in the
Gospel,[1] but the emphasis laid on " believing " is a prime
feature of Johannine doctrine (see on 1^7). Finally, Paul's
" Christ in me " (Rom. 8^{10}, 2 Cor. 13^5, Gal. 2^{20}) and " I in
Christ " (Rom. 16^7, 2 Cor. 5^{17}, Gal. 1^{22}) are conjoined as
inseparable in Jn. 15$^{4. 5}$. Paul's ἐν Χριστῷ is not less mystical
than anything in Jn. descriptive of the Christian life (see on
Jn. 14^{20} 15^{16} 17^{23}).

The Epistles to the Ephesians and Colossians belong to a
later period in Paul's career.[2] We should expect to find
resemblances in Jn. to their Christology, associated as they
are by name with Churches in that portion of Asia Minor
where Jn.'s literary activity was put forth. These Epistles
specially illustrate the doctrine of the Prologue of the Gospel
as to the Person of Christ. His Pre-existence (Jn. 1^1) is laid
down, " He is before all things " (Col. 1^{17}). He is the Creative
Word (Jn. 1^3), and, as Jn. says, " That which has come into
being was, in Him, life " (1^4), so in Col. 1^{17} we have, " In Him
all things hold together or cohere." [3] The Pauline ἐν μορφῇ
θεοῦ ὑπάρχων (Phil. 2^6) is the doctrine of Jn. 1^1,[4] even as οὐκ
ἁρπαγμὸν ἡγήσατο τὸ εἶναι ἴσα θεῷ is brought out at Jn.
5^{18} 10^{33}.

The teaching of Jn. 1^{16} as to Christ's πλήρωμα which His
disciples share is anticipated in Col. 1^{19}, " It was the good

---

[1] Cf. p. lxv.
[2] We take them as Pauline ; but in any case they are later in date
than those already cited.
[3] See on Jn. 1^4.
[4] Cf. also Jn. 1^{14} for the δόξα which the μονογενής receives from
the Father.

pleasure [of the Father] that in Him should all the πλήρωμα dwell " (cf. Eph. 4¹³). Again, " In Him dwelleth all the πλήρωμα of the Godhead." σωματικῶς (Col. 2⁹) brings us very near to the cardinal thesis, " the Word was made flesh " (Jn. 1¹⁴). And with this, both in Paul and Jn., is combined the doctrine of the *invisibility* of God. God is ἀόρατος, and Christ is His εἰκών, the πρωτότοκος πάσης κτίσεως (Col. 1¹⁵) ; cf. Jn. 1¹⁸ : " No man hath seen God . . . but the μονογενής, who is God . . . hath declared Him."

These are more than verbal coincidences. They show that hardly anything is missing from the doctrine of Christ as set out in the Prologue (except the actual term λόγος), which is not implicit in the Epistles to the Colossians, Ephesians, Philippians. Much that is enunciated in the Prologue was not a new discovery of the writer; it had been familiar to the Churches of Asia Minor for some time before it was put into the words which were thenceforth accepted by Christendom as the supreme philosophical statement and charter of its deepest faith.[1]

(iii) The Doctrine of the Logos and the Prologue to the Fourth Gospel

The thesis of the Gospel is that Jesus is the Revealer of God (1¹⁸), its practical aim being given at the end (20³¹). The Prologue, however, is more than a mere preface, for it offers a philosophical explanation of the thesis. Jesus is the Revealer of God, because He is the Logos of God. This is a proposition which does not appear at all in the body of the Gospel, any more than the theological words and phrases, πλήρωμα, σκηνοῦν, μονογενὴς θεός, εἶναι εἰς τὸν κόλπον, ἐξηγεῖσθαι, which are found in the Prologue. Not only does Jesus never claim the title " Logos " for Himself, but Jn. never applies it to Him in the evangelical narrative.

The Prologue is undoubtedly by the same hand that wrote the Gospel, but it is written from a different point of view, entirely consistent with the Gospel but not derived from the history which the Gospel narrates. Jn. prefixes a short Preface to his hortatory First Epistle, and there again he introduces the conception of Jesus as the Logos (1 Jn. 1¹; cf. p. lxi), while he does not in this later passage elucidate his meaning. But the Prologue is, as I have said, more than a Preface. It is a summary restatement of the Christian gospel from the philosophical side; and was probably written after the narrative was completed,[2] not now to record or summarise the words of

[1] See p. cxliii.   [2] Cf. p. cxliv.

Jesus, but to express the writer's conviction that Jesus the Christ was Himself the Divine Logos.

The influences which contributed to the formulation for the first time in the Prologue of the Christian Doctrine of the Word were, no doubt, various.

1. The Hebrew Scriptures have much about the Divine Voice in creation, the Creative Word (see on 1³). In the Targums, or paraphrases of the Old Testament, the action of Yahweh is constantly described as His "Word" (מימרא), the term *Memra* being sometimes used as of a Person. Thus the Targum of Onkelos on Gen. 28²¹ says that Jacob's covenant was that "the Word of Yahweh should be his God." This kind of quasi-personification extends to the Psalms, and particularly to the Book of Proverbs, where personal qualities are repeatedly ascribed to Wisdom (חכמה); cf. Prov. 3¹³ᶠ· 4⁵ᶠ· 7⁴, the most remarkable passage being Prov. 8²² : "Yahweh possessed me in the beginning of His way, before His works of old. I was set up from everlasting, from the beginning, or ever the earth was." This is poetry, not metaphysical prose ; but it treats *Wisdom* as the expression of God, co-eternal with Him. This quasi-personification of Wisdom is continued in the teaching of the son of Sirach, Ecclus. 24³, which has much about Creative Wisdom, actually claiming for her, "I came forth from the mouth of the Most High."

2. When we turn from Palestine to Alexandria, from Hebrew sapiential literature to that which was written in Greek, we find this creative wisdom identified with the Divine λόγος, Hebraism and Hellenism thus coming into contact. God is addressed as ὁ ποιήσας τὰ πάντα ἐν λόγῳ σου (Wisd. 9¹). The λόγος is the universal healer (Wisd. 16¹²). This Almighty λόγος is said to have leaped down from heaven, as a warrior, bringing God's commandment as a sharp sword . . . "it touched the heaven, but stood upon the earth " (Wisd. 18¹⁵· ¹⁶). This last pronouncement suggests the personification of the λόγος who came to earth, but so much is not consciously present to the writer's thought. The language of the Book of Wisdom betrays Stoic influence at several points,[1] but with the Stoics λόγος was not personal.

3. The doctrine of the λόγος in Philo's writings has been frequently examined; and here it can receive only a brief notice. We have already called attention to some striking verbal parallels between Philo and the Fourth Gospel,[2] and such may be traced also in what Philo says about the λόγος;

[1] Cf. Rendel Harris, "Stoic Origins of St. John's Gospel " (*Bulletin of John Rylands Library,* Jan. 1922).
[2] F. xciii above.

but the differences in the underlying thoughts as to this are manifest, and far-reaching. Some of these must now be summarised :

(a) The doctrine of the *Personality* of the Logos is vague in Philo, and especially so when he comes to the association of the Logos with Creation (see on 1³). Thus Philo has the expressions ὄργανον δὲ λόγον θεοῦ, δι᾽ οὗ κατεσκευάσθη (*de Cherub.* 35): τὸ μὲν δραστήριον ὁ τῶν ὅλων νοῦς (*de mund. opif.* 3): when God was fashioning the world (ὅτε ἐκοσμοπλάστει), He used the Word as a tool (χρησάμενος ὀργάνῳ τούτῳ, *de migr. Abr.* 1): Philo speaks of the creative power (ποιητική), according to which the Creator made the world with a word (λόγῳ τὸν κόσμον ἐδημιούργησε, *de prof.* 18). In other passages the λόγος is εἰκὼν θεοῦ (cf. Col. 1¹⁵)[1] : εἰκὼν θεοῦ, δι᾽ οὗ σύμπας ὁ κόσμος ἐδημιουργεῖτο (*de monarch.* ii. 5; cf. *de confus. ling.* 20 and 28, where he speaks of τὸν εἰκόνα αὐτοῦ, τὸν ἱερώτατον λόγον).[2]

The earliest Christian writers [3] take up the Jewish thought of the Creative Word from a different standpoint, while they employ language similar to that of Philo. To Jn. the Word is a personal Divine Agent who co-operated with the Creator in the work of Creation, even Jesus Christ, the Son of the eternal Father. Paul does not use the term λόγος, but his language about the work of Christ in creation is almost identical with that of the Prologue to the Fourth Gospel. Cf. εἷς κύριος Ἰησοῦς Χριστός, δι᾽ οὗ τὰ πάντα (1 Cor. 8⁶); τὰ πάντα δι᾽ αὐτοῦ . . . ἔκτισται (Col. 1¹⁶); cf. also δι᾽ οὗ καὶ ἐποίησεν τοὺς αἰῶνας (Heb. 1²). Like Philo, and like Jn., these writers employ the preposition διά to describe the mediating work of the Word (or the Son) in Creation; but in ascribing Divine personality to this mediating Agent, they agree with each other and with Jn., while they differ from Philo. Paul and Jn. do not borrow from Philo, nor are they directly dependent on his speculations; but they and Philo represent two different streams of thought, the common origin of which was the Jewish doctrine of the *Memra* or Divine Word.[4]

(b) The *pre-existence* of the Logos is not explicit in Philo, whereas it is emphatically declared in the opening words of the Prologue to the Gospel. Philo applies, indeed, the epithet πρεσβύτατος to the λόγος more than once (*de confus. ling.* 28, *quod det. pot.* 22); but such a phrase does not imply eternal pre-existence. See on 1¹.

(c) The Johannine doctrine of the connexion between Life and Light, which appears in the Logos teaching of the

[1] See p. cxli n.
[2] Cf. for a full discussion, Drummond, *Philo Judæus*, ii. 185 ff.
[3] See Lightfoot on Col. 1¹⁶.   [4] Cf. p. cxxxix.

Prologue (1⁴; cf. also 8¹²), does not appear in Philo, although it suggests a line of speculation which would, one supposes, have been congenial to him.

(d) Most significant of all differences between Jn. and Philo, is that Jn.'s philosophy rests avowedly on the doctrine of the Incarnation (see on 1¹⁴), while this is absolutely precluded by the principles of Philo. "There are," he says, "three kinds of life: one which is πρὸς θεόν, another πρὸς γένεσιν, and a third which is a mixture of both. But the ζωὴ πρὸς θεόν has not descended to us (κατέβη πρὸς ἡμᾶς), nor has it come as far as the necessities of the body" (*Quis rer. div. hær.* 9).

4. In addition to these various philosophies, with which the Christian doctrine of the Logos has been associated by scholars, attention has been directed of recent years to the Mandæan and Hermetic literature, as possible homes of the Logos idea. Many parallels to Johannine phraseology have been collected from the writings of Lidzbarski, Reitzenstein, and others by Walter Bauer in the last edition of his commentary on the Fourth Gospel. Some of these are striking, especially those from the Mandæan Liturgies: "I am a Word, a Son of Words"; "the Word of Life"; "the Light of Life"; "the First Light, the Life, which was out of the Life"; "the worlds do not know thy Names, nor understand thy Light." [1] There is, however, no evidence that Mandæan teachings had any influence on Christian philosophy in its beginnings. Christian or Jewish belief may have affected the development of Mandæism, but Mandæism was not a *source* from which Christian doctrine derived any of its features.[2] Probably, as in other cases, the parallels that have been cited are only verbal. To build up community or similarity of doctrine upon coincidences of language between two writers is highly precarious; and when the Johannine doctrine of the Logos is compared with that of Philo or the Stoics or the Sapiential Books, or even that of the Mandæan Liturgies, this should always be borne in mind.[3]

[1] Bauer, pp. 8–13.
[2] For the Mandæan doctrines and their growth, see W. Brandt, in *E.R.E.* viii. p. 380 f.
[3] A passage may be cited from Plato to illustrate this : καὶ δὴ καὶ τέλος περὶ τοῦ παντὸς νῦν ἤδη τὸν λόγον ἡμῖν φῶμεν ἔχειν· θνητὰ γὰρ καὶ ἀθάνατα ζῷα λαβὼν καὶ συμπληρωθεὶς ὅδε ὁ κόσμος οὕτω, ζῷον ὁρατὸν τὰ ὁρατὰ περιέχον, εἰκὼν τοῦ ποιητοῦ, θεὸς αἰσθητός, μέγιστος καὶ ἄριστος κάλλιστός τε καὶ τελεώτατος γέγονεν, εἷς οὐρανὸς ὅδε μονογενὴς ὤν (*Timæus*, § 44, sub fin.). To find here any relation to the Johannine doctrine of the μονογενής or the Pauline thought of Christ as the εἰκών of God, would be very perverse ; but the coincidences in language are almost startling.

It is now apparent that the doctrine of a Divine λόγος was widely distributed in the first century. The Hebrew Targums or paraphrases of the ancient scriptures; the Wisdom literature of Judaism,[1] both in Palestine and Alexandria; the speculations of Philo; the philosophy of Heraclitus, and that of the later Stoics, all use the idea of the Logos to explain the mysterious relation of God to man. We may be sure that the Logos of God was as familiar a topic in the educated circles of Asia Minor as the doctrine of Evolution is in Europe or America at the present day, and was discussed not only by the learned but by half-instructed votaries of many religions.

Christian disciples, Docetic and Ebionite no less than simple, unspeculative followers of Jesus, were conscious of the wonder of His life. It was inevitable that the Pauline teaching of the Epistles to the Colossians and Ephesians [2] should quicken deep thoughts as to the relation of Jesus to the Eternal God. The Epistle to the Hebrews uses language about the "Word of God" (Heb. 4[12]) which naturally provoked questionings as to the relation of this energising and heart-searching Logos to the great High Priest Himself. An earlier writer, the Seer of the Apocalypse, actually gives the title "the Word of God" (Rev. 19[13]) to the Leader of the Christian host, probably having the conception of the Logos as a Warrior (Wisd. 18[15]) in his mind. Jn. must have been not only conversant in some degree with the philosophical speculations of Ephesus as to the Divine Logos, and with such teaching as that of Heb. 4[12], but above all with the application of the title "the Word of God," by the author of the Apocalypse, whose disciple he was.[3] Such a phrase in the Apocalypse did not solve problems, but it must have suggested a remarkable problem to the followers of Jesus in the next generation, who asked what it meant. To call Jesus the λόγος of God without further explanation might well suggest that Docetic theory of His Person which it is one of the purposes of the Fourth Gospel to dispel as wholly irreconcilable with His earthly life.[4]

Jn.'s chief aim was to show (it was his deepest conviction) that Jesus is the Revealer of God. But the philosophers, whether Hebrew or Greek, whether they took Logos as meaning *speech* or as meaning *reason*, had for centuries been occupied with the idea that the Divine Word is the Revealer, and had

[1] See on 1[10] for a parallel to Jn.'s Logos doctrine in *Enoch* xlii. 1 on the Divine Wisdom.
[2] Cf. p. cxxxvii
[3] Cf. p. lxviii. See on 5[38] for a simpler use of the phrase, "the Logos of God."
[4] See on 1[14].

not found it possible thus completely to bridge the gulf between God and man. How can we reconcile Spirit and Matter, the One and the Many, the Infinite and the Finite ? It was left for Christian philosophy to proclaim that the only solution of these problems, which metaphysics had failed to solve, was *historical*. And the first statement of this is in the Prologue to the Fourth Gospel, ὁ Λόγος σὰρξ ἐγένετο. The philosophers had said that the Word is the Revealer of God. That is true, for Jesus is the Word.

Whether any one before Jn. had said explicitly, " The Word became flesh," we do not know; nor can we say that this express and fundamental proposition was present to his mind when he penned the narrative of the Fourth Gospel. It may have been so, but it nowhere appears explicitly except in the Prologue, as has been pointed out already.[1] When Loisy wrote, " La théologie de l'incarnation est la clef du livre tout entier, et qu'elle le domine depuis la première ligne jusqu'à la dernière," [2] he was not accurate if he meant that the Logos doctrine of the Prologue dominated the entire Gospel. On the contrary, the Prologue is the recommendation of the Gospel to those who have approached it through metaphysics rather than through history; but the evangelist never allows his metaphysics to control his history.[3] He appeals to no " witness " to corroborate the doctrine of the Word which he sets out in the Prologue, while the appeal to " witnesses," Divine and human, appears in every part of the evangelical narrative.[4] He puts it forth as the philosophical solution of the great problem, " How can God reveal Himself to man ? "—a solution latent in the Wisdom literature of the Hebrews, although not perceived by the philosophers of Greece. This is Jn.'s great contribution to Christian philosophy, that *Jesus is the Word* ; but nowhere, as Harnack has pointed out, does he deduce any formula from it. It was for later ages to do this, and to treat the Johannine presentation in the Prologue of *the Word* who *became flesh*, as the secure basis for far-reaching thoughts and hopes as to the destiny of man. " He became what we are that He might make us what He is," is the saying of Irenæus,[5] not of Jn.

For Jn. it is sufficient to preach as gospel that " God so loved the world that He sent His Son "; he does not put forward

---

[1] P. cxxxviii.   [2] *La Quatrième Évangile*, p. 98.
[3] Cf. Harnack s important article on the " Prologue " in *Zeitschr. f. Theol. und Kirche*, 1892, No. 3.
[4] Cf. p. xc.
[5] *Adv. Hær.* v. Pref., "Qui propter immensam suam dilectionem actus est quod sumus nos, uti nos perficeret esse quod est ipse."

the tremendous paradox, " the Word became flesh," as the gospel which he has received, although it supplies for him as he ponders it the *rationale* of the revelation of God in Jesus Christ. In the Sapiential Books of the O.T., the praises of Wisdom are several times put into poetry or rhythmic form; Prov. 8 is a familiar example. The hymn on *Sophia* in Wisd. 7[22f.] points back to that of Prov. 8, and the traces of its use in Heb. 1[3] 4[12] are apparent. Yet another Wisdom hymn, Ecclus. 24[3-22], takes up some thoughts from the two earlier hymns, and may have influenced the language of Jn. 1[3. 14] (cf. Ecclus. 24[8. 9. 12]). It is, then, not without precedent if it be found that the doctrine of the Logos in the Prologue to Jn., like the doctrine of Sophia in the Sapiential Books, should have been put into the form of an Ode or Hymn, the profundity of the subject being better suited to poetry than to prose. The following arrangement of the Logos Hymn embodied in the Prologue is here offered for examination:

THE LOGOS HYMN

1. Ἐν ἀρχῇ ἦν ὁ Λόγος,
   καὶ ὁ Λόγος ἦν πρὸς τὸν θεόν,
   καὶ θεὸς ἦν ὁ Λόγος.

2. οὗτος ἦν ἐν ἀρχῇ πρὸς τὸν θεόν.

3. πάντα δι' αὐτοῦ ἐγένετο,
   καὶ χωρὶς αὐτοῦ ἐγένετο οὐδὲ ἕν.

4. ὃ γέγονεν ἐν αὐτῷ ζωὴ ἦν,
   καὶ ἡ ζωὴ ἦν τὸ φῶς τῶν ἀνθρώπων.

5. καὶ τὸ φῶς ἐν τῇ σκοτίᾳ φαίνει,
   καὶ ἡ σκοτία αὐτὸ οὐ κατέλαβεν.

10. ἐν τῷ κόσμῳ ἦν,
    καὶ ὁ κόσμος δι' αὐτοῦ ἐγένετο,
    καὶ ὁ κόσμος αὐτὸν οὐκ ἔγνω.

11. εἰς τὰ ἴδια ἦλθεν,
    καὶ οἱ ἴδιοι αὐτὸν οὐ παρέλαβον.

14. καὶ ὁ Λόγος σὰρξ ἐγένετο,
    καὶ ἐσκήνωσεν ἐν ἡμῖν,

    καὶ ἐθεασάμεθα τὴν δόξαν αὐτοῦ,
    δόξαν ὡς μονογενοῦς παρὰ πατρός,

    πλήρης χάριτος καὶ ἀληθείας.

18. θεὸν οὐδεὶς ἑώρακεν πώποτε·
μονογενής, θεός, ὁ ὢν εἰς τὸν κόλπον τοῦ πάτρος,
ἐκεῖνος ἐξηγήσατο.

The hymn is a philosophical *rationale* of the main thesis of the Gospel. It begins with the proclamation of the Word as Pre-existent and Divine (vv. 1, 2). Then appear the O.T. thoughts of the Word as creative of all (v. 3), life-giving (v. 4), light-giving (v. 5). But the whole universe (v. 10), including man (v. 11), was unconscious of His omnipresent energy. He became Incarnate, not as a momentary Epiphany of the Divine, but as an abiding and visible exhibition of the Divine Glory, even as the Son exhibits the Father (v. 14). Thus does the Word as Incarnate reveal the Invisible God (v. 18).

Two parenthetical notes as to the witness of John the Baptist, to the coming Light (vv. 6–9), and His pre-existence (v. 15), are added. We have also two exegetical comments by the evangelist,[1] at vv. 12, 13, to correct the idea which v. 11 might convey, that no one received or recognised the Word when He came; and again at vv. 16, 17, to illustrate the " grace and truth " of v. 14.

The great theme of a Divine Revealer of God is implicit in the first and last stanzas of the hymn (vv. 1, 18), the rest being concerned with the method of the revelation.

The Hebraic style of the hymn is plain. The repetition in the second line of a couplet of what has been said already in the first line (vv. 3, 5); the elucidation of the meaning of the first line by the emphatic word being repeated in the next (vv. 4, 5, 11, 14), which provides an illustration of what has been called " climactic parallelism " (cf. Ps. 29⁵ 93³); the threefold repetition in the first three lines of v. 14, all of which involve the bodily visibility of the Logos—sufficiently show that the model is not Greek but Hebrew poetry.

It will be noticed that the hymn moves in abstract regions of thought. The historical names—John, Moses, Jesus Christ—are no part of it: they are added in the explanatory notes of the evangelist. Nevertheless, v. 14 states an historical fact, and points to an event in time; but the history is told *sub specie æternitatis*.

The treatment of the Prologue as embodying a hymn on the Logos has been suggested more than once in recent years. An analysis of it from this point of view was published by C. Cryer in 1921.[2] In 1922 C. F. Burney treated the Prologue

---

[1] This is in the manner of Jn. ; cf. p. xxxiv.
[2] *Expository Times*, July 1921, p. 440.

k

as a hymn (with comments) originally composed in Aramaic ;[1] and Rendel Harris suggested that it was based on a Hymn to Sophia, although he did not work out the details of any rhythmic arrangement. He developed the parallels between the Prologue and the Sapiential literature of the O.T., comparing also some Stoic phrases.[2]

The arrangement of the stanzas which is printed above is not identical with those adopted by Burney or Cryer, an important difference being that the hymn proper does not embody argument (cf. vv. 12, 13, 16, 17) or contain the Personal Name of Jesus Christ. It is a Logos hymn of a triumphant philosophy, directly Hebrew in origin, but reflecting the phrases which had become familiar in Greek-speaking society. In the Christian literature of the first two centuries a good many traces of rhythm and verse arrangement may be found in impassioned passages of prose.[3] Eusebius (*H.E.* v. 28. 5) cites a writer who remarks on the number of Christian Psalms and Odes which from the beginning (ἀπ' ἀρχῆς) sung of Christ as the Word (τὸν λόγον τοῦ θεοῦ τὸν Χριστὸν ὑμνοῦσι θεολογοῦντες). Such a collection of Christian hymns were those known as the *Odes of Solomon*, which present so many points of contact with the Johannine writings, and especially with the Prologue to the Gospel, that they demand mention at this point.

The *Odes of Solomon* were first published from the Syriac by Rendel Harris in 1909.[4] He regarded them as of first-century date, and to this Harnack gave his adhesion. I have given reasons elsewhere [5] for regarding this date as too early, and for treating them as Christian hymns composed about 160 or 170 A.D.

These beautiful hymns are composed in cryptic fashion, and they contain no avowed verbal quotations either from the O.T. or the N.T. But the doctrine of the Logos is repeatedly dwelt on, in a way which recalls Johannine teaching. The Word is the Thought (ἔννοια) of God (Odes xvi. 20, xxviii. 18, xli. 10); this Thought is Life (ix. 3) and Light (xii. 7). " Light dawned from the Word that was beforetime in Him " (xli. 15), so that the pre-existence of the Word is recognised (cf. xvi. 19). He is the Agent of Creation, for " the worlds

---

[1] *Aramaic Origin, etc.*, p. 41.

[2] " Athena Sophia and the Logos " (*Bulletin of John Rylands Library*, July 1922). See also Rendel Harris, *The Origin of the Prologue* (1917).

[3] See the article " Hymnes " in Cabrol's *Dict. d'archéol. chrétienne*, vi. 2839.

[4] His final edition appeared in 1920 (Manchester University Press).

[5] Cambridge, *Texts and Studies*, " The Odes of Solomon " (1913) ; cf. also *Theology*, Nov. 1920.

were made by His [God's] Word and by the Thought of His heart " (xvi. 20). The Incarnation of the Word is expressed by saying " the dwelling-place of the Word is man " (xii. 11 ; cf. xxii. 12); and God continually abides with man, for " His Word is with us in all our way " (xli. 11). Were these sublime phrases as early as the first century, we should have to treat the Odes not only as arising in an environment like that which was the birthplace of the Fourth Gospel, but as being actually one of the sources from which its distinctive doctrines were derived. This, however, cannot be maintained. The Odes, nevertheless, provide a welcome illustration of that mystical aspect of Christian teaching which has sometimes been erroneously ascribed to Hellenic rather than to Hebrew influences. They catch the very tone of Jn.,[1] and show how deep-rooted in Christian devotion was the Johannine doctrine of the Word, within seventy years of the publication of the Fourth Gospel.

CHAPTER VI

DOCTRINAL TEACHING OF THE FOURTH GOSPEL

  (i) The Authority of the O.T.
 (ii) The Johannine Doctrines of Life and Judgment.
(iii) The Kingdom of God and the New Birth.
 (iv) The Eucharistic Doctrine of Jn.
  (v) The Johannine Miracles.

(i) THE AUTHORITY OF THE O.T.

(i) THE Old Testament was, for a Jew, the fount of authority, and in the Fourth Gospel it is frequently quoted to establish a fact, or to clinch an argument, or to illustrate something that has been said.

Thus the people by the lake-side (6^{31}) quote Ex. 16^{15} to confirm their statement that their fathers had been given bread from heaven. The O.T. was their book of national history.

Jesus is represented in Jn. as appealing to the Law (Deut.

---

[1] This is not only true of their Logos doctrine. With 1 Jn. 4^{19} we may compare, " I should not have known how to love the Lord if He had not loved me " (Ode iii. 3). In the note on 17^6 below, I have cited another parallel from Ode xxxi. 4, 5. See also notes on 1^{32} 5^{17} 6^{27} $7^{37. 38}$ 8^{12}. The Odist dwells continually on the great Johannine themes — Love, Knowledge, Truth, Faith, Joy, Light; he never mentions sin, repentance, or forgiveness (cf. p. xcv).

19^{15}) and to the Psalms (Ps. 82^6) in support of His arguments with the Jews (8^{17} and 10^{34}). The Synoptic narrative agrees with this representation of His mode of argument (Mk. 12^{35} and parallels; Mt. 4$^{4.\ 6.\ 11}$=Lk. 4$^{4.\ 8.\ 12}$). Paul appealed to the O.T. in the same fashion, as every Rabbi did (Rom. 3^{10}, 1 Cor. 15^{45}, Gal. 3^{11}, etc.).

Again, the Fourth Gospel represents Jesus as illustrating His teaching by the citation of Scripture passages; *e.g.* He quotes Isa. 54^{13} at 6^{45}, and His quotation (7^{38}), " Out of his belly shall flow rivers of living water," seems to be illustrative rather than argumentative. There are many instances in the Pauline Epistles of this use of the O.T. (*e.g.* Rom. 4^6); and the Synoptists ascribe it to Jesus just as Jn. does (Mt. 9^{13} 21$^{16.\ 42}$, etc.). So far there is no difficulty in the report of the Fourth Gospel as to the use said to have been made of the O.T. by Jesus and His hearers.

(ii) The Jews, however, did not only hold that the O.T. was authoritative; they held that it pointed forward to Messiah, and to His Kingdom which was one day to be established among them. It was a *prophetic* volume, and for them prophecy included *prediction*. They believed that the actual words of the O.T. were intended by God to have a future as well as a present application.

Thus Jn. represents the people [1] as expecting that Messiah would come one day, because the prophets had so predicted; and expecting Him to be born at Bethlehem (7^{42}; cf. Mt. 2^5), of the seed of David; to vindicate Himself by wonderful works (6$^{14.\ 30}$) because the Scriptures of the prophets had assured them that so it would be; and to "abide for ever" (12^{34}) because so it had been indicated in "the law." The Synoptists do not give any details as to the nature of the Messianic expectation, but they are clear that Messiah was looked for, by the priests (Mk. 14^{61}); by pious folk such as Simeon, Anna, the two at Emmaus (Lk. 2$^{26.\ 36}$ 24^{21}); by John the Baptist, who expected Messiah to work miracles (Mt. 11^2, Lk. 7^{20}); and by the people generally (Lk. 3^{15}). The hope that the Messianic prophecies would one day be fulfilled was in every pious Jewish heart, and Jn.'s report that this expectation was vivid is borne out by all the other evidence we have.

(iii) The evangelists, Jn. as well as the Synoptists, were convinced that this expectation had been satisfied, for they believed that in Jesus the Messiah had been found. The purpose of Jn. in writing his gospel was that his readers might believe that " Jesus is the Christ " (20^{31}); and he is quite assured that Isaiah (12^{41}) as well as Zechariah spoke of Jesus. He applies,

[1] Cf. p. lxxxii.

e.g., Zech. 12¹⁰ to the piercing of the Lord's side on the Cross
(19³⁷). Jn. tells of John the Baptist applying to himself the
prophecy of the Forerunner (1²³; cf. Mk. 1², Lk. 3⁴; cf. 7²⁷,
Mt. 3³), and accepting unhesitatingly Jesus as the Messiah
(1²⁹. ³⁴); and he ascribes the same belief to other disciples
(1⁴¹. ⁴⁵. ⁴⁹ 6⁶⁹, etc.). Martha makes the same confession
(11²⁷). The disciples are represented as applying Messianic
Scriptures to Jesus both before (2¹⁷) and after His Resurrection (2²² 12¹⁶).

The author of *Hebrews* finds Jesus as the Christ frequently
(1⁵ 2¹² 5⁵ 10⁵) in the Psalms and in the Law; and in one passage
at least Paul elaborates an argument (Eph. 4⁸) which depends
for its force upon a mystical and forward reference to Jesus
in Ps. 68¹⁸.

Indeed, that Jesus is the Messiah of O.T. prophecy is the
burden of the earliest gospel sermons (Acts 2³¹. ³⁶ 3²⁰ 5⁴², etc.).

(iv) Jn. agrees with the Synoptists in representing Jesus as
accepting this position, and as claiming therefore to be the
subject of O.T. prophecy. The difference is [1] that Jn. puts the
recognition by His disciples of Jesus as the Messiah (1⁵⁰),
and His acceptance of their homage, earlier than the Synoptists
formally do (Mk. 8²⁹); but it is not to be overlooked that
Lk. (4⁴¹) represents Him as conscious of His Messiahship at a
date prior to the call of Peter and James and John by the
lake-side. Jn. also puts into His mouth the plain affirmation
to the Woman of Samaria that He was the Christ (4²⁶). At a
later stage the Synoptists tell that He said the same thing to
the high priest (Mk. 14⁶²; cf. Lk. 22⁶⁷, Mt. 26⁶⁴), which is not
told explicitly by Jn., who does not go into full details about
this examination by Caiaphas (18²⁴ ; but cf. 19⁷). There can be
no doubt that, according to Jn. and the Synoptists alike, it was
implied in Jesus' claim and explicitly asserted once and again
that He was the Messiah of the O.T. " Moses wrote of me,"
and the Scriptures " bear witness of me " (5³⁹. ⁴⁶) are words
that Jn. places in His mouth.

(v) Hence we are not surprised to come upon the expression
that in Jesus and His ministry " the Scripture was fulfilled "
(ἐπληρώθη). It does not seem to say more than, as we have
seen, was accepted *ex animo* by all His early disciples. Yet
the expression is not found in Paul or in Hebrews or in the
Apocalypse or in the Johannine or Petrine Epistles. The idea
of the " fulfilment " of the Scriptures in Jesus appears but
once in Mk., four times in Lk. and the Acts (as well as twice
with the verb τελεῖν instead of πληροῦν), six times in Jn. (and
once with τελεῖν), and twelve times in Mt. It occurs once in

[1] Cf. p. cxxxiv.

James (2²³), but with no Messianic reference, being applied to the fulfilment of Gen. 15⁶ in the later promise of Gen. 22¹⁶ᶠ. These passages from the Gospels must presently be examined separately, but it is plain from their distribution that the idea of the " fulfilment " of a particular Scripture as an incident of Christ's Ministry and Passion is more conspicuous in the later writings of the N.T. than in the earlier. Whatever the dates of Jn. and Mt. may be, they are later, in their present form, than the Epistles of Paul or than Mk. and Lk.; and it is in these later Gospels that the phrase becomes frequent, either in the form " the Scripture was fulfilled," or " in order that the Scripture might be fulfilled."

This way of speaking of the " fulfilment " of Scripture does not appear at all in the sub-apostolic age, although the belief was universal in Christian circles that the O.T. rites and prophecies pointed onward to Christ. Barnabas, for instance, who is full of " types," and who finds Christ in the most unlikely places in the O.T. (see § 9, where he finds in the number of Abraham's servants a forecast of the Cross of Jesus), never speaks of the πλήρωσις or " fulfilment " of a Scripture. The same is true of Justin Martyr. Nor is the formula of citation " then was fulfilled " a formula which Irenæus used, except when (as in *Hær.* iii. 9. 2) he reproduced it from the Gospels (Mt. 1²³). The only instances of πληροῦν being used of Scripture in his writings are in *Hær.* iii. 10. 4, where he says that the angels proclaimed the promise made to David as a promise fulfilled (. . . ὑπόσχεσιν . . . πεπληρωμένην εὐαγγελίσωνται), and perhaps in *Dem.* 38, where he writes that " This " (*i.e.* Amos 9¹¹) " our Lord Jesus Christ truly fulfilled." But in neither of these passages is the formula of citation " then was fulfilled " used by Irenæus. The earliest appearance of the phrase, subsequent to the First and Fourth Gospels, is in Hegesippus, who wrote about 160–180 A.D. In a passage where Hegesippus (quoted by Eusebius, *H.E.* ii. 23. 15) is describing the martyrdom of James the Just by the Jews, he adds, καὶ ἐπλήρωσαν τὴν γραφὴν τὴν ἐν τῷ Ἡσαΐᾳ γεγραμμένην, Ἄρωμεν τὸν δίκαιον (Isa. 3¹⁰; cf. Wisd. 2¹²). The passage he quotes has not any such reference, but Hegesippus has been attracted by the word δίκαιος, and so he ventures to say that the Jews " fulfilled " this Scripture.[1] In every Christian age it has been a fault of piety, when searching the O.T., to mistake verbal coincidence with fact for a veritable fulfilment of prophetic words.

[1] Barnabas (§ 6) applies the words to Christ's Passion; and Cyprian quotes Wisd. 2¹²ᶠ. to illustrate a general thesis, " Quod ipse sit iustus, quem Iudaei occisuri essent " (*Test.* ii. 14).

It should be added that this formula of citation is not used (except when reproducing Mt. 2¹⁵· ¹⁷) by the authors of any of the earlier Apocryphal Gospels. It is not found in them until we come to *Evangelium Pseudo-Matthæi*, a work of the fifth or sixth century; and its presence here is probably to be explained by the fact that this apocryphal writer aims at imitating the manner of the canonical Matthew.[1]

The probable reason that the phrase "then was fulfilled the Scripture " is frequent in Jn. and Mt., but does not appear again until Hegesippus, and then rarely until post-Nicene times, is that the phrase was peculiarly Jewish. Jn. and Mt. are full of Hebraisms, and Hegesippus was a Jew. In the O T. "to fulfil" is used of a petition (Ps. 20⁵) or a Divine promise (1 Kings 8¹⁵), but rarely of a prophecy (1 Kings 2²⁷, 2 Chr. 36²¹, Dan. 4³³, 1 Esd. 1⁵⁷). It seems that the word came into use in the Rabbinical schools after the O.T. canon had been closed. "To fulfil that which was said " and "then was fulfilled " are formulæ of citation that are occasionally found in Jewish writings (so Bacher, *Exeg. term.* i. 171).

It has often been thought that there existed in Apostolic days a Jewish collection of O.T. passages held to be predictive of Messiah.[2] If this were the case, it would be natural that it should be utilised by the writers of the Gospels, at any rate of the later Gospels, Mt. and Jn. Allen has suggested [3] that the quotations in Mt. introduced by a formula are derived from a written source of this kind, and not directly from the canonical Old Testament. The same might be true of the quotations in Jn.; but the existence of such a collection of *testimonia* in the first century has not yet, as it seems to the present writer, been established.

To return to the phrase "the Scripture was fulfilled," as it appears in the Gospels. It always has reference to a particular verse of the O.T. (ἡ γραφή), the words of which fit the incident that the evangelist has recorded. There are two notable instances in Mt. The evangelist finds (Mt. 2¹⁷) in Jer. 31¹⁵ words prophetic of the Massacre of the Innocents; and again (Mt. 27⁹) he says that in the buying of the Potter's

---

[1] This apocryphon says "then was fulfilled " of Hab. 3², Isa. 1³ (the Nativity), of Ps. 148⁷ (the dragons adoring Jesus), of Isa. 11⁶ (a legend of the Flight into Egypt), of Isa. 19¹ (the prostration of the idols), and of Ps. 65⁹ (the wisdom of the Child Jesus). It is curious that it does *not* cite Jer. 31¹⁵ or Hos. 11¹, which are cited as *testimonia* in the canonical Matthew.

[2] See, in particular, Rendel Harris, *Testimonia,* who holds that the existence of such a collection of Messianic prophecies has been proved.

[3] W. C. Allen, *St. Matthew,* p. lxii.

Field with the blood money "was fulfilled that which was spoken by Jeremiah" (Zech. 11¹³; cf. Jer. 32⁶ᶠ·). In both of these cases we are dealing only with the comment of the evangelist, and it is probable that he was misled by verbal coincidences, just as Hegesippus was when he quoted Isa. 3¹⁰ of the martyrdom of James the Just (see p. cl). Having regard to the historical contexts both of Jer. 31¹⁵ and of Zech. 11¹³ (Jer. 32⁶ᶠ·), it cannot be maintained that they are more than vaguely descriptive or suggestive of incidents in the Gospel history.

The case of Lk. 4²¹ is different. Here the evangelist tells that Jesus read aloud in the synagogue the passage Isa. 61¹·², and that He began His comment upon it by saying, "To-day hath this Scripture been fulfilled in your ears." There is no improbability in this, and it is entirely in agreement with the claim which, as we have seen, Jesus made repeatedly for Himself, that He was the subject of O.T. prophecy.

(vi) We come next to a more difficult conception, yet one which is logically connected with the belief in prophecy as understood by a Jew. Jn. represents Jesus as saying "the Scripture cannot be broken," οὐ δύναται λυθῆναι ἡ γραφή (10³⁵). This is not said in reference to the fulfilment of prophecy, but parenthetically as an assertion of the permanent authority of O.T. words. But where prophecy was in view, it was held that the prediction once made carried with it the assurance of its accomplishment. The more strictly the verbal inspiration of the sacred books was taught by the Rabbinical schools, the more deeply would it be felt that the punctilious fulfilment of the Messianic predictions was fore-ordained of God. This was believed by every pious Jew, and the belief emerges distinctly in the Fourth Gospel, the evangelist ascribing this conviction to Jesus Himself. We may recall here some Synoptic passages which show that the belief that "the Scripture *cannot* be broken" was shared by Mt., Mk., and Lk. (especially by Lk.), and that all three speak of it as having the authority of their Master.

(a) At Mk. 10³² (cf. Mt. 20¹⁸) Jesus predicts His condemnation and death at Jerusalem, τὰ μέλλοντα αὐτῷ συμβαίνειν, or, as Lk. (18³¹) more explicitly puts it, "all the things that are written by the prophets shall be accomplished (τελεσθήσεται) unto the Son of Man."

(b) According to Mk. 14²¹, Mt. 26²⁴, Jesus said at the Last Supper, "The Son of Man goeth, even as it is written of Him," or as Lk. has it, "as it hath been determined," κατὰ τὸ ὡρισμένον (Lk. 22²²). Cf. also Lk. 21²².

(c) Lk. (22³⁷) alone records that Jesus said after the Last

Supper τοῦτο τὸ γεγραμμένον δεῖ τελεσθῆναι ἐν ἐμοί, τό Καὶ μετὰ ἀνόμων ἐλογίσθη (Isa. 53¹²).

(*d*) Lk (24²⁶) represents Jesus as asking the disciples on the way to Emmaus, οὐχὶ ταῦτα ἔδει παθεῖν τὸν Χριστὸν; and then interpreting the Messianic prophecies to them. (*e*) So again, according to Lk. 24⁴⁴, Jesus said to the company in the Upper Room, δεῖ πληρωθῆναι πάντα τὰ γεγραμμένα ἐν τῷ νόμῳ Μωσέως καὶ τοῖς προφήταις καὶ ψαλμοῖς περὶ ἐμοῦ : it was *necessary* that all that had been written should be fulfilled.

In like manner Luke ascribes to Peter (Acts 1¹⁶) the saying that it was *necessary* that the Scripture about Judas should be fulfilled.

This conception, then, of the *inevitableness* of the fulfilment of O.T. prophecies is ascribed by all the evangelists to Jesus, but it comes out most frequently in Lk. and Jn., the Fourth Evangelist generally expressing it, as we shall see presently, in another way.[1]

(vii) We have now to consider the meaning of the expression, common in Mt. and Jn., that certain things happened *in order that* the Scripture might be fulfilled.

A similar expression is found two or three times in the O.T. " Solomon thrust out Abiathar from being priest . . . *that he might fulfil* the word of the Lord which He spake concerning the house of Eli " (1 Kings 2²⁷). The LXX has here πληρωθῆναι τὸ ῥῆμα Κυρίου. It may be that in this passage we need not suppose Solomon's motive to be that he might fulfil 1 Sam. 2²⁷ᶠ·, but that the writer only means that the event corresponded with what had been predicted. In like manner it has been suggested that in some passages where ἵνα πληρωθῇ ἡ γραφή is found in the Gospels, we need not give ἵνα a telic force. It may be used loosely on occasion with πληρωθῇ, as it is certainly used loosely, without telic force, in other contexts (*e.g.* Mk. 5⁴³, 6²⁵, 9⁹, in all of which cases the other Synoptists discard Mark's ἵνα; cf. Jn. 1²⁷ 11⁵⁰ etc.). But thus to evacuate ἵνα of its telic force in the phrase ἵνα πληρωθῇ ἡ γραφή, however agreeable to our modern ideas of the Bible, is to do violence to the contexts, and to fail in appreciation of the Jewish doctrine of prophecy.

(viii) When the Chronicler places the rise of Cyrus " after the word of the Lord by the mouth of Jeremiah had been accomplished " (μετὰ τὸ πληρωθῆναι ῥῆμα κυρίου, 2 Chron. 36²²), he means more than that the event corresponded with what had been predicted. He means that the event was overruled by God with a view to the fulfilment of His own

---
[1] For the use of δεῖ in Jn., see on 3¹⁴.

eternal purpose, which had been proclaimed by Jeremiah the prophet.

Both Mt. and Jn. express themselves in the same way. Mt. uses the phrase ἵνα πληρωθῇ, or ὅπως πληρωθῇ, eight times of a *testimonium* quoted from the O.T., viz.: 1²³ (Isa. 7¹⁴), 2¹⁵ (Hos. 11¹), 2²³ ("He shall be called a Nazarene," the source of which is uncertain), 4¹⁴ (Isa. 9¹· ²), 8¹⁷ (Isa. 53⁴), 12¹⁷ (Isa. 42¹ᶠ·), 13³⁵ (Ps. 78²), 21⁴ (Zech. 9⁹). This was his doctrine, that the *words* of the prophets, quite apart from their context, had a forward Messianic reference, and that the incidents of the ministry of Jesus were divinely overruled, *in order that* the prophecies might be fulfilled. And in one remarkable passage, where he is following Mk., Mt. places this doctrine in the mouth of Jesus. Mark (14⁴⁹; cf. Mt. 26⁵⁶) reports that Jesus said at His betrayal that the manner of His violent arrest was ἵνα πληρωθῶσιν αἱ γραφαί. No special "Scripture" is quoted, and it may be that only the general trend of O.T. prophecy about Messiah and His sufferings was in the mind of the Speaker, or in that of the evangelist who reported His words. Yet that the evangelist believed Jesus to have said that an incident took place, "in order that the Scriptures might be fulfilled," is significant.

We now come to the use in Jn. of this phrase. It occurs four times in a comment by the evangelist upon something which he has recorded, and he attributes the use of it to Jesus three times.

(*a*) Jn. says (12³⁷· ³⁸) that the people did not believe on Jesus, despite His signs, ἵνα ὁ λόγος Ἡσαίου τοῦ προφήτου πληρωθῇ, quoting Isa. 53¹, "Lord, who hath believed our report?" etc. The same prophecy is quoted in Rom. 10¹⁶, a similar interpretation being given to it, except that Paul does not use the formula ἵνα πληρωθῇ.

Jn. makes it clear that ἵνα here has a telic force, for he proceeds διὰ τοῦτο οὐκ ἠδύναντο πιστεύειν, ὅτι πάλιν εἶπεν Ἡσαίας, quoting Isa. 6¹⁰, "He hath blinded their eyes," etc. This *testimonium* from the O.T. is also cited by Mt. (13¹⁴) in the form "unto them is fulfilled the prophecy of Isaiah," words which Mt. ascribes to Jesus Himself.

The other instances in which Jn. comments thus on a recorded incident occur in the narrative of the Passion.

(*b*) In Jn. 19²⁴ the parting of Jesus' garments among the soldiers is said to have been ἵνα ἡ γραφὴ πληρωθῇ, the words of Ps. 22¹⁸ being cited, "They parted my garments among them, and upon my vesture did they cast lots." The Synoptists mention the parting of the garments, but do not expressly quote Scripture for it. See note *in loc.*

(c) In Jn. 19²⁸ the saying of Jesus on the cross, " I thirst," is recorded, and Jn. adds that it was said ἵνα τελειωθῇ ἡ γραφή, presumably having Ps. 69²¹ in his mind. The Synoptists do not record this word from the cross. See note *in loc.*

(d) Jn. 19³⁶, " These things came to pass, ἵνα ἡ γραφὴ πληρωθῇ, *A bone of Him shall not be broken* " (Ex. 12⁴⁶; cf. Ps. 34²⁰), Jesus being the true Paschal Lamb.

It is noteworthy that Jn. twice comments on recorded words of Jesus in the same way; that is, he speaks of them as if they were inevitable of fulfilment, like words of Scripture. In 18⁸, ⁹ we read: " Jesus answered . . . If ye seek me, let these go their way, that the word might be fulfilled (ἵνα πλ. ὁ λόγος) which He spake, Of those whom Thou hast given me I lost not one " (referring back to 17¹²); and again, 18³¹, ³²: " the Jews said unto him, It is not lawful for us to put any man to death : that the word of Jesus might be fulfilled (ἵνα ὁ λόγος τοῦ Ἰησοῦ πλ.), which He spake, signifying by what manner of death He should die " (referring back to 12³²). For Jn., the words of his Master were possessed of authority and inspired by foreknowledge; the event necessarily corresponded to what Jesus had said.

(ix) In two or three passages Jn. seems to go beyond a statement of his own belief as to the inevitableness of the fulfilment of O.T. prophecy; for he has been thought to ascribe the same opinion to Jesus Himself.

In 13¹⁸ we have: " I know whom I have chosen : but that the Scripture may be fulfilled, *He that eateth my bread lifteth up his heel against me* " (Ps. 41⁹); and again in 17¹²: " I guarded them, and not one of them perished, but the son of perdition ; that the Scripture might be fulfilled," allusion probably being made to the same passage, Ps. 41⁹ (but cf. Ps. 109⁸, Acts 1¹⁶). These phrases, as they stand, suggest that Jesus taught not only that the treachery of Judas was a " fulfilment " of Scripture, but that its progress was overruled in its incidents, so that " the Scripture might be fulfilled." It may be so, but this is not necessarily the true interpretation, for in both passages the recalling of O.T. prophecy may be but an editorial addition or a comment of the evangelist after his habit.[1]

In like manner, ἵνα πληρωθῇ ὁ λόγος in 15²⁵ (where see note) may be added to the report of the Lord's words by Jn., who found it apposite to cite ἐμίσησάν με δωρεάν from Ps. 35¹⁹ or Ps. 69⁴. In any case, in this particular passage, some doubt must rest upon the accuracy of the report, which makes Jesus speak of " *their* Law," as if to separate Himself from Judaism.

---

[1] See p. xxxiv, and also the notes *in loc.*

Otherwise we have to suppose that Jesus taught that the cause-
less hatred with which He was rejected had been fore-ordained
in words of the Psalmist which had to be fulfilled.

(II) The Johannine Doctrines of Life and Judgment

In Jewish thought the conception of a Day of Judgment
when the future destiny of men shall be determined does not
appear until after the Exile. One of the earliest allusions to
this is in Dan. 12[2, 3] : " Many of them that sleep in the dust
of the earth shall awake, some to eternal life and some to shame
and eternal contempt," a passage which (although it does not
speak of a *general* resurrection) contemplates a separation of
men into the righteous and unrighteous, and so presupposes
judgment.

The growth of the idea is intimately connected with the
growth of the Messianic hope. Judgment is the prerogative
of kings, and so it was the office of the Messianic King. " A
throne shall be established in mercy, and one shall sit thereon
in truth, in the tent of David, judging and seeking judgment "
(Isa. 16[5]; cf. Isa. 32[1]). The theocratic King of Ps. 72[1] executes
judgment in response to the petition, " Give the King Thy
judgments, O God, and Thy righteousness unto the King's
son "; or as the Targum has it, " Give the precepts of Thy
judgment to King Messiah." It is noteworthy that the vision
of Dan. 7[13], which tells of One to come " with the clouds of
heaven like unto a son of man," does *not* ascribe the office of
judgment to this Coming One, but rather to the Ancient of
6ays, Who is the fount of all true judgment (cf. Deut. 1[17]).

However, when we come to the Book of Enoch, we find
the doctrine of world judgment clearly expressed, and the
office of judgment committed to the Son of Man.[1] The various
forms which the doctrine of judgment takes in this book are
summarised by Charles on *Enoch* 45[3]: " The Elect One will sit
on the throne of His glory, 45[3], 55[4], 62[3, 5] . . . being placed
thereon by the Lord of Spirits, 61[8], 62[2]; and His throne is
likewise the throne of the Head of Days, 47[3] 51[3]," a typical
passage being : " He sat on the throne of His glory, and the
sum of judgment was committed unto Him, the Son of Man "
(69[27]). How far the eschatology of this book was prevalent in
Palestine in the first century we do not know precisely; but
it is clear that the orthodox believed that the dead, or at
any rate the righteous dead, would rise again. The *Book of
Jubilees* (23[11]) speaks of " the day of the Great Judgment,"

---

[1] Cf. p. cxxvii.

and the *Apocalypse of Baruch* (50³·⁴ 51 f.) tells of a resurrection
at the Advent of Messiah for the purpose of judgment. The
Second Book of Esdras belongs to the latter half of the first
century, and is tinged with Christian thought; but its testimony is relevant here. In 2 Esd. 12³³ it is said of the wicked
that Messiah " shall set them alive in His judgment, and when
He hath reproved them, He shall destroy them."

By Mk., Jesus is represented as saying of Himself :
" Ye shall see the Son of Man sitting at the right hand
of power, and coming with the clouds of heaven " (Mk.
14⁶²; cf. Mk. 13²⁶ 8³⁸). The picture of Him as the Judge
at the Last Judgment is explicit in Mt. 25⁴⁰ᶠ·, His judgment being : " These shall go away into eternal punishment ; but the righteous into eternal life." The office
of Judge is assigned to Him by the apostolic preachers :
" This is He which was ordained of God to be the Judge of
quick and dead " (Acts 10⁴²); and again: " God hath appointed a day in the which He will judge the world in righteousness by the man whom He hath ordained " (Acts 17³¹). Paul
has the same doctrine; he speaks of " the Day when God
shall judge the secrets of men by Jesus Christ " (Rom. 2¹⁶;
cf. 2 Cor. 5¹⁰).

It is, therefore, highly probable that Jewish doctrine in the
first century conceived of Messiah as the Judge at the Last
Judgment; and it is certain that in Mt., in the Acts, and in
Paul it is taught that Jesus is to be that Judge. In claiming
to be the Messiah of Jewish hopes, He claimed, as it would
seem, to be the Judge of mankind at the Last Assize.

Thus the language in which Jesus spoke to His Jewish
disciples about the final judgment of mankind was the language
of Jewish Apocalyptic. The images and the figures which He
employed to bring home to His hearers the severity and certainty of the Divine judgments were not unfamiliar to them.
He always spoke to men in the language which they could best
understand; and, as the first disciples were Jews, He spoke to
them as a Jew would speak, conveying to them at the same
time deeper and more spiritual truths than any of which Jews
had dreamed. He was, in truth, the Messiah of their ancient
traditions.

In the first years of bewildered hope after His Ascension,
the expectation was strong in many hearts, as the Pauline
Epistles show, that the Son of Man would speedily come again
in judgment to vindicate the Divine righteousness, and to
fulfil the Divine purpose of the ages. But time went on; and,
as the first generation of Christian believers passed away, it
became evident that the Promise of the Lord's Coming, as

they had understood it, was not certainly to be fulfilled all at once. Jerusalem had fallen. The Temple was destroyed. Christianity was no longer a phase of Judaism. The thought of Jesus as the Messiah ceased to be the dominating thought of those who called Him Master. He was Messiah, but He was more. And it was the task of the last of the evangelists to remind the Church how much there was in the teaching of Jesus Himself as to the Judgment of Mankind, and the Coming of His Kingdom, that had been neglected in the eager faith of the little community which had so unerringly perceived in the Risen Lord the Christ of their fathers.

Accordingly, we find in the Fourth Gospel, on the one hand, phrases entirely in the manner, so to speak, of Mt. and of the Acts and of Paul, as to Messiah and Messiah's judgment at the last; and, on the other hand, a wider and more catholic presentation of Jesus as the world's King and Saviour, whose Kingdom is already established in some degree.

(a) To Jn., Jesus is the Christ, the Son of God, just as He is to the Synoptists. Indeed, Jn. is the only evangelist who reproduces the Jewish title *Messiah* (1^{42} 4^{25}). If Jesus had not been Messiah, He could not have been the Light of the World, of Jew as well as of Greek. To Jn., as to the Synoptists, Jesus was the Son of Man of Daniel's vision.[1] The words addressed to Nathanael (1^{51}) could not have been understood by any one not a Jew: " Ye shall see the heaven opened, and the angels ascending and descending upon the Son of Man." That recalls the vision of the Son of Man of the Synoptists (Mk. 14^{62} and parls.). Jn. is not unmindful of this aspect of the teaching of Jesus, viz. that He proclaimed Himself as the Jewish Messiah, of whose judgment the Jewish Apocalypses had spoken.

Further, Jn. is explicit in the announcement of a Great Assize at last, when all men shall be judged by the Son of Man. " The hour cometh in which all that are in the tombs shall hear His voice, and shall come forth, they that have done good, unto the resurrection of life ; and they that have done ill, unto the resurrection of judgment " (5^{29}). For this παρουσία[2] cf. 1 Jn. 2^{28}; it is a Christian privilege that " we may have boldness in the Day of Judgment " (1 Jn. 4^{17}). That this doctrine appears in Jn. is only what we expect to find in writings which go back to the reminiscences of a Jewish disciple.

(b) But, for Jn., Christianity has broken its Jewish fetters once for all. The aged apostle remembers, as he looks back, that there were teachings of Jesus which transcended all the hopes and thoughts of Judaism, and these are now reproduced

---

[1] Cf. p. cxxx.　　　　　　　　　　[2] Cf. p. lxii.

(through the medium of a disciple) for the instruction of the Church. The rigid ecclesiastical polity of the Jews was a thing of the past. And Jesus had said that it would not be permanent; that the time was coming when neither Samaria nor Jerusalem would be the spiritual home of the true worshippers of God (4²¹ᶠ·). He had spoken, too, of His flock as embracing not only Jews but Gentiles (10¹⁶). Here were master thoughts, denying any exclusive privilege to the Jew, inconsistent or seemingly inconsistent with any millennial reign of Messiah on Mount Sion. In fact, when the Fourth Gospel was being written, Christianity was being accepted by Greek and Roman as well as Jew. And the catholicity of its appeal is perceived by the evangelist to be agreeable to the mind of Christ, as disclosed in sayings of His not yet recorded and only imperfectly understood.

Moreover, it was becoming clear that the expectation of an Advent of the Son of Man and of the establishment in its fulness of the Kingdom of God in the near future was a mistaken expectation. There will, indeed, be a final consummation. Jn. is the only evangelist who uses the expression " the Last Day " (see on 6³⁹); he does not deny, rather he explicitly declares, the doctrine of a Great Assize, while he does not look for any immediate Advent of Christ in majesty, such as the first generation of Christians had expected. But the outlook of the Last Discourses (cc. 14–16) is directed to the future of the Church on earth rather than to any sudden and glorious Coming of the Master from heaven (cf., however, 14³). And this surprised the Apostles: " Lord, what is come to pass, that Thou wilt manifest Thyself to us, and not unto the world ? " (14²²). They had been told, " I will manifest myself unto him that loveth me " (14²¹); this was an Advent of Jesus to the faithful soul. But they were hardly content. And Jn. reports that Christ gave no other answer to their curiosity about His Coming than the quiet promise, " If a man love me, he will keep my words . . . and we will make our abode with him " (14²³).

Thus Jn. will not dwell on the prospect of the Final Judgment of the world as it had presented itself to Jewish minds. He knows that it was involved in the teaching of Christ, and he says so in the Gospel, stating it with greater explicitness in the First Epistle.[1] But there was another element in that teaching which needed fresh emphasis. The judgment of the individual is determined in the present by his own attitude to Christ : " he that believeth not is judged already " (3¹⁸, where see note). This judgment is not arbitrary, but inevitable,

[1] See p. lxii.

and is the issue of a moral necessity.   In the sight of God, to whom a thousand years are as one day, the predestined future is as certain as the past, and it may be discerned in the present. *Die Weltgeschichte ist das Weltgericht*: " he that believeth not is judged already."   And so, on the other hand, with the believer in Christ: " he comes not into judgment, but has passed from death into life " (5^{24}).   Those who believe in Him shall be safe at the last (11^{26}; cf. 17^{12}), and He will ' 'raise them up " ($6^{39. 40}$, etc.).   In virtue of the Life which they share with Him, they will be sharers of the Resurrection unto eternal life.

A third doctrine which Jn. expounds with greater fulness than the Synoptists is the doctrine of *life* here and hereafter. In the Synoptists, indeed, the teaching of Jesus is explicit as to a future life and a resurrection to judgment both of righteous and unrighteous, while at the same time He points out that the conditions of this future existence are necessarily dissimilar to those of our bodily life here (Mk. $12^{25f.}$).   In Jn. the thought emerges that the ζωὴ αἰώνιος of the future may begin in the present.   It is already possessed by him who believes in Jesus ($3^{15. 16. 36}$ $6^{40. 47}$) or in the Father who sent Him (5^{24}).   It is both a present possession and a hope of the future.   This is the reason why Jn. can speak of *judgment* being already determined; it begins here and is fulfilled hereafter, as *life* also is.

It is to be observed, however, that this doctrine of ζωὴ αἰώνιος is not peculiar to Jn., but is also found in the Synoptists, although it is by them expressed in a different way, in terms of the Jewish concept of the Kingdom of God to which the Synoptic references are so frequent.   In Jn., "eternal life," the life of the citizenship of the "Kingdom of God," is that on which a man enters after he has been born ἄνωθεν (3^3). The Kingdom of God, according to the Synoptist presentation, is at once present and future.   It is future, if we contemplate its complete fulfilment (*e.g.* Mt. 8^{12} 13^{43} 25^{34}, Mk. 9^{47}, Lk. 13^{28}) and pray " Thy Kingdom come " (Mt. 6^{10}).   But, in another sense, it is present now.   "The Kingdom of God is within you " (Lk. 17^{21}; cf. Lk. 6^{20} 11^{20}).   And to enter into it one must become like a little child (Mt. 18^3, Mk. 10^{15}, Lk. 18^{17}), a condition which should be compared with Jn. 3^3.   To enter into the Kingdom of God and to enter into life are, indeed, treated by Mk. as identical expressions (Mk. $9^{45. 47}$).   It thus appears that the spiritual doctrine of ζωὴ αἰώνιος of which Jn. is so full, is implicit in the Synoptic Gospels, which speak of the Kingdom of God coming and come, just as in Jn. we read of eternal life as both future and already present.[1]

[1] See, further, p. clxii.

Hence there is no inconsistency, as has sometimes been suggested, between the two sides of the Johannine teaching about eternal life. " He that believeth on me hath eternal life," and " I will raise him up at the last day," express the same doctrine, viz. that whether in this world or in the world to come, *life*, that is, the spiritual life, which is " life indeed," is found in Christ alone. This is the perpetual theme of the Fourth Gospel.

In Christ is life (1^4). This He has in Himself as God has (5^{26}). He has the words of eternal life (6^{68}). His words are life (6^{63}). To know Him is eternal life (17^3). He is *the* Life (14^6). He gives the living water which continually and eternally vivifies the energies of the spirit (4^{14} 7^{38}). He came that His flock might have life (10^{10}). He is the Bread of Life (6^{35}), the Bread which sustains life. The Bread which He gives is His Flesh, given for the life of the world (6^{51}). Without this no one has life (6^{53}); but he that eats of it abides in Christ (6^{56}; cf. 15^4). They who follow Him have the light of life (8^{12}). That is the secret of eternal life in this present stage of being. (See further on 11^{25}.)

So, too, is it after death. Christ quickens the dead, as the Father does. ὁ υἱὸς οὓς θέλει ζωοποιεῖ (5^{21}). Those who keep His word shall not taste of death (8^{51}). He is not only the Life ; He is at once " the Resurrection *and* the Life " (11^{25}). Those to whom He gives eternal life never perish ; no one plucks them out of His hand (10^{28}).

Others will perish (3^{16}); those who are rebellious shall not see life, but God's wrath rests upon them (3^{36}). " If ye will not believe that I am He, ye shall die in your sins " (8^{24}). " If a man abide not in me, he is cast forth as a branch and is withered; and they gather them and cast them into the fire, and they are burned " (15^6).

Such is the doctrine of Judgment and of Life expounded in the Fourth Gospel. The evangelist is at once Hebraist and Hellenist. He wrote " that ye may believe that Jesus is the Messiah, the Son of God " (a Jewish belief, for Greeks and pagans had no thought of Messiah), and also " that believing ye may have life in His Name," a universal message which it is of supreme consequence to all men to apprehend.

There are, then, in Jn. these two contrasted views of the future life, one pointing back to Hebraism, the other more akin to Hellenism, but both accepted by the evangelist. To rule out either as foreign to his thought is not scientific criticism. Thus Wendt [1] has been followed by some scholars in his view

[1] *St. John's Gospel*, p. 136.

l

that the phrase ἡ ἐσχάτη ἡμέρα is an interpolation added by an editor in 6[39. 40. 44. 45] 11[24] 12[48]; his reason apparently being that the doctrine of a "last day" or "day of judgment" is inconsistent with the spiritual doctrine of eternal life which Jn. unfolds. But there is nothing in the style of these verses to suggest that they are not Johannine. If we extrude from the text of a book every phrase which does not seem to us to be congenial to the argument, we may indeed reduce the residuum to a consistent whole, but it does not follow that we are doing justice to the author's opinions or that we have got nearer to what he originally set down. We may think it strange that a Hellenist should be a Hebraist in certain regions of thought. But the writer of the Fourth Gospel was both.

(iii) The Kingdom of God and the New Birth

The Kingdom of God, coming and come, is a principal topic in the Synoptic reports of the teaching of Jesus. Many of His parables are concerned with the explanation of its significance. In a sense, it is a present reality (Lk. 17[21]), but it is more frequently named in the Synoptic Gospels as an ideal to be realised in the future (Mt. 6[10], Mk. 9[1], etc.), the signs of its approach not being always apparent (Lk. 17[20]).[1] The phrases, "the Kingdom of Heaven," "the Kingdom of God" were not unfamiliar to the Jews, of whom some looked for a political and social Utopia, a happy future for their race and nation; while others, more spiritually minded, understood that righteousness rather than prosperity was the ideal of a community over whom Yahweh was King. Of this Kingdom Jesus taught that no one could become a citizen without a spiritual change, without turning away from material things, and approaching God with the simplicity and single-heartedness of a little child (Mt. 18[3], Mk. 10[15], Lk. 18[17]). It is this last conception that is expounded with startling emphasis in the discourse of Jesus with Nicodemus: "Except a man be *born from above*, he cannot see the Kingdom of God " (Jn. 3[3]).

The idea of rebirth is not peculiar to Christianity. The Brahman, the spiritual aristocrat of India, is "twice born." In the *Novella* of Justinian (lxxviii.) it is asserted of a manumitted slave that he has τὸ τῆς παλιγγενεσίας δίκαιον. Wetstein, who quotes this, quotes also the saying of Apuleius that the day of a convert's initiation is his birthday. The idea, indeed, is frequent in the Mystery religions which had a vogue at the end of the first century. Mithraism may have been affected by Christian phraseology, but in any case the

---

[1] See above, p. clx.

expression used of one who has been initiated, *renatus in æternum*, is noteworthy.[1]

More to the point, when examining Jn. 3[3], is the language used in Rabbinical writings of Gentile proselytes who have accepted Judaism. " A man's father only brought him into this world; his teacher, who taught him wisdom, brings him into the life of the world to come." [2]   Wetstein quotes: "The stranger who is proselytised is like a child newly born, because he must break away from his former teachers and principles, as well as from the ties of kinship." [3]   The germ of this metaphor, which is a very natural one, appears in such passages as Ps. 87[4]; and it may have been familiar to the Rabbis of the first century, although the Talmud, as we have it, being of later date, does not prove this to demonstration.   The narrative of the discourse with Nicodemus (3[10]) *seems* to represent Jesus as expressing surprise that he, a master of Israel, should not be acquainted with the doctrine of rebirth, but this is not quite certain.   See notes on 3[4. 10].

In any case, Nicodemus, as one of the Sanhedrim, must have been familiar with the phrase " the Kingdom of God," which he and his fellows were accustomed to interpret in terms of the Messianic expectation of future prosperity and peace. It was for the future, rather than the present; and its ideals were political and social rather than spiritual, although spiritual ideals were not wholly absent from it.   But he was hardly prepared to be told that he was not following the path which led to the Kingdom, and that without a complete change of attitude he could not enter it.   He must become like a child before its Heavenly Father; he must be " born again."

This phrase, however, is expanded in v. 5, where it takes the form " born (or begotten) of water and the Spirit."   This has generally been interpreted of baptism, and the interpretation demands careful analysis.

It must first be observed that the representation of baptism as a new birth is infrequent in the N.T.   We find it, perhaps, in 1 Pet. 1[3. 23], where Christians are described as " begotten again not of corruptible seed but of incorruptible "; and it appears in the phrase λουτρὸν παλιγγενεσίας (Tit. 3[5]).   Paul generally speaks of baptism, not as a new birth, but as a " burial with Christ " in the baptismal waters followed by a rising

---

[1] This phrase, which refers to the *taurobolium*, appears first in the fourth century (*C.I.L.* vi. 510).

[2] *Mishna*, Surenhus. iv. 116, quoted by Schürer, *Hist. of Jewish People*, i. 317 (Eng. Tr.).

[3] *Yebamoth*, 62a.

again therefrom (Rom. 6³, Col. 2¹²).¹ But, at the same time, for Paul a man in Christ is "a new creation" (2 Cor. 5¹⁷), and this thought is not far from that of the "regeneration" of the Christian believer, and the image of baptism as a new birth.

At any rate, this image is used in the literature of the second and third centuries, more frequently than any other, to illustrate baptism. In the note on 3⁵ passages are quoted from "2 Clement" (about 140 A.D.) and Hermas, which treat 3⁵ as having a baptismal reference. So Justin says: We bring the catechumens "where there is water, and after the same manner of regeneration as we also were regenerated ourselves, they are regenerated"; and he proceeds to cite 3³ (loosely, after his wont).² Christ, he says in another place, "was made the beginning of a new race which is regenerated by Him through water and faith and wood, which contains the Mystery of the Cross."³ Both Hippolytus⁴ and Irenæus⁵ speak of the "laver of regeneration"; and Irenæus more than once describes baptism as "the power of regeneration unto God."⁶ Clement of Alexandria in like manner uses the verb "to be regenerated" as equivalent to "to be baptized."⁷

Hence, although the doctrine of baptism as a new birth is not prominent in the N.T., it was probably recognised by the end of the first century, as it certainly was in the second century; and if we are to take Jn. 3⁵ as accurately reporting a saying of Jesus, He gave to the image the seal of His authority.

There are, however, grave difficulties in the way of this, the usual, interpretation of the passage. That Jesus is the Author of the terse and pregnant aphorism, "Except a man be begotten from above (ἄνωθεν) he cannot see the Kingdom of God" (Jn. 3³), need not be doubted; it is, as we have seen, but a picturesque and arresting statement of the Synoptic saying, "Except ye become as little children, ye cannot enter the Kingdom of Heaven" (Mt. 18³). But if, in His discourse with Nicodemus, He explained "being begotten from above" (v. 3) as "being begotten of water and the Spirit" (v. 5), and this latter phrase is to be understood of baptism, it can only be John's baptism⁸ which was indicated, for Christian baptism was not yet instituted as an initiatory rite. As Jn. observes (7³⁹, where see note), "the Spirit was not yet given because

---

¹ I have discussed the symbolism of baptism more fully in *Studia Sacra*, p. 51 f.
² *Apol.* i. 61.
³ *Tryph.* 138.
⁴ *Theoph.* 10.
⁵ *Hær.* v. 15. 3.
⁶ *Hær.* iii. 17. 1 ; cf. i. 21. 1.
⁷ *Pæd.* vi. *sub init.*
⁸ The Pharisees did not accept John's baptism (Lk. 7³⁰).

Jesus was not yet glorified." But John's baptism could hardly have been described as " being born of water *and the Spirit.*" It is true that Ezekiel (36²⁵) speaks of the new spirit that comes by sprinkling (cf. Ps. 51². ⁷, Zech. 13¹); but Jn. expressly distinguishes the baptism of John which was ἐν ὕδατι only from that of Jesus which was to be ἐν πνεύματι ἁγίῳ (1³³). At a later date it was reported that John's adherents did not know of the Holy Spirit (Acts 19²). If Jesus in the words of Jn. 3⁵ recommended to Nicodemus that he should submit himself to baptism by John, He ascribed a spiritual efficacy to that baptism which was unknown to John's own adherents.

It is difficult to resist the inference that the words ἐξ ὕδατος were not part of the original Saying of Jesus which is reproduced by Jn., but that the form which the Saying takes in 3⁵ is due to the evangelist (or to a later editor) who is expressing it in the language of the next generation, and with an application wider than, and differing from, that which it bore when addressed to Nicodemus. That Jesus enforced upon Nicodemus the necessity for a spiritual change, for " regeneration," is, indeed, highly probable ; but that as the road to this He should have recommended the baptism of John, and above all that He should have described this as " being born of water and of the Spirit," is improbable.

What has happened here is that Jn. has taken a great Saying of Jesus (v. 3), addressed, it may be, to Nicodemus in the first instance, and that he has restated it in v. 5, in terms of the doctrine of Christian baptism which was beginning to take shape at the end of the first century. The Saying of Jesus, it can hardly be doubted, laid stress on the spiritual change which candidates for the Kingdom of Heaven must undergo; they must be born ἄνωθεν (v. 3); and it was natural in early days of persecution and trial that the critical moment should be identified with the moment of baptism, when the new convert deliberately professed faith in Jesus as the Son of God, and accepted the resulting obligations and perils.

We have to reckon, of course, with the doctrine of baptism as applicable to *adult* proselytes. When it became customary (as it did at an early date) to baptize infants, the doctrine underwent necessary modifications. In the beginning, *conversion—* the change of mind and heart consequent on a conviction of the unique claims of Jesus—was indistinguishable from *regeneration*, the new birth into a world of larger and freer opportunity. But once the practice of baptizing infants was adopted, as agreeable to the mind of Christ, it became obvious that the initial *regeneration* was not a *conversion*, in any intelligible sense, for an infant has no settled purpose or habit of mind or mental outlook which needs to be changed; and thus the term *conversion* was reserved for that subsequent awakening of a spiritual sense and of a turning to God, which may be either sudden or gradual, according to the life-history of the individual concerned. The neglect of these elementary considerations has been mischievous in keeping alive controversies about baptismal regeneration which have sometimes been only disputes about words.

At v. 16 the discourse with Nicodemus passes into an exposition of the doctrine of eternal life, which is apparently (see on v. 16) due to the evangelist himself. The topic is, however, not a new one. It is the same topic as that of the " Kingdom of God " with which the discourse opens; but the evangelist expounds it after his own manner and in language which may appeal to Greek no less than to Jew. " Eternal life " is the desire of all mankind; and the spiritual movement which is requisite if the desire is to be satisfied is an act of faith in Jesus as the Son of God. This is the perpetual theme of the Fourth Gospel.

(IV) THE EUCHARISTIC DOCTRINE OF JN.

A

The author of the Fourth Gospel gives no explicit account of the institution of the Lord's Supper. That he knew of it is certain, for at the earliest date to which the Gospel can be assigned the Eucharist was an established Christian rite (1 Cor. 10[16f.], Acts 2[42] 20[7]) whose significance was fully realised. Jn. tells of the Last Supper (c. 13), but he does not identify it with the Paschal Feast as the Synoptists do, placing it on the eve of the Passover. He has in this particular departed from the Synoptic tradition, which, seemingly, he wishes to correct.[1] For Jn. the Passover Victim was Jesus on the Cross, and it may be that his omission to record the institution of the Lord's Supper is due to his desire to avoid the suggestion that the Eucharist is the Christian Passover; just as, unlike the Synoptists, he avoids sacramental language (see on 6[11]) in his account of the Feeding of the Five Thousand, which took place shortly before a Passover celebration.

B

We next observe that the discourse which, in Jn.'s narrative, follows the Feeding of the Five Thousand is reminiscent

[1] See p. cvi.

of sacramental language, more particularly towards its close; and this must be examined in some detail.

That some words were spoken at Capernaum (6[26. 42. 59]) which told of the heavenly Bread as superior to the loaves provided for the hungry multitude is not difficult of credence. But that the whole discourse, as it is found in 6[26-58], belongs to this occasion is improbable. It falls into three sections, vv. 26–40, vv. 41–51ᵃ, vv. 51ᵇ–58. The *first* section tells of the Bread from heaven which God gives to those who believe in Jesus, and it announces that Jesus is, Himself, the Bread of Life. The *second* section is introduced by objections raised by " the Jews," and speaks further of Jesus as the Bread of Life, but does not say explicitly that this Bread is the gift of the Father. The objectors seem to be Galilæans (v. 42), although they are called " Jews," the term that is used through-out the Gospel for the opponents of Jesus. In the *third* section the terminology is changed, and not only the terminology but the doctrine as well. For Jesus speaks now, not of Himself as the heavenly Bread continually given by the Father to believers, but of the Bread which He is, *Himself*, to give them *in the future* (δώσω, v 51). This gift is described as His flesh and His blood, which He will give for the life of the world, and which when appropriated by the believer will be the source and the guarantee of eternal life.

The three sections of this discourse are bound together by Jn., and he represents them as forming a whole. The refrain " I will raise him up at the last day " occurs in all three sections (vv. 39, 40, 44, 54). The same is true of the expression, " who (or which) came down from heaven," which occurs seven times (vv. 33, 38, 41, 42, 50, 51, 58). And the reference to the manna in the wilderness (v. 31) is answered in v. 49 and again in v. 58. There is a general unity of theme, the doctrine expounded from beginning to end being the main Johannine doctrine, viz. that the only way to life is belief in Jesus, a belief which involves continuous " feeding " on Him, *i.e.* the refreshment and invigoration of man by perpetual communion with the Son of Man.

C

The discourse as a whole, and especially its third section, is couched in Eucharistic language. Jn.'s doctrine of " feed-ing " on Christ is, indeed, a spiritual and mystical doctrine; but it is not doubtful that he means, in vv. 51ᵇ–58, to suggest that at any rate one mode of thus " feeding " on Christ is through the sacrament of the Holy Communion. To speak of eating Christ's flesh and drinking His blood is a metaphor intensely realistic and quite extraordinary,[1] going far beyond the teaching about the heavenly bread in the verses which precede. Perhaps the emphasis laid here upon the "flesh" and "blood" of Christ is in polemical reference to the Docetism which Jn. always had in view.[2] But, in any case, the language is Eucharistic and was recognised as such so soon as the Fourth Gospel began to be read. Two or three witnesses may be cited here in proof of this.

1. The Eucharistic language of Ignatius (about 110 A.D.) is clearly influenced by Jn. 6.

(a) ἄρτον θεοῦ θέλω, ὅ ἐστιν σὰρξ τοῦ χριστοῦ . . . καὶ πόμα θέλω τὸ αἷμα αὐτοῦ, ὅ ἐστιν ἀγάπη ἄφθαρτος (Rom. vii.). Here we have the ἄρτος θεοῦ of Jn. 6[33] identified with the σάρξ of Jn. 6[51], and the words about the drinking of Christ's blood go back to the same source. Despite his realism, Ignatius is a mystic like Jn. (cf. also Trall. viii., Philad. i.); and his doctrine of the Eucharist is like Jn.'s in this, that he does not state it so as to exclude other methods of approach to God.

(b) In Philad. iv., the reference to the Eucharist is explicit. σπουδάσατε οὖν μιᾷ εὐχαριστίᾳ χρῆσθαι· μία γὰρ σὰρξ τοῦ κυρίου ἡμῶν Ἰησοῦ Χριστοῦ, καὶ ἓν ποτήριον εἰς ἕνωσιν τοῦ αἵματος αὐτοῦ. The point to be noted is the use of σάρξ for the Body of Christ in the Eucharist, as in Jn. 6, a phraseology not found elsewhere in the New Testament.

(c) The same inference may be drawn from Smyrn. vi., where Ignatius says that the Docetæ εὐχαριστίας καὶ προσευχῆς ἀπέχονται διὰ τὸ μὴ ὁμολογεῖν τὴν εὐχαριστίαν σάρκα εἶναι τοῦ σωτῆρος ἡμῶν Ἰησοῦ Χριστοῦ, a passage as startling in its realism as Jn. 6.

2. Justin (about 145 A.D.) uses similar language. He says (Apol. i. 66) that as the Word was made flesh, and as Jesus had both flesh and blood for our salvation, so also the Eucharistic food is, we are taught, the σάρξ and αἷμα of Christ. The reference is, again, to Jn. 6[51, 54].

That Ignatius and Justin should have applied the language of Jn. 6[51b-58] to the Eucharist is not surprising, for this has been done in every Christian age. But inasmuch as they provide the earliest patristic allusions to Jn. 6, their testimony is especially apposite, as indicating the obvious interpretation of "eating the flesh and drinking the blood" of Christ.[3]

[1] In Ezek. 39[18, 19] there is mention of eating the flesh and drinking the blood of men ; but this refers to the slaughter and destruction of enemies.

[2] Cf. Pfleiderer, Prim. Christianity, iv. 38 f. So Ignatius (Smyrn. vi.) uses the argument that the Eucharist implies the reality of Christ's flesh.

[3] This is the interpretation adopted in the Prayer of Humble Access

It will be observed that the promise of eternal life which
is attached in vv. 54, 58, to the eating of the flesh and drinking
of the blood of Christ, did not deter the second-century Fathers
from giving this passage a Eucharistic reference. For Ignatius
the Eucharist was a means of union with Christ, and so of
sharing in His Passion and Resurrection. A strong passage is
Eph. xx : ἕνα ἄρτον κλῶντες ὅ ἐστιν φάρμακον ἀθανασίας, ἀντίδοτος
τοῦ μὴ ἀποθανεῖν ἀλλὰ ζῆν ἐν Ἰησοῦ Χριστῷ διὰ παντός. Irenæus
(*Hær.* iv. 18. 5, v. 2) even argues that our fleshly bodies must
inherit eternal life because they partake of the Eucharistic food.
The date of the *Didache* is uncertain,[1] but if it were of the
second century, then the language of the Post-Communion
prayer would be noteworthy here : " Thou didst bestow upon
us πνευματικὴν τροφὴν καὶ πότον καὶ ζωὴν αἰώνιον."

3. Both the Old Syriac (about 200 A.D.) and the Peshitta
Syriac (about 450 A.D.) render σάρξ in the seven places where
it occurs in Jn. 6 (vv. 51–56, 63) by the Syriac word *pagar*,
which is the rendering of σῶμα in the Synoptic accounts of the
Institution of the Lord's Supper. That is, the Syriac version
of Jn. 6⁵¹ᵇ runs: " The bread which I will give is my Body,
for the life of the world," which at once suggests Lk. 22¹⁹:
τοῦτό ἐστι τὸ σῶμά μου [τὸ ὑπὲρ ὑμῶν διδόμενον] or 1 Cor. 11²⁴ :
τοῦτό μού ἐστι τὸ σῶμα τὸ ὑπὲρ ὑμῶν. As early, then, as 200 A.D.
the Syriac Church translated Jn. 6 in such a way as to make a
Eucharistic reference explicit and unmistakable. To this translation we shall come back presently.

Thus a Eucharistic reference in Jn. 6⁵¹ᵇ⁻⁵⁸ is not to be evaded.
This does not mean that a non-sacramental explanation might
not be placed by a Christian reader upon the mystical phraseology of the passage. No one would deny that there may be
ways of " eating the flesh and drinking the blood " of Christ
in a spiritual manner which do not involve sacramental feeding.
But the *language* is sacramental, and was so understood
throughout the second century.

D

If we accept literally the Johannine statement that the
words of Jn. 6⁵¹ᵇ⁻⁵⁸ were addressed to Jews in the synagogue of
Capernaum, after the Feeding of the Five Thousand, then the
further statement that they were treated by the hearers as
incredible and as a " hard saying " (v. 60) follows as of course.
It could not have been otherwise. Even those who had

in the Anglican Liturgy, where it is derived from the *Order of Communion* of 1548.
[1] Cf. p. lxxvii.

been disciples of Jesus would naturally be shaken in their allegiance.

It is true that in Jn. (see on 3¹⁴) the prediction of Jesus that death would be the end of His ministry is placed at an earlier period than in the Synoptists, and therefore such a prediction at this point is consistent with the Johannine narrative as a whole. But it is specially perplexing to find a prediction addressed to " the Jews," who were outside the circle of His immediate followers, to the effect that He would give His flesh for the world's life. This can hardly be historical. And, again, the language in which this momentous announcement is couched is definitely sacramental. It would thus appear that Jesus took this opportunity, before the Eucharist was instituted, of making prophetic reference to it as a means of grace and as the appointed way of communion with Him. This has been held by many expositors, but it is very difficult to accept, having regard to the audience and the occasion of the discourse.

The conclusion which seems to emerge is that the discourse of Jn. 6²⁶⁻⁵⁸, either in whole or in part, is placed out of its historical context. We have seen that, at any rate, vv. 51ᵇ–58 are reminiscent of the words spoken by Jesus at the institution of the Eucharist on the eve of His Passion. Very little is told by the Synoptists of what was said by Him on that occasion, and it may well be that, as in other cases, the Fourth Gospel here supplies what is not to be found in the narratives of its predecessors. An examination of the word σάρξ, as represented in Syriac, provides, as we shall see, reason for accepting Jn. 6⁵¹ᵇ as the Johannine version of the actual words used at the institution of the Lord's Supper.

E

Let us ask the question, " Is the Aramaic word behind σάρξ in Jn. 6⁵¹ᵇ the same as the Aramaic word behind σῶμα in Mk. 14²², Lk. 22¹⁹ ? "

The general distinction between σάρξ and σῶμα in the N.T. is no more than this, that σῶμα is the organised σάρξ, the bodily nature regarded as an organic whole. In Eph. 2¹⁵ the σάρξ of Christ is mentioned where we should expect σῶμα, probably because σῶμα is used in v. 16 of His *mystical* body. In Col. 1²² we find the expression τὸ σῶμα τῆς σαρκὸς αὐτοῦ, both words being employed to describe the body of Christ. Jn. avoids the word σῶμα, using it only (see on 2²¹) of a *dead* body; and prefers σάρξ (cf. 1¹⁴), probably because he wishes to emphasise the fact of the Incarnation, as against the nascent

Docetism of the age.[1]   And so the word σῶμα, which is common
to the Synoptic and the Pauline narratives of the institution
of the Eucharist, does not occur in Jn. 6.

In the LXX σάρξ and σῶμα are both used to render the
Hebrew בָּשָׂר, a word which is nearly always behind σάρξ and
more frequently than any other word behind σῶμα.   And if the
Aramaic form of בְּשַׂר were the word used by Jesus when He
said "This is my Body," it might be rendered σῶμα or σάρξ
according to the idiosyncrasy of the translator.

There is, however, another Aramaic word which may
have been that actually used at the institution of the Lord's
Supper, viz. the Aramaic form of the Hebrew פֶּגֶר.   In the
O.T. פֶּגֶר is rendered only three times by σῶμα, and then always
in the sense of *dead* body (Gen. 15[11], 2 Kings 19[35], Isa. 37[36]);
but by the first century of our era it is quite possible that it
may have been used to denote a *living* body.   As we have
already seen, the Syriac versions of Jn. 6 always give *pagar*
as their translation of σάρξ ; viz. the same word as they use in
rendering "This is my Body."   And this Syriac *pagar* in
Jn. 6 may well be a reversion to the actual word used by Jesus
at the institution of the Eucharist.

In any case, whether the original word used at the Last
Supper was the Aramaic בְכַר = Hebr. בְּשַׂר, or the Aramaic form
of פֶּגֶר, it is clear that it might have been rendered by σῶμα or
by σάρξ according to the habit of the translator.[2]

F

That the memory of the Aramaic word actually used by
Jesus should not have been preserved may be thought surprising, but it is not more surprising than the variety of the
forms which the Greek version of the words of institution
has assumed.[3]

The words following the blessing of the bread are as follows
in the various reports:

      (1) In Mk.: "Take ; this is my Body."
      (2) In Mt.: "Take, eat ; this is my Body."

---

[1] Thus, in the Apostles' Creed, the earlier versions have " resurrection of the *flesh*," which afterwards became " resurrection of the
body," no doctrinal difference being intended.

[2] Abbott (*Diat.* 1326 ff.) holds that τὸ σῶμά μου in the words of
institution is to be interpreted as " myself " ; but this does not
adequately represent σῶμα.

[3] See, for textual discussion of these passages, Sanday in *D.B.* ii.
636 f.

(3) In the Western text of Lk.: " This is my Body."
(4) In the later and fuller text of Lk.: " This is my Body, which is given for (ὑπέρ) you ; this do in remembrance of me."
(5) In Paul : " This is my Body, which is for (ὑπέρ) you ; this do in remembrance of me."
(6) In Jn.: " The bread which I will give is my Body (so the Syriac has it), for (ὑπέρ) the life of the world."

It may be taken as certain that the words " This (bread) is my Body " were used; and also that, either in connexion with the Bread or the Cup, it was said by Jesus that what was given was " on behalf of " men. Thus Mk., Mt., Lk., connect the words τὸ ὑπὲρ πολλῶν (or ὑμῶν) ἐκχυννόμενον with the giving of the Cup, while Paul and the longer text of Lk. have also ὑπὲρ ὑμῶν of the σῶμα which is given; the allusion to the impending sacrifice on the Cross being obvious. We have the same in Jn., who reports that Jesus said, " The bread which I will give is my Body, for the life of the world." The universal efficacy of Christ's sacrifice is a favourite doctrine of Jn. In 1²⁹ the Baptist points to Jesus as taking away τὴν ἁμαρτίαν τοῦ κόσμου. In 1 Jn. 2² he is not content with stating that Christ is a propitiation (ἱλασμός) for (περί) our sins, but he adds, " and not for ours only," ἀλλὰ καὶ περὶ ὅλου τοῦ κόσμου. So in his account of the eucharistic words he goes beyond the ὑπὲρ ὑμῶν of Lk. and Paul, and even beyond the ὑπὲρ πολλῶν of Mk.; the content of these sacred words to him was ὑπὲρ τῆς τοῦ κόσμου ζωῆς.

The idea that the Eucharistic rite was instituted as a memorial, εἰς τὴν ἐμὴν ἀνάμνησιν, is peculiar in the N.T. to Paul and the longer text of Lk. It does not appear in Mk., Mt., or the Western text of Lk., nor do we find it in Jn. The earliest appearance of this belief outside the N.T. seems to be in Justin, who quotes (*Apol.* i. 66) τοῦτο ποιεῖτε εἰς τὴν ἀνάμνησίν μου, τοῦτό ἐστι τὸ σῶμά μου, apparently from Lk. 22¹⁹. Cf. also Justin, *Tryph.* 41, 70. We have to bear in mind throughout the examination of sacramental passages in Jn., that (like Mk.) he gives no hint of the Pauline and Lucan doctrine that the Eucharist was instituted as a *memorial*.[1] It is, for him, a means of spiritual " feeding " on Christ, the assimilation of His humanity.

---

[1] This must be taken in connexion with the fact that he probably knew the text of Lk. (p. xcix), as well as the Pauline Epistles (p. cxxxvii).

G

So far, we have had under review the eucharistic language in c. 6 only. But an examination of 15^{1-12} also discloses allusions to the Eucharist.

It is argued elsewhere [1] that cc. 15, 16 are out of place in the traditional texts of the Fourth Gospel, and that c. 15 should follow immediately after 13^{30}. Judas has left the Upper Room, and it appears that this is the point in the narrative (see on 13^4) at which we must suppose the Eucharist to have been instituted.[2] Now there are only two passages in which Jesus is said to have mentioned the *vine*, although in two or three parables He spoke of vineyards. The first is Mk. 14^{25} (see the parallels Mt. 26^{29}, Lk. 22^{18}): "I will no more drink of the fruit of the vine (τὸ γέννημα τῆς ἀμπέλου) until that day when I drink it new with you in the kingdom of God." The words are full of difficulty, but they mean at least that Jesus announced to His disciples His approaching death: He would never drink wine again on earth with them. But for "wine" the unexpected and unusual paraphrase "fruit of the vine" or "juice of the vine" is used, the thoughts of the hearers being directed to the source from which the wine on the table was derived. It is remarkable that the discourse which for other reasons we have placed at this point should begin "I am the True Vine," and should proceed to develop the lesson that the life of the branches is dependent on their sharing the life of the Vine.

The eucharistic wine is described by Clement of Alexandria as τὸ αἷμα τῆς ἀμπέλου τοῦ Δαβίδ (*Quis diues saluetur*, § 29); and one of the eucharistic thanksgivings in the *Didache* (§ 9) is Εὐχαριστοῦμέν σοι . . . ὑπὲρ τῆς ἁγίας ἀμπέλου Δαβὶδ τοῦ παιδός σου, ἧς ἐγνώρισας ἡμῖν διὰ Ἰησοῦ τοῦ παιδός σοι. Origen, too, uses the words "before we are inebriated with the blood of the *true vine*, which rises up from the root of David." [3] These passages only show that the idea of Jesus as the Vine was associated with eucharistic thoughts. But in another passage (on Ps. 104^{15}) Origen brings together the two verses Mk. 14^{25} and Jn. 15^1, when he is speaking again (in allusion to Ps. 23^5) of the spiritual inebriation of the eucharistic Cup, τὸ γέννημα τῆς ἀληθινῆς ἀμπέλου μεθύσκον ὡς κράτιστον [4] (see also p. clxxv below).

We have seen that the language of the latter part of c. 6, while definitely sacramental, does not exclude the possibility of a spiritual feeding on Christ by the faithful soul. It is

---

[1] P. xx.   [2] Tatian places the institution after 13^{32}.
[3] Lommatzsch, xi. 258.   [4] *Ibid.* xi. 456.

equally true that the allegory of the Vine and the branches which are sustained by its life permeating and quickening them, does not refer (and was never taken to refer) solely to the Eucharist; but that it was suggested in the first instance by the words of institution seems probable, nevertheless.

As we have already pointed out, there is no trace in Jn. of that aspect of the Eucharist in which it is a Memorial, εἰς ἀνάμνησιν. He reproduces "This is my Body" at 6⁵¹, and proceeeds to lay stress on the necessity for the Christian of feeding on it. He speaks in like manner and in the same sentence of "drinking" the "Blood" of Christ, (6⁵³), and records words of Jesus signifying that without such "eating" and "drinking" the Christian disciple has no "life in himself." The wine represents the Blood of Christ and of this all His disciples are to drink, thus assimilating His Life. Now this is the same teaching as in 15¹ᶠᶠ·. Jesus is the Vine, through which and from which the wine of life flows, and this wine must be assimilated by the branches of the vine, or they will die.

Just as Jesus claimed to be ὁ ἄρτος ὁ ἀληθινός (6³²), so He claims (15¹) to be ἡ ἄμπελος ἡ ἀληθινή. He is the Real Bread (as contrasted with the earthly bread which typified it), and so He is the Real Vine (as contrasted with the vine of whose juice [1] the disciples had partaken at the Last Supper). In c. 6, the immediate consequence of the disciple's feeding on this Bread and drinking this Wine is, "he abideth in me and I in him" (6⁵⁶). And so too in 15⁴, this mutual abiding is the secret of the branch's life and fertility. "He that abideth in me, and I in him, the same beareth much fruit, for apart from me you can do nothing" (15⁵). This doctrine of the mutual indwelling of Christ and the believer, "that we may dwell in Him and He in us," [2] is found in the Fourth Gospel only at 15⁴ and 6⁵⁶ (where see note), which is an indication that in both passages it is to be interpreted in the same way.

Again, the teaching of 15¹⁻⁸ leads up to the doctrine of the mutual love (ἀγάπη) which Christian disciples should have for each other, and to the New Commandment (15¹² 13³⁴). This springs out of the thought that they are all alike branches of the True Vine, whose mystical "juice" is assimilated by all. There is no trace of this idea of the *unity* of communicant disciples, or of their mutual *love*, in c. 6, where stress is laid rather on their *faith* (vv. 35, 40, 47), and on the gift of *life* which they

[1] Note that wine is repeatedly called the *blood* of the grape (Deut. 32¹⁴, Ecclus. 39²⁶ 50¹⁵, 1 Macc. 6³⁴).

[2] No emphasis seems to have been laid on this indwelling in most of the early Liturgies ; it appears, however, in the Liturgy of the Syrian Jacobites (see Brightman, *Eastern Liturgies*, p. 106).

receive in eating the Heavenly Bread (v. 51). The Flesh and Blood of Christ are both indeed the subject of vv. 53–57; but the teaching of vv. 32–58 is mainly occupied with drawing out the meaning and the power of that *Bread* which is His Flesh, as distinct from the *Wine* which is His Blood.

Here must be cited some additional passages from Ignatius, whose eucharistic doctrine resembles that of Jn. very closely, both in the apparent crudeness of the language in which it is expressed (he prefers, like Jn., to use the word σάρξ instead of σῶμα) and in the fact that he does not confine the promised blessings to those who actually receive the eucharistic elements. Both are mystics, with a profound and awful sense of the mystery of the Eucharist.

In *Trall.* 8, Ignatius describes the bread and wine as representing, respectively, *faith* and *love*: ἐν πίστει, ὅ ἐστιν σάρξ τοῦ κυρίου, καὶ ἐν ἀγάπῃ, ὅ ἐστιν αἷμα Ἰησοῦ Χριστοῦ. " Faith is the flesh, the substance of the Christian life; love is the blood, the energy coursing through its veins and arteries " (Lightfoot). It will be observed that Ignatius, at any rate *in loc.*, associates *faith* with the Bread (as in Jn. 6), while he associates ἀγάπη with the Wine (as in Jn. 15). So he says again (*Rom.* 7): ἄρτον θεοῦ θέλω ὅ ἐστιν σάρξ τοῦ Χριστοῦ . . . καὶ πόμα θέλω τὸ αἷμα αὐτοῦ, ὅ ἐστιν ἀγάπη ἄφθαρτος. It is therefore no passing idea but a settled thought with Ignatius that the Blood of Christ is *Love*. Once more, when speaking of the unity of the eucharistic feast, he says that as there is μία σάρξ of the Lord, so there is also ἓν ποτήριον εἰς ἕνωσιν τοῦ αἵματος αὐτοῦ (*Phil.* 4), which Lightfoot renders " so that all may be one by partaking of His own blood." All this is very like the doctrine of Jn. 15¹⁻¹², in its association of mutual love and common life with the sacrament of Christ's Blood, once the eucharistic reference is perceived; although Ignatius does not allude directly to Jn. 15.

Origen,[1] however, brings the similitude " I am the Bread of Life " into direct comparison with " I am the True Vine." He says, after his curious manner, that to understand the latter similitude, you must go back to Ps. 104¹⁵, where it is said that while bread strengthens man's heart, wine gladdens it (ἄρτος στηρίζει, οἶνος εὐφραίνει). And elsewhere he pursues the same idea, identifying the inebriating Cup of Ps. 23⁵ with the eucharistic chalice, and adding, " This drink is the fruit of the True Vine, who said, *I am the True Vine*.[2] Origen's identifications are often fantastic, but the passages that have

---

[1] *In Ioann.* 33.
[2] Comm. *in Matt.* 85 (Lommatzsch, iv. 416). Cf. Cyprian, *Epist.* lxiii. 2, on the association of the " True Vine " with the Cup.

now been cited show that the eucharistic reference of Jn. 15^1 is not a modern fancy.

(v) The Johannine Miracles

A

The Fourth Evangelist teaches explicitly that Jesus exhibited in His works the Divine glory (cf. 2^{11}), which had been His from eternity (17^5); and not only so, but also that Jesus Himself claimed that His works bore witness to His august origin and mission (5^{36} 10^{25} 15^{24}). Jn. does not suggest that the faith which is evoked by miracle is of the highest type (cf. 2^{23}); and in one place he represents Jesus as deprecating an appeal to " signs and wonders " (4^{48}), which is in correspondence with the Marcan tradition (cf. Mk. 8^{12}). But nevertheless Jn. lays stress on " signs " as truly witnessing to the claims of Jesus.

The common opinion of the first century was that the doing of wonderful works, such as an ordinary human being could not do, showed that the wonder-worker had been sent by God, whose help he had (3^2). Jn. shared this opinion, and he likes to call the works of Jesus His σημεῖα, as significant of His superhuman personality (2^{11} 4^{54} 6^{14} 12^{18}, etc.). There were many such signs (2^{23} 3^2 6^2 7^{31} 11^{47} 12^{37}), but Jn. has selected only a few for detailed record, choosing such as, to his mind, show in a special manner that Jesus was the Son of God (20^{31}).

Jn. uncompromisingly attributes to Jesus the power of working miracles, but he omits many which the Synoptists describe, some being so remarkable that the omission is surprising; and in one or two instances he seems deliberately to alter a Synoptic story so that it no longer implies miracle. Thus Jn. says nothing of Jesus stilling the storm by a word of authority, which Mk. narrates as an extraordinary instance of Jesus' control of inanimate nature (cf. Mk. 4^{39-41}), even more convincing, as it would seem, than the turning of water into wine at Cana. Jn. does not tell of Peter walking on the sea (cf. Mt. 14^{28}); and his story of the great draught of fishes [1] seems to give a version of that incident which is wholly devoid of a miraculous element ($21^{6f.}$). So too (see note on 6^{21}), Jn. retells Mk.'s story of Jesus " walking on the sea " in such a manner as to correct it, by omitting any suggestion of miracle.

There is a further omission by Jn. in his report of the miracles of Jesus which is in striking contrast with the Synoptic records. Jn. tells nothing of any cure by Jesus of demoniacs, such as

[1] Jn. does not call it a σημεῖον.

the cures which appear so prominently in Mk. (cf. Mk. $1^{23.34}$ 3^{11} 5^2 7^{25} 9^{17}; cf. 6^7). That disorder of the brain is due to demoniac possession was believed by the Jews of the first century generally, and Jn. mentions such a belief (7^{20} $8^{48f.}$ $10^{20f.}$), but he does not imply, as the Synoptists do, that Jesus believed it. Nor does he adduce any cure of mental disturbance by the word of Jesus as a proof of His supernatural power. Jn. does not exaggerate the supernatural element in the works of Jesus, while he sometimes refuses to assert its presence where the Synoptists fasten on it as of deepest moment.

B

Only six of the wonderful ἔργα of Jesus are described by Jn.—three in Galilee, and then three in Jerusalem and Bethany —as follows:

    i. The turning water into wine (2^{1-11}).
    ii. The healing of the nobleman's son (4^{46-54}).
    iii. The feeding of the five thousand (6^{4-13}).
    iv. The healing of the impotent man (5^{2-9}).
    v. The healing of the blind man (9^{1-7}).
    vi. The raising of Lazarus (11^{1-44}).

Of these, i., ii., iii., and vi. are explicitly called σημεῖα (cf. 2^{11} 4^{54} 6^{14} 12^{18}). The allusion in 9^{16} marks v. also as a σημεῖον; while iv. is not thus spoken of at all, although it may be included in the ἔργα to which Jesus alludes at 5^{36}.[1]

In each of these six cases the evangelist describes the σημεῖον as arising out of the circumstances of the case. Jesus does not deliberately set Himself to perform any wonderful work the occasion for which has not been suggested by human need. All of these miracles may be regarded as signs of *pity*, as well as of *power*, with the single exception of the first. As described by Jn., the magnitude of the miracle at Cana seems to be quite disproportionate to its immediate purpose, viz. that of relieving some awkwardness at a village wedding. It can hardly be called a " sign " of the infinite compassion of Jesus, as the other Johannine miracles may be called. It was such a sign of His δόξα, that it stabilised the faith of disciples (2^{11}); but Jn. says no more about it.

C

It has been suggested by some scholars[2] that the *signs* of Jesus which are described by Jn. were chosen by him so

---

[1] The incident of Jesus walking by the sea is not, of course, called a σημεῖον by Jn. ; see on 6^{17-21}.
[2] Cf. E. F. Scott, *The Fourth Gospel*, p. 3.

as to bring out the force of some special discourse or saying of Jesus with which they are associated. That is possible in some instances, to which we shall return; but it cannot be said of Nos. i., ii., or iv. The sign at Cana is a sign of nothing except the δόξα which Jesus exhibited in this display of His power (2^{11}), nor is any word of Jesus associated with its lesson (see on 2^9). So, too, the healing of the nobleman's son, although an indication of the compassion of Jesus as well as of His power, is not associated by Jn. with any commendation by Jesus of the man's faith, such as concludes the similar story in Lk. 7^9. Jn. does not hint in his narrative (4$^{46\text{-}54}$) at anything more than an exhibition of power. Nor, again, does the healing of the impotent man at Bethesda (5$^{2\text{-}17}$) clearly lead up to any discourse disclosing the spiritual meaning of his cure. It excited immediately a dispute about Sabbath observance, the formal breach of which suggested to the Pharisees the charge of impiety. Jesus answers them by claiming to be in the same relation to the Sabbath that God is: " My Father worketh hitherto, and I work " (5^{17}). In other words, He compares His own beneficent activity on a Sabbath day to that of God, who is always and every day exerting His omnipotence for the benefit of mankind. And the rest of c. 5 draws out the relation of the Son to the Father. But no stress is laid on the miraculous character of the healing (if, indeed, that was its nature), and the discourses of c. 5 do not discuss this at all.

The healing of the man born blind, on the other hand, leads up, although by a circuitous route, to a saying of Jesus. The story begins, like that in c. 5, with a charge of Sabbath-breaking (9^{16}), and the Pharisees, having failed to disprove the alleged cure, reiterate the charge that the healer must be a sinner. The long and elaborate disputation of 9$^{13\text{-}34}$ may have been related in order to exhibit to the reader how blind the Pharisees really were; and at 9^{39} a single sentence of Jesus suggests that the miracle symbolised the mission of Him who came to impart the faculty of spiritual vision to those who were spiritually blind. The story, in short, may have been inserted at this point to illustrate the claim of Jesus to be the Light of the World (8^{12}). But that is not to be taken as the evangelist's sole purpose in narrating it. He wishes also to impress upon the reader that the hatred with which Jesus inspired the Pharisees had its roots in His refusal to accept the Sabbatical Law as a final statement of the will of God.

The feeding of the five thousand is closely connected by Jn. with a long discourse on the Bread of Life (6$^{26\text{-}58}$). The miracle is treated as leading up to the discourse at Capernaum,

although this association presents serious exegetical difficulties.[1]
The miraculous feeding is not treated by Jn. as sacramental
(see on 6^{11}), while the eucharistic reference of $6^{51\text{-}58}$ is unmistakable. This part of the discourse suggests the institution
of the Eucharist ($6^{51f.}$) more definitely than it recalls the feeding
of the five thousand. The discourse is probably placed by
Jn. out of its historical setting, but its position as following
the σημεῖον (6^{14}) of the miraculous feeding has, no doubt,
been deliberately chosen by the evangelist.

Lastly, it is to be observed that no formal discourse is
associated with the raising of Lazarus, which, nevertheless,
is also called a σημεῖον (12^{18}). This, as is usual with Jn.,
means a sign of Divine power (cf. $11^{4.\ 40}$) rather than of Divine
compassion, although the pity of Jesus for the sisters of Lazarus
has a prominent place in the story. The spiritual teaching
of the miracle is, no doubt, clearly expressed at 11^{25}, " I am the
Resurrection and the Life." But it would be going beyond
the evidence to claim that such teaching *suggested* to Jn. the
story of the raising of Lazarus from the dead; nor is such a
literary method that of the Fourth Gospel.[2]

D

Something must now be said about the " miraculous "
element in the " signs " of Jesus, which Jn. reports in detail.

The healing of the impotent man at Bethesda is not called
a " miracle " or a " sign " by Jn. (see on 7^{21}). The man's
infirmity was chronic, having lasted thirty-eight years, like
that of the woman in Lk. 13^{11} who " had a spirit of infirmity
eighteen years "; although Jn. does not ascribe the man's
bodily condition to the influence of a " spirit," as Lk. does.[3]
Probably Jn. thought the cure to be so extraordinary that
it could not have been effected by any means short of the exercise of Divine power. It was indeed one of the beneficent
" works " of Jesus (5^{36}), but not all of these suggest " miracle."
And we are not compelled to suppose any miracle in the
incident of $5^{5\text{-}9}$. The cure has many parallels in the modern
treatment of some forms of nervous infirmity. *Possunt quia
posse uidentur.*

The healing of the nobleman's son ($4^{46\text{-}54}$) is called a σημεῖον
by Jn. (4^{54}; cf. 4^{48}), who regards it apparently as an instance
of telepathic healing, as is more expressly indicated in the
parallel story of Mt. $8^{5f.}$, Lk. $7^{2f.}$ (see on 4^{46}). Telepathic
healings can hardly be ruled out as impossible by those who

---

[1] See p. clxx.   [2] See p. lxxxvi.
[3] See p. clxxvii.

recognise the extraordinary spiritual power of Jesus, even if they do not accept His Divine claims. But it is generally overlooked that Jn. does not say that Jesus spoke an effective word of healing. All He is represented as saying is, " Thy son liveth," *i.e.* " he will recover." We may assume that the symptoms had been described by the father, who believed his son to be dying. Jesus told him that his son would live. There is no record of a " miracle " here. Many a physician, having heard detailed the course which a disease has taken, would be able to predict either that it would end fatally, or that the moment for anxiety had passed. Jn. would have regarded such prescience as superhuman, and therefore a " sign " of Divine knowledge; so would most Orientals at the present day. But those who have experience of the scientific diagnosis of disease would be slow to treat such prescience as beyond human powers.

The cure of the man blind from birth is more difficult to interpret. Jn. represents it as a $\sigma\eta\mu\epsilon\hat{\iota}ον$ (9^{16}), and as miraculous (cf. 11^{37}). Yet he tells that it was effected after the use of natural remedies such as those which were used at the time by practitioners of the healing art (see on $9^{6.\ 7}$, and cf. Mk. 7^{33}). The cure may not, indeed, have been brought about as simply as this. The patient, after his cure, claimed that the healer must have been more than an ordinary man ($9^{32.\ 33}$), the point of the story being that the blindness was congenital (see on $9^{18f.}$). The only case in the Synoptists which seems to be a cure of blindness from birth is that of Mk. $8^{22f.}$, and there the language used is not quite explicit. We cannot be sure of what happened in the case described by Jn.[1] No one can assert with confidence that congenital blindness, whether complete or partial, could *never* be relieved by the use of natural remedies; and it must be remembered that the cure in Jn. 9^{6-11} is not said to have been instantaneous. The border line between possible and impossible is not easy to define in such cases.

The story of the feeding of the five thousand is deep rooted in the evangelical tradition, being found in all the Gospels; in Mk. it is a " miracle," outside the ordinary course

---

[1] Holtzmann (*Life of Jesus*, Eng. Tr., p. 193) cites a case of cure of " atrophy of the optic nerve of many years' standing," resulting when the Holy Coat of Treves was displayed in 1891. There were ten other cures for which physicians of repute could find no medical explanation, including those of arms and legs impotent through rheumatism. Holtzmann thinks that these cures were due to " suggestion " made by the spiritual authorities of the Roman Catholic Church, who exhibited the relic as efficacious to cure; and he cites them as possible parallels to some of the Gospel miracles.

of nature, quite as much as in Jn. Jn. calls it a σημεῖον (6¹⁴)
which suggested to the people that Jesus was a prophet, because
He was able to do such wonderful things. Nothing is said
expressly by Jn. of this " sign " being a manifestation of the
Divine δόξα which was disclosed in the works of Jesus (cf. 2¹¹),
but that is substantially what is implied. No Gospel suggests
any doubt as to what happened. Jesus literally multiplied the
loaves, so that five of them fed five thousand; and yet, after
the multitude had eaten, more bread was left (for the fragments
filled twelve baskets) than had originally been provided.

Many explanations have been offered of this extraordinary
incident with the motive of rendering it more credible; [1] but
no naturalistic hypothesis is completely satisfying. Strauss
urged that the tradition grew out of Old Testament stories
about miraculous meals (see note on 6¹⁵). Others think that
the narrative of the feeding of the multitude arose out of the
institution of the Eucharist, which is thus placed at an early
period in the public ministry of Jesus; but this is to rewrite
the narrative of the Last Supper (see further on 6¹¹). Others,
again, appeal to some hypnotic power of suggestion possessed
by Jesus, which enabled Him to persuade people that they had
seen what they had *not* seen. This will not commend itself
to any who find in Him the Divine attribute of truth as well
as that of power. He did not deceive men by illusory pretence,
or by a trick which would impress the simple folk who came
to hear Him. If, as we hold, the narratives of Jn. and Mk.
alike go back to those who were eye-witnesses of the scene, it
is not easy to dispose of the available evidence, scanty as it is,
by supposing this miracle story to rest on a mistaken tradition
of what really happened.

The story of the miracle at Cana is even more difficult to
believe, and it is not at all so well attested as the miraculous
feeding. It rests upon the Johannine tradition *alone*; and, as
has been observed above (p. clxxvii), the occasion for working
so stupendous a miracle was hardly adequate, as compared
with that which is apparent in the feeding of the multitude.
The latter was a work of kindly charity; the former only
relieved a little awkwardness at a village wedding. The
miracle at Cana is described as a sign of power over inanimate
nature, in that water was literally turned into wine ; and the
only motive assigned by Jn. is that Jesus thus " manifested His
glory, and His disciples believed on Him " (2¹¹). There is
nothing quite like this anywhere else in the Gospels, and in the
τέρας or prodigy which Jesus is said to have performed we

[1] See, for various hypotheses, Schweitzer, *Quest of the Historical
Jesus*, pp. 41, 52, 60, 84, 326.

can find no inner meaning, except in so far as it indicated superhuman power.

Various ways of escape from the literal truth of the narrative have been mentioned in the Additional Note on 2^{10} (see also on 2^9), but none of them carries complete conviction. The most plausible of these is that suggested by Wendt who thinks that the story grew up round some traditional saying, such as that of keeping the good wine until the end. It is noticeable, indeed, that Jn. does not tell the story as if he were telling it for the first time (see on 2^9); he tells it as a story already in currency. But, nevertheless, its particularity of detail, its psychological interest, its reference to the setting aside of the authority of Mary, its coherence, all indicate that an actual incident lies behind 2^{1-11}, rather than that it has been developed out of a single terse saying.

That there was a feast at Cana, and that Jesus unexpectedly supplied the needs of a wedding party, is in no way unlikely. That some of His disciples who were present (and it is probable that John the son of Zebedee was one) discerned in His action a sign of His superhuman power is expressly stated. But it is not said that Jesus Himself claimed to do anything miraculous on the occasion, or that He acquiesced in any such interpretation of His intervention. His complete power over nature can hardly be challenged by those who recognise His personality as Divine, and believe that He afterwards rose from the dead. But the question of His power over nature and its limits does not arise for us here, unless we can be sure that what some disciples (the other guests do not seem to have been specially impressed) interpreted as miracle would have been interpreted in the same way by ourselves had we been there.

In regard to the raising of Lazarus, we must first examine an alleged difficulty which does not present itself in the case of the other Johannine miracles.

It is asked, How could Mk. be silent about so notable a miracle, if he knew that it had taken place? The argument *e silentio* is always precarious, and in this particular instance it is especially so. None of the Synoptists mentions the raising of Lazarus, but they pay little attention to the development of the ministry of Jesus at Jerusalem. On the other hand, from c. 5 onward Jn. devotes himself to describing the increasing hostility of the Pharisees to Jesus, and in his narrative the climax of their opposition was reached when the Lazarus miracle attracted the attention and inspired the enthusiasm of many people at Jerusalem and its neighbourhood.[1] The point

[1] Cf. Richmond, *The Gospel of the Rejection*, p. 141.

in the story, as told by Jn., is not, primarily, that the miracle was a stupendous one, but that it did, in fact, hasten the final decision of the Jewish authorities to secure the death of Jesus (11[53]). The Synoptists tell nothing of the words or works of Jesus which are reported in cc. 5, 7–12 of the Fourth Gospel. For some reason, this whole ministry and not merely the raising of Lazarus is omitted in the narrative of Mk., upon which Lk. and Mt. primarily depend, and which is the framework of their Gospels.

No serious examination of Mk. can fail to observe the fragmentary character of his Gospel. It consists of a number of incidents and discourses, which, as is generally held, owe their preservation to the reminiscences or the preaching of Peter. There is no pretence that the Marcan Gospel is a complete narrative. Now Peter does not appear once in Part II. of the Fourth Gospel (cc. 5, 7–12). He is not represented as having been present in Jerusalem or Bethany until the Last Supper (13[6]), although it is probable that he was present at the supper at Bethany of which Jn. tells 12[1f.] (cf. Mk. 14[3f.]). He appears to have come up to Jerusalem for the Passover. More particularly, Peter is replaced by Thomas as the leader and chief spokesman in the story of Lazarus, and there is no reason to suppose that he was present on the occasion of the dead man being raised, or for some little time afterwards (see on 11[16]). If he were not an eye-witness of what happened, it is not surprising that he did not include the story among his reminiscences. He had been present when Jairus' daughter was raised from the dead, and this was duly recorded by Mk. (5[37f.]), as one of Peter's experiences. There was no special reason why a second miracle of revivification should be mentioned, if Peter did not see it; indeed, it would weaken the credibility of any man's reminiscences if he included in them an incident so extraordinary, of which he had not first-hand knowledge.

But more than this should be said about Mk.'s omission to note the miracle of the raising of Lazarus, in which he is followed by Mt. and Lk. The Synoptic account of the triumphal entry of Jesus into Jerusalem provides no explanation of the extraordinary enthusiasm with which He was received on this His last visit Up to c. 11, Mk. tells of no visit of Jesus to Jerusalem. How then did it come to pass that the people of the city treated His entry as a royal progress ? " Many spread their garments upon the way . . . they cried, Hosanna, Blessed is He that cometh in the name of the Lord " (Mk. 11[8. 9]). The only evangelist who gives a sufficient reason for this is Jn., who says explicitly that it was the report of the raising of Lazarus at Bethany which so excited the people that even the Pharisees had to confess "the world is gone after Him." It is Jn.'s habit to correct Mk. where he deems it necessary (see p. xcvii); and at this point, by rectifying a serious omission in Mk., he makes the story of the triumphal entry coherent for the first time.[1]

We now come to the details of the miracle as told by Jn., for miracle (whether rightly or wrongly) he held it to be. As compared with the Synoptic miracles of reviving the dead, from one point of view it is much more surprising. For the revivification of a corpse more than three days dead would be more impressive than the raising up of a child only just dead (Mk. $5^{35f.}$), or of a young man brought out for burial (Lk. 7^{11}), as that speedily follows death in the East. Indeed, in these Synoptic stories the hypothesis that death had not actually taken place before Jesus spoke the word which restored them, is not formally excluded. Jesus said that the daughter of Jairus was not dead, although no one believed Him ; and instances are not lacking of persons being prepared for burial who were really alive. Even those who reject all *miracula* need find no difficulty in Mk. 5^{35} or Lk. 7^{11}.

There is a certain similarity in Jn.'s narrative of the raising of Lazarus to these stories in Mk. and Lk. The revivification was brought about in all cases by the *voice* of Jesus (11^{43}). Again, Jesus is made by Jn. to say that the sickness of Lazarus was *not* unto death (11^4) and that His friend had fallen asleep (cf. Mk. 5^{39}): "I go that I may awake him out of *sleep*" (11^{11}, where see note). It has often been suggested that Lazarus was in a kind of death-like trance, which his sisters had mistaken for death,[2] which persisted for three days in the tomb, but which was dispelled when the tomb was opened, and the loud voice of authority was heard. Martha, indeed, said that the body was decomposed (11^{39}), but that is only what she would expect on the fourth day after death, and there is no hint in the narrative that she was right about it. Vv. 41, 42, would, on such a theory, represent the joy of Jesus in finding that His friend was still alive.

There is no doubt that, even if this naturalistic explanation represents the truth of the matter, the effect produced on the spectators would be overwhelming. They would conclude that one possessed of such powers in recalling a buried man to

---

[1] Cf. Headlam, *Miracles of the N.T.*, p. 226, and Garvie, *The Beloved Disciple*, p. 129 ; *contra*, Burkitt, *The Gospel History and its Transmission*, p. 222, and Moffatt, *Introduction to Lit. of N.T.*, p. 539.

[2] Renan held that the supposed resuscitation was a fraud arranged by the sisters, with the connivance of Jesus Himself (*Vie de Jesus*, c. 22). But this is now upheld by few critics, if by any ; and it is inconsistent with all that we know of Jesus.

life must be superhuman. Their report would draw to Jesus many adherents, and the enthusiasm with which His entry into Jerusalem was received would be a natural consequence.

But the narrative of c. 11, *as it stands*, is not consistent with such a theory. Jn.'s comments on the words of Jesus (cf. v. 13) cannot always be regarded as final (see on 2^{21}); but here at v. 14 he records that Jesus had said plainly, "Lazarus is dead." The evangelist accepted this as a fact, and he depicts the demeanour of Jesus throughout, not as that of one who was serene in His consciousness that His friend was still living, but as that of one who knew that Lazarus was dead, and who proposed to use the supernormal forces which He possessed to restore him to life, in order that the disciples and the other bystanders might " believe " (vv. 15, 42). We cannot, indeed, claim on any hypothesis that we have in c. 11 the *exact* words which Jesus used in speaking about the death of Lazarus and in His consolation of Martha. There is no trace of the story having been written down until half a century or more after the event; and if, as we hold, it represents an historical incident, it depends on the memory of a very old man, who has all his life pondered on it as the greatest of his Master's works of mercy, and as a signal illustration of His words of mystery, " I am the Resurrection and the Life " (v. 25).

It has been thought, indeed, that the whole story was built up round this saying. But it cannot be treated as a mere invention or as a parable constructed to convey spiritual truth, like the parable of Dives and Lazarus, which has been regarded by some critics as its germ. The literary method of Jn. is quite different (cf. p. lxxxiii). He means to narrate something that really happened, and he has drawn a vivid picture. The distinction, *e.g.*, of the characters of Martha and Mary is remarkably exposed (see on v. 20). The description of the agitation of Jesus (vv. 34, 35) is not such as a romancer would have ventured to set down. The Jews at v. 37, instead of referring to the Synoptic raisings from the dead, as they would certainly have been made to do by a writer of fiction, refer instead to the recent healing of the blind man at Jerusalem (see note *in loc.*).

We conclude, then, that the narrative of c. 11 describes a remarkable incident in the ministry of Jesus. It may be that the details are not reproduced by Jn. with such precision as a modern historian would desiderate. In that case, there is room for the hypothesis that Lazarus was raised from a death-like trance by an extraordinary effort of will, and exercise of spiritual power, by Jesus. Those who do not accept " miracle " in any form may be inclined to adopt some such hypothesis. But that Jesus could literally recall the dead to life is not impossible of credence by any one who believes that He Himself "rose from the dead." The miracle of Lazarus is on a different level from the recorded miracle at Cana, where it is not the spiritual forces at the command of Jesus that are in question, but the transformation of water into wine by a mere fiat of His word, comparable to the *Fiat lux* in the ancient story of Creation. But he is a bold dogmatist who, in the present condition of our knowledge, will venture to set precise limits to the exercise of *spiritual* force even by ordinary human beings, still less when He who sets it in action has all the potentialities of the spiritual world at His command.

CHAPTER VII

COMMENTARIES

OF patristic commentaries on the Fourth Gospel, the earliest is that by *Heracleon*,[1] of which only fragments, dealing mainly with cc. 1, 4, are extant. It illustrates the Gnostic applications of the text. *Origen's* commentary [2] is strikingly original, but, after his manner, is often fantastic; it is essential to the student of the exegesis of the third century. *Chrysostom* [3] is eloquent and vigorous, but, full as his homilies are, I have not found his exposition of much service. The Fathers were generally better theologians than critics, and this is especially true of Chrysostom. He does not reach the heights of *Augustine*, who can pack a sermon into an epigram and who has always been reckoned among the very greatest of commentators; but even his commentaries are valuable rather for his insight into great spiritual truths than for their precise exposition of the text. The metrical paraphrase of the Fourth Gospel by *Nonnus* (*circa* 400 A.D.) is a remarkable feat, its Homeric hexameters following the text closely enough, but it is not instructive to the modern reader. As a translation, *Jerome's* Vulgate is in no need of praise. I have found the writings of *Ignatius*, *Justin*, and *Irenæus* more valuable than any of the set commentaries by the Fathers : Ignatius for his theological

---

[1] See p. lxxiii.

[2] The best edition is that by A. E. Brooke (Cambridge University Press, 2 vols., 1896).

[3] Chrysostom's *Homilies on St. John* are accessible in English in the Oxford "Library of the Fathers."

presuppositions, which are markedly like those of the Fourth Evangelist,[1] Justin [2] and Irenæus for their use of the Gospel, which is often of great value as bringing out the original meaning.

I have made no attempt to collect or collate the views of modern commentators,[3] although I am very sensible of obligations to many of them. During the last quarter of a century great commentaries on the Fourth Gospel, such as those of Brückner, Meyer, Westcott, Godet, of former generations, have not been produced.[4] Scholars have devoted themselves rather to the historical and critical problems of the " Gospel according to St. John " than to the exposition in detail of the text. I have given references in the Introduction and Notes to many essays and treatises on these problems, published both in Europe and in America, which are full of valuable and illuminating comment. It is needless to dwell on the aids to Johannine study to be found in the learned Biblical Dictionaries and Encyclopædias of our time. Particular mention should be made of E. A. Abbott's *Johannine Grammar*, which is now as indispensable to the expositor for its grammatical distinctions (sometimes too subtle) as Wetstein's great work is still indispensable for its classical parallels to the language of the N.T.

The treatment of the historical and critical problems involved is very difficult. Perhaps we have not data for their complete solution. But all such inquiries are subsidiary to the exposition of the sacred text itself. This is at once more important and more difficult. It is vastly more important to learn what the evangelist meant to teach, and what was the picture of our Lord that was present to his mind, than to know whether the book was written by an apostle or by the pupil of an apostle, important as this is in its place. Again, the expositor's task is specially difficult, if he tries to place himself in the position of those who read the Gospel when it was first published. Its appeal to the twentieth century cannot be unfolded until the lesser task has been in some measure accomplished, of setting forth its appeal to the second century. Before we venture to appraise the permanent value of the writer's teaching, we must first discover what he meant to say. And this discovery is sometimes disconcerting, perhaps because the author moves in spiritual regions of thought

---

[1] See p. lxxi.   [2] See p. lxxv.
[3] A full list will be found in Moffatt's *Introd. to the N.T.*
[4] A recent commentary by Walter Bauer, *Das Johannes Evangelium* (Tübingen, 1925), is packed with scholarly comment, although it is not on a large scale.

too high for us, perhaps because his convictions are unwelcome to the scientific temper of our time. The most profound book of the New Testament can be truly interpreted, as it was written, only by a disciple, by one who is willing to learn.

THE GOSPEL ACCORDING TO
ST. JOHN

————◆————

THE PROLOGUE (I. 1-18)

1. Ἐν ἀρχῇ ἦν ὁ Λόγος,

THE Prologue to the Gospel is in the form of a hymn,[1] whose theme is the Christian doctrine of the Logos, explanatory comments being added at various points. Speculations about the Logos of God were current among Greek thinkers, and Jn. does not stay to explain the term, which was in common use at the time. But he sets out, simply and without argument, what he believes the true doctrine to be; and he finds its origin in the Jewish teaching about the Word of God rather than in the theosophy of Greek Gnosticism. Its final justification is the Life and Person of Jesus Christ.

Paul had declared that " a man in Christ is a new creation " (καινὴ κτίσις, 2 Cor. 5[17]). This thought is connected by Jn. with the Jewish doctrine of the creative Word, and accordingly he begins by stating his doctrine of the Logos in phrases which recall the first chapter of Genesis.

The Divine Pre-existent Word (vv. 1, 2)

I. 1. ἐν ἀρχῇ ἦν ὁ λόγος. The book of Genesis opens with ἐν ἀρχῇ ἐποίησεν ὁ θεὸς τὸν οὐρανὸν καὶ τὴν γῆν. But Jn. begins his hymn on the creative Logos even farther back. Before anything is said by him about creation, he proclaims that the Logos was in being originally—ἐν ἀρχῇ ἦν, not ἐν ἀρχῇ ἐγένετο (see for the distinction on 8[58]). This doctrine is also found in the Apocalypse. In that book, Christ is also called the Word of God (19[13]), and He is represented (22[13]) as claiming pre-existence : " I am the Alpha and the Omega, the first and the last, the beginning and the end." Paul, who does not apply

[1] Cf. Introd., p. cxliv.

καὶ ὁ Λόγος ἦν πρὸς τὸν Θεόν,
καὶ Θεὸς ἦν ὁ Λόγος.

the title " Logos " to Christ, yet has the same doctrine of His pre-existence: " He is before all things " (Col. 1¹⁷). With this cf. the words ascribed to Jesus in 17⁵. Philo does not teach the pre-existence of the Logos (see Introd., p. cxl); but a close parallel to Jn.'s doctrine is the claim of Wisdom (σοφία) in Prov. 8²³, κύριος . . . πρὸ τοῦ αἰῶνος ἐθεμελίωσέ με ἐν ἀρχῇ, πρὸ τοῦ τὴν γῆν ποιῆσαι. Jn. never employs the word σοφία (or σόφος), while he uses λόγος of the Personal Christ only here and at v. 14; but it is the Hebrew doctrine of the Divine Word going forth (λόγος προφορικός) rather than the Greek doctrine of immanent Divine Reason (λόγος ἐνδιάθετος) which governs his thought of the relation of the Son to the Father.

λόγος is apparently used of the Personal Christ at Heb. 4¹² (this difficulty need not be examined here); as we hold it to be in 1 Jn. 1¹, ὃ ἦν ἀπ' ἀρχῆς ὃ ἀκηκόαμεν . . . περὶ τοῦ λόγου τῆς ζωῆς (see for ἀπ' ἀρχῆς on 15²⁷ below, and cf. Introd., p. lxi).

καὶ ὁ λόγος ἦν πρὸς τὸν θεόν. εἶναι πρός τινα is not a classical constr., and the meaning of πρός here is not quite certain. It is generally rendered apud, as at Mk. 6³ 9¹⁹ 14⁴⁹, Lk. 9⁴¹; but Abbott (Diat. 2366) urges that πρὸς τὸν θεόν carries the sense of " having regard to God," " looking toward God " (cf. 5¹⁹). This sense of direction may be implied in 1 Jn. 2¹ παράκλητον ἔχομεν πρὸς τὸν πατέρα, but less probably in 1 Jn. 1², τὴν ζωὴν τὴν αἰώνιον ἥτις ἦν πρὸς τὸν πατέρα, which provides a close parallel to the present passage. In Prov. 8³⁰, Wisdom says of her relation to God, ἤμην παρ' αὐτῷ: and in like manner at Jn. 17⁵, Jesus speaks of His pre-incarnate glory as being παρὰ σοί. It is improbable that Jn. meant to distinguish the meanings of παρὰ σοί at 17⁵ and of πρὸς τὸν θεόν at 1¹. We cannot get a better rendering here than " the Word was with God."

The imperfect ἦν is used in all three clauses of this verse, and is expressive in each case of continuous timeless existence.

καὶ θεὸς ἦν ὁ λόγος, " the Word was God " (the constr. being similar to πνεῦμα ὁ θεός of 4²⁴). θεός is the predicate, and is anarthrous, as at Rom. 9⁵, ὁ ὢν ἐπὶ πάντων θεός. L reads ὁ θεός, but this would identify the Logos with the totality of divine existence, and would contradict the preceding clause.

This, the third clause of the majestic proclamation with which the Gospel opens, asserts uncompromisingly the Divinity of the Logos, His Pre-existence and Personality having been first stated; cf. 10³⁰ 20²⁸, and Phil. 2⁶

2. οὗτος ἦν ἐν ἀρχῇ πρὸς τὸν Θεόν.

3. πάντα δι' αὐτοῦ ἐγένετο,
   καὶ χωρὶς αὐτοῦ ἐγένετο οὐδὲ ἕν.

2. This verse reiterates, after a fashion which we shall find Jn. to favour, what has been said already in v. 1, laying stress, however, upon the fact that the relationship with Deity implied in πρὸς τὸν θεόν was eternal; it, too, was " in the beginning." That is to say, v. 2 is a summary statement of the three propositions laid down in v. 1, all of which were true ἐν ἀρχῇ. For the emphatic use of οὗτος, cf. 1¹⁵ 6⁴⁶ 7¹⁸ 15⁵.

The Creative Word (v. 3)

3. πάντα (all things severally, as distinct from ὁ κόσμος, the totality of the universe, v. 10) δι' αὐτοῦ ἐγένετο, " all things came into being (for creation is a *becoming*, as contrasted with the essential *being* of the Word) through Him."

In the Hebrew story of creation, each successive stage is introduced by " And God said " (Gen. 1³). The Psalmist personifies in poetical fashion this creative word: " By the word of Yahweh were the heavens made " (Ps. 33⁶; cf. Ps. 147¹⁵, Isa. 55¹¹). In later Judaism, this doctrine was consolidated into prose; cf., *e.g.*, " Thou saidst, Let heaven and earth be made, and Thy Word perfected the work " (2 Esd. 6³⁸; cf. Wisd. 9¹). This was a Jewish belief which Philo developed in his own way and with much variety of application, sometimes inclining to the view that the λόγος was a mere passive instrument employed by God, at other times, under Greek influence, regarding it as the cosmic principle, the formative thought of God.[1]

3, 4. καὶ χωρὶς αὐτοῦ ἐγένετο οὐδὲ ἕν. This expresses negatively what has been said positively in the previous line, a common construction in Hebrew poetry (cf. Ps. 18³⁶, ³⁷ 39⁹, etc). Jn. uses this device several times (*e.g.* 1²⁰ 3¹⁶ 6⁵⁰, 1 Jn. 1⁵ 2⁴). " Apart from Him nothing came into being." The sentence excludes two false beliefs, both of which had currency, especially in Gnostic circles: (*a*) that matter is eternal, and (*b*) that angels or æons had a share in the work of creation.

The interpretation of this passage during the first four centuries implies a period or full-stop at ἕν, whereas since Chrysostom the sentence has been generally taken as ending with ὃ γέγονεν : " apart from Him nothing came into being that did come into being." ὃ γέγονεν, if we adopt the later view of the constr., is redundant and adds nothing to the sense.

[1] See Introd., p. cxl.

4. ὃ γέγονεν ἐν αὐτῷ ζωὴ ἦν,

But this kind of emphatic explicitness is quite in accordance with the style of Jn. It is also the case that Jn. favours ἐν with a dative at the beginning of a sentence, e.g. 13³⁵ 15⁸ 16²⁶, 1 Jn. 2⁴ 3¹⁰·¹⁶·¹⁹ 4², so that to begin with ἐν αὐτῷ in v. 4 would be in his manner.

The early uncials, for the most part, have no punctuation, while the later manuscripts generally put the point after γέγονεν. But the evidence of MSS. as to punctuation depends upon the interpretations of the text with which scribes were familiar, and has no independent authority. In the present passage the Old Syriac,[1] Latin, and Sahidic versions, as well as the Latin Vulgate, decidedly favour the placing of the point after ἔν, the O.L. *b* putting this beyond doubt by inserting *autem* in the next clause : " quod autem factum est, in eo uita est." The interpretation which places the point after ἔν was adopted by Catholics and Gnostics alike in the early centuries; cf. Irenæus (*Hær.* II. ii. 4, III. viii. 3), Hippolytus (*c. Noetum*, 12), Origen (*in Ioann.* 36, etc.), Clem. Alex. (*Pæd.* i. 11, *Strom.* vi. 11), and, apparently, Tertullian (*adv. Prax.* 21). It is difficult to resist their witness to the construction of the Greek, provided that the next sentence as read by them yields an intelligible meaning.

Harris [2] defends the construction " without Him was not anything made that was made," by citing a passage from the Stoic Chrysippus which is alike redundant in form: Fate is " the λόγος according to which all things that have been made have been made, and all things that are being made are being made, and all things that are to be made will be made."

The Word issuing in Life and Light (vv. 4, 5)

4. ὃ γέγονεν ἐν αὐτῷ ζωὴ ἦν, " That which has come into being was, in Him, Life," *i.e.* the life which was eternally in the Word, when it goes forth, issues in created life, and this is true both of (*a*) the *physical* and (*b*) the *spiritual* world. (*a*) Jesus Christ, the Son and the Word, is the *Life* (11²⁵ 14⁶), the Living One (ὁ ζῶν, Rev. 1¹⁷); and it is through this Life of His that all created things hold together and cohere (τὰ πάντα ἐν αὐτῷ συνέστηκεν, Col. 1¹⁷). (*b*) In the spiritual order, this is also true. The Son having life in Himself (5²⁶) gives life to whomsoever he wishes (οὓς θέλει ζωοποιεῖ, 5²¹). Cf. 1 Jn. 5¹¹, and

---

[1] Also the Peshitta ; see Burkitt, *J.T.S.*, April 1903, p. 436.
[2] " Stoic Origins of St. John's Gospel," in *Bulletin of John Rylands Library*, Jan. 1922, quoting Stobæus, *Phys.* 180.

καὶ ἡ ζωὴ ἦν τὸ φῶς τῶν ἀνθρώπων·

5. καὶ τὸ φῶς ἐν τῇ σκοτίᾳ φαίνει,
καὶ ἡ σκοτία αὐτὸ οὐ κατέλαβεν.

see on 17²⁴. The children of God are those who are quickened by a spiritual begetting (see on v. 13). See also on 6³³. If ἐν αὐτῷ is the true reading at 3¹⁵ (where see note), we have another instance there of ἐν αὐτῷ being awkwardly placed in the sentence.

Presumably because of this awkward position of ἐν αὐτῷ, some Western authorities אD, many Old Latin texts, and the Old Syriac, replace ἦν by ἐστίν ; interpreting, as it seems, the sentence to mean " that which has come into being in Him *is* life." But this reading and rendering may safely be set aside as due to misapprehension of the meaning.

καὶ ἡ ζωὴ ἦν τὸ φῶς τῶν ἀνθρώπων. The first movement of the Divine Word at the beginning was the creation of Light (Gen. 1³). This was the first manifestation of Life in the κόσμος, and the Psalmist speaks of the Divine Life and the Divine Light in the same breath: " With Thee is the fountain of life, and in Thy light shall we see light" (Ps. 36⁹). God is *Light* (1 Jn. 1⁵) as well as *Life*, if indeed there is any ultimate difference between these two forms of energy (see on 8¹²).

In this verse, Jn. does not dwell on the thought of the Word's Life as the Light of the κόσμος, but passes at once to the spiritual creation; the Life of the Word was, at the beginning, the Light of *men*. Cf. 12⁴⁶ 9⁵, and see especially on 8¹² for the Hebrew origins and development of this thought, which reaches its fullest expression in the majestic claim ἐγώ εἰμι τὸ φῶς τοῦ κόσμου (8¹²).

Philo speaks of the sun as a παραδεῖγμα of the Divine Word (*de somn.* i. 15); but he does not, so far as I have noticed, connect *life* and *light* explicitly.

5. τὸ φῶς ἐν τῇ σκοτίᾳ φαίνει. The guiding thought is still the story of the creation of light, which dissipated the darkness of chaos. But this is a story which ever repeats itself in the spiritual world; Jn. does not say " the Light *shone*," but " the Light *shines*." In 1 Jn. 2⁸ he applies the thought directly to the passing of spiritual darkness because of the shining of Christ, the true light (ἡ σκοτία παράγεται καὶ τὸ φῶς τὸ ἀληθινὸν ἤδη φαίνει).

καὶ ἡ σκοτία αὐτὸ οὐ κατέλαβεν. καταλαμβάνειν generally means to " seize " or " apprehend," whether physically (Num. 21³², Mk. 9¹⁸, [Jn.] 8⁴), or intellectually (Acts 10³⁴ 25²⁵, Eph. 3¹⁸, etc.). Thus we may translate " the darkness apprehended it not," *i.e.* did not understand or appreciate it; and so

the vulg. has *tenebrae eam non comprehenderunt*, the note of
tragedy being struck at once, which appears again, vv. 10, 11
(where, however, the verb is παραλαμβάνειν); see on 3¹⁹.
But καταλαμβάνειν often means also to "overtake"
(Gen. 31²³, Ex. 15⁹, Ecclus. 11¹⁰, 1 Thess. 5⁴); Moulton-
Milligan illustrate from the papyri this use of the verb, viz. of
evil "overtaking" one. This is its meaning in the only other
place where it occurs in Jn., viz. 12³⁵, ἵνα μὴ σκοτία ὑμᾶς
καταλάβῃ, "lest darkness overtake you."¹ Origen (with other
Greek interpreters) takes κατέλαβεν in this sense here, explaining that the thought is of darkness perpetually pursuing
light, and never overtaking it.² The meaning "overtake in
pursuit" readily passes into "overcome"; *e.g.* 2 Macc. 8¹⁸,
where it is said that God is able "to overcome those who come
upon us" (τοὺς ἐρχομένους ἐφ᾽ ἡμᾶς . . . καταλαβεῖν). A classical parallel is cited by Field from Herod. i. 87, ὡς ὥρα πάντα
μὲν ἄνδρα σβεννύντα τὸ πῦρ, δυναμένους δε οὐκέτι καταλαβεῖν, *i.e.*
"when he saw . . . that they were unable to *overcome* the fire."
That this is the meaning of the verb in the present verse is
supported by the fact that the thought of Christ's rejection does
not appear, and could not fitly appear, until after the statement
of His historical "coming into the world" (vv. 9, 10). We
have not yet come to this, and it is the spiritual interpretation of
the Creation narrative that is still in view. Thus in the Hymn
of Wisdom (Wis. 7²⁹) we have : "Night succeeds the Light,
but evil does not overcome wisdom" (σοφίας δὲ οὐκ ἀντισχύει
κακία). The darkness did not overcome the light at the
beginning, and the light still shines. This is not the note of
tragedy, but the note of triumph. Good always conquers evil.
"The darkness did not overcome the light" (so R.V. *marg.*).

Philo's commentary on Gen. 1³ is in agreement with this
interpretation. He says that τὸ νοητὸν φῶς is the image of
θεῖος λόγος, which is the image of God. This may be called
παναύγεια, "universal brightness" (cf. 8¹²). On the first day
of creation this light dispelled the darkness : ἐπειδὴ δὲ φῶς μὲν
ἐγένετο, σκότος δὲ ὑπεξέστη καὶ ὑπεχώρησεν,³ *i.e.* "darkness
yielded to it and retreated." Jn. applies this thought to Christ
as the Light of the world. There is never an eclipse of this
Sun.

C. J. Ball suggested ⁴ that behind κατέλαβεν lies a confusion
of two Aramaic verbs, קַבֵּל, "take, receive," and אַקְבֵּיל,
"darken." He holds that, both here and at 12³⁵, the original

¹ See also the reading of אD at 6¹⁷ and the note there.
² *In Ioann.* 76 ; cf. also Brooke's edition, ii. 214.
³ *de opif. mundi*, 9.
⁴ Quoted by Burney, *Aramaic Origin, etc.*, p. 30.

6. Ἐγένετο ἄνθρωπος ἀπεσταλμένος παρὰ Θεοῦ, ὄνομα αὐτῷ

Aramaic (which he finds behind the Greek) was לָא אקבליה, "obscured it not," and that this was misread לָא קבליה, "received it not."[1] This is ingenious, but, as we have seen, κατέλαβεν is good Greek for "overcome," so that there is no need to suppose any corruption of the original text.

Explanatory Comment: John the Baptist was not the Light
(vv. 6–9)

A feature of the style of Jn. is his habit of pausing to comment on words which he has recorded (cf. Introd., p. xxiv). Here we have a parenthetical note to explain that the Light of which the Logos hymn sings is not John the Baptist. It has been suggested that this was inserted as necessary to combat the pretensions of some Christians who exalted the Baptist unduly (cf. Acts 18²⁵ 19³ᶠ·); but see on v. 20 below.

For Jn., as for Mk., the "gospel of Jesus Christ, the Son of God" (Mk. 1¹), began with the preaching of the Baptist. Jn. does not stay to record stories of the Birth of Jesus, as Lk. and Mt. do. He opens his Gospel with a mystical hymn about the Logos, which reminds the reader that the true beginnings of the wonderful life are lost in the timeless and eternal Life of God. But in the Gospel Jn. is to describe the historical manifestation of the Word, and this was prepared for, and introduced by, the preaching of the Baptist. Upon this Jn. dwells more fully than any other evangelist, probably because his informant, the aged son of Zebedee, was himself one of the Baptist's disciples. For the use made by Jn. of Mk., see Introd., pp. xcvi, c; and the correspondences between Mk. 1 and Jn. 1 in regard to what they tell about the Baptist and his sayings are remarkable.

Mk. 1² introduces the Baptist by quoting Mal. 3¹, "I send my messenger before my face"; Jn. introduces him as a man "sent from God." Both Mk. 1² and Jn. 1²³ apply to him the prophecy of Isa. 40³. Mk. 1⁷ gives two utterances of the Baptist about Christ which reappear Jn. 1¹⁵· ²⁷· ³⁰. Mk. 1⁸ and Jn. 1²⁶ both report the emphasis laid by the Baptist on his baptism being *with water*. And the allusions to the baptism of Jesus in Jn. 1³³· ³⁴ are reminiscent of Mk. 1¹⁰· ¹¹.

6. ἐγένετο ἄνθρωπος κτλ. ("There arose a man," etc.). There is no introductory particle connecting this with v. 5. It is a sentence quite distinct from the verse of the Logos Hymn which goes before.

[1] Cf. F. C. Burkitt in *Theology*, July 1922, p. 49, for a criticism of Ball's emendation.

Ἰωάνης· 7. οὗτος ἦλθεν εἰς μαρτυρίαν, ἵνα μαρτυρήσῃ περὶ τοῦ

ἀπεσταλμένος παρὰ θεοῦ. The Baptist made this claim for himself (3²⁸); cf. Mal. 3¹. Cf. 9¹⁶· ³³ for a similar use of παρὰ θεοῦ, and see on 6⁴⁵.

ὄνομα αὐτῷ Ἰωάνης. For the constr. cf. 3¹ and Rev. 6⁸ 9¹¹. Burney urges that this is a Semitic constr.,[1] and represents an Aramaic or Hebrew שמו ; but it is also good Greek, e.g. Ἀριστοφῶν ὄνομα αὐτῷ (Demosth. contra Zenoth. 11).

The spelling Ἰωάνης is preferred to Ἰωάννης by most modern editors, being almost universally found in B. "It belongs to the series of Hellenised names which treat the an of the Hebrew termination (Ioanan) as a variable inflection" (Blass, Gram. 11).[2]

Jn. is prone to distinguish carefully people who have the same name, e.g. Judas (6⁷¹ 13² 14²²), Mary (11² 19²⁵), Joseph (19³⁸); in this being more scrupulous than the Synoptists. It is, perhaps, worthy of note, therefore, that Jn. never writes "John the Baptist," but always "John," as if there were no other John who could be confused with him. On this has been based an argument to prove that John the son of Zebedee is, in some sense, the author (if not the actual scribe) of the Fourth Gospel; for the one person to whom it would not occur to distinguish John the Baptist from John the son of Zebedee would be John the son of Zebedee himself. On the other hand, the Synoptists only occasionally give the full description "John the Baptist," "John" being quite sufficient in most places where the name occurs. It would not be as necessary for an evangelist writing for Christian readers at the end of the first century to say explicitly "John the Baptist," when introducing the John who bore witness to Jesus at the beginning of His ministry, as it was for Josephus when writing for Roman readers to distinguish him as "John who is called the Baptist" (Antt. XVIII. v. 2).

7. οὗτος ἦλθεν εἰς μαρτυρίαν. This was the characteristic feature of the Baptist's mission, "to bear witness" to the claims of Him who was to come. The Fourth Gospel is full of the idea of "witness" (see Introd., p. xc), the words μαρτυρία, μαρτυρεῖν, being frequent in Jn., while they occur comparatively seldom in the rest of the N.T. The cognate forms μαρτύς, μαρτύριον, are, on the other hand, not found in Jn., although they occur in the Apocalypse.

ἵνα μαρτυρήσῃ. ἵνα with a finite verb, in a telic sense, where in classical Greek we should expect an infinitive, is a

---

[1] Aramaic Origin, etc., p. 31.
[2] Cf. Westcott-Hort, Appx., p. 59, and E.B. 2504.

φωτός, ἵνα πάντες πιστεύσωσιν δι' αὐτοῦ. 8. οὐκ ἦν ἐκεῖνος τὸ φῶς, ἀλλ' ἵνα μαρτυρήσῃ περὶ τοῦ φωτός. 9. ἦν τὸ φῶς τὸ ἀληθινὸν ὃ common constr. in κοινή Greek, and is specially frequent in Jn.[1] Burney[2] held that this linguistic feature is due to the Aramaic origin of Jn., and that behind ἵνα is the particle ךְ or דִי. But the colloquial character of Jn.'s style provides a sufficient explanation (cf. 11[50] and 18[14]).

περὶ τοῦ φωτός. John Baptist says (v. 33) that it was revealed to him that Jesus was the Coming One.

ἵνα πάντες πιστεύσωσιν δι' αὐτοῦ ("that all might believe through him," i.e. through, or by means of, the testimony of John the Baptist). Ultimately the Baptist's mission would affect not Israel only, but all men (πάντες). As the Divine Law is said to have come διὰ Μωυσέως (v. 17), so there is a sense in which Christian faith came δι' Ἰωάνου. Abbott (Diat. 2302 f.) inclines to the view that αὐτοῦ refers here to Christ, αὐτός throughout the Prologue being used for the Word ; but Jn. never uses the expression πιστεύειν διὰ Ἰησοῦ (see on 3[15]). Jesus, for him, is the end and object of faith, rather than the medium through which it is reached (see on 1[12]).

Jn. uses the verb πιστεύειν about 100 times, that is, with nine times the frequency with which it is used by the Synoptists, although the noun πίστις, common in the Synoptists, never occurs in Jn., except at 1 Jn. 5[4].[3]   See further on v. 12.

Here πιστεύειν is used absolutely, the object of faith being understood without being expressed; cf. 1[50] 4[42. 53] 5[44] 6[64] 11[15] 12[39] 14[29] 19[35] 20[8. 25].

8. ἐκεῖνος is used substantially, whether as subject or obliquely, with unusual frequency in Jn., the figures for its occurrence is the four Gospels being (according to Burney[4]) Mt. 4, Mk. 3, Lk. 4, Jn. 51. Jn. uses it often to express emphasis, or to mark out clearly the person who is the main subject of the sentence, as here.   It is used of Christ, 1[18] 2[21] 5[11], 1 Jn. 2[6] 3[5. 7. 16].

οὐκ ἦν ἐκεῖνος τὸ φῶς. The Baptist was only ὁ λύχνος, the lamp; cf. 5[35].

ἀλλ' ἵνα μαρτυρήσῃ περὶ τοῦ φωτός. This is an elliptical constr. of which somewhat similar examples occur 9[3] 13[18] 15[25], 1 Jn. 2[19] (Abbott, Diat. 2106 f.).   The meaning is, " but he

---

[1] Cf. Abbott, Diat. 2093, 2687.

[2] Aramaic Origin, etc., p. 70.

[3] Per contra, πιστεύειν never occurs in the Apocalypse, while πίστις occurs 4 times.   See Introd., p. lxv.

[4] Aramaic Origin, etc., p. 82.

came that he might bear witness, etc. The repetition of the whole phrase ἵνα μαρτυρήσῃ περὶ τοῦ φωτός is thoroughly Johannine.

Burney suggests [1] that here (as also at 5⁷ 6⁵⁰ 9³⁶ 14¹⁶) ἵνα is a mistranslation of an Aramaic relative, ךְּ, "who." The rendering then is simple, "he was not the Light, but one who was to bear witness of the Light"; but the correction is unnecessary.

9. ἦν τὸ φῶς κτλ. The constr. of the sentence has been taken in different ways, and the ambiguity was noticed as far back as the time of Origen.[2]

(1) The Latin, Syriac, and Coptic versions take ἐρχόμενον with ἄνθρωπον. The Light enlightens every man who comes into the world. But if this were the meaning, (*a*) we should expect παντὰ τὸν ἐρχόμενον rather than παντὰ ἄνθρωπον ἐρχόμενον; (*b*) these words are wholly redundant, for they do not add anything to "every man"; (*c*) the expression "coming into the world" is not used elsewhere by Jn.[3] of a *man* being born (16²¹ is no exception). This last consideration excludes also the rendering "every man, *as* he comes into the world," apart from the fact that, although Wordsworth suggests it in his *Ode*, the idea of any special Divine enlightenment of infants is not Scriptural.

(2) It is better to take ἐρχόμενον with φῶς (so R.V.). Jn. several times uses the phrase "coming into the world" of the Advent of Christ (6¹⁴ 11²⁷ 16²⁸ 18³⁷); and elsewhere (3¹⁹, 12⁴⁶) in the Gospel Christ is spoken of as "light coming into the world." And if we render "the Light, which lighteth every man, was coming into the world," the constr. of ἦν with the present participle as used for the imperfect is one which appears frequently in Jn. (see on 1²⁸ below). ἦν . . . ἐρχόμενον means "was in the act of coming."

Westcott, while retaining this meaning, endeavours to combine with it the conception of the Light having a permanent existence (ἦν, the verb used in v. 1). "There was the Light, the true Light which lighteth every man; that Light was, and yet more, that Light was coming into the world." This seems, however, to attempt to get too much out of the words, and on our view of the whole passage the meaning is simpler.

We are still occupied with Jn.'s comment (vv. 6–9) on what the Logos Hymn has said about the Light (vv. 4, 5). The Baptist was not the perfect Light, but he came to bear witness to it; and this perfect Light was then coming into the world.

---

[1] *Aramaic Origin, etc.*, pp. 32, 75.   [2] *In Ioann.* (ed. Brooke, ii. 216).
[3] It is found, however, several times in the Talmud; see Lightfoot, *Hor. Hebr.*, in loc.; and cf. Schlatter, *Sprache u. Heimat.*, *u.s.w.*, p. 18.

φωτίζει παντὰ ἄνθρωπον ἐρχόμενον εἰς τὸν κόσμον.

When Jn. wrote the First Epistle he could say, " The true Light already shineth " (1 Jn. 2⁸), but it was only coming at the time when the Baptist's mission began. Jesus had come into the world, indeed; but He had not yet manifested Himself as the Light. ἀληθινόν. Christ is τὸ φῶς τὸ ἀληθινόν, not to be interpreted as " the *true* Light " (although such a rendering is convenient), for that suggests that all other lights are misleading, which is not implied; cf. 5³⁵. ἀληθινός is distinguished from ἀληθής as the *genuine* from the *true*. The opposite of ἀληθινός is not necessarily false, but it is imperfect, shadowy, or unsubstantial. " The ἀληθής fulfils the promise of his lips, but the ἀληθινός the wider promise of his name. Whatever that name imports, taken in its highest, deepest, widest sense, whatever according to that he ought to be, *that* he is to the full " (Trench, *Synonyms of N.T.*). Thus ἀληθινός here is significant. Christ is not " the true *and only* Light," but rather " the *perfect* Light," in whose radiance all other lights seem dim, the Sun among the stars which catch their light from Him.

There are indeed a few passages where ἀληθινός cannot be sharply distinguished from ἀληθής : thus ἀληθινός at 19³⁵ stands for the veracity of the witness, just as ἀληθής does at 21²⁴. Moreover, the fact that ἀληθής and its cognates are not found in the Apocalypse, while ἀληθινός occurs in it 10 times, might suggest that the choice of the one adjective rather than the other was only a point of style. In the same way, ψεύστης is used 7 times in Jn. for a *liar*, but the word in the Apocalypse is ψευδής.

Nevertheless the distinction between ἀληθής and ἀληθινός in Jn. is generally well marked. We have τὸ φῶς τὸ ἀληθινόν here (cf. 1 Jn. 2⁸); οἱ ἀληθινοὶ προσκυνηταί, 4²³ ; ὁ ἄρτος ὁ ἀληθινός, 6³² ; ὁ μόνος ἀληθινὸς θεός, 17³ (cf. 7²⁸ 1 Jn. 5²⁰); ἡ ἀληθινὴ κρίσις, 8¹⁶ ; ἡ ἄμπελος ἡ ἀληθινή, 15¹. In all these passages the meaning " genuine " or " ideal " will bear to be pressed, as also in the only place where the word occurs in the Synoptists, for τὸ ἀληθινόν of Lk. 16¹¹ is the *genuine* riches. Even at 4³⁷, where ἀληθινός is applied to a proverb, something more is implied than veraciousness (see note *in loc.*).

Less clearly, but still with some plausibility, can the distinctive sense of ἀληθινός be pressed in the Apocalypse, where it is applied to God's ways (15³), His judgments (16⁷ 19²), His words (19⁹ 21⁵ 22⁶), to Himself (6¹⁰), and to Christ (3⁷· ¹⁴ 19¹¹). See further on 17³.

φωτίζει. This verb does not occur again in Jn., but cf. Lk. 11³⁵· ³⁶.

ὁ φωτίζει παντὰ ἄνθρωπον. That the Servant of Yahweh would be a "light to the Gentiles" as well as to the Jews was the forecast of Deutero-Isaiah (42⁶ 49⁶); but this passage suggests a larger hope, for the Coming Light was to enlighten *every* man. It was this great conception upon which the early Quakers fixed, urging that to every man sufficient light was offered; and some of them called this passage "the Quaker's text." The Alexandrian theologians, *e.g.* Clement, had much to say about the active operation of the Pre-Incarnate Word upon men's hearts; and it is interesting to observe that they did not appeal to this text, which is in fact not relevant to their thought, as it speaks only of the universal enlightenment which was shed upon mankind *after* the Advent of Christ.

εἰς τὸν κόσμον. The term κόσμος is used of the universe by Plato (*Gorg.* 508) and Aristotle (*de mund.* 2), Plutarch (*Mor.* 886 B) affirming that Pythagoras was the first to use the word thus, the order of the material world suggesting it.[1] This idea of a totality of the natural order is thoroughly Greek, and is without early Hebrew counterpart, עוֹלָם not being used in this meaning until the later days of Jewish literature.[2] In the LXX κόσμος appears in the sense of "ornament," and occasionally to describe the ordered host of the heavenly bodies, but it is not used for "universe" until we reach the later Hellenistic books, *e.g.* Wisd. 11¹⁷. Paul has κόσμος 46 times, and the Synoptists 14 times ; but Jn. has it 100 times. Primarily, in the N.T. it is used of the material universe as distinct from God (cf. 21²⁵). But man is the chief inhabitant of the world as we know it, and thus κόσμος usually in Jn. includes the world of moral agents as well as the sum of physical forces. That is, it stands for mankind at large, as well as for the earth which is man's habitation (6⁵¹ 7⁴ 12¹⁹).

When, however, a term which was the product of Greek philosophy began to be used in connexion with the Hebrew doctrine of God and man, it inevitably gathered to itself the associations connected with Hebrew belief as to the Fall. To the Stoic, the κόσμος was perfect. This could not be held by a Jew. Inasmuch, then, as the Fall introduced disorder into that which in the beginning was "good" (Gen. 1³¹), the term κόσμος when used of the visible order frequently carries with it a suggestion of imperfection, of evil, of estrangement from the Divine. The κόσμος cannot receive the Spirit of Truth (14¹⁷); it hates Christ (7⁷); it hates His chosen (15¹⁹ 17¹⁴); they are forbidden to love it (1 Jn. 2¹⁵). The world which is aloof from

---

[1] Cf. Trench, *Synonyms of N.T.*
[2] Dalman, *Words of Jesus*, pp. 162, 171.

10. ἐν τῷ κόσμῳ ἦν,
καὶ ὁ κόσμος δι' αὐτοῦ ἐγένετο,
καὶ ὁ κόσμος αὐτὸν οὐκ ἔγνω.

God may easily pass into an attitude of hostility to God, and the phrase " this world " (see on 8²³) calls special attention to such enmity. According to Philo (*quod deus imm.* 6 and *de mund* 7), the κόσμος is the father of time, God being the Father of the κόσμος; a picturesque expression which brings out his view that the universe was created by God, who brought Cosmos out of Chaos, while its genesis goes back beyond the beginning of time.

A striking parallel to this verse is found in the *Testaments of the Twelve Patriarchs* (Levi, c. 14): τὸ φῶς τοῦ νόμου τὸ δοθὲν ἐν ὑμῖν εἰς φωτισμὸν πάντος ἀνθρώπου.   Charles, indeed (note *in loc*), holds that Jn. 1⁹ is *based* on this passage; but the date of the Greek versions of the *Testaments* is by no means certain, and there is no sufficient evidence of their existence in their present form before the time of Origen.[1]

There are unmistakable allusions to the verse in the Christian Apocalypse known as " The Rest of the Words of Baruch," where Jeremiah addresses God as τὸ φῶς τὸ ἀληθινὸν τὸ φωτίζον με (ix. 3).   In the same section the writer calls Christ τὸ φῶς τῶν αἰώνων πάντων, ὁ ἄσβεστος λύχνος (ix. 13), and speaks of Him as ἐρχόμενον εἰς τὸν κόσμον ἐπὶ τὸ ὄρος τῶν ἐλαιῶν (ix. 18). See Introd., p. lxxii.

For the citation of the verse by Basilides, as quoted by Hippolytus, see Introd., p. lxxiii.

The Logos Hymn resumed (vv. 10, 11)

10. ἐν τῷ κόσμῳ ἦν. ἦν, as in vv. 1–4, stands for continuous existence.   The Logos was immanent in the world before the Incarnation, which has not yet been mentioned in the hymn, although suggested in the evangelist's comment in v. 9.

καὶ ὁ κόσμος δι' αὐτοῦ ἐγένετο, repeated from v. 3, " the world came into being through Him," the creative Logos being personal all through the hymn.

καὶ ὁ κόσμος αὐτὸν οὐκ ἔγνω.   The paratactical constr. καὶ . . . καί is continued, as in vv. 1, 4, 5.   At this point καί is used adversatively, " and yet," the world not recognising the Word although the Word was immanent in it.

This use of καί for καίτοι (which Jn. never employs) is

---

[1] Cf. Burkitt, *J.T.S.*, Oct. 1908 ; Plummer, *Comm. on St. Matthew*, p. xxxiv. f.

11. εἰς τὰ ἴδια ἦλθεν,

characteristic of the Fourth Gospel, *e.g.* 3[11] 5[43] 6[70] 7[28. 30] 8[21] 9[30] 10[25] 16[32]. Burney [1] claims this as a Semitic usage, but it occurs in classical Greek; *e.g.* Thucyd. v. 6. 1, Σταγείρῳ προσ-βάλλει . . . καὶ οὐκ εἷλε, and Eurip. *Herakl.* 508, ὁρᾶτ᾿ ἔμ᾿ ὅσπερ ἦν περίβλεπτος βροτοῖς ὀνομαστὰ πράσσων, καί μ᾿ ἀφείλεθ᾿ ἡ τύχη.

ὁ κόσμος αὐτὸν οὐκ ἔγνω. Primarily, the reference is to the world's ignorance of the Pre-Incarnate Logos, immanent continuously in nature and in man.

Pfleiderer points out the similarity of this language to what Heraclitus says about the eternal Reason: τοῦ δὲ λόγου τοῦδ᾿ ἐόντος αἰεὶ ἀξύνετοι γίνονται ἄνθρωποι . . . γινομένων γὰρ πάντων κατὰ τὸν λόγον τόνδε ἀπείροισιν ἐοίκασι, *i.e.* " men are without under-standing of this Logos, although it is eternal, . . . although everything happens in accordance with this Logos, men seem to be ignorant (of it)." [2] Heraclitus was one of those whom Justin accounted a Christian before his time, having lived μετὰ λόγου,[3] and his writings were probably current in the circles where the Fourth Gospel was written. But although Jn. used similar language to Heraclitus when writing of the Word, his thought goes far beyond the impersonal Reason of the Greek sage.

Even here, the meaning of " the world knew Him not " cannot be confined to the Immanent Logos. Jn. several times comes back to the phrase, applying it to the world's failure to recognise the Incarnate Christ; *e.g.* ὁ κόσμος . . . οὐκ ἔγνω αὐτόν (1 Jn. 3[1]); οὐκ ἔγνωσαν . . . ἐμέ (16[3]). Cf. 14[7] 17[25], 1 Cor. 1[21]. And in the next verse (v. 11) the Incarnate Word is clearly in view, for the aorist ἦλθεν expresses a definite point of time, although the Incarnation of the Word is not explicitly asserted until v. 14.

A saying about Wisdom very similar to the thought of this verse is in *Enoch* xlii. 1: " Wisdom found no place where she might dwell ; then a dwelling-place was assigned to her in the heavens. Wisdom came to make her dwelling among the children of men and found no dwelling-place; then Wisdom returned to her place and took her seat among the angels." What the Jewish apocalyptist says of *Wisdom*, the Prologue of the Fourth Gospel repeats of the Logos.

11. εἰς τὰ ἴδια ἦλθεν. This (see on 19[27]) is literally " He came to His own home." And the following words, " His own

---

[1] *Aramaic Origin, etc.*, p. 66.

[2] See Hippol. *Ref.* ix. 9, cited by Pfleiderer, *Primitive Christianity,* iv. 7.

[3] *Apol.* i. 46.

καὶ οἱ ἴδιοι αὐτὸν οὐ παρέλαβον.

12. ὅσοι δὲ ἔλαβον αὐτόν, ἔδωκεν αὐτοῖς ἐξουσίαν τέκνα Θεοῦ γενέ-

received Him not," would well describe His rejection by His own kinsfolk and neighbours in Galilee, according to the saying that a prophet has no honour in his own country (Mk. 6⁴, Mt. 13⁵⁷, Lk. 4²⁴; cf. Jn. 4⁴⁴). But the thought of this verse is larger. The world did not know Him, did not recognise Him for what He was (v. 10). But when He came in the flesh, He came (ἦλθεν) to "the holy land" (2 Macc. 1⁷, Wisd. 12³), to the land and the people which peculiarly belonged to Yahweh and were His own (Ex. 19⁵, Deut. 7⁶). In coming to Palestine, rather than to Greece, the Word of God came to His own home on earth. Israel were the chosen people; they formed, as it were, an inner circle in the world of men; they were, peculiarly, " His own." He was " not sent but to the lost sheep of the house of Israel " (Mt. 15²⁴). " His own " intimate disciples did indeed receive him (see 13¹ 17⁶· ⁹· ¹¹ for οἱ ἴδιοι), but the thought here is of His own people, Israel. The Fourth Gospel is the Gospel of the Rejection; and this appears thus early in the Prologue (cf. 3¹¹ 5⁴³).

It is not said that Israel did not " know " Him, as is said of the " world " (v. 10); but Israel did not receive Him in welcome (cf. 14³ for this shade of meaning in παραλαμβάνω). Like the Wicked Husbandmen in the parable (Mk. 12¹, Mt. 21³³, Lk. 20⁹), Israel knew the Heir and killed Him.

Comment to avoid misunderstanding of v. 11 (vv. 12, 13)

12. " His own received Him not " might suggest that *no* Jew welcomed Him for what He was. Accordingly (cf. Introd., p. cxlv), the evangelist notes that there were *some* of whom this could not be said. ὅσοι δέ κτλ.=*but* (δέ must be given its full adversative force), at the same time, as many as received Him (and this would include Jews as well as Greeks) were endowed with the capacity and privilege of becoming children of God. For λαμβάνειν used of " receiving " Christ, cf. 5⁴³ 13²⁰.

ὅσοι δὲ ἔλαβον αὐτόν, ἔδωκεν αὐτοῖς κτλ. This is the first appearance of a constr. which is very frequent in Jn., viz. the reinforcement of a *casus pendens* by a pronoun. It is a common, if inelegant, form of *anacoluthon*, more often met with in colloquial than in literary Greek. Jn. employs it 27 times (as against 21 occurrences in all three Synoptists). Burney suggests that this is due to the Aramaic original which he finds behind Jn., the *casus pendens* being a favourite Semitic idiom.[1]

The Jews rejected Christ; but His message was addressed to all mankind. He gave to " as many as received Him " the right to become children of God. ἐξουσία occurs again 5^{27} 10^{18} 17^2 $19^{10.\ 11}$; it stands for *authority* rather than *power*. The privilege and right of those who "receive" Christ, *i.e.* those who " believe on His Name," is that they may become τέκνα θεοῦ; but this (Jn. suggests) is not an inherent human capacity.

The conception of the faithful as " children of God " has its roots deep in Jewish thought. Israel conceived of herself as in covenant with Yahweh (see on 3^{29}), and the prophets speak of her as Yahweh's wife (Hos. 1, 2). " Thy sons whom thou hast borne to me " are words ascribed to Yahweh when addressing the nation (Ezek. 16^{20}). Thus the Jews were accustomed to think of themselves as peculiarly the children of God (see on 8^{41}). But the teaching of Jesus did not encourage any such exclusive claim of Judaism. He taught the doctrine of the Fatherhood of God as having a more catholic range. To enter the kingdom of God is to become the child of God and the possessor of eternal life (for all these phrases mean the same thing; cf. $3^{3f.}$), and the gate of the kingdom is the gate of faith in Christ. This is the message of the Fourth Gospel (20^{30}), and it is addressed to all who will hear it. We have here (in vv. 12, 13) a summary of the teaching of c. 3 about the New Birth and Eternal Life.

The phrase τέκνα θεοῦ is not placed either by Synoptists or by Jn. in the mouth of Jesus Himself: He is represented as speaking of υἱοὶ θεοῦ (Mt. 5^9); and this is also the title for believers generally used by Paul (Gal. 3^{26}), who employs the notion of *adoption*, as recognised by Roman law, to bring out the relation of God to the faithful.[2] But τέκνα θεοῦ is thoroughly Johannine (cf. 11^{52} and 1 Jn. $3^{1.\ 2.\ 10}$ 5^2), and the phrase implies a community of life between God the Father and His children, which is described in v. 13 as due to the fact that they are " begotten " of God (cf. $3^{3f.}$). τέκνον is from the root τεκ—, " to beget."

The " children of God " are all who " believe in the Name " of Christ. The idea of the Fatherhood of God as extending to all mankind alike, heathen or Jewish, *prior* to belief in Christ, is not explicit in the Gospels (cf. Acts 17^{28}), however close it may be to such a pronouncement as that of the Love of God for the world at large (3^{16}). But for Jn., the " children " are those who " believe."

---

[1] *Aramaic Origin, etc.*, p. 64.
[2] Paul has τέκνα θεοῦ at Rom. $8^{16.\ 17.\ 21}$, Phil. 2^{15} (from Deut. 32^5).

σθαι, τοῖς πιστεύουσιν εἰς τὸ ὄνομα αὐτοῦ, 13. οἳ οὐκ ἐξ αἱμάτων οὐδὲ ἐκ θελήματος σαρκὸς οὐδὲ ἐκ θελήματος ἀνδρὸς ἀλλ' ἐκ Θεοῦ ἐγεννήθησαν.

τοῖς πιστεύουσιν εἰς τὸ ὄνομα αὐτοῦ. The frequency of the verb πιστεύειν in Jn. has been already noted (1⁷). Here we have to mark the form πιστεύειν εἰς . . . The phrase "to believe in Christ," in Him as distinct from believing His words or being convinced of certain facts about Him, is, with one exception (Mt. 18⁶), not found in the Synoptists; but in Jn. we find πιστεύειν εἰς . . . 35 times,[1] always referring to God or Christ, except εἰς τὴν μαρτυρίαν (1 Jn. 5¹⁰). The phrase πιστεύειν εἰς τὸ ὄνομα αὐτοῦ occurs again 2²³, 3¹⁸ (cf. 1 Jn. 5¹³), but not in the speeches of Jesus Himself. In the O.T. the "Name" of Yahweh is often used as equivalent to His Character or Person, as He manifests Himself to men (cf. 2 Sam. 7¹³, Isa. 18⁷; see on 5⁴³ below). It is possible that this usage of ὄνομα in the N.T. is an Aramaism. We have it several times in the expression βαπτίζειν εἰς τὸ ὄνομά τινος (cf. Mt. 28¹⁹).[2] But, whether it is Aramaic or no, to believe in "the Name" of Jesus for Jn. is to believe "in Him" as the Son of God and the Christ.

13. For οἳ . . . ἐγεννήθησαν, the O.L. version in b gives qui natus est, the verse being thus a reference to the Virgin Birth of Christ. Irenæus (adv. Haer. III. xvii. 1 and xx. 2), and possibly Justin (Tryph. 61 ; cf. Apol. i. 32, 63 and ii. 6), bear witness to the existence of this (Western) reading. Tertullian (de carne Christi, 19) adopts it formally, adducing arguments against the common text "who were born," which he says is an invention of the Valentinians. In recent years the reference of the verse to Christ, and the reading qui natus est, have been approved by Resch (Aussercanonische Paralleltexte, iv. 57) and by Blass (Philology of the Gospels, p. 234).[3] But the MS. evidence is overwhelming for ἐγεννήθησαν, which moreover, as we shall see, is in accordance with the characteristic teaching of Jn.

The children of God are "begotten" by Him by spiritual generation, as contrasted with the ordinary process of physical generation.

---

[1] Note that πιστεύουσιν is the present participle, and expresses the continual life of faith, not an isolated act of faith (see on 6²⁹). See, further, for the unclassical constr. πιστεύειν εἰς, Abbott, Diat. 1470 f.

[2] I have discussed this expression in Studia Sacra, p. 66 f. A similar use of the construction εἰς τὸ ὄνομά τινος occurs in papyri; e.g. ἔντευξις εἰς τοῦ βασιλέως ὄνομα is a "petition to the king's majesty," the name of the king being the essence of what he is as ruler. Cf. Deissmann, Bible Studies, Eng. Tr., 146 f., 196 f.

[3] Cf. also Burney, Aramaic Origin, etc., p. 43.

οὐκ ἐξ αἱμάτων κτλ. It was a current doctrine in Greek physiology that the human embryo is made from the *seed* of the father, and the *blood* of the mother. Thus Wisd. 7², " In the womb of a mother was I moulded into flesh in the time of ten months, being compacted in blood (παγεὶς ἐν αἵματι) of the seed of man and pleasure that came with sleep." Cf. 4 Macc. 13²⁰ and Philo (*de opif. mundi* 45).[1]

The plural αἱμάτων is unexpected, but Brückner quoted the parallel ἄλλων τραφεὶς ἀφ' αἱμάτων (Eurip. *Ion*, 693). Augustine (*Serm.* cxxi. 4) explains αἱμάτων, " mixtis sanguinibus, masculi et feminae, commixtione carnis masculi et feminae," which may be right ; but more probably the plural is used to indicate drops of blood.

οὐδὲ ἐκ θελήματος σαρκός, " nor yet of the will of the flesh," *i.e.* of sexual desire. θέλημα is used once or twice in the LXX in the sense of *delectatio, e.g.* Isa. 62⁴ and Eccles. 12¹. Hippolytus (*Ref.* vi. 9) has the phrase ἐξ αἱμάτων καὶ ἐπιθυμίας σαρκικῆς, καθάπερ καὶ οἱ λοιποὶ, γεγεννημένος, which is apparently a reminiscence of this verse, of which at any rate it gives the meaning, identifying θέλημα with ἐπιθυμία (cf. 1 Jn. 2¹⁶).

The passage is also recalled by Justin (*Tryph.* 63), ὡς τοῦ αἵματος αὐτοῦ οὐκ ἐξ ἀνθρωπείου σπέρματος γεγεννημένου ἀλλ' ἐκ θελήματος θεοῦ.

οὐδὲ ἐκ θελήματος ἀνδρός, " nor yet of the will of a man," *i.e.* a *male*, for so ἀνήρ is always used in Jn., as distinct from ἄνθρωπος.

The threefold negation emphasises the point that the " begetting " of the children of God has nothing to do with the normal begetting of children.

ἀλλ' ἐκ θεοῦ (God being the immediate cause of the new spiritual life which begins in the believer). The metaphor of God as " begetting " children is strange to a modern ear, but it is frequent in Jn. Cf. also 1 Pet. 1³, ὁ . . . ἀναγεννήσας ἡμᾶς εἰς ἐλπίδα ζῶσαν, and see J. B. Mayor on Jas. 1¹⁸.

The verb γεννᾶν in the active voice generally means " to beget," and is used of the father, *e.g.* Ἀβραὰμ ἐγέννησε τὸν Ἰσαάκ (Mt. 1²). Sometimes this is followed by ἐκ and the mother's name, *e.g.* ἐγέννησα ἐξ αὐτῆς Τωβίαν (Tobit 1⁹).

γεννᾶν is also, but rarely, used of the " bearing " of children by a woman, *e.g.* μία μήτηρ ἐγέννησεν ἡμᾶς διδύμους (*Acta Philippi*, 115).

In Jn. the verb (with one exception, 1 Jn. 5¹) is only found in the passive γεννᾶσθαι. Sometimes this means " to be born," *e.g.* 9²ᶠ· 16²¹ 18³⁷; cf. Μαρίας, ἐξ ἧς ἐγεννήθη Ἰησοῦς (Mt. 1¹⁶).

---

[1] See H. J. Cadbury (*Expositor*, Dec. 1924, p. 432), to whom these references are due.

14. καὶ ὁ Λόγος σὰρξ ἐγένετο,

But usually in Jn. γεννᾶσθαι means "to be begotten," and the phrase "to be begotten by God" is thoroughly Johannine. Jn. does not shrink from drawing out the metaphor, e.g. πᾶς ὁ γεγεννημένος ἐκ τοῦ θεοῦ ἁμαρτίαν οὐ ποιεῖ, ὅτι σπέρμα αὐτοῦ ἐν αὐτῷ μένει (1 Jn. 3⁹). God's σπέρμα is in the man, who is thus (the phrase occurs in the next verse, 1 Jn. 3¹⁰) τέκνον θεοῦ. An even closer parallel to vv. 12, 13, is πᾶς ὁ πιστεύων ὅτι Ἰησοῦς ἐστιν ὁ Χριστὸς ἐκ τοῦ θεοῦ γεγέννηται (1 Jn. 5¹·⁴), where it is again said that those who believe in Christ are "begotten of God." Cf. also 1 Jn. 2²⁹ 4⁷ 5¹⁸. This mystical language goes back to Ps. 2⁷, where Yahweh says of the king of His favour, ἐγὼ σήμερον γεγέννηκά σε. Indeed, to say that believers are "begotten of God" is only to stretch a little farther the metaphor involved in the words, "Our Father which art in heaven." See on v. 12.

The rendering of ἐγεννήθησαν here by *nati sunt* in the Latin versions cannot be taken to exclude the translation "were begotten"; for in the several passages in 1 Jn. where we have the phrase γεγεννημένος ἐκ τοῦ θεοῦ (2²⁹ 3⁹ 4⁷ 5¹·¹⁸), and where it must bear the meaning "begotten by God" (see especially 1 Jn. 3⁹), the Latin versions similarly have *natus*.

The Incarnation (v. 14)

14 καὶ ὁ λόγος σὰρξ ἐγένετο. The repeated καὶ introducing the next three clauses should be noticed.

Here we have the climax of the Johannine doctrine of Christ as the Word. That the Son of God became man is unmistakably taught by Paul (Rom. 1³ 8³, Gal. 4⁴, Phil. 2⁷·⁸): He was "manifested in the flesh" (1 Tim. 3¹⁶). So, also, according to Heb. 2¹⁴, He partook of our flesh and blood. But the contribution of Jn. to this exalted Christology is that he expressly identifies Christ with the "Word of God," vaguely spoken of in the Wisdom literature of the Hebrews and also in the teaching of Philo and his Greek predecessors. The Logos of philosophy is, Jn. declares, the Jesus of history (cf. v. 11); and this is now stated in terms which cannot be misunderstood. That "the Word became flesh" must have seemed a paradox to many of those who read the Prologue to the Fourth Gospel when it was first made public; but the form of the proposition is deliberate. It would have been impossible for Philo (see Introd., p. cxli).

The heresy of Docetism was always present to the mind of Jn. (while it is most plainly in view in the First Epistle); the

καὶ ἐσκήνωσεν ἐν ἡμῖν,

idea of Christ as a mere phantasm, without human flesh and blood, was to him destructive of the Gospel. " Every spirit that confesseth that Jesus Christ is come in the flesh is of God " (1 Jn. 4²). But it is the deceiver and the antichrist who " confess not that He is come in the flesh " (2 Jn.⁷). The lofty teaching of the Prologue identifies Jesus with the Word, and the explicit declaration that *the Word became flesh* was necessary to exclude Docetic teaching.[1] A characteristic feature of the Fourth Gospel is its frequent insistence on the true humanity of Jesus. He is represented as tired and thirsty (4⁶·⁷; cf. 19²⁸). His emotion of spirit is expressed in His voice (see on 11³³). He wept (11³⁵). His spirit was troubled in the anticipation of His Passion (12²⁷ 13²¹). And the emphasis laid by Jn. on His " flesh " and " blood " (6⁵³), as well as on the " blood and water " of the Crucifixion scene, shows that Jn. writes thus of set purpose. Cf. also 20²⁷. At one point (8⁴⁰) Jn. attributes to Jesus the use of the word ἄνθρωπος as applied to Himself.

ὁ λόγος σὰρξ ἐγένετο. Here σάρξ signifies man's nature as a whole, including his rational soul (cf. 1 Thess. 5²³). Thus the rendering here in the Old Syriac (although not in the Peshitta) of σάρξ by *pagar*,[2] *sc.* " the Word became a body "— a rendering known to Ephraim [3] and Aphrahat [4]—is inadequate and might mislead. The Logos did not became " *a* man," but He became " man " in the fullest sense; the Divine Person assuming human nature in its completeness. To explain the exact significance of ἐγένετο in this sentence is beyond the powers of any interpreter.

καὶ ἐσκήνωσεν ἐν ἡμῖν. This sentence has generally in modern times been understood to mean " and He pitched His tent among us," or *dwelt among us*, ἡμῖν referring to those who witnessed the public ministry of Jesus, and more particularly to those who associated with Him in daily intercourse. ἐν ἡμῖν, on this rendering, would be equivalent to *apud nos* or *inter nos*, a use of ἐν with the dative which may be defended by 10¹⁹ 11⁵⁴. A σκήνη or *tent* is a temporary habitation, and ἐσκήνωσεν might thus indicate the sojourn on earth for a brief season of the Eternal Word. In the N.T., however, the verb does not connote *temporary* sojourning in any other place where it is found.

Origen [5] and Chrysostom [6] understand the clause differently,

---

[1] Cf. Introd., p. clxx.   [2] Cf. Introd., p. clxix.
[3] Cf. Burkitt, *Ephraim's Quotations from the Gospel*, p. 50.
[4] *Of the Resurrection*, § 15.
[5] Comm. *in Ioann*. 20, 142, 202.   [6] *In loc.*

καὶ ἐθεασάμεθα τὴν δόξαν αὐτοῦ,

For them, it is parallel to the preceding clause, "the Word became flesh," and is another statement of the Incarnation.[1] The Word took humanity as His *tabernacle*, ὥσπερ ὁ ναὸς δόξαν εἶχε θεοῦ κατασκηνοῦσαν ἐν αὐτῷ (Origen, *l.c.* 202). This would be in harmony with Paul's great phrase ναὸς θεοῦ ἐστέ (1 Cor. 3[16]), and gives its proper force to ἐν ἡμῖν. Cf. Ecclus. 24[8] ἐν Ἰακὼβ κατασκήνωσον, as addressed to Wisdom. In the N.T. the verb only occurs again Rev. 7[15] 12[12] 13[6] and 21[3], where it is said that in the New Jerusalem God σκηνώσει μετ᾽ αὐτῶν. So the prophets had foretold, *e.g.* κατασκηνώσω ἐν μέσῳ σου, λέγει κύριος (Zech. 2[10]); ἔσται ἡ κατασκήνωσίς μου ἐν αὐτοῖς (Ezek. 37[27]). Cf. Lev. 26[11], Ezek. 43[7]. Such language goes back to the thought of the σκήνη or tabernacle in the desert (Ex. 25[8. 9]), where Yahweh dwelt with Israel. The verb σκηνοῦν would always recall this to a Jew. Philo says that the sacred σκήνη was a symbol of God's intention to send down to earth from heaven the perfection of His Divine virtue (*Quis div. hær.* 23).

The language of this verse recalls Ps. 85[9. 10]:

His salvation is nigh them that fear Him,
That glory (δόξα) may dwell (κατασκηνῶσαι) in our land:
Mercy (ἔλεος) and truth (ἀλήθεια) have met together,
Righteousness and peace have kissed each other.

The connexion of δόξα and the verb σκηνοῦν will presently be examined more closely.

ἐθεασάμεθα τὴν δόξαν αὐτοῦ. θεᾶσθαι is never used in the N.T. of spiritual vision, while it is used 22 times of "seeing" with the bodily eyes. Cf. 1[32. 38] 4[35] 6[5] 11[45], 1 Jn. 4[12. 14] (θεὸν οὐδεὶς πώποτε τεθέαται . . . ἡμεῖς τεθεάμεθα . . . ὅτι ὁ πατὴρ ἀπέσταλκεν τὸν υἱόν), and 1 Jn. 1[1. 2] ὃ ἑωράκαμεν τοῖς ὀφθαλμοῖς ἡμῶν, ὃ ἐθεασάμεθα κτλ. Neither here nor at 1 Jn. 1[1] is there any question of a supersensuous, mystical perception of spiritual facts, in both passages the claim being that the author has "seen" with his eyes (the aorist points to a definite moment in the historic past) the manifested glory of the Incarnate Word.

The use of the first person plural when speaking of his Christian experience is characteristic of Jn., and runs all through the First Epistle (cf. 1 Jn. 1[1] 3[2. 14] 5[15. 19. 20]) He speaks not only for himself but for his fellow-believers (cf. 3[11]); and in this passage for such of these (whether living or departed) as

[1] Burkitt (*Ev. da Mepharreshê,* ii. 307) favours this mode of render-ing the Syriac.

had been eye-witnesses of the public ministry of Jesus. (Cf. also 2 Pet. 1¹⁷, and see Introd., p. lx).

δόξα, δοξάζειν are favourite words with Jn. (although they are not found in the Johannine Epistles). Certain shades of meaning must be distinguished.

As in Greek authors generally, δόξα often means no more than "honour," and δοξάζειν means "to honour greatly"; e.g. 5⁴¹ 7¹⁸ 8⁵⁰· ⁵⁴ 9²⁴ 11⁴ 12⁴³ 14¹³ 15⁸ 16¹⁴ 17¹· ⁴· ¹⁰ 21¹⁹ (see on 4⁴⁴). But Jn. uses these words sometimes with special reference to that δόξα which belongs to God alone, e.g. 17⁵ recalls the glory of the *Eternal* Word. According to one interpretation (see above) of ἐσκήνωσεν ἐν ἡμῖν, δόξα here (cf. 2¹¹ 11⁴⁰) stands for the Divine glory exhibited in the earthly life of Jesus which was perceived by those who companied with Him, and this must in any case be *part* of the meaning of ἐθεασάμεθα τὴν δόξαν αὐτοῦ. The crisis of this "glorification" in Jn. is the Passion (7³⁹ 12¹⁶· ²³) consummated in the Risen Life (13³²). See especially on 13³².

We must, at this point, recall the later Jewish doctrine of the *Shekinah* or visible dwelling of Yahweh with His people. The word שְׁכִינָה, "that which dwells," is appropriated in later Judaism to the Divine presence. When in the O.T. Yahweh is said to dwell in a place, the Targums, to avoid anthropomorphism, preferred to say that He "caused His *Shekinah* to dwell." The *Shekinah* was the form of His manifestation, which was glorious; but the *glory* is distinct from the *Shekinah*, which is used as equivalent to the Divine Being Himself. Thus the Targum of Isa. 60² is: "In thee the *Shekinah* of Yahweh shall dwell, and His *glory* shall be revealed upon thee." Again, Lev. 26¹², "I will walk among you and be your God," becomes in the Targum "I will place the *glory* of my *Shekinah* among you, and my *Memra* shall be with you." Or again, Isa. 6¹, "I saw the Lord," becomes in the Targum "I saw the *glory* of the Lord" (see on 12⁴¹).¹

Now by bilingual Jews the representation of *Shekinah* by σκήνη was natural, and when σκηνοῦν or κατασκηνοῦν is used in the later books of the LXX or the Apocalypse of the *dwelling* of God with men, the allusion is generally to the doctrine of the *Shekinah* (cf. Rev. 7¹⁵). Accordingly, ἐσκήνωσεν ἐν ὑμῖν καὶ ἐθεασάμεθα τὴν δόξαν αὐτοῦ also carries a probable allusion to the glory of the *Shekinah* which was the manifestation on earth of God Himself.²

---

¹ Cf. Marshall in *D.B.*, *s.v.* "Shekinah"; and see Burney, *Aramaic Origin, etc.*, pp. 35–37.
² Generally in the LXX, δόξα is the rendering of כָּבוֹד (as in Ps 85⁹,

δόξαν ὡς μονογενοῦς παρὰ πατρός,

δόξαν ὡς μονογενοῦς παρὰ πατρός. The glory of the Word is described as "a glory as of the Only-begotten from the Father." Neither Son nor Father has yet been mentioned, and the sentence is a parenthesis explanatory of the δόξα of the Word. We may connect παρὰ πατρός either (a) with μονογενοῦς or (b) with δόξαν.

If (a) be adopted, then we have the parallels 6[46] 7[29] 16[27] 17[8], in all of which passages Jesus says of Himself that He is παρὰ θεοῦ or the like, a phrase which means more when applied to Him thus than it means in 1[6], where John Baptist has been described as ἀπεσταλμένος παρὰ θεοῦ, or in 9[16. 33], where the Pharisees say that Jesus was not παρὰ θεοῦ. But μονογενὴς παρά would be an unusual combination, especially in Jn., who always has ἐκ θεοῦ, not παρὰ θεοῦ, when he wishes to say "begotten of God "[1] (cf. 1 Jn. 2[29] 3[9] 4[7] 5[1. 4. 18]). It is true, indeed, that the distinctions between παρά, ἀπό, and ἐκ were being gradually obliterated in the first century, and that we cannot always distinguish παρά from ἐκ (see on 6[46]), but the point is that Jn. never uses παρά with γεννᾶσθαι.

(b) If we connect δόξαν with παρὰ πατρός, the meaning is "the glory such as the only Son receives from his Father." Cf. 5[41. 44] for δόξαν παρὰ τοῦ μόνου θεοῦ. "No image but the relation of a μονογενής to a father can express the twofold character of the glory as at once derivative and on a level with its source."[2] The manifested glory of the Word was as it were the glory of the Eternal Father shared with His only Son. Cf. 8[54] ἔστιν ὁ πατήρ μου ὁ δοξάζων με, where see note.

The word μονογενής is generally used of an only child (e.g. Judg. 11[34], Tob. 3[15] 6[10. 14], Lk. 7[12] 8[42] 9[38], Heb. 11[17]), the emphasis being on μονο—rather than on γενής. Thus Plato speaks of μονογενὴς οὐρανός (Tim. 31); and Clement of Rome (§ 25) describes the legendary bird, the *phœnix*, as μονογενές, sc. it is the only one of its kind, *unique* (cf. the LXX of Ps. 25[16]). Some of the O.L. texts (a e q) render μονογενής here by *unicus*, which is the original meaning, rather than by *unigenitus*, which became the accepted Latin rendering so soon as controversies arose about the Person and Nature of Christ.

An only child is specially dear to its parents; and μονογενής is used to translate יָחִיד in Ps. 22[20],[3] 35[17], where we should

---

Isa. 60[1]); but in Esth. 1[1] 6[8] it represents יְקָר, which is the word commonly used in the Targums.

[1] So the original Nicene Creed ran, γεννηθέντα ἐκ τοῦ πατρὸς μονογενῆ.

[2] Hort, *Two Dissertations*, p. 13. Cf. Phil. 2[6] ἐν μορφῇ θεοῦ ὑπάρχων.

[3] Justin (*Tryph.* 105) associates Ps. 22[20] with Jn. 1[14], using the term μονογενής.

πλήρης χάριτος καὶ ἀληθείας.

expect ἀγαπητός. Conversely ἀγαπητός is used for an *only* son, Gen. 22²; cf. Amos 8¹⁰.[1] And in every place where Jn. has μονογενής (except perhaps in this verse), viz. 1¹⁸ 3¹⁶·¹⁸, 1 Jn. 4⁹, we might substitute, as Kattenbusch has pointed out, ἀγαπητός for it, without affecting the sense materially.[2] At this point, however, the meaning is clear. The glory of the Incarnate Word was such glory as the only Son of the Eternal Father would derive from Him and so could exhibit to the faithful.

πλήρης χάριτος καὶ ἀληθείας. If καὶ ἐθεασάμεθα . . . πατρός is parenthetical, as we take it to be, then πλήρης is in apposition to λόγος at the beginning of the verse, and the construction is regular and simple. If the adj. πλήρης were always treated as declinable (as it is, *e.g.*, Mk. 8¹⁹, Mt. 14²⁰ 15³⁷, Acts 6³), this would be the only possible construction of the passage.

πλήρης, however, is often treated as *indeclinable* by scribes, in the N.T., the LXX, and the papyri; [3] and it is possible, therefore, to take it in the present passage (the only place where it occurs in Jn.) as in apposition either to δόξαν or to αὐτοῦ or μονογενοῦς in the previous line. For πλήρης here D reads πλήρη, which apparently was meant by the scribe to be taken with δόξαν. Turner has shown [4] that Irenæus, Athanasius, Chrysostom, and later Greek Fathers did not connect πλήρης with ὁ λόγος, but (generally) with δόξαν. And the Curetonian Syriac (Syr. sin. is deficient at this point) will not permit πλήρης to be taken with λόγος.[5]

On the contrary, Origen seems to favour the connexion of πλήρης with λόγος or μονογενής.[6] The O.L. (followed by vulg.) has *plenum* in apposition with *uerbum*; and internal evidence seems to favour this construction, despite the authority of most Greek Fathers. For to speak of the *glory* of Christ as being "full of grace and truth" is not as intelligible as to speak of Christ Himself being πλήρης χάριτος καὶ ἀληθείας; cf. Acts 6⁸, Στέφανος πλήρης χάριτος καὶ δυνάμεως, and for this constr. of πλήρης as descriptive of a man's quality, see Acts

---

[1] See J. A. Robinson, *Ephesians*, p. 229 f.
[2] See *D.C.G.*, *s.v.* " Only-Begotten " ; and for a different line of reasoning reaching the same conclusion, cf. Harris, *Bulletin of John Rylands Library*, July 1922.
[3] See Hort, *Select Readings*, p. 24 ; Blass, *Gram.*, p. 81 ; Turner, *J.T.S.*, 1899, p. 121 f., and 1900, p. 561, for many examples.
[4] *J.T.S.*, 1899, p. 123 f., 1900, p. 561.
[5] See Burkitt, *J.T.S.*, 1900, p. 562.
[6] See Origen, Comm. *in Ioann.*, ed. Brooke, ii. 219, 220.

6³·⁵ 7⁵⁵ 11²⁴. Further, in v. 16 the πλήρωμα from which Christians receive grace is that of Christ Himself, which shows that πλήρης here refers to Him.

The problem is one of grammar rather than of exegesis, for on any rendering *grace* and *truth* are specified as characteristic attributes of the Incarnate Word, or of His manifestation of Himself in the world. These two words χάρις and ἀλήθεια must now be examined.

The characteristically Christian word χάρις does not appear in Jn. except at 1¹⁴·¹⁶·¹⁷, in the Prologue. It is never placed in the mouth of Jesus by any evangelist (except in the sense of *thanks*, Lk. 6³²·³⁴ 17⁹), and is not used at all by Mk. or Mt. In Lk. it is applied occasionally to the special favour of God to individuals (1³⁰ 2⁴⁰·⁵²), as it is several times in the LXX (*e.g.* Gen. 6⁸). But its Christian use as *grace* is derived from Paul,[1] who habitually employs it to designate the condescending love of God in redemption, as contrasted with the legalism of the Mosaic economy (Rom. 5²¹ 6¹⁴ and *passim*); and the influence of Paul's terminology appears in Acts (*e.g.* 20²⁴ τὸ εὐαγγέλιον τῆς χάριτος τοῦ θεοῦ), Heb. 10²⁹, 1 Pet. 1¹³, etc. So we have χάρις in the specially Christian sense in Barnabas, § 5, and Ignatius (*Magn.* 8), and thenceforth in all Christian writers. But Jn. never uses χάρις except here and vv. 16, 17, and this is an indication of the faithfulness with which the primitive Christian phraseology is preserved in the Fourth Gospel. He does not even speak of the *grace* of God, when he writes ἠγάπησεν ὁ θεὸς τὸν κόσμον (3¹⁶), although what Paul meant by χάρις is behind his thought.

On the other hand, ἀλήθεια is one of the keywords of the Fourth Gospel. The question of Pilate, "What is truth?" (18³⁸) has received its answer. It was the purpose of Christ's mission that He should "bear witness to the truth" (18³⁷; cf. 5³³). The Word of the Father which He came to proclaim is truth (17⁸). He emphasises the truth of His pronouncements to His disciples (16⁷) and to the multitude (8⁴⁵). He is "a man that hath told you the truth" (8⁴⁰). Truth came through Him (1¹⁷); He is "full of truth" (1¹⁴); He is the Truth itself (14⁶). So He will send the Spirit of truth (15²⁶ 14¹⁷; cf. 1 Jn. 4⁶ 5⁷), who is to guide the faithful into all the truth (16¹³). Christ's disciples will "know the truth, and the truth shall make them free" (8³²); "he that doeth the truth cometh to the light" (3²¹; cf. 1 Jn. 1⁶); and Christ's prayer for His chosen is that they

---

[1] J. A. Robinson (*Ephesians*, p. 224), in a valuable note on χάρις, does not think that Paul *introduced* the word in its new sense to the Christian vocabulary, but that he did much to develop its use, especially in connexion with the extension of the Gospel to the Gentiles.

may be "sanctified in the truth" (17¹⁷·¹⁹). Every one that is of the truth hears His voice (18³⁸).

The word ἀλήθεια occurs 25 times in the Gospel and 20 times in the Johannine Epp., while it is only found 7 times in the Synoptists and not at all in the Apocalypse. The distribution of ἀληθής and ἀληθῶς is similar, while that of ἀληθινός (see on v. 9) is somewhat different, as it is common in the Apocalypse. These figures show that the idea of *Truth* is dominant with Jn.,[1] and that the truth of Christ's teachings is one of his deepest convictions. He represents Christ as claiming to teach and to be the Truth; and although the Synoptists do not dwell upon it, yet this feature of Christ's claim appears in their account of His controversy with the Pharisees at Jerusalem during the last week of His public ministry (Mk. 12¹⁴, Mt. 22¹⁶, Lk. 20²¹). "We know," they said, "that thou art true, and teachest the way of God in truth"; *i.e.* they began by a verbal recognition of the claim that He had made for Himself, a claim directly recorded by Jn. alone. While then, the emphasis laid in the Fourth Gospel upon the truth of Christ's teaching is partly due to the circumstances in which the book was produced, and the desire of Jn. to assure his readers not only of the spiritual beauty but also of the solid foundations of Christian doctrine, we need not doubt that it gives a representation faithful to historical fact, when it describes Jesus as Himself claiming to be the Ambassador and Revealer of the Truth. In the Galilæan discourses we should not expect to find this topic prominently brought forward, and the Synoptists are mainly occupied with Galilee. But when they bring Jesus to the critical and intellectual society of Jerusalem, they indicate that His claims to the possession of absolute truth had been noticed by those who wished to disparage and controvert His teaching.

Various explanations have been offered of the combination "grace and truth" as the two pre-eminent attributes of the Incarnate Logos. As we have seen, *grace* is what Jn. prefers to describe as *love* (God's love descending on men), and *truth* brings *light* (cf. Ps. 43³)); accordingly some exegetes refer back to v. 4, where the Divine *life* issues in *light*. But even if we equate χάρις with ἀγάπη, we cannot equate it with ζωή ; and further Jn. does not represent ἀλήθεια as *issuing from* χάρις. Rather are χάρις and ἀλήθεια co-ordinate.

The combination is found again in v. 17, where *grace and truth*, which came through Christ, are contrasted with the *Law*, which was given through Moses. In the O.T. χάρις and ἀλήθεια are not explicitly combined, but ἔλεος and ἀλήθεια occur often in combination as attributes of Yahweh (Ps. 40¹¹

---

[1] As it is with Paul (cf. 2 Thess. 2¹⁰).

15. Ἰωάνης μαρτυρεῖ περὶ αὐτοῦ καὶ κέκραγεν λέγων Οὗτος ἦν
ὃν εἶπον Ὁ ὀπίσω μου ἐρχόμενος ἔμπροσθέν μου γέγονεν, ὅτι πρῶτός

89¹⁴; cf. Ex. 34⁶), and in Ps. 61⁷ as attributes of the Messianic
King. As we have seen above (p. 21), the meeting of ἔλεος
and ἀλήθεια is associated in Ps. 85⁹·¹⁰ with the dwelling
(κατασκηνῶσαι) in the Holy Land of the Divine δόξα. And it
is to this passage in the Psalter, more than to any other passage
in the O.T., that the words and thoughts of Jn. 1¹⁴ are akin.
The idea of the Divine compassion (ἔλεος), of which the O.T. is
full, is enlarged and enriched in the N.T. by the idea of Divine
grace (χάρις).[1]

*The Baptist's witness to the pre-mundane existence of
the Word (v. 15)*

15. The verse is parenthetical, interpolating at this point
the Baptist's witness to the pre-existence of Christ, which has
been implied in v. 14.

μαρτυρεῖ, the historic present. What John said is, and
remains, a witness to the pre-mundane dignity of Christ.

καὶ κέκραγεν, " and he hath cried aloud "; his voice was
still sounding when the Fourth Gospel was written. For
κράζειν, see on 7²⁸. א*D om. λέγων after κέκραγεν.

οὗτος. See on 1².

οὗτος ἦν ὃν εἶπον, " this was He of whom I spake "; cf.
8²⁷ 10³⁵ for the constr. ὃν εἶπον. At v. 30 we have the more
usual ὑπὲρ οὗ εἶπον. The awkwardness of the constr. is
responsible for variant readings. ὁ εἰπών is read by א^aB*C*,
but this is impossible; ὃν εἶπον is found in א^cbAB³DLΘ, and
must be accepted despite the inferiority of its attestation.[2]

ὃν εἶπον. It would seem from all four Gospels that the
Baptist proclaimed "the Coming One" (ὁ ἐρχόμενος) before he
had identified Him with Jesus. The terms of John's proclamation are repeated in v. 30, almost verbally, and must be placed
beside the Synoptic forms. We have seen on v. 6 above that the
correspondences between Jn. and Mk. as to the Baptist's witness are very close; [3] and it is clear that at this point ἔμπροσθέν
μου γέγονεν is intended by Jn. to express what Mk. (and also
Mt., Lk.) meant by ἰσχυρότερός μου (see also on v. 27). Thus
ἔμπροσθεν does not indicate priority in *time* as at 3²⁸ (that is

---

[1] Cf. Augustine (*de pecc. mer.* ii. 31), who notes that when you
compare Jn. 1¹⁴ with Ps. 85¹⁰, you have to substitute *gratia* for
misericordia.

[2] See further, for the variants, Abbott, *Diat.* 2507a.

[3] See Introd., p. ci.

μου ἦν. 16. ὅτι ἐκ τοῦ πληρώματος αὐτοῦ ἡμεῖς πάντες ἐλάβομεν,

brought out in the next clause), but in *dignity*, as at Gen. 48²⁰, where it is said that Jacob made Ephraim ἔμπροσθεν τοῦ Μανασσῆ. "He that comes after me has come-to-be before me " (cf. 6²⁵ for a like use of γέγονε).

ὅτι πρῶτός μου ἦν. This is a Johannine addition to the Synoptic proclamation of the Baptist. It has been rendered in two different ways. (*a*) To render πρῶτός μου as "my Chief," "my Superior," is defensible, and Abbott (*Diat.* 2665) cites some authorities for a similar use of πρῶτος. But " He was my Chief " would be a tame addition to the great saying, " He that cometh after me is preferred before me." (*b*) The usual interpretation treats πρῶτος as equivalent to πρότερος, " He was *before* me," *sc.* in His pre-Incarnate life, although He was born into the world six months after the Baptist. The verb ἦν favours this (cf. 8⁵⁸ and vv. 1, 2, 4, 10 above). πρῶτός μου, then, is parallel to πρῶτον ὑμῶν at 15¹⁸, in both cases πρῶτος meaning *anterior*. This use of a superlative for a comparative may be supported by classical examples, *e.g.* Xenophon, *Mem.* I. ii. 46 δεινότατος σαυτοῦ ταῦτα ἦσθα, and we may compare Justin, *Apol.* i. 12, where οὗ βασιλικώτατον καὶ δικαιότατον . . . οὐδένα οἴδαμεν means " than whom we know no one *more* regal and just." On this rendering of πρῶτος " because He *was* before me," Jn. ascribes to the Baptist a knowledge of Christ's Pre-existence, which it is improbable that he had realised. But it is quite in the manner of Jn. to attribute to the Baptist that fuller understanding of Christ's Person which was not appreciated even by the apostles until after His Resurrection (see on v. 29).

Explanation of v. 14: *Christ the Giver of grace* (*vv.* 16, 17)

16. ὅτι . . . ὅτι introduces vv. 16, 17, v. 16 being explanatory of v. 14, and v. 17 elucidating v. 16 further. ὅτι is here read by אBC*DL 33, and must be preferred to the rec. καί (AWΘ),which is probably due to scribes not understanding that v. 15 is a parenthesis.

ὅτι ἐκ τοῦ πληρώματος αὐτοῦ κτλ. The Incarnate Word is indeed " full " of grace and truth, *for* (ὅτι) out of His " fulness " we have all received. Stephen is described (Acts 6⁸) as πλήρης χάριτος as well as his Master, although in a lesser degree; but he was only one of many disciples of whom this might be said.

ἡμεῖς πάντες ἐλάβομεν, " we, all of us," ἡμεῖς being prefixed for emphasis, *i.e.* all Christian disciples. The subject of

καὶ χάριν ἀντὶ χάριτος· 17. ὅτι ὁ νόμος διὰ Μωϋσέως ἐδόθη, ἡ χάρις καὶ ἡ ἀλήθεια διὰ Ἰησοῦ Χριστοῦ ἐγένετο.

ἐλάβομεν is wider than that of ἐθεασάμεθα in v. 14, where the thought is of contemporary witnesses of the public ministry of Jesus. It is, however, not only they who receive of His fulness, but every true believer.

πλήρωμα[1] does not occur again in Jn., but is used in the same way of the " fulness " of Christ at Eph. 4¹³, Col. 1¹⁹. The thought of Eph. 1²³ that the Church is His πλήρωμα is a different one; cf. also Rom. 15²⁹. See p. cxxxvii.

καὶ χάριν ἀντὶ χάριτος. ἀντί does not appear again in Jn.; it is a preposition which was going out of use in the first century.

Chrysostom understands the sentence to mean that Christians have received the higher χάρις of Christ *in exchange* for the χάρις of the law, " for even the things of the law were of grace." If this were the meaning intended, viz. that the lesser favour were replaced by the greater, there is a parallel to the thought in Philo, who says that God always limits His first favours (τὰς πρώτας χάριτας), and then bestows others in their stead (ἀεὶ νέας ἀντὶ παλαιοτέρων, *de post. Caini*, 43). But the point of v. 17 is that χάρις did *not* come through the Mosaic law, the word being explicitly confined to the grace of Christ (see on v. 14).

A better suggestion is that of J. A. Robinson,[2] viz. that ἀντί implies *correspondence* rather than *substitution* here, and that the idea is that the χάρις which the Christian receives corresponds to the source of the χάρις in Christ.[3]

17. The paratactic construction (see p. lxxix) is unmistakable; we should expect ὁ νόμος μὲν . . . ἡ χάρις δὲ καὶ ἡ ἀλήθεια κτλ.

In v. 16 the evangelist exults in the "grace for grace," *i.e.* the grace after grace, which all believers have received in Christ. This is, indeed, in marked contrast with the spiritual condition of those who were " under the law," as Paul would have expressed it, for it is pre-eminently through Christ that "grace" comes into play. χάρις is never spoken of in the LXX as a privilege of the Jew, and the contrast between *law* and *grace* is a master-thought of Paul (Rom. 4¹⁶ 6¹⁴· ¹⁵, Gal. 5⁴).

---

[1] For πλήρωμα, see Lightfoot, *Colossians*, p. 255 f., and J. A. Robinson, *Ephesians*, p. 255 f.

[2] *Ephesians*, p. 223.

[3] The LXX of Zech. 4⁷ has the difficult phrase ἰσότητα χάριτος χάριτα αὐτῆς, but the resemblance to χάριν ἀντὶ χάριτος here seems to be only verbal.

18. Θεὸν οὐδεὶς ἑώρακεν πώποτε·

Here it is explicit; it had become a Christian commonplace by
the time that the Prologue came to be written, but Jn.
never returns to it in the body of his Gospel.
The contrast is between νόμος and χάρις, as in Paul, but
καὶ ἡ ἀλήθεια was added by Jn. after χάρις, the two having
been combined in v. 14. The thought of the freedom which
truth brings appears again at 8³², and ἀλήθεια is very apposite
here. Its addition to χάρις is Jn.'s contribution to Paul's
contrast of law and grace. It is not that the Mosaic law was
not true, as far as it went; but that the truth of Christ emanci-
pates the believer from the bondage of the law.
That the law was *given* through Moses is repeated 7¹⁹
(cf. 6³²); but *the grace* and *the truth* (ἡ ἀλήθεια ; cf. 14⁶) *came*
through Jesus Christ. Moses was only the mediator through
whom God gave the law; but Christ is Himself the source of
grace and truth.
The full historical name "Jesus Christ" appears here for
the first time in Jn. It was not used by the contemporaries of
Jesus in His public ministry, and is only found in the Synoptists
Mk 1¹, Mt. 1¹. It appears again Jn. 17³, and also 1 Jn. 1³ 2¹ 3²³ 4²
5²⁰. In the Acts it occurs 2³⁸ 3⁶ 4¹⁰ 10³⁶ 16¹⁸, five times in the
Apocalypse, and often in Paul (see Introd., p. cxxxvi).

*The Logos Hymn concluded : The Logos the Revealer of
God (v. 18)*

18. θεὸν οὐδεὶς ἑώρακεν πώποτε. That God is invisible to the
bodily eye was a fundamental principle of Judaism (Ex. 33²⁰,
Deut. 4¹²). The Son of Sirach asks, τίς ἑόρακεν αὐτὸν καὶ
ἐκδιηγήσεται; (Ecclus. 43³¹), to which Jn. supplies the answer
here (cf. ἐξηγήσατο at the end of the verse). Philo, as a good
Jew, has the same doctrine. God is ἀόρατος (*de post. Caini*, 5),
even though Moses in a sense may be called θεόπτης (*de mut.
nom.* 2), and the name "Israel" means *uir uidens deum* (see
on 1⁵¹ below).[1] ἀόρατος is applied to God in like manner, Col.
1¹⁵, 1 Tim. 1¹⁷.[2]
The doctrine that God is invisible is not, indeed, peculiar to
Hebrew thought; cf. the verse from the Orphic literature
quoted by Clement Alex. (*Strom.* v. 12) :

οὐδέ τις αὐτὸν
εἰσοράᾳ θνητῶν, αὐτὸς δέ γε πάντας ὁρᾶται.

[1] See Drummond's *Philo Judæus*, ii. 9, 206.
[2] See Introd., p. cxxxviii.

μονογενής, Θεός, ὁ ὢν εἰς τὸν κόλπον τοῦ Πάτρος,

But we incline to a *Hebrew* origin for the Prologue, rather than a *Greek*. Jn. is specially insistent on the doctrine that God is invisible. Cf. 5³⁷, οὔτε εἶδος αὐτοῦ ἑωράκατε, and (a passage closely parallel to 1¹⁸) 6⁴⁶, οὐχ ὅτι τὸν πατέρα ἑώρακέν τις, εἰ μὴ ὁ ὢν παρὰ τοῦ θεοῦ, οὗτος ἑώρακεν τὸν πατέρα. See note on 14⁷, and cf. 1 Jn. 4¹². ²⁰. In the Greek Bible πώποτε always occurs with a negative. Jn. has it again 5³⁷ 6³⁵ 8³³, 1 Jn. 4¹²; cf. also Lk. 19³⁰. μονογενὴς θεός. This is the reading of אBC*L 33 (the best of the cursives), Peshitta, Clem. Alex., Origen, Epiphanius, etc., while the rec. ὁ μονογενὴς υἱός is found in all other uncials (D is lacking from v. 16 to 3²⁶) and cursives, the Latin vss. and Syr. cur. (Syr. sin. is lacking here) Chrysostom and the Latin Fathers generally. An exhaustive examination of the textual evidence was made by Hort,[1] and his conclusion that the true reading is μονογενὴς θεός has been generally accepted. There can be no doubt that the evidence of MSS., versions, and Fathers is overwhelmingly on this side.

μονογενής occurs again in Jn. only at 1¹⁴ 3¹⁶. ¹⁸, 1 Jn. 4⁹, and in the last three instances in connexion with υἱός, so that the tendency of scribes would be to replace the more difficult θεός here by the more familiar υἱός, as they have done; while there would be no temptation to replace υἱός by θεός. μονογενὴς θεός[2] was an expression adopted by Arius and Eunomius as freely as by the orthodox Catholics, so that its occurrence in a Gospel text would hardly have been used for polemical purposes by either party. It is an expression unfamiliar to the modern ear, and is therefore hard of acceptance by any to whom the cadence "only begotten Son" seems inevitable. However, it is probable—although the patristic testimony does not altogether favour this view—that μονογενής is not to be taken as an adjective qualifying θεός, but that μονογενής, θεός, ὁ ὢν εἰς τὸν κόλπον τοῦ πατρός are three distinct designations of Him who is the Exegete or Interpreter of the Father (cf. Abbott, *Diat.* 1938).

That the Word is θεός (not ὁ θεός) has already been stated without qualification in v. 1. In v. 14 His glory is said to be like the glory which a μονογενής receives from his father, which prepares the way for giving Him the title of μονογενής. This title suggests that relation of Christ to God, as the Son to the

---

[1] *Two Dissertations* (1876), the most valuable of commentaries on Jn. 1¹⁸.

[2] μονογένεια θεά is cited by Harris from the Orphic literature as a title of Persephone (*Bulletin of John Rylands Library*, July, 1922).

Father, which has not yet been mentioned, but which is prominent in the Fourth Gospel. And, finally (as is also suggested
by μονογενής, see on v. 14 above), this relation is one of eternal
love. The Word may be described as ὁ ὢν εἰς τὸν κόλπον τοῦ
πατρός.

We translate, therefore:

" God hath no man seen at any time:
The Only-Begotten, who is God, who dwells in the
Father's bosom,
This is He who revealed God."

θεὸν οὐδεὶς κτλ. Jn. generally *begins* such a sentence with
οὐδείς, but here θεόν is put first for special emphasis; cf. 3³²
13²⁸ 15¹³ 16²², where similarly οὐδείς is not put in the forefront.

εἰς τὸν κόλπον. " The wife of one's bosom " is a phrase,
used in many languages, for " beloved wife." Cf. Num. 11¹²,
Deut. 13⁶. The metaphor is even applied to friendship between
man and man; *e.g.* Cicero (*ad Fam. Ep.* xiv. 4. 3), " Cicero
meus quid aget ? iste uero sit in sinu semper et complexu meo,"
and Plutarch, *Cato minor*, 33 *fin.*, Γαβίνιον Αὖλον, ἐκ τῶν
Πομπηΐου κόλπων ἄνθρωπον.

Hence ὁ ὢν εἰς τὸν κόλπον τοῦ πατρός expresses the intimate
relationship of love between the Son and the Father; the Word
shares in the secrets of Deity. ὢν stands for *eternal* being
(cf. 8⁵⁸ and Rev. 1⁴); it is the relation between Son and Father
prior to the Incarnation, that is in the writer's thought.

εἰς τὸν κόλπον, *without a verb of motion*, occurs elsewhere
neither in the Greek Bible nor in Greek literature generally
(Abbott, *Diat.* 2712), the more usual constr. being ἐν τῷ κόλπῳ
(as at 13²³, which does not, however, help us). It is possible
that εἰς is used here in the same sense as ἐν (cf. 19¹³), as it often
is in Mk.;[1] on the other hand, ὢν εἰς τὸν κόλπον τοῦ πατρός
recalls ὁ λόγος ἦν πρὸς τὸν θεόν (v. 1), where πρός may carry a
sense of *direction* (see note *in loc.*).

Ignatius has a phrase which may be reminiscent of v. 18,
viz. Ἰησοῦν Χριστὸν τὸν ἀφ᾽ ἑνὸς πατρὸς προελθόντα καὶ εἰς ἕνα ὄντα
καὶ χωρήσαντα (*Magn.* 7); see on 13³.

For ὁ ὢν εἰς τὸν κόλπον τοῦ πάτρος, Harris[2] appositely quotes
Spenser's *Hymn to Heavenly Beauty*:

" There in His bosome Sapience doth sit,
the soueraine dearling of the Deitie,"

where Spenser seemingly identifies the σοφία of the Sapential
Books of the O.T. with the λόγος of the N.T.

---

[1] See Turner, *J.T.S.*, Oct. 1924, p. 14.
[2] *Bulletin of John Rylands Library*, July 1922.

ἐκεῖνος ἐξηγήσατο.

ἐκεῖνος ἐξηγήσατο   For ἐκεῖνος, see on v. 8; here it is very emphatic: " It is *He* who interpreted (the Father)." The object of ἐξηγήσατο is not stated, but it is not doubtful.   It was God *as Father* that He who was " in the bosom of the Father " revealed to men.   The aorist indicates a particular period in time, *i.e.* that of the life of Christ on earth.

ἐξηγεῖσθαι is used elsewhere in the N.T. by Lk. alone (Lk. 24³⁵, Acts 10⁸ 15¹². ¹⁴ 21¹⁹), and in the sense of " to rehearse," for the benefit of others, words or incidents of sacred significance.   It is the verb technically used in Greek literature of a declaration or exposition of Divine mysteries (see Wetstein for many examples).   Thus, in Job 28²⁷ it is said that God " declared " (ἐξηγήσατο) wisdom, which was otherwise hidden from man; and the official interpreters of dreams in Gen. 41⁸. ²⁴ are called ἐξηγηταί.

Here we have the climax of the Prologue.   The significance of the doctrine of the Logos is expressed in two words, ἐκεῖνος ἐξηγήσατο, " It is He who interpreted the Father."   In v. 17 it has been affirmed that " the truth came through Jesus Christ," and the highest form of truth is the knowledge of God. This He declared with a precision which could only be exhibited by One whose dwelling was " in the bosom of the Father."   " What He hath seen and heard, of that He beareth witness " (3³²).   Cf. Mt. 11²⁷, Lk. 10²².

The last words of the Prologue (v. 18) set out briefly the theme of the Gospel which is to follow.   It is the ἐξήγησις or Exhibition to the world of God in Christ.[1]

PART I.   (I. 19–IV. 54 and VI.).

The Baptist's witness as to the Coming One (I. 19–28)

19. This is the beginning of the Gospel, as distinct from the Prologue, and it opens, as Mk. does, with the witness of John the Baptist, differing, however, from Mk. in that the Baptism of Jesus is already over, reference being made to it at vv. 32, 33.

The indications of time in cc. 1, 2 are remarkable and precise.   If the incident described vv. 19–28 is dated Day i., then Day ii. (ἐπαύριον) is taken up with vv. 29–34.   Again,

[1] See Introd., p. cxlv.

19. Καὶ αὕτη ἐστὶν ἡ μαρτυρία τοῦ Ἰωάνου, ὅτε ἀπέστειλαν πρὸς αὐτὸν οἱ Ἰουδαῖοι ἐξ Ἱεροσολύμων ἱερεῖς καὶ Λευείτας ἵνα ἐρωτήσωσιν

Day iii extends from v. 35 (ἐπαύριον) to v. 39. Then, if we read πρωί for πρῶτον (see note *in loc.*) at v. 41, the incident of vv. 40–42 belongs to Day iv. Day v. extends from v. 43 (ἐπαύριον) to the end of the chapter. Nothing is told of Day vi., but Day vii. (τῇ ἡμέρᾳ τῇ τρίτῃ) is the day of the Marriage at Cana (see further on 2[1]). That is, the Gospel opens with the detailed report of a momentous week.

καὶ αὕτη ἐστὶν κτλ. "Now the witness of John is this . . .," αὕτη being the predicate of identification, and καί referring back to v. 7 or v. 15, where John's witness has been mentioned. We have now a threefold testimony of John, given on three consecutive days (vv. 19, 29, 35), the first being the *announcement* of the Coming One, the second the *designation* of Jesus as He who was to come, and the third having as its consequence the *following* of Jesus by two of John's disciples. The particularity of detail points to the story coming ultimately from an eye-witness, probably from John the son of Zebedee, whose reminiscences lie behind the Fourth Gospel (see on vv. 35, 40). For the idea of μαρτυρία in Jn., cf. Introd., p. xci, and see on v. 7.

ὅτε ἀπέστειλαν πρὸς αὐτὸν οἱ Ἰουδαῖοι κτλ. So BC* 33, but אC[3]LΔW om. πρὸς αὐτόν. AΘ *fam.* 13 add πρ. αὐτόν after Λευείτας.

John the Baptist was now carrying on his ministry, and his work had aroused intense interest (Lk. 3[15]). It was natural that the Sanhedrim (see on 7[32]) should send representatives to inquire into his purpose and personal claims. John the Baptist's father being a priest, his activities would be of special interest to the whole priestly order. Accordingly the authorities at Jerusalem sent "priests and Levites," a combination that does not occur again in the N.T. Levites are mentioned elsewhere only at Lk. 10[32], Acts 4[36]; and Jn. does not employ the term ἱερεύς again, although he often has ἀρχιερεύς.

οἱ Ἰουδαῖοι. The use of this term in Jn. is remarkable. Except in the phrase, "the King of the Jews," the Synoptists only use the word Ἰουδαῖος five times (Mt. 28[15], Mk. 1[5] 7[3], Lk. 7[3] 23[51]), while it occurs more than 70 times in Jn. When Jn. refers to the social or religious customs of "the Jews" (*e.g.* 2[6. 13] 4[9] 5[1] 6[4] 7[2] 11[55] 19[40. 42]), he does not exclude Galilæans, who were at one in religion and habits of life with the inhabitants of Judæa. But he generally means by "the Jews," the people of Judæa and particularly of Jerusalem, the scene of so large a part of his narrative. The Fourth Gospel is pre-eminently the

αὐτόν Σὺ τίς εἶ; 20. καὶ ὡμολόγησεν καὶ οὐκ ἠρνήσατο, καὶ ὡμολό-

story of the rejection of Jesus by these "Jews," who were deeply imbued with national sentiment, intensely conservative in religious matters, bigoted and intolerant in their pride of race (cf. 5¹⁰). Their popular leaders were the Pharisees, and we find from v. 24 that the commission of inquiry about John the Baptist's doings had been sent by them. In v. 19 οἱ Ἰουδαῖοι are not to be distinguished from οἱ Φαρισαῖοι of v. 24. It is the "Jews" and the "Pharisees" who are represented throughout the Fourth Gospel as especially the opponents of Jesus and His claims.

In one passage (6⁴¹·⁵²), indeed, objectors who appear from the context to have been Galilæans are explicitly called "the Jews," perhaps because they represented the Jewish party of hostility; but see note *in loc.* In the present verse, there is no doubt that οἱ Ἰουδαῖοι are the leaders of religious thought in Jerusalem.

ἐξ Ἰεροσολύμων. The Hebrew יְרוּשָׁלַם is transliterated Ἰερουσαλήμ in the LXX, whence we have "Jerusalem." This primitive form of the name is not found in Mt. (except 23³⁷), Mk., or Jn., while it is nearly always used by Lk., and always in the Apocalypse (3¹² 21²·¹⁰, of the New Jerusalem).

The Hellenistic form Ἰεροσόλυμα came into vogue about 100 B.C., and is the form usually employed in the Books of the Maccabees (cf. 2 Macc. 3⁹) and in Josephus. It is generally treated as a neuter plural, but in Mt. 2³ and Tob. 14⁴ it appears as a feminine singular, perhaps being taken to represent "the sacred Solyma." [1] This is the form (Ἰεροσόλυμα, as a neuter plural) which is *always* used in Jn., as well as in Mt. and Mk. See further on 2²³.

ἵνα ἐρωτήσωσιν αὐτόν, "that they should interrogate him." They asked him, Σὺ τίς εἶ; "Who are you?" not meaning thereby to ask him his name or parentage, for that his father was Zacharias the priest must have been well known to the authorities. But they meant to ask him who he claimed to be, and he understood their meaning, for he disclaimed at once any pretence of being the Christ.[2]

For the answer given by Jesus to the same question, Σὺ τίς εἶ; see 8²⁵.

---

[1] Westcott-Hort do not adopt the rough breathing, "as due to a false association with ἱερός"; but see Moulton-Milligan, *s.v.* Ἰεροσόλυμα.

[2] For the vagueness, and also the prevalence, of the expectation in the first century that a divinely appointed leader, popularly called Messiah, should appear, see G. F. Moore in *The Beginnings of Christianity*, i. 356.

γησεν ὅτι Ἐγὼ οὐκ εἰμὶ ὁ Χριστός.   21. καὶ ἠρώτησαν αὐτόν
Τί οὖν; Ἠλείας εἶ; καὶ λέγει Οὐκ εἰμί.   Ὁ προφήτης εἶ σύ; καὶ

The pronoun σύ is used with extraordinary frequency in
Jn., his tendency being to lay stress on personality (cf. Abbott,
Diat. 1726, 2402).

20. καὶ ὡμολόγησεν καὶ οὐκ ἠρνήσατο καὶ ὡμολόγησεν, a good
example of *parataxis*, or the habit of using co-ordinate sentences
conjoined by καί, which is so marked a feature of Jn.'s style.
See above on v. 10.

The alternation of affirmative and negative statements, so as
to make explicit what is meant, is also thoroughly Johannine;
cf. 1 Jn. 1⁵ 2⁴·²⁷. See above on v. 3.

With "confessed and denied not," cf. Josephus, *Antt.* VI.
vii. 4, Σαοῦλος δὲ ἀδικεῖν ὡμολόγει καὶ τὴν ἁμαρτίαν οὐκ ἠρνεῖτο.

Jn. has ὁμολογεῖν again 9²² 12⁴², 1 Jn. 1⁹ 2²³ 4²·¹⁵.

John the Baptist is bold and direct in his reply to them,
saying ἐγὼ οὐκ εἰμὶ ὁ Χριστός, ἐγώ being emphatic, "*I* am not
the Christ," the form of his answer suggesting that they might
have to reckon with the Christ, nevertheless. Lk. (3¹⁵) tells
in like manner of John's disclaimer, which is mentioned again
3²⁸ below (cf. also Acts 13²⁵).

ἐγὼ οὐκ εἰμί. So אABC*LW 33; rec. has οὐκ εἰμὶ ἐγώ
(C³Θ). In c. 1, the Baptist's use of ἐγώ is a feature of the
narrative (vv. 23, 26, 27, 30, 31, 33), his distinctive ministry
being thus brought into clear view.

Jn. dwells with special emphasis on the acceptance by John
the Baptist of a ministry quite subordinate to that of Jesus
(cf. 3²⁸⁻³⁰ 5³³ᶠ. 10⁴¹). Disciples of the Baptist had been found
by Paul at Ephesus (Acts 19¹⁻⁷); and there is some evidence that
by the end of the first century a Baptist community was prominent there, whose members offered allegiance to their founder
rather than to Christ. As late as the middle of the third
century, the *Clementine Recognitions* mention such a sect
explicitly: "ex discipulis Johannis qui . . . magistrum suum
ueluti Christum praedicarunt" (i. § 54 and § 60).[1] The necessity of refuting such claims made for the Baptist in Ephesus
and its neighbourhood sufficiently explains the importance
which the Fourth Gospel attaches to John the Baptist's confession, "I am not the Christ."

21. καὶ ἠρώτησαν αὐτόν, Τί οὖν; The argumentative τί οὖν;
quid ergo? appears in Rom. 6¹⁵ 11⁷.

The variants are puzzling. B has σὺ οὖν τί; which can
hardly be right; אL om. σύ; C* 33 insert σύ before Ἠλείας;
while AC³ΓΔΘ with the Latin vss. have Ἠλείας εἶ σύ. Perhaps

---

[1] Cf. Lightfoot, *Colossians*, p. 401 f.

ἀπεκρίθη Οὔ. 22. εἶπαν οὖν αὐτῷ Τίς εἶ; ἵνα ἀπόκρισιν δῶμεν τοῖς

σύ has been interpolated from the next clause ; it is not necessary for the sense. We omit it, with Tischendorf, accordingly.

Ἡλείας εἶ; There was a general belief that Elijah would return to earth to prepare the way of the Messiah. This was founded on Mal. 4⁵. In Mk. 9¹¹ it is mentioned, as commonly recognised, that " Elijah must first come " (cf. Mk. 6¹⁵ 8²⁸ and parallels). His mission was to be the establishment of order (Mk. 9¹²), as is also explained in the Mishna.[1] Justin quotes (*Tryph.* 8) Jewish doctrine to the effect that Messiah was to be hidden until pointed out and anointed by Elijah.

In a sense, John the Baptist was the Elijah of Jewish expectation, and so Jesus declared (Mt. 11¹⁴; cf. Lk. 1¹⁷), but in the sense in which the Jewish emissaries put the question, " Art thou Elijah ? " the true answer was *No*; for, while the Baptist fulfilled the preliminary ministry of which Malachi had spoken, he was not Elijah returned to earth in bodily form.[2]

ὁ προφήτης εἶ σύ ; This was another alternative. The Jews held that not only Elijah, but others of the great prophets, would return before Messiah's appearance. Cf. 2 Esd. 2¹⁷, " For thy help will I send my servants Isaiah and Jeremiah," a passage which may be pre-Christian. One of the rumours about Jesus during His Galilæan ministry was that He was " Jeremiah or one of the prophets " (Mt. 16¹⁴; cf. Mk. 8²⁸). See 9¹⁷ below. But more specific than this expectation of the return of one of the older prophets was the expectation of one who was pre-eminently " *the* prophet," whose coming was looked for on the ground of Deut. 18¹⁵. This idea is not in the Synoptists, but appears three times in Jn. (1²¹ 6¹⁴ 7⁴⁰). Christian exegesis from the beginning (Acts 3²² 7³⁷) found the fulfilment of Deut. 18¹⁵ in the Christ; but pre-Christian, *i.e.* Jewish, comment distinguished " the prophet like unto Moses " from the Messiah, as is clear from the present passage and from 7⁴⁰; see on 6³¹. To the question, " Art thou the prophet ? " the only answer was *No*, for the Jews were mistaken in distinguishing ὁ προφήτης ὁ ἐρχόμενος from the Christ, whose herald John was.

22. εἶπαν οὖν κτλ., " And so they said to him, *Who* are you ? " οὖν is a favourite connecting particle in the Fourth Gospel, seldom expressing logical sequence, but generally historical transition only (as in Homer). It occurs 195 times,

[1] *Edujoth*, viii. 7, quoted by Schürer, *Hist. of Jewish People*, II. ii. 156.
[2] Cf. Headlam, *Life and Teaching of Jesus Christ*, p. 166.

πέμψασιν ἡμᾶς· τί λέγεις περὶ σεαυτοῦ; 23. ἔφη, Ἐγὼ φωνὴ βοῶντος ἐν τῇ ἐρήμῳ Εὐθύνατε τὴν ὁδὸν Κυρίου, καθὼς εἶπεν Ἡσαίας ὁ προφήτης. 24. Καὶ ἀπεσταλμένοι ἦσαν ἐκ τῶν Φαρισαίων. 25. καὶ ἠρώτησαν αὐτὸν καὶ εἶπαν αὐτῷ Τί οὖν βαπτίζεις εἰ σὺ οὐκ εἶ ὁ

and is used as εὐθύς is used in Mk.[1] In a few passages Jn. places it in the mouth of Jesus, indicating logical consequence, e.g. 6⁶² 12⁵⁰ 13¹⁴ 16²². It does not occur in 1 Jn. at all.

ἵνα ἀπόκρισιν κτλ. The constr. is elliptical, as at 9³⁶, where see note. ἀπόκρισις occurs again 19⁹.

23. ἔφη, Ἐγὼ φωνὴ κτλ. The Synoptists (Mk. 1³, Mt. 3³, Lk. 3⁴) apply the words of Isa. 40³ to the Baptist and his mission; but Jn. represents him as applying the text to himself [2] when answering the interrogation of the Jews. The *source* of the citation, viz. the prophecy of Isaiah, is explicitly given in all four Gospels.

The Synoptists quote from the LXX, but Jn. seems to reproduce a citation made *memoriter* from the Hebrew. Instead of ἑτοιμάσατε τὴν ὁδὸν κυρίου, he has εὐθύνατε, from the second clause of Isa. 40³, where the LXX has εὐθείας ποιεῖτε.[3]

Theologians, both Eastern and Western, have noted the contrast between φωνή and λόγος. John "was the Voice, but not the Word" (Ephraim, *Epiphany Hymns*, i. 9). So also Augustine (*serm.* 293. 3): "Johannes uox ad tempus, Christus uerbum in principio aeternum." Cf. Origen, *Comm.* (ed. Brooke, II. 233).

24. The rec. text (so NWΘ) inserts οἱ before ἀπεσταλμένοι, *i.e.* "And certain had been sent from among the Pharisees," as distinct from the questioners of v. 19. But οἱ is omitted by א*A*BC*L; and we must render "And *they*," *i.e.* the priests and Levites of v. 19, "had been sent from the Pharisees." And, in fact, v. 25 shows that the argument is carried on from v. 21.

The Pharisees (mentioned again 4¹ 7⁴⁵ 8¹³ 9¹³ 11⁴⁶ 12¹⁹·⁴²) were the true representatives of the old Jewish spirit (see on v. 19). Strictly conservative, they were intolerant of all innovation, whether of doctrine or ritual, and the baptizing ministry of John aroused their suspicions. See on 7³².

25. τί οὖν βαπτίζεις; Hitherto, no hint has been given that

---

[1] Cf. Burkitt, *Evangelion da-Mepharreshê*, ii. 89, and Abbott, *Diat.* 1883, 2640. Jn.'s usage of οὖν corresponds somewhat to the Hebrew "wāw consecutive."

[2] Justin reproduces (*Tryph.* 88) this peculiar feature of the Fourth Gospel, and represents the Baptist as saying οὐκ εἰμὶ ὁ Χριστός, ἀλλὰ φωνὴ βοῶντος (vv. 20, 23).

[3] See Lightfoot, *Biblical Essays*, p. 139, and Burney, *Aramaic Origin, etc.*, p. 114.

Χριστὸς οὐδὲ 'Ηλείας οὐδὲ ὁ προφήτης; 26. ἀπεκρίθη αὐτοῖς ὁ 'Ιωάνης λέγων 'Εγὼ βαπτίζω ἐν ὕδατι· μέσος ὑμῶν στήκει ὃν ὑμεῖς

the ministry of John the herald was one of *baptism*. It is assumed that all readers of the Gospel will know that. The question, " Why are you baptizing ? " is put to him by the Pharisees of the deputation from Jerusalem, who were the conservative guardians of orthodox practice.

The baptism of proselytes from heathenism was a recognised, if not a universal, practice in Jewry at this time. But why should *Jews* be baptized ? And what authority had John to exercise this ministry ? Baptism, that is a symbolic rite of purification, would indeed be a token of the approach of the Messianic kingdom; " I will sprinkle clean water upon you, and ye shall be clean " (Ezek. 36[25]) were prophetic words (cf. Zech. 13[1]). But John had admitted that he was not Messiah; he was not even Elijah or " the prophet " (v. 21). His claim to be the Voice in the wilderness of Isa. 40[3] did not satisfy the Pharisees as to his authority for exercising so novel and irregular a ministry as that of baptizing Jews seemed to be.

26. The attitude of the Baptist to Jesus is explained more clearly in vv. 25-34 than it is in the Synoptists, whose source of knowledge about him was tradition and not personal acquaintance. This is what we should expect if the ultimate author of the Fourth Gospel were John the son of Zebedee, for he seems to have been one of the Baptist's disciples (see on v. 35). Jn. does not narrate the Baptism of Jesus directly, but what he tells is consistent with the Marcan story.

We have, first, the Proclamation of the Coming One (Mk. 1[7], Mt. 3[11], Lk. 3[16]), to which reference is made several times in this chapter. But when the proclamation was first made, the Baptist did not know (except in Mt.'s account; see on v. 31) that Jesus was the Predestined One for whose Advent he looked. Both in the Synoptists and in Jn. is the contrast drawn out between baptism ἐν ὕδατι (which was all that John offered) and baptism ἐν πνεύματι ἁγίῳ (which was to be the work of the Christ). When Jesus presented Himself for baptism, the Baptist noticed a dove alighting on His head (v. 32); and as he looked he became conscious that this was the sign of the Spirit, and that Jesus was the expected One who should baptize ἐν πνεύματι ἁγίῳ. All this is now to be set out in detail.

ἀπεκρίθη αὐτοῖς ὁ 'Ιωάνης λέγων. In Jn. we nearly always have the constr. ἀπεκρίθη καὶ εἶπεν (see on v. 50 below), but here and at 12[23] ἀπεκρ. λέγων seems to be the true reading.

The Baptist had been asked, " Why do you baptize ? " What authority have you ? (v. 25). He gives no direct answer ;

οὐκ οἴδατε, 27. ὁ ὀπίσω μου ἐρχόμενος, οὗ οὐκ εἰμὶ ἐγὼ ἄξιος ἵνα
but before he speaks of Him whose herald he was, he admits
that he did baptize, but only "with water." ἐγὼ βαπτίζω ἐν
ὕδατι. ἐγώ is emphatic : " Yes, *I* baptize, I administer a symbolic rite of purification, of cleansing with water." The words
are in all the Synoptic accounts of the Proclamation, where the
contrast with the baptism with the Holy Spirit (v. 33) immediately follows (Mk. 1⁸ and parallels). Here, at v. 26, ἐγὼ βαπτίζω
ἐν ὕδατι is only a reiteration of the claim for himself which he
was accustomed to make as he predicted the Coming of a
Greater One (see on v. 33).

μέσος ὑμῶν. The rec. text (so NΘ) inserts δέ after μέσος,
but om. אBC*LTᵇ. It is not required by the sense. A new
sentence begins with μέσος, in Johannine style without any
connecting particle. We should have expected ἐν μέσῳ ὑμῶν,
but Jn. never uses this constr.; cf. 19¹⁸ μέσον δὲ τὸν Ἰησοῦν, and
see on [8]³· ⁹.

στήκει is read by BLTᵇ, and א has ἑστήκει: the rec. with
ACΔWNΘ gives the more usual ἕστηκεν. But στήκει, "standeth
up " or "standeth fast," is more dramatic, and well attested.

μέσος ὑμῶν στήκει. Apparently Jesus was actually present
on this occasion, which is subsequent to His Baptism, as appears
from the fact that the Baptist now knows Him for what He is,
although the questioners did not : ὃν ὑμεῖς οὐκ οἴδατε, ὑμεῖς
being emphatic. Perhaps the Baptist's statement that the
Coming One was even in their midst was treated as of no
serious importance; there is no record, at any rate, of his being
further questioned as to what he meant, or to which person of the
company his words were applicable.

οἴδατε. εἰδέναι is a favourite verb with Jn., occurring three
times as often in the Fourth Gospel as in the Synoptists. It
is not easy to distinguish it in meaning from γινώσκειν (see
on 1⁴⁸), although Westcott (on Jn. 2²⁴) has made a subtle analysis of the two verbs. Probably we might say that γινώσκειν
generally stands for relative, acquired knowledge, gradually
perfected, while εἰδέναι indicates a complete and absolute
knowledge of the object. The latter would be the natural verb
to express Divine knowledge (but cf. 17²⁵), although it would
include also human certainty (see 2⁹). But it is doubtful if the
two verbs can be differentiated with any precision.[1] Both are
frequently used in the LXX to render יָדַע; and the following
list of passages shows that they are often used in Jn. without
any perceptible difference of meaning.

Both verbs are used of Christ's knowledge of the Father;

[1] Cf. R. Law, *The Tests of Life* (p. 364), for γινώσκειν and εἰδέναι.

λύσω αὐτοῦ τὸν ἱμάντα τοῦ ὑποδήματος. 28. Ταῦτα ἐν Βηθανίᾳ

γινώσκω at 10¹⁵ 17²⁵, οἶδα at 7²⁹ 8⁵⁵. Both are used of the world's knowledge (or ignorance) of God, or of that possessed by the Jews : γινώσκω at 1¹⁰ 17²³· ²⁵ 8⁵⁵ 16³, 1 Jn. 3¹· ⁶; οἶδα at 7²⁸ 8¹⁹ 15²¹. Both are used of man's knowledge of God and Christ : γινώσκω at 14⁷· ⁹ 17³, 1 Jn. 2⁴· ¹³· ¹⁴ 4⁶· ⁷· ⁸ 5²⁰, and οἶδα at 1³¹· ³³ 4²² 14⁷. Both are used of Christ's knowledge of men or of ordinary facts, e.g. γινώσκω at 2²⁵ 5⁶· ⁴² 6¹⁵ 10¹⁴· ²⁷, and οἶδα at 6⁶⁴ 8³⁷ 13³. The word used for the Father's knowledge of the Son is γινώσκω (10¹⁵), and not οἶδα as we should have expected. With this array of passages before us, we shall be slow to accept conclusions which are based on any strict distinction in usage between the two verbs.

27. ὁ ὀπίσω μου ἐρχόμενος κτλ. This clause (see v. 15) is in apposition to μέσος ὑμῶν στήκει κτλ. of the previous verse. Through misunderstanding of this, variants have arisen. The rec. with AC³ΓΔ prefixes αὐτός ἐστιν (as if v. 27 began a new sentence), and adds (with Θ) ὃς ἔμπροσθέν μου γέγονεν (from v. 15); but neither of these insertions is found in אBC*LNTᵇW. א*B also omit ὁ before ὀπίσω, but ins. ACא³NWΘ; the omission of the article is awkward, and is explicable from itacism, ὁ . . . ὀπ.

For the Synoptic forms of the Baptist's proclamation, see Introd., p. c. Mt.'s alteration of "loosen the thong of His sandals " to " carry His sandals " (βαστάσαι for λῦσαι) may point back to the form in Q. Either duty was that of a slave; and Wetstein (Mt. 3¹¹) cites a Rabbinical maxim (Cetuboth, f. 90. 1) to the effect that a disciple might offer any service to his teacher which a slave did for his master, except that of unfastening his shoes, which was counted as a menial's duty.

ἄξιος does not occur elsewhere in Jn. (cf. Lk. 15¹⁹), and the constr. ἄξιος ἵνα . . . is not found elsewhere in the N.T. Jn. never uses ἱκανός (οὐκ εἰμὶ ἱκανὸς ἵνα . . . is found again Mt. 8⁸, Lk. 7⁶). Perhaps ἄξιος is the more appropriate adj. here (cf. Acts 13²⁵, where it is found in the citation of the Baptist's proclamation, instead of the Synoptic ἱκανός); but cf. 2 Cor. 2¹⁶ πρὸς ταῦτα τίς ἱκανός;

28. The situation of the place is uncertain, and the variety of reading perplexes the topographical problem still more.

Βηθανίᾳ is read by א*ABC*WNΘ and must be accepted, although a " Bethany beyond Jordan " is not mentioned elsewhere. The rec. reading Βηθαβαρᾷ was adopted by Origen on geographical grounds (Comm. vi. 40). The Sinai Syriac has Beth Abré, which Burkitt thinks must rest on local tradition similar to that followed by Origen.

ἐγένετο πέραν τοῦ Ἰορδάνου, ὅπου ἦν ὁ Ἰωάνης βαπτίζων.

29. Τῇ ἐπαύριον βλέπει τὸν Ἰησοῦν ἐρχόμενον πρὸς αὐτόν, καὶ

Conder identified *Bethabara* with the ford called 'Abârah, N.E. of Bethshean.[1] Jordan had many fords and ferries, and the name Bethabara would suit any place near a ford, its root being עבר "to cross"; but it is in favour of Conder's identification that the name is not found elsewhere (cf. *Beth-barah*, Judg. 7[24]). 'Abârah is barely 20 miles from Cana as the crow flies, but would be about 40 miles by road, so that it would be a *possible* site, if we take into account the time spent on the journey (2[1]). It is, however, too far from Jerusalem to suit the Synoptic narrative (Mk. 1[5], Mt. 3[5]), and the traditional site is much farther south, near Jericho.[2]

Beth-Nimrah, on the E. side of Jordan, N.E. of Jericho, will meet all the conditions of the problem. In Josh. 13[27] (B) Beth-Nimrah becomes Βαιθαναβρά, and this form might be corrupted either into Bethany *or* Bethabara. We incline to accept this identification, which, made at the first by Sir George Grove, was accepted by Sir Charles Wilson,[3] and favoured by Cheyne.

ὅπου ἦν Ἰωάνης βαπτίζων. This coupling of a participle with the verb εἶναι, where we should expect an imperfect (ἐβάπτιζε) denoting continued action, is common in Jn. We have the phrase ἦν Ἰωάνης βαπτίζων repeated 3[23] 10[40]; cf. also 5[5] 11[1] 13[23]. It is also found in the Synoptists (*e.g.* Lk. 5[16], Mt. 19[22]). This may be an Aramaic constr., but it is also found in classical Greek.

Abbott notes (*Diat.* 2171) that ὅπου after the name of a place (a constr. which appears again 12[1] 19[18], and in Mk., Mt. occasionally) is not in accordance with classical usage. Milligan cites from a second-century papyrus, εἰς Λιβύην ὅπου Ἄμμων . . . χρησμῳδεῖ, an excellent parallel.

The Baptist's designation of Jesus as the Christ (vv. 29–34)

29. τῇ ἐπαύριον. We now come to the second day of this spiritual diary (see on v. 19). One of the characteristics of the Fourth Gospel is the precision with which the author gives dates (see Introd., p. cii).

βλέπει τὸν Ἰησοῦν. The name Ἰησοῦς generally takes the article in Jn. (as in the Synoptists), except where an apposi-

---

[1] *D.B., s.v.* "Bethabara."
[2] Eusebius, *Onom.*
[3] See Smith's *D.B.*[2], *s.v.* "Beth-Nimrah"; cf. also *E.B., s.v.* "Bethany," and see Rix, *Tent and Testament*, p. 175 f.

λέγει Ἴδε ὁ Ἀμνὸς τοῦ Θεοῦ ὁ αἴρων τὴν ἁμαρτίαν τοῦ κόσμου.

tional phrase with the article is introduced, or in a quotation (4¹· ⁴⁷ 6²⁴), or in the phrase ἀπεκρίθη Ἰη. (see on 1⁵⁰), or before οὖν (see on 6¹⁵). There are a few other exceptions to the rule (e.g. 11⁵¹ 12⁴⁴), but where the article is missing before Ἰη. the text always calls for scrutiny. B is more prone to omit ὁ before Ἰη. than the other great uncials. (See Introd., p. lxvi.)

ἐρχόμενον πρὸς αὐτόν, "coming towards him." According to the Johannine narrative, Jesus had been baptized already, and probably the Temptation in the Wilderness had taken place. It would be natural that He should come back to John's neighbourhood, where many earnest inquirers were gathered. There is no mention of any conversation between Him and John on this occasion; but John, as He passes, designates Him publicly as the Christ.

Ἴδε κτλ. This is a favourite word with Jn.; cf. 1³⁶· ⁴⁷ 3²⁶ 5¹⁴ 7²⁶· ⁵² 11³· ³⁶· 12¹⁹ 16²⁹ 18²¹ 19⁴· ⁵· ¹⁴ 20²⁷. The Apocalyptist prefers ἰδού.

ὁ ἀμνὸς τοῦ θεοῦ, i.e. the Lamb provided by God (see on 6³³). The word ἀμνός, common in LXX, appears in N.T only here, v. 36, 1 Pet. 1¹⁹, and Acts 8³² (a quotation from Isa. 53⁷), in each instance being applied to Christ, and with a sacrificial connotation. On the other hand, the diminutive ἀρνίον (occurring occasionally in the LXX, e.g. Ps. 114⁴· ⁶, Jer. 11¹⁹ 50⁴⁵, but not as often as ἀμνός) is found in the N.T. only at 21¹⁵ and in the Apocalypse, where it is applied to Christ 29 times. Although the distribution of ἀμνός and ἀρνίον is thus markedly different, no distinction of meaning can be traced when they are applied to Christ.

ὁ ἀμνὸς τοῦ θεοῦ κτλ. We have, first, to ask what the evangelist understood by the unique title "the Lamb of God," and what connotation it had for him.

(a) In Jer. 11¹⁹ we have: "I was as a gentle lamb (ἀρνίον) led away to be slaughtered," the emphasis being on the innocence of the victim; and Isaiah's "as a lamb (ἀμνός) before her shearers is dumb" (Isa. 53⁷) conveys the same idea. The two passages are brought together by Origen,[1] and the point of the comparison need not be missed. But the thought of the gentleness of a lamb is insufficient to explain the "Lamb of God which takes away the sin of the world."

(b) In 1 Pet. 1¹⁹ the Redemption of Christ is likened to that wrought on a lower plane by the sacrifice of a lamb without blemish. The deliverance from Egypt is the type of deliverance from the bondage of sin, and so the blood of the Paschal

[1] In Ioann. vi. 53.

lamb was typical of the blood of Christ. At the institution of
the Passover, indeed, the blood of the Paschal lamb was not
primarily piacular or redemptive; it was sprinkled on the door-
posts, that the destroying angel might " pass over " the house
(Ex. 12¹³). Nevertheless, the conception of its redemptive
efficacy prevailed in later Jewish thought; and Hort quotes
(on 1 Pet. 1¹⁹) an apposite Midrash on Ex. 12²² : " With two
bloods were the Israelites delivered from Egypt, the blood of
the Paschal lamb and the blood of circumcision." The reference in 1 Pet. 1¹⁹, then, relates to the Paschal lamb rather than
to the lamb of Isa. 53⁷.

In the Apocalypse, the application of ἀρνίον to Christ has
primary reference to the idea of a lamb as a *victim* [1] (Rev.
5⁶. ⁹ 7¹⁴), whose death is an expiatory sacrifice, efficacious for all
mankind. And the association in Rev. 15³ of the " Song of
Moses " with the " Song of the Lamb " suggests that, as in
1 Pet. 1¹⁹, the slain Lamb of the Apocalypse is compared with
the Paschal lamb, rather than with the lamb of the daily sacrifice.

The comparison of Christ with the Paschal lamb appears also
in a document earlier than either 1 Peter or the Apocalypse,
viz. 1 Cor. 5⁷, " Christ our Passover has been sacrificed for us."
And, inasmuch as this thought is conspicuously present in the
Johannine narrative of the Passion (see on 19³⁶), it would be
legitimate to interpret " the Lamb of God " in the present
passage in the same way, and to find here the thought that " the
Lamb of God, that taketh away the sins of the world," is the
true Paschal Lamb, of whom the Passover victims of the past
had been a type.

(c) It seems, however, that in the Johannine use of the title,
" the Lamb of God," there is a reference to Isa. 53⁶. ⁷ : " Yahweh hath laid on Him the iniquity of us all . . . as a lamb that
is led to the slaughter . . . He opened not His mouth." [2]
The passage is directly applied to Christ in Acts 8³², and other
phrases from the same prophecy are treated as having a
Messianic reference in Mt. 8¹⁷, 1 Pet. 2²²ᶠ·, Heb. 9²⁸. It is
certain that, soon after the Passion, Christian believers found
in Isa. 53 a forecast of the sufferings and the redemption of
Jesus Christ. And the author of the Fourth Gospel, writing
at the end of the first century, could not have been unaware
of this Christian interpretation of Hebrew prophecy,[3] which

[1] Secondarily, as Charles shows, the Apocalyptist conceives of the
Lamb as *leader*, an idea prominent in Jewish apocalyptic, but not
present in the Fourth Gospel (*Revelation*, i. cxiii).

[2] Cyprian's *Testimonia* (ii. 15) for Jn. 1²⁹ include *both* Ex. 12³ᵗ· and
Isa. 53⁷.

[3] Clement of Rome (§ 16), writing in the same decade, cites Isa. 53
in full, applying it all to Christ.

would be quite sufficient to explain the majestic title, "The Lamb of God, that taketh away the sin of the world." Indeed, Jn. treats Isa. 53 as a Messianic chapter at 12[38]; see on 19[30].

Such considerations help us to understand Jn.'s use of the title. But it is the *Baptist's* use of the title that presents difficulty. That he had been led to identify Jesus with Messiah who was to come, whether by private converse with Him before His baptism, or by the sign at the baptism which he believed himself to have received (v. 33), is in accordance with all the evidence that is available.[1] But that John the Baptist should have spoken of *the Christ* as "the Lamb of God, that taketh away the sin of the world," and have done so, not only before His Passion, but before His public ministry had begun, requires explanation.

The idea of a Suffering Messiah was not prevalent among the Jews of the first century[2] (see on 12[34]). The apostles never reconciled themselves to the idea that Jesus was to die by violence (Mk. 9[32] and *passim*; cf. Lk. 24[21]). Yet here we find the Baptist represented as foreseeing from the beginning that the climax of the ministry of Jesus would be death, and as announcing this publicly by acclaiming Him as the true Lamb of sacrifice, foreordained of God. It has been urged, in explanation, that the Baptist was the son of a priest, familiar with sacrificial ideas all his life. He certainly thought of himself as the Forerunner of the Christ, and Jn. represents him as believing that he was the herald of Isa. 40[3] (see on v. 23). He was, therefore, a student of the Isaianic prophecies which tell of the ideal Servant of Yahweh, the chosen One in whom Yahweh delights (Isa. 42[1]). Later he was reassured, when in perplexity, by learning that the mighty works of Jesus were such as had been predicted of this Servant of Yahweh (Mt. 11[5], Lk. 7[22]; cf. Isa. 35[5. 6] 42[7] 61[1]). And so what more natural than that he should apply to Jesus the most striking of all the prophecies about Yahweh's Servant, viz. Isa. 53? If he identified in his thoughts this great prophetic ideal with the person of Jesus, it would be explicable that he should call Jesus "the Lamb of God, which taketh away the sin of the world."

Dr. C. J. Ball[3] held that the title "Lamb of God" has an even closer connexion with Isa. 53 than is indicated by the word ἀμνός in Isa. 53[6]. The Hebrew word טָלֶה "lamb" came in its Aramaic form טַלְיָא to mean "child," "boy," "servant"; and he suggested that what the Baptist really said in Aramaic

---

[1] See Introd., p. ci.
[2] Cf. also Justin, *Tryph.* 32, and Introd., p. cxxxiii.
[3] See Burney, *Aramaic Origin, etc.*, p. 108.

was, " Behold the Servant of God, who takes away the sin of the world," the Greek rendering in Jn. 1²⁹ being an excusable mistranslation. Ball urged further that ὁ υἱὸς τοῦ θεοῦ in v. 34 is a more correct rendering of the same Aramaic phrase, in both cases the explicit reference being to the παῖς of Isa. 42¹ 52¹³, Acts 3¹³ 4²⁷.

The main difficulty in the way of all such explanations is that there is no good evidence that the Messianic application of Isa. 53 was current among the Jews in pre-Christian times. As has been said above, it became current among Christians immediately *after* the Passion of Christ; but it does not appear that either the Jews or the early disciples during the earthly ministry of Jesus conceived of Isa. 53 as foretelling a suffering Christ.[1] It is, therefore, hard to believe that John the Baptist, alone among the witnesses of the ministry of Jesus, and before that ministry had begun, should have associated Him with the central figure of Isa. 53; and that he should have so markedly anticipated the conclusions reached by those who, after the Passion, looking back upon the life and death of Jesus, found them to fulfil the predictions of the Hebrew prophet.

To sum up. John Baptist believed Jesus to be the Christ of Jewish expectation, and announced Him as such, probably in the hearing of John, the son of Zebedee. Looking back, the aged apostle in after years realised how momentous an announcement this was, even more momentous than the Baptist had understood. And when dictating his recollections of an incident on which he had pondered long and deeply, it is intelligible that he should state the Baptist's cry, " Behold the Christ," in terms which unfolded all that Jesus had come to mean for himself. Jesus was " the Lamb of God, who takes away the world's sin." We do not suppose that the speeches in the Fourth Gospel were all spoken exactly as they are set down, although they may have been in some instances. But here, whether we attribute the form of the Baptist's announcement to John the son of Zebedee, or to the scribe and editor of the Gospel who put in order the old man's reminiscences, we must recognise the probability that the Baptist's actual words were simpler, and a less perfect expression of the Gospel of Redemption. Cf. Introd., p. cii.

ὁ αἴρων τὴν ἁμαρτίαν τοῦ κόσμου. In 1 Jn. 3⁵ we have ἐκεῖνος ἐφανερώθη ἵνα τὰς ἁμαρτίας ἄρῃ. Here the " taking away " is in the present tense, the *futurum instans* (like μαρτυρεῖ in v. 15). ὁ αἴρων is He who takes away and is always taking away the

---

[1] Burkitt, *Christian Beginnings*, p. 39, points out that the application of Isa. 53 to the Passion was made by *Greek*-speaking Christians in the first instance. Cf. *Theology*, July 1922, p. 50.

30. οὗτός ἐστιν ὑπὲρ οὗ ἐγὼ εἶπον Ὀπίσω μου ἔρχεται ἀνὴρ ὃς ἔμπροσθέν μου γέγονεν, ὅτι πρῶτός μου ἦν. 31. κἀγὼ οὐκ ᾔδειν αὐτόν, ἀλλ᾽ ἵνα φανερωθῇ τῷ Ἰσραήλ, διὰ τοῦτο ἦλθον ἐγὼ ἐν ὕδατι

world's sin, a profound Christian conception, formulated first in this verse, and reproduced with fidelity in the liturgical "Lamb of God, which *takest away* (not which *took away* once for all at Calvary, although that also is true) the sins of the world." For the Atonement is not only an event in time, but an eternal process.

The *sin* of the world—not *sins* in the plural, as at 1 Jn. 3⁵ —is here contemplated. Western liturgies have followed 1 Jn. 3⁵ rather than Jn. 1²⁹ in pleading "Agnus Dei qui tollis *peccata mundi, miserere nobis.*" But *the sin of the world* is a deeper stain than the sins of individual men and women; and the Fourth Evangelist, who views the mission of Jesus *sub specie æternitatis*, sees that it is the sin of the κόσμος (cf. v. 9), the lawlessness and rebellion of all created being, that is the subject of redemption. This includes, indeed, the sins of all men, but it is the sin of the κόσμος, which knew not Jesus (v. 10), that is in view in this tremendous phrase.

αἴρειν is used of *taking away* sin at 1 Sam. 15²⁵ 25²⁸, as at 1 Jn. 3⁵; at Isa. 53⁴ we have οὗτος τὰς ἁμαρτίας φέρει, the image being of the *bearing* of another's sin.

30. This verse is almost verbally identical with v. 15, and illustrates well Jn.'s habit of repeating a phrase which he regards as specially significant after a short interval, in a slightly different form (see on 3¹⁶).

οὗτός ἐστιν κτλ. "*This* One," pointing to Jesus, *is* He of whom I spake. The reference is not merely to vv .26, 27, but to Jn.'s proclamation of the Coming of Jesus, before He began His ministry, which is common to the Synoptists and Jn. (see on v. 15, and Introd., p. c).

The rec. text has οὗτός ἐστι περὶ οὗ ἐγὼ εἶπον, with אᶜAC³LNΔΘ; but א*BC*W give ὑπὲρ οὗ, "in whose behalf," the Baptist always regarding himself as the herald of Jesus. Blass points out that λέγειν ὑπέρ = λέγειν περί, "to speak about," is common in classical Greek, and that ὑπέρ for περί is found in Paul (*e.g.* 2 Cor. 8²³). But in Jn. (with whom it is a favourite preposition) ὑπέρ always means "in behalf of." Cf. 6⁵¹ 10¹¹. ¹⁵ 11⁴. ⁵⁰. ⁵¹. ⁵² 13³⁷. ³⁸ 15¹³ 17¹⁹ 18¹⁴, 1 Jn. 3¹⁶. See on 1¹⁵ for ὃν εἶπον, which seems to be the true text in that place.

ἀνήρ is applied, as here, to Jesus, Acts 2²² 17³¹; see on 1¹³ above for its Johannine usage.

31. κἀγὼ οὐκ ᾔδειν αὐτόν, repeated v. 33, "even I did not know Him" (cf. v. 26), *sc.* as the Messiah. That John the

βαπτίζων.   32. Καὶ ἐμαρτύρησεν Ἰωάνης λέγων ὅτι Τεθέαμαι τὸ

Baptist knew Jesus in their early years is hardly doubtful, but
the statement here made is that he did not recognise Him
for what He was before His Baptism.   The account in Mt.
3[14f.] is different, and represents John as unwilling to baptize
Jesus because he was aware of His Messiahship.   Jn's narrative, here as at other points (see v. 32), is more primitive than
the Matthæan tradition.

ἵνα φανερωθῇ τῷ Ἰσραήλ.   John knew that his ministry was
one of preparation only; its ultimate purpose was that in its
exercise the Expected One should be made manifest.

φανεροῦν, "to reveal," is a late Greek word, occurring in
LXX only at Jer. 33[6].   In the Synoptic Gospels it appears once
only (Mk. 4[22]), but is used in the Marcan Appendix (16[12. 14])
of the "manifestation" of the Person of Jesus, as in Jn. (7[4]
21[1. 14]; cf. 1 Jn. 1[2]).   The verb always indicates emergence from
mysterious obscurity, and a sudden breaking forth into clear
light.   Cf. 2[11] where it is used of the manifestation of the
glory of Jesus; and 3[21] of the manifestation in Him of the
works of God.   At 1 Tim. 3[16] it suggests Divine pre-existence,
and of this there may be a hint here (cf. v. 15), as there certainly
is in 1 Jn. 3[5], ἐκεῖνος ἐφανερώθη ἵνα τὰς ἁμαρτίας ἄρῃ.

τῷ Ἰσραήλ.   The "manifestation" for which the Baptist
looked was only to Israel.   The exhortation of the brethren of
Jesus was, indeed, φανέρωσον σεαυτὸν τῷ κόσμῳ (7[4]), but even
there no more is suggested than a public manifestation to the
Jews.   Jn. is fond of the term κόσμος (see on v. 9), and the
thought that Jesus manifested Himself to the whole order of
created life is deep-rooted in his thought; but he does not suggest that the Baptist had any such wide vision.

ἦλθον ἐγὼ ἐν ὕδατι βαπτίζων.   This was the most conspicuous
feature of his ministry; cf. v. 26, and see further on v. 33.

32. John now explains how and when it was that he came
to recognise Jesus as the Christ.

ἐμαρτύρησεν.   This testimony, as the aorist denotes, was
delivered at a definite moment; cf. contra μαρτυρεῖ in v. 15.
The testimony is to the effect that John saw a dove or pigeon
alight on Jesus at His baptism.   There is no hint that we are
to think of a spiritual vision; the verb θεᾶσθαι (see on 1[14]) is
always used in the N.T. of seeing with the bodily eyes.   The
incident is related differently by Mk. (1[10]), who implies (as does
Mt. 3[16]) that Jesus Himself saw the Spirit descending like a
dove.   Lk. 3[22] does not say who saw it, but all agree that a
dove was seen, the words of Lk., σωματικῷ εἴδει, laying
emphasis on the objective and physical nature of the incident.

Πνεῦμα καταβαῖνον ὡς περιστερὰν ἐξ οὐρανοῦ, καὶ ἔμεινεν ἐπ' αὐτόν.

All the evangelists, that is, agree in recording that a dove alighted upon Jesus when presenting Himself for baptism. The dove was regarded in Palestine as a sacred bird. Xenophon (*Anab.* i. iv. 9) reports that it was not lawful in Syria to hunt doves; and this is suggested by Tibullus (i. 7. 17):

Quid referam ut uolitet crebras intacta per urbes
Alta Palaestino sancta columba Syro.

So Lucian explains that to the Syrians a dove is *tabu*, and that any one unwittingly touching a dove is counted unclean (*de Dea Syria*, 54; cf. 14). Philo [1] comments on the great number of doves at Ascalon, and upon their tameness, due to the circumstance that from ancient times the people were not allowed to eat them, so that they were never caught (ap. Euseb. *Praep. Evangel.* viii. 14. 64).[2]

Furthermore, the dove was regarded among the Semites as a symbol of the Spirit. Of φωνὴ τῆς τρυγόνος, "the voice of the turtle" (Cant. 2¹²), there is a Chaldee interpretation, reported by Wetstein, "the Voice of the Spirit." And by the Jewish doctors the Spirit hovering over the primeval waters (Gen. 1²) was compared to a dove: "Spiritus Dei ferebatur super aquas, sicut columba, quae fertur super pullos suos nec tangit illos." [3]

Hence we can understand why a dove alighting upon Jesus should have been regarded as symbolic of a descent of the Divine Spirit.[4] The words ascribed to the Baptist are explicit. He saw the dove, and forthwith recognised it as the sign which he had been expecting (v. 33).

For the expression καταβαίνειν ἐξ οὐρανοῦ, see on 3¹³.

Some other divergences from the Synoptic accounts of the Baptism should be observed. Jn. says nothing of the heavens being opened (Mk. 1¹⁰ and parallels), or of the Voice from heaven (see on 12²⁸ below); and having regard to his knowledge of Mk.,[5] with whose account of the Baptist he has so much in

---

[1] Iu *Quis rer. div. hær.* § 25, Philo, when discoursing on Gen. xv. 9, interprets the turtle dove and pigeon (τρυγόνα καὶ περιστεράν) of divine and human wisdom respectively, the περιστερά standing for human wisdom, as being gentle (ἥμερος) and fond of the haunts of men.

[2] Clement of Alexandria says that the Syrians venerate doves, as the Eleans venerate Zeus (*Protrept.* ii. 35).

[3] Quoted by Wetstein on Mt. 3¹⁶ from *Chagiga*, 15A.

[4] Students of the fantastic science of *Gematria* have not failed to note that the arithmetical value of the letters in περιστερά is 801, the same total as that represented by αω (Alpha and Omega). Cf. Irenæus, *Hær.* i. 14. 6, who gives this as a Gnostic fancy.

[5] See Introd., p. c.

33. κἀγὼ οὐκ ᾔδειν αὐτόν, ἀλλ' ὁ πέμψας με βαπτίζειν ἐν ὕδατι,

common (see on v. 6), it would seem that these omissions are deliberate. Here, as in v. 31, the Johannine narrative appears to be more primitive than that of the Synoptists.

καὶ ἔμεινεν ἐπ' αὐτόν (cf. for the constr. 3³⁶). This is, on the other hand, a detail not found in the Synoptic narratives, perhaps added here with a reminiscence of Isa. 11², where it is said of the Messianic King, ἀναπαύσεται ἐπ' αὐτὸν πνεῦμα τοῦ θεοῦ.[1] Jerome (on Isa. 11²) quotes the following from the *Gospel of the Hebrews*: "When the Lord was come up out of the water, the whole fount of the Holy Spirit descended and rested upon Him, and said to Him: My Son, in all the prophets was I waiting for thee that thou shouldest come, and I might rest in thee. For thou art my rest, thou art my first-begotten Son that reigneth for ever." This is a doctrinal combination of the Synoptic and Johannine narratives, probably intended to teach the *permanence* of the spiritual gift here vouchsafed through Christ to mankind.[2]

The form in which the Dove and the Voice from heaven at the Baptism of Jesus are mentioned in the *Odes of Solomon* [3] is curious. Ode xxiv. begins: "The Dove fluttered over the Christ, because He was her head, and she sang over Him and her voice was heard," sc. in the Underworld. The singing or cooing of the dove is as it were a Heavenly Voice; and "fluttering" recalls the verb used by Justin, ὡς περιστερὰν τὸ ἅγιον πνεῦμα ἐπιπτῆναι ἐπ' αὐτόν (*Dial.* 88). The verb ἐπιπτῆναι is also found, in reference to the Baptism of Christ, in the Sibylline Oracles (vii. 67) and in Origen (*c. Cels.* i. 40, 41), and its rendering *volare* or *devolare* in Tertullian (*adv. Val.* 27) and in Hilary (in *Ps.* liv. 7), showing that it had a place in some extra-canonical record. This idea of the dove "fluttering" is, as we have seen, associated in Hebrew thought with the idea of the Spirit "brooding" over the waters; cf. Gen. 1², Deut. 32¹¹.

33. κἀγὼ οὐκ ᾔδειν αὐτόν, repeated from v. 31. John the Baptist repeats, as an essential part of his witness, that he did not recognise Jesus for what He was until the dove lit upon Him; and he recognised Him then only because he had been divinely warned that there would be a sign. The Baptist is not represented as saying that he knew that the sign would be forthcoming in the case of a candidate for baptism.

---

[1] Irenæus (*Hær.* iii. 17. 1) associates Isa. 11² with the Baptism of Jesus.
[2] See Abbott, *Diat.* 712 ff., for speculations as to why Jn. avoided the word *rest* and preferred *abide*.
[3] Cf. Introd., p. cxlvi.

ἐκεῖνός μοι εἶπεν Ἐφ' ὃν ἂν ἴδῃς τὸ Πνεῦμα καταβαῖνον καὶ μένον ἐπ' αὐτόν, οὗτός ἐστιν ὁ βαπτίζων ἐν Πνεύματι Ἁγίῳ. 34. κἀγὼ

ὁ πέμψας με. Cf. v. 6. John's mission to baptize was from God.

ἐκεῖνός (explicit and emphatic, see on v. 8) **μοι εἶπεν κτλ.** The Hebrew prophets had claimed that " the word of Yahweh " came to them, and John, the last of them, makes the same claim. " God said to me "; of that he was assured.

ἐφ' ὃν ἂν ἴδῃς τὸ πνεῦμα καταβ. κτλ. Upon whomsoever the Spirit descended and abode, He would be the minister of a greater baptism than that of John. John had doubtless (although this is not recorded) had many opportunities of observing the intense spirituality of the early life of Jesus, and his intercourse with Jesus previous to His baptism (according to Mt. 3¹⁴) had led John to see something of His unique personality. But, as the story is told, the Baptist was not finally assured of the Messiahship of Jesus until the dove rested upon Him. He had not been told that the descent of the Spirit would thus be indicated; but the sign was sufficient, and he accepted it joyfully.

οὗτός ἐστιν ὁ βαπτίζων ἐν πνεύματι ἁγίῳ. For οὗτος, cf. 1², and note that βαπτίζων is a prophetic present (cf. αἴρων in v. 29). The Spirit descended on Jesus, so that He might baptize men therewith, and that the Spirit might rest on them as it rested on Him, although not in the same plenitude (cf. 3³⁴).

ἐν ὕδατι . . . ἐν πνεύματι ἁγίῳ. Baptism as administered by John was, according to the Synoptists, symbolical of purification of the soul. It was, according to Mk. 1⁴, βάπτισμα μετανοίας εἰς ἄφεσιν ἁμαρτιῶν. There may be a hint at 3²⁵ of some association of John's ministry with the idea of purification, but there is no suggestion anywhere in the Fourth Gospel that his baptism was one " of repentance with a view to the remission of sins." It has been pointed out[1] that the language of Josephus (*Antt.* xviii. 5. 2) about John's ministry of baptism suggests that it was not addressed so much to penitents as to those who were dedicating themselves very specially to an ascetic life of virtue. That it was symbolical, at any rate, of *dedication*, as well as of *purification*, is plain from the circumstance that Jesus submitted, at the beginning of His ministry, to be baptized by John.

In all the Gospels the primary contrast between the ministry of John and the ministry of Jesus is that the first was ἐν ὕδατι, the second ἐν πνεύματι ἁγίῳ. Jn. makes the Baptist insist three times (vv. 26, 31, 33) that his baptism was *only* ἐν ὕδατι—that

[1] Jackson and Lake, *The Beginnings of Christianity*, i. 102.

ἑώρακα, καὶ μεμαρτύρηκα ὅτι οὗτός ἐστιν ὁ Υἱὸς τοῦ Θεοῦ.

is, it was only the symbol of a baptism ἐν πνεύματι which he could not minister. In the prophets water is used several times as an image of the Spirit (cf. Isa 44³, Ezek. 36²⁵, and note the verb in Joel 2²⁸, "I will *pour out* my Spirit upon all flesh"). Jn. is fond of this image (cf. 4¹⁴ 7³⁸); and the contrast of "water" and "spirit" in the Baptist's references to his ministry of baptism is intended to convey that it was only preparatory to, and symbolical of, a greater ministry that was at hand.

Mt. 3¹¹ and Lk. 3¹⁶ (but not Mk. 1⁸ or Acts 1⁵) speak of the ministry of Jesus as a baptizing "with the Holy Spirit *and with fire.*" But Jn. says nothing about a baptism with fire. Fire is the symbol of judgment, and Jesus "came not to judge the world, but to save the world" (12⁴⁷; cf. 9³⁹), in the Johannine presentation of His teaching.

34. κἀγὼ ἑώρακα, καὶ μεμαρτύρηκα. John's testimony was that of an eye-witness. He had seen the sign of the dove, and he bears witness accordingly, the perfect μεμαρτύρηκα indicating that his testimony was continuous up to the time of speaking, that Jesus was the Son of God.

In Jn., ὁ υἱὸς τοῦ θεοῦ is a recognised title of Messiah, Nathanael (1⁴⁹) and Martha (11²⁷) employing it as the Baptist does here. With this the Synoptists agree (Mk. 3¹¹, Mt. 14³³ 26⁶³ 27⁴⁰, Lk. 22⁷⁰); the title had a definite meaning to Jewish ears, and was applied in the sense of "Messiah."[1] In this sense it had its roots in the O.T.; cf., *e.g.*, Ps. 2⁷, where the theocratic king is Yahweh's Son, and Ps. 89²⁷. The evidence for its use in Apocalyptic literature is scanty, only one instance being found in *Enoch* (cv. 2) of Messiah being called "my Son"; cf. 2 Esd. 7²⁸ 13³². ³⁷. ⁵² 14⁹.

Jn is the only evangelist who represents Jesus as using this title of Himself (5²⁵ 10³⁶ 11⁴, where see notes). In these passages, if they stood alone, no higher meaning than "Messiah" need be ascribed to it; but when they are taken in connexion with the peculiar claims of sonship made by Jesus, in the Synoptists as well as in Jn. (see on 3¹⁷), the phrase "the Son of God" seems intended by Jn. to have a deeper significance (cf. 3¹⁸ 5²⁵ 19⁷ 20³¹).

For ὁ υἱὸς here there is a Western reading, ὁ ἐκλεκτός (א* *e* Syr. cur., probably supported by *Pap. Oxy.* 208). Cf. Mt. 27⁴⁰ with Lk. 23³⁵.

[1] Cf. *contra*, Dalman, *Words of Jesus*, Eng. Tr., p. 275; Burkitt (*Christian Beginnings*, p. 25) regards "Son of God" as the most primitive of the Christological titles.

35. Τῇ ἐπαύριον πάλιν εἱστήκει ὁ Ἰωάνης καὶ ἐκ τῶν μαθητῶν αὐτοῦ δύο, 36. καὶ ἐμβλέψας τῷ Ἰησοῦ περιπατοῦντι λέγει Ἴδε ὁ Ἀμνὸς τοῦ Θεοῦ. 37. καὶ ἤκουσαν οἱ δύο μαθηταὶ αὐτοῦ λαλοῦντος καὶ

The first disciples of Jesus (vv. 35–39)

35. τῇ ἐπαύριον (cf. v. 29). This is the third day of the story (see on 1¹⁹), and the first day of the ministry of Jesus: " primae origines ecclesiae Christianae " (Bengel).

πάλιν is a favourite word with Jn., occurring over 40 times, while it only occurs twice in Lk. (Mk. has it 27 times, and Mt. 17 times). Jn. uses it as a sort of resumptive conjunction, where a new section is introduced (*e.g.* 8¹². ²¹ 10⁷. ¹⁹ 21¹, etc.), the idea of *repetition* not being prominent in such cases.

πάλιν εἱστήκει.[1] The next incident is that the Baptist was standing awaiting Jesus, whom he had acclaimed on the previous day. On this occasion he had two of his own disciples with him.

ἐκ τῶν μαθητῶν αὐτοῦ δύο. For the constr. δύο ἐκ τῶν . . ., see on 1⁴⁰. A μαθητής is one who learns from, and associates himself with, a respected teacher. The μαθηταί of John the Baptist are mentioned again 3²⁵ 4¹ (cf. Mk. 2¹⁸, Mt. 11² 14¹², Lk. 7¹⁸ 11¹). See on 2².

One of these two disciples of the Baptist (cf. 3²⁵ 4¹) was Andrew (v. 40); the other is not named, and nothing more is said about him. But the Synoptic account of the call of the first disciples of Jesus (Mk. 1¹⁹, Mt. 4¹⁸) indicates that the first pair, Andrew and Peter, were quickly followed by the second pair, the sons of Zebedee. These are never mentioned explicitly in Jn., except in 21¹, but it is natural to infer that the unnamed disciple of v. 35 was one of them, viz. either James or John; and it would be in harmony with the reticence in regard to himself displayed throughout by the eye-witness whose reminiscences lie behind the Fourth Gospel, that he should here be referred to, *i.e.* that the unnamed disciple was John the son of Zebedee (see on vv. 19, 40).[2]

36. καὶ ἐμβλέψας. The verb (only again in Jn. at v. 42) signifies an intent, earnest gazing; cf. Mk. 10²¹ 14⁶⁷.

Jesus was not coming towards the Baptist (cf. v. 29) on this occasion, but moving away. John again designates him as " the Lamb of God " or the Christ, in the hearing of the two disciples who were in his company.

---

[1] This form (plpft. with sense of impft.), "was standing," occurs again 7³⁷ 18⁵. ¹⁶ 20¹¹. The MSS. vary between εἱστήκει and ἱστήκει, the latter being always adopted by Westcott-Hort.

[2] Cf. Introd., p. xxxvi.

ἠκολούθησαν τῷ 'Ιησοῦ. 38. στραφεὶς δὲ ὁ 'Ιησοῦς καὶ θεασάμενος αὐτοὺς ἀκολουθοῦντας λέγει αὐτοῖς Τί ζητεῖτε; οἱ δὲ εἶπαν αὐτῷ 'Ραββεί (ὃ λέγεται μεθερμηνευόμενον Διδάσκαλε), ποῦ μένεις;

37. אB place αὐτοῦ after μαθηταί, but αὐτοῦ comes first in C*LT^b 33, and even before οἱ δύο in AC³NΓΔΘW.

The two disciples heard John's words, and heard them with understanding and appreciation, for such (see on 3⁸) is the force in Jn. of ἀκούειν followed by a genitive.

καὶ ἠκολούθησαν τῷ 'Ιησοῦ, "and went after Jesus." Here was no decision to follow Him throughout His ministry and attach themselves to His Person, for the aorist only indicates their action at one definite moment. Jesus had not "called" them, or invited them to be His companions and disciples (cf. Mk. 1¹⁷ and parallels); nor were they constrained to go after Him by anything that they had seen Him do. John's striking and repeated designation of Him as the Expected One arrested their attention, and His own Personality did the rest.

38. στραφεὶς δέ κτλ. He turned round (cf. 20¹⁴), for He had heard their steps behind Him.

For θεασάμενος, always used of bodily vision, see on v. 14.

He asks, τί ζητεῖτε; "What do you seek? what are you looking for?" Their answer is, "Where are you staying?" for they desired an opportunity of private conversation with Him. They had not yet reached the stage of discipleship; they wished to know a little more about Him.

Abbott (*Diat.* 2649*b*) finds an illustration of τί ζητεῖτε; in Philo (*quod. det. pot.* 8) who, commenting on τί ζητεῖς; of Gen. 37¹⁵, explains it as the utterance of the ἔλεγχος to the wandering soul. Later on (c. 40) the ἔλεγχος is identified with the λόγος. But the parallel is not close enough to prove that Jn. is *indebted* to Philo for the use of so familiar a phrase as τί ζητεῖτε; Cf. 18⁴ 20¹⁵.

The disciples address Jesus as *Rabbi*, a title which Jn., writing for Greek readers, at once interprets, ὃ λέγεται μεθερμηνευόμενον, Διδάσκαλε. For similar interpretations of Aramaic or Hebrew words, cf. vv. 41, 42, 4²⁵ 5² 9⁷ 11¹⁶ 19¹³· ¹⁷, 20¹⁶.

They may have addressed Jesus thus because they took Him for a Rabbi travelling alone, but more likely they used *Rabbi* as an ordinary title of respect. It was the title which the Baptist's disciples were accustomed to use when addressing their master (3²⁶); and it appears from 13¹³ that afterwards the disciples of Jesus habitually addressed Him either as *Rabbi* (teacher) or as *Mari* (lord). The distinction is only this, that the antithesis to *Rabbi* is "scholar," and to *Mar* is "servant" or "slave" (cf. 15¹⁵); the terms being often used without any

clear sense of a difference between them. Either might be
rendered " Sir," without going wrong. Thus, in the Synoptic
narratives of the Transfiguration, where Mk. (9⁵) has *Rabbi*,
Lk. (9³³) renders it by ἐπιστάτα, and Mt. (17⁴) by κύριε. So in
the story about the storm on the lake, where Mk. (4³⁸) has
διδάσκαλε, Lk. (8²⁴) has ἐπιστάτα, and Mt. (8²⁵) has κύριε.
But while κύριε may thus sometimes represent *Rabbi*, or be
used (as at 12²¹ 21¹⁵) merely as the equivalent of the English
" Sir," it generally points to an original מָרִי or *Mari*.[1]

The Johannine usage of these terms is interesting. In the
early part of the Gospel the disciples are always represented as
saying *Rabbi*, while others,[2] such as the woman of Samaria
(4¹¹), the nobleman of Capernaum (4⁴⁹), the sick man at Bethesda
(5⁷), the blind man after his cure (9³⁶), Mary and Martha of
Bethany (11³. ²¹. ²⁷. ³², but cf. 11²⁸ and note there), say κύριε.
The multitude who were fed with the five loaves first say *Rabbi*
(6²⁵); but, after they have heard the discourse about the
heavenly bread, say κύριε (6³⁴). The first occasion on which a
disciple is represented as saying κύριε is at the conclusion of
this discourse, when Peter says, " Lord, to whom shall we go ? "
(6⁶⁸). We have Ῥαββεί used again by the disciples at 11⁸, but
κύριε at 11¹²; and thenceforward *Rabbi* disappears from their
speech, and they say *Lord* (13⁶. ²⁵ 14⁵. ⁸. ²² 21¹⁵, etc.), the change
in address indicating a growing reverence. The title *Rabbi*
was not employed after the Resurrection of Jesus, who was
afterwards spoken of as *Maran* or ὁ κύριος (cf. 1 Cor. 16²²,
and see note on 4¹).

Thus Jn.'s report as to the use of these titles by the disciples
is not only consistent, but is probably historical. Nothing of
this kind can be traced in the Synoptists, who do not distinguish between διδάσκαλε and κύριε as modes of address,
both being in use, as they represent the facts, at all stages of
the association of the Twelve with Jesus. Indeed, Lk. (11¹)
puts the phrase κύριε δίδαξον ἡμᾶς into the mouth of
the disciples. In this regard, a more primitive tradition is
preserved in the Fourth Gospel.

The Aramaic *Rabbi* is not found in Lk., and in Mt. only
in the greeting of Judas to his Master (26²⁵. ⁴⁹). Mk. has it in
the corresponding place (Mk. 14⁴⁵), and also places it twice
in Peter's mouth (Mk. 9⁵ 11²¹). *Rabboni* is found in Mk. 10⁵¹.
With these exceptions, the Synoptists always translate רַבִּי,
and do not reproduce the title itself.

---

[1] See on the whole subject, Dalman, *Words of Jesus*, Eng. Tr.,
pp. 324–340, and Burkitt, *Christian Beginnings*, pp. 43 ff.

[2] Nicodemus, naturally, says *Rabbi* (3²).

39. λέγει αὐτοῖς Ἔρχεσθε καὶ ὄψεσθε. ἦλθαν οὖν καὶ εἶδαν ποῦ
μένει, καὶ παρ' αὐτῷ ἔμειναν τὴν ἡμέραν ἐκείνην· ὥρα ἦν ὡς δεκάτη.

Lk. and Jn., both of whom wrote for Greek readers, thus
differ markedly as to the title *Rabbi*, Lk. never mentioning it,
while Jn. has it again and again, giving the Greek rendering
of it on its first occurrence. Probably the explanation is that
behind Jn. we have the report of one who spoke Aramaic, and
who was present at many of the scenes which he describes;
while Lk. rests on documents and on information gained at
second hand. In the reminiscences of his first intercourse with
Jesus, as John the son of Zebedee dictated them, he employed
the term *Rabbi*, which he remembers that he used; and his
interpreter, Jn., naturally translated it for the benefit of his
Greek readers, but preserved the original word.

39. Ἔρχεσθε καὶ ὄψεσθε. For ὄψεσθε (BC*LTᵇW and syrr.),
the rec. has ἴδετε with אAC³NΔΘ and latt. Lightfoot (*Hor.
Hebr.* in loc.) and Schlatter note that "Come and see" is
a common formula of authoritative invitation in Talmudic
authors; but parallels are unnecessary to cite for so simple
a phrase. Cf. 1⁴⁶ 11³⁴, ἔρχου καὶ ἴδε.

"Come and ye shall see." This is the method of discovery
which Jesus commended to the first inquirers, and it is still the
method by which He is revealed. Not by dialectic or argument, although these have their place, is the soul's quest
satisfied. For that there must be the personal following, the
"abiding" in His presence. Cf. 8³¹, and see on 6³⁵.

ἦλθαν καὶ εἶδαν ποῦ μένει. Observe the historic present
following "they saw" (cf. 21⁴).

Accordingly, the two inquirers παρ' αὐτῷ ἔμειναν τὴν ἡμέραν
ἐκείνην, "abode with Jesus that day," *sc.* that eventful day
which the narrator recalls (see on 11⁴⁹ for a like use of
ἐκεῖνος). Perhaps it was the Sabbath day (see on 2¹). The
addition "it was about the tenth hour" is, no doubt, a personal
reminiscence. That is, it was ten hours after sunrise, or about
4 p.m., when the two disciples reached the place where Jesus
was lodging.

The evangelists uniformly follow the practice, common
throughout the Roman world, of counting the hours from
sunrise. Thus Josephus reports (*Vita*, 54) that it was a Jewish
custom to dine (ἀριστοποιεῖσθαι) on the Sabbath day at the
sixth hour. Now the ἄριστον was the usual midday meal
(δεῖπνον being *supper*), so that "the sixth hour" means *noon*,
i.e. the day began about 6 a.m. The parable of the Discon-
tented Labourers shows this clearly (Mt. 20⁵· ⁶). So, in the
present passage, "the tenth hour" was about 4 p.m. There

40. Ἦν Ἀνδρέας ὁ ἀδελφὸς Σίμωνος Πέτρου εἷς ἐκ τῶν δύο τῶν ἀκουσάντων παρὰ Ἰωάνου καὶ ἀκολουθησάντων αὐτῷ· 41. εὑρίσκει

were "twelve hours in the day" (11⁹), but as the day was reckoned from sunrise to sunset, the length of an "hour" depended on the time of year. No doubt, the precision of reckoning habitual to people with watches and clocks is not to be looked for among Orientals of the first century; but it is remarkable how prone Jn. is to note the time of day (cf. 4⁶· ⁵² 18²⁸ 19¹⁴ 20¹⁹), and his exactitude suggests that he is reproducing the report of an observer of the events recorded.[1]

The call of Peter (vv. 40-42)

40. Ἀνδρέας. Jn. alone tells that Andrew was a disciple of the Baptist (v. 35). The Synoptic story of the call of Peter and Andrew (Mk. 1¹⁶ᶠ· and parls.) may be another version of vv. 40-42, but it probably narrates a more formal call to apostleship which came later (see on v. 37, and Introd., p. xxxv). Andrew is introduced as "Simon Peter's brother," being the less famous of the two (cf. also 6⁸ and Mk. 1¹⁶, Mt. 4¹⁸ 10², Lk. 6¹⁴); and, except at 12²², he is always associated with Peter. Jn. assumes that every one will know who Simon Peter was, a similar assumption being made by Lk., who mentions "the house of Simon" and "Simon's wife's mother" (Lk. 4³⁸), before anything is told about Simon himself. See, further, on 6⁸ for the prominence of Andrew in the Fourth Gospel.

εἷς ἐκ τῶν δύο κτλ. Jn. prefers to write εἷς ἐκ rather than εἷς simpliciter when speaking of one of a number of persons (cf. 6⁸· ⁷⁰· ⁷¹ 7⁵⁰ 11⁴⁹ 12² 13²¹· ²³ 18²⁶ 20²⁴). The Synoptists generally omit ἐκ, as Jn. does on occasion (7¹⁹ 12⁴).

τῶν ἀκουσάντων παρὰ Ἰωάνου, sc. v. 35. The constr. παρά τινος occurs again 6⁴⁵ 7⁵¹ 8²⁶· ⁴⁰ 15¹⁵; it is quite classical.

41. The text is uncertain. ℵ*LWΓΔ give πρῶτος. This would mean that Andrew was the first to find his brother Peter; implying that the unnamed disciple had also set out to find his brother (i.e., presumably, James, the elder son of Zebedee), and that he did find him, but later. But if the sentence means all this, it is very obscurely expressed.

πρῶτον, accepted by most modern editors, is supported by ℵᶜABTᵇΘ fam. 13, and the vss. generally. This would mean that Andrew found Peter first, before he did anything else, there

---

[1] The idea (adopted by Westcott) that Jn. follows a method of counting the hours from midnight has been shown by W. M. Ramsay (D.B., 475-479) to be untenable ; cf. A. Wright, N.T. Problems, pp. 147 ff.

οὗτος πρωὶ τὸν ἀδελφὸν τὸν ἴδιον Σίμωνα καὶ λέγει αὐτῷ Εὑρήκαμεν τὸν Μεσσίαν (ὅ ἐστιν μεθερμηνευόμενον Χριστός). 42. ἤγαγεν

being no suggestion of John looking for any one, or of any other disciple being found by either of them. The emphasis on ἴδιον, "his *own* brother," would be consistent with this. Whether we read πρῶτος or πρῶτον, a good deal of time elapses between v. 39 and v. 43. Andrew and the *innominatus*, presumably, have a full and convincing conversation with Jesus, staying with Him for the afternoon and night ; Andrew goes out and finds Peter, who is brought back to Jesus, welcomed, and renamed Kephas. Modern editors (Alford is an exception) try to find time for all this between 4 p.m. and the next morning (ἐπαύριον, v. 43), although this is not stated. It would be easier to understand the sequence of events if we suppose "that day" (v. 39) to mean a full day of twenty-four hours, from sunset to sunset, and allow two nights, instead of one only, to intervene between ἐπαύριον of v. 35 and ἐπαύριον of v. 43. This would be consistent either with πρῶτος or πρῶτον, both being awkward on any hypothesis.

But there is another reading, πρωί, supported by the O.L. texts *b*, *e*, and (apparently) *r*, all of which have *mane*.[1] An original πρωιτοναδελφον would readily be corrupted to πρω- τοναδελφον, which leads to πρωτοντοναδελφον. We conclude that πρωί is the true reading. Jn. uses this form (not πρωΐα) again at 18²⁸ 20¹; and it gives an excellent sense here. "He finds early in the morning his own brother Simon," having stayed the night at the lodging where Jesus was. Then ἐπαύριον in v. 43 stands for the day after the finding of Simon, which occupies Day iv. of the spiritual diary covered by this chapter (see on v. 29 above). This is certain if πρωί be accepted as the true reading, and even if we read πρῶτον it is highly probable.

εὑρήκαμεν τὸν Μεσσίαν. This was (and is) the Great Discovery. Andrew speaks for his unnamed companion as well as for himself: "*We* have found the Messiah."

τὸν Μεσσίαν. The Aramaic title מָשִׁיחַ is found in the N.T. elsewhere only at 4²⁵. See on v. 38 for the preservation of such Aramaic forms in Jn., although not in the Synoptists, the Greek interpretation being added. Cf. Ps. 2², Dan. 9²⁵. ²⁸.

According to Jn., the recognition of Jesus as the Christ by Andrew, by Philip (v. 45), and by Nathanael (v. 49) was swift and unhesitating; although it is noteworthy that nothing of this kind is told of Peter, whose confession of faith is not

[1] The Old Syriac does not reproduce here any word like πρῶτον or πρωί.

αὐτὸν πρὸς τὸν Ἰησοῦν. ἐμβλέψας αὐτῷ ὁ Ἰησοῦς εἶπεν Σὺ εἶ Σίμων ὁ υἱὸς Ἰωάνου, σὺ κληθήσῃ Κηφᾶς (ὃ ἑρμηνεύεται Πέτρος).

recorded until 6[68, 69]. The Synoptists suggest, as is probable *a priori*, that the disciples did not reach full conviction all at once, but that it came to them gradually, the critical point being Peter's confession (Mk. 8[29], Mt. 16[16], Lk. 9[20]). Perhaps we should regard the full assurance which Jn. ascribes to Andrew, Philip, and Nathanael on their first meeting with Jesus as antedated. It is, however, legitimate to treat their utterances (vv. 41, 45, 49) as the expressions of an enthusiasm which became dulled, as the novelty of their intercourse with Jesus passed away, and which did not become a reasoned conviction until later.[1]

42. The rec. has Ἰωνᾶ (with AB[3]ΓΔ) for the better supported Ἰωάνου (אB*LW 33, etc.). A similar variation appears at 21[15-17].

ἐμβλέψας, *sc.* "having looked intently on him." This verb has already (v. 36) been used of the Baptist's earnest look at Jesus; it is used by the Synoptists of the piercing, scrutinising gaze of Jesus (Mt. 19[26], Mk. 10[21, 27], Lk. 20[17]), and of His "looking" upon Peter after his denial.

It is plain from this verse (cf. 21[15-17] and Mt. 16[17]) that Simon was known as "Simon, son of John," to distinguish him from others bearing the common personal name "Simon." By the Synoptists he is generally called "Peter," but often simply "Simon"; in the lists of the apostles it being added that he was surnamed "Peter" (Mt. 10[2], Mk. 3[16], Lk. 6[14]), this addition being necessary to distinguish him from the other apostle called Simon. The designation "Simon Peter" marks a later date than "Simon" simply; and it is noteworthy that while in Jn. he is described as Σίμων Πέτρος 17 times (see further on 18[15]), this double name appears in the Synoptists only at Mt. 16[16] (a passage peculiar to Mt. and later than the Marcan tradition) and at Lk. 5[8].[2]

Jn. states here that Jesus gave Simon the Aramaic name or nickname of *Kephas*, which became Πέτρος in Greek, when He saw him for the first time, discerning his strong character at a glance. Mk. (3[16]) rather suggests (although he does not say expressly) that Simon was given the name of Peter when he was selected as one of the Twelve, much as John and James were called *Boanerges* or "sons of thunder." This is not suggested, however, in the lists of the apostles in Lk. (6[14f.]) and

[1] Cf. Introd., p. cxxxiv.
[2] See a full note on "The Names of St. Peter" in Hort, 1 *Peter*, p. 152.

43. Τῇ ἐπαύριον ἠθέλησεν ἐξελθεῖν εἰς τὴν Γαλιλαίαν, καὶ εὑρίσκει Φίλιππον. καὶ λέγει αὐτῷ ὁ Ἰησοῦς Ἀκολούθει μοι. 44. ἦν

Mt. (10²; Mt. has Σίμων ὁ λεγόμενος Πέτρος). It is obviously appropriate that Mt. should call the apostle "Simon Peter" (16¹⁶) when relating his great confession, and that Jesus, addressing him on that occasion as "Simon, son of John," should have reminded him of the name Kephas: σὺ εἶ Πέτρος, καὶ ἐπὶ ταύτῃ τῇ πέτρᾳ οἰκοδομήσω μου τὴν ἐκκλησίαν. Jn. may have ante-dated the giving of the new and significant name, but there is no proof of this.

To give a new name in the O.T. history sometimes marked the beginning of a new relation to God; e.g. Jacob was called Israel (Gen. 32²⁸), and Abram became Abraham (Gen. 17⁵), after a spiritual crisis (cf. also Isa. 62² 65¹⁵). When adult converts from heathenism are baptized, they are given a new name for a similar reason. But there is no evidence that it is in Jn.'s mind to suggest this when he recalls that Jesus called Simon, Kephas, "the rock man," [1] although such an inference might be drawn from Mt. 16¹⁶ᶠ· if it stood alone. Jn.'s narrative here is quite simple, and there is no subtlety in the telling. See, however, on 6⁶⁹.

The Aramaic name Kephas (perhaps the same as Kaiaphas) is familiar in Paul, who uses it to designate Simon always in 1 Cor. (1¹² 3²² 9⁵ 15⁵) and generally in Gal. (1¹⁸ 2⁹· ¹¹· ¹⁴; but cf. 2⁷· ⁸). It appears in no other Gospel but Jn., and the retention of the Aramaic כיפא is a touch that could hardly have occurred to any one whose mother speech was not Aramaic (see on vv. 38, 41, and cf. p. lxxix). By the end of the first century Simon was best known as Πέτρος, and he has been generally called by this name ever since.

The call of Philip and Nathanael (vv. 43-51)

43. τῇ ἐπαύριον, i.e. on Day v. of this eventful week (see on v. 9), Jesus resolved to go forth into Galilee; for ἐξελθεῖν εἰς τὴν Γαλιλαίαν cf. 4⁴³, and note that Jesus is now on the E. side of Jordan. Either as He was starting, or on the way, He found Philip, who was a Galilæan like Andrew and Peter, and who was probably brought into touch with Him by their means.

The rec. text adds ὁ Ἰησοῦς after ἠθέλησεν, omitting the name after αὐτῷ, but the better reading (אABWΘ) omits it after ἠθέλησεν and inserts it after αὐτῷ.

Thus, we might suppose from the order of the words that

[1] See Moffatt, Introd., p. 524.

δὲ ὁ Φίλιπος ἀπὸ Βηθσαϊδά, ἐκ τῆς πόλεως Ἀνδρέου καὶ Πέτρου.
45. εὑρίσκει Φίλιππος τὸν Ναθαναὴλ καὶ λέγει αὐτῷ Ὃν ἔγραψεν

the subject of ἠθέλησεν and εὑρίσκει is not ὁ Ἰησοῦς, but Πέτρος,
who has been mentioned immediately before. Then we should
have the attractive sequence: Andrew finds Peter, Peter finds
Philip, Philip (in his turn) finds Nathanael (v. 45), all being
fellow-Galilæans and friends. But if Πέτρος is the subject of
εὑρίσκει, it must also be the subject of ἠθέλησεν.

44. Philip is said to be ἀπὸ Βηθσαϊδά, *i.e.* from Bethsaida
Julias, at the N.E. end of the Lake of Galilee (see on $6^{1.\ 16}$ 12^{21}).
Bethsaida had been rebuilt by Philip, tetrarch of Ituræa
(Lk. 3^1), as Josephus records (*Antt.* xviii. 2. 1); and it is pos-
sible that the apostle Philip was named after the ruler of the
district.

After Βηθσαϊδά, Jn. adds ἐκ τῆς πολέως Ἀνδρέου καὶ Πέτρου.
The house of Andrew and Peter was not at Bethsaida, but at
Capernaum (Mk. $1^{21.\ 29}$), a town which Jn. mentions, 2^{12} 4^{46}
$6^{17.\ 24.\ 59}$, and of which he knew the situation precisely. The
discrepancy is unimportant.

Attempts have been made to distinguish in Jn. between
ἀπό, as indicating habitation, and ἐκ, birthplace (see Abbott,
Diat. 2289). If this could be sustained, we might say that
Philip was a native of Capernaum, whose home was at Bethsaida.
But it appears from $6^{33.\ 38.\ 41}$ 7^{42}, that ἀπό and ἐκ are used almost
interchangeably, as they were beginning to be in Greek authors
generally. Cf. Ps. 140^1,

ἐξελοῦ με ἐξ ἀνθρώπου πονηροῦ
ἀπὸ ἀνδρὸς ἀδίκου ῥῦσαί με,

where no distinction can be traced. Moulton-Milligan, *s.v.*
ἐκ, quote from papyri the phrase οἱ ἐκ τῆς κώμης of the *inhabitants* (not necessarily the *natives*) of a village. See further
on 11^1.

ἀκολούθει μοι. This probably means no more, in this context, than that Jesus asked for Philip's company on the journey
into Galilee. The same call was afterwards addressed to others
with a more exacting meaning (cf. Mk. 2^{14}, Mt. 8^{22} 19^{21}, and
especially Jn. 21^{19}).

It has been suggested that Philip is to be identified with the
disciple who wished to bury his father before he obeyed the call
to follow (Mt. 8^{22}), but this is mere conjecture.

45. Nathanael is a Hebrew name, נְתַנְאֵל, meaning "God
has given," the equivalent of the Greek *Theodore*. He was of
Cana of Galilee (21^2), and it was perhaps there that Philip
found him, as Cana is the next place mentioned (2^1).

Μωῦσῆς ἐν τῷ νόμῳ καὶ οἱ προφῆται εὑρήκαμεν, Ἰησοῦν υἱὸν τοῦ Ἰωσὴφ τὸν ἀπὸ Ναζαρέτ. 46. καὶ εἶπεν αὐτῷ Ναθαναήλ Ἐκ Ναζαρὲτ δύναταί τι ἀγαθὸν εἶναι; λέγει αὐτῷ ὁ Φίλιππος Ἔρχου καὶ ἴδε. 47. εἶδεν Ἰησοῦς τὸν Ναθαναὴλ ἐρχόμενον πρὸς αὐτὸν καὶ

Nathanael has been identified, e.g. by Renan and Zahn, with Bartholomew, because (1) in the Synoptic lists of the apostles, Philip is associated with Bartholomew as he is here with Nathanael, and (2) while the name Nathanael does not occur in the Synoptists, Bartholomew (which is only a patronymic, *Bar Tholmai*) is not found in Jn.

This group of disciples are represented as students of the O.T. As Andrew says, " We have found the Messiah " (v. 41), so Philip says, " We have found Him of whom Moses and the prophets wrote." This is what was explained to the disciples at Emmaus (Lk. 24[27]). The reference to " Moses " includes at any rate Deut. 18[15].

The Person in whom these prophecies were fulfilled is described by Philip as " Jesus, a son of Joseph (not *the* son, τὸν υἱόν of the rec. text being erroneous), the man from Nazareth." It is certain that the author of the Fourth Gospel did not regard Jesus as a " son of Joseph "; for him Jesus was μονογενὴς θεός (v. 18). But he does not stay to explain that Philip's confession fell short of the truth, just as he does not comment on the query, " Is not this Jesus the son of Joseph ? " (6[42]). Jn. is sure that his readers are of one mind with himself as to the Divinity of Jesus, and that they will not misunderstand. This characteristic of Jn.'s style has been called " the irony of St. John," [1] and it appears several times. (Cf. 6[42] 7[35] 18[28] 19[19].)

τὸν ἀπὸ Ναζαρέτ. " The man from Nazareth " (so Acts 10[37]) was the natural designation of Jesus by those who only knew where He lived (see on 18[5]). " Jesus of Nazareth " is still a descriptive phrase on the lips of many who are assured that He was θεὸς ἐκ θεοῦ.

46. Nathanael's rejoinder has been taken by some to be a meditative comment on what Philip has said rather than a question, viz. " Some good *might* come out of Nazareth." But the order of the words is in favour of it being taken interrogatively, " Can any good thing come out of Nazareth? " Nazareth is not mentioned in the O.T., so that there was nothing to connect the place with the prophecies of Messiah. See on 7[41. 52]. But Nathanael's question has something of scorn in it, as if Nazareth had a bad name; however, of this there is no evidence. Nathanael was of Cana, and the rivalry between neighbouring villages might account for his expression of

---

[1] Salmon, *Introd. to N.T.*, p. 280; cf. p. xxxiv above.

λέγει περὶ αὐτοῦ Ἴδε ἀληθῶς Ἰσραηλείτης, ἐν ᾧ δόλος οὐκ ἔστιν.
48. λέγει αὐτῷ Ναθαναήλ Πόθεν με γινώσκεις; ἀπεκρίθη Ἰησοῦς
καὶ εἶπεν αὐτῷ Πρὸ τοῦ σε Φίλιππον φωνῆσαι ὄντα ὑπὸ τὴν συκῆν

incredulity as to Nazareth being a prophet's home. That he
does not seem to have heard of Jesus before shows how retired
His life had been before He began His public ministry.

47. There is no suggestion that Jesus overheard Nathanael's
incredulous query. He speaks from His previous knowledge
of the man (v. 48).

ἴδε. See on v. 29.

ἀληθῶς Ἰσραηλείτης ἐν ᾧ δόλος οὐκ ἔστιν. Isaac complained
of Jacob's guile (δόλος, Gen. 27³⁵) ; but that was before he
received the new name of Israel and had a vision of heavenly
things. The Psalmist hails as blessed the man "in whose
spirit there is no guile " (Ps. 32²); and of the ideal Servant of
Yahweh it was declared, "neither was any guile found in his
mouth " (Isa. 53⁹). Thus he who is truly an Israelite (cf.
Rom. 2²⁹), representing Israel at its best, must be without guile,
and such a man Nathanael was declared by Jesus to be.

Jn. has ἀληθῶς again, 4⁴² 6¹⁴ 7²⁶. ⁴⁰ 8³¹, 1 Jn. 2⁵.

48. πόθεν με γινώσκεις; "Whence do you know me?"
Nathanael had overheard the remark of Jesus, and expresses
wonder that He should have known anything about him.

γινώσκειν is a favourite word with Jn., occurring about
twice as frequently as it does in the Synoptists, which is all the
more remarkable as Jn. never uses the noun γνῶσις (Lk. 1⁷⁷ 11⁵²,
and often in Paul). For the supposed distinction between
εἰδέναι and γινώσκειν, see on v. 26; cf. 2²⁴.

ἀπεκρ. Ἰη. ℵΘ insert ὁ before Ἰησοῦς, but om. ABLWΓΔ;
see on vv. 29, 50.

πρὸ τοῦ σε Φίλιππον φωνῆσαι. φωνεῖν is the word used in
Jn. for calling any one by his personal name or usual title;
cf. 10³ 11²⁸ 12¹⁷ 13¹³ 18³³.

ὑπὸ τὴν συκῆν εἶδόν σε, "I saw thee under the fig tree."
ὑπό is not found with the acc. elsewhere in Jn. (see on ὑποκάτω in
v. 50). Perhaps it indicates here that Nathanael had withdrawn
to the shelter of the fig tree, under which Jesus had seen him.

ὑπὸ τὴν συκῆν. The fig tree is a very familiar object in
Palestine, where it was specially valued for the grateful shade
of its leaves. National tranquillity is often pictured by the
image of every man sitting "under his vine and under his fig
tree" (1 Kings 4²⁵, Mic. 4⁴, 1 Macc. 14¹²). When Jesus says to
Nathanael, "When thou wast under the fig tree," i.e. probably
the fig tree in the precincts of his own house, He alludes to some
incident of which the evangelist gives no explanation. What-

εἰδόν σε.   49. ἀπεκρίθη αὐτῷ Ναθαναήλ 'Ραββεί, σὺ εἶ ὁ υἱὸς τοῦ Θεοῦ, σὺ βασιλεὺς εἶ τοῦ Ἰσραήλ.   50. ἀπεκρίθη Ἰησοῦς καὶ εἶπεν

ever it was, the fact that Jesus should have known it impressed Nathanael so much that he broke out into the confession, " Thou art the Son of God, Thou art the King of Israel." The power which Jesus had of reading the secrets of men's hearts is alluded to again, 2²⁴· ²⁵ 4¹⁹· ²⁹.

This episode has been compared [1] with the story of the prolonged meditation of Gautama under the Bodhi tree, where he attained Buddha-hood, and thenceforward began to gather disciples. But there is no real parallel. It was not Jesus, but His disciple Nathanael, who meditated under the fig tree, nor is there any hint (as in the Buddha legend) that Jesus received " enlightenment " thus.

Cheyne [2] gets rid of the fig tree by the supposition that there has been a misreading of an Aramaic original, the words וְאַתָּה מִתְחַנֵּן, " when thou wast making supplication," being mistaken for וְאַתָּה תַּחַת הַתְּאֵנָה, " when thou wast under the fig tree." This is not convincing.

Other fanciful hypotheses about Nathanael are that the incident indicated here is another version of the story of Zacchæus in the sycamore tree (Abbott, *Diat.* 3375 f.); or that in him we are to see a figure symbolical of Paul, an Israelite who broke through the prejudices of his early training (sufficiently answered by Moffatt, *Introd. to N.T.*, p. 565) ; or that we are to equate him with the Beloved Disciple (cf. Introd., p. xxxvii). But the simplest interpretation is the best. Nathanael was a real figure, and his call was vivid in the mind of the aged disciple whose recollections are behind the Fourth Gospel.

49. 'Ραββεί. See on v. 38.

σὺ εἶ ὁ υἱὸς τοῦ θεοῦ. Cf. Peter's σὺ εἶ ὁ ἅγιος τοῦ θεοῦ (6⁶⁹), and Martha's σὺ εἶ ὁ Χριστός, ὁ υἱὸς τοῦ θεοῦ (11²⁷); and see below on v. 51. Nathanael sees in Jesus One who has displayed a wonderful knowledge of his past life (cf. 4¹⁹· ²⁹), and so he identifies Him with the expected Messiah. For the title ὁ υἱὸς τοῦ θεοῦ, see on v. 34 above.

σὺ βασιλεὺς εἶ τοῦ Ἰσραήλ. This, to us, is a lesser title than ὁ υἱὸς τοῦ θεοῦ, but not so to Nathanael; see on 12¹³. Nathanael has been hailed by Jesus as an "Israelite," a worthy and representative son of Israel, and he replies out of the fulness of his heart, " Thou art the King of Israel," and therefore Nathanael's King. Both Messianic titles, " Son of God " and " King of Israel," have their roots in Ps. 2.

[1] By Seydel. See *D.C.G.*, ii. 288.
[2] *E.B.*, *s.v.* " Nathanael."

αὐτῷ Ὅτι εἶπόν σοι ὅτι εἶδόν σε ὑποκάτω τῆς συκῆς, πιστεύεις; μείζω τούτων ὄψῃ. 51. καὶ λέγει αὐτῷ Ἀμὴν ἀμὴν λέγω ὑμῖν, ὄψεσθε

50. ἀπεκρίθη Ἰη. καὶ εἶπεν. In the Synoptists (except at Mk. 7²⁸) the formula is ὁ ἀποκριθεὶς εἶπεν, but in Jn. the almost invariable use is "answered and said," two co-ordinate verbs being used (see on v. 26). In the LXX both constructions are found.

Burney (*Aramaic Origin, etc.*, p. 53) claims ἀπεκρίθη Ἰη. καὶ εἶπεν as a literal rendering of an Aramaic original, as it is in Theodotion's Daniel. The constr., however, is common in the LXX, where the original is Hebrew (not Aramaic), *e.g.* 1 Sam. 14²⁸ 19²², 2 Chron. 29³¹ 34¹⁵, Joel 2¹⁹ (of Yahweh). A more plausible argument for an Aramaic original of Jn. is found by Burney in the large number of *asyndeton* sentences. This is a specially Aramaic (not a Hebrew) characteristic. If, however, the narrative parts of the Gospel were dictated (as we hold to be probable) by one to whom Aramaic was his native language, we should expect to find them reproduced sometimes in Greek with an Aramaic flavour.

Ἰησοῦς often—perhaps generally—takes the def. art. in Jn. (see on v. 29); but the phrase ἀπεκρίθη Ἰησοῦς is common, *e.g.* 4¹⁰ 8¹⁴· ⁵⁴ 9³ 13⁷· ³⁶ 18³⁴· ³⁶, etc.

ὅτι εἶπόν σοι ὅτι κτλ. The second ὅτι introduces the words actually said. The first ὅτι is "because," a favourite use with Jn., and is here employed *suspensively* at the beginning of the sentence, as again at 14¹⁹ 15¹⁹ 16⁶ 20²⁹ (and also in the Apocalypse; cf. Abbott, *Diat.* 2176).

ὑποκάτω is not found again in Jn.; it is more emphatic than ὑπό of v. 48, and perhaps indicates concealment "under the cover of the fig tree." But the variation ὑπὸ τὴν συκῆν . . . ὑποκάτω τῆς συκῆς is thoroughly Johannine; when repeating a phrase, Jn. is apt to alter it slightly, either by a change in the order of the words, or by using a different word.

μείζω τούτων ὄψῃ. Perhaps there is an allusion here to the designation of Nathanael as ἀληθῶς Ἰσραηλείτης (v. 47). Jacob, to whom the name of "Israel" was given, was pre-eminently a man of vision. The ancient (although erroneous) interpretation of his new name equated it with אִישׁ רֹאֶה אֶל, *uir uidens Deum*. This etymology was adopted by Philo, who, commenting on the story of Jacob at Peniel (Gen. 32), says (*de somn.* i. 21): "He compels him to wrestle, until He has imparted to him irresistible strength, having changed his ears into eyes, and called this newly modelled type, *Israel*, i.e. *one who sees*" (Ἰσραήλ, ὁρῶντα).

Nathanael, who is "an Israelite indeed," must also be a man

of vision, and the vision which is promised him is greater even than that which he has already recognised, viz. that Jesus is " the King of Israel " (v. 49).

51. καὶ λέγει αὐτῷ, 'Αμὴν ἀμὴν λέγω ὑμῖν. Despite the singular αὐτῷ, the plural ὑμῖν suggests that the words which follow were addressed to others besides Nathanael. When Jesus prefaces a saying addressed to an individual by this solemn introduction, He is represented by Jn. as putting it in the form ἀμὴν ἀμὴν λέγω σοι (3³· ⁵· ¹¹ 21¹⁸). Further, although the promise is in the singular μείζω τούτων ὄψῃ, the vision is described as to be seen by more than one, ὄψεσθε κτλ. Nathanael is only one of those who are to see " the heaven opened and the angels ascending and descending," etc.

ἀμὴν ἀμὴν λέγω ὑμῖν. The authority with which Jesus was accustomed to speak has been noted above (Introd., p. cx). His authoritative manner of speech is indicated sometimes in the Synoptists by the mere addition of λέγω σοι or λέγω ὑμῖν, e.g. Mk. 2¹¹ 11²⁴, Lk. 5²⁴ 6²⁷ 7²⁸ 10¹²· ²⁴ 11⁸· ⁹ etc., Mt. 5⁴⁴ 16¹⁸ 21⁴³ 23³⁹ etc. This is often found in the expanded form ἀμὴν λέγω ὑμῖν (30 times in Mt., 13 in Mk., and 6 in Lk., who also translates אָמֵן by ναί, ἀληθῶς or ἐπ' ἀληθείας). Jn. always gives it in the form ἀμὴν ἀμὴν λέγω ὑμῖν (25 times; cf. 4³⁵ 13³³ for λέγω ὑμῖν simply). In Jn. the formula is usually associated with sayings not given by the Synoptists; but cf. 3⁵ 13¹⁶· ²⁰. It is clear from the Gospels that this was a characteristic *usus loquendi* of the Lord (Himself *the Amen*, Rev. 3¹⁴; cf. Isa. 65¹⁶), who never rested His sayings on the authority of other masters, as the Rabbinical habit was, but spoke as One possessed of the secrets of life.

Why the ἀμήν is doubled in the Johannine reports cannot be confidently explained. There are instances in the other Gospels of Jesus repeating at the beginning of a sentence the name of the person addressed, for greater emphasis, *e.g. Martha, Martha* (Lk. 10⁴¹), *Simon, Simon* (Lk. 22³¹), *Eloi, Eloi* (Mk. 15³⁴); but this does not provide an exact parallel. It would appear that ἀμήν was for Him a form of solemn attestation (see also on 4²¹); and it may be that the solemnity was emphasised by Him sometimes by doubling the ἀμήν. He forbade oaths (cf. 4²¹), but where people wished to be emphatic He allowed them to say *Yea, yea*, ναὶ ναί (Mt. 5³⁷), and this is *Verily, verily.*[1] See Lk. 7²⁶ 11⁵¹ for ναί as equivalent to ἀμήν. Hence, in Mt. 5³⁷, Jesus recommends as a form of solemn affirmation ἀμὴν ἀμήν, which we find from the report of

---

[1] Allen, in *Matthew* 5³⁷, writes : " The Talmud *Sanhed.* 36ᵃ discusses whether Yes and No are oaths, and decides that they are oaths if repeated twice."

τὸν οὐρανὸν ἀνεῳγότα καὶ τοὺς ἀγγέλους τοῦ Θεοῦ ἀναβαίνοντας καὶ καταβαίνοντας ἐπὶ τὸν Υἱὸν τοῦ ἀνθρώπου.

Jn. to have been frequently adopted by Himself. The duplication of ἀμήν impressed the disciple, who remembered it, the Synoptic record having lost this characteristic feature.

In Jn. (as in the Synoptic Gospels, where λέγω ὑμῖν only or ἀμὴν λέγω ὑμῖν is found) ἀμὴν ἀμὴν λέγω ὑμῖν, while special emphasis is laid on the words which follow, always carries a reference to what has gone before—either a reply to an observation (e.g. 3³ 6²⁶· ³² 5¹⁹ 8³⁴· ⁵⁸ 13³⁸; cf. Mk. 10²⁹, Mt. 26³⁴), or an explanation and expansion of something that has already been said (e.g. 1⁵¹ 5²⁴· ²⁵ 10¹· ⁷ 12²⁴ 13¹⁶· ²⁰· ²¹ 16²⁰· ²³ 14¹²; cf. Mk. 13³⁰, Mt. 26¹³). Even 8⁵¹ goes back to 8⁴³, 6⁴⁷ to 6⁴⁰, 5²⁵ to 5²⁴, although the connexion is not so obvious. But it is important to observe that in Jn. the prelude ἀμὴν ἀμὴν λέγω ὑμῖν never introduces a new saying unrelated to what precedes (see on 10¹). In like manner in the O.T. we find ἀμήν prefacing a responsive agreement to something that has been already said (1 Kings 1³⁶, Neh. 5¹³, Jer. 11⁵); or in its doubled form, ἀμὴν ἀμήν, as concluding a sort of liturgical response (Num. 5²², Judith 13²⁰, Ps. 41¹³). But in the O.T. we do not find ἀμήν used at the beginning of a sentence, to strengthen what is to follow.

The phrase ἀπ᾽ ἄρτι (for which see on 13¹⁹) is prefixed to ὄψεσθε by ΑΓΔΘ and the Syriac vss., but is omitted by אBLW latt., etc., and must be rejected. It has been added by scribes because of a misunderstanding of the meaning of the words which follow (cf. Mt. 26⁶⁴). The vision which is described is not one which was to be revealed *henceforth, i.e.* from the time of speaking; it was for the future, perhaps the distant future.

ὄψεσθε. ὄπτομαι (but not ὁρᾶν in the pres. or perf. tenses) is always used in Jn. (3³⁶ 11⁴⁰ 16¹⁶, 1 Jn. 3²) of the vision of heavenly or spiritual realities, as distinct from a seeing with the eyes of the body. The same usage is common in the rest of the N.T., but there are exceptions (e.g. Acts 7²⁶ 20²⁵). For the difference in usage between ὄπτομαι and θεωρεῖν, see on 2²³, and cf. Abbott (*Diat.* 1307, 1597 f.).

ὄψεσθε τὸν οὐρανὸν ἀνεῳγότα κτλ. We can hardly doubt that some words here are taken from the story of Jacob's vision at Bethel, viz. κλίμαξ ἐστηριγμένη ἐν τῇ γῇ, ἧς ἡ κεφαλὴ ἀφικνεῖτο εἰς τὸν οὐρανόν, καὶ οἱ ἄγγελοι τοῦ θεοῦ ἀνέβαινον καὶ κατέβαινον ἐπ᾽ αὐτῆς. ὁ δὲ κύριος ἐπεστήρικτο ἐπ᾽ αὐτῆς καὶ εἶπεν κτλ. (Gen. 28¹²· ¹³). It is, however, remarkable that no Christian writer before Augustine seems to have noticed that Jn. 1⁵¹ is, in part, a quotation (see, for the patristic interpretations of the passage, Additional Note, p. 70 f.). The promise to Nathanael, as an " Israelite indeed," that he (with others) shall see angelic visions, is couched in terms which recall the vision of Jacob, the father of his race, of whom Nathanael is no unworthy descendant. That the vision of Bethel was seen by Jacob *before* he received the new and pregnant name of Israel does not constitute a difficulty, for we are not concerned with the *details* of Jacob's vision. The evangelist's report does not indicate that he thought of it as *fulfilled* in Nathanael. The words ascribed to Jesus have to do with Jacob's vision only in so far as they suggest to Nathanael that he was not the first Israelite to have visions of heaven and the angels.

What is to be the occasion of the vision promised to Nathanael and his companions ? The direction in which an answer must be sought is indicated by the use, for the first time, in the Gospel of the strange designation of Jesus as " the Son of Man." We have already seen (Introd., p. cxxvii) that the title " the Son of Man," applied by Jesus to Himself, most frequently appears in eschatological passages, which have reference to His final and glorious Advent, after which His indestructible kingdom is to be fully established (cf. Dan. 7¹³). The vision of this Advent seems to be what is promised to Nathanael and his believing companions. Nathanael is represented as acknowledging that Jesus is " the Son of God, the King of Israel " (v. 49), *i.e.* that He is the Messiah as looked for under the aspect of King, the " political " Messiah (see on v. 34) of Israel's hope. But there was a higher conception than this, a more spiritual picture than that of an earthly prince; and it was to this (as suggested by the words of Dan 7¹³) that Jesus pointed His followers, when He spoke of Himself as the Son of Man. It was a greater thing to see Him as the Son of Man than as the King of Israel. The vision which would be the condemnation of the high priest who presumed to condemn Jesus, viz. ὄψεσθε τὸν υἱὸν τοῦ ἀνθρώπου ἐκ δεξίων καθήμενον τῆς δυνάμεως καὶ ἐρχόμενον μετὰ τῶν νεφελῶν τοῦ οὐρανοῦ (Mk. 14⁶²), would be the reward of disciples who faithfully accepted Him as the Messiah.

The parallel to this passage in the Synoptists is the promise which followed upon the confession of Peter and the rest. Peter's confession, like that of Nathanael, was σὺ εἶ ὁ Χριστός, and in making it he was the spokesman of the others. And the promise which follows is the counterpart of the promise to Nathanael, viz.: " The Son of Man shall come in the glory of His Father with His angels. . . . Verily I say unto you, There be some of them that stand here which shall in no wise taste of

death, till they see the Son of Man coming in His Kingdom"
(Mt. 16[27. 28]; cf. Mk. 8[38] 9[1], Lk. 9[26. 27]). The parallelism with
Jn. 1[51] is remarkable, and the difficulty of explaining both
passages (for they are left unexplained by the evangelists)
shows that, alike in the Synoptists and in Jn., they embody a
genuine reminiscence or tradition.[1] See on 6[69] for Jn.'s version
of Peter's confession.

There is in Jn. a third confession of faith, which should be
placed beside that of Nathanael and that of Peter, viz. that of
Martha (11[27]), who says σὺ εἶ ὁ Χριστός, ὁ υἱὸς τοῦ θεοῦ, ὁ εἰς τὸν
κόσμον ἐρχόμενος. No reply of Jesus is recorded until we
reach v. 40, when He says, with apparent reference to her
previous confession, " Said I not unto thee, that if thou be-
lievedst, thou shouldest see the glory of God ? " That is,
again, as in the case of Nathanael, *Vision* is the reward of
Faith: the vision of the Divine glory, as exhibited in the power
over death which Jesus had (see note on 11[40]).

The attempts which have been made to trace a detailed
correspondence between what is said about Jacob's vision
at Bethel and the vision promised to Nathanael are quite
unsuccessful. Nathanael, it must be borne in mind, is here
typified by Jacob or Israel as " the man who sees." It is,
therefore, impossible to take Jacob as the type of Christ or the
Son of Man; and this rules out several modern interpretations.
E.g., to take (see Meyer) the angels ascending and descending
as typical of the continuous intercourse between God and Christ,
the Father and the Son (see on 5[19] 6[57]), presupposes that Jacob at
Bethel typifies Christ, not to mention that the idea of the intercourse between the Father and the Son being carried on by the
ministry of angels is quite foreign to the Gospels.

Burney [2] points out that the Hebrew בּוֹ, which is rendered
at Gen. 28[13] ἐπ' αὐτῆς by the LXX, and by the English versions
" on it," *sc.* on the ladder, might also be rendered " on him,"
sc. on Jacob. He cites a Midrash where this interpretation is
proposed, and where it is said of the angels at Bethel that they
were ascending on high and looking at Jacob's εἰκών (which
was in heaven), and then descending and finding his sleeping
body. Burney suggests that the heavenly εἰκών of Israel was
the Son of Man, and that Gen. 28[13] is quoted here by Jn. from
the Hebrew, בּוֹ being rendered " on Him," *i.e.* the heavenly
Ideal of Israel. If the heavens were opened, Nathanael would

---

[1] Both Justin (*Apol.* i. 6) and Irenæus (*Dem.* 10) speak of angels
as following and attending the Son. Cf. J. A. Robinson, *St. Irenæus
and the Apostolic Preaching*, pp. 27 ff.

[2] *Aramaic Origin, etc.*, p. 116 ; cf. for Rabbinical speculations
about the angels and Jacob's ladder, Abbott, *Diat.* 2998 (xiii.).

then see the angels of God " ascending and descending upon
the Son of Man." But, as we have said, Jn. certainly does
not intend Jacob at Bethel to be taken as the type of the Son of
Man, and so this interesting interpretation does not help us.

ADDITIONAL NOTE ON THE PROMISE TO NATHANAEL

I. 51. No commentator before Augustine suggests any
connexion between Gen. 28[13] and Jn. 1[51]. When the proneness
of the early exegetes to seek O.T. *testimonia* is remembered,
this is remarkable. A few passages may be cited to illustrate
the various interpretations that were placed on both texts.

(*a*) Philo, as one would expect, has much to say about
Jacob's vision at Bethel (*de somn.* i. 22). Between heaven and
earth, he says, there is the air, the abode of incorporeal souls,
immortal citizens. The purest of the beings who pass to and
fro are angels, who report the Father's orders to His children,
and their needs to Him. Here (§ 23) is an image of man's soul,
of which the foundation, as it were, is earthly (αἴσθησις), but the
head is heavenly (νοῦς). And the λόγοι of God move in-
cessantly up and down, ascending that they may draw the
soul heavenwards, condescending that they may impart life
from above. This, despite some verbal similarities, has no
bearing on the exegesis of Jn. 1[51].

(*b*) Origen (*c. Celsum*, vi. 21) recalls the Platonist doctrine,
favoured by Celsus, that souls can make their way to and from
the earth through the planets, and speaks with approval of
Philo's exposition of Gen. 28[13] which has been cited above.
He says that Gen. 28[13] either refers to the Platonic view or to
" something greater," but he does not explain what this is.

(*c*) Origen quotes Jn. 1[51] several times. In *Hom. in Luc.*
xxiii. (Lommatzsch, v. 178) he quotes it to show that visions of
angels are seen only by those to whom special grace is given;
and similarly in *de Orat.* 11 (Lommatzsch, xvii. 128) he says
that the angels ascending and descending are visible only to
eyes illuminated by the light of knowledge (γνῶσις). In another
place (*c. Celsum*, i. 48) he interprets the phrase τὸν οὐρανὸν
ἀνεῳγότα of the opening of the heavens at the Baptism of Christ,
forgetting that Jn. represents the Baptism as prior to the call
of Nathanael. In none of these passages is it suggested that
Gen. 28[13] had occurred to him as a parallel.

(*d*) Tertullian refers twice to Jacob's ladder. Just as some
men behave badly in time of persecution, and others well, so in
Jacob's dream some mount to higher places, others go down to
lower (*de Fuga*, 1). More interesting is his comment in another
place (*c. Marcion.* iii. 24): By the vision of Jacob's ladder, with

God standing above, is shown the way to heaven, which some
take and others fall from. "This," said Jacob, "is the gate of
heaven," and the gate is provided by Christ. Tertullian never
mentions Jn. 1^{51}. It may be added that Cyprian quotes neither
Gen. 28^{13} nor Jn. 1^{51}.

(e) Irenæus (*Dem.* 45) says that Jacob's ladder signifies
the Cross, "for thereby they that believe on Him go up to the
heavens," adding that "all such visions point to the Son of
God, speaking with men and being with men." He does not
quote Jn. 1^{51} anywhere.

(f) Justin (*Tryph.* 58, 86) quotes in full the story of Jacob
at Bethel. He urges that it was not God the Father who
stood above the ladder (Gen. 28^{13}), but the Angel of His
presence; and he finds the type of Christ, not in the ladder,
but in the stone which Jacob had used for a pillow, and which
he anointed (Gen. 28^{18}). He does not allude to Jn. 1^{51}.

(g) Chrysostom (*in loc.*) regards the ministry of angels in
Gethsemane (Lk. 22^{43}) and the Resurrection (Jn. 20^{12}) as a
fulfilment of Jn. 1^{51}, an inadequate explanation. In an obscure
passage (*in Col.* ii. 5), he refers to Gen. 28^{13} as a sign of the
Divine Sonship of Christ, but he does not associate it with
Jn. 1^{51}.

(h) Jerome alludes to Jacob's ladder several times (*e.g.*
Epp 98. 3, 118. 7, 123. 15, and *Tract. de Ps.* cxix.). It
represents, he says, the Christian life, the Lord standing above
holding out His hand to help those going up, and casting
down the careless. Like Justin, he takes the stone of Jacob as
a type of Christ the cornerstone; but he does not quote Jn. 1^{51}
in this context.

(i) Augustine is the first exegete to find in Jn. 1^{51} an allusion
to Gen. 28^{13}. He, too, regards Jacob's stone as a type of
Christ; and he suggests that the confession of Nathanael that
Jesus is the Christ was like the anointing of the stone by Jacob
(Gen. 23^{18}). The "angels, ascending and descending,"
typify the preachers of the Gospel. Augustine, however, intro-
duces two ideas not altogether consistent with each other.
First the angels "ascend and descend upon the Son of Man,"
because He is at once above and below, in heaven and on earth.
"Filius enim hominis sursum in capite nostro, quod est ipse
Salvator; et Filius hominis deorsum in corpore suo, quod est
Ecclesia." Secondly, he explains that the Ladder is a type of
Christ, who said, "I am the Way"; and it is notable that
Augustine is the first Christian writer to suggest this thought
(*c. Faustum*, xii. 26). He refers again to the association
between Gen. 28^{13} and Jn. 1^{51} in *de Civ. Dei*, xvi. 39, and in
Serm. cxxiii. 3, 4; but he does not elsewhere speak of Jacob's

II. 1. Καὶ τῇ ἡμέρᾳ τῇ τρίτῃ γάμος ἐγένετο ἐν Κανᾶ τῆς Γαλιλαίας, καὶ ἦν ἡ μήτηρ τοῦ Ἰησοῦ ἐκεῖ· 2. ἐκλήθη δὲ καὶ ὁ Ἰησοῦς καὶ οἱ

ladder as typifying Christ. Augustine does not seem to be clear as to the correspondence between the details of Jacob's vision and the promise to Nathanael; and, in fact, the correspondence cannot be set out precisely. But his general idea has left its mark on modern exegesis.

The First Sign : the Marriage at Cana (II. 1–12)

II. 1. Cana of Galilee, to which the narrative now brings us, is named twice again in Jn. (4⁴⁶ 2¹²), but nowhere else in the N.T. It is mentioned by Josephus (*Vita*, § 16) κώμη τῆς Γαλιλαίας ἡ προσαγορεύεται Κανά, and is not to be confounded with another Cana in Cœlo-Syria. Its exact situation is not certain. The traditional site is *Kefr Kenna*, 3½ miles N.E. of Nazareth; but *'Ain Kânâ*, a little nearer Nazareth, and *Khirbet Kânâ*, 8 miles N. of Nazareth, have also been suggested.

τῇ ἡμέρᾳ τῇ τρίτῃ. So אALΔW, but BΘ and *fam.* 13 have τῇ τρίτῃ ἡμέρᾳ.

Jesus reached Cana on the third day after the call of Philip and Nathanael (1⁴³), when a start was made from the neighbourhood of Bethabara for Galilee. This is a journey that would occupy two days (1²⁸), and no incident is recorded of the last day of travel.

It has been pointed out (on 1¹⁹) that we have in the first section of the Gospel (1¹⁹ to 2¹¹) a record of six or (more probably) of seven eventful days at the beginning of the public ministry of Jesus. Which of these days was the Sabbath? Most probably it was the day of the call of Andrew and John, who " abode with Him that day " (1³⁹). There was no travelling, such as there was on the days of the journey from Bethany to Cana. If this be so, we reach an interesting coincidence, for then the day of the Marriage at Cana would be the fourth day of the week; and a Talmudical direction ordained that the marriage of a virgin should be on the fourth day,[1] or our Wednesday. Marriage feasts in Palestine were, and are, generally held in the afternoon or evening.

ἡ μήτηρ τοῦ Ἰη. Jn. never gives her name (cf. 2¹² 6⁴² 19²⁵), just as he does not mention the name of John the son of Zebedee or that of James his brother. Mary, who had apparently some special interest in the wedding (2³· ⁵), had come over to Cana

---

[1] So Lightfoot, *Hor. Hebr.*, in loc. ; so too there is an old English rhyme which declares that for weddings Wednesday " is the best day of all."

from the neighbouring village, Nazareth, or from Capernaum (see 2¹²). Perhaps it was the wedding of a relative, which would account for Jesus being invited to attend.

Joseph is not mentioned, and it is probable that he was dead at this time.

In a Sahidic apocryphal fragment edited by Forbes Robinson,[1] Mary is said to be the sister of the bridegroom's parents. The fragment (which seems to be part of a sermon on the Marriage at Cana) adds that the parents told Mary that the wine was failing, and asked her to use her influence with Jesus, who replied to her " in a kindly voice, Woman, what wilt thou with me ? " (see on v. 4 below). According to this account, the waterpots were prepared that the guests might wash *before* the meal (see on v. 6).

The Monarchian *Preface* to the Gospel (see Introd., p. lvii) begins: " Hic est Iohannes euangelista unus ex discipulis dei, qui uirgo electus a deo est, quem de nuptiis uolentem nubere uocauit deus, etc." This legend that the bridegroom was John the son of Zebedee (whose mother Salome was sister of Mary) had much currency in later times. That Jesus had dissuaded John from marriage is told in the second-century Gnostic *Acts of John* (§ 113).

2. μαθηταί. In all the Gospels the followers of Jesus are so described, the title sometimes indicating members of the apostolic Twelve or all of them, sometimes being used in a wider sense. Thus in Mk. 2¹⁵ 3⁷, Mt. 8²¹, Lk. 6¹³, Jn. 6⁶⁰· ⁶¹· ⁶⁶ 20³⁰, μαθηταί is not restricted to the Twelve.

At first the followers of Jesus were called οἱ μαθηταὶ αὐτοῦ, thus distinguishing them from the disciples of other Rabbis (cf. on 1³⁵); but as time went on they began to be described absolutely as οἱ μαθηταί, " *the* disciples " being a Christian phrase which no one would mistake. The earlier description is found in Mk., as is natural, much oftener than the later, and the same habit of phrase is found in Jn.[2]

Thus οἱ μαθηταὶ αὐτοῦ stands for the general body of the apostles in 6³· ⁸· ¹²· ¹⁶· ²²· ²⁴ 12⁴· ¹⁶ 13²³ 16¹⁷· ²⁹ 18¹· ¹⁹· ²⁵ 20²⁶, and perhaps 21². The phrase is used in a wider sense at 2¹⁷· ²² 4² 6⁶⁰· ⁶¹· ⁶⁶, and perhaps 3²². At 4⁸· ²⁷ 9² it is not clear which or how many of οἱ μαθηταὶ αὐτοῦ were present, and the same is true of the present verse.

The later phrase, οἱ μαθηταί, used absolutely, is only applied once in Jn. to the collected Twelve (13⁵, followed consequentially by 13²²). It often stands for the disciples *already mentioned*, e.g. 20¹⁰ (two), 21⁴· ¹² (seven), 20¹⁹· ²⁰ (ten). At 4³¹· ³³ and

---

[1] *Coptic Apocryphal Gospels*, p. 164.
[2] Cf. Turner, *J.T.S.*, April 1925, p. 236.

μαθηταὶ αὐτοῦ εἰς τὸν γάμον. 3. καὶ ὑστερήσαντος οἴνου λέγει ἡ

11⁷. ⁸. ¹². ⁵⁴ (and perhaps 20¹⁸), in like manner, οἱ μαθηταί indicates only the disciples present on the occasion, whose number is not specified. οἱ μαθηταί is used in the widest sense at 20³⁰, as including all the eye-witnesses of Jesus' works. It is plain from a comparison of these passages that not only does Jn. follow the earlier rather than the later phrase when speaking of the Twelve, but that μαθηταί is often used by him when the Twelve are not in the picture.

Jn. tells nothing of the selection of the Twelve, although he has οἱ δώδεκα as a distinctive description of them (6⁶⁷. ⁷⁰. ⁷¹ 20²⁴; cf. 6¹³). He never gives the title ἀπόστολοι to the Twelve, the word ἀπόστολος only occurring 13¹⁶ in its general sense of " one that is sent "; cf. 20²¹.

There is nothing to indicate that οἱ μαθηταὶ αὐτοῦ in this verse is meant to include *all* the new disciples, five in number, that have been named in the preceding chapter. Jesus asked Philip (1⁴³) to accompany Him to Galilee, and Nathanael was himself of Cana. These two may be assumed to have been present. Perhaps, also, John the son of Zebedee, whom we have identified with the unnamed disciple of 1³⁷, was there; for there are hints that the narrative goes back to an eye-witness (see on v. 6). But there is nothing to suggest that the brothers Andrew and Peter were present. And the absence of any mention of this incident in Mk., which is based on Peter's reminiscences, would be natural if Peter was not a witness of it.

In any case, as Jesus had not yet declared Himself for what He was, and as the " disciples " had been attracted only during the previous week, it is not likely that they were invited to the wedding in their capacity *as* His disciples. They were probably present as friends of the bride and bridegroom. Nothing in the narrative supports the suggestion of some commentators that they were *unexpected* guests, and that the failure of the wine was due to this sudden addition to the wedding party.

ἐκλήθη is perhaps to be rendered "there had been bidden," as if it were a pluperfect.

3. For ὑστερήσαντος οἴνου (אᵃABLWΔΘ) is found in א* *a b ff²* a Western paraphrase, οἶνον οὐκ εἶχον, ὅτι συνετελέσθη ὁ οἶνος τοῦ γάμου, εἶτα . . . For οἶνον οὐκ ἔχουσιν at the end of the verse, א* has accordingly substituted οἶνος οὐκ ἔστιν.

Wine was always provided on occasions of rejoicing (cf. Gen. 14¹⁸); and there was a Jewish saying, " Without wine there is no joy " (*Pesachim*, 109ᵃ). That there should not be enough for the guests would be deemed unfortunate; and Mary,

μήτηρ τοῦ Ἰησοῦ πρὸς αὐτόν Οἶνον οὐκ ἔχουσιν. 4. καὶ λέγει αὐτῇ
ὁ Ἰησοῦς Τί ἐμοὶ καὶ σοί, γύναι; οὔπω ἥκει ἡ ὥρα μου. 5. λέγει ἡ

who is represented as having some kind of authority in the
house, or at any rate as sufficiently intimate to give orders to the
servants (v. 5), calls the attention of Jesus to the deficiency.
That she should tell *Him* of this, rather than the host or the
" governor of the feast," suggests at least that she had un-
bounded trust in His resourcefulness. But probably something
more is meant. Jesus had now for the first time gathered
disciples round Him, and Mary may well have thought that the
time had come for Him to show Himself for what she knew
Him to be.

λέγει . . . πρὸς αὐτόν. The more usual constr. λέγει αὐτῇ
occurs in the next line. The constr. πρός τινα after λέγειν is
not found in Mk., Mt., the Apocalypse, or the Johannine
Epistles, but it is often found in Jn. (3⁴ 4¹⁵· ⁴⁸· ⁴⁹ 6⁵ 7⁵⁰ 8³¹) as
well as in Lk.

4. τί ἐμοὶ καὶ σοί; is a phrase, translated from the Hebrew,
occurring several times in the Greek Bible, and always suggestive of diversity of opinion or interest. Thus in Judg. 11¹²
Jephthah says τί ἐμοὶ καὶ σοί; in hostile challenge to the King
of the Ammonites. David (2 Sam. 16¹⁰) says τί ἐμοὶ καὶ ὑμῖν;
to the sons of Zeruiah, meaning that he does not agree with
their advice. The Woman of Sarepta (1 Kings 17¹⁸) reproaches
Elijah with the same phrase. Elisha uses it in declining to help
King Jehoram (2 Kings 3¹³). Neco, King of Egypt, says to
Josiah, τί ἐμοὶ καὶ σοί; meaning, " Why should we fight?
I am not marching against *you* " (2 Chron. 35²¹). And in Mk. 5⁷
the man with the unclean spirit says the same thing to Jesus,
"Why do you concern yourself with me? Let me alone "
(cf. Mk. 1²⁴, Mt. 8²⁹).

The phrase does not always imply reproach, but it suggests
it. Here it seems to be a gentle suggestion of misunderstanding:
" I shall see to that; it will be better that you should leave it to
me." This is the view of Irenæus: " Dominus repellens eius
intempestivam festinationem, dixit, etc." (*Hær.* iii. 17. 7).

γύναι, as a vocative, does not convey any idea of rebuke
or reproach, as is clear from the tender γύναι, ἴδε ὁ υἱός σου of
19²⁶. It was thus that Augustus addressed Cleopatra (Dio, li.
12. 5) and Ulysses addressed Penelope (*Odyssey*, 19. 555). But,
nevertheless, that Jesus should call His mother γύναι, and not
μῆτερ, as would be natural, indicates that the time is past for
the exercise of any maternal authority on her part.

οὔπω ἥκει ἡ ὥρα μου means primarily, in this context, that
the moment had not come for Jesus to intervene; that He was

μήτηρ αὐτοῦ τοῖς διακόνοις Ὅ τι ἂν λέγῃ ὑμῖν, ποιήσατε. 6. ἦσαν δὲ ἐκεῖ λίθιναι ὑδρίαι ἓξ κατὰ τὸν καθαρισμὸν τῶν Ἰουδαίων κείμεναι, χωροῦσαι ἀνὰ μετρητὰς δύο ἢ τρεῖς. 7. λέγει αὐτοῖς ὁ Ἰησοῦς conscious of the failure of the wine, and did not need to be reminded of it. At the proper moment, He would act, if necessary. The evangelist, however, means something more by the record of this saying of Jesus. He places similar words in His mouth more than once. ὁ καιρὸς ὁ ἐμὸς οὔπω πάρεστιν (πεπλήρωται) (7⁶· ⁸) means that the time had not come for the public manifestation of Himself as Messiah. At 12²³ Jesus says that the hour of His Death has come : ἐλήλυθεν ἡ ὥρα ἵνα δοξασθῇ ὁ υἱὸς τοῦ ἀνθρώπου (cf. 12²⁷); and, again, Πάτερ, ἐλήλυθεν ἡ ὥρα (17¹; cf. 13¹). Jn. in his own person speaks similarly of the appointed hour of the manifestation and death of Jesus, e.g. οὔπω ἐληλύθει ἡ ὥρα αὐτοῦ (7³⁰; cf. 8²⁰).

Twice in Mt.'s account of the Passion, similar phrases are used, viz. ὁ καιρός μου ἐγγύς ἐστι (Mt. 26¹⁸) and ἤγγικεν ἡ ὥρα (Mt. 26⁴⁵, Mk. 14⁴¹); and Jesus frequently in the Synoptic narrative predicts death as the conclusion of His public ministry. But the Fourth Gospel is written from beginning to end *sub specie æternitatis*; the predestined end is foreseen from the beginning. (See on 3¹⁴ for Jn.'s use of δεῖ.) It is as inevitable as is the hour of a woman's travail (16²¹). Bearing this in mind, it is probable that Jn. meant his readers to understand by the words " Mine hour is not yet come " spoken at the Marriage Feast at Cana, that the moment had not yet come for the public manifestation by Jesus of Himself as Messiah, the first sign of this Epiphany being the miracle of the water turned into wine.

5. Mary did not take amiss the words of Jesus. She has been assured that He is aware of all the facts, and that is enough for her. So she bids the servants to execute promptly any order that He gives, for she feels certain that He will intervene, when the time has come. She is represented in the story as expectant of some " sign " that will show Jesus for what He is.

ποιήσατε. In Jn., the aorist imperative often occurs, as " more authoritative than the pres. imper., which may denote continuous action." [1] Cf. vv. 7, 8 γεμίσατε . . . ἀντλήσατε, and also 2¹⁶· ¹⁹ 4¹⁶· ³⁵ 6¹⁰ 7²⁴ 9⁷ 11³⁹ 12²⁷ 13²⁷ 15⁹ 21¹⁰.

6. ἦσαν δὲ ἐκεῖ κτλ. Jn. often uses δέ to introduce a new point: " *Now* there were six waterpots, etc." Cf. 6¹⁰ 18⁴⁰.

χωροῦσαι ἀνὰ μετρητάς κτλ., " containing two or three firkins apiece." ἀνά does not occur again in Jn.; cf. Rev. 4⁸. For

[1] Abbott, *Diat.* 2437.

Γεμίσατε τὰς ὑδρίας ὕδατος. καὶ ἐγέμισαν αὐτὰς ἕως ἄνω. 8. καὶ
λέγει αὐτοῖς 'Αντλήσατε νῦν καὶ φέρετε τῷ ἀρχιτρικλίνῳ. οἱ δὲ
this classical use of χωρεῖν (see on 8[37]) cf. 2 Chron. 4[5] χωροῦσαν
μετρητὰς τρισχιλίους.

ὑδρίαι. It was customary to have large water-jars of stone
in or near the room where a feast was being held, in order
that water might be available for the ceremonial washing of
hands prescribed before and after meals. The water was
carried from the jars in pitchers or basins, and was poured over
the fingers, so that it ran down to the wrist (cf. Mk. 7[3]); and it
was a special duty of one's servant to see to this (cf. 2 Kings
3[11], where Elisha is described as he " who poured water on the
hands of Elijah," *i.e.* as his servant). A " firkin " or *bath*
(μετρητής; cf. 2 Chron. 4[5]) was about 8½ gallons, so that
the huge water-pots of the narrative (quite distinct from wine
vessels) contained about 20 gallons each. A smaller sized
ὑδρία was used for carrying water from a well (cf. 4[28]).

κατὰ τὸν καθαρισμὸν τῶν 'Ιουδαίων (cf. 3[25]). The Fourth
Gospel was written for Greek, not for Jewish, readers; and so,
as at many other points, an explanatory note of this kind is
added (cf. v. 13). The Jewish customs as to ceremonial
washings were common to Galilee, as to the rest of Palestine;
and no special emphasis should be laid here on the term " Jews "
as distinguished from Galilæans. See above on 1[19], and cf.
2[13] 6[41].

7. ἕως ἄνω, " up to the brim " (cf. Mt. 27[51] for ἕως κάτω,
" down to the bottom "). This is mentioned to show that no
room was left for adding anything to the water in the jars.

8. ἀντλήσατε νῦν κτλ., " Draw out now, and bear to the
governor of the feast." The ἀρχιτρίκλινος is called the ἡγούμενος
in Ecclus. 32[1]. It was customary for one of the principal
guests to preside as *arbiter bibendi* (Horace, *Od.* ii. 7) or
συμποσίαρχος, and it is this person who is indicated here by
ἀρχιτρίκλινος, a word which elsewhere means a butler who
arranged the *triclinium*, or three couches, each for three, at
the table.

ἀντλήσατε νῦν has been generally taken to mean that the
servants were bidden to draw water *from the great jars* and
convey it in pitchers to the ruler of the feast. Westcott argues
that ἀντλήσατε νῦν means rather " draw out now *from the
well*," whence water had previously been taken to fill the jars
" up to the brim "; and that no miracle was wrought upon the
water in the jars, but only upon water freshly drawn from the
well in response to the command of Jesus. It is true that
ἀντλεῖν is naturally used of drawing water from a well (cf.

ἤνεγκαν. 9. ὡς δὲ ἐγεύσατο ὁ ἀρχιτρίκλινος τὸ ὕδωρ οἶνον γεγενημένον, καὶ οὐκ ᾔδει πόθεν ἐστίν, οἱ δὲ διάκονοι ᾔδεισαν οἱ ἠντληκότες

4[7] and Gen. 24[20], Ex. 2[19], Isa. 12[3]). But the difficulties of this
interpretation are considerable :
 (1) If Westcott's view be taken, the act (v. 7) of filling
the large jars with water was quite otiose and has nothing to do
with the story. There was no reason to mention the waterpots at all, if the miracle consisted in the conversion to wine of
water freshly drawn from the well in pitchers [1] and brought
direct to the ἀρχιτρίκλινος.
 (2) ἀντλεῖν can quite properly be used of drawing or
pouring a liquid from a large vessel into a smaller one; and in
its compounds ἐξαντλεῖν, καταντλεῖν, it means " to pour out,"
" to pour over." The drawing from the large *hydriæ* in the
story would have been done by ladles (κύαθοι).[2]
 (3) That ἀντλεῖν could be used of drawing *wine* appears
from a passage in the comic poet Pherecrates (see *D.C.G.* ii.
815); and that a *hydria* was sometimes used to hold *wine* can
be shown from Pollux, *Onomasticon*, x. § 74, . . . ἔφη Ὑδρίαν
δανείζειν πεντέχουν ἢ μείζονα, ὥστ᾽ οὐ μόνον ὕδατος ἀλλὰ καὶ οἴνου
ἂν εἴη ἀγγεῖον ἡ ὑδρία. This last quotation shows that the
ἀρχιτρίκλινος would have had no reason for being surprised at
wine being brought from the waterpots.
 Jn. clearly means his readers to believe that what was
served to the ruler of the feast was drawn from the water-jars;
and that it was then served as a beverage. Had it been brought
by the attendants for the purpose of pouring it on the hands
of the ἀρχιτρίκλινος, it would have been brought in a different
kind of vessel, and he would not have proceeded to taste it.
 We must further notice that Jn. does not say that either
the ruler of the feast, or the wedding guests generally, found
anything miraculous in the wine that was served at the end.
It was the disciples only who are said to have " believed " in
Jesus, in consequence of this " sign." See Introd., p. clxxxii.
 9. ὡς δὲ ἐγεύσατο ὁ ἀρχιτρ. κτλ., the aorist being used like
a pluperfect: "when the ruler of the feast had tasted, etc."
Cf. 7[10].
 τὸ ὕδωρ οἶνον γεγενημένον. The words have been generally
understood to imply that *all* the water in the six waterpots,
amounting to about 120 gallons (see on v. 6), had been turned
into wine. Jn. may have meant this; but if so, the new supply

---

[1] See Abbott, *Diat.* 2281-2.
[2] Dr. L. C. Purser refers me to illustrations of *hydriæ* and *cyathi*
in Daremberg and Saglio's *Diction. des antiq.*, Figs. 3921-3926, 2235-
2239 ; and also to the passages next cited.

would have been a large over-provision for the needs of the guests at the end of the feast, when they had already consumed what had been provided by the host.   In the story of Bel and the Dragon, six firkins, or 50 gallons of wine, offered daily to the idol are regarded as sufficient for 70 priests with their wives and families.   A hundred and twenty gallons would be so unnecessarily large a supply that the residue of the twelve baskets left after the Feeding of the Five Thousand (6[13]) does not furnish any analogy.   Here there would have been a prodigality, not indeed inconceivable in the case of One whom the narrator describes as the Agent of creation (1[3]), but without parallel in the record of the other " signs " of Christ.

The difficulty arising from the quantity of wine that would have been left over perhaps affects modern readers more than it would have affected contemporaries.   Wine might be abused, and drunkenness was always blameworthy; but the idea that it is wrong to use wine in moderation, like any other gift of God, would have been foreign to primitive Christianity or to Judaism.[1]   The modern notion that "wine" in the N.T. means unfermented, non-intoxicating wine is without foundation.[2] Indeed, it was just because Jesus did not condemn the use of wine that He was reproached as a " winebibber " (Mt. 11[19], Lk. 7[34]) by those who wished to disparage Him.   Unlike John the Baptist, Jesus was not an ascetic.

It must, however, be observed that Jn. does not say explicitly that the *entire* contents of the water-jars were turned into wine.   " The water which had become wine " was that which was served to the ruler of the feast, and Jn. says nothing of any other.   Nor is it clear that he means us to understand that the servants had noticed any change in the beverage which they served.   They knew that they had taken it from the waterpots (or from one of them); that is all.

To change one pitcher of water into wine is no less " supernatural " than to change 120 gallons; and we do not escape difficulty by refusing to exaggerate the story as it stands.   Jn. certainly implies that some objective change took place in the water served for drinking purposes (cf. 4[46]).   To reduce the powers of Christ to human standards was no part of his design. It has been thought, indeed, by some that a suggestion made by Jesus that the water had become wine may have wrought so powerfully on the minds of those present that they were convinced that it was even so.   The belief of the ἀρχιτρίκλινος that he had been drinking wine, when he had only been drinking

---

[1] There is a reference to the Marriage at Cana in a characteristic discussion of drunkenness by Clem. Alex. (*Pæd.* ii. 2. 184 P).

[2] Cf. *Unfermented Wine*, by H. E. Ryle and others (1917).

τὸ ὕδωρ, φωνεῖ τὸν νυμφίον ὁ ἀρχιτρίκλινος, 10. καὶ λέγει αὐτῷ
Πᾶς ἄνθρωπος πρῶτον τὸν καλὸν οἶνον τίθησιν, καὶ ὅταν μεθυσθῶσιν
τὸν ἐλάσσω· σὺ τετήρηκας τὸν καλὸν οἶνον ἕως ἄρτι. 11. Ταύτην

water, may have been an illusion due to the magnetic and compelling force of the words of Jesus. But we cannot tell precisely what happened, and must be content here with the
endeavour to discover what Jn. meant his readers to believe.

The indirect manner in which the statement of the miracle
is made should be observed. " When the ruler of the feast
had tasted the water that had become wine." The story is not
told for the first time. It is recorded as if the facts were well
known. The ἀρχιτρίκλινος on tasting the beverage served
to him, not knowing anything of its source, says, " It is very
good, even better than that which was served first." It is this
observation of the ruler of the feast that is emphasised by the
narrator, rather than the extraordinary character of the " sign "
which he records.

Another feature of this story is that it does not lead up to
any great saying of Jesus or to any discourse like that which Jn.
appends to the Feeding of the Five Thousand. Nor does the
evangelist draw any moral from it. He notes it as the first
of the " signs " of Jesus by which He exhibited His glory
(v. 11), but he says no more. In short, the way in which the
story is told goes far to support the view that it is a genuine
reminiscence, or tradition, of an actual occurrence, although
it is impossible now to discern exactly what took place. See
Additional Note p. 81, and cf. Introd., p. clxxxii.

10. τὸν ἐλάσσω. The rec. text, with ℵᶜΑΝΓΔΘ, prefixes τότε,
but om. ℵ*BLTᵇW.

The ἀρχιτρίκλινος speaks of a common practice at feasts as he
knew them; viz. that when men's palates had become dull by
drinking—*cum inebriati fuerint* (vg.), " when men be dronke,"
as Tyndale and Cranmer translate—inferior wine was served.

Schlatter quotes a Rabbinical tradition as to the wine drunk
on the occasion of a boy's circumcision: the father says to the
guests as he offers it, " Drink from this good wine; from this
I will give you to drink also at his wedding." In the present
case, the surprise of the ruler of the feast was due, not to good
wine being served, but to its being served last. It was kept
ἕως ἄρτι (cf. 5¹⁷ 16²⁴ and 1 Jn. 2⁹ for this phrase).

For the adj. καλός, see further on 10¹¹. καλός is used of
wine, as here, in a fourth-century papyrus quoted by Moulton-
Milligan, *s.v.*

τὸν καλὸν οἶνον τίθησιν. This suggests that the wine was
placed on the table, as is our modern custom.

ἐποίησεν ἀρχὴν τῶν σημείων ὁ Ἰησοῦς ἐν Κανᾷ τῆς Γαλιλαίας καὶ
ἐφανέρωσεν τὴν δόξαν αὐτοῦ, καὶ ἐπίστευσαν εἰς αὐτὸν οἱ μαθηταὶ
αὐτοῦ.

11. ταύτην ἐποίησεν ἀρχὴν τῶν σημείων. We have now
passed from the "witness" of the Baptist to the "witness"
of the works of Jesus (see on 1[7]). The Miracle of Cana was
the first of the "signs" which Jesus wrought during His
earthly ministry. By them, according to Jn., "He made
manifest His glory" (see on 1[14]). They were not merely
wonders or prodigies (τέρατα), but "signs" by which men
might learn that He was the Christ (20[31]) and "believe on
Him." (For the phrase πιστεύειν εἰς αὐτόν, see on 1[12].)
The highest faith is that which can believe without a sign
(20[29]), but signs have a useful function as bearing their
witness to the glory of Jesus. This aspect of His signs is
asserted by Jesus Himself (5[36]). When the tidings reached
the disciples that Lazarus was dead, He said that it was
well, for the miracle of his recovery would be all the greater
(11[15]). He rebuked the multitudes, because they followed
Him for what they might get, and *not* because of His signs
(6[26]). Cf. 10[38] 14[11]. And the same aspect of miracles
appears in the Synoptists (Mk. 2[10], Mt. 11[20], etc.).[1] See on
4[48] and 10[25].

The "disciples" who are here said to have "believed on
Him" as a consequence of what they saw at Cana, or rather
whose new faith was thus confirmed, were, as yet, few in
number, Philip and Nathanael and John being among them
(see on v. 2).

ADDITIONAL NOTE ON THE MIRACLE AT CANA

Some exegetes have supposed that this incident foreshadowed (or was intended by the evangelist to indicate) the
replacement of the inferior dispensation by the superior, the
Law by the Gospel. Such a view of Jn.'s literary method has
been discussed in the Introduction (p. lxxxv); but it may be
pointed out that the arguments assembled to prove that this
particular narrative is an invention of the evangelist, designed
to teach spiritual truth in an allegorical way, seem peculiarly
weak.

(1) *Six*, it is said, is a significant number—the perfect
number—and so there are 6 waterpots. But there is no number
from 1 to 10 which could not be given a mystical interpretation;
and the idea that 6 represents the 6 days of creation, which

[1] See further *s.v.* "Miracles" in *D.B.* iii. 388.

is the best that Origen [1] can do with the waterpots, is not very convincing.

Origen also suggests that the " two or three firkins " in each waterpot of purification intimate that the Jews are purified by the word of Scripture, receiving sometimes " two firkins," *i.e.* the *psychical* and *spiritual* sense of the Bible, and sometimes " three firkins," *i.e.* the *psychical, spiritual,* and *corporeal* senses. That is, he thinks that on occasion the literal or corporeal sense is not edifying, although it generally is (see Introd., p. lxxxv). But Origen does not say that he abandons the literal or historical sense of Jn. 2[1-11], and it is probable that he did not mean this, while he found allegorical meanings in some details of the story.[2] In the same way, Gregory of Nyssa is not to be taken as questioning the historicity of the narrative when he says that " the Jewish waterpots which were filled with the water of heresy, He filled with genuine wine, changing its nature by the power of His faith." [3] That an incident can be treated by a commentator in an allegorical manner does not prove that he regards it as unhistorical, and still less that the narrator had invented it to serve a spiritual purpose.

For example, there must be few preachers who have not drawn out lessons of a spiritual sort from the incident of the wine that was served at the end of the wedding feast being the best. It is a law of nature, and therefore a law of God, that the best comes last, being that for which all that goes before has prepared. So it is, to take the illustration suggested by the story, in a happy marriage. The best wine of life comes last. The fruits of autumn are richer than the flowers of spring. So perhaps it will be in the next life:

" . . . the best is yet to be,
The last of life for which the first was made."

Such reflexions are legitimate. But there is nothing to show that they were in the mind of the evangelist, or that the story of the Marriage at Cana was invented to teach them.

(2) A modern attempt to explain the story of the Sign at Cana as merely a parable of edification is that of E. A. Abbott.[4] He finds the germ of the story in the account of Melchizedek given by Philo, as bringing forth " wine instead of water " (*Leg. Alleg.* iii. 26); and he explains that " the six

[1] *De princ.* iv. 1. 12.
[2] Hippolytus (*Ref.* v. 3) reports that the Naassenes allegorised the water turned into wine, but he gives no details.
[3] *Orat. in Meletium.*
[4] *S.v.* " Gospels " in *E.B.*, 1796, 1800.

12. Μετὰ τοῦτο κατέβη εἰς Καφαρναοὺμ αὐτὸς καὶ ἡ μήτηρ

waterpots represent the inferior dispensation of the weekdays, *i.e.* the Law, preparing the way for the perfect dispensation of the Sabbath, *i.e.* the Gospel, of which the wedding feast at Cana is a type." He adds a Philonic quotation about the number 6 " being composed of 2 × 3, having the odd as male and the even as female, whence originate those things which are according to the fixed laws of nature. . . . What the number 6 generated, that the number 7 exhibited in full perfection " (*de septem.* 6).

Moffatt[1] favours yet a third Philonic explanation of the number 6, suggesting that the six ὑδρίαι correspond to Philo's principle that six is the " most productive " (γονιμωτάτη) of numbers (*decal.* 30).

These are desperate expedients of exegesis, and if Jn. really had any such notions in his mind when he said there were *six* waterpots prepared for the use of the wedding guests, he wrote more obscurely than is his wont. The truth is that mention of this unusually large number of ὑδρίαι is more reasonably to be referred to the observation of an eye-witness, who happened to remember the circumstance, than to elaborate symbolism of the narrative.

(3) The case for treatment of the whole story as due to a misunderstanding of some figurative saying can be put more plausibly. Wendt[2] puts it thus: " It is quite possible that an utterance which the apostle originally made in a figurative sense—Jesus turned the water of legal purification into the wine of marriage joy—was afterwards interpreted by the circle of Johannine disciples as recording an actual conversion of such water of purification into wine for a marriage." This is not to say that Jn. did not mean to narrate the incident as historical; it is to say, on the contrary, that he was mistaken in doing so, and that the story, in all its intimate detail, has been built up from vague hearsay. Quite different is such a theory from that which would regard the narrative as invented in order to teach that the wine of the Gospel, which Jesus provides, is better than the unsatisfying water of the Law; but it has its own difficulties. See Introd., p. clxxxii.

Interlude at Capernaum (*v.* 12)

12. μετὰ τοῦτο. This phrase does not occur in the Synoptists, but appears 4 times in Jn. (cf. 11[7, 11] 19[28]), and always connotes strict chronological sequence, as distinct from

[1] *Introd. to N.T.*, p. 524.   [2] *St. John's Gospel*, p. 241.

αὐτοῦ καὶ οἱ ἀδελφοὶ καὶ οἱ μαθηταὶ αὐτοῦ, καὶ ἐκεῖ ἔμειναν οὐ
πολλὰς ἡμέρας.

the vaguer μετὰ ταῦτα (see Introd., p. cviii). μετὰ ταῦτα is
read here in the fourth century Pap. Oxy. 847 and also in
M 124* with *b f ff*² *q*.

κατέβη εἰς Καφαρναούμ (this is the best attested spelling).
Jesus "went down" to Capernaum, Cana being on higher
ground: Jn. uses the same phrase again (4⁴⁷) for the journey
from Cana to Capernaum. The distance by road is about
20 miles. To assume that the party walked by way of Nazareth
(which is in a different direction), and that this journey to
Capernaum is to be identified with that mentioned Mt. 4¹³,
lacks evidence.

Capernaum is to be located at *Tell Hum* (more properly,
Telhum); or, less probably, at *Khan Minyeh*.[1] These places
are about 3 miles apart, both on the N. shore of the Sea of
Galilee.

Nothing is told about this short visit to Capernaum, so that
mention of it has no allegorical significance. V. 12 is merely
an historical note.

It will be noticed that the mother and "brethren" of Jesus
were with Him now, on the return of the wedding guests from
Cana; but thenceforth they do not travel about with Him.
His public mission has begun.

They stayed at Capernaum "not many days" (οὐ πολλὰς
ἡμέρας), the note of time being characteristic (see Introd., p. cii)
of the Fourth Gospel.

After ἀδελφοί, BLTᵇW, with Pap. Oxy. 847, omit αὐτοῦ, but
ins. אΑΝΓΔΘ, and most vss. א *a b e ff*² *l q*, with some cursives
and the Coptic Q, omit καὶ οἱ μαθηταὶ αὐτοῦ.

ADDITIONAL NOTE ON THE BRETHREN OF JESUS

The mother and "brethren" of Jesus accompanied Him
on this journey. The "brethren" are always (except in Jn.
7³ᶠ·) mentioned in the Gospels in connexion with Mary (cf.
Mk. 3³¹, Mt. 12⁴⁶, Lk. 8¹⁹ and Mk. 6³, Mt. 13⁵⁵); and it is not
unlikely that she shared their home until (see 19²⁷) she was
entrusted to the care of her nephew, John the son of Zebedee.
The evangelists consistently represent them as incredulous of
the claims of Jesus (see reff. above), and as regarding Him as
out of His mind (Mk. 3²¹, for "His friends" here are apparently to be identified with "His mother and His brethren"

[1] Cf. Rix, *Tent and Testament*, pp. 285 ff., and Sanday, *D.C.G.*,
i. 269.

in v. 31). Their names were James, Joseph, Simon, and Jude
(some of the commonest names in Palestine), and they had
sisters (Mt. 13[55], Mk. 6[3]). James, "the Lord's brother,"
became a believer after the Resurrection of Jesus (Acts 1[14]);
St. Paul reports that the Risen Lord appeared to him (1 Cor.
15[7]); and he was the first bishop of Jerusalem (see Acts
12[17] 15[13]). Grandsons of Jude (who probably also confessed
Christ afterwards, Acts 1[14]) were leaders of the Church in
the time of Domitian (Eus. *H.E.* iii. 19, 20, 32).

The ancient problem as to the "brethren of the Lord"
cannot be fully discussed here. (1) The theory known as the
Hieronymian, because it was started by Jerome, is that they
were the sons of Alphæus, who is identified with Clopas, and
Mary, who is regarded as the Virgin's sister (but see on 19[25]
as to both these equations). Thus they were maternal cousins
of Jesus, and were loosely called His "brethren." This would
involve the identification of "James the Lord's brother"
with James the son of Alphæus, who was one of the Twelve.
But the Lord's brethren remained incredulous throughout His
public ministry, and could not therefore have been numbered
among the Twelve (see on 7[5]). That James the Lord's brother
is called an "apostle" at Gal. 1[19] is nothing to the point, for
the circle of "apostles" was much larger than the circle of the
Twelve. Further, despite the vague use of ἀδελφός in a few
passages in the LXX, where a cousin is addressed or indicated
(cf. 2 Sam. 20[9], 1 Chron. 23[21. 22], Tobit 7[2. 4]), we cannot equate
ἀδελφός and ἀνεψιός or give any reason for the evangelists' use of
the word "brethren" when "cousins" would have been more
literally exact. (2) The *Helvidian* theory, against which
Jerome's polemic was addressed, is that these "brethren" were
sons of Joseph and Mary, born later than Jesus, and appeal is
made by its advocates to the phrasing of Mt. 1[25] as indicating
that Mary did not remain a virgin. But it is difficult to understand how the doctrine of the Virginity of Mary could have
grown up early in the second century if her four acknowledged
sons were prominent Christians, and one of them bishop of
Jerusalem. (3) The most probable, as it is the most ancient,
view is that expounded by *Epiphanius*, viz. that the "brethren
of the Lord" were sons of Joseph by a former wife. Thus
they were really the stepsons of Mary, and might naturally
be called the "brothers" of Jesus; the fact, too, that Mary
shared their home would be accounted for. Hegesippus
(*fl.*150; cf. Eus. *H.E.* iii. 11, iv. 22) stated that Clopas (Jn. 19[25])
was a brother of Joseph, a view which Epiphanius adopted.

It thus appears that we have to distinguish three groups of
persons bearing the same names, viz.:

i. James the son of Zebedee, James the son of Alphæus; Simon Peter, Simon Zelotes; Judas the son of another James, also called Thaddæus, and Judas Iscariot, were all of the Twelve (Mt. 10²ᶠ·, Mk. 3¹⁶ᶠ·, Lk. 6¹⁴ᶠ·).

ii. James called the Just, the first bishop of Jerusalem, Simon, Judas, and Joseph, the Lord's brethren, were sons of Joseph by his first wife (Mk. 6³, Mt. 13⁵⁵).

iii. James the Little (ὁ μικρός), of whom we know nothing more, and Joses were sons of Clopas and another Mary (Mk. 15⁴⁰, Mt. 27⁵⁶; see on Jn. 19²⁵). They had another brother, Symeon, who was second bishop of Jerusalem, and was appointed to that office, according to Hegesippus, because he was the Lord's " cousin " (Eus. *H.E.* iii. 11, iv. 22). This phrase is used because Clopas was brother of Joseph, the foster father of Jesus.

Hence it would seem that James, Joses, and Symeon in Group iii. were first cousins of James, Joseph, Simon, and Judas in Group ii.[1]

The Cleansing of the Temple (vv. 13–22)

13 ff. This incident is placed in the traditional text of Jn. at the beginning of the ministry of Jesus (2¹³⁻¹⁷), while the Synoptists place it at the end (Mk. 11¹⁵⁻¹⁷, Mt. 21¹². ¹³, Lk. 19⁴⁵. ⁴⁶). Before examining this discrepancy, we must review the differences between the Synoptic and Johannine narratives, and also come to some conclusion as to the significance of the action of Jesus on this occasion.

The Synoptic tradition is based on Mk.; Mt. and Lk. having no details that are not in Mk., and omitting some of his. It is convenient, then, to begin by comparing Jn. with Mk.; and it appears at once that Jn. (as often elsewhere [2]) knows Mk.'s narrative, which he amplifies and alters in some details.

Both evangelists tell of the upsetting of the tables of the moneychangers. Jn. omits, as do Mt. and Lk., a point preserved by Mk., viz. that Jesus forbade the carrying of goods or implements through the Temple courts, a practice probably due to the desire to make a short cut between the city and the Mount of Olives (Mk. 11¹⁶). Jn. alone states that sheep and oxen were being sold in the precincts (τὸ ἱερόν), the sale of pigeons only being mentioned by Mk. Jn. adds that Jesus

---

[1] For full treatment of this problem, see especially Lightfoot, *Galatians*, pp. 252–291 ; J. B. Mayor, *Ep. of St. James*, Introd., c. 1 ; and C. Harris, *D.C.G.*, *s.v.* " Brethren of the Lord." Dom Chapman defends the Hieronymian view in *J.T.S.*, April 1906.

[2] Cf. Introd., p. xcvii.

used a whip to drive out the beasts, while he ordered their
owners to take the pigeons away, with the rebuke, " Make not
my Father's house a house of business." The rebuke in Mk.
is different, being made up of quotations from Isa. 56[7] and
Jer. 7[11], " *My house shall be called a house of prayer for all the
nations*, but you have made it *a den of thieves*." That is to
say, Mk. represents Jesus as denouncing the dishonesty of the
traffic which was carried on within the Temple precincts; while
from Jn. it would seem as if the traffic itself, apart from its
honesty or dishonesty, were condemned. The Scripture which
the burning zeal of Jesus recalls to Jn. is Ps. 69[9]; and he notes
that the Jews asked for a sign of His authority, to which Jesus
replied by saying, " Destroy this temple, and I will raise it
up in three days "—enigmatical words which (according to
Jn.) the Jews misinterpreted. None of this is in Mk., who
adds, however, that the chief priests and scribes began to seek
the death of Jesus, fearing Him and being alarmed at the effect
of His words upon the people.

What was the meaning of the action of Jesus in " cleansing "
the Temple ? It does not seem to have been suggested by any
special incident. According to all the accounts, it was quite
spontaneous.

Perhaps the best answer is that the action of Jesus was a
protest against the whole sacrificial system of the Temple.[1]
The killing of beasts, which was a continual feature of Jewish
worship, was a disgusting and useless practice. The court of
slaughter must have been like a shambles, especially at Passover
time. And Jesus, by His bold action, directed public attention
not only to the impropriety of buying and selling cattle in the
sacred precincts, with the accompanying roguery which made
the Temple a den of thieves, but also to the futility of animal
sacrifices. He had declared Himself against Jewish Sabba-
tarianism. He now attacks the Temple system. This it was
which set the temple officials against Him. The cry, " Thou
that destroyest the temple," disclosed the cause of their bitter
enmity.

There is, indeed, no hint that Jesus interfered *directly* with
the work of the priests.[2] He quoted a prophetic passage
(Hos. 6[6]) which deprecated the offering of animal victims
(Mt. 9[13] 12[7]), but not on this occasion. Nor is He said to have
prevented any animal from being led to sacrifice. What He
interfered with was a market, not held in the court where the
altars were, but in the outer Court of the Gentiles. Yet some

---

[1] So Oesterley in *D.C.G.*, ii. 712 ; cf. Caldecott, *J.T.S.*, July 1923,
p. 382.
[2] So Burkitt, *J.T.S.*, July 1924, p. 387 f.

such market was necessary, if animal sacrifices were to go on. It was inevitable that oxen and sheep and pigeons should be available for purchase, in or near the precincts of the Temple, by the pilgrims who came up to worship at the great feasts, and particularly at the Passover. If this practice were stopped, the whole system of sacrificial worship would disappear. It may therefore have been the purpose of Jesus, by His action of " cleansing the Temple," to aim a blow at the Temple system in general (cf. 4²¹). But if so, it was not immediately perceived to be His purpose by His own disciples, who continued to attend the Temple worship after His Passion and Resurrection (Acts 2⁴⁶ 3¹; cf. 6⁷).

Whether this be the true explanation of the drastic action of Jesus, or whether we should attach a lesser significance to it by supposing that His purpose was merely to rebuke those who profaned the Temple courts by chaffering and bargaining, it is not possible to decide with certainty. We pass on to consider whether it is more probable that the incident occurred at the beginning or at the end of His ministry. Mk. (followed by Mt. and Lk.) places it at the end; Jn. seems to place it at the beginning. Which is more likely ?

It is true that Mk. only tells of *one* visit of Jesus to Jerusalem; and so, if he mentioned the Cleansing of the Temple at all, he had to put it at the end of the ministry. Nor is the Marcan dating of events in the last week always to be accepted as accurate. As to the date of the Day of the Crucifixion, *e.g.*, Jn. is to be preferred to Mk. (see Introd., p. cvi). So that it is not to be taken for granted that, in a matter of this sort, Mk. must be right and Jn. wrong. But if we reflect how deep must have been the indignation aroused by such an act as that recorded in Jn. 2¹⁵, how the vested interests of the cattle-dealers must have been affected by it, how little disposed men are to yield to opposition which will bring them financial loss, we shall find it hard to believe that Jesus was a comparatively unknown person in Jerusalem when He " cleansed " the Temple. The one moment at which such an action could have been carried through without instant retaliation was, apparently, the moment after His triumphal entry, when even the Pharisees began to despair of diverting the crowds from following Him (12¹⁹). On psychological grounds, the incident is hardly credible, if it is to be put at the beginning of the ministry of Jesus. At that time the Temple officials would have made short work of any one who attempted to stop the business of the Temple courts by violence.

Our conclusion accordingly is that there is some mistake (which cannot now be explained) in that account of the Cleansing

13. Καὶ ἐγγὺς ἦν τὸ πάσχα τῶν Ἰουδαίων, καὶ ἀνέβη εἰς Ἱεροσόλυμα ὁ Ἰησοῦς. 14. καὶ εὗρεν ἐν τῷ ἱερῷ τοὺς πωλοῦντας βόας καὶ

of the Temple which places it immediately after the miracle of
Cana, as the traditional text of Jn. places it.[1] Some expositors
have postulated two cleansings, one at the beginning, the other
at the close of Jesus' ministry; but, apart from the fact that
this duplication of similar incidents is improbable, we find it
difficult to suppose that this particular incident, or anything
like it, could have happened at so early a stage in the ministry
of Jesus as is suggested by the traditional order of the chapters
in the Fourth Gospel.[2]

13. ἐγγὺς ἦν τὸ πάσχα τῶν Ἰουδαίων. ἐγγύς is used again
6^4 7^2 11^{55} of the approach of a feast; elsewhere in the Gospel
it is used of proximity in *space*, not *time*.

τὸ πάσχα τῶν Ἰουδαίων. Jn. is accustomed to describe
the Passover festivals which he mentions as " of the Jews "
(cf. 5^1 6^4 11^{55}), and he speaks in the same way of the Feast of
Tabernacles (7^2). The Synoptists never speak thus. Westcott
suggested that the qualifying phrase " of the Jews " implies the
existence at the time of writing of a recognised *Christian* Passover, from which Jn. wishes to distinguish those which he
records ... ...t this explanation will not cover the language of
7^2, for there was no Christian Feast of Tabernacles. It is
simpler to say that Jn. is writing for Greek readers, and that
the qualifying clause is explanatory for them (cf. v. 6 and 19^{40}).
Paul was proud of being a Jew, but he speaks nevertheless
of Ἰουδαϊσμός (Gal. 1^{13}) as something quite foreign to his
present religious convictions; and so there is nothing in the
addition " of the Jews " inconsistent with the nationality of
John the son of Zebedee, even if we were to suppose that he
wrote these words with his own hand, at the end of a long
Christian life, lived for the most part out of Palestine, during
which he had dissociated himself from his Jewish past.

ἀνέβη εἰς Ἱεροσόλυμα. ἀναβαίνειν is the verb regularly
used of " going up " to Jerusalem for the feasts (5^1 7^8 11^{55} 12^{20}).
In this context it does not connote the idea of ascending from
lower to higher ground (as in v. 12), but of journeying to the
metropolis.

14, 15. The ἱερόν, or sacred precinct, must be distinguished from the ναός, or Temple itself. Here, the ἱερόν is the
Outer Court, or Court of the Gentiles, where the animals needed
for sacrifice or offering were bought. To those coming from a

[1] See Introd., p. xxx.
[2] See Drummond (*Character and Authorship, etc.*, p. 61) and Cadoux
(*J.T.S.*, July 1919).

πρόβατα καὶ περιστερὰς καὶ τοὺς κερματιστὰς καθημένους, 15. καὶ
ποιήσας φραγέλλιον ἐκ σχοινίων πάντας ἐξέβαλεν ἐκ τοῦ ἱεροῦ, τά τε
πρόβατα καὶ τοὺς βόας, καὶ τῶν κολλυβιστῶν ἐξέχεεν τὰ κέρματα
καὶ τὰς τραπέζας ἀνέτρεψεν, 16. καὶ τοῖς τὰς περιστερὰς πωλοῦσιν

distance, as well as to Jews of Jerusalem, it was a convenience
to be able to buy on the spot the oxen or sheep or pigeons
(Lev. 5⁷ 15¹⁴. ²⁹ 17³, etc.) that were required for sacrifice or for
offerings of purification. So, too, the trade of the moneychangers was a necessary one, because Roman money could
not be paid into the Temple treasury. The capitation tax or
" atonement money " of half a shekel (see Ex. 30¹³, Neh. 10³²,
Mt. 17²⁴) had to be tendered in the orthodox coinage.

κέρμα signifies a small coin, and hence we have κερματιστής,
" a moneychanger." So too, κόλλυβος, κολλυβιστής, with
like meanings (v. 15). Lightfoot quotes ¹ a Talmudic rule:
" It is necessary that every one should have half a shekel to
pay for himself. Therefore, when he comes to the exchange
to change a shekel for two half-shekels he is obliged to allow
him some gain, which is called קולבון or κόλλυβος." That is,
the κόλλυβος was the discount charged by the moneychanger
for exchanging a shekel into two half-shekels.

For τὰ κέρματα (BLTᵇW 33, with Pap. Ox_, ⁰ ·⁻ˎ the
rec. has τὸ κέρμα with אANΔΘ, apparently treating it as a
collective noun: " He poured out the coin (pecuniam) of the
moneychangers."

For ἀνέτρεψεν (BWΘ, with Pap. Oxy. 847) the rec. has
ἀνέστρεψεν with ALNΔ, א fam. 13 having κατέστρεψεν (from
Mk. 11¹⁵). ἀναστρέφειν is not used in the N.T. in the sense of
" upsetting "; for ἀνατρέπειν, cf. 2 Tim. 2¹⁸.

τράπεζα is classical for a moneychanger's table, and we
have τὴν τράπεζαν ἀνατρέπειν " to upset the table " in Demosthenes (403. 7).

For the redundant ἐκβάλλειν ἐκ, see on 6³⁷.

σχοινιά means " a bunch of rushes," while σχοινίον is a
" cord "; and some have thought that the scourge or whip
used by Jesus was made from the rushes used for bedding for
the cattle. It may have been so, but φραγέλλιον ἐκ σχοινίων
is adequately translated by " a whip of small cords." The
whip is not mentioned by the Synoptists, and the detail is
suggestive of the recollections of an eye-witness.

πάντας ἐξέβαλεν . . . τά τε πρόβατα καὶ τοὺς βόας. It
would seem that the whip was used on the owners of the
cattle as well as on the sheep and oxen. πάντας ἐξέβαλιν
in the Synoptist accounts (Mt. 21¹²; cf. Mk. 11¹⁵, Lk. 19⁴⁵ˎ

¹ Hor. Hebr., ii. 275.

εἶπεν Ἄρατε ταῦτα ἐντεῦθεν, μὴ ποιεῖτε τὸν οἶκον τοῦ Πατρός μου οἶκον ἐμπορίου. 17. ἐμνήσθησαν οἱ μαθηταὶ αὐτοῦ ὅτι γεγραμμένον ἐστίν

certainly applies to the *men*; the Synoptists do not mention the driving out of the *cattle*.

Jerome (in Mt. 21[15]) says that the cattle-dealers did not resist Jesus: "a certain fiery and starry light shone from His eyes and the majesty of Godhead gleamed in His face."[1]

16. The doves or pigeons could not be driven out as the cattle were; but the order to those who sold them is peremptory : ἄρατε ταῦτα ἐντεῦθεν, "take them hence." For the aor. imper. ἄρατε, see on v. 5.

The reason given for this action is different from that given by the Synoptists. They represent Jesus as indignant at the *dishonesty* of the traffic pursued in the Temple: "Ye have made it a den of thieves." According to Jn., Jesus seems to object to the traffic in itself, honest or dishonest, as secular business that ought not to be transacted in a sacred place: "Make not my Father's house a house of merchandise" (but see above, at p. 87). The remarkable phrase "*my* Father"—not "*our* Father"—is not found in Mk., but it occurs 4 times in Lk., 16 times in Mt., and 27 times in Jn. We have thus the authority of Mt. and Lk., as well as that of Jn., for regarding it as a phrase which Jesus used habitually. It indicates a peculiar relationship between Him and God, the Father of all, which is not shared by the sons of men (cf. Jn. 20[17]).

ὁ οἶκος τοῦ Πατρός μου is the earthly Temple. So the Lord is represented by Lk. (2[49]) as saying, "Wist ye not that I must be in my Father's house ?" (ἐν τοῖς τοῦ Πατρός μου). But ἡ οἰκία τοῦ Πατρός μου (14[2]), "the Dwelling Place of my Father," in which are many mansions, is the heavenly temple, the Eternal and Changeless Home of the Eternal.

The Temple is often described in the O.T. as "the house of God," and Jesus so described it (Mk. 2[26], Mt. 12[4], Lk. 6[4]). It was to make an unmistakable claim for Himself to substitute for this familiar expression the words "the house of My Father." Here is an express assertion that He was Messiah, the Son of God, as Nathanael had already perceived Him to be (1[49]). Cf. 5[17].

17. οἱ μαθηταὶ αὐτοῦ, sc. who were present (see on 2[2]). They saw in the action of Jesus in purifying the Temple courts an illustration of that burning zeal of which the Psalmist had sung, "The zeal of thy house hath consumed me" (Ps. 69[9]). No Psalm is so frequently quoted in the N.T. as this. The rest of v. 9, "The reproaches of them that reproach thee are fallen

---

[1] See James, *Apocryphal N.T.*, p. 8.

Ὁ ζῆλος τοῦ οἴκου σου καταφάγεταί με. 18. ἀπεκρίθησαν οὖν οἱ Ἰουδαῖοι καὶ εἶπαν αὐτῷ Τί σημεῖον δεικνύεις ἡμῖν, ὅτι ταῦτα ποιεῖς; 19. ἀπεκρίθη Ἰησοῦς καὶ εἶπεν αὐτοῖς Λύσατε τὸν ναὸν τοῦτον, καὶ ἐν τρισὶν ἡμέραις ἐγερῶ αὐτόν. 20. εἶπαν οὖν οἱ Ἰουδαῖοι

upon me," is applied by Paul to the Christ (Rom. 15³). Jn. represents Jesus as citing v. 4, "They hated me without a cause," as fulfilled in His own experience (15²⁵), and as saying, "I thirst," on the Cross in fulfilment of v. 21.[1] It appears, then, that Ps. 69 was regarded as prophetic of Messiah, and the disciples, as they watched Jesus, seem to have regarded His Cleansing of the Temple as a Messianic action (cf. Mal. 3¹⁻⁵). They foresee that the fiery energy which He displays will wear Him out at last, and they substitute for the past tense of the Psalmist, "hath consumed me" (κατέφαγεν), the future καταφάγεται, "will consume me."

The rec. text here has κατέφαγε, but the uncials give καταφάγεται. The true text of the LXX at Ps. 69¹⁰ seems to be κατέφαγε (following the Hebrew), but B reads καταφάγεται.

Other citations from Ps. 69 are found, Acts 1²⁰ (v. 25), Rom. 11⁹·¹⁰ (vv. 22, 23). Cf. also Mt. 27³⁴·⁴⁸.

The Synoptists always have γέγραπται for citations from the O.T. ; Jn. prefers γεγραμμένον ἐστίν (as here and at 6³¹·⁴⁵ 10³⁴ 12¹⁴; but see 8¹⁷ and critical note there).

18. The Jews (see on 1¹⁹ 5¹⁰) did not view the action of Jesus as His disciples did. They wished to know by what authority He had taken upon Himself the rôle of a reformer (cf. Mk. 11²⁸, Mt. 21²³, Lk. 20²). If He had authority, what "sign" could He perform in proof of it ? It has always been true of un-educated people that "except they see signs and wonders, they will not believe" (4⁴⁸). And even the educated Pharisees and scribes asked Jesus for "signs," although, probably, they asked because they did not think that He could gratify their request (cf. Mk. 8¹¹, Mt. 16¹). See on v. 11 for the value of the witness of such signs.

Jesus gave no sign such as the crowds asked for. His words (see on v. 19) did not provide anything more than a fresh assertion of His power. This is quite consistent with the Synoptic reports of His refusal to work "signs" for Herod (Lk. 23⁸) or for the scribes and Pharisees (Mt. 12³⁹).

19. λύσατε τὸν ναὸν τοῦτον κτλ. We must distinguish this saying of Jesus from the interpretation which the evangelist puts upon it in v. 21. That it is an authentic saying is plain from the fact that, perhaps in a distorted form, it was made a topic of accusation against Jesus at His trial before the high

[1] Cf. Introd., p. clv.

priest (Mk. 14⁵⁸, Mt. 26⁶¹; cf. Mk. 15²⁹, Acts 6¹⁴). That by the ναός which would be destroyed Jesus was understood to mean Herod's Temple is certain from the retort of the Jews (see on v. 20). But the precise form of words is uncertain, nor were the witnesses at the trial agreed about this. According to Mk., the witnesses falsely reported the saying in the form, " *I will destroy* this temple made with hands, and in three days (διὰ τριῶν ἡμερῶν) I will build another made without hands " (Mk. 14⁵⁸). This is softened down by Mt., according to whom the witnesses alleged that Jesus said, " *I can destroy* the temple of God and build it in three days " (Mt. 26⁶¹). According to Jn. in the present passage, Jesus only said that *if the Jews destroyed* the Temple, in three days He would raise it up. It is a question whether any of these reports precisely reproduces the words of Jesus at the Cleansing of the Temple. On another occasion He is reported by the Synoptists (Mk. 13², Mt. 24², Lk. 21⁶) to have predicted the downfall of the Temple, and this is undoubtedly authentic. But it is not probable that He should have declared that *He* would rebuild it or raise it up again.[1] A rebuilding of the Temple would mean the restoration of the old Jewish system of ritual and sacrifice, and we know that this was not the purpose of Jesus (see above, pp. 87, 88). He told the Samaritan woman that He did not accept the principle which she attributed to Him, that Jerusalem was the special place where men ought to worship (4²⁰· ²¹). The worship of the future was to be of a spiritual sort, and not to be confined to any one centre. To the vision of the seer of the Apocalypse, there was no temple in the New Jerusalem (Rev. 21²²). That Jesus should have said that He would rebuild the Temple at Jerusalem if it were destroyed, is not credible. The Temple was, indeed, the chief obstacle to the acceptance of His gospel by the Jews.

But the Marcan version of His words, or rather the Marcan version of the witnesses' report of His words (Mk. 14⁵⁸), has no such improbability. It lays stress on the contrast between the temple made with hands and the temple made without hands (cf. Acts 7⁴⁸ 17²⁴, Heb. 9¹¹), between the temple built by Herod, which was the centre of Jewish worship, and the " spiritual house " of Christian believers, which was to offer up " spiritual sacrifices " (1 Pet. 2⁵; cf. 2 Cor. 6¹⁶). That Jesus foresaw the passing of the Temple, and its replacement by a less exclusive and less formal worship is certain, however we try to explain His prescience.

Next, we observe that it is common to all the reports of this

---

[1] Notwithstanding a suggestion in *Enoch* xc. 28 that Messiah was to reconstruct the Temple (based on Hag. 2⁷ᶠ·).

saying of His that He asserted that the replacement of the old by the new would be "in three days." Salmon suggested [1] that Jesus may have had in His thoughts the words of the prophet about reconstruction after apparent destruction: "After two days will He revive us: on the third day He will raise us up, and we shall live before Him" (Hos. 6²). The Synoptists, however, tell again and again that Jesus predicted that His Death would be followed by His Resurrection "on the third day" (Mk. 8³¹, Mt. 16²¹, Lk. 9²²; Mk. 9³¹, Mt. 17²³; Mk. 10³⁴, Mt. 20¹⁹, Lk. 18³³; cf. also Mt. 27⁶³). It is more natural to bring the "three days" of Mk. 14⁵⁸, Mt. 26⁶¹, Jn. 2¹⁹ into connexion with these passages than to presuppose a reminiscence of Hos. 6²—a prophetic text which, it is curious to note, is never quoted of the Resurrection in the Apostolic age.[2]

We conclude, then, that Jesus at the Cleansing of the Temple declared (1) that the Temple, the pride and glory of Jerusalem, would be destroyed at no distant date, and that the Temple worship would pass away; (2) that He would Himself replace it by a spiritual temple; and (3) that the transition from the old order to the new would occupy no more than "three days." His hearers were at once indignant and incredulous, for they understood His words as a threat, and that the rebuilding of which He spoke was a literal rebuilding with stones and mortar.

The *Epistle of Barnabas* (§ 16) states explicitly that the spiritual temple then being built up was the company of Christian believers: "I will tell you concerning the temple how these wretched ones [*i.e.* the Jews] being led astray set their hope on the building, and not on their God that made them, as if it were the house of God." He quotes Isa. 49¹⁷ and *Enoch* lxxxix. 56 as predictive of the destruction of the Temple, and proceeds, "Let us inquire whether there be any temple of God." He concludes that there is, quoting words of *Enoch* (xci. 13), "When the week is being accomplished, the temple of God shall be built gloriously." He goes on, "Before we believed in God, the abode of our heart was corrupt and weak, a temple truly built by hands"; but the temple of the Lord is now built gloriously, for "having received the remission of sins and having set our hope on the Name, we became new, being created again from the beginning, wherefore God truly dwelleth in our habitation within us. . . . This is a spiritual temple built for the Lord." The allusion to "the temple made with hands" is reminiscent of Mk. 14⁵⁸, and the whole passage shows

---

[1] *Human Element in the Gospels*, p. 218.
[2] Tertullian (*ad. Judæos* 13) and Cyprian (*Test.* ii. 25) both cite it.

Τεσσεράκοντα καὶ ἓξ ἔτεσιν οἰκοδομήθη ὁ ναὸς οὗτος, καὶ σὺ ἐν
τρισὶν ἡμέραις ἐγερεῖς αὐτόν; 21. ἐκεῖνος δὲ ἔλεγεν περὶ τοῦ ναοῦ

that the antithesis between the Jewish temple of stone and the
Christian temple of faithful hearts was familiar to the sub-
Apostolic age. We have it again in Justin (*Tryph.* 86), who
says that Jesus made His disciples to be "a house of prayer
and worship" (οἶκος εὐχῆς καὶ προσκυνήσεως). The idea
probably goes back to sayings of Jesus such as Mk. 14[58] and
the present passage, although it is not suggested here that
Barnabas knew the Fourth Gospel.

"In three days I will raise it up." The Agent of the
revival is to be Jesus Himself. This suggests at once that it
was not to His own bodily Resurrection that Jesus referred
here. For by the N.T. writers God the Father is *always*
designated as the Agent of Christ's Resurrection (Acts 2[24] 3[15]
4[10] 10[40] 13[30], Rom. 4[24] 8[11] 10[9], 1 Cor. 6[14] 15[15], 2 Cor. 4[14], Gal. 1[1],
Eph. 1[20], 1 Thess. 1[10], Heb. 13[20], 1 Pet. 1[21]). Jesus is not
represented as raising Himself. Hence we have a confirmation of the conclusion already reached, that it was not the
resuscitation of the Body of Jesus from the tomb that was in
His thought here, but rather the passing of the old (and material)
temple and the beginning of the new (and spiritual) temple of
Christian believers. See on v. 21, and note the passive ἠγέρθη
at v. 22; but cf. also 10[18].

20. Jn. relates several conversations of Jesus, cast in somewhat similar form to this. That is, there is first a difficult saying
of His. It is misunderstood and its spiritual significance is not
discerned, a too material interpretation being given to it by His
hearers. Then either He Himself, or the evangelist, adds an
explanatory statement. Cf., for instances of this, 3[4] 4[11, 33]
6[42, 51f]. See Introd., p. cxi.

ἐν τρισὶν ἡμέραις, "*within* three days," not "*after* three
days," the preposition perhaps being significant.[1]

τεσσεράκοντα καὶ ἓξ ἔτεσιν κτλ. Abbott (*Diat.* 2021-4)
would refer these words to the original building of the Temple
in the time of Ezra. If, with the LXX, we omit the words "of
Babylon" after "Cyrus the king" at Ezra 5[13], and assume
that "Cyrus king of Persia" (Ezra 1[1]) is intended, we may take
the first year of Cyrus king of Persia, *i.e.* 559 B.C., for the year in
which the edict to build the Temple was issued. But according
to Josephus (*Antt.* XI. i. 1), it was completed in 513 B.C., *i.e.*
forty-six years after; and so it is stated in the chronology of
Eusebius. This is a summary of Abbott's argument, which
seems, however, to depend on too many subsidiary hypotheses

---

[1] Cf. Abbott, *Diat.* 2331.

to be satisfactory. Heracleon refers the words to Solomon's Temple,[1] which Origen refutes, but gives no satisfactory explanation of his own. It seems more likely, as has generally been held by modern editors, that Herod's building is the subject of the allusion in this verse.

τεσσεράκοντα καὶ ἓξ ἔτεσιν οἰκοδομήθη κτλ. The aor. οἰκοδομήθη does not imply that the building was completed, as may be seen from a parallel sentence in Ezra 5[16] (appositely cited by Alford) describing the building of Ezra's Temple, ἀπὸ τότε ἕως τοῦ νῦν ᾠκοδομήθη καὶ οὐκ ἐτελέσθη : it only implies that building operations had been in progress for forty-six years. In fact, Herod's Temple was not completed until 64 A.D., in the time of Herod Agrippa.

According to Josephus, Herod the Great began to repair and rebuild the Temple in the eighteenth year of his reign (*Antt.* xv. xi. 1), *i.e.* 20–19 B.C. This would give either 27 A.D. or 28 A.D. as the year of the Passover indicated in these verses.[2] The year of the Crucifixion is not certain, but it was probably 29 A.D. or 30 A.D. It is not possible to draw *exact* chronological inferences from the " forty and six years " of this verse, but the phrase agrees well enough with the probable date, as gathered from other considerations. It is difficult to account for the attribution of so definite a statement of time to the Jewish objectors if it did not embody a reminiscence of fact. As to the fact itself, the Jews must have been well informed.

As at other points in the Gospel (v. 6 5[5] 21[11]), some critics have supposed that the number mentioned here is to be interpreted in an esoteric fashion, after the methods of *Gematria*. The name Ἀδάμ has 46 as its numerical equivalent, and thus the occult reference [3] in " forty-six years hath this Temple been in building " would be to some contrast between the first and second Adam. It is unnecessary to dwell upon such extravagances.[4] Hardly less fanciful is it to suppose, as Loisy does, that the forty-six years refer to the actual age of Jesus at the time, He being taken for a man forty-nine years old (8[57]), near the end of His ministry.

21. ἐκεῖνος δὲ ἔλεγεν κτλ., "but He was speaking about the temple of His body." ἐκεῖνος is emphatic, " but He, on the contrary . . ." See on 1[8] 19[35].

For Jn.'s habit of commenting on sayings of Jesus, cf. Introd., p. xxxiv. This comment seems to convey that by the

---

[1] So also ps.-Cyprian, *de montibus Sina et Sion,* 4.
[2] Turner (*D.B.* i. 405*b*) gives 27 A.D., and von Soden (*E.B.* 804) gives 28 A.D.
[3] This is suggested in ps.-Cyprian, *de mont. Sina, etc.,* 4.
[4] Cf. Introd., p. lxxxvii.

τοῦ σώματος αὐτοῦ. 22. ὅτε οὖν ἠγέρθη ἐκ νεκρῶν, ἐμνήσθησαν οἱ μαθηταὶ αὐτοῦ ὅτι τοῦτο ἔλεγεν, καὶ ἐπίστευσαν τῇ γραφῇ καὶ τῷ λόγῳ ὃν εἶπεν ὁ Ἰησοῦς.

words " Destroy this temple," Jesus meant " Destroy this body of mine." But this is hardly possible (see on v. 19). Had He meant that, He would have spoken with less ambiguity. He plainly meant Herod's Temple, and was so understood. Christian believers are, indeed, spoken of as the " Temple of God " (2 Cor. 6¹⁶), but not Christ Himself. He was " greater than the Temple " (Mt. 12⁶). But the comment is much condensed, and may mean only that the " temple of His body " of which Jesus spoke was the " spiritual house " of Christian believers (1 Pet. 2⁵), who are collectively the Body of Christ (1 Cor. 12²⁷); the " three days " carrying an allusion to the interval between the Death and Resurrection of Jesus, which marked, as it seems to the evangelist looking back, the watershed between Judaism and Christianity.

τοῦ σώματος αὐτοῦ. Jn. is not fond of the word σῶμα (see p. clxxi); he always uses it of a *dead* body, not of a living one (cf. 19³¹·³⁸·⁴⁰ 20¹²).

22. ἐμνήσθησαν οἱ μαθηταί (see on v. 2) in v. 17 recalls what the disciples remembered *at the time, i.e.* they thought of Ps. 69⁹ when they saw the burning zeal of their Master; in this verse it recalls what they thought *after His Resurrection* of the meaning of His words recorded in v. 19. So, again, in 12¹⁶ Jn. tells that it was not until after Jesus was glorified that the disciples understood the forward reference of Zech. 9⁹; [1] cf. Lk. 24⁸ and Jn. 13¹⁹ 14²⁹.

ἐπίστευσαν τῇ γραφῇ. ἡ γραφή seems to refer in Jn. to a definite passage of Scripture,[2] as it does throughout the N.T., rather than to the O.T. generally (which would be αἱ γραφαί). At Jn. 10³⁵ 13¹⁸ (17¹²) 19²⁴·²⁸·³⁶·³⁷ the actual passage is quoted; at Jn. 7³⁸·⁴² (which see) the reference is not quite certain; while here and at 20⁹ no clue is given to the passage to which allusion is made. But as it is plain from Acts 2³¹ 13³⁵ that Ps. 16¹⁰, " Neither wilt thou suffer thy Holy One to see corruption," was cited by Peter and Paul alike as predictive of the Resurrection of Christ, we may conclude that this is the verse in the evangelist's mind when he says that the disciples after the Resurrection " believed the Scripture."

---

[1] Irenæus lays down the principle that no prophecy is fully understood until after its fulfilment : πᾶσα γὰρ προφητεία πρὸ τῆς ἐκβάσεωι αἴνιγμά ἐστι (*Hær.* iv. 26).

[2] Abbott, *Diat.* 1722 *a–l*, argues, but unconvincingly, that ἡ γραφή means here " the general tenor of the Scriptures."

23. Ὡς δὲ ἦν ἐν τοῖς Ἱεροσολύμοις ἐν τῷ πάσχα ἐν τῇ ἑορτῇ, πολλοὶ ἐπίστευσαν εἰς τὸ ὄνομα αὐτοῦ, θεωροῦντες αὐτοῦ τὰ σημεῖα ἃ ἐποίει· 24. αὐτὸς δὲ Ἰησοῦς οὐκ ἐπίστευεν αὐτὸν αὐτοῖς διὰ τὸ

Ps. 16[10] was the "proof text" to which the Apostolic age referred.

καὶ τῷ λόγῳ ὃν εἶπεν ὁ Ἰη., "and the saying which Jesus spake," i.e. the saying in v. 19. ὁ λόγος is often thus used of a "saying" of Jesus; e.g. ἐπίστευσεν ὁ ἄνθρωπος τῷ λόγῳ ὃν εἶπεν αὐτῷ ὁ Ἰη. (4[50]); cf. 6[60] 7[36] 15[20] 18[9]. [32] 21[23]. ὅν is read by אBLT[b], the rec. having ᾧ with ΑΝWΓΔΘ.

Sojourn at Jerusalem (vv. 23-25)

23. ἐν τοῖς Ἱεροσολύμοις. This is the true reading here, although rec. text with a few minuscules omits τοῖς, in accordance with Jn.'s usual practice. He has the article with Ἱεροσόλυμα (see on 1[19] for this form) 3 times only, viz. 2[23] 5[2] 11[18] (see on 10[22]). No other N.T. writer has this usage, but it appears 2 Macc. 11[8] 12[9]. Perhaps τὰ Ἱεροσόλυμα means "the precincts of Jerusalem" in these exceptional passages.

If the traditional order of the verses 2[13]-3[21] be correct, then the statement of v. 23 is not easy to interpret. Nothing has been said hitherto of "signs" at Jerusalem, and yet both here and at 3[2] they are mentioned as notorious. The only "sign" that has been mentioned is the "sign" at Cana of Galilee. There would be no difficulty if we could assume that vv. 2[13]-3[21] belong to the last week in the ministry of Jesus. The "signs" would then be those which were wrought at Jerusalem or in its neighbourhood on His last visit, "the signs which He was doing" (ἐποίει). The Raising of Lazarus is given by Jn. special prominence among these (12[18]), and there was also the Blasting of the Fig Tree (Mk. 11[14]), as well as others not described in detail (12[37]; cf. 7[31]).

But, as the text stands, we must suppose that Jn. refers here to "signs" at Jerusalem wrought at the beginning of the ministry of Jesus, which he does not describe (cf. 3[2] 4[45]).

πολλοὶ ἐπίστευσαν, including not only inhabitants of Jerusalem, but some from among those who had come up to the feast from the country parts.

For the phrase ἐπίστευσαν εἰς τὸ ὄνομα, see on 1[12]. Although these people had been attracted to Jesus because of the "signs" that they saw, their belief was neither stable nor adequate. A similar thing happened in Galilee, ἠκολούθει αὐτῷ ὄχλος πολύς, ὅτι ἐθεώρουν τὰ σημεῖα ἃ ἐποίει (6[2]), the same phrase that we have here.

αὐτὸν γινώσκειν πάντας, 25. καὶ ὅτι οὐ χρείαν εἶχεν ἵνα τις μαρτυρήσῃ περὶ τοῦ ἀνθρώπου· αὐτὸς γὰρ ἐγίνωσκεν τί ἦν ἐν τῷ ἀνθρώπῳ.

θεωρεῖν is a favourite verb with Jn., occurring 23 times;
cf also 1 Jn. 3[17]. It only occurs twice in the Apocalypse
(11[11. 12]), and never in Paul. It may be used either of bodily
vision (20[6. 14]) or of mental contemplation (12[45] 14[17]), but
always connotes intelligent attention. The English word
which most nearly represents θεωρεῖν, as used by Jn., is " to
notice." Here and at 6[2] 7[3] it indicates the notice which the
observers took of the " signs " of Jesus. See for the difference
between θεωρεῖν and ὄπτομαι on 1[51], and cf. 16[16].

24, 25. οὐκ ἐπίστευεν αὐτὸν αὐτοῖς, " He was not trusting
Himself to them." The kind of faith that is generated by
" signs " is not very stable; cf. 4[48] and 6[14. 15].

διὰ τὸ αὐτὸν γινώσκειν πάντας, " because He knew all
men." See 1[48] 5[42] for other instances of this penetrating insight
into men's characters (γινώσκειν being used in both cases),
and 6[61. 64] 13[11] (where οἶδα is used in the same way; see on
1[26] above). Another illustration of the same faculty of insight
is found in 4[19. 29]. Cf. Mt. 9[4], Jn. 21[17].

αὐτὸς γὰρ ἐγίνωσκεν τί ἦν ἐν τῷ ἀνθρώπῳ, " He knew what
was in man," ὁ ἄνθρωπος being used generically (cf. 7[51]). This,
to be sure, is a Divine attribute, and is so represented in the
O.T., e.g. Jer. 17[10] 20[12], where Yahweh is said to " search the
heart and try the reins." But it is also, in its measure, a
prerogative of human genius; and (with the possible exception
of 1[48]) it is not clear that Jn. means us to understand that the
insight of Jesus into men's motives and characters was different
in kind from that exhibited by other great masters of mankind.

The Discourse with Nicodemus (III. 1–15)

III. 1. Nicodemus appears three times in the Fourth Gospel
(see on 7[50] 19[39]), but is not mentioned by any other evangelist,
unless we may equate him with the ἄρχων of Lk. 18[18] (see
below on v. 3). The attempt to identify him with Joseph of
Arimathæa has no plausibility (see on 19[39]); and the suggestion
that he is a fictitious character invented by Jn. to serve a literary
purpose is arbitrary and improbable (see Introd., p. lxxxiii f.).
Νικόδημος is a Greek name borrowed by the Jews, and appears
in Josephus (*Antt.* XIV. iii. 2) as that of an ambassador from
Aristobulus to Pompey. In the Talmud (*Taanith*, 20. 1)
mention is made of one Bunai, commonly called Nicodemus
ben Gorion, and it is possible (but there is no evidence) that he
was the Nicodemus of Jn. He lived until the destruction of

III. 1. *Ην δὲ ἄνθρωπος ἐκ τῶν Φαρισαίων, Νικόδημος ὄνομα αὐτῷ, ἄρχων τῶν Ἰουδαίων· 2. οὗτος ἦλθεν πρὸς αὐτὸν νυκτὸς καὶ εἶπεν

Jerusalem, which would accord very well with the idea that Jn. has the " young ruler " of Lk. 18¹⁸ in his mind, although in that case γέρων of v. 4 must not be taken to indicate that the person in question was really " old " at the time of speaking. All that can be said with certainty of the Nicodemus of the text is that he was a Pharisee, and a member of the Sanhedrim (7⁵⁰), and apparently a wealthy man (19³⁹). He seems to have been constitutionally cautious and timid (see on 7⁵⁰).

Some points in the narrative of 3¹⁻¹⁵ would suggest that the incident here recorded did not happen (as the traditional text gives it) at the beginning of the ministry of Jesus. First, at v. 2, mention is made of σημεῖα at Jerusalem which had attracted the attention of Nicodemus; but we have already noted on 2²³ that no σημεῖον in that city has yet been recorded. On the other hand, the " signs " which had been wrought at Jerusalem during the weeks before the end had excited much curiosity. That Nicodemus should have come secretly during the later period would have been natural, for the hostility of the Sanhedrim to Jesus had already been aroused (7⁵⁰) ; but that there should have been any danger in conversing with the new Teacher in the early days of His ministry does not appear. Again, at v. 14 (where see note), Jesus predicts His Passion; but if this prediction be placed in the early days of His ministry, we are in conflict with the Synoptists, who place the first announcement of His Death after the Confession of Peter. No doubt, Jn. is often in disagreement with the earlier Gospels, but upon a point so significant as this we should expect his record to agree with theirs.

However, there is not sufficient evidence to justify us in transposing the text here; and we leave the story of Nicodemus in its traditional position, although with a suspicion that the original author of the Gospel did not intend it to come so early.[1]

For the constr. Νικόδημος ὄνομα αὐτῷ, see on 1⁶.

2. For the rec. τὸν Ἰησοῦν (N), אABLTᵇWΘ have αὐτόν.

οὗτος ἦλθεν πρὸς αὐτὸν νυκτός. This was the feature of the visit of Nicodemus which attracted attention : he came by night. Cf. 7⁵⁰ 19³⁹. He was impressed by what he had heard, and he gradually became a disciple; cf. 12⁴².

The form into which the conversation is thrown is similar to that in c. 4.[2]   There is a mysterious saying of Jesus (3³ 4¹⁰),

[1] See Introd., p. xxx.
[2] See, for a fuller discussion, Introd., p. cxi.

αὐτῷ Ῥαββεί, οἴδαμεν ὅτι ἀπὸ Θεοῦ ἐλήλυθας διδάσκαλος· οὐδεὶς γὰρ δύναται ταῦτα τὰ σημεῖα ποιεῖν ἃ σὺ ποιεῖς, ἐὰν μὴ ᾖ ὁ Θεὸς μετ᾽ αὐτοῦ. 3. ἀπεκρίθη Ἰησοῦς καὶ εἶπεν αὐτῷ Ἀμὴν ἀμὴν λέγω

at which the interlocutor expresses astonishment (3^4 $4^{11.\ 12}$), whereupon the saying is repeated ($3^{5f.}$ $4^{13.\ 14}$), but still in a form difficult to understand. That, in both cases, there was an actual conversation is highly probable; but the report, as we have it, cannot in either case be taken to represent the *ipsissima verba*. Nothing is said in c. 3 of any one being present at the interview between Jesus and Nicodemus; but, on the other hand, there is nothing to exclude the presence of a disciple, and hence the account of the interview may be based, in part, on his recollections.

καὶ εἶπεν αὐτῷ Ῥαββεί. See on 1^{38}. Nicodemus was ready to address Jesus as *Rabbi*, because he recognised in Him a divinely sent διδάσκαλος. This was not to recognise Him as Messiah; but Nicodemus and others of his class (note the plural οἴδαμεν, " we all know," as at 9^{31} and Mk. 12^{14}),[1] like the blind man of 9^{33}, were convinced by the signs which Jesus did that He had come ἀπὸ Θεοῦ (cf. 13^3 16^{30}). That " signs " are a mark of Divine assistance and favour was a universal belief in the first century; and Jn. repeatedly tells that this aspect of His signs was asserted by Jesus Himself (see on 2^{11} above, and cf. Introd., p. xcii). The declaration of Nicodemus that no one could do the miracles which Jesus did, ἐὰν μὴ ᾖ ὁ Θεὸς μετ᾽ αὐτοῦ, however foreign to modern habits of thought, expressed the general belief of Judaism. That Jesus went about doing good and healing, ὅτι ὁ Θεὸς ἦν μετ᾽ αὐτοῦ, is the declaration ascribed to Peter in Acts 10^{38}. The σημεῖα to which Nicodemus referred were those mentioned 2^{23} as having inspired faith at Jerusalem. See note *in loc.*

3. For the phrase ἀπεκρίθη Ἰησοῦς καὶ εἶπεν, see on 1^{50}. ℵΔΘΑΝ read ὁ Ἰησοῦς, but BLT[b]W omit ὁ : see on 1^{29}. For " Verily, verily," see on 1^{51}.

Jesus answers the thought of Nicodemus, rather than his words. Nicodemus was prepared to accept Him as a prophet and a forerunner of the Messianic kingdom; but he misunderstood the true nature of that kingdom. It was a spiritual kingdom, " not of this world," as it is described in the only other place in Jn. where it is mentioned (18^{36}). It did not come " with observation " (Lk. $17^{20.\ 21}$), and no appreciation of signs or miracles would bring a man any nearer the understanding of it. A new faculty of spiritual vision must be acquired before it can be seen. The answer of Jesus is startling

---

[1] Cf. also the use of οἴδαμεν in 20^2.

σοι, ἐὰν μή τις γεννηθῇ ἄνωθεν, οὐ δύναται ἰδεῖν τὴν βασιλείαν τοῦ Θεοῦ. 4. λέγει πρὸς αὐτὸν ὁ Νικόδημος Πῶς δύναται ἄνθρωπος

and decisive : ἀμὴν ἀμὴν (see on 1⁵¹) λέγω σοι (the saying is of general application, but it is personally addressed to Nicodemus), ἐὰν μή τις γεννηθῇ ἄνωθεν, οὐ δύναται ἰδεῖν τὴν βασιλείαν τοῦ θεοῦ. This saying is the Johannine counterpart of Mk. 10¹⁵ ἀμὴν λέγω ὑμῖν, ὃς ἐὰν μὴ δέξηται τὴν βασιλείαν τοῦ θεοῦ ὡς παιδίον, οὐ μὴ εἰσέλθῃ εἰς αὐτήν (cf. the parallels Mt. 18³, Lk. 18¹⁷). It is to be observed that this saying in Mk. and Lk. comes immediately before the colloquy with the rich young man, whom Lk. describes as a "ruler," and it is not impossible that this " ruler " is to be identified with Nicodemus (see on v. 1).[1] In any case, " the kingdom of God" or " the kingdom of heaven " is a main topic in the teaching of Jesus as reported by the Synoptists; and it is noteworthy that in this passage (the only passage where Jn. reproduces the phrase in full) the saying which introduces it is terse and epigrammatic, quite in the Synoptic manner. That we have here a genuine saying of Jesus is certain, given in another shape at Mk. 10¹⁵. It is repeated in an altered form at v. 5 (cf. v. 7), and reason is given in the note there for regarding the form in v. 3 as the more original of the two. For the *repetitions* in Jn., see further on 3¹⁶.

ἄνωθεν, in the Synoptists (generally) and always in the other passages (3³¹ 19¹¹· ²³) where it occurs in Jn., means " from above," *desuper*; so also in James 1¹⁷ 3¹⁵· ¹⁷. This is its meaning here, the point being not that spiritual birth is a *repetition*, but that it is being born into a higher life. To be begotten ἄνωθεν means to be begotten from heaven, " of the Spirit." [2]

No doubt, to render ἄνωθεν by *denuo*, " anew," " again," as at Gal. 4⁹, gives a tolerable sense, and this rendering may be defended by Greek usage outside the N.T. Wetstein quotes Artemidorus, *Onirocr.* i. 13, where a man dreams that he is being born, which portends that his wife is to have a son like himself: οὕτω γὰρ ἄνωθεν αὐτὸς δόξειε γεννᾶσθαι. So Josephus, *Antt.* i. xviii. 3, φιλίαν ἄνωθεν ποιεῖται πρὸς αὐτόν, "he made friends with him again." But *desuper* suits the context in the present passage better than *denuo*.

οὐ δύναται ἰδεῖν τὴν βασιλείαν τοῦ θεοῦ. " To see " the kingdom of God is to participate in it, to have experience of it, as at Lk. 9²⁷. For this use of ἰδεῖν, cf. Acts 2²⁷ " to see corruption," Lk. 2²⁶ and Jn. 8⁵¹ " to see death (cf. Ps. 89⁴⁸,

[1] This view is taken by Bacon, *Fourth Gospel*, pp. 382, 520.
[2] See Abbott, *Diat.* 2573.

γεννηθῆναι γέρων ὤν; μὴ δύναται εἰς τὴν κοιλίαν τῆς μητρὸς αὐτοῦ δεύτερον εἰσελθεῖν καὶ γεννηθῆναι; 5. ἀπεκρίθη Ἰησοῦς Ἀμὴν ἀμὴν

Heb. 11⁵), Rev. 18⁷ " to see mourning," 1 Macc. 13³ " to see distresses," Eccl. 9⁹ " to see (that is, to *enjoy*) life." ¹ No doubt, a distinction may be drawn linguistically between " seeing the kingdom of God " and " entering into the kingdom of God," which is the phrase used in v. 5. Thus in Hermas, *Sim.* ix. 15, the wicked and foolish women *see* the kingdom while they do not *enter* it. But no such distinction can be drawn here; v. 5 restates v. 3, but it is not in contrast with it. " Seeing the kingdom of God " in Jn.'s phraseology is " entering into it "; it is identical with the " seeing " of " life " in v. 36, where see note.²

4. λέγει πρὸς αὐτὸν ὁ N. For this constr. of λέγειν, see on 2³. Nicodemus is represented as challenging the idea of rebirth. From one point of view this is easy to understand. He was probably familiar with the Jewish description of a proselyte as " one newly born " (see Introd., p. clxiii). But for Jews a Gentile was an alien, outside the sheltering providence of Yahweh. Certainly, *he* must begin his spiritual life anew, if he would be one of the chosen people. But it was incredible that any such spiritual revolution should be demanded of an orthodox Jew.

Yet this is not the objection which Nicodemus is represented as urging. The words placed in his mouth rather suggest that he took the metaphor of a new birth to mean literally a physical rebirth. " How can a man be born again, when he is old ? " (as may have been his own case, but see on vv. 1, 3). " Can he enter a second time into his mother's womb ? " This would have been a stupid misunderstanding of what Jesus had said, but yet it is to this misunderstanding that the reply of Jesus is directed. It is not a fleshly rebirth that is in question, but a spiritual rebirth, which is a different thing.

Nicodemus says δεύτερον, where Jesus had said ἄνωθεν, thus mistakenly understanding by ἄνωθεν, *denuo* rather than *desuper*; see on v. 3 above.

πῶς δύναται κτλ. ; This is a favourite turn of phrase in Jn. Cf. 3⁹ 5⁴⁴ 6⁵² 9¹⁶.

5. ὁ must be omitted before Ἰησοῦς, as in v. 3. See on 1²⁹.

For γεννηθῇ nearly all the Latin versions have *renatus* (*f* alone has *natus*), which may point to a Western reading

¹ Cf. also Dalman, *Words of Jesus*, Eng. Tr., 108.
² Cf. Tertullian, *de bapt.* 12 : " nisi natus ex aqua quis erit, non habet uitam."

λέγω σοι, ἐὰν μή τις γεννηθῇ ἐξ ὕδατος καὶ Πνεύματος, οὐ δύναται εἰσελθεῖν εἰς τὴν βασιλείαν τοῦ Θεοῦ. 6. τὸ γεγεννημένον ἐκ τῆς

ἀναγεννηθῇ. But probably the Latin rendering is of the nature of an interpretation (with a reminiscence of γεννηθῇ ἄνωθεν in v. 3), the verb ἀναγεννάω occurring in N.T. only at 1 Pet. 1³. ²³.

Another Western variant[1] is τὴν βασιλείαν τῶν οὐρανῶν for the rec. τὴν βασ. τοῦ θεοῦ, which is supported by אᶜABLNWΓΔΘ. א* 511 e m support τῶν οὐρανῶν, which is also read in Justin (*Apol.* i. 61), Hippolytus (*Ref.* viii. 10), Irenæus (*Frag.* xxxiii., ed. Harvey), and ps.-Cyprian *de Rebaptismate* 3. Tertullian has *in regnum caelorum* (*de Bapt.* 13); but in another place *in regnum dei* (*de Anima* 39). Origen's witness is alike uncertain, his Latin translation giving both *caelorum* (*Hom.* xiv. *in Lucam*, and *Comm. in Rom.* ii. 7) and *dei* (*Hom.* v. *in Exod.*). Perhaps, as Hort says, the Western reading was suggested by the greater frequency of the phrase εἰσέρχεσθαι εἰς τὴν βασιλείαν τῶν οὐρανῶν in Mt.

The seal of the baptismal waters is thrice mentioned by Hermas (*Sim.* ix. 15, 16) as a pre-requisite to entering the *kingdom of God*; and in 2 Clem. 6 (before 140 A.D.) we have "if we keep not our baptism pure and undefiled, with what confidence shall we enter into the *kingdom of God?*" It is possible that here we have reminiscences of the language of v. 5. See Introd., p. lxxvi.

The reference in the word ὕδατος is clearly to *Christian* baptism (see Introd., p. clxiv). But, so far as Nicodemus was concerned, this would have been an irrelevant reference; the argument being darkened by the presence of ὕδατος καὶ before πνεύματος. Jesus explains that Nicodemus must be "begotten from above" before he can enter the kingdom of God, *i.e.* that a spiritual change must pass upon him, which is described in v. 6 as being "begotten of the Spirit." The words ὕδατος καί have been inserted in v. 8 by א *a b e*, etc. (see note *in loc.*), although they form no part of the true text; and it has been suggested that, in like manner, in the verse before us they are only an interpretative gloss.[2] There is, however, no MS. evidence for their omission here (although the Sinai Syriac transposes the order of words and testifies to a reading "begotten of Spirit and of water"), nor is there extant any patristic citation of the verse which speaks of "being begotten of the

---

[1] Many examples of this are given by Ezra Abbot, *Fourth Gospel*, p. 33.

[2] See Kirsopp Lake, *Influence of Textual Criticism on Exegesis of N.T.* (1904), p. 18, and Wendt's *St. John's Gospel*, p. 120.

Spirit " and does not mention the water. The passage from Justin (*Apol.* i. 61) by which Lake supports his argument is as follows : ἔπειτα ἄγονται ὑφ' ἡμῶν ἔνθα ὕδωρ ἐστί, καὶ τρόπον ἀναγεννήσεως, ὃν καὶ ἡμεῖς αὐτοὶ ἀνεγεννήθημεν, ἀναγεννῶνται . . . καὶ γὰρ ὁ Χριστὸς εἶπεν, Ἂν μὴ ἀναγεννηθῆτε, οὐ μὴ εἰσέλθητε εἰς τὴν βασιλείαν τῶν οὐρανῶν. Justin is quoting loosely (after his manner), and it is not certain whether it is Jn. 3³ or Jn. 3⁵ that he has in his mind. But there is nothing to suggest that the reading before him was ἐὰν μή τις γεννηθῇ ἐκ Πνεύματος κτλ. Indeed, in another place (*Tryph.* 138) he has the phrase τοῦ ἀναγεννηθέντος ὑπ' αὐτοῦ δι' ὕδατος καὶ πίστεως καὶ ξύλου.

We conclude that the words ὕδατος καί cannot be extruded from the text of Jn., but that they are not to be regarded as representing precisely the saying of Jesus. They are due to a restatement by Jn. of the original saying of v. 3, and are a gloss, added to bring the saying of Jesus into harmony with the belief and practice of a later generation.[1]

ἐὰν μή τις γεννηθῇ κτλ. We have seen (on 1¹³) that those who believe on the name of Christ are described as " begotten of God," ἐκ θεοῦ γεγεννημένοι, and the references given in the note show that this is a characteristic Johannine phrase. It is necessary to interpret the words ὁ γεγεννημένος ἐκ τοῦ πνεύματος (vv. 5, 6, 8) in similar fashion, and to understand them as describing the man who " is begotten of the Spirit." " God is Spirit " (4²⁴), and the phrases " begotten of God " and " begotten of the Spirit " mean the same thing. At 1 Jn. 3⁹ we have πᾶς ὁ γεγεννημένος ἐκ τοῦ θεοῦ ἁμαρτίαν οὐ ποιεῖ, ὅτι σπέρμα αὐτοῦ ἐν αὐτῷ μένει, but a few verses later (1 Jn. 3²⁴) it is said of those who keep God's commandments γινώσκομεν ὅτι μένει ἐν ἡμῖν, ἐκ τοῦ πνεύματος οὗ ἡμῖν ἔδωκεν. The " seed of God " is the " Spirit," whereof believers are made partakers by a spiritual begetting. That is to say, the words ἐκ τοῦ Πνεύματος in this verse point to the Spirit as the Begetter of believers.

To translate " born of the Spirit " suggests that the image is of the Spirit as the *female* parent of the spiritual child, whereas Johannine usage (and O.T. usage also, as we have seen on 1¹³) shows that the image is that of the Spirit as the Begetter. It has been pointed out already (on 1¹³) that the Latin rendering *natus* must not be taken as excluding the meaning *begotten*.

In Semitic languages the Spirit, *Ruḥ*, is feminine; *e.g.* the Old Syriac of 14²⁶ runs, " The Spirit, the Paraclete, *she* shall teach you all things." Thus the phrase " begotten of the Spirit," which we have found reason for accepting as Johannine,

---

[1] Cf. Introd., p. clxv.

σαρκὸς σάρξ ἐστιν, καὶ τὸ γεγεννημένον ἐκ τοῦ πνεύματος πνεῦμά
ἐστιν. 7. μὴ θαυμάσῃς ὅτι εἶπόν σοι Δεῖ ὑμᾶς γεννηθῆναι ἄνωθεν.
8. τὸ πνεῦμα ὅπου θέλει πνεῖ, καὶ τὴν φωνὴν αὐτοῦ ἀκούεις, ἀλλ᾽ οὐκ

would be inconsistent with the Aramaic origin of the Fourth
Gospel. If, as Burney held, Jn. were originally written in
Aramaic, then the original behind τὸ γεγεννημένον ἐκ τοῦ
Πνεύματος must have meant "*born* of the Spirit." But this
does not harmonise with 1[13] or 1 Jn. 3[9].

6. After σάρξ ἐστιν, 161 Syr. cur. and some O.L. texts
add the explanatory gloss ὅτι ἐκ τῆς σαρκὸς ἐγεννήθη. After
πνεῦμά ἐστιν, a similar group with Syr. sin. add ὅτι ἐκ τοῦ πνεύματός ἐστιν.

Flesh and *Spirit* are distinct, and must not be confused.
They are contrasted with each other in 6[63], where the property
of "quickening" is ascribed to *spirit*, while *flesh* has no such
quality, where eternal life is in question. Both are constituent
elements of man's nature, and so of the nature of Christ (Mk.
14[38], 1 Pet. 3[18] 4[6]). They represent the two different orders of
being, the lower and the higher, with which man is in touch.
Flesh can only beget flesh, while spirit only can beget spirit.

7. μὴ θαυμάσῃς κτλ. "Marvel not that I said to thee,
You must be begotten from above." The aphorism is repeated
in the original form (v. 3), which we have shown reason for supposing to have been amplified in v. 5. ὑμᾶς includes all men,
and not Nicodemus only; observe that it is not ἡμᾶς, for Jesus
Himself did not need re-birth. Of *His* natural birth it could be
said τὸ γὰρ ἐν αὐτῇ γεννηθὲν ἐκ πνεύματός ἐστιν ἁγίου (Mt. 1[20]).

μὴ θαυμάσῃς : cf. 5[28], 1 Jn. 3[13]. θαυμάζειν in Jn. generally
indicates *unintelligent* wonder.

δεῖ ὑμᾶς . . . See on 3[14] (cf. 2[4] 4[24]) for the thought of the
Divine necessity involved in Jn.'s use of δεῖ.

8. ἐκ τοῦ πνεύματος. א *a b e ff*[2] *m* Syr. sin. and Syr. cur. give
ἐκ τοῦ ὕδατος καὶ τοῦ πνεύματος, an expansion of the true text
from v. 5.

τὸ πνεῦμα ὅπου θέλει πνεῖ, καὶ τὴν φωνὴν αὐτοῦ ἀκούεις.

πνεῦμα may be translated either "wind" or "Spirit."
It is true that elsewhere in the N.T. πνεῦμα never has its
primitive meaning "wind" (except in the quotation of Ps. 104[4],
in Heb. 1[7]; cf. 2 Esd. 8[22]); but this meaning is often found in
the LXX, e.g. Gen. 8[1], 1 Kings 18[45] 19[11], 2 Kings 3[17], Isa. 7[2]
11[15], Ps. 148[8], Ecclus. 43[17], Wisd. 5[23].

The verb πνεῖν occurs 5 times elsewhere in the N.T. and is
always applied to the blowing of the wind (cf. 6[18]). In the
LXX it is found 5 times with the same application, there always
being in the context some allusion to the Divine action. Cf.

Bar. 6⁶¹ τὸ δ᾽ αὐτὸ καὶ πνεῦμα ἐν πάσῃ χώρᾳ πνεῖ, and esp
Ps. 147¹⁸ πνεύσει τὸ πνεῦμα αὐτοῦ καὶ ῥυήσεται ὕδατα.

φωνή is properly articulate speech, but is often equivalent
to " sound." In the LXX " the Voice of God " is a common
form of expression, and φωνή is often used of thunder as God's
Voice in nature (Ex. 9²³, 1 Sam. 7¹⁰, Ps. 18¹³, etc.). It is twice
used of the sound of wind, in Ps. 29⁸ (of a tempest, as the Voice
of Yahweh) and 1 Kings 19¹² (φωνὴ αὔρας λεπτῆς, "the still
small voice " which Elijah heard). In Jn. it is always used of
a Divine or heavenly voice (except 10⁵ where the " voice " of
strangers is contrasted with the " voice " of the Good Shepherd).
There is no etymological objection to translating " The
wind blows where it will, and thou hearest its sound "; but we
may equally well translate " The Spirit breathes where He will,
and thou hearest His Voice." There is a like ambiguity in
Eccles. 11⁵, ἐν οἷς οὐκ ἔστιν γινώσκων τις ἡ ὁδὸς τοῦ πνεύματος,
where the " way " which is unknown by man may be the " way
of the Spirit " or the " way of the wind." To the Hebrew
mind the wind, invisible yet powerful, represented in nature
the action of the Divine Spirit, as is indicated in Gen. 1² and
often in the O.T.; and so in some places the precise rendering
of πνεῦμα may be doubtful. That, however, it *never* stands
for "wind " in the N.T. elsewhere is a weighty consideration
for the translator of the verse before us. φωνή may mean, as we
have seen, " the sound " of wind; but it is also to be remembered that the φωνή from heaven of Rev. 14¹³ was the Voice of
the Spirit. The ἦχος from heaven on the Day of Pentecost
was said to be like a " rushing mighty wind " (Acts 2²).

The context, however, seems to remove all ambiguity in the
present passage. Πνεῦμα at the beginning of the verse must
refer to the same subject as πνεύματος at its close, and in
vv. 5, 6. The argument is that, as the Divine Spirit operates as
He will, and you cannot tell whence or whither (οὐκ οἶδας
πόθεν ἔρχεται καὶ ποῦ ὑπάγει), so it is with every one begotten
of the Spirit. That which is begotten of the Spirit shares
in the quality of spirit (v. 6). Thus Christ, who was pre-
eminently ὁ γεννηθεὶς ἐκ πνεύματος (Mt. 1²⁰), said of Himself,
in words identical with those of this verse, ὑμεῖς οὐκ οἴδατε
πόθεν ἔρχομαι, ἢ ποῦ ὑπάγω (8¹⁴; cf. 9²⁹). So it is in his
measure of every child of God who is begotten of the Spirit
(cf. 1¹³). Not only do the laws of physical generation not
govern spiritual generation (for natural law does not always
hold in the spiritual world), but you cannot standardise or
reduce to law the manifestations of spiritual life. It is the
teaching of Jn. (8³²), just as clearly as of Paul, that " where the
Spirit of the Lord is, there is liberty " (2 Cor. 3¹⁷).

οἶδας πόθεν ἔρχεται καὶ ποῦ ὑπάγει· οὕτως ἐστὶν πᾶς ὁ γεγεννημένος ἐκ τοῦ πνεύματος. 9. ἀπεκρίθη Νικόδημος καὶ εἶπεν αὐτῷ Πῶς δύναται ταῦτα γενέσθαι; 10. ἀπεκρίθη Ἰησοῦς καὶ εἶπεν αὐτῷ Σὺ εἶ ὁ διδάσκαλος τοῦ Ἰσραὴλ καὶ ταῦτα οὐ γινώσκεις; 11. ἀμὴν ἀμὴν

The rendering of πνεῦμα as *Spirit* rather than *wind* is supported by the Latin versions,[1] which have " spiritus ubi uult spirat "; and it is noteworthy that the earliest patristic allusion to the passage, viz. Ign. *Philad.* 7, is decisive for it. Ignatius says: " Even though certain persons desired to deceive me after the flesh (κατὰ σάρκα) yet the Spirit (τὸ πνεῦμα) is not deceived, being from God, οἶδεν γὰρ πόθεν ἔρχεται καὶ ποῦ ὑπάγει," the last phrase being an exact quotation from the verse before us.[2] Other early authorities for the same view are Origen (Fragm. *in loc.*, ed. Brooke, ii. 252), and the author of the third-century treatise *de rebaptismate*, 15, 18. It is not until we reach the later Fathers that the interpretation " the wind blows where it lists " makes its appearance.

For the use of ὑπάγειν in Jn., see on 7³³, 16⁷.

τὴν φωνὴν αὐτοῦ ἀκούεις. The construction of ἀκούειν in Jn. is remarkable. When it governs the acc., as here (cf. 5³⁷ 8⁴³, etc.), it means merely " to perceive by hearing "; but when it takes the gen. it generally means " to hearken to," *i.e.* to hear and appreciate (cf. 1³⁷ 5²⁵. ²⁸ 6⁶⁰ 9³¹ 10³. ¹⁶. ²⁰ 18³⁷).[3] In the present passage " thou hearest His voice " does not connote obedience to the Spirit's teaching. See on 1⁴⁰ for the constr. ἀκούειν παρά τινος.

9. πῶς δύναται ταῦτα γενέσθαι; Here is no repetition of the former question (v. 4). Nicodemus is puzzled by the teaching of vv. 6–8 about the spiritual birth and the freedom and unexpectedness of the spiritual life in one who has been " begotten of the Spirit."

10. אN 69 read ὁ Ἰησοῦς, but om. ὁ ABLΔΘW.

ὁ διδάσκαλος τοῦ Ἰσραήλ. Both articles are significant :

---

[1] So, too, the early Armenian version ; see *J.T.S.*, 1924, p. 237.

[2] The words following ὑπάγει in Ignatius are καὶ τὰ κρυπτὰ ἐλέγχει, and Schmiedel (*E.B.* 1830) argues that Ignatius is dependent, not on Jn., but on a Philonic interpretation of Gen. 16⁸. Philo (*de Prof.* 37) comments on the story of Hagar thus : " Conviction (ὁ ἔλεγχος) speaking to the soul, says to her πόθεν ἔρχῃ καὶ ποῦ πορεύῃ ; " But this is not so verbally like the Ignatius passage as Jn. 3⁸ is, and there is no similarity whatever in thought between Ignatius and Philo here.

[3] Charles (*Revelation*, p. cxl.) observes that this distinction is not observed in the Apocalypse. Cf. Blass, *Gram.*, p. 103, and Abbott, *Diat.* 1614. The usage of ἀκούειν in Acts 9⁷ 22⁹ seems to be the reverse, viz., with φωνήν it means " to hear the articulate words," but with φωνῆς, to hear a sound only.

λέγω σοι ὅτι ὃ οἴδαμεν λαλοῦμεν καὶ ὃ ἑωράκαμεν μαρτυροῦμεν, καὶ
"Art thou the authorised (*or*, the well-known) teacher of the
Israel of God ? "
καὶ ταῦτα οὐ γινώσκεις; He might have been expected
to recognise, when he was told it, the doctrine of the various
manifestations of the Spirit in man's life.
11. For the introductory ἀμὴν ἀμήν, see on 1[51].
With this verse v. 32 is closely parallel : ὃ ἑώρακεν καὶ ἤκουσεν,
τοῦτο μαρτυρεῖ· καὶ τὴν μαρτυρίαν αὐτοῦ οὐδεὶς λαμβάνει. We
should expect καίτοι rather than καί in the second member of the
sentence in both cases, but Jn. never uses καίτοι. See on 1[10].
ὃ οἴδαμεν λαλοῦμεν. Cf. 8[38] 12[50] 16[18].
The verb λαλεῖν is used with special frequency in Jn. It
occurs nearly 60 times in the Gospel; and 30 times it is placed
in the mouth of Jesus in the first person singular, the only
Synoptic instance of this latter use being Lk. 24[44]. The general
distinction between λέγειν and λαλεῖν, viz. that λέγειν relates
to the substance of what is said, while λαλεῖν has to do
with the fact and the manner of utterance, holds good to a
certain extent in Jn., as it does in classical Greek. But in Jn.
the two verbs cannot always be distinguished in their usage
and meaning, any more than " say " and " speak " can
always be distinguished in English. Here ὃ οἴδαμεν λαλοῦμεν
should be rendered " we speak of what we know," the words
spoken not being given; but then ταῦτα τὰ ῥήματα ἐλάλησεν
(8[20]) means," He spoke these words," viz. the very words that
have just been cited (cf. 16[25] 17[1. 13], etc.). See, in particular,
10[6] 14[10] 12[49] 16[18], in which passages the verb λαλεῖν is used
exactly as λέγειν might be; cf. 8[43].
If there is any special tinge of meaning in λαλεῖν as compared with λέγειν in Jn., it is that λαλεῖν suggests frankness
or openness of speech. Jn. " assigns it to Christ 33 times in the
first person, whereas it is never thus used by the Synoptists,
except at Lk. 24[44] after the Resurrection " (Abbott, *Diat.*
2251*b*). See on 18[20].
The plural forms οἴδαμεν, λαλοῦμεν, etc., arrest attention.
The verse is introduced by the solemn ἀμὴν ἀμήν, and so is
represented by Jn. as spoken by Jesus. Now the plural of
majesty is not ascribed to Jesus anywhere, and in v. 12 He
employs the singular εἶπον. Abbott (*Diat.* 2428) suggests
that the plurals here associate the Father's witness with that of
the Son (cf. 5[32. 37]); but this would be foreign to the context.
Further, v. 32, ὃ ἑώρακεν καὶ ἤκουσεν, τοῦτο μαρτυρεῖ is clearly
a repetition of what is said in this verse.
The plurals οἴδαμεν are, therefore, explained (cf. 4[22]) by

τὴν μαρτυρίαν ἡμῶν οὐ λαμβάνετε. 12. εἰ τὰ ἐπίγεια εἶπον ὑμῖν καὶ οὐ πιστεύετε, πῶς ἐὰν εἴπω ὑμῖν τὰ ἐπουράνια πιστεύσετε; 13. καὶ

some exegetes (e.g. Godet, Westcott) as associating His disciples with Jesus in the testimony with which He confronts Nicodemus. "We," i.e. my disciples and I, "speak of what we know." But this is markedly unlike the authoritative tone of the rest of the discourse. Nor is there any other instance of the disciples' testimony being mentioned in the same breath as His own testimony. They bore witness, indeed, because they had been with Him from the beginning (15²⁷), but He did not rely on this while He was in the flesh. Even if we adopt the reading ἡμᾶς for ἐμέ at 9⁴ (where see note), we do not get a true parallel to ὃ ἑωράκαμεν μαρτυροῦμεν of the present verse.

The similarity of the language used here to that which Jn., in other passages, uses to associate his own witness with that of his fellow-disciples is very close: e.g. ὃ ἀκηκόαμεν, ὃ ἑωράκαμεν . . . ὃ ἐθεασάμεθα . . . ἀπαγγέλλομεν ὑμῖν (1 Jn. 1ᶠ·; cf. 1 Jn. 4¹⁴), or ἐθεασάμεθα τὴν δόξαν αὐτοῦ (1¹⁴), or the use of οἴδαμεν in 1 Jn. 3². ¹⁴ 5¹⁵· ¹⁹· ²⁰. And, having regard to the way in which commentary and free narrative are intermingled in this chapter (see on v. 16), we seem to be driven to the conclusion that in v. 11 Jn. is not reproducing the actual words of Jesus so much as the profound conviction of the Apostolic age that the Church's teaching rested on the testimony of eye-witnesses (cf. 1 Jn. 4¹⁴). He has turned the singular ἑώρακα (see v. 32) into the plural ἑωράκαμεν (v. 11), just as in v. 5 he has added ἐξ ὕδατος to the original saying of the Lord about the need of spiritual birth.

καὶ τὴν μαρτυρίαν ἡμῶν οὐ λαμβάνετε. This is repeated (v. 32), and is a frequent theme in the Fourth Gospel. Cf. 1¹¹ 5⁴³ 12³⁷.

12. The contrast between τὰ ἐπίγεια and τὰ ἐπουράνια appears again, 1 Cor. 15⁴⁰, 2 Cor. 5¹, Phil. 2¹⁰ 3¹⁹, James 3¹⁵; the word ἐπίγειος appearing in these passages only in the Greek Bible. The thought of this verse is like Wisd. 9¹⁶· ¹⁷, "Hardly do we divine the things that are on earth, and the things that are close at hand we find with labour; but the things that are in the heavens who ever yet traced out . . . except thou gavest wisdom and sentest thy Holy Spirit from on high?"

The ἐπίγεια or "earthly things" as to which Jesus has already spoken include the doctrine of the kingdom of God, which was to be set up on earth, and accordingly of the New Birth which Nicodemus found it difficult to accept. Such matters are wonderful in the telling, although ἐπίγεια all the time, in contradistinction to the deep secrets of the Divine

οὐδεὶς ἀναβέβηκεν εἰς τὸν οὐρανὸν εἰ μὴ ὁ ἐκ τοῦ οὐρανοῦ καταβάς,

nature and purpose (ἐπουράνια), of which no one could tell except " He that cometh from heaven " (v. 32). πιστεύσετε. So אABL. πιστεύσητε is read by ΓΔΘW *fam.* 13, etc.

13. οὐδεὶς ἀναβέβηκεν εἰς τὸν οὐρανόν κτλ. The argument is that none can speak with authority of τὰ ἐπουράνια, except one who has been ἐν οὐρανῷ, and has come down from thence. And of no one can this be said but the " Son of Man " (see Introd., p. cxxx), for no man has ever ascended thither. To the question of Prov. 30⁴ τίς ἀνέβη εἰς τὸν οὐρανὸν καὶ κατέβη; the suggested answer is " God alone " (cf. Deut. 30¹² and the reference thereto in Rom. 10⁶). So too in Bar. 3²⁹, " Who hath ascended to heaven and taken her (*sc.* Wisdom), and brought her down from the clouds ? " the answer is " No one." There is a Talmudic saying which taught this explicitly: " R. Abbahu said: If a man says to thee, I ascend to heaven, he will not prove it," [1] *i.e.* the thing is impossible. This was the accepted Jewish doctrine.

On the other hand, the Jewish apocalypses have legends of saints being transported to heaven that they might be informed of spiritual truth, *e.g.* Enoch (*Enoch* lxx. 1, etc.), Abraham (in the *Testament of Abraham*), Isaiah (*Ascension of Isaiah,* 7), etc.[2] But of such legends the Fourth Gospel has no trace. " *No one* has ascended into heaven, save He who descended from heaven, viz. the Son of Man."

There is no reference to the Ascension of Christ in this passage (cf. 6⁶² 20¹⁷), which merely states that no *man* has gone up into heaven to learn heavenly secrets. It is only the Son of Man who came down from heaven, which is His home, who can speak of it and of τὰ ἐπουράνια with the authority of knowledge.[3]

The phrase καταβαίνειν ἐκ τοῦ οὐρανοῦ is used again of Christ's coming in the flesh at 6³³. ³⁸. ⁴¹. ⁴². ⁵⁰. ⁵¹. ⁵⁸, but in that sense nowhere else in the N.T. In 1 Thess. 4¹⁶ κατ. ἐξ οὐρανοῦ is used of the Advent of Christ in glory, and in 1³² above of the Descent of the Spirit at the Baptism of Jesus. καταβαίνειν is also used Eph. 4⁹ of the Descent into Hades. The phrase here, however, undoubtedly refers to the Descent of Christ to

---

[1] Quoted by Schürer from *Jer. Taanith,* ii. 1.
[2] See my article, " Assumption and Ascension," *E.R.E.* ii. 151.
[3] A curious passage in Irenæus (*Hær.* IV. xii. 4) speaks of the Word of God being in the habit of ascending and descending for the welfare of men (" ab initio assuetus Verbum Dei ascendere et descendere "), with allusion to Ex. 3⁷. ⁸.

ὁ Υἱὸς τοῦ ἀνθρώπου. 14. καὶ καθὼς Μωϋσῆς ὕψωσεν τὸν ὄφιν ἐν

earth in His Incarnation, and the use of the title " the Son of Man " in this context has no Synoptic parallel (see Introd., p. cxxx).

It may be added that the pre-existence of the Son of Man in heaven is a tenet of the Book of Enoch: " That Son of Man was named in the presence of the Lord of Spirits and His name before the Head of days. And before the sun and the signs were created, before the stars of the heaven were made, His name was named before the Lord of Spirits " (xlviii. 2. 3). See on 6⁶².

ὁ υἱὸς τοῦ ἀνθρώπου. So אBLTᵇW 33, but the clause ὁ ὢν ἐν τῷ οὐρανῷ is added by ΑΝΓΔΘ, with the Lat. and some Syr. vss. (not *Diatessaron*). If the clause were part of the original text, it is not easy to account for its omission. It does not contain any doctrine different from that of the Prologue as to the pre-existence of the Son; cf. ὁ ὢν εἰς τὸν κόλπον τοῦ πατρός (1¹⁸). Nor does it add anything to the argument, which is complete in itself, if the verse ends with ὁ υἱὸς τοῦ ἀνθρώπου. Indeed, it makes the argument more difficult to follow. The point is that the Incarnate Son of Man is the only person on earth who can speak with authority of heavenly things, and that because He has come down from heaven itself. If we retain ὁ ὢν ἐν τῷ οὐρανῷ we must interpret the phrase of the timeless existence of the Son in the heavenly places, while yet He is manifested on earth. But this thought suggests later developments of Christology. The clause is probably an interpretative gloss, added at an early period, possibly in the second century.[1]

It may be doubted whether vv. 13–15 really belong to the discourse of Jesus to Nicodemus, or whether they should not ᵣather be taken as part of the commentary which Jn. subjoins (see on v. 16 below). If the latter alternative be accepted, the report of the discourse ends quite naturally with the question of v. 12. But the title " the Son of Man " is never used in the Gospels in narrative, or in evangelistic comment, being found only in the report of words of Jesus Himself.[2] This consideration is conclusive for taking the comment of Jn. as beginning with v. 16, and not with v. 13.

14. καθὼς Μωϋσῆς ὕψωσεν τὸν ὄφιν κτλ.

ὑψοῦν means " to lift up," either literally or figuratively, when it is equivalent to " exalt." In Acts 2³³ (τῇ δεξιᾷ τοῦ θεοῦ ὑψωθείς) and Acts 5³¹ (τοῦτον ὁ θεὸς . . . ὕψωσεν τῇ δεξιᾷ αὐτοῦ) it is used of the exaltation by God of Jesus to His

[1] See Hort, *Select Readings*, in loc.   [2] Cf. Introd.. p. cxxii.

right hand, *i.e.* of the Ascension. Cf. Phil. 2⁹ and Isa. 52¹³, where it is said of the Servant of Yahweh ὑψωθήσεται καὶ δοξασθήσεται σφόδρα.

But the word is not used thus in the Fourth Gospel, where it is always applied to the " lifting up " of Jesus on the Cross, and is always found in connexion with the title " Son of Man " (see Introd., p. cxxxii). Jesus said to the incredulous Jews (8²⁸) ὅταν ὑψώσητε τὸν υἱὸν τοῦ ἀνθρώπου, τότε γνώσεσθε ὅτι ἐγώ εἰμι, " When ye shall have lifted up the Son of Man, then ye shall know, etc." This " lifting up " is to be the act of the Jews, not of God (as in Acts 2³³ 5³¹), and it is therefore clear that it does not refer to the Ascension, but to the Crucifixion. Again in 12³² we have ἐὰν ὑψωθῶ ἐκ τῆς γῆς, πάντας ἑλκύσω πρὸς ἐμαυτόν, on which Jn.'s comment is, "this He said, signifying by what death He should die." And that the people understood the word thus appears from their rejoinder (12³⁴); while they knew that the Christ " abides for ever," they were puzzled by the saying that the " Son of Man " was to be " lifted up." If ὑψωθῆναι were to be understood merely as "exaltation " (as the Ascension was) they would have had no difficulty in admitting δεῖ ὑψωθῆναι τὸν υἱὸν τοῦ ἀνθρώπου (see note *in loc.*).

In the present passage, there can in like manner be no reference to the Ascension of Jesus, as in that case the type of the brazen serpent would not be applicable. In the story in Num. 21⁹ᶠ·, Moses set his brazen serpent " upon the standard," or, as the LXX turns it, ἔστησεν αὐτὸν ἐπὶ σημείου, so that those who had been bitten by the poisonous serpents might look upon it and live. As the story is explained in Wisd. 16⁶· ⁷, the brazen serpent was a σύμβολον σωτηρίας : " he that turned towards it was not saved because of that which was beheld, but because of thee, the Saviour of all (τὸν παντῶν σωτῆρα)." The word ὑψοῦν is not used anywhere in the LXX of the act of Moses in "lifting up " the serpent and exposing it to the gaze of the people, nor is the word used anywhere in the N.T. outside Jn. of the "lifting up " of Jesus on the Cross. But this is undoubtedly the parallel which is drawn in the words of Jesus in 3¹⁴. Those who looked in faith upon the brazen serpent uplifted before them were delivered from death by poison; those who look in faith upon the Crucified, lifted up on the Cross, shall be delivered from the death of sin.

The early Greek interpreters are quite unanimous about this. Thus Barnabas (§ 12) says that Moses made a brazen serpent, the τύπος of Jesus, that he set it up conspicuously (τίθησιν ἐνδόξως), and bade any man that had been bitten " come to the serpent which is placed on the tree (ἐπὶ τοῦ ξύλου ἐπικείμενον) and let him hope in faith that the serpent being himself dead can yet make him alive (αὐτὸς ὢν νεκρὸς δύναται ζωοποιῆσαι), and straightway he shall be saved." This is but an elaboration of the idea in Jn. 3[14], going beyond what is there said, for Barnabas emphasises the point that the brazen serpent is a type of Jesus, while all that is said in Jn. 3[14] is that as the first was " lifted up," so must the Son of Man be " lifted up."

Origen (*Exhort. ad martyr.* 50, arguing that death by martyrdom may be called ὕψωσις), and Cyprian (*Test.* ii. 20) apply Jn. 3[14] to the Crucifixion of Jesus; cf. Justin, *Tryph.* 94. Claudius Apollinaris (about 171 A.D.) writes of Jesus as ὑψωθεὶς ἐπὶ κεράτων μονοκέρωτος, where ὑψοῦν evidently means to lift up on the Cross; cf. Ps. 22[21] (Routh, *Reliq. Sacr.*, i. 161). See also the passage from Artemidorus quoted on 21[18. 19] below, for the connexion between the ideas of ὕψος and of crucifixion.

We have then here a prediction placed in the mouth of Jesus, not only of His death, but of the *manner* of that death. The Synoptists represent Jesus as more than once foretelling His death by violence (Mk. 8[31] 9[31] 10[33] and parallels), but only in Mt. 20[19] is death by crucifixion specified; cf. Lk. 24[7]. But by the use of the word ὑψοῦν (cf. also 8[28] and 12[32]) Jn. consistently represents Jesus as predicting that He would be crucified, which would carry with it the prediction that He would suffer at the hands of the Roman authorities, and not by the Jews (cf. Jn. 18[31. 32]).

It is not consistent with the Synoptic tradition (cf. Mk. 8[31], Mt. 16[21], Lk. 9[22]) to represent Jesus as foretelling His Passion so early in His Ministry. We should expect not to find any indication of this until after the Confession of Peter (6[68. 69]). And if vv. 11–15 are intended by the evangelist to be taken as words of Jesus, rather than as reflexions of his own (see on v. 13), then it is probable that they are recorded here out of their historical context. See on v. 1 above.

It has been suggested, however (*e.g.* by Westcott and E. A. Abbott) that we must see a deeper significance in the word ὑψοῦν as placed in the lips of Jesus. Abbott holds[1] that the Aramaic word which is rendered by ὑψοῦν was זְקַף, and that this actually has the double meaning (1) to exalt, (2) to crucify. But Burkitt has shown that this cannot be accepted because זְקַף could not be used of a " lifting up " such as the Ascension was.[2] In short, (*a*) Jn. clearly states his own view of what Jesus meant by the words which he ascribes to Him here; (*b*) all the early Greek exegetes agree with him; (*c*) if we try to get back to the Aramaic word lying behind ὑψοῦν, we cannot find one which has this special ambiguity. אָרִים will fit ὑψοῦν

---

[1] *Diat.* 2998 (xxiii)*e*.   [2] *J.T.S.*, July 1919, p. 337.

τῇ ἐρήμῳ, οὕτως ὑψωθῆναι δεῖ τὸν Υἱὸν τοῦ ἀνθρώπου, 15. ἵνα πᾶς ὁ πιστεύων εἰς αὐτὸν ἔχῃ ζωὴν αἰώνιον.

in the sense of "exalt," but not in that of "crucify." יָקַר will fit ὑψοῦν in the sense of "crucify," but not in that of "exalt." We cannot therefore accept Westcott's view that "the *lifting up* includes death and the victory over death." There does not seem to be any hint of this in any of the passages in which ὑψοῦν occurs in Jn.

The Jewish commentators on Num. 21[9f.] give little help as to the significance of the brazen serpent, being perplexed by the inconsistency of the story with the general prohibition of all images in the religion of Israel. Indeed, Hezekiah found it necessary to destroy "the brazen serpent that Moses had made" (2 Kings 18[4]) because it had led to idolatrous practices. Philo (*Legg. All.* ii. 19) allegorises the narrative after his manner. As the poisonous serpents signify the pleasure (ἡδονή) which is dangerous to the soul, so the brazen serpent signifies temperance (σωφροσύνη) ; then the man who sees psychically the beauty of σωφροσύνη, καὶ διὰ τούτου τὸν θεὸν αὐτόν, ζήσεται.

Jesus, however, explicitly takes this story as a type of His Cross, which *must* have fulfilment : δεῖ, " it is necessary " that so " the Son of Man shall be lifted up," as Jn. reports His words here. Something has already been said (see note on 2[4]) of what may be called the Predestinarian Doctrine of Jn.; see also Introd., p. clii, where Jn.'s use of the phrase " that it might be fulfilled " is examined. A similar Divine necessity is indicated several times elsewhere in this Gospel by the word δεῖ. The evangelist uses it, when writing in his own person, of the inevitableness of the Resurrection of Christ. But he also ascribes the employment of this way of speech to Jesus Himself. " I *must* work the works of Him that sent me, while it is day " (9[4]); " Other sheep I *must* bring " (10[16]); and again at 12[34] the people charge Jesus with saying, as here, δεῖ ὑψωθῆναι τὸν υἱὸν τοῦ ἀνθρώπου. Cf. also 3[30]. There is nothing peculiar to the Fourth Gospel in this.[1] The Synoptists and Paul alike share the belief that it is not Fate but Providence that rules the world, that God foreknows each event because He has predetermined it, and that therefore it must come to pass. To reconcile this profound doctrine with human free will was the problem of a later age.

See note on 12[32].

15. Before ἔχῃ the rec. text interpolates μὴ ἀπόληται ἀλλ'

[1] See a discussion of the predestinarian teaching of Jn. in Westcott, *Epistles of St. John*, p. 91.

(from v. 16) with ΑΓΔΘ, but the words are omitted here by אBLTᵇW 33 *fam.* 1, etc.

The rec. has εἰς αὐτὸν after πιστεύων (a common constr in Jn. ; see on 1¹²) with אΓΔΘ ; but recent editors have generally followed BTᵇW in reading ἐν αὐτῷ. Yet the constr. πιστεύειν ἔν τινι *never* appears in Jn., so that if we read ἐν αὐτῷ, πιστεύων must be taken in an absolute sense (see on 1⁷ for this usage), and we must translate, with the R.V., " Whosoever believeth may in Him have eternal life." (Cf. for the constr. 1⁴.) The thought of the believer being " in Christ " is thoroughly Johannine (15⁴, 1 Jn. 5²⁰) as well as Pauline. But we prefer the reading εἰς αὐτόν, which has good MS. support. See on v. 16.

The connexion between faith and eternal life runs through the Gospel, the purpose of its composition being ἵνα πιστεύοντες ζωὴν ἔχητε ἐν τῷ ὀνόματι αὐτοῦ (20³¹). Cf. 6⁴⁷ ὁ πιστεύων ἔχει ζωὴν αἰώνιον and 3³⁶ ὁ πιστεύων εἰς τὸν υἱὸν ἔχει ζω. αἰώ., where see note.

The adj. αἰώνιος is always associated in Jn. with ζωή (*never*, as in Mt. or Mk., with " sin " or " fire "), the expression ζωὴ αἰώνιος occurring 17 times in the Gospel and 6 times in 1 Jn. (in the form ἡ ζωὴ ἡ αἰώνιος in 1 Jn. 1² 2²⁵). ζωὴ αἰώνιος as the portion of the righteous is mentioned Dan. 12², and thereafter the expression is found in the Psalter of Solomon (iii. 16) and in *Enoch*.[1] It occurs frequently in the Synoptists and in Paul, and always in the sense of the future life after death (but see on 12⁵⁰). This significance it has also in Jn. many times; *e.g.* in the present passage this is the primary meaning. Cf. esp. 12²⁵, and see note on 4¹⁴. But for Jn , and for him alone among N.T. writers (although cf. 1 Tim. 6¹⁹), ζωὴ αἰώνιος may be a present possession of the believer (3³⁶ 5²⁴ 6⁴⁷, 1 Jn. 5¹³), which continues and abides after the shock of death (6⁵⁴). " To have eternal life " means more than " to live for ever "; the stress is not so much upon the duration of the life, as upon its quality. To have eternal life is to share in the life of God (5²⁶) and of Christ (1⁴), which is unfettered by the conditions of time. And so it is defined as the *knowledge* of God and of Christ (17³), for true knowledge cannot be without affinity. Thus ὁ ἔχων τὸν υἱὸν ἔχει τὴν ζωήν (1 Jn. 5¹²). See Introd., p. clx.

[1] See Dalman, *Words of Jesus*, Eng. Tr., p. 157, for illustrations from the later Jewish literature.

16. Οὕτως γὰρ ἠγάπησεν ὁ Θεὸς τὸν κόσμον, ὥστε τὸν Υἱὸν τὸν

The Evangelist's comment on the preceding Discourse
(vv. 16–21, 31–36)

16. This " comfortable word " is described in the Anglican Liturgy as one of those which " our Saviour Christ saith." But it would seem that Jn. does not mean to place vv. 16–21 in the mouth of Jesus; these verses are rather reflexions and comments by the evangelist on the words which he has already ascribed to Jesus in His discourse with Nicodemus. The dialogue framework is dropped; past tenses, ἔδωκεν, ἀπέστειλεν, ἐλήλυθεν, are used, as would be natural if the writer is meditating on the great events of the past; the word μονογενής, which occurs twice, vv. 16, 18, is not elsewhere placed on the lips of Jesus, while it is thoroughly Johannine (see 1[14. 18] and 1 Jn. 4[9]). Indeed v. 16 is repeated almost verbatim 1 Jn. 4[9]: ἐν τούτῳ ἐφανερώθη ἡ ἀγάπη τοῦ θεοῦ ἐν ἡμῖν, ὅτι τὸν υἱὸν αὐτοῦ τὸν μονογενῆ ἀπέσταλκεν ὁ θεὸς εἰς τὸν κόσμον ἵνα ζήσωμεν δι' αὐτοῦ.

The passage vv. 16–21 is introduced by οὕτως γάρ . . ., which is quite in Jn.'s style when he is making a comment: cf. αὐτὸς γάρ . . . (2[25]), οἱ γὰρ μαθηταί (4[8]), ὁ γὰρ Ἰησοῦς . (5[13]), ὁ γὰρ πατήρ (5[20]), αὐτὸς γὰρ ᾔδει . . . (6[6]), ᾔδει γάρ . . . (6[64] 13[11]), οὔπω γὰρ ἦν . . . (7[39]), οὐδέπω γὰρ ᾔδεισαν . . . (20[9]). Further, it is to be observed that ὥστε does not occur again in Jn., and that the constr. οὕτως . . . ὥστε with indicative, although classical, does not appear elsewhere in the N.T. (see Abbott, *Diat.* 2203, 2697). No new theme is introduced at v. 16, but the teaching of the discourse with Nicodemus is recapitulated, the opening sentence being a summary of the " Gospel according to St. John."

It is the constant teaching of Jn. that in the order of redemption God's Love precedes the movement of man's soul to him. " We love because He first loved us " (1 Jn. 4[19]; cf. 1 Jn. 4[10]). Cf. " Ye did not choose me, but I chose you " (15[16]) and also 13[18]. See Rom. 5[8]. In this verse the Love of God is represented as prior to the faith of man. Indeed, God *is* Love (1 Jn. 4[8]).

The verb ἀγαπάω is generally used by the Synoptists for the love which man has for man or for God (Mk. 12[30]); and Jn. in like manner uses it of the love of man for his fellows (13[34] 15[12. 17]), or for Jesus (8[42] 14[15. 21. 23] 21[15]) or for God (1 Jn. 4[10]). It is used once in the Synoptists for the love of Jesus for man (Mk. 10[21]), and this is frequent in Jn. (11[5] 13[1. 23. 34] 14[21] 15[9. 12] 21[7. 20]). ἀγαπάω is never used in the

μονογενῆ ἔδωκεν, ἵνα πᾶς ὁ πιστεύων εἰς αὐτὸν μὴ ἀπόληται ἀλλ᾽ ἔχῃ ζωὴν αἰώνιον. 17. οὐ γὰρ ἀπέστειλεν ὁ Θεὸς τὸν Υἱὸν εἰς τὸν

Synoptists of the Love of God for man, although this central fact is behind many of the parables; but Jn. employs it thus, not only here but at 14²³, 17²³, 1 Jn. 3¹ 4¹⁰ (cf. Rom. 5⁸, Eph. 2⁴, 2 Thess. 2¹⁶). The mutual love of God and Christ is implicit in the Synoptists (cf. ὁ υἱός μου ὁ ἀγαπητός, Mk. 1¹¹ 9⁷, Mt. 3¹⁷ 17⁵, Lk. 3²²), but Jn. is explicit in using ἀγαπάω to describe it, e.g. 3³⁵ 10¹⁷ 15⁹ 17²³. ²⁴. ²⁶, and 14³¹. See, further, Additional Note on 21¹⁵ on ἀγαπᾶν and φιλεῖν.

Here the Love of God for man is an all-embracing love: ἠγάπησεν ὁ θεὸς τὸν κόσμον (for κόσμος see on 1⁹). It was manifested by His giving "His only begotten Son" (for μονογενής see on 1¹⁴), "His Beloved Son," ὁ υἱὸς ὁ ἀγαπητός (Mt. 3¹⁷). The language is perhaps reminiscent of Gen. 22¹⁶, where it was said to Abraham οὐκ ἐφείσω τοῦ υἱοῦ σου τοῦ ἀγαπητοῦ, the simple ἔδωκεν conveying the sense of a complete "giving up"; cf. Rom. 8³².

τὸν υἱὸν τὸν μονογενῆ. So ℵ*BW, but ℵ*CALTᵇΘ add αὐτοῦ after υἱόν.

ἵνα πᾶς ὁ πιστ. κτλ. This was the motive of the Gift, that all men might have eternal life (see on v. 15) through faith in Christ. For the phrase πιστεύων εἰς αὐτόν, see on 1¹².

"To perish" (ἀπολλύναι) is contrasted again with "to have eternal life" at 10²⁸ (cf. 17¹²). It is the word used for "losing" one's soul; and it refers here to a man's final destiny (cf. Mt. 10²⁸ σῶμα ἀπολέσαι ἐν γεέννῃ). Hence ζωὴ αἰώνιος in this verse must be interpreted of the future (see on 3¹⁵) rather than of the present, although it includes this.

The repetition of the phrase ἵνα πᾶς ὁ πιστεύων εἰς αὐτὸν ἔχῃ ζωὴν αἰώνιον from v. 15, with a slight change (viz. the addition after αὐτόν of μὴ ἀπόληται ἀλλά), is a feature of Johannine style.[1] Jn. frequently repeats phrases or themes of special import, often with slight verbal changes, as if they were a refrain. Cf., e.g., 3³. ⁵ 4²³. ²⁴ 6³⁵. ⁴¹. ⁴⁸. ⁵¹ 6³⁹. ⁴⁰ 8²⁴ 10⁸. ⁹. ¹¹. ¹⁵ 15¹. ⁵ 16¹⁴. ¹⁵.

17. ἀπέστειλεν ὁ θεὸς τὸν υἱόν κτλ. The "sending" of Jesus by God is a conception common to the Synoptists, to Paul, and to Jn. Two verbs are used, πέμπω and ἀποστέλλω, the former being more frequent in Jn., and the latter in the Synoptists, no distinction of meaning between them being traceable (cf. 17¹⁸ and 20²¹). Paul has πέμπω only (Rom. 8³); Lk. has πέμπω once (Lk. 20¹³), but the parallels Mk. 12⁶, Mt. 21³⁷ have ἀποστέλλω. Elsewhere the Synoptists always

---

[1] Cf. Introd., p. cxvi.

have ἀποστέλλω of God sending His Son, *e.g.* Mk. 9[37],
Mt. 10[40] 15[24], Lk. 4[43] 9[48] 10[16]. It may be added that πέμπω
is infrequent in the LXX, which generally has ἀποστέλλω.
There is a fine passage in the *Ep. to Diognetus* (§ 7) about
God " sending " His Son, in which both verbs are used.[1]
Westcott attempts to distinguish Jn.'s usage of πέμπω and
ἀποστέλλω (see his Additional Note on 20[21]), and so does
Abbott (*Diat.* 1723*d–g*), who reverses the meanings that
Westcott proposes. No distinction can safely be drawn.

For ἀποστέλλω in Jn. in similar contexts to the present
(*i.e.* of God sending His Son), cf. 3[34] 5[36. 38] 6[29. 57] 7[29] 8[42] 10[36]
11[42] 17[8. 18. 21. 23. 25] 20[21] and 1 Jn. 4[9. 10. 14]. For πέμπω cf.
4[34] 5[23. 24. 30] 6[38. 39. 44] 7[16. 28. 33] 8[16. 18. 26. 29] 9[4] 12[44. 45. 49] 13[20]
14[24] 15[21] 16[5].

τὸν υἱόν. The rec. text adds αὐτοῦ, with ΑΓΔΘ, but om.
אBLT[b]W *fam.* 1.

This usage of ὁ υἱός absolutely, as contrasted with ὁ πατήρ,
is common to all the evangelists, and by all of them is attributed
to Jesus when speaking of Himself. See Mk. 13[32], Mt. 11[27],
Lk. 10[22], and Jn. 5[19] 6[40] 8[36] 14[13] 17[1], besides Jn. 3[36], 1 Jn. 2[22]
4[14], where the evangelist thus describes Jesus. He uses
ὁ υἱός absolutely, at this point for the first time. Cf. 1 Cor. 15[28].

This verse is in close connexion with v. 16. The Divine
purpose in redemption embraces all humanity. It is not
confined to Jews only, or to elect nations or individuals, but
embraces the whole world. This Divine intention may be
thwarted by man's abuse of his free will, but none the less it
is directed to all mankind (cf. 1 Tim. 2[4], Tit. 2[11]).

But in the current Jewish eschatology[2] Messiah was to
come as the Judge of mankind, and so Jesus taught, both
according to the Synoptists (Mt. 25[31f.]) and to Jn.: cf. Jn. 5[27],
where we have the Son given "authority to execute judgment,
because He is the Son of man," the context showing that the
Last Judgment is indicated. So, again, in 9[39] we have εἰς
κρίμα ἐγὼ εἰς τὸν κόσμον τοῦτον ἦλθον, the reference being
indeed to a present rather than a future judging, but still the
coming of Jesus being represented as εἰς κρίμα, as issuing in
judgment. See further on 8[15].

How, then, is this to be reconciled with the universal
purpose of love in the mission of Christ ? Jn. is quick to
supply the answer. The purpose of this mission in the mind
of God was that *every one* who believed in Christ should have
eternal life. Christ, as the Son of Man, is to be the Judge of
mankind; he does not question that, and later on he says it
explicitly (5[27]). But His primary office is that of Saviour,

---

[1] Cf. Introd., p. lxxvi.   [2] *Ibid.* p. clvi.

κόσμον ἵνα κρίνῃ τὸν κόσμον, ἀλλ' ἵνα σωθῇ ὁ κόσμος δι' αὐτοῦ. 18. ὁ πιστεύων εἰς αὐτὸν οὐ κρίνεται· ὁ μὴ πιστεύων ἤδη κέκριται,

and it was to *save* that He was sent. That some should reject Him is no part of the Father's will; but if they do reject Him, they bring judgment on themselves. And so Jn. declares οὐ γὰρ ἀπέστειλεν ὁ θεὸς τὸν υἱὸν εἰς τὸν κόσμον ἵνα κρίνῃ τὸν κόσμον, ἀλλ' ἵνα σωθῇ ὁ κόσμος δι' αὐτοῦ. This is repeated 12⁴⁷, where Jesus is represented as saying οὐ γὰρ ἦλθον ἵνα κρίνω τὸν κόσμον, ἀλλ' ἵνα σώσω τὸν κόσμον. ἵνα σώσω, not ἵνα κρίνω (as Jewish-Apocalyptic believed), expresses the final cause of the mission of the Son of Man. Cf. Zech. 9⁹ ὁ βασιλεύς σου ἔρχεταί σοι δίκαιος καὶ σώζων.

For the universality of this redemptive purpose, see 4⁴² ὁ σωτὴρ τοῦ κόσμου, and the note there. It was one of the last prayers of Jesus that the world should come to recognise at last that God loved it, and that therefore He had sent His Son (17²³).

σωθῇ. σώζειν occurs only 6 times in Jn., σωτηρία once (4²²), and σωτήρ twice (4⁴², where see note, and 1 Jn. 4¹⁴).

In the LXX it generally represents ישע, which primarily means " enlargement " and hence " deliverance," ישועה being, at last, almost equivalent to " victory," and often used in the O.T. of the final Messianic Deliverance. In the N.T. σώζειν sometimes stands for deliverance from bodily sickness, or healing (see 11¹² and cf. Mk. 5²⁸ 6⁵⁶ 10⁵² etc.); frequently it carries with it the idea of rescue from physical death (*e.g.* 12²⁷, Mk. 3⁴ 15³⁰); and in other passages the thought is of spiritual deliverance (*e.g.* 5³⁴ 10⁹ 12⁴⁷, Mk. 10²⁶ 13¹³), *i.e.* of the transition from death to life, conceived of either as present or as future (in an eschatological reference), wrought by the life-giving power of Christ, and applied to the individual soul by an act of faith. This, the deepest meaning of σωτηρία, is constantly present to the mind of Jn. See on 4⁴² for σωτήρ.

18. To the thought of Jn., ζωὴ αἰώνιος begins in the present, and is not only a hope of the future (see on 3¹⁵ above); so also the κρίσις, or the inevitable distinction between man and man, determined by the use or abuse of his free will, begins in the present life.

Here for Jn. is the supreme test of the human spirit, whether the man " believes in " Christ or does not believe. ὁ πιστεύων εἰς αὐτὸν οὐ κρίνεται, or, as it is expressed later on, εἰς κρίσιν οὐκ ἔρχεται, ἀλλὰ μεταβέβηκεν ἐκ τοῦ θανάτου εἰς τὴν ζωήν (5²⁴). The believer *has* eternal life in Christ; he has passed into life. There is no uncertainty as to the final judgment for him.

ὅτι μὴ πεπίστευκεν εἰς τὸ ὄνομα τοῦ μονογενοῦς Υἱοῦ τοῦ Θεοῦ.
19. αὕτη δέ ἐστιν ἡ κρίσις, ὅτι τὸ φῶς ἐλήλυθεν εἰς τὸν κόσμον καὶ

But there is also the man who is not willing to come to
Christ that he may have life (5⁴⁰), i.e. not willing to "believe "
Of him Jn. says ὁ μὴ πιστεύων ἤδη κέκριται, "he has been
judged already" by his unfaith, the present judgment being
anticipatory of the future. This is, indeed, the judgment
which will declare itself at the Last Day (12⁴⁸). But that the
judgment will be manifested at the Last Day is not inconsistent
with its having been already determined in the present life by
the unbelief and blindness and disobedience of the man. So
it is said of the prince of evil that he "has been judged"
(16¹¹), although the exhibition of this tremendous judgment
is not yet.

The rec. text has ὁ δὲ μὴ πιστ. κτλ. with ALTᵇΓΔΘ; but
אBW ff² l om. δέ. The two sentences ὁ πιστεύων . . . and ὁ μὴ
πιστεύων are co-ordinate and complementary; and it is quite
in the Johannine manner to place them side by side without any
adversative or connecting particle.

Jn. uses μή with a pres. part. over 20 times.

ὅτι μὴ πεπίστευκεν . . ., "because he has not believed," a
continuing movement of unbelief being indicated by the pft.
tense. Abbott (Diat. 2187) compares with ὁ μὴ πιστεύων . . .
ὅτι μὴ πεπίστευκεν . . . of this verse, the passage 1 Jn. 5¹⁰ . . .
ὁ μὴ πιστεύων . . . ὅτι οὐ πεπίστευκεν . . . "In the latter ὅτι οὐ
states the fact objectively ; in the former ὅτι μή states it
subjectively, as the judgment pronounced by the Judge."
ὅτι μή is a very unusual construction (see Diat. 2695), and
demands some such explanation here.[1]

For the phrase πιστεύειν εἰς τὸ ὄνομα, see on 1¹².

For μονογενής, see on 1¹⁴. It is possible that the repetition
of the adjective here is intended to mark, not only the greatness
of the Father's love (as in v. 16), but also the uniqueness of
Jesus as a Saviour. There is no other (cf. Acts 4¹²).

19. αὕτη δέ ἐστιν ἡ κρίσις. The form of the sentence, introducing an explanation, is thoroughly Johannine; cf. 1 Jn. 1⁵
5¹¹·¹⁴. "This is the judging," sc. not the sentence of judgment (κρίμα), but the way in which the judgment is accomplished. It is no arbitrary sentence, but the working out of
a moral law. The root of unbelief in Christ is the refusal
to turn to His Light, because the man's conduct will not bear
scrutiny. Jn. traces unbelief to moral causes.

"The Light came into the world "; so he has already in the

---

[1] The uncial fragment Tʷ has the unique reading ὅτι οὐ μὴ πεπίστευκεν,
which indicates that the scribe felt the difficulty.

ἠγάπησαν οἱ ἄνθρωποι μᾶλλον τὸ σκότος ἢ τὸ φῶς· ἦν γὰρ αὐτῶν
πονηρὰ τὰ ἔργα. 20. πᾶς γὰρ ὁ φαῦλα πράσσων μισεῖ τὸ φῶς καὶ
οὐκ ἔρχεται πρὸς τὸ φῶς, ἵνα μὴ ἐλεγχθῇ τὰ ἔργα αὐτοῦ· 21. ὁ δὲ
ποιῶν τὴν ἀλήθειαν ἔρχεται πρὸς τὸ φῶς, ἵνα φανερωθῇ αὐτοῦ τὰ
ἔργα ὅτι ἐν Θεῷ ἐστιν εἰργασμένα.

Prologue described the Advent of Christ (1⁴· ⁵· ⁹); "and men
loved the darkness rather than the Light, for evil were their
works" (see on 1⁹). The comparison of wickedness to darkness and of virtue to light is, of course, found elsewhere, *e.g.*
Philo, *Quaest. in Gen.* ii. 22, and *Test. of XII. Patr.*, Naph. ii.
10, "neither while ye are in darkness can ye do the works of
light." So Job says of the wicked that they "are of them
that rebel against the light" (Job 24¹³). The image occurs
with special frequency in Jn., *e.g.* 8¹² 12³⁵· ⁴⁶, 1 Jn. 1⁶ 2⁸· ⁹· ¹¹;
that Jesus is τὸ φῶς τοῦ κόσμου (8¹²) is one of his central
thoughts.

With ἦν γὰρ αὐτῶν πονηρὰ τὰ ἔργα cf. 7⁷, where Jesus is
represented as saying that the κόσμος hated Him, ὅτι τὰ ἔργα
αὐτοῦ πονηρά ἐστιν. The same phrase appears in 1 Jn. 3¹², of
the deeds of Cain. Jn. always takes the darkest view of the
world apart from Christ ; cf. ὁ κόσμος ὅλος ἐν τῷ πονηρῷ
κεῖται (1 Jn. 5¹⁹). Cf. also Col. 1²¹, 2 Tim. 4¹⁸, for τὰ ἔργα τὰ
πονηρά.

20. Jn. proceeds to explain the psychology of this shrinking
of the world from Christ the Light.

πᾶς γὰρ ὁ φαῦλα πράσσων κτλ., "for every one who prac-
tises base things hates the Light." Both in this passage and
at 5²⁹ (the only two places where Jn. has the adj. φαῦλος or
the verb πράσσειν), we have φαῦλα πράσσειν, but ἀγαθά (τὴν
ἀλήθειαν, v. 21) ποιεῖν. πράσσειν does not carry with it the
idea of anything accomplished, or abiding as the result of
action, whereas ποιεῖν is to *make* as well as to *do*; and perhaps some such difference is intended by Jn., although in
Rom. 7¹⁵· ¹⁹ the verbs cannot be distinguished.

The base liver does not come to the Light, lest his works be
reproved. We have ἐλέγχειν again 8⁴⁶ 16⁸; cf. Eph. 5¹³ τὰ δὲ
πάντα ἐλεγχόμενα ὑπὸ τοῦ φωτὸς φανεροῦται.

We should expect μήποτε for ἵνα μή, but μήποτε never occurs
in Jn., who employs the constr. ἵνα μή 18 times. Burney points
out [1] that ἵνα μή corresponds exactly with the Aramaic דְּלָא.

21. א* omits from ὁ δὲ ποιῶν to τὰ ἔργα, because of the
homoioteleuton τὰ ἔργα αὐτοῦ v. 20 and v. 21 (as read in its
exemplar, instead of αὐτοῦ τὰ ἔργα).

ὁ δὲ ποιῶν τὴν ἀλήθειαν (cf. 1 Jn. 1⁶) ἔρχεται πρὸς τὸ φῶς

---

[1] *Aramaic Origin, etc.,* p. 100.

31. Ὁ ἄνωθεν ἐρχόμενος ἐπάνω πάντων ἐστίν· ὁ ὢν ἐκ τῆς γῆς ἐκ τῆς γῆς ἐστιν καὶ ἐκ τῆς γῆς λαλεῖ. ὁ ἐκ τοῦ οὐρανοῦ ἐρχόμενος

This is a universal saying, not to be confined to those who are already believers in Christ. As Christ Himself said: πᾶς ὁ ὢν ἐκ τῆς ἀληθείας ἀκούει μου τῆς φωνῆς (18³⁷). Jn. states that every honest doer of the truth comes into the light, and (as Christ is *the* Light) he therefore approaches Christ; he does so "that his works may be made manifest" (cf. 9³). See on 8³⁴.

ὅτι ἐν θεῷ ἐστιν εἰργασμένα. ὅτι may mean "because" or "that." The latter rendering seems preferable. The honest man ("in whom is no guile," 1⁴⁷) comes to the light that it may be made plain that his deeds have been done ἐν θεῷ, a remarkable expression for which there is no exact parallel; cf. κοπιώσας ἐν κυρίῳ (Rom. 16¹²). See Ps. 139²³· ²⁴ for the prayer of the righteous man, who does not shrink from the closest scrutiny of his life.

The evangelist's commentary continued (vv. 31–36)

31–36 Reasons have been given in the Introduction (p. xxiii) for taking these verses in sequence to vv. 16–21, vv. 22–30 having been displaced from their original position.

The argument of this paragraph is as follows: He that is of the earth can testify only to earthly things (v. 31; cf. v. 12). Christ, who is from heaven, in testifying of heavenly things, testifies to that which He has seen and heard, but His witness is not accepted (v. 32; cf. v. 11). Nevertheless, he who does accept it, agrees that Jesus was the promised Messenger of God (v. 33; cf. v. 17). He speaks the message of God, and thereby shows that He was sent by God (v. 34). He speaks this message in its completeness, for the Spirit is not granted to Him in part only (v. 34); He is the Beloved Son (v. 35; cf. v. 16).

31. ℵ*D *fam*.1 *a b e ff*² and Syr. cur. om. the second ἐπάνω πάντων ἐστίν at the end of the verse; but ins. ℵᶜABLTᵇΔΘW. Jn. is fond of repeating phrases, with a slight verbal change (see on v. 16).

ὁ ἄνωθεν ἐρχόμενος, *i.e.* Christ. ἄνωθεν has its usual Johannine significance of *desuper*, "from above" (but see on 3³); cf. ἐγὼ ἐκ τῶν ἄνω εἰμί (8²³) and 1 Cor. 15⁴⁷.

ἐπάνω πάντων ἐστίν. This is expressed by Paul in the same way ὁ ὢν ἐπὶ πάντων (Rom. 9⁵; cf. Eph. 1²¹).

ὁ ὢν ἐκ τῆς γῆς . . . λαλεῖ. There is a similar thought in 1 Jn. 4⁵: αὐτοὶ ἐκ τοῦ κόσμου εἰσί· διὰ τοῦτο ἐκ τοῦ κόσμου λαλοῦσιν,

ἐπάνω πάντων ἐστίν· 32. ὃ ἑώρακεν καὶ ἤκουσεν, τοῦτο μαρτυρεῖ, καὶ τὴν μαρτυρίαν αὐτοῦ οὐδεὶς λαμβάνει. 33. ὁ λαβὼν αὐτοῦ τὴν μαρτυρίαν ἐσφράγισεν ὅτι ὁ Θεὸς ἀληθής ἐστιν. 34. ὃν γὰρ ἀπέ-

the only difference being that κόσμος carries the idea of the moral condition of the world (see on 1⁹), while γῆ is the physical "earth" simply. Cf. 2 Esd. 4²¹: "Qui super terram inhabitant quae sunt super terram intellegere solummodo possunt, et qui super caelos quae super altitudinem caelorum." See on 3¹².

ἐκ τῆς γῆς ἐστιν. Jn. is inclined to the constr. εἶναι ἐκ . . . as indicating origin and affinity; cf. 8²³ and *passim*. The constr. γεγεννῆσθαι ἐκ has already been discussed (3⁵ and 1¹³). For λαλεῖ, see on 3¹¹.

32. ΑΓΔΘ read καὶ ὃ ἑώρακεν, but אBDLTᵇW om. καί. In this verse the words of v. 11 are repeated, the evangelist taking them up and amplifying them.

ὃ ἑώρακεν. This is one of the few passages in Jn. where ὁρᾶν in the perf. tense is used of *spiritual* vision (see also 8³⁸ 14⁷ 15²⁴, and cf. 1¹⁸).

ὃ . . . ἤκουσεν, τοῦτο μαρτυρεῖ. It is the constant teaching of Jn. that Jesus proclaimed what He had "heard" from the Father (8⁴⁰ 15¹⁵; cf. 12⁴⁹). Jesus is the "Faithful Witness," according to the Apocalypse (Rev. 1⁵). Cf. Introd., p. xcii.

καὶ τὴν μαρτυρίαν αὐτοῦ οὐδεὶς λαμβάνει. This is reproduced from v. 11, where see note. In the traditional order of the text, this sentence would be inconsistent with v. 26, which tells of the crowds that flocked to hear Jesus; but it is plain that John the Baptist is not the speaker here (see Introd., p. xxiii).

Jn. hastens in v. 33 to correct the rhetorical οὐδείς, just as he corrects 1¹¹ by 1¹²; cf. also 8¹⁵· ¹⁶ 12⁴⁴ᶠ·.

For the position of οὐδείς in the sentence, see on 1¹⁸.

33. ὁ λαβὼν αὐτοῦ τὴν μαρτυρίαν κτλ., *i.e.* who has accepted as convincing the witness of Christ about eternal life and God's love; cf. vv. 3–15, upon which all this is commentary.

σφραγίζειν here and at 6²⁷ (where see note) is the equivalent of "to attest," the metaphor of *sealing* being a common one. He who accepts the witness of Jesus thereby attests that Jesus speaks the words of God as His accredited Messenger, and in this attestation virtually testifies to his belief that God is true (ὁ θεὸς ἀληθής ἐστιν). So at 8²⁶ it is urged that God, who sent Jesus, is true (ὁ πέμψας με ἀληθής ἐστιν), and that Jesus speaks what He has heard from God, the implied conclusion being that the hearers of Jesus may believe in Him and trust what He says. The argument of 1 Jn. 5¹⁰ puts the same

στειλεν ὁ Θεὸς τὰ ῥήματα τοῦ Θεοῦ λαλεῖ· οὐ γὰρ ἐκ μέτρου δίδωσιν τὸ Πνεῦμα. 35. ὁ Πατὴρ ἀγαπᾷ τὸν Υἱόν, καὶ πάντα δέδωκεν ἐν τῇ

thing in another way, viz. God has testified of His Son, and so he who does not believe this testimony makes God a liar. Lightfoot (*Hor. Hebr.* in loc.) quotes the Rabbinical maxim that "the seal of God is truth."

34. ὃν ἀπέστειλεν ὁ θεός. See, on this Divine mission of the Son, the note on v. 17 above.   He whom God has sent speaks God's words; cf. 8²⁶ and 17⁸ τὰ ῥήματα ἃ ἔδωκάς μοι.

In Jn. ῥῆμα never occurs in the singular ; we always have τὰ ῥήματα (no art. at 6⁶⁸), and in Jn. they are always "the" words of God (cf. 8⁴⁷) or of Christ Himself. In contradistinction to this, τὰ ῥήματα never occurs in the Apocalypse, while we have instead οἱ λόγοι, used for Divine words or sayings (cf. Introd., p. lxvi). In Jn., λόγος is always in the singular, except 10¹⁹ 14²⁴ (see on 10¹⁹).

τὰ ῥήματα τοῦ θεοῦ λαλεῖ, *sc.* Christ speaks the sayings, the full message, of God Himself ; He does not merely proclaim fragments of that message. Cf. 17⁸, and see on 3¹¹ for λαλεῖν.

οὐ γὰρ ἐκ μέτρου δίδωσιν τὸ πνεῦμα, "for [God] does not give the Spirit [to Him] by measure," but in its fulness.

The rec., with AC²DΓΔΘ, adds ὁ θεός after δίδωσιν, but om. אBC*LTᵇW 33; it supplies, however, the correct interpretation of the words. Origen rightly understands "God" to be the subject of δίδωσιν, although some have supposed "Christ" to be the subject and the meaning to be that Christ gives the Spirit in its fulness to those who believe in Him: but this latter interpretation destroys the argument of the passage, and introduces a thesis which is very questionable. Christ gives the Spirit to His own (cf. 7³⁸ 15²⁶), but could it be said that He gives it οὐκ ἐκ μέτρου? Only of One could it be said that the Spirit was given in its fulness. The Talmudical saying that "the Spirit of God did not dwell upon the prophets, *nisi mensura quadam*,"[1] is true, whether it be an original Jewish saying, or one which owes its form to Christian influence.

ἐκ μέτρου is, apparently, equivalent to μέτρῳ, "by measure"; but the constr. ἐκ μέτρου is not found again in the Greek Bible, nor has any parallel been produced from Greek literature.[2]

God the Father gives the Spirit in its fulness, and not "by measure," to Christ, because He is His Beloved Son, as v. 35 explains.

35. ὁ πατὴρ ἀγαπᾷ τὸν υἱόν. It is characteristic of Jn. to

---

[1] *Vajikra*, R. xv., quoted by Wetstein.
[2] See Abbott, *Diat.* 2324, 2714. Dr. L. C. Purser compares Soph. *Phil.* 563 ἐκ βίας, *violently*, and *El.* 279 ἐκ δόλου, *treacherously*.

χειρὶ αὐτοῦ. 36. ὁ πιστεύων εἰς τὸν Υἱὸν ἔχει ζωὴν αἰώνιον· ὁ δὲ ἀπειθῶν τῷ Υἱῷ οὐκ ὄψεται ζωήν, ἀλλ' ἡ ὀργὴ τοῦ Θεοῦ μένει ἐπ' αὐτόν.

use the verb ἀγαπᾶν of the mutual love of God the Father and Christ (see on 3¹⁶ above). In 5²⁰ we find ὁ γὰρ πατὴρ φιλεῖ τὸν υἱόν, in a context similar to that of the present passage ; but it does not seem probable that, in describing the inmost mystery of the Divine Love, Jn. would have ventured to differentiate between φιλεῖν and ἀγαπᾶν. As to the alleged distinction between them, see on 21¹⁷.

For the absolute use of ὁ υἱός in Jn., see on 3¹⁷ above.

πάντα δέδωκεν ἐν τῇ χειρὶ αὐτοῦ. So in 13³ (where see note) πάντα ἔδωκεν αὐτῷ ὁ πατὴρ εἰς τὰς χεῖρας. It is a favourite thought in Jn., that the Father has *given* all things to the Incarnate Son ; *e.g.* judgment 5²²· ²⁷, to have life in Himself 5²⁶, authority 17², glory 17²⁴, His Name 17¹¹, His commandments 12⁴⁹ (cf. 14³¹ 17⁴), and even His disciples 6³⁷ (where see note). The parallel in the Synoptists is πάντα μοι παρεδόθη ὑπὸ τοῦ πατρός μου (Lk. 10²², Mt. 11²⁷) ; and there can be little hesitation in accepting the saying that " the Father gave all things " to His Son as a genuine saying of Jesus. " What *grace* is in the Pauline Epistles, *giving* is in the Fourth Gospel " (Abbott, *Diat.* 2742).

36. ὁ πιστεύων εἰς τὸν υἱὸν ἔχει ζωὴν αἰώνιον (see on 6²⁷· ²⁹). We have had almost the same sentence above, 3¹⁵, where see note, and cf. also 6⁴⁷. The present participles πιστεύων . . . ἀπειθῶν are noteworthy, as indicating continuous belief or disobedience. A single *Credo* does not gain " eternal life," nor for a single act of disobedience or faithlessness does " the wrath of God " necessarily " abide " on a sinner. It is the temper and trend of the life that count with God.

ἀπειθέω does not occur again in Jn. It is, strictly, " to be disobedient," as opposed to πείθομαι, " to allow oneself to be persuaded "; but rather implies a rebellious mind than a series of disobedient acts. Sometimes it expresses unbelief rather than disobedience, as at Acts 14². In the present passage there is a variant ἀπιστῶν for ἀπειθῶν found in a few cursives, and the Vulgate, following the " European " and " Italian " O.L. versions, has accordingly *incredulus*. But the African O.L. follows the better reading ἀπειθῶν, understanding by it *dis-obedience* rather than unbelief. That this is the meaning is confirmed by the remarkable parallel in Eph. 5⁶: ἔρχεται ἡ ὀργὴ τοῦ θεοῦ ἐπὶ τοὺς υἱοὺς τῆς ἀπειθείας.

It is not always possible to distinguish the two shades of meaning in ἀπειθεῖν. To " believe " is to have " eternal life,"

22. Μετὰ ταῦτα ἦλθεν ὁ Ἰησοῦς καὶ οἱ μαθηταὶ αὐτοῦ εἰς τὴν Ἰουδαίαν γῆν, καὶ ἐκεῖ διέτριβεν μετ' αὐτῶν καὶ ἐβάπτιζεν. 23. ἦν

and this " eternal life " is God's commandment (ἡ ἐντολὴ αὐτοῦ ζωὴ αἰώνιός ἐστιν, 12⁵⁰) ; so that " to believe " is " to obey."

οὐκ ὄψεται ζωήν. Cf. v. 3, οὐ δύναται ἰδεῖν τὴν βασιλείαν τοῦ θεοῦ, and also 8⁵¹. ⁵², where " seeing " death is equivalent to " tasting " death. The rebel (ἀπειθῶν) will not " see " life, because he cannot appreciate or assimilate it. Cf. 6⁵³, and esp. 1 Jn. 5¹², ὁ μὴ ἔχων τὸν υἱὸν τοῦ θεοῦ τὴν ζωὴν οὐκ ἔχει.

ἡ ὀργὴ τοῦ θεοῦ is not mentioned again in Jn., although often in Paul (Rom. 1¹⁸, Eph. 5⁶ ; and cf. Rev. 19¹⁵ etc.). It is a thoroughly Hebraic conception, the phrase being common in the LXX; and John the Baptist spoke of "the wrath to come " (Mt. 3⁷, Lk. 3⁷). The expression does not appear in the Synoptic reports of the words of Jesus, and He may never have used it, preferring to dwell on the fatherly love of God rather than on His hatred of sin. The phrase ἡ ὀργὴ τοῦ θεοῦ has nothing in common with Greek philosophy or religion, but it has its roots in that conception of God as essentially a moral Being, to whom therefore sin is hateful, which is behind all the teaching of Christ.

μένει is the pres. tense, not the future (μενεῖ), as some Latin authorities take it to be. Not only in the world to come, but in this world, the " wrath of God " abides upon him who is continuously rebellious, in will and deed, against the heavenly vision.

The second witness of John the Baptist (vv. 22–30)

22. μετὰ ταῦτα, the phrase with which Jn. is accustomed to introduce new chapters to his story (see Introd., p. cviii). After the ministry of Jesus in Jerusalem at the Passover and the interview with Nicodemus (2²²ff.), He moved with the disciples whom He had gathered round Him (see on 2²) into the country districts of Judæa, εἰς τὴν Ἰουδαίαν γῆν (the only occurrence in the N.T. of this descriptive phrase; cf. Mk. 1⁵), and He stayed there with them, baptizing. Probably the locality was somewhere near the fords in the neighbourhood of Jericho.

διατρίβειν occurs in N.T. elsewhere only in Acts (but see on 11⁵⁴). The imperfect tenses διέτριβεν . . . ἐβάπτιζεν imply that Jesus and His disciples made a stay of some duration in the district. Here, and at 3²⁶ 4¹, it is said that Jesus baptized people; but the editor's correction at 4² states that Jesus did

δὲ καὶ Ἰωάνης βαπτίζων ἐν Αἰνὼν ἐγγὺς τοῦ Σαλείμ, ὅτι ὕδατα πολλὰ ἦν ἐκεῖ, καὶ παρεγίνοντο καὶ ἐβαπτίζοντο· 24. οὔπω γὰρ ἦν

not baptize in person, that being the work of His disciples. This is the only ascription in the N.T. of a ministry of baptism to Jesus, whether in person or with the aid of others (see on 4²). But there is no historical improbability about it. He had Himself submitted to baptism at the hands of John, thus (at the least) giving the seal of His approval to the ministry which John was exercising. His first disciples were taken from among the disciples of John. There is no question, at this stage, of *Christian* baptism, *i.e.* of baptism as a sacramental rite. That was only to be instituted after His Resurrection (Mt. 28¹⁹); cf. 7³⁹. The baptism of John was symbolic of a cleansing of the soul (cf. 3²⁵ below), and making a fresh start in the spiritual life. " Repent ye " was an early message of Jesus (Mk. 1¹⁵), as it was the chief message of John Baptist. See further on 4².

23. For the constr. ἦν . . . Ἰω. βαπτίζων, where we would expect ἐβάπτιζεν (as in the preceding verse), see on 1²⁸. παραγίγνομαι does not occur again in Jn.

John also was carrying on his ministry of baptism in the same neighbourhood, viz. at Aenon.

Αἰνὼν ἐγγὺς τοῦ Σαλείμ. These places cannot be identified with certainty. There is a *Salim* to the E. of Shechem, and a village called '*Ainun* to the N.E.; but (1) there is no water at 'Ainun, and Αἰνών was a place of ὕδατα πολλά; (2) 'Ainun is 7 miles from Salim, and this could hardly be described as " near " (cf. 11¹⁸ 19²⁰·⁴²); and (3) it is not likely that John the Baptist was labouring among the Samaritans (cf. 4⁹). The site assigned by Eusebius and Jerome (and shown to the pilgrim Aetheria in the fourth century) is probably the true site, viz. in the Jordan valley about 7½ miles south of Beisan, the ancient Scythopolis. " Aenon near to Salim " is marked at this point on the mosaic map of Madeba. There is still here " a remarkable group of seven springs, all lying within a radius of a quarter of a mile, which answers well to the description ὕδατα πολλά." ¹ It is on the W. bank of the Jordan, and this is confirmed by v. 26. Cheyne would read " Jerusalem " for " Salim," and finds Aenon in 'Ain Karim, which is near Jerusalem on the W. side.² But this is merely guess-work.

Those who find allegory in Jn.'s place-names, interpret " Aenon near to Salim " as indicating " fountains near to

¹ Sir C. W. Wilson in Smith's *D.B.²*, *s.v.* " Aenon."
² See *E.B.*, *s.v.* " John the Baptist."

βεβλημένος εἰς τὴν φυλακὴν Ἰωάνης. 25. Ἐγένετο οὖν ζήτησις ἐκ

peace," the Baptist preparing for the higher purification by Christ the King of peace (Melchi-zedek).[1]

24. This verse is a parenthetical comment of Jn. (see Introd., p. xxxiv), which indicates the time at which the events happened which he records (see p. cii). The Synoptists tell nothing of this ministry of Jesus in Judæa, and Jn. is careful to remark that it was exercised in the earlier days of His public activity, before John the Baptist had been imprisoned. It is quite in his manner to assume that his readers know of the arrest of John and his martyrdom (cf. Introd., p. xciv). See also on 5[35].

All that has been mentioned in the Fourth Gospel up to this point seems to be precedent to the wonderful ministry in Galilee (Mk. 1[14]–6[6]), which culminated in the choice of the Twelve (Mk. 3[13]) and their subsequent mission (Mk. 6[7]). Indeed Mk. expressly says that all this was " after John was delivered up " (Mk. 1[14]). When, therefore, Jn. speaks of the " disciples " who were with Jesus in this early ministry in Judæa, we cannot assume that the " Twelve " are indicated, the presumption being the other way (see on 2[2] above). That episodes like those in c. 3 and the beginning of c. 4 are not recorded by Mk. may be due to the fact that Peter, upon whose reminiscences Mk. has largely based his narrative, was not present; while their appearance in the Fourth Gospel is explicable, if the authority behind it was one of the disciples who witnessed the ministry in Judæa and Samaria. He may have been John the son of Zebedee.

25, 26. ἐγένετο οὖν κτλ. " So there arose a questioning on the part of (ἐκ) John's disciples with Jews about purifying," *sc.* about the purificatory baptisms which Jesus, as well as John, was encouraging.[2] The turn of the sentence (ἐκ) shows that it was the Baptist's disciples who began the dispute; they were puzzled that Jesus, to whom John had pointed as One far superior to himself, should carry on a ministry, outwardly similar to John's, and thus divert disciples from their own master, who was pre-eminently " the Baptist." Naturally, they would cross-examine the Jews who flocked to Jesus' ministry of baptism, and would ask them what was its special virtue.

Finally, they came to John with their complaint, addressing him as their Rabbi (see on 1[38]): " He who was with thee on the

---

[1] So Abbott, *E.B.*, 1796.

[2] Abbott (*Diat.* x. iii. 332) thinks that the dispute must have had reference to the association of *fasting* with baptism.

τῶν μαθητῶν Ἰωάνου μετὰ Ἰουδαίων περὶ καθαρισμοῦ. 26. καὶ
ἦλθον πρὸς τὸν Ἰωάνην καὶ εἶπαν αὐτῷ 'Ραββεί, ὃς ἦν μετὰ σοῦ
πέραν τοῦ Ἰορδάνου, ᾧ σὺ μεμαρτύρηκας, ἴδε οὗτος βαπτίζει καὶ
πάντες ἔρχονται πρὸς αὐτόν. 27. ἀπεκρίθη Ἰωάνης καὶ εἶπεν Οὐ
δύναται ἄνθρωπος λαμβάνειν οὐδὲν ἐὰν μὴ ᾖ δεδομένον αὐτῷ ἐκ τοῦ
οὐρανοῦ. 28. αὐτοὶ ὑμεῖς μοι μαρτυρεῖτε ὅτι εἶπον Οὐκ εἰμὶ ἐγὼ ὁ
Χριστός, ἀλλ' ὅτι Ἀπεσταλμένος εἰμὶ ἔμπροσθεν ἐκείνου. 29. Ὁ
ἔχων τὴν νύμφην νυμφίος ἐστίν· ὁ δὲ φίλος τοῦ νυμφίου, ὁ ἑστηκὼς

other side of the Jordan (sc. at Bethany or Bethabara; cf. 1[28]),
to whom thou hast borne witness (1[32]), behold (see on 1[29]), He
(οὗτος, perhaps implying hostility; cf. 6[42]) is baptizing and all
are coming to Him." They were jealous and angry that what
they counted their master's prerogative should be invaded.

ζήτησις does not occur again in the Gospels, but we find
the word in 1 Tim. 6[4], suggesting meticulous dispute rather
than legitimate and profitable inquiry.

The rec. reading Ἰουδαίων (א*Θ fam. 13, the Latin vss., and
Syr. cu.) seems preferable to Ἰουδαίου (אᶜABLNWΓΔ), which
the R.V. has adopted. If the dispute were only with an
individual Jew, we should expect Ἰουδαίου τινος.[1]

We have had the word καθαρισμός, of ritual or ceremonial
purification, at 2[6] above.

27, 28. ἀπεκρ. Ἰω. καὶ εἶπεν. For the construction, see on 1[26].
John's reply to his disciples' outburst of jealousy was to
remind them of a great principle of life: " A man can receive
nothing, except it have been given him from heaven." As Paul
says, " What hast thou, that thou didst not receive ? " (1 Cor.
4[7]). The same principle is enunciated, in different forms,
Jn. 6[65] 19[11]. As to John's baptism, it became a puzzle to the
Jews whether it was " from heaven or of men " (Mk. 11[30]);
John would certainly have claimed that his commission to
baptize was " from heaven," but he could not go beyond its
limitations. " Ye yourselves," he answers, " are my witnesses
that I said *I am not the Christ* (1[20. 23]), but that *I am sent
before* (1[15]) *Him* (ἐκείνου, sc. Jesus, whom you know that I
acclaimed as the Christ)."

After λαμβάνειν, LΘ fam. 13 add ἀφ' ἑαυτοῦ.

29. ὁ ἔχων τὴν νύμφην νυμφίος ἐστίν. This is the only reference in Jn. to the representation of Christ as the Church's
Bridegroom, which has its origin in the mystic phraseology of
the O.T. (see on 1[12]). Yahweh is described as the jealous
husband of Israel (Ex. 34[15], Deut. 31[16], Ps. 73[27]), or as betrothed

---

[1] Bentley suggested that μετὰ Ἰουδαίου was a corruption of μετὰ τῶν
Ἰησοῦ, a violent and unnecessary emendation, although Loisy seems to
view it with favour.

καὶ ἀκούων αὐτοῦ, χαρᾷ χαίρει διὰ τὴν φωνὴν τοῦ νυμφίου. αὕτη οὖν ἡ χαρὰ ἡ ἐμὴ πεπλήρωται. 30. ἐκεῖνον δεῖ αὐξάνειν, ἐμὲ δὲ ἐλαττοῦσθαι.

to Israel (Hos. 2[19]), and we have the explicit statement, "Thy Maker is thy husband: Yahweh of hosts is His Name" (Isa. 54[5]). The Rabbis held that Moses was the paranymph or "friend of the bridegroom." In the N.T. Christ is represented as the Bridegroom, and the Church, the spiritual Israel, as the Bride. The image appears in Paul (Eph. 5[32] and 2 Cor. 11[2]; in the latter passage, Paul regarding himself as the paranymph), and also in the Apocalypse, where the New Jerusalem descends from heaven as a bride adorned for her husband, the Lamb (Rev. 19[7] 21[2]). This doctrine, according to the Synoptists, goes back to the teaching of Jesus Himself. The parables of the Marriage Feast and of the Ten Virgins (Mt. 22[1] 25[1]) imply as much; and, above all, there is the reply of Jesus to the question why His disciples did not practise fasting, while the disciples of John the Baptist did: "Can the sons of the bridechamber fast, while the Bridegroom is with them?" (Mk. 2[19]). In this saying Jesus claims to be the mystical Bridegroom Himself, and thus answers those who would put Him on a level with John the Baptist.

The answer of John in the present passage is similar. His disciples complain because his work is being invaded by Jesus; but he reminds them that while Jesus is the νυμφίος, who naturally has the Bride for His own, he, John, is only ὁ φίλος τοῦ νυμφίου, the Bridegroom's friend, the paranymph, whose office it was to bring the Bride and the Bridegroom together. That being done, his task is accomplished.

The *shoshben*, or παρανύμφιος, was a well-recognised personage in Judæa (not in Galilee, and there is no mention of him in the account of the marriage at Cana). He stands expectant (ὁ ἑστηκώς ; cf. 12[29]), and rejoices when he hears the voice of the bridegroom in converse with his bride (for ἡ φωνὴ τοῦ νυμφίου, cf. Jer. 7[34] 16[9], Rev. 18[23]).

χαρᾷ χαίρει does not occur again in Jn., but is found Isa. 66[10], 1 Thess. 3[9]. It is not necessarily a Hebraism; cf. Plato, *Sympos.* 195 B, φεύγων φυγῇ τὸ γῆρας.

ἡ χαρὰ ἡ ἐμὴ πεπλήρωται. Cf. for the same phrase, 15[11].

ἐμός is a favourite possessive pronoun with Jn., occurring 40 times, as against one appearance in the Apocalypse (Rev. 2[20]). Cf. Introd., p. lxvi.

30. ἐκεῖνον δεῖ αὐξάνειν κτλ. Again (see on 3[14]) we have δεῖ, "it *has* to be." The herald's task is over when He who has been proclaimed is come. It was divinely ordered that John

IV. 1. Ὡς οὖν ἔγνω ὁ Κύριος ὅτι ἤκουσαν οἱ Φαρισαῖοι ὅτι Ἰησοῦς

the Baptist's ministry should recede into the background, while that of Jesus drew "all men" (v. 26) more and more. ' He must increase, while I must decrease," is the final message of the Baptist. So Jesus had said, " The least in the kingdom of heaven is greater than he " (Mt. 11[11]).

Jesus leaves Judæa for Galilee by way of Samaria (IV. 1–4)

IV. 1. ὁ κύριος. This is read by ABCLT[b]W, but the Western reading (אDΘ *fam.* 1, with *a b c e ff*[2] *l* Syr. cur.) is ὁ Ἰησοῦς. It is plain that the text has been tampered with. The verse is clumsily expressed and seems to have been re-written, ὁ κύριος having probably been inserted in the later draft to remove any ambiguity as to the subject of the sentence.

It has been pointed out (on 1[38]) that His disciples were accustomed to address Jesus either as *Rabbi* (Teacher) or as *Mari* (Lord). And in His absence, according to the Synoptists, they used both terms, either saying ὁ διδάσκαλος (as Jesus bade them do, Mk. 14[14]) or ὁ κύριος (Mk. 11[3]), an appellation which He approved (Mk. 5[19]). In Jn., Martha says ὁ διδάσκαλος (11[28]); Mary Magdalene says ὁ κύριος (20[2, 18]), and so do the disciples (20[25] 21[7]).

In direct narrative, when the evangelists are using their own words and not reporting the words of others, a distinction must be made. In Lk. (7[13] 10[1] 11[39] 12[42] 17[5] 22[61]), " the Lord " is often used by the evangelist. So in the Marcan Appendix (16[19, 20]) we have " the Lord " twice. This also is the usage of the Gospel of Peter. But Mk. (followed by Mt.) *never* writes " the Lord," but always " Jesus." The primitive narratives, that is, took the form " Jesus said . . .," " Jesus did . . ." The form " the Lord said " is later.

Now in the direct narrative of the Fourth Gospel we find " Jesus " as in Mk., and not " the Lord " as in Lk., with five exceptions which are instructive. In 4[1] 6[23] 11[2], ὁ κύριος is the true reading; but these verses are all explanatory glosses, not from the hand of Jn., but written after the first draft of the story had been completed. In 20[20] 21[12], where we have ὁ κύριος, we are in the middle of the post-Resurrection narrative, and it is not unnatural that special reverence should be exhibited in writing of Him who had risen.

Soon after the Resurrection, the title began to imply that larger and deeper meaning of ὁ κύριος as the representative of יהוה which is frequent in Paul and is found in the Acts (2[36] 9[11]). That " Jesus is Lord " (1 Cor. 12[3]; cf. Phil. 2[11]) has become

πλείονας μαθητὰς ποιεῖ καὶ βαπτίζει ἢ Ἰωάνης,—2. καίτοιγε Ἰησοῦς
αὐτὸς οὐκ ἐβάπτιζεν ἀλλ᾽ οἱ μαθηταὶ αὐτοῦ,—3. ἀφῆκεν τὴν Ἰουδαίαν

the central thought of the Christian profession; but now the
predicate means more than "Master," for it expresses the
doctrine of the Incarnation. Perhaps we may say that the
passage from the lower to the higher sense begins with the
citation of Ps. 110¹ by the Master Himself (Mk. 12³⁶).

Thus the use by Jn. of the form of narrative in which the
central figure is designated as "Jesus" (save in the exceptional passages cited) rather than as "the Lord," illustrates
well the primitive characteristics which the Fourth Gospel
exhibits.

Probably some time had elapsed since Jesus had begun His
ministry in Judæa (cf. διέτριβεν, 3²²); and it is possible
that His departure was subsequent to John's imprisonment
(cf. 3²⁴). The Pharisees (see on 1²⁴) had begun to take notice
of Him, being perhaps even more suspicious of Him than they
had been of John (1²⁴), because they had heard that (ὅτι
recitantis) "Jesus is making more disciples than John";
and so He moved to another place (cf. 7¹ 10³⁹). At this stage
He was anxious to avoid open collision with the Pharisees. It
will be noticed that we have the "making of disciples" and
"baptizing" associated closely thus early, long before the
charge is said to have been given to the apostles μαθητεύσατε
. . . βαπτίζοντες αὐτούς (Mt. 28¹⁹).

The art. is omitted before Ἰησοῦς πλείονας μαθ. ποιεῖ, contrary to the general usage of Jn., who prefers to write
ὁ Ἰησοῦς (see on 1²⁹). We have the same omission at 4⁴⁷ 6²⁴,
and for the same reason as here, viz. that ὅτι introduces the
words which were actually spoken : the construction is not
oblique, but that of ὅτι *recitantis*.

2. If this verse is part of the original draft of the Gospel,
it is a parenthetical comment or correction by Jn., and is quite
in his manner (see on 2²¹). He wishes to prevent his readers
from making any mistake; the Pharisees had heard that Jesus
was baptizing disciples in large numbers, but Jn. pauses to
explain that the report which reached them was inaccurate
in so far as it suggested that Jesus baptized in person. And it
may be that this correction of ἐβάπτιζεν in 3²² (where see note)
is well founded.

But it is probable that the verse 4² is not from the hand of
Jn.,¹ but was added at a revision of the text, because of the
idea that it would detract from the dignity of Jesus to perform
the ministry of baptism, which even Paul was accustomed as a

¹ See Introd., p. xxxiii.

καὶ ἀπῆλθεν πάλιν εἰς τὴν Γαλιλαίαν. 4. Ἔδει δὲ αὐτὸν διέρχεσθαι διὰ τῆς Σαμαρίας.

5. Ἔρχεται οὖν εἰς πόλιν τῆς Σαμαρίας λεγομένην Συχάρ, πλησίον τοῦ χωρίου ὃ ἔδωκεν Ἰακὼβ Ἰωσὴφ τῷ υἱῷ αὐτοῦ· 6. ἦν δὲ ἐκεῖ πηγὴ

rule to leave to others. There are slight indications, too, that the *style* of the verse is not Johannine. καίτοιγε does not occur elsewhere in the N.T., and Jn. is apt to use καί where another would use καίτοι (see on 1¹¹). Again, Ἰησοῦς is not preceded by the def. article, as is the general usage of Jn. (see on 1²⁹). For οἱ μαθηταὶ αὐτοῦ, see on 2².

3. ἀφῆκεν τὴν Ἰουδαίαν, " He forsook Judæa." ἀφίημι is an unusual word to use of leaving a *place*, but cf. 16²⁸. DΘ *fam.* 13 with Latin texts read τὴν Ἰουδαίαν γῆν (cf. 3²²).

καὶ ἀπῆλθεν πάλιν εἰς τὴν Γαλιλαίαν, " He departed *again* into Galilee," the first ministry in Galilee having been already described (1⁴³–2¹²); see on 3²⁴. We should not have expected the aor. ἀπῆλθεν, as the journey is not yet completed, and the Samaritan episode comes next. But it is quite good Greek, εἰς meaning " towards." " He left again for Galilee," is the exact rendering.

πάλιν is a favourite word with Jn., as with Mk. It is used of going *back* to a place, as it is here, 4⁴⁶ 6¹⁵ 10⁴⁰ 11⁷ 18³³· ³⁸ 19⁴· ⁹ 20¹⁰. AB*ΓΔ omit πάλιν, but ins. אB²CDLTᵇWΘ *fam.* 13 with the O.L. and Old Syriac vss.

4. ἔδει δὲ αὐτὸν κτλ., *sc.* " He had to go through Samaria," unless He wished to make a detour. Josephus mentions (*Antt.* xx. 6. 1) that it was the habit of the Galilæans going to Jerusalem to pass through Samaria, this being the direct route (cf. Lk. 9⁵¹· ⁵²). But apparently Jesus did not start from Jerusalem, but from Jericho (cf. 3²²); and the road that He took was probably the north-western road from thence to Ai and Bethel, where He would strike the great northern road used by caravans.

ἔδει does not stand here for any Divine necessity, although Jn. often uses it thus (see on 2⁴ 3¹⁴).

Discourse at the well with the Samaritan woman (vv. 5-26)

5. Συχάρ. " Near to the plot of ground (χωρίον; cf. Mt. 26³⁶) that Jacob gave to Joseph," *i.e.* to the E. of Shechem (Gen. 33¹⁸ 48²²), the modern *Nablûs.* Some have thought that Sychar and Shechem are identical, but they have been distinguished since Eusebius. Sychar is probably to be identified with the village ʼAskar (ע having displaced א, a linguistic change which is also observable in the Arabic form

τοῦ ᾿Ιακώβ. ὁ οὖν ᾿Ιησοῦς κεκοπιακὼς ἐκ τῆς ὁδοιπορίας ἐκαθέζετο
οὕτως ἐπὶ τῇ πηγῇ· ὥρα ἦν ὡς ἕκτη. 7. ἔρχεται γυνὴ ἐκ τῆς Σαμα-

of Ascalon). 'Askar is situated about five furlongs N.E. of
Jacob's Well.[1]

E. A. Abbott finds *Sychar* in the root שׁכר, " drunkenness "; *i.e.* it is an opprobrious name for Shechem (cf. Isa. 28[1]):
this, he suggests, is suitable to the moral of the dialogue, which
has to do with drinking.[2] But there is no need to find such
subtle and obscure allegory in a place-name.

6. κεκοπιακώς. The verb is used again by Jn. only at
v. 38. ὁδοιπορία appears elsewhere in the N.T. only at
2 Cor. 11[26].

ἐκαθέζετο, " He was seated "; cf. 11[20] 20[12]. καθέζομαι in
the N.T. is always used in a *durative* sense. T[w] has the unique
variant ἐκάθισαν.

οὕτως may mean " just as He was," *sc.* without waiting to
select a place deliberately; but more probably it refers to
κεκοπιακὼς ἐκ τῆς ὁδοιπορίας, " tired with His journey, He was
seated by the well." Cf. 1 Kings 2[7] for a somewhat similar
use of οὕτως. οὕτως is omitted here in some cursives and in
Latin, Syriac, and Coptic vss.

For **κεκοπιακώς,** see on 1[14] for Jn.'s emphasis on the true
humanity of Jesus. He saw nothing in speaking of Jesus as
" tired " which was inconsistent with His oneness with Him
of whom the prophet wrote, " The Everlasting God, the Lord,
fainteth not, neither is weary " (Isa. 40[28]).

" Jacob's Well "[3] is at a fork in the northern road to
Samaria; one branch, the ancient caravan road, going N.E. to
Scythopolis, the other going W. by Nablûs and thence N. to
Engannim. The well is about 100 feet deep, and at the bottom
the water collects, probably by infiltration. The double title
πηγή (v. 6) and φρέαρ (vv. 11, 12) is thus explicable. Why
any one should have taken pains to sink a deep pit, when there
is abundance of water both at Nablûs and 'Askar, we cannot
tell; any more than we can explain why a woman should come
half a mile from 'Askar to draw water which she could have
got in the village. But, at any rate, the well is there, and
probably has been there since the days of Jacob. In the
absence of knowledge of the exact position of the woman's

---

[1] See, for a full discussion of the site, G. A. Smith, *Hist. Geogr. of
Holy Land*, ch. 18.
[2] *E.B.*, 1801.
[3] For difficulties in the way of accepting the tradition that the well
of Sychar was " Jacob's Well," cf. *Pal. Explor. Fund Quarterly Statement*, April 1910, p. 131.

ρίας ἀντλῆσαι ὕδωρ.   λέγει αὐτῇ ὁ Ἰησοῦς Δός μοι πεῖν.   8. οἱ γὰρ
μαθηταὶ αὐτοῦ ἀπεληλύθεισαν εἰς τὴν πόλιν, ἵνα τροφὰς ἀγοράσωσιν.

house, it would be idle to speculate as to the motive which drew
her to this, which was even then a sacred well, rather than to the
'Ain at 'Askar.

"It was about the sixth hour," that is, about noon (see
on i. 39), the natural time to rest while the sun was at its height.
The account given by Josephus of Moses resting by a well in
Midian (Ex. 2¹⁵) provides a striking parallel : καθεσθεὶς ἐπί
τινος φρέατος ἐκ τοῦ κόπου καὶ τῆς ταλαιπωρίας ἠρέμει μεσημβρίας
οὔσης οὐ πόρρω τῆς πόλεως (Antt. II. xi. 1).   As in the Gospel
story, Moses was sitting by the well at midday, weary with
his journey, when the women came to draw water for their
flocks.   No doubt, the usual time for this was in the evening,
but there is no improbability in water being drawn sometimes
at noon, as Josephus represents it, and as Jn. says that the
woman came to do.

7. "A woman of Samaria" (ἐκ τῆς Σαμαρίας: cf. 1⁴⁴).
In later days she was commemorated as St. Photina, on
March 20.

For ἀντλεῖν, the regular word for drawing water from a
well, see on 2⁸· ⁹ above.

δός μοι πεῖν.   So א*B*C*DL; the rec. has πιεῖν.   This is
a common Greek constr.; cf. Xen. Cyrop. VII. i. 1, τῷ δὲ Κύρῳ
. . . προσήνεγκαν ἐμφαγεῖν καὶ πιεῖν, and see v. 33.

8. οἱ γὰρ μαθηταὶ αὐτοῦ κτλ., "For His disciples had gone
into the city (sc. Sychar, vv. 5, 39) to buy food."   Had they
been with Him, they would have been the natural persons
to draw water for their Master, and He would not have had
need to ask of a stranger.   Probably they carried with them
an ἄντλημα, or skin-bucket, as part of their travelling equip-
ment, in which water could be drawn.   The woman notices
that Jesus has no ἄντλημα (v. 11).

We do not know which of His disciples were with Jesus
on this journey (see on 2²), or how many there were.   See
further on v. 18.

Syr. sin. places this clause in its chronological order after
πηγῇ (v. 6), a rearrangement of the text made for the sake of
clearness; ¹ but the use of parenthesis is quite in Jn.'s style
(see, e.g., 2⁶).

τροφάς, victuals, only here in pl. number.

That the disciples should buy victuals in a Samaritan town
shows that the barrier between Jew and Samaritan was not
impassable.   The rule as to food seems to have varied from

¹ See Introd., p. xxvii.

9. λέγει οὖν αὐτῷ ἡ γυνὴ ἡ Σαμαρεῖτις Πῶς σὺ Ἰουδαῖος ὢν παρ' ἐμοῦ πεῖν αἰτεῖς γυναικὸς Σαμαρείτιδος οὔσης; οὐ γὰρ συνχρῶνται Ἰουδαῖοι Σαμαρείταις. 10. ἀπεκρίθη Ἰησοῦς καὶ εἶπεν αὐτῇ Εἰ ᾔδεις τὴν δωρεὰν

time to time. One Rabbinical precept is, " Let no man eat the bread of the Cuthæans, for he that eateth their bread is as he that eateth swine's flesh " (M. Shebhiith, viii. 10), and Samaritan wine was forbidden to a Jew. But, on the other hand, " the victuals of the Cuthæans are permitted if not mixed with wine or vinegar " (Jerus. Ab. Zar. v. 4), and their unleavened bread was allowed (Bab. Kidd. 76a).[1] There was continuous traffic of Jews through Samaria—from Galilee to Jerusalem, and from Jerusalem to Galilee—and it is unlikely, except at moments of intense theological excitement, that a hungry traveller would have scrupled to buy bread in a Samaritan village, or that a Samaritan villager would have scrupled to sell it.

9. Πῶς σὺ Ἰουδαῖος ὢν κτλ. The Samaritan woman affects surprise—for her words are ironical—that a Jew should ask her for water. There was nothing strange in asking a woman for water, as it was women who generally drew it from the wells; cf. Gen. 24[17]. However bitter the feeling between Jew and Samaritan, we cannot suppose that a draught of cold water in the noontide heat would be likely to be refused by either to other. It was counted the mark of a wicked man " not to have given water to the weary to drink " (Job. 22[7]); and the precept of kindness was universal: " If thine enemy be thirsty, give him water to drink " (Prov. 25[21]). Yet the woman makes her little gibe—half-jest, half-earnest—recalling to Jesus the old feud between Jews and Samaritans. She recognised Jesus as a Jew, perhaps by His dress or perhaps by His manner of speech (cf. Mt. 26[73]). The narrative does not say explicitly that she granted the request of Jesus, Δός μοι πεῖν, but the reader is intended to understand that she did so.

The explanatory comment οὐ γὰρ συγχρῶνται Ἰουδαῖοι Σαμαρείταις, " for Jews do not treat familiarly with Samaritans," is omitted by ℵ*D a b e, but it must be retained with ℵ[a]ABCLT[b]WNΘ. συγχρᾶσθαι does not occur again in N.T., but it appears in Ignat. Magn. 3, ὑμῖν δὲ πρέπει μὴ συγχρᾶσθαι τῇ ἡλικίᾳ τοῦ ἐπισκόπου, " it becomes you not to presume upon the youth of your bishop," to treat him with undue familiarity.

If συνχρῶνται is translated " have dealings with," co-utuntur, the comment would not be accurate; for although Jews and Samaritans were intolerant of each other (cf. Lk. 9[53], Jn. 8[48]), of necessity there was much business intercourse. As v. 8

[1] See, for these Talmudical references, D.C.G., s.v. " Samaria."

τοῦ Θεοῦ, καὶ τίς ἐστιν ὁ λέγων σοι Δός μοι πεῖν, σὺ ἂν ᾔτησας αὐτὸν καὶ ἔδωκεν ἄν σοι ὕδωρ ζῶν.   11. λέγει αὐτῷ ἡ γυνή· Κύριε,

indicates, Jews could trade with Samaritans, as indeed they could do with heathen (cf. Neh. 13[16]). The comment is not that of the Samaritan woman, but of the evangelist, and is quite in his manner (cf. Introd., p. xxxiv).

10. ἀπεκρ. καὶ εἶπ. For the constr., see on 1[50].

εἰ ᾔδεις τὴν δωρ. κτλ., "If thou knewest the gift of God"; cf. 8[19]. δωρεά, a free gift, occurs in the Gospels adverbially (Mt. 10[8]), and is always used in the Acts and Epistles of a *divine* gift. It refers here to the "living water" mentioned in the next sentence, *i.e.* to the gift of the Holy Spirit (which δωρεά always indicates in the Acts). Some commentators have referred to 3[16], and have interpreted it of the gift which God gave of His Son, and the revelation of salvation through Him.

τίς ἐστιν ὁ λέγων σοι. The woman had taken Him for a Jew. But He was no ordinary Jew, and if she had understood who He was, *she* would have been the suppliant (σὺ ἂν ᾔτησας αὐτόν, "It is *you* who would have asked *Him*), and He would have granted her request (cf. Mt. 7[7]); He would have given her "living water."

ἔδωκεν ἄν σοι ὕδωρ ζῶν. This saying was paradoxical in its form, like the saying with which the attention of Nicodemus was arrested (3[3]). The woman did not understand it (v. 11), nor could she have been expected to do so. But Jesus is here following the method by which He was accustomed to convey instruction to simple people who were willing to learn; and the discourse which follows may be particularly compared with 6[26f.]. The plan of these instructions, for which there are Synoptic parallels, has been discussed in the Introduction, p. cxi.

ὕδωρ ζῶν. "Living water" is water issuing from a spring or fountain, unlike the water in Jacob's Well, which was due to percolation and rainfall,[1] being collected in a kind of cistern or pit (τὸ φρέαρ, v. 12). This was good water, but had not the virtues of "running" or "living" water, such as was always preferred, especially for purposes of purification (Gen. 26[19], Lev. 14[5], Num. 19[17]).

Water was full of symbolism to Eastern thought, and in the O.T. it is often symbolic of the Divine Wisdom which is the source of life. Thus "the law of the wise" is πηγὴ ζωῆς (Prov. 13[14]; cf. Prov. 14[27]). The Son of Sirach declares that he that possesses the law shall obtain wisdom: "with bread of understanding shall she feed him, and give him water of

---
[1] See *D.C.G.* ii. 40a.

οὔτε ἄντλημα ἔχεις καὶ τὸ φρέαρ ἐστὶν βαθύ· πόθεν οὖν ἔχεις τὸ ὕδωρ τὸ ζῶν; 12. μὴ σὺ μείζων εἶ τοῦ πατρὸς ἡμῶν Ἰακώβ, ὃς ἔδωκεν ἡμῖν

wisdom to drink " (Ecclus. 15². ³). Zechariah's vision of hope is that " living waters shall go out from Jerusalem " (Zech. 14⁸; cf. Ezek. 47¹, Joel 3¹⁸), *i.e.* that in the glorious future the blessings of the Law shall be extended far and wide. The promise of Isaiah (12³) is " with joy shall ye draw water out of the wells of salvation," a passage specially parallel to the declaration of Christ here.

" If thou hadst known who it is that speaketh to thee, thou wouldest have asked Him, and He would have given thee living water." To appreciate the depth of this saying, it must be remembered that, according to the O.T., it is Yahweh Himself who is the Fountain of living waters (Ps. 36⁹, Jer. 2¹³ 17¹³; cf. Cant. 4¹⁵, where the mystic Bride is described as φρέαρ ὕδατος ζῶντος). So also in the Apocalypse, the river of the Water of Life proceeds from the throne of God and of the Lamb (Rev. 22¹; cf. Rev. 7¹⁷). Thus the statement of Jesus to the Woman of Samaria that, had He been asked, He would have given her living water, implies His claim to be One with the Lord of the O.T. prophets, who is alone the Source and Spring of the living waters which refresh the soul and assuage the spiritual thirst of men. See further on v. 14.

Note that Jesus does not call Himself the Living Water, although He calls Himself the Living Bread (6⁵¹). It is from Him that the Living Water proceeds, for this is the symbol of the Spirit which He was to send (7³⁹).

There is no exact parallel in Philo to this doctrine of the Living Water which flows from the Word, although the similar idea expounded by St. Paul (1 Cor. 10⁴) of the mystical meaning of the Rock in the Desert from which water flowed forth for the refreshment of Israel is found in *Leg. Alleg.* ii. 21 : ἡ γὰρ ἀκρότομος πέτρα ἡ σοφία τοῦ θεοῦ ἐστιν, ἣν ἄκραν καὶ πρωτίστην ἔτεμεν ἀπὸ τῶν ἑαυτοῦ δυνάμεων, ἐξ ἧς ποτίζει τὰς φιλοθέους ψυχάς.

In the Messianic forecast of Isa. 35⁷ one of the promised blessings was εἰς τὴν διψῶσαν γῆν πηγὴ ὕδατος, and at v. 26 below (where see note) Jesus is represented as declaring that He was Messiah. See on 9¹ for a quotation of this Messianic passage by Justin Martyr.

11. κύριε. She is impressed by the Speaker, and so addresses Him now (cf. vv. 15–19) in terms of respect (see on 1³⁸). How could He provide spring water, or water of any kind, without a bucket (ἄντλημα ; cf. v. 8) ?

For **φρέαρ** and its depth, see on v. 6. The broken constr. οὔτε . . . καί is found only once again in N.T., at 3 Jn.¹⁰.

τὸ φρέαρ, καὶ αὐτὸς ἐξ αὐτοῦ ἔπιεν καὶ οἱ υἱοὶ αὐτοῦ καὶ τὰ θρέμματα
αὐτοῦ; 13. ἀπεκρίθη Ἰησοῦς καὶ εἶπεν αὐτῇ Πᾶς ὁ πίνων ἐκ τοῦ
ὕδατος τούτου διψήσει πάλιν· 14. ὃς δ᾽ ἂν πίῃ ἐκ τοῦ ὕδατος οὗ ἐγὼ

λέγει αὐτῷ ἡ γυνή. B, with the Coptic Q and Syr. sin.,
omits ἡ γυνή; but ins. אᶜACDLTᵇWΘ.

12. It could not be from the well, that Jesus would provide
living water. Whence then could He get it? Even Jacob
got water for himself and his household from this well. Was
the Speaker greater than Jacob, who had to draw the water
from the well like any one else?

μὴ σὺ μείζων εἶ τοῦ πατρὸς ἡμῶν Ἰακώβ; See 6³¹ and cf. the
similar question put by the Jews (8⁵³), "Art thou greater than
our father Abraham?"

"Our father Jacob." The Samaritans claimed descent
from Joseph, through Ephraim and Manasseh (Josephus,
Antt. xi. 8. 6).

ὃς ἔδωκεν ἡμῖν τὸ φρέαρ. Field compares Pausan. iii. 25. 3:
ἔστι δὲ ἐν τῇ Πυρρίχῳ φρέαρ ἐν τῇ ἀγορᾷ, δοῦναι δέ σφισι τὸν
Σιληνὸν νομίζουσι.

θρέμμα is a word occurring nowhere else in the Greek Bible.
τὰ θρέμματα means "cattle," a usage of which Wetstein gives
many instances; etymologically, it might include also Jacob's
servants or retainers, all who were fed by him.

13, 14. Jesus explains to the puzzled woman that He does
not speak of ordinary spring water. Those who drink of it will
thirst again; but the Living Water satisfies eternally (οὐ μὴ
διψήσει εἰς τὸν αἰῶνα: cf. 6³⁵). The parallels between this
discourse and that of 6²⁶ᶠ· have been exhibited in the Introduction, p. cxi.

14. "It shall become in him a fountain of water springing
up unto eternal life." In v. 10 the thought is of God as the
Eternal Fountain; but it was also a Hebrew thought that the
man who has assimilated the Divine Wisdom becomes himself,
as it were, a fountain from which streams of the water of life
proceed. Thus the promise of Isa. 58¹¹ is, "Thou shalt be
like a spring of water, whose waters fail not." Schoettgen
quotes an apposite saying from the Talmud: "Quando homo
se convertit ad dominum suum, tanquam fons aquis uiuis
impletur, et fluenta eius egrediuntur ad omnis generis homines
et ad omnes tribus." And similarly Wetstein quotes from
Tanchuma, f. 17. 1: "Unde Abrahamus didicit legem? R.
Simeon filius Jochai dixit: bini renes eius tanquam binae
lagenae aquarum factae sunt, ex quibus lex promanavit."
See on 7³⁸ below.

The passage in Ecclus. 24²¹⁻³¹ about the Divine Wisdom

δώσω αὐτῷ, οὐ μὴ διψήσει εἰς τὸν αἰῶνα, ἀλλὰ τὸ ὕδωρ ὃ δώσω
αὐτῷ γενήσεται ἐν αὐτῷ πηγὴ ὕδατος ἀλλομένου εἰς ζωὴν αἰώνιον.

presents some parallels to these thoughts. The stream of the
waters of Wisdom comes originally from God: "Her thoughts
are filled from the sea, and her counsels from the great deep"
(v. 29). Of the wise man increasing in wisdom it may be
said, "My stream became a river, and my river became a sea"
(v. 31); these waters of Wisdom lose themselves at last in the
same eternal Ocean whence they sprang. Cf. Ps. 36⁹ παρὰ
σοὶ πηγὴ ζωῆς. The water of life is, as Jesus says here, πηγὴ
ὕδατος ἀλλομένου εἰς ζωὴν αἰώνιον, *leaping forth to eternal life.*
C. Wesley puts it all in familiar words:

> "Thou of life the Fountain art,
> Freely let me take of Thee;
> *Spring Thou up within my heart,*
> Rise to all eternity."

The verb ἅλλομαι does not seem to be applied elsewhere
to the action of water. But water in this passage is symbolic of
the Spirit (cf. 7³⁸ᶠ·); and "ἅλλομαι or ἐφάλλομαι in LXX is
applied to the action of a 'spirit of God,' forcing its way or
falling violently on Samson, Saul, and David."[1] It may be,
therefore, as E. A. Abbott has suggested, that ἀλλομένου is
used here with special reference to the action of the Holy Spirit,
vehement like that of rushing waters. If that be so, εἰς ζωὴν
αἰώνιον expresses the *purpose* of this spiritual torrent of grace;
it is " with a view to eternal life."

There seems to be a reminiscence of this passage in Ignatius,
Rom. 7, ὕδωρ δὲ ζῶν καὶ λαλοῦν† ἐν ἐμοί, where Lightfoot
supposes the MS. reading to be a corruption of ὕδωρ δὲ ζῶν καὶ
ἀλλόμενον. It is possible that there is also a trace of it in
Justin (*Tryph.* 69). Commenting on Isa. 35⁷ he says: πηγὴ
ὕδατος ζῶντος παρὰ θεοῦ . . . ἀνέβλυσεν (*i.e.* has gushed forth)
οὗτος ὁ Χριστός. Cf. also *Tryph.* 114, and see on 7³⁸.

Verses 10 and 14 are quoted explicitly in *Pistis Sophia*, c.141.

In one important particular, at least, the promise of Jesus
about the Living Water transcends what is said about the
Water of Wisdom by the Son of Sirach. "They that drink
me shall yet be thirsty" are the words of Ecclus. 24²¹; the
spiritual thirst is insatiable, so far as the Hebrew sage knew.
But Jesus said: "Whosoever shall drink of the water that I
shall give him shall never thirst" (cf. 6³⁵). To him who has
appropriated the revelation of God in Christ, there is no sense of
imperfection in the Divine gift, no dissatisfaction with it as
insufficient. The Living Water is always quickening, always

[1] Abbott, *Diat.* 2315; cf. Judg. 14⁶· ¹⁹ 15¹⁴, 1 Sam. 10¹⁰ 16¹³.

15. λέγει πρὸς αὐτὸν ἡ γυνή Κύριε, δός μοι τοῦτο τὸ ὕδωρ, ἵνα μὴ διψῶ μηδὲ ἔρχωμαι ἐνθάδε ἀντλεῖν. 16. λέγει αὐτῇ Ὕπαγε φώνησον

flowing in correspondence with human need. As Bengel puts it: "ubi sitis occurrit, hominis non aquae defectus est." The promise of Jesus is that those who "thirst after righteousness shall be filled" (χορτασθήσονται, Mt. 5⁶).

With ἐκ τοῦ ὕδατος οὗ ἐγὼ δώσω αὐτῷ cf. ὁ ἄρτος ὃν ἐγὼ δώσω of 6⁵¹. אDT^bWN, with the Lat. and Syr. vss. generally, insert ἐγώ before the second δώσω; but om. ABCLΓΔΘ.

εἰς τὸν αἰῶνα, "for ever." This is a common phrase in the LXX and occurs elsewhere in the N.T.; but it is especially frequent in Jn. (6⁵¹· ⁵⁸ 8³⁵· ⁵¹· ⁵² 10²⁸ 11²⁶ 12³⁴ 13⁸ 14¹⁶, 1 Jn. 2¹⁷, 2 Jn.²).

The phrase εἰς ζωὴν αἰώνιον first appears in 4 Macc. 15³, where a mother prefers to the temporal safety of her sons τὴν εὐσέβειαν ... τὴν σώζουσαν εἰς αἰώνιον ζωὴν κατὰ θεόν. It appears again in Jn. 4³⁶ 6²⁷ 12²⁵, Rom. 5²¹, 1 Tim. 1¹⁶, and Jude²¹, and in each case the reference is to the future life, the life after death (see note on 3¹⁵).

15. λέγει πρὸς αὐτόν. For the constr., see on 2³. For κύριε. cf. v. 11.

δός μοι τοῦτο τὸ ὕδωρ. Cf. 6³⁴ δὸς ἡμῖν τὸν ἄρτον τοῦτον. The woman did not understand Jesus' words about the Water which assuages thirst for ever; and her reply is a puzzled request: "Give me this water, that I may not be thirsty, and need not come hither continually to draw from the well." She speaks half in irony; for she does not believe in any πηγὴ ὕδατος such as Jesus had incomprehensibly spoken of as being "in" the recipient of His gift.

The rec. text has ἔρχωμαι with ACDWΓΔΘ; but א*B support διέρχωμαι. As Field points out, διέρχωμαι may have arisen from a mistake in transcribing ΜΗΔΕΕΡΧΩΜΑΙ; but in any case the prep. διά does not add special force to the verb here (cf. Lk. 2¹⁵).

ἵνα μὴ διψῶ κτλ. For ἵνα with the pres. subj., cf. 6²⁹, 1 Jn. 1³ 2²⁷ 5³.

16. The exact bearing of the words of Jesus, "Go, call thy husband, and come hither," is not easy to determine. Perhaps the woman was going off, after her last retort, and Jesus bade her come back again with her "husband," as He wished to carry on His ministry at Sychar (v. 39). He had observed her intelligence, and He knew her need. Another interpretation of the words is that Jesus wished, by mentioning her "husband," to recall her to a sense of her sad condition, that thus the way might be opened for a fuller presentation to her

τὸν ἄνδρα σου καὶ ἐλθὲ ἐνθάδε. 17. ἀπεκρίθη ἡ γυνὴ καὶ εἶπεν
Οὐκ ἔχω ἄνδρα. λέγει αὐτῇ ὁ Ἰησοῦς Καλῶς εἶπες ὅτι Ἄνδρα οὐκ
ἔχω· 18. πέντε γὰρ ἄνδρας ἔσχες, καὶ νῦν ὃν ἔχεις οὐκ ἔστιν σου
ἀνήρ· τοῦτο ἀληθὲς εἴρηκας. 19. λέγει αὐτῷ ἡ γυνή Κύριε, θεωρῶ

of His message. We cannot in any case assume that more
than a fragment of the conversation has been preserved, and
much that was said is, no doubt, omitted in the narrative of
Jn. (see on v. 18).

For the verb ὑπάγειν, see on 16⁷; and for the aor. imper.
φώνησον, see on 2⁵.

17. καὶ εἶπεν. So אᶜADLNΓΔΘ, but BCW Syr. sin. and
Syr. cur. add αὐτῷ.

The woman, by this time, feels that she is in the presence of
One to whom she cannot lie, and she confesses, " I have no
husband." Jesus gently shows her that He knows all about
that, and about her past. " You had five husbands, and he
whom thou hast now is not thy husband." Jn. frequently lays
stress on the power which Jesus had of reading men's hearts
(cf. 1⁴⁸, 2²⁴· ²⁵). If the report of His words here is precise, He
showed more than natural insight, and this the evangelist
evidently means to suggest. But (see on v. 18) we have to
remember that the record of this conversation probably depends
on the subsequent report of the woman (v. 27), and in regard
to some details she may have confused what her own guilty
conscience told her with what Jesus saw in her face. On the
other hand, to have had five husbands in succession would be
an unusual experience, and the woman may have been notorious
for the number of her marriages. But there is no hint in the
narrative that Jesus had heard of her before, although there is
nothing to exclude this possibility.

18. πέντε ἄνδρας. It is remarkable that Heracleon (according to Origen) read ἐξ ἄνδρας, a reading unknown elsewhere.
Origen, himself, finds allegory in the number *five*, and says
that it refers to the fact that the Samaritans only recognised
as canonical the five books of Moses.[1]

For ἀληθές, א has ἀληθῶς.

Upon the words πέντε γὰρ ἄνδρας ἔσχες κτλ. has been
built a theory that the narrative of the Samaritan woman at
the well is an allegory from beginning to end, and that the
woman is a symbol of the Samaritan people. It is recorded
(2 Kings 17²⁴ᶠ·) that the King of Assyria brought colonists from
Babylon, Cuthah, Avva, Hamath, and Sepharvaim, and planted
them in Samaria; and that each set of colonists brought with
them the cult of their former national deities, who were wor-

[1] Comm. *in Jn.* (ed. Brooke), ii. 271.

shipped side by side with Yahweh. Here then are the five " husbands " of the Samaritan woman, while the husband who was " not a husband " stands for the spurious cult of Yahweh, which to the Jews was little better than heathenism.[1] But this ingenious interpretation will not bear analysis. It appears from the narrative in 2 Kings 17[30, 31] that not five, but seven, strange deities were introduced into Samaria from Assyria.[2] Further, these were not the objects of worship in succession, but simultaneously, so that the supposed analogy to the successive husbands of the Samaritan woman breaks down. Again, the allegory would imply that the heathen deities had been the legitimate gods of Samaria, while Yahweh whom she came to worship was not a true " husband " at all, and that therefore Samaria's relation to Yahweh was that of an illegitimate and shameful sort, shame equally resting on her and Him who was not her " husband."   No Christian writer of the first century, or of any century, would have ventured to construct an allegory so blasphemous when its implications are examined. This fancy may safely be rejected.

Another suggestion is that " he whom thou hast is not thy husband " alludes to Simon Magus, who had a great influence in Samaria (Acts 8[9-11]).

But the simplest interpretation is the best. The narrative is a genuine reminiscence of an incident that actually happened, recorded many years after the event, and probably—so far as the words of the conversation are concerned—with much freedom. That Jesus expressed Himself so tersely and even enigmatically, to an ignorant woman, as the deep saying of v. 14 would suggest, without explaining what He said more fully, is improbable. On the other hand, the vividness and simplicity of the story have the note of actuality. The narrative brings out clearly the main features of the interview between Jesus and the woman, and it is easy to follow the general lines of their conversation.

When the woman got back to her friends (v. 29) she reported in eager haste what her experience had been, and told them what Jesus had said to her. She may have exaggerated or confused words here and there, but that the incident became known to any one was probably due to her own talk about it. Jesus seems to have been alone with her (v. 27), but this is not certain. If we could suppose that one of the disciples remained with his Master at the well, while the others went into Sychar to make their purchases (which would *a priori* be probable), then we should be able to refer the report of the conversation

---

[1] So Pfleiderer, *Primitive Christianity*, iv. 30.
[2] Nevertheless, Josephus (*Antt.* ix. 14. 3) counts them as *five*.

ὅτι προφήτης εἶ σύ. 20. οἱ πατέρες ἡμῶν ἐν τῷ ὄρει τούτῳ προσε-
κύνησαν· καὶ ὑμεῖς λέγετε ὅτι ἐν Ἱεροσολύμοις ἐστὶν ὁ τόπος ὅπου

to the disciple's recollection, as well as to the woman's account
of it. And that the disciple who remained with his Master is
not mentioned by the evangelist would not surprise us if he
were John the son of Zebedee, who is kept so much out of sight
in the Fourth Gospel, while at the same time his reminiscences
are behind large parts of it. But this only can be affirmed with
certainty, that the woman told the story to her fellow-villagers,
and with such emphasis that many of them "believed on"
Jesus, so that He (and no doubt His disciples) stayed at Sychar
for two days (v. 40). All the disciples who were present (see
on v. 8) must have become thoroughly familiar with her report.

19. For κύριε, see v. 11, and for the shades of meaning of
θεωρεῖν see on 2²³.

κύριε, θεωρῶ κτλ., "Sir, I perceive," sc. from what you
have said, "that you are a prophet" (cf. 9¹⁷, Lk. 7¹⁶, "a
prophet" not "the prophet"). A prophet was one who had
special powers of insight, as well as of foresight. Cf. Lk. 7³⁹,
where the Pharisee objects that if Jesus were really a prophet
He would have known that the woman with the cruse of oint-
ment was a sinner. The Samaritan woman was astonished at
the knowledge of her personal history which Jesus displayed,
and, by her reply, she virtually confesses that it is witl her
even as He had said.

20. The woman diverts the conversation to another subject,
and proceeds to raise a theological difficulty, either to evade the
personal issue, or because she was honestly anxious to learn
what a prophet with such wonderful insight would say about
the standing controversy between Jews and Samaritans.
Probably both motives affected her.

οἱ πατέρες ἡμῶν κτλ., "Our fathers worshipped in this
mountain," i.e. Mount Gerizim, at the foot of which Jacob's
Well is situated. Abraham (Gen. 12⁷) and Jacob (Gen. 33²⁰)
had set up altars at Shechem; and the Samaritan Pentateuch
at Deut. 27⁴ recorded the setting up of an altar in Mount
Gerizim (the true reading being Mount Ebal); cf. also Deut.
11²⁹ 27¹². After the Return from the Babylonian Captivity,
the Jews and Samaritans parted company, and a temple was
erected on Mount Gerizim about 400 B.C. It was destroyed
by John Hyrcanus about 129 B.C.; but the *odium theologicum*
grew more bitter thereafter, and in the first century the hatred
between Jew and Samaritan was ready to break out at any
moment.

καὶ ὑμεῖς λέγετε κτλ., "and you (i.e. the Jews) say that

προσκυνεῖν δεῖ. 21. λέγει αὐτῇ ὁ Ἰησοῦς Πίστευέ μοι, γύναι, ὅτι ἔρχεται ὥρα ὅτε οὔτε ἐν τῷ ὄρει τούτῳ οὔτε ἐν Ἱεροσολύμοις προσκυνή-

in Jerusalem is the place where one ought to worship." ὁ τόπος is " the place (Deut. 12⁵) which the Lord your God shall choose . . . to put His Name there " (cf. Deut 16² 26³), but the name of the place is not given in the Books of the Law, and the Samaritans recognised no later Scriptures (as they deemed them). Thus such passages as 2 Chron. 6⁶ 7¹², Ps. 78⁶⁸, to which Jews appealed as justifying their claim for Jerusalem as the appointed religious centre, were not recognised as authoritative by Samaritans. For τόπος as indicating the Temple, see 11⁴⁸.

J. Lightfoot [1] illustrates this passage by the following from *Bereshith Rabba*, § 32 : "R. Jochanan going to Jerusalem to pray, passed by Mount Gerizim. A certain Samaritan, seeing him, asked him, 'Whither goest thou?' 'I am,' saith he ' going to Jerusalem to pray.' To whom the Samaritan, ' Were it not better for thee to pray in this holy mountain than in that cursed house '?" Cf. Lk. 9⁵³ and Jn. 8⁴⁸.

The verb προσκυνεῖν is used absolutely here and at 12²⁰; it may be followed either by a dative, 4²¹. ²³ 9³⁸ (as always in Mk. and Paul), or by an accusative, 4²². ²³ (as in Lk. 24⁵²). It is noteworthy that in the Apocalypse, where it occurs 25 times, there is the same variety of construction as in Jn. Cf. Rev. 5¹⁴ for the same absolute use as here.[2] The word always stands in Jn. for *divine* worship, while elsewhere it sometimes signifies no more than respect (cf. Mt. 18²⁶ and perhaps Mt. 8²).

21. πίστευέ μοι, γύναι, is read by אBC*LW; the rec. has γύναι, πίστευσόν μοι (ADNΓΔΘ).

πίστευέ μοι, a unique phrase in the Greek Bible, calls attention to the fact that what follows is deliberately said: the more usual ἀμὴν ἀμήν does not occur in this chapter (see on 1⁵¹). In a monastic Rule formerly ascribed to St. Benedict it was laid down that no stronger form of asseveration than this is to be used : " iuramentum aliud nemo proferat, nisi *Crede mihi*, sicut in euangeliis legimus dominum Samaritanae affirmasse, aut *Certe* aut *Sane*." [3]

γύναι; see on 2⁴.

ἔρχεται ὥρα, " an hour is coming ": so v. 23, 5²⁵. ²⁸

[1] *Horæ Hebr.* iii. 279.
[2] Abbott (*Diat.* 1647 ff.) distinguishes προσκυνεῖν with dat. as a Jewish constr. meaning "to prostrate oneself," from προσκ. followed by acc. as a Greek constr. indicating a more spiritual form of " worship." But this is not really involved.
[3] From the document called *Ordo qualiter* (Migne, P.L. lxvi. 938), an eighth-century supplement to the Benedictine Rule.

σετε τῷ Πατρί. 22. ὑμεῖς προσκυνεῖτε ὃ οὐκ οἴδατε, ἡμεῖς προσ·

16². ²⁵. ³². That the phrase occurs 7 times exactly is noted by Abbott (*Diat.* 2625).

It is not ἡ ὥρα, for the thought of the inevitableness of the predestined hour (see on 2⁴) is not present here; cf. Lk. 17²².

οὔτε . . . οὔτε . . ., "not (only) in Gerizim and not (only) in Jerusalem." These ancient rivalries will disappear when the spirituality of true religion is fully realised. The prophets had already taken this wide view. "Men shall worship Yahweh, every one from his place," was the vision of Zephaniah (2¹¹): "in every place incense is offered unto my Name, and a pure offering," was Malachi's forecast (1¹¹). The words ascribed to Jesus here are in entire harmony with His saying about the destruction of the Temple, and its replacement by the spiritual temple of believers (see on 2¹⁹). Cf. Acts 7⁴⁸ 17²⁴. ²⁵.

"The Father," not as contrasted with "the Son" (see 3³⁵), but as the Father of all men. The Samaritan woman had referred to "our father Jacob," and "our fathers (who) worshipped" in Gerizim (vv. 12, 20); but pride of ancestry is to be replaced by the thought of the universal Fatherhood of God, when questions pertaining to worship are being answered.

ὁ πατήρ is a very frequent designation of God in Jn.; but it nearly always occurs in connexion with the thought of the Sonship of Christ. Here, however, it is rather "the Universal Father"; perhaps we may compare 8²⁷ 16²⁶ᶠ. (see on 6²⁷).

22. This verse is an assertion of the superiority of the Jewish religion to the Samaritan, not based on any difference as to the *place* of worship, but rather on the difference as to their knowledge of the *Object* of worship. "Ye," *i.e.* the Samaritans, "worship that which ye know not" (cf. ἣν ὑμεῖς οὐκ οἴδατε in v. 32). They accepted Yahweh for the true God, indeed, but they knew little about Him. By refusing to recognise the writings of the prophets and psalmists they had shut themselves off from all revelation of God except that which was contained in the Law. The Athenian inscription ᾿Αγνώστῳ θεῷ quoted in Acts 17²³ provides no parallel to the ignorance of the Samaritans. The Samaritans knew, as the Athenians professedly did not know, the Name of the God to whom they erected their altar on Mount Gerizim; but their ignorance was an ignorance of His character and purposes.

"We," on the other hand, *i.e.* the Jews, "worship that which we know" (but cf. 7²⁸), the same God as the God of the Samaritans, but known to Jews as He was not known to

κυνοῦμεν ὃ οἴδαμεν, ὅτι ἡ σωτηρία ἐκ τῶν Ἰουδαίων ἐστίν· 23. ἀλλὰ

Samaritans; cf. Ps. 147[19. 20].[1] The Jews were the chosen people, "whose is the adoption and the glory and the covenants, and the giving of the law, and the service (of God), and the promises" (Rom. 9[4]). Paul's enumeration of their prerogatives is not more emphatic than the calm statement, "We worship that which we know." The woman of Samaria is not permitted to suppose that the Speaker believes the Samaritan religion to be as good as the Jewish, although He tells her that in the future their poor rivalries as to their respective sanctuaries will be disregarded as of no consequence. He gives the reason why the Jewish religion is, and must be, superior: ἡ σωτηρία ἐκ τῶν Ἰουδαίων ἐστίν.

ἡ σωτηρία, "*the* salvation," the Messianic deliverance (see on 3[17]), was the central thought of Jewish national expectation (cf. Lk. 1[69. 71. 77], Acts 13[26. 47]). It was to come from the tribe of Judah, ἐκ τῶν Ἰουδαίων, as distinct from the other tribes; cf. Gen. 49[10] (a passage which Samaritans accepted as canonical, although they do not seem to have taken it as Messianic), Isa. 59[20] (quoted Rom. 11[26]). Later Judaism held firmly to this conviction of Jewish prerogative. Cf. *Test. of XII. Patr.*, Dan. v. 10, "There shall arise unto you from the tribe of [Judah and] Levi the salvation of Yahweh"; see also Gad viii. 1, Naph. viii. 2). See further for σωτήρ, σωτηρία, on 4[42]. Here the point is that the Messianic deliverance was to be ἐκ τῶν Ἰουδαίων. For the constr. εἶναι ἐκ . . . cf. 1[46] 7[22. 52] 10[16]; and for "the Jews" in the Fourth Gospel, see on 1[19].

The force of ἡμεῖς must be observed: "*We* worship that which we know." Jesus, here, definitely associates Himself with the Jews; He *is* a Jew. Their God is His God. Nowhere in the Gospels is there another passage so emphatic as this, in its assertion of the common nationality of Jesus and the Jews who rejected Him; cf. Mt. 15[24]. Here He associates Himself with Jews in a common worship. The plural οἴδαμεν in 3[11] (see note) is not a true parallel to this. See on 15[25].

In this verse are expressed the worthiness of Jewish worship and the supreme privilege of the Jewish race; but in v. 23 we have on the other hand the simplicity of the ideal worship of God and the catholicity of true religion. Both aspects are included in the Fourth Gospel. The evangelist is not forgetful of the debt which Christianity owes to Judaism, while he views Christianity *sub specie æternitatis* as for all men and for all time.

23, 24. The repetition of τοὺς προσκυνοῦντας seems to have misled scribes and translators, so that there are a good many

[1] Cf., however, 8[54].

ἔρχεται ὥρα καὶ νῦν ἐστιν, ὅτε οἱ ἀληθινοὶ προσκυνηταὶ προσκυνήσουσιν τῷ Πατρὶ ἐν πνεύματι καὶ ἀληθείᾳ· καὶ γὰρ ὁ Πατὴρ τοιούτους ζητεῖ τοὺς προσκυνοῦντας αὐτόν· 24. Πνεῦμα ὁ Θεός, καὶ τοὺς

minor variants, but none calling for special notice. Syr. cur. exhibits extraordinary confusion here, for in it v. 24 runs as follows: " For God is a Spirit, and those that worship Him in spirit, and to worship for them it behoves, even those that in spirit and in truth worship Him." [1]

23. ἔρχεται ὥρα, repeated from v. 21 (where see note), the theme of that verse, which has been temporarily abandoned in v. 22, being resumed. It is a question whether καὶ νῦν ἐστίν, both here and at 5²⁵, should not be treated as an editorial comment on the words of Jesus. But probably the words " and now is " are appended to " an hour is coming," to obviate any misunderstanding. Jesus has told the Samaritan woman that the old rivalries as to sanctuary are passing away, and that in the future " the true worshippers shall worship the Father in spirit and in truth." But that is not confined to the future; it may be equally asserted of the present, that true worshippers worship thus. See on 5²⁵.

For the word ἀληθινός, " genuine," see on 1⁹. Here οἱ ἀληθινοὶ προσκυνηταί is equivalent to " the genuine worshippers ": at whatever altar they worship, they worship ἐν πνεύματι καὶ ἀληθείᾳ.

The πνεῦμα is the highest in man, for it associates him with God who *is* Spirit. In so far as a man walks κατὰ πνεῦμα, does he realise the dignity of his being (cf. Rom. 8⁵). To worship ἐν πνεύματι is, then, to worship in harmony with the Divine Spirit, and so to worship in truth (cf. 16¹³ τὸ πνεῦμα τῆς ἀληθείας). This is a general statement, and we must not bring in here thoughts which are peculiar to Christian doctrine, because of that fuller revelation of God which was granted in the Incarnation. Indeed, Philo has a passage precisely parallel: γνήσιοι [θεραπεῖαι] δὲ εἰσὶν αἱ ψυχῆς ψιλὴν καὶ μόνην θυσίαν φερούσης, ἀλήθειαν, *sc.* " Genuine religious services are those of a soul offering the plain and only sacrifice, viz. truth " (*quod. det. pot. insid.* 7). Cf. Ps. 145¹⁸.

καὶ γάρ only occurs again in Jn. at 4⁴⁵; it seems to mean " for indeed " (but cf. Abbott, *Diat.* 2167).

ὁ πατήρ, the Universal Father; see on v. 21.

ζητεῖ, " seeks." It is not only that the true worshippers are accepted of God, but that He seeks for such. The approach

---

[1] See Burkitt, *Evangelion da Mepharreshê*, ii. 219, and cf. Rendel Harris, *Cod. Bezæ*, p. 246, who would trace the error to the Western colometry of D.

προσκυνοῦντας ἐν πνεύματι καὶ ἀληθείᾳ δεῖ προσκυνεῖν. 25. λέγει αὐτῷ ἡ γυνή Οἶδα ὅτι Μεσσίας ἔρχεται, ὁ λεγόμενος Χριστός· ὅταν

of man to God is not initiated by man; the first movement of love is on the side of God. This is the constant teaching of Jn.; cf. 1 Jn. 4¹⁰, and Jn. 3¹⁶ 6⁴⁴ 15¹⁶. It is a phase of that doctrine of pre-destination which underlies the Fourth Gospel; see note on 3¹⁴. The *gift* of the Spirit is a necessary preliminary to spiritual worship.

24. πνεῦμα ὁ θεός. The spirituality of God was an essential tenet of Judaism (cf. 1 Kings 8²⁷, Isa. 31³), although all its implications were not recognised. It was a tenet common to Jews and Samaritans, but it is here for the first time put into three words, and its bearing on the nature of worship drawn out. The similar phrases ὁ θεὸς φῶς ἐστίν, ὁ θεὸς ἀγάπη ἐστίν (1 Jn. 1⁵ 4⁸), show that we must render " God is Spirit," not " God is *a* spirit." It is the Essential Being, rather than the Personality, of God which is in question.

The consequence of this, as regards worship, is repeated from v. 23. For true worship there must be affinity between the Worshipped and the worshipper.

ἐν πνεύματι καὶ ἀληθείᾳ. ℵ* has the aberrant reading ἐν πνεύματι ἀληθείας (from 14¹⁷).

For the repetition of the phrase "worship in spirit and in truth " from v. 23, see on 3¹⁶ above. Such refrains or repetitions are a special feature of Johannine style.

25. Little is known about the Messianic doctrine of the Samaritans, but that they cherished Messianic hopes, although less clearly than the Jews did, is known from other sources. Josephus (*Antt.* XVIII. iv. 1) tells of a rising in Samaria, quelled by Pilate, which was evidently due to a kind of fanaticism, similar to that of Simon Magus in the same district (Acts 8⁹) who gave himself out to be " some great one." [1] The Samaritan woman thought of Messiah as a prophet, like the prophet foretold in Deut. 18¹⁸ (cf. v. 29 below). This was common to Jew and Samaritan, that Messiah was to be a Revealer of new truths about God and man: ὅταν ἔλθῃ ἐκεῖνος, ἀναγγελεῖ (cf. 16¹³) ἡμῖν ἅπαντα. Thus in the *Similitudes of Enoch* (xlvi. 3) there is a description of the Son of Man " who reveals all the treasures of that which is hidden, because the God of spirits hath chosen Him."

οἶδα. ℵᶜL *fam.* 13 have οἴδαμεν.

The Samaritan woman had already confessed that Jesus was " a prophet " (v. 19); but now she begins to wonder if He

[1] Cf. Justin, *Apol.* i. 53, for a vague statement of Samaritan doctrine as to Messiah, similar to Jewish belief.

ἔλθῃ ἐκεῖνος, ἀναγγελεῖ ἡμῖν ἅπαντα. 26. λέγει αὐτῇ ὁ Ἰησοῦς
Ἐγώ εἰμι, ὁ λαλῶν σοι.
27. Καὶ ἐπὶ τούτῳ ἦλθαν οἱ μαθηταὶ αὐτοῦ, καὶ ἐθαύμαζον ὅτι

may not be more. "I know," she says it wistfully,
"that Messiah is coming; when He comes, He will declare
all things to us." Her words are almost a query; they in-
vite a further declaration on the part of Jesus, which He gives
forthwith.

Messiah is here without the article, and the title may have
been used as a kind of proper name. At 1⁴¹ (where see note)
it has the article, and there as here is explained by Jn. for
his Greek readers (cf. 1³⁸). ὁ λεγόμενος is not "which is
interpreted" (ὅ ἐστιν μεθερμηνευόμενον, 1⁴¹), but is equivalent
to "which is commonly called," Χριστός being used like a
proper name by the time that the Fourth Gospel was written.
See, for a similar usage, 11¹⁶ and cf. 5².

26. Jesus declares Himself. "I who am talking to you
(λαλῶν) am He." So, to the blind man whose sight had been
restored, He said ὁ λαλῶν μετὰ σοῦ ἐκεῖνός ἐστιν (9³⁷). The
usage of the phrase ἐγώ εἰμι in Jn. has been discussed in the
Introduction, p. cxx; and it is probable that this is one of the
cases where, although the predicate is not expressed, it is implied
in the context: "I that talk to you am the Christ." See on
v. 10.

Nevertheless, the phrase ἐγώ εἰμι αὐτὸς ὁ λαλῶν is placed
in the mouth of Yahweh at Isa. 52⁶, and it may be that Jn. here
intends ἐγώ εἰμι to indicate the style of Deity, as at other points
(see Introd., p. cxxi). Cf. esp. 8⁵⁸.

ἐγώ εἰμι, ὁ λαλῶν σοι, then, if not an assertion of the
Speaker's Divinity, is at any rate an assertion of His Messiahship. That it should have been made so early in His public
ministry is not in accordance with what we should gather from
the Synoptists. Perhaps Jn. has antedated this momentous
declaration; or perhaps it was actually made on this occasion,
although unheard or unnoticed by Peter, who may not have
been present with Jesus on His journey through Samaria
(see on v. 8 above).

The disciples wonder (v. 27)

27. ἐπὶ τούτῳ κτλ., "upon this came His disciples," *i.e.*
at this point in the story. ἐπὶ τούτῳ is not used elsewhere in
the N.T. in this sense, but the reading is well attested, only
א*D having ἐν τούτῳ.

ἐθαύμαζον, "began to wonder" or "kept wondering."

μετὰ γυναικὸς ἐλάλει· οὐδεὶς μέντοι εἶπεν Τί ζητεῖς ἢ τί λαλεῖς μετ᾽ αὐτῆς;
28. Ἀφῆκεν οὖν τὴν ὑδρίαν αὐτῆς ἡ γυνὴ καὶ ἀπῆλθεν εἰς τὴν πόλιν, καὶ λέγει τοῖς ἀνθρώποις 29. Δεῦτε ἴδετε ἄνθρωπον ὃς εἶπέν μοι πάντα ἃ ἐποίησα· μήτι οὗτός ἐστιν ὁ Χριστός; 30. ἐξῆλθον ἐκ τῆς πόλεως καὶ ἤρχοντο πρὸς αὐτόν.

This is the true reading (אABCDW⊙) as against the rec. ἐθαύμασαν.

To talk with a woman in a public place was not consonant with the grave dignity of a Rabbi; Lightfoot quotes the Rabbinical precept, " Let no one talk with a woman in the street, no, not with his own wife." [1]

Yet the disciples had learnt by this time that Jesus had good reason for what He did, and they did not venture to expostulate. They did not ask the woman Τί ζητεῖς; "What do you want ? " nor did they ask Jesus Τί λαλεῖς μετ᾽ αὐτῆς; "Why are you talking with her ? " That they did *not* ask these questions, which they were tempted to ask, is the reminiscence of some one who was of the company. For μέντοι, see on 12⁴².

The Samaritan woman tells her friends about Jesus
(*vv.* 28-30)

28. The woman was so much impressed that she went off to tell her friends in Sychar. She left her waterpot, or ὑδρία, which was a large, heavy vessel (cf. 2⁶), behind her, as she intended to return speedily. Probably it had not yet been filled, as she had been engrossed with the conversation (cf. v. 7), and it was useless to carry it backwards and forwards.

29. During the heat of the day, the men of the village were not working in the fields, and so she found them readily. In her excitement, she uses the exaggerated language of an uneducated woman, " Come and see a man who told me all things that ever I did."

πάντα ἅ. So אBC* Syr. sin. Syr cur., as against πάντα ὅσα of the rec. text (cf. v. 39).

μήτι οὗτός ἐστιν ὁ Χριστός; " Is this, perhaps, the Christ ? " (see on v. 25). Cf. Mt. 12²³ μήτι οὗτός ἐστιν ὁ υἱὸς Δαυείδ; and Jn. 8²² (for the form of sentence) μήτι ἀποκτενεῖ ἑαυτόν; The question is put tentatively, with just a shade of hope that the answer may turn out to be in the affirmative. But cf. 18³⁵ and 21⁵, where μήτι introduces a question to which it is assumed that the answer will be " No."

30. We have seen above (v. 25) that the Samaritans had

[1] *Hor. Hebr.*, iii. 287.

31. Ἐν τῷ μεταξὺ ἠρώτων αὐτὸν οἱ μαθηταὶ λέγοντες Ῥαββεί, φάγε. 32. ὁ δὲ εἶπεν αὐτοῖς Ἐγὼ βρῶσιν ἔχω φαγεῖν ἣν ὑμεῖς οὐκ οἴδατε. 33. ἔλεγον οὖν οἱ μαθηταὶ πρὸς ἀλλήλους Μή τις ἤνεγκεν

Messianic hopes. The men of Sychar were so much impressed by what the woman told them that they left the village and "were coming" (ἤρχοντο) to Him. The impft. tense is used as indicating that they were on their way while the conversation between Jesus and His disciples which follows was being carried on.

The rec. text has οὖν after ἐξῆλθον, which is rejected by ABLΓΔΘ. But אNW have it, and it would be quite in Jn.'s style. The omission of οὖν by a scribe after ἐξῆλθον would be a natural slip, ΕΞΗΛΘΟΝΟΥ passing into ΕΞΗΛΘΟΝ. The redundant ἐξῆλθον ἐκ occurs again 8⁴². ⁵⁹ 10³⁹, 1 Jn. 2¹⁹; and cf. 18²⁹.

Discourse with the Disciples (vv. 31-38)

31. ἐν τῷ μεταξύ (subaud. χρόνῳ), "in the meanwhile," sc. before the Samaritan villagers arrived. There is no exact parallel to this use of μεταξύ in the Greek Bible; but cf. Acts 13⁴² and Lk. 8¹.

ἠρώτων αὐτόν κτλ., "the disciples begged Him, saying, Rabbi, eat." For οἱ μαθηταί used absolutely of the disciples who were present, see on 2². For ἐρωτᾶν, "to beseech," cf. vv. 40, 47. The disciples (see vv. 8, 31) were apprehensive lest He should be overcome by hunger and fatigue (cf. v. 6). See on 1³⁸ for "Rabbi" as a title of address.

32. Jesus had been fatigued, but He was sustained by spiritual support of which the disciples did not know (v. 34). ἐγώ and ὑμεῖς are both emphatic.

βρῶσις occurs again 6²⁷. ⁵⁵, in the same sense as the more correct form βρῶμα (see v. 34), viz. that of the thing eaten, not of the act of eating (as in 1 Cor. 8⁴). The only other occurrence of βρῶσις in the Gospels is in Mt. 6¹⁹. ²⁰, where it means "rust."

33. The conversation pursues the course usual in Jn.'s narrative. Jesus utters a profound saying (v. 32). It is misunderstood and its spiritual meaning is not discerned (v. 33). Then He enlarges the saying and explains it to some extent.[1]

Here the puzzled disciples say to each other (πρὸς ἀλλήλους; cf. 16¹⁷), "Did some one perhaps bring Him something to eat?"

[1] See Introd., p. cxi, as to this method of discourse.

αὐτῷ φαγεῖν; 34. λέγει αὐτοῖς ὁ Ἰησοῦς Ἐμὸν βρῶμά ἐστιν ἵνα ποιήσω τὸ θέλημα τοῦ πέμψαντός με καὶ τελειώσω αὐτοῦ τὸ ἔργον.

μή τις ἤνεγκεν αὐτῷ φαγεῖν; For constr., see on 4⁷; and cf. v. 29 for the form of the sentence. 34. ποιήσω is read by BCDLNTᵇΘW ; the rec. text has ποιῶ, with אΑΓΔ. Yet ποιήσω may be due to assimilation of tense with τελειώσω which follows.

Jesus answers the disciples by reminding them that it was in the fulfilment of His mission that He had His strength and His joy. He had been tired and, no doubt, hungry; but the joy of perceiving the receptiveness of the Samaritan woman and the eager welcome which the villagers gave Him was sufficient to renew His vigour of body as well as of spirit.

To do God's will is the supreme obligation of man at every moment of life, and to it is attached the supreme reward (Mk. 3³⁵, Mt. 7²¹, Jn. 7¹⁷ 9³¹ and *passim*). The condition " Thy will be done " (Mt. 6¹⁰) governs all Christian prayer, as it governed the prayer of Christ (Lk. 22⁴², Mt. 26⁴²) at Gethsemane. Christ's " meat " was to do the will of God, the metaphor being similar to that suggested by " Man doth not live by bread alone, but by every word of God " (Deut. 8³), which was the Scripture thought that supported Him in His Temptation (Mt. 4⁴, Lk. 4⁴); cf. Job 23¹², Ps. 119¹⁰³. It was in Him that the words of the Psalm, " Lo, I come to do thy will, O God," received their complete fulfilment (Ps. 40⁷ˑ ⁸, Heb. 10⁷).

ἐμὸν βρῶμά ἐστιν ἵνα ποιήσω κτλ. : ἵνα has no telic force here (cf. 6²⁹ 15⁸ 17³), " My meat is to do, etc." Wetstein quotes a good parallel from Thucyd. i. 70 μήτε ἑορτὴν ἄλλο τι ἡγεῖσθαι ἢ τὸ τὰ δέοντα πρᾶξαι.

βρῶμα is found in Jn. only in this verse; see above (v. 32) on βρῶσις. The thought is one which appears many times in Jn.; *e.g.* " I seek not mine own will, but the will of Him that sent me " (5³⁰), and " I am come down from heaven not to do mine own will, but the will of Him that sent me " (6³⁸); cf. 14³¹ and Acts 13²².

τοῦ πέμψαντός με. For the conception of Jesus as " sent " by God, see on 3¹⁷.

καὶ τελειώσω αὐτοῦ τὸ ἔργον, " and to accomplish His work." " To do God's will " is, in a measure, within the reach of any man, but " to accomplish His work," to perform it perfectly and completely, was possible only for the Son of Man. This perfection of achievement bore witness to the uniqueness of His mission : " The works that the Father hath given me to accomplish bear witness that the Father hath sent me " (5³⁶). So at the close of His ministry He could say, " I have accom-

35. οὐχ ὑμεῖς λέγετε ὅτι Ἔτι τετράμηνός ἐστιν καὶ ὁ θερισμὸς
ἔρχεται; ἰδοὺ λέγω ὑμῖν, ἐπάρατε τοὺς ὀφθαλμοὺς ὑμῶν καὶ θεάσασθε

plished the work which Thou hast given me to do" (17⁴);
and from the Cross came the word τετέλεσται (19³⁰).

35. The illustration of the harvest used by Jesus to unfold
to the disciples the significance of the incident just narrated
brings Jn. into line with the Synoptists, who repeatedly tell of
His parables of the seed.

He was the Great Sower (cf. Mk. 4¹⁴ff·), and the seed just
now sown in the heart of the Samaritan woman was springing
up already. The harvest of souls at Sychar followed forthwith
upon the sowing, contrary to the natural order in which he who
wishes to reap must have patience and wait. Natural law does
not always prevail in the spiritual world. The spiritual harvest
was ready to be reaped with joy (v. 35), so that Sower and reaper
might rejoice together (v. 36). But the reaping would not be
for Him. It was the apostles who were to reap at a later date
the harvest which originally sprang from the seed that He had
sown in Samaria.

τετράμηνος. So ℵABCDLNTᵇ⊛, as against the rec. τετράμηνον. τετράμηνος does not occur again in the Greek Bible,
although τετράμηνον (used as a substantive) is read by A at
Judg. 19² 20⁴⁷. The meaning "four months long" is not
doubtful, and the words τετράμηνός ἐστιν καὶ ὁ θερισμὸς ἔρχεται
mean "the harvest comes in four months' time." But
we cannot interpret this as indicating that the harvest of the
fields of Sychar would not be ready for four months from the
date of the interview of the woman of Samaria with Jesus, for
that would involve the scene being laid in January or early in
February. That was the rainy season, and there would have
been no difficulty in getting water to drink, such as is suggested (vv. 6, 7). The words οὐχ ὑμεῖς λέγετε, "Do you
not say?" which introduce the sentence, suggest that it was a
proverbial phrase.

J. Lightfoot (*Hor. Hebr.*, in loc.) quotes a passage from
a Rabbinical writer, showing that the agricultural year was
divided into six periods of two months each, viz. seed-time,
winter, spring, harvest, summer, and the season of extreme
heat, so that the interval between sowing and harvest would be
reckoned roughly as four months, although actually it might
be a little longer. Thus Jesus here reminds His disciples of a
rural saying, "Harvest does not come for four months," and
then he points to the contrast with the spiritual harvest already
ripe for gathering in the hearts of the Samaritan villagers,
although the seed had been sown only that day.

156 THE GOSPEL ACCORDING TO ST. JOHN [**IV. 35.**

The words of this proverbial saying, with a trifling change, form a line of iambic verse:[1]

$$\tau\epsilon\tau\rho\acute{a}\mu\eta\nu\acute{o}s \ \acute{\epsilon}\sigma\tau\iota \ \chi\acute{\omega} \ \theta\epsilon\rho\iota\sigma\mu\grave{o}s \ \acute{\epsilon}\rho\chi\epsilon\tau\alpha\iota.$$

If Jn. represented Jesus as quoting Greek iambics, then there would be some ground for treating the narrative of c. 4 as an allegory rather than as an historical reminiscence, freely edited. But this would be at variance with the general lines on which the Gospel is written. The disciples elsewhere (see on 1[38]) address Jesus in Aramaic, and doubtless He spoke in the same language to them. That Jn. should represent them as familiar with a Greek proverb in verse is incredible. Further, not only is this proverb unknown in Greek literature, but it would be hard for it to have currency among Greeks. There is no evidence that the Greeks had a sixfold division of the agricultural year as the Hebrews had; and if they did not adopt this division, *four* months would not be as likely an interval to be contemplated as normal between seed-time and harvest as *five* or even *six* months.

Again, ἔτι precedes τετράμηνός ἐστιν κτλ. in אABCNT[b]WΔΘ, and has to be retained, although it is omitted by DL *fam.* 13 Syr. cur. But ἔτι spoils the iambic *senarius*, and yet it must be reckoned with; for the saying which Jesus quotes as familiar to the disciples is, " There are *yet* four months (*sc.* from the time of sowing), and then comes the harvest."

We conclude, therefore, that the rhythm of ὁ θερισμὸς ἔρχεται is an accident, and that we are to regard the whole phrase as the Greek rendering of an Aramaic agricultural proverb. See 5[14] for another accidental Greek verse.

With the paratactic constr. ἔτι τετράμηνός ἐστιν καὶ ὁ θερισμὸς ἔρχεται, Milligan[2] compares the illiterate P Par. 18[14] ἔτι δύο ἡμέρας ἔχομεν καὶ φθάσομεν εἰς Πηλοῦσι.

ἰδοὺ λέγω ὑμῖν. ἰδού is unusual in Jn., occurring again only in 16[32] 19[5] (12[15] is a LXX quotation). Jn. generally has ἴδε (see on 1[29]). ἰδού here and at 16[32] is almost equivalent to "but"; it introduces a contrast with what has gone before.

ἐπάρατε τοὺς ὀφθαλμούς is an expressive phrase, suggesting careful and deliberate gaze, which we have both in O.T. (Gen. 13[10], 2 Sam. 18[24], 1 Chron. 21[16], Ezek. 18[6]) and in N.T. (Lk. 16[23] 18[13], Mt. 17[8]). See on 6[5] (cf. 11[41] 17[1]), where, as here, the phrase is followed by the verb θεᾶσθαι, which in the N.T. (see on 1[14]) is always used of seeing with the bodily eyes.[3]

---

[1] See Westcott, *St. John,* i. 179.
[2] *Vocabulary of Greek Testament,* p. 314.
[3] Abbott (*Diat.* 2616–7) attaches a spiritual significance to Jn.'s mention of our Lord's " lifting up " His eyes.

τὰς χώρας, ὅτι λευκαί εἰσιν πρὸς θερισμὸν ἤδη. 36. ὁ θερίζων μισθὸν λαμβάνει καὶ συνάγει καρπὸν εἰς ζωὴν αἰώνιον, ἵνα ὁ σπείρων

The disciples could see for themselves that the fields (cf. Lk. 21²¹ for this use of χώρα) were whitening for the harvest already. Jesus does not say that the material harvest of the fields of Sychar was springing up immediately after it had been sown; the harvest of which He speaks is expressly contrasted with the harvest that takes months to grow and ripen. The allusion is to the spiritual receptiveness of the Samaritan woman, the measure of faith which she has already exhibited (v. 29), and the eagerness with which her friends and neighbours were even now coming to inquire of Jesus for themselves. These were the fields for the spiritual harvest, which was patent not to the eye of faith only, but to the bodily eyes of the disciples, for these people were hastening to meet them even at the moment of speaking.

ἤδη may be taken either with what precedes, or with what follows. But the word "already" seems to go more impressively with what has just been said than with the saying of v. 36.

Nothing, then, can be certainly inferred as to the time of year from this verse. The fields may have, literally, been ready for the reapers, and if so, it was the harvest season. That, in itself, would bring home to the disciples the meaning of the Lord's words about the spiritual harvest; but it is clear that it is the spiritual harvest which is primarily referred to in v. 35ᵇ, while it is the natural harvest which is the subject of the proverb of v. 35ᵃ.

36. The terse, pithy aphorisms of vv. 35-37 recall the sayings of Jesus recorded in the Synoptists, by their form no less than by the use of the illustration of sowing and reaping. See Introd., p. cx.

ὁ θερίζων μισθὸν λαμβάνει. Cf. the more general saying, true of all labour and not only of that in the fields, ἄξιος γὰρ ὁ ἐργάτης τοῦ μισθοῦ αὐτοῦ (Lk. 10⁷); and also 2 Tim. 2⁶. Here the reaper reaps in spiritual fields, and his reward is that he gathers fruit unto life eternal. (For this phrase, see on 4¹⁴.) The reaping is itself the reward, because of the joy which it brings; the "fruit" which is gathered is that of the spiritual harvest, the outlook being not that only of the present life, but of that which is to come.

Jn. does not use the word μισθός again, but of καρπός he has much (15²ᶠ·) to say. The apostles were chosen (15¹⁶) ἵνα ὑμεῖς ὑπάγητε καὶ καρπὸν φέρητε, καὶ ὁ καρπὸς ὑμῶν μένῃ. Just as Paul speaks of his converts as καρπός (Rom. 1¹³), so here

ὁμοῦ χαίρῃ καὶ ὁ θερίζων. 37. ἐν γὰρ τούτῳ ὁ λόγος ἐστὶν ἀληθινὸς

the "fruit" which the disciples were to gather εἰς ζωὴν αἰώνιον was the harvest of souls in Samaria.[1] אADΓΔΘ and most vss. have καί after ἵνα, but om. BCLNTᵇW.

ἵνα ὁ σπείρων κτλ., "so that the sower may rejoice together with the reaper." This is quite contrary to the natural order. In nature the rule is that men sow in tears, if they are afterwards to reap in joy (Ps. 126⁵·⁶). The labour of the sower is heavy, and it precedes by a long interval (cf. v. 35) the joy of the reapers at harvest-time (Isa. 9³). But the prophet had sung of the wonderful days of Messiah, when "the plowman shall overtake the reaper, and the treader of grapes him that soweth the seed" (Amos 9¹³; cf. Lev. 26⁵), so fertile should the land be. Something like this had happened at Sychar. The Sower was rejoicing along with the reapers, who were already gathering fruit unto life eternal. See on 11¹⁵.

ὁμοῦ is found again in N.T. only at 20⁴ 21² and Acts 2¹; and it is infrequent in the LXX.

37. The rec. text has ὁ before ἀληθινός, but om. אBC*LNTᵇWΔ.

ἐν γὰρ τούτῳ κτλ., "Herein is the saying true (ἀληθινός, for which see on 1⁹), One soweth, and another reapeth." Another proverb is cited here, for which many parallels can be found. Wetstein quotes ἄλλοι μὲν σπείρουσιν, ἄλλοι δ᾽ ἀμήσονται.

That the sower should not have the joy of reaping is regarded in the O.T. as a sad thing (Job 31⁸), and is spoken of as a punishment for sin (Deut. 28³⁰, Mic. 6¹⁵). Yet this often happens, not through sin but through the unselfishness of the sower or the inevitable conditions of his work. So here, Jesus was the Sower, but He permitted His disciples to reap. And the labourer in the field of the spirit must be ready to acknowledge that "One sows, another reaps," may be a condition of his highest usefulness. "Sic uos, non uobis" is his Master's challenge.

But more was involved here, and a greater paradox than is suggested by the reaper being a different person from the sower. That a man should reap where he had not sown is, indeed, ordinarily a matter for peculiar thankfulness on his part (Deut. 6¹¹, Josh. 24¹³); but this privilege is the natural prerogative of the lord of the fields, who sends his servants to sow, but takes the harvest for himself (Mt. 25²⁶). Yet Jesus, who was here

---

[1] The similarity between this passage and Gal. 6⁸ ὁ σπείρων εἰς τὸ πνεῦμα ἐκ τοῦ πνεύματος θερίσει ζωὴν αἰώνιον, is only verbal, although remarkable; cf. Rom. 6²².

ὅτι ἄλλος ἐστὶν ὁ σπείρων καὶ ἄλλος ὁ θερίζων. 38. ἐγὼ ἀπέστειλα
ὑμᾶς θερίζειν ὃ οὐχ ὑμεῖς κεκοπιάκατε· ἄλλοι κεκοπιάκασιν, καὶ ὑμεῖς
εἰς τὸν κόπον αὐτῶν εἰσεληλύθατε.

the Lord of the harvest, had Himself done the sowing, while
He permitted His servants to gather the fruits.
Hence ἀληθινός means more than ἀληθής here. The proverb is not only accurate, if cynical, in regard to the physical
harvest; but the highest illustration of its truth is seen in the
spiritual region. Cf. Abbott, *Diat.* 1727*i*.

38. This is to repeat what has already been said, but puts
it into plainer language. ἐγώ is emphatic; it was *I* who sent
you to reap in a field which you had not sown.

If we confine the words ἐγὼ ἀπέστειλα ὑμᾶς κτλ. to the
incident just narrated, the verse yields a quite intelligible sense.
The disciples had not "laboured" in Sychar; the seed was
sown there by Jesus Himself, and in some measure by the
Samaritan woman. Primarily, Jesus and the woman were the
ἄλλοι into whose labours the disciples had entered, not to speak
of every prophet and pious teacher of the past who had prepared
the way in Samaria for the message of Christ.

The verb ἀποστέλλειν is frequent in Jn. (see on 3¹⁷); but
it is only used once again by Jn. of Jesus sending forth His
disciples, viz. at 17¹⁸, nor does Jn. use the title ἀπόστολος of
them (cf. 13¹⁶). But ἐγὼ ἀπέστειλα ὑμᾶς at once suggests a
mission such as those recorded Mk. 3¹⁴ 6⁷, although Jn. has
not described anything of the kind; and it might be thought
that these words placed by Jn. in the mouth of Jesus here have
reference to a former sending forth of the Twelve, such as
the Synoptists report, rather than to any mission confined to the
disciples (see on v. 8) who were with Jesus at Sychar. But the
missions of the Twelve and of the Seventy were of men who
were sent to *sow* rather than to *reap*, nor could they be fitly
described by the words, "I sent you to reap where you had
not laboured." Nor can we be sure that the missions of Mk.
3¹⁴ 6⁷ had been initiated before this Samaritan journey took
place (see on 6¹).

Pfleiderer [1] suggests that the words of this verse, which
might fitly be applied to the later work of the apostles (*e.g.*
Acts 8⁵⁻⁷· ¹⁴ᶠ·), are carelessly applied here by Jn. to an early
incident in Jesus' ministry. But the fact is that the words
"others have laboured and you have entered into their labours"
will fit every period of the Church's life, as they would fit every
era of scientific discovery. That, however, does not supply any
ground for refusing credence to the statement that they, or

[1] *Primitive Christianity*, Eng. Tr., iv. 33.

39. Ἐκ δὲ τῆς πόλεως ἐκείνης πολλοὶ ἐπίστευσαν εἰς αὐτὸν τῶν Σαμαρειτῶν διὰ τὸν λόγον τῆς γυναικὸς μαρτυρούσης ὅτι Εἶπέν μοι πάντα ἃ ἐποίησα. 40. ὡς οὖν ἦλθον πρὸς αὐτὸν οἱ Σαμαρεῖται, ἠρώτων αὐτὸν μεῖναι παρ' αὐτοῖς· καὶ ἔμεινεν ἐκεῖ δύο ἡμέρας. 41. καὶ πολλῷ πλείους ἐπίστευσαν διὰ τὸν λόγον αὐτοῦ, 42. τῇ τε γυναικὶ

words like them (for Jn. writes freely), were addressed by Jesus to His disciples at Sychar, as conveying a lesson which it was good for them to learn.

The faith of the Samaritan villagers (vv. 39–42)

39. The Samaritan villagers who, on another occasion, rejected Jesus and His disciples had not heard Him teach; their objection to His presence was not personal, but rested on the fact that, as a Jew, He was going to Jerusalem to keep a feast (Lk. 9[52]). The people of Sychar, on the other hand, were won by His words (v. 42).

πολλοὶ ἐπίστευσαν εἰς αὐτόν. The phrase is a favourite with Jn., occurring six times (cf. 7[31] 8[30] 10[42] 11[45] 12[42]). The aorist seems to indicate a definite, but not necessarily lasting, movement of faith evoked by special words or deeds of Jesus. For the constr. πιστεύειν εἴς τινα, see on 1[12].

The first believers at Samaria were won, not by visible miracles or signs (cf. 2[23] 7[31] 10[42] 11[45] 12[42]), but by the woman's report of what Jesus had said to her. Many more believed because of His sayings which they themselves had heard (v. 42; cf. 8[30]). But v. 39 illustrates the normal way in which men are drawn to Christ in the first instance; cf. His prayer for those who were to be led to Him through the apostles' teaching : ἐρωτῶ . . . περὶ τῶν πιστευόντων διὰ τοῦ λόγου αὐτῶν εἰς ἐμέ (17[20]).

For ὅσα of the rec. text the better reading (אBC*L) is ἅ, as at v. 29.

40. ὡς οὖν ἦλθον κτλ. For Jn.'s frequent use of οὖν, see on 1[22]. He likes the introductory ὡς οὖν (cf. 11[6] 18[6] 20[11] 21[9]), which is not found in the Synoptists.

The Samaritans who had been impressed by the woman's story desired to listen themselves to the teaching of Jesus, and at their request he lodged in Sychar ιwo days. For Jn.'s habit of recording dates, or intervals of time, see Introd., p. cii. He repeats in v. 43 that the stay of Jesus in this village was for two days only, τὰς δύο ἡμέρας (cf. 11[6]).

41. πολλῷ πλείους ἐπίστευσαν . . ., "many more believed because of His word." Cf. ταῦτα αὐτοῦ λαλοῦντος πολλοὶ ἐπίστευσαν εἰς αὐτόν (8[30]).

IV. 41-42.] FAITH OF THE SAMARITAN VILLAGERS 161

ἔλεγον ὅτι Οὐκέτι διὰ τὴν σὴν λαλιὰν πιστεύομεν· αὐτοὶ γὰρ ἀκηκόαμεν, καὶ οἴδαμεν ὅτι οὗτός ἐστιν ἀληθῶς ὁ Σωτὴρ τοῦ κόσμου.

N⊙ *fam.* 13 add εἰς αὐτόν after ἐπίστευσαν (as at 8³⁰), but
om. the greater uncials. πιστεύειν is here used in an absolute
sense, " to believe," as often in Jn. See on 1⁷.

42. ἀκηκόαμεν. The gloss παρ' αὐτοῦ is added by א *fam.* 13.
After κόσμου, the rec. text, with ADLNΓ⊙, inserts ὁ Χριστός,
but, again, this explanatory gloss is not found in אBC*TᵇW,
and must be rejected.

λαλιά, "way of speech," "manner of talking," occurs
again in N.T. only at Mt. 26⁷³ and 8⁴³ (where see note).

οὐκέτι διὰ τὴν σὴν λαλιάν κτλ., "No longer do we believe
because of thy speaking, for we have heard and know, etc."
οὐκέτι always means "no longer" in Jn. (cf. 6⁶⁶ 11⁵⁴ 14¹⁹· ³⁰
15¹⁵ 16¹⁰· ²¹· ²⁵ 17¹¹ 21⁶). The initial stages of belief may be
brought about by the report of others (see on v. 39), but the
belief which is complete and assured depends on personal
contact and association with Christ (see on 1³⁹ and cf. Lk. 24³⁹,
"Handle me and see ").

That the Samaritan villagers rose to the conception of Jesus
as not only Messiah, but as "the Saviour of the world," is not
probable. This great title reflects the conviction of a later
moment in Christian history, and of a more fully instructed
faith. Jn. in writing the story of Jesus at Sychar tells it in
his own phraseology, as will become apparent if the history of
the terms "saviour," "salvation," is recalled.

In O.T. theology, Yahweh is the Author of salvation (see
on 3¹⁷), and to Him it is always ascribed. He is repeatedly
called מוֹשִׁיעַ, σωτήρ (Ps. 24⁵ 62⁷, Isa. 12², Bar. 4²², 3 Macc.
7¹⁶), the "Saviour" of Israel or of individual Israelites.
σωτήρ is also used in the LXX of human deliverers, e.g. of the
judges (Judg. 3⁹), just as in Egypt the Ptolemies, and in Greece
Brasidas and Philip of Macedon, were so designated. But in
the O.T., *Messiah* is never called מוֹשִׁיעַ or σωτήρ, the nearest
approach to such a description being Zech. 9⁹ ὁ βασιλεύς σου
ἔρχεται δίκαιος καὶ σώζων. To O.T. Judaism, Messiah was but
the instrument of the true σωτήρ, Yahweh, who is described
(Ps. 28⁸) as ὑπερασπιστὴς τῶν σωτηρίων τοῦ χριστοῦ αὐτοῦ.

In the later literature, there are faint traces of the conception
of Messiah as Saviour; e.g. it is said of the Son of Man in
Enoch xlviii. 7, "The righteous are saved in his name, and he is
the avenger of their life "; cf. l. 3. The Messianic deliverance was pre-eminently the "salvation of Israel " for which
pious Hebrews looked (see on v. 22 above); but that in the
first century Messiah was given the title σωτήρ is not proven.

In the Synoptists, σωτήρ occurs only twice, Lk. 1⁴⁷ (where it is applied to God, as in the O.T.), and Lk. 2¹¹ σωτὴρ ὅς ἐστι Χριστὸς κύριος, "a Saviour (not *the* Saviour) who is Christ the Lord." Cf. Acts 13²³ and Acts 5³¹ ἀρχηγὸς καὶ σωτήρ, which suggests ὁ ἀρχηγὸς τῆς σωτηρίας of Heb. 2¹⁰. The first unambiguous instance of the application of the title in its full sense to our Lord is Phil. 3²⁰ σωτῆρα . . . κύριον Ἰησοῦν Χριστόν. See also 2 Tim. 1¹⁰, Tit. 1⁴ 3⁶, 2 Pet. 1¹¹ 2²⁰ 3². ¹⁸; and cf. Eph. 5²³, 1 Tim. 1¹⁵.

The evidence shows that σωτήρ, as a title, began to be applied to Christ as readily as to God the Father, as soon as the Gospel message of redemption was understood and appropriated. The title has its roots in the O.T., and there is no need of the hypothesis that it is imported into the N.T. from the pagan mysteries or from the Emperor cults.[1] But that it was recognised as a Messianic title before Christ came is unproved and improbable.

The universality of salvation (at any rate so far as Jews were concerned) had already been declared by the prophets; cf. Joel 2³² ἔσται πᾶς ὅς ἂν ἐπικαλέσηται τὸ ὄνομα κυρίου σωθήσεται (quoted Acts 2²¹, Rom. 10¹³). God is called τὸν πάντων σωτῆρα (Wisd. 16⁷); cf. 1 Tim 4¹⁰ σωτὴρ πάντων ἀνθρώπων. But the magnificent title ὁ σωτὴρ τοῦ κόσμου is found in the Greek Bible only in the verse before us, and at 1 Jn. 4¹⁴. It is one of the distinctive phrases of the Johannine writings; cf. 12⁴⁷ and especially 3¹⁷, where the purpose of Christ's mission is declared to be ἵνα σωθῇ ὁ κόσμος δι' αὐτοῦ. See note on 3¹⁷, and for κόσμος on 1⁹.

It has been suggested by G. Vos [2] that a parallel for ὁ σωτὴρ τοῦ κόσμου may be seen in 2 Esd. 13²⁶, where it is said of Messiah *liberabit creaturam suam*. But it is doubtful if *creatura* is equivalent to "the universe of creation," and further the passage may be affected by Christian influence.

A nearer parallel is Philo's ὁ σωτὴρ τοῦ παντός (*quod deus imm.* 34), which he applies to God. The passage presents some superficial resemblance to the story of the Samaritan woman at the well. Philo has quoted Num. 20¹⁷ᶠᶠ·, where the Israelites seek permission to pass through Edom, promising not to drink water from the wells, or, if they did, to pay for it. To be able to pass by the attractions of earth befits the heavenly soul; such is Philo's reflexion, and he adds that it is folly to drink from cisterns contrived by the distrustfulness of man, when the Saviour of the Universe has opened to us His heavenly treasury

[1] The title is often bestowed on the Emperors, and especially on Hadrian, in inscriptions. See Deissmann, *Light from the East*, p. 369.
[2] *D.C.G.*, ii. 573.

43. Μετὰ δὲ τὰς δύο ἡμέρας ἐξῆλθεν ἐκεῖθεν εἰς τὴν Γαλιλαίαν.
44. αὐτὸς γὰρ Ἰησοῦς ἐμαρτύρησεν ὅτι προφήτης ἐν τῇ ἰδίᾳ πατρίδι τιμὴν οὐκ ἔχει. 45. ὅτε οὖν ἦλθεν εἰς τὴν Γαλιλαίαν, ἐδέξαντο αὐτὸν

(cf. Deut. 28¹²), in comparison with which all the wells in the world are not worth looking at. This suggests Jn. 4¹⁴, but then the σωτήρ in the Philo passage is not the Logos, but God Himself. The resemblance between Philo's language and Jn.'s is not sufficient to indicate any literary connexion.

It may, however, be noted as a curious point that a reference in Jn. 4⁴² to Num. 20¹⁷ᵗ. is actually traced by Ephraim Syrus. In a baptismal hymn (*Epiphany Hymns*, vii. 7) he has: " To the sons of Lot Moses said, ' Give us water for money, let us only pass by through your border.' They refused the way and the temporal water. Lo ! the living water freely given and the path that leads to Eden."

Departure from Sychar and reception in Galilee (vv. 43–45)

43. τὰς δύο ἡμέρας, *sc.* the two days mentioned in v. 40.

After ἐκεῖθεν the rec. text, with ΑΝΓΔ, adds καὶ ἀπῆλθεν from v. 3, but the addition is not found in אBCDTᵇW, and is unnecessary. Θ substitutes καὶ ἀπῆλθεν for ἐκεῖθεν.

Jesus had left Judæa because of the attention with which the Pharisees were suspiciously regarding His work there (v. 1), and was moving into Galilee (v. 3). The teaching at Sychar was only an episode of His journey (vv. 4–42), and the narrative is now resumed.

44. προφήτης ἐν τῇ ἰδίᾳ πατρίδι τιμὴν οὐκ ἔχει. The writer does not say that Jesus quoted this familiar proverb[1] when He was passing from Samaria into Galilee. The verse is an editorial comment, illustrative of the context, and only notes that Jesus quoted the saying either then or on some other occasion. The aor. ἐμαρτύρησεν seems to be used like an English pluperfect; cf. the similar aorists ἐποίησεν and ἦλθον in v. 45, "He had done," "they had come"; cf. also ἐξένευσεν at 5¹³. For the verb as applied to explicit sayings of Jesus, cf. 13²¹.

The saying is placed in the mouth of Jesus in the Synoptic narratives, at Mk. 6⁴, Mt. 13⁵⁷, in the form οὐκ ἔστιν προφήτης ἄτιμος εἰ μὴ ἐν τῇ πατρίδι αὐτοῦ, and in Lk. 4²⁴ as οὐδεὶς προφήτης δεκτός ἐστιν ἐν τῇ πατρίδι αὐτοῦ. In these passages the πατρίς of Jesus is Nazareth, where He was teaching and where His friends and kinsfolk were amazed that " the car-

[1] Its equivalent is found in Plutarch, Pliny, and Seneca ; see D. Smith, *s.v.* " Proverbs," *D.C.G.*, ii. 445.

penter, the Son of Mary," should exhibit such wisdom as His
words revealed.

As Jn. applies the proverb, the circumstances were wholly
different from those at Nazareth. Jesus had left Judæa, where
the Pharisees were beginning to watch Him with suspicion
(4¹⁻³), and was moving *via* Samaria into Galilee. What does
the writer mean here by His having "no honour in His own
country"? Alternative explanations have been offered.

(1) If 4⁴⁴ refers to the departure of Jesus from Judæa,
because His mission was not sufficiently welcomed there, then
by His πατρίς Jn. must mean Jerusalem or Judæa. Origen
(*in Joann.* p. 268, and Fragm. *in Joann.* 4⁴⁴) adopts this view.
He says that Jerusalem was the πατρίς of all the prophets,
and of Jesus as well. Thus 1¹¹ εἰς τὰ ἴδια ἦλθεν, καὶ οἱ ἴδιοι
αὐτὸν οὐ παρέλαβον would provide a parallel for the present
verse. But (*a*) Jesus had made many disciples in Jerusalem
already (2²³), and it was His success that had aroused the
suspicion of the Pharisees (4¹). And (*b*) Jn. knew quite well
that Jesus was "of Galilee," which implies that His home or
πατρίς was there (see 1⁴⁵ and 7⁴²·⁵²). It is unlikely that Jn.
should allude to Jerusalem as Christ's πατρίς, more particularly
as there are good reasons for holding that he was familiar with
Mk.,[1] who applies the word to Nazareth.

(2) Some commentators apply 4⁴⁴, not to what precedes
but to what follows. Jesus had been attracting much notice in
Judæa; it was His habit to withdraw Himself, at least in the
early stages of His ministry, from a hostile environment (7¹ 10³⁹),
and to seek retirement. He wished, then (so it is urged), to
go from Judæa to some place where He might escape unwelcome attention, and He knew from former experience that His
old friends in Galilee would not be likely to make too much
of Him. According to this view, the citation of the proverb
here is a suggestion of the writer that Jesus deliberately chose
to go into a territory where He expected that His mission would
not arouse public interest. This is highly improbable; and,
besides, Jesus was, in fact, cordially received by the people of
Galilee (v. 45), and the miracle of the healing of the nobleman's
son is recorded immediately (vv. 46 ff.).

The verse, then, is a gloss the applicability of which to the
context is not immediately clear. Perhaps it has been misplaced, but there is no evidence for this. Jn. is prone to insert
explanatory reflexions [2] or glosses in the body of his narrative,
which are not always convincing to modern readers; and this
gloss seems to be Johannine. μαρτυρεῖν and ἴδιος are favourite
words with Jn.; he is apt to introduce his explanations with

[1] Introd., p. xcvi.   [2] Cf. Introd., p. xxxiv.

οἱ Γαλιλαῖοι, πάντα ἑωρακότες ὅσα ἐποίησεν ἐν Ἱεροσολύμοις ἐν τῇ ἑορτῇ· καὶ αὐτοὶ γὰρ ἦλθον εἰς τὴν ἑορτήν.

γάρ (cf. esp. 5¹³ ὁ γὰρ Ἰησοῦς ἐξένευσεν, where, as here, the aor. stands for the pluperfect). τιμή, indeed, is not in Jn.'s vocabulary, and instead of it he always uses δόξα when he would speak of the honour paid by one man to another (see on 1¹⁴); but the proverb as quoted by Mk. has ἄτιμος (although τιμή only occurs in the Synoptists in the sense of "price"; cf. Mt. 27⁶·⁹). It is remarkable that the true text of the verse before us gives αὐτὸς γὰρ Ἰησοῦς κτλ. (אABCDWΓΔΘ) without ὁ, while Jn.'s use is to prefix the def. article to the name Ἰησοῦς (as the rec. text does here); see on 1²⁹.

We conclude that v. 44 is a gloss, introduced by Jn. or by some later editor from Mk. 6⁴, suggested by the mention of Galilee, but not apposite in this place.

45. ὅτε is the true reading, but א*D have ὡς.

For ὅσα (אᶜABCLNWΘ), ἅ is read by the rec. with א*DTᵇΓΔ. See, for a similar variant, vv. 29, 39.

ὅτε οὖν ἦλθεν κτλ., "When, then, He had come into Galilee," οὖν not connoting causation but sequence only (see on 1²²).

The Galilæans, among whom He came, had seen His "signs" at Jerusalem at the feast (2²³ 3²), καὶ αὐτοὶ γὰρ ἦλθον εἰς τὴν ἑορτήν, sc. "for (note the introduction of the explanation by γάρ) they also had come for the feast" (the aor. ἦλθον, as well as the preceding ἐποίησεν, being used with a pluperfect sense). The Samaritans did not go up to Jerusalem for the feasts, and so Jesus and His activities there were not known to them; but the Galilæans were orthodox and went up regularly. The words of Jesus alone, without "signs," were sufficient to convince the villagers of Sychar of His claims.

αὐτοὶ γὰρ ἦλθον εἰς τὴν ἑορτήν. ἔρχεσθαι is naturally used of coming up to the feast, when the standpoint of the writer is *Jerusalem* (e.g. 11⁵⁶ 12¹²); but when the scene is in Galilee, as here, and mention is made of worshippers "going up" to the feast, we should expect ἀναβαίνειν (as at 7⁸). In this sentence of explanation the writer seems to be recalling what he had noticed at Jerusalem, viz. that the Galilæans came up for the Passover mentioned in c. 2.

Healing of the nobleman's son (vv. 46–54)

46. Despite the differences between the story of the healing of the centurion's servant (Mt. 8⁵ᶠᶠ·, Lk. 7⁶ᶠᶠ·) and Jn.'s story

of the healing of the nobleman's son, the two narratives probably recall the same incident. The differences are obvious.
In Jn. the anxious inquirer is βασιλικός ; in Mt., Lk., he is
ἑκατόνταρχος. In Jn. the patient is sick of a fever; in Mt. he
is παραλυτικός. In Mt., Lk., Jesus is asked only to speak the
word of healing, but He offers to go down to the man's house.
In Jn. He is asked to go down, but he only says that the boy
will recover (v. 50); nor does Jesus express surprise at the
man's faith, as He does in Mt., Lk. In Mt., Lk., the patient
is the servant (Mt. has παῖς, Lk. has both παῖς and δοῦλος),
while in Jn. he is the man's son (υἱός, παιδίον). Further, it
has been argued that the strong faith of the centurion in Mt.,
Lk., " becomes intelligible, without ceasing to be admirable,
when we reflect that he was evidently aware of the miracle
formerly wrought for another inhabitant of the same city, an
eminent person, one of the court which his own sword
protected." [1]

It has also been supposed that while the centurion of Mt.,
Lk., was a Gentile (Mt. 8[10]), the nobleman of Jn. was probably
a Jew; but of this latter conjecture there is no evidence. There
is no hint in Jn. as to the nationality or religious belief of the
βασιλικός.

Yet the stories are not so dissimilar that they could not
have been confused. Irenæus actually treats them as one and
the same: " Filium centurionis absens verbo curavit dicens,
Vade, filius tuus vivit," are his words (Hær. ii. 22. 3). In both
cases the patient's home was at Capernaum, and in both cases
it is suggested (although not expressly stated by Jn.) that he was
healed from a distance; that is, that the healings were " telepathic " in modern phrase. The only other instance of this in
the Gospels is the case of the Syrophœnician woman's daughter
(Mk. 7[29, 30], Mt. 15[28]). The faith of the nobleman, as indicated in v. 50, " the man believed the word which Jesus spake
to him," was very strong, and he cannot be placed, in this
respect, on a lower level than the centurion of Mt., Lk. It is
probable that one of the most obvious discrepancies in the two
narratives, " servant " and " son," is due to the ambiguity of
the word παῖς, which may mean either. That Jn. uses παῖς
in v. 51 (and there alone in the Gospel), although he has υἱός
in vv. 46, 47, 50, 53, may be significant in this connexion.[2]

[1] Chadwick, Expositor, IV. v. 443 f. ; so Westcott, in loc.
[2] There is a miracle story in the Babylonian Talmud (Ber. 34b)
which looks like another version of this. When a son of Gamaliel
was sick, the father sent messengers to Rabbi Chanina ben Dosa to
ask for his intercessions. He prayed, and then said, " Go, for the
fever has now left him." They marked the time, and going back found

46. Ἦλθεν οὖν πάλιν εἰς τὴν Κανὰ τῆς Γαλιλαίας, ὅπου ἐποίησεν τὸ ὕδωρ οἶνον. Καὶ ἦν τις βασιλικὸς οὗ ὁ υἱὸς ἠσθένει ἐν Καφαρναούμ· 47. οὗτος ἀκούσας ὅτι Ἰησοῦς ἥκει ἐκ τῆς Ἰουδαίας εἰς τὴν Γαλιλαίαν, ἀπῆλθεν πρὸς αὐτὸν καὶ ἠρώτα ἵνα καταβῇ καὶ ἰάσηται αὐτοῦ τὸν υἱόν· ἤμελλεν γὰρ ἀποθνήσκειν. 48. εἶπεν οὖν ὁ Ἰησοῦς

See, for the "miraculous" element in the story, Introd., p. clxxix.

ἦλθεν οὖν κτλ. οὖν expresses sequence, not causation (see on 1²²). It was not *because* the Galilæans welcomed Him that Jesus moved on to Cana. πάλιν, a favourite word with Jn. (see on 4³), reminds the reader that He had been there before.

Κανᾶ . . . ὅπου ἐποίησεν τὸ ὕδωρ οἶνον. An explanatory note reminding the reader of the narrative of 2¹ff..

καὶ ἦν. So ABCΓΔΘW; אDLNTᵇ have ἦν δέ.

βασιλικός, *i.e.* one of the courtiers of Herod, tetrarch of Galilee; D has βασιλισκός, *regulus*, which would convey the erroneous idea that this courtier was a petty king. Some have identified him with Chuza, Herod's steward (Lk. 8³), or with Manaen (Acts 13¹); but this is only guess-work. The man was eager to invoke any help that might cure his son, quite independently of his religious principles or position.

47. ἀκούσας ὅτι . . . ὅτι *recitantis* is followed by the actual words which reached the anxious father, viz. " Jesus is coming from Judæa into Galilee "; hence, in accordance with Jn.'s practice, ὁ is omitted before Ἰησοῦς (see on 4¹).

ἀπῆλθεν πρὸς αὐτόν. The man left his son for a time, in his eagerness to secure the aid of a healer.

After ἠρώτα the rec. has αὐτόν, but om. אBCDLTᵇW.

καταβῇ. See on 2¹² for " going down " from Cana to Capernaum.

καὶ ἰάσηται αὐτοῦ τ. υ. ἰᾶσθαι occurs in Jn. only once again (5¹³), except in a quotation where it is used metaphorically (12⁴⁰). Presumably the " signs " which had impressed the people at Jerusalem (2²³) were works of healing, but Jn. does not say so explicitly. He assumes that his readers will know *why* it was that a man whose son was sick should seek Jesus, *sc.* because of His reputation as a healer.

ἤμελλεν ἀποθνήσκειν, *incipiebat mori*. The phrase is used at 11⁵¹ 12³³ 18³² of the impending death of Jesus; but in the present passage there is no suggestion in ἤμελλεν of the *inevitability* or *predestined* certainty of the boy's death; it expresses futurity only, " was going to die."

that in that hour the boy had been cured. See Trench, *Miracles*, p. 123.

πρὸς αὐτόν Ἐὰν μὴ σημεῖα καὶ τέρατα ἴδητε, οὐ μὴ πιστεύσητε.
49. λέγει πρὸς αὐτὸν ὁ βασιλικός Κύριε, κατάβηθι πρὶν ἀποθανεῖν
τὸ παιδίον μου. 50. λέγει αὐτῷ ὁ Ἰησοῦς Πορεύου· ὁ υἱός σου ζῇ.

48. εἶπεν ὁ Ἰ. πρὸς αὐτόν. For the constr. of λέγειν here and
at v. 49, see on 2³.

The answer of Jesus was neither "Yes" nor "No." It
almost conveys a feeling of disappointment that the working
of "signs" should be expected of Him. The Samaritan
villagers had accepted Him because of His words alone, without
any signs (4⁴¹·⁴²).

The collocation σημεῖα καὶ τέρατα does not occur again in
Jn., but it is frequent in the Greek Bible (Ex. 7³, Isa. 8¹⁸ 20³,
Dan. 4²·³ 6²⁷, Mt. 24²⁴, Mk. 13²², Acts 2¹⁹·²²·⁴³ 4³⁰ 5¹² 6⁸ 7³⁶
14³ 15¹², Rom. 15¹⁹, 2 Cor. 12¹², 2 Thess. 2⁹, Heb. 2⁴). τέρας,
"a prodigy," never occurs in the N.T. except in conjunction
with σημεῖον. No doubt a σημεῖον need not be miraculous, but
the Jews, like all the peoples of early ages, were more ready
to see the Divine power in what seemed to be "supernatural"
than in the "natural" order; and it is not likely that they
would have distinguished sharply a σημεῖον from a τέρας. Jn.
is specially prone to use the word σημεῖον when speaking of the
"works" of Jesus (see Introd., p. clxxvi, and also on 2¹¹,
where the relation between faith and "signs" in the Fourth
Gospel is considered).

οὐ μὴ πιστεύσητε. This might be interrogative: "Will
you not believe without signs?" But more probably it is
categorical: "You will not believe, etc." That the Jews
"seek signs" (1 Cor. 1²²) was as true at Cana as in
Jerusalem. The plural πιστεύσητε may indicate that the
words, although addressed to an individual, include in their
reference a whole class of people to which the nobleman
belonged.

49. κύριε. "Sir." For this mode of address, see on 1³⁸.

κατάβηθι. The man perceives that his request has not
been definitely refused, despite what Jesus had said to him
and to the bystanders as to the imperfection of a faith based on
"signs."

πρὶν ἀποθανεῖν τὸ π. μ. In like manner, Martha and Mary
(11²¹·³²) thought that for Jesus to rescue their sick brother
from death, He must be by his bedside. "Duplex imbecillitas
rogantis, quasi Dominus necesse haberet adesse, nec posset
aeque resuscitare mortem. Atqui etiam ante quam descendit
parens, vitae restitutus est filius eius" (Bengel).

τὸ παιδίον μου. A *fam.* 13 have υἱόν for παιδίον. But not
only is παιδίον the word in the best texts; it is obviously

ἐπίστευσεν ὁ ἄνθρωπος τῷ λόγῳ ὃν εἶπεν αὐτῷ ὁ Ἰησοῦς, καὶ ἐπορεύετο. 51. ἤδη δὲ αὐτοῦ καταβαίνοντος οἱ δοῦλοι ὑπήντησαν αὐτῷ λέγοντες ὅτι ὁ παῖς αὐτοῦ ζῇ. 52. ἐπύθετο οὖν τὴν ὥραν παρ' αὐτῶν

right. "My little child," the father says in his anguish; cf Mk. 9²⁴ ὁ πατὴρ τοῦ παιδίου.

50. The answer of Jesus tests the father severely. "Go thy way ; thy son lives." When the father had left the boy, he was at the point of death (v. 47); but the only assurance that Jesus gave was that the boy was still living. See Introd., p. clxxx.

Before ἐπίστευσεν the rec. inserts καί (ACNΓΔΘ), but om. אBDW.

ἐπίστευσεν τῷ λόγῳ. For the constr., cf. 5⁴⁷; and note that the man believed without any corroboration of Jesus' words. See 20²⁹.

καὶ ἐπορεύετο. The impft. marks the continuous progress of the man's journey, and not any sudden movement of departure. Cf. Mt. 24¹, Lk. 2³ 7⁶ 19²⁸ 24²⁸, for ἐπορεύετο.

By some commentators a difficulty has been found in the statement of v. 52, that the anxious father did not reach home until the next day, although Jesus' words of assurance had been addressed to him at 1 p.m. (see on v. 52). But even if we are to apply such strict tests of time and circumstance to the Johannine stories, there is no special difficulty here. It is 20 miles or more, the way being rough and hilly, from Cana to Capernaum. Presumably the βασιλικός had a retinue with him, and it would take some time to get them together for the journey. Even if an immediate start had been made in the midday heat, it would not have been easy to reach Capernaum the same evening. If we are to speculate about such a matter, it seems probable that the father got home early the next morning, for his anxiety would have prevented him resting at night on the way. If he left Cana at 3 p.m. and got home at 2 a.m. next morning, all the time conditions of the story would be satisfied.

51. ὑπήντησαν. So אBCDLNΘW; the rec. has ἀπήντησαν. Cf. 11²⁰· ³⁰ 12¹⁸.

After αὐτῷ the rec. adds καὶ ἀπήγγειλαν (אD have ἤγγειλαν); om. BLN.

ὁ παῖς. This is the only appearance of παῖς in Jn., and it is replaced (wrongly) by υἱός in DL fam. 13. See on v. 49.

For αὐτοῦ (אABCW), the rec. has σου (with DLΔΘ), as if ὅτι after λέγοντες were ὅτι recitantis, introducing the actual words of the servants.

ἐν ᾗ κομψότερον ἔσχεν· εἶπαν οὖν αὐτῷ ὅτι Ἐχθὲς ὥραν ἐβδόμην ἀφῆκεν αὐτὸν ὁ πυρετός. 53. ἔγνω οὖν ὁ πατὴρ ὅτι ἐκείνῃ τῇ ὥρᾳ ἐν ᾗ εἶπεν αὐτῷ ὁ Ἰησοῦς ὁ υἱός σου ζῇ· καὶ ἐπίστευσεν αὐτὸς καὶ ἡ οἰκία αὐτοῦ ὅλη. 54. Τοῦτο δὲ πάλιν δεύτερον σημεῖον ἐποίησεν ὁ Ἰησοῦς ἐλθὼν ἐκ τῆς Ἰουδαίας εἰς τὴν Γαλιλαίαν.

52. ἐπύθετο. This is the best attested reading. *Fam.* 13 give the more usual form ἐπυνθάνετο. πυνθάνομαι does not occur again in Jn.

τὴν ὥραν παρ᾽ αὐτῶν. So אACDNW⊕; the rec. has παρ᾽ αὐτῶν τὴν ὥραν; B omits παρ᾽ αὐτῶν, and has τὴν ὥραν ἐκεινήν.

ἐν ᾗ κομψότερον ἔσχεν, "in which he got better," the aor. marking a definite change in his condition. κομψότερον is not found again in the LXX or N.T., but the phrase κομψῶς ἔχεις, "you are doing finely," occurs in Arrian, *Epict.* iii. 10. 13, an apposite passage cited by Wetstein. κομψότερον ἔσχεν is good, idiomatic Greek, and does not read like a translation from the Aramaic. Cf. Introd., p. lxvii.

εἶπαν οὖν. So BCLNW; the rec. has καὶ εἶπον (אAD⊕).

ὅτι (*recitantis*) introduces the actual words of the servants.

The spelling ἐχθές (אAB*CDW⊕) must be preferred to the rec. χθές (cf. Acts 7²⁸, Heb. 13⁸).

ὥραν ἐβδόμην, *sc. about* the seventh hour, the acc. being less definite than the dat. of v. 53; see Ex. 9¹⁸ ταύτην τὴν ὥραν αὔριον, "to-morrow *about* this hour" (cf. Rev. 3³ ποίαν ὥραν). The seventh hour was 1 p.m. (see on 1³⁹). The point may be, however, that it was common belief that the seventh hour of fever was the critical hour. Clement of Alexandria (*Strom.* vi. 16) thought that the seventh *day* of any disease marked the crisis.

ὁ πυρετός, "the fever". The word occurs again in N.T. only at Mt 8¹⁵, Mk. 1³¹, Lk. 4³⁸· ³⁹, Acts 28⁸.

53. ἐκείνῃ τῇ ὥρᾳ, "that very hour," the dat. fixing the hour definitely. The rec. text prefixes ἐν, but א*BC omit. In this was the σημεῖον, that the fever left the boy at the exact time that Jesus said, "Thy son lives."

ἐπίστευσεν, "believed," the verb being used absolutely, to express complete faith (see on 1⁷).

καὶ ἡ οἰκία αὐτοῦ ὅλη. Cf. Acts 18⁸.

54. πάλιν δεύτερον. This tautologous phrase occurs again 21¹⁶; cf. πάλιν ἐκ δευτέρου, Mt. 26⁴², Acts 10¹⁵.

The sentence points back to the miracle at Cana, which Jn. says was the first of the "signs" of Jesus; and it calls attention to the fact that the healing of the nobleman's son was, like the earlier sign, wrought after Jesus had left Judæa for Galilee

The Feeding of the Five Thousand (VI. 1–13)

VI. 1 ff. The incident of the Feeding of the Five Thousand is the only one in the public ministry of Jesus before the last visit to Jerusalem which is found in all four Gospels; Mk., Mt., and Jn. (but not Luke) adding an account of the Storm on the Lake. The Synoptists (Mk. 6³¹f·, Mt. 14¹³f·, Lk. 9¹⁰f·) agree in placing the miraculous feeding after the return of the Twelve from their mission, and after the beheading of John the Baptist. The labours which the apostles had undertaken made a period of rest desirable (Mk. 6³¹); and also it was but prudent to go into retirement for a time, as Herod's suspicions had been aroused, and he was desirous of seeing Jesus (Lk. 9⁹). The setting of the miracle in Jn. is not inconsistent with these some-what vague indications of the period in the ministry of Jesus at which it was wrought.

Reasons have been given already for the conclusion (see Introd., p. xvii) that cc. 5 and 6 have been transposed, so that in the original draft of Jn., c. 6 followed directly after c. 4. At the end of c. 4 Jesus and His disciples are at Cana, and we now find them crossing the Sea of Galilee to its north-eastern side. They probably followed the road familiar to them (2¹²), and went down from Cana to Capernaum, where they had their heavy [1] fishing-boat (τὸ πλοῖον, Mk. 6³²). Mk. (followed by Mt.) says that the place to which they went by boat was " a desert place," as Jesus wished to retire for a time from public view, but that the crowd followed them by road, evidently being able to observe the course the boat was taking, and arrived before them (Mk. 6³². ³³). Jn. rather implies that Jesus and His disciples arrived first (6³). Lk. (9¹⁰) gives the name of the place as Bethsaida, by which he must mean Bethsaida Julias (et Tell) at the extreme north end of the lake, on the eastern side, for no other Bethsaida is known.[2] These data are all fairly consistent with each other, if we suppose that the place was the little plain on the north-eastern shore (about a mile south of Bethsaida Julias) which is now called *el-Baṭîhah*. This was grazing ground, and there would be abundance of grass there at the Passover season (cf. 6⁴. ¹⁰, Mk. 6³⁹).[3] A hill (6³) rises up behind it. This plain is about 4 miles by boat from Tell Hûm (the most probable site of Capernaum; see on

---

[1] As it held thirteen persons, it must have been a large boat.

[2] The supposition that there was another Bethsaida on the western shore lacks evidence, and is improbable. Cf. 12²¹.

[3] It is said that grass is found there at all seasons (W. M. Christie, *D.C.G.* ii. 589) ; cf. Rix (*Tent and Testament*, pp. 265 ff.) for the geo-graphical problem.

1. Μετὰ ταῦτα ἀπῆλθεν ὁ Ἰησοῦς πέραν τῆς θαλάσσης τῆς Γαλιλαίας τῆς Τιβεριάδος. 2. ἠκολούθει δὲ αὐτῷ ὄχλος πολύς, ὅτι ἐθεώρουν τὰ σημεῖα ἃ ἐποίει ἐπὶ τῶν ἀσθενούντων. 3. ἀνῆλθεν δὲ

2¹²), and perhaps 9 miles from it by following the path along the western shore and crossing the fords of Jordan, where it flows into the lake from the north. It was the latter route that the crowds took who followed Jesus. See further 6¹⁵ᶠ.

1. μετὰ ταῦτα. For this phrase, see Introd., p. cviii.

ἡ θάλασσα τῆς Γαλιλαίας is the name given in Mt. and Mk. to the lake called in the O.T. the " Sea of Chinnereth " (Num. 34¹¹, etc.). It is called ἡ λίμνη Γεννησαρέτ in Lk. 5¹, and ἡ θάλασσα τῆς Τιβεριάδος in Jn. 21¹. Tiberias was a town on the western shore, founded A.D. 22 by Herod Antipas, and named after Tiberius, which shows that the designation " the Sea of Tiberias " could hardly have been current during our Lord's ministry.[1] Accordingly the double designation found here, τῆς θαλάσσης τῆς Γαλιλαίας τῆς Τιβεριάδος, shows the use of the contemporary name " the Sea of Galilee," followed by the explanatory gloss " that is, of Tiberias," added to identify the lake for Greek readers at the end of the first century. If we ascribe τῆς θαλάσσης τῆς Γαλιλαίας to the aged apostle, John the son of Zebedee, when telling his reminiscences, the addition τῆς Τιβεριάδος would naturally be made by the evangelist, whom we call Jn. Cf. v. 23 for the town of Tiberias.

2. ἠκολούθει δέ. So אBDLNW. But the rec. καὶ ἠκολούθει (ΑΓΔΘ) is quite in Jn.'s manner, who often uses καί for δέ (see below, v. 21).

" A great crowd was following Him " (cf. Mt. 14¹³, Lk. 9¹¹; and see Mk. 6³³), i.e. not only did they follow Him now, when He wished to be in retirement, but they had been following Him about before He crossed the lake; ἠκολούθει is the impft. of continued action. Their reason was " because they were noticing the signs that He was doing on the sick." ἐθεώρουν (BDLNΘ) is the better reading, as preserving the idea that they had been continually observing His powers of healing (for θεωρεῖν in a like context, cf. 2²³), but אΓΔ have ἑώρων. W has θεωροῦντες.

As Jn. represents the matter, it was *previous* works of healing that had attracted the attention of the crowds; e.g., presumably, the cure of the nobleman's son, which has just been narrated (4⁴⁶ᶠᶠ.). Cf. also the works of healing narrated in Mk. 1²⁹· ³²· ⁴⁰ 2¹ 3¹ 6⁵, but not described by Jn. Mt. 14¹⁴

[1] Josephus (B.J. iii. 3, 5) has τῆς πρὸς Τιβεριάδα λίμνης, which Niese notes as having been altered in inferior MSS. to Τιβεριάδος.

εἰς τὸ ὅρος Ἰησοῦς, καὶ ἐκεῖ ἐκάθητο μετὰ τῶν μαθητῶν αὐτοῦ. 4. ἦν
δὲ ἐγγὺς τὸ πάσχα, ἡ ἑορτὴ τῶν Ἰουδαίων. 5. ἐπάρας οὖν τοὶς

and Lk. 9[11], however, record that Jesus began the day on this
occasion by healing the sick. This is not mentioned by Mk.
On the other hand, Mk. 6[34] (followed by Lk. 9[11], but not by
Mt.) says that the earlier part of the day was spent in *teaching*
the people; but neither for this nor for works of healing is there
room in the Johannine narrative (see below on v. 5). Jn.
seems to know the Marcan story (see on v. 7), but he corrects
it as he proceeds. See Introd., p. xcvii.

3. ἀνῆλθεν δὲ εἰς τὸ ὅρος Ἰη., "Jesus went up to the hill,"
i.e. the hill rising out of the little plain by the shore. Mk.
(6[46]), followed by Mt., mentions the hill *after* his narrative
of the miracle; but Mt. (15[29]), in telling what preceded the
parallel miracle of the Feeding of the Four Thousand, says,
as Jn. does here, ἀναβὰς εἰς τὸ ὅρος ἐκάθητο ἐκεῖ. Perhaps Jn.
has borrowed here from Mt., but this is unlikely.[1]

It was the habit of Jesus to *sit* when He taught, as the
Rabbis were accustomed to do (cf. Mk. 4[1] 9[35], Mt. 26[55], Lk. 4[20]
5[3] [Jn.] 8[2]); and He was wont to go up to the hills, whether for
teaching (Mt. 5[1] 24[3]) or for prayer (Mk. 6[46], Lk. 6[12] 9[28]).

The verb ἀνέρχομαι occurs again in N.T. only at Gal. 1[18];
and א*D give ἀπῆλθεν here.

This narrative represents Jesus and His disciples as having
arrived at the eastern side of the lake before the crowd, who
according to Mk. (6[33]) had arrived there first. According to
Mk. 6[30], Lk. 9[10], the disciples who were with Jesus were the
"apostles"; and this is implied in Jn.'s narrative, though
not explicitly stated, for the twelve baskets of fragments of
v. 13 indicate that the number of disciples present was twelve.
See on 2[2].

4. It has been pointed out [2] that, although τὸ πάσχα is
read here by all MSS. and vss., yet there are patristic comments
on the verse which suggest that some early writers did not
treat "the feast" of 6[4] as a Passover, and that therefore the
texts before them did not include the words τὸ πάσχα at this
point. Thus Irenæus (*Hær.* II. xxii. 3) is silent as to this
Passover, although it would have been apposite to his argument to use it.[3] If τὸ πάσχα were omitted here, it would be
natural to identify the feast of this verse with the Feast of

---

[1] See Introd., p. **xcvi.** Streeter, *The Four Gospels*, p. 413, hazards
the guess that the words ἀναβὰς εἰς τὸ ὅρος ἐκάθητο ἐκεῖ originally stood
in the text of Mk.

[2] Most explicitly by Hort, *Select Readings*, p. 77.

[3] See Introd., p. xviii.

ὀφθαλμοὺς ὁ Ἰησοῦς καὶ θεασάμενος ὅτι πολὺς ὄχλος ἔρχεται πρὸς

Tabernacles noted in 7². Having regard to the importance
of the σκηνοπηγία, it might properly be described as pre-
eminently ἡ ἑορτὴ τῶν Ἰουδαίων (see on 7²). But it would
be precarious to omit words so fully attested as τὸ πάσχα,[1]
and on the hypothesis, which has been adopted in this Commentary, that c. 5 comes after c. 6 (see Introd., p. xviii), all is
clear. The Passover mentioned here as " near " is the feast
whose celebration is narrated in 5¹; *i.e.* it was the second
Passover of the public ministry of Jesus (that mentioned in 2¹³
being the first), and was probably the Passover of the year
28 A.D.

For the phrase " feast of *the Jews,*" see on 2¹³; and cf.
2⁶ 19²¹. ⁴².

It has been suggested that this note about the approaching
Passover was introduced into the narrative to explain the large
concourse of persons who were present on the occasion of the
miracle, and who are supposed to have been thronging the
roads on the way to Jerusalem for the observance of the feast.
But the north-eastern corner of the lake is hardly a point at
which we should expect to find thousands of such travellers.
Jn. is fond of introducing notes of time into his narrative (see
p. cii), and he has similar notes about approaching festivals at
2¹³ 7² 11⁵⁵. ἐγγύς is a favourite word with him, both in relation
to time and to distance.

5. ἐπάρας οὖν τοὺς ὀφθαλμοὺς ὁ Ἰη. For this phrase, see on
4³⁵, where, as here, it is followed by the verb θεᾶσθαι. It is
used again of Jesus at 17¹; cf. also 11⁴¹ and Lk. 6²⁰. For
θεᾶσθαι see on 1¹⁴.

πολὺς ὄχλος, *i.e.* apparently the ὄχλος πολύς of v. 2 (see on
12⁹), who had followed Jesus and His disciples round the head
of the lake. But, no doubt, once it was known where He was,
people would flock to the place from the neighbouring villages
to see and hear Him. According to the Synoptists (see on
v. 2), the crowd came upon Jesus early in the morning, and
the day was spent teaching or healing their sick. Then,
towards evening, the disciples suggest that the people should
be sent away that they might buy food for themselves. Jn.
tells nothing of teaching or healing on this occasion, and he
represents Jesus as having foreseen, as soon as the crowd began
to gather, the difficulty that would arise about food. When He
saw the great multitude coming, He asked Philip, " Whence
are we to buy loaves ? "

---

[1] Burkitt (*Ev. da Mepharreshê,* ii. 313) shows that the Syriac
tradition is against omitting τὸ πάσχα.

αὐτόν, λέγει πρὸς Φίλιππον Πόθεν ἀγοράσωμεν ἄρτους ἵνα φάγωσιν
οὗτοι; 6. τοῦτο δὲ ἔλεγεν πειράζων αὐτόν· αὐτὸς γὰρ ᾔδει τί

It is to be observed that in the narratives of the Feeding of
the Four Thousand (Mk. 8⁴, Mt. 15³³), although *not* in the
parallel narratives of the Feeding of the Five Thousand, the
disciples put this question (πόθεν) to Jesus. The question is
the same as that which Moses puts to Yahweh (Num. 11¹³),
πόθεν μοι κρέα δοῦναι παντὶ τῷ λαῷ τούτῳ; and the misgivings
of Moses, when he reflects that he had 600,000 footmen
to feed, are expressed in terms not unlike those which Philip
uses here, πᾶν τὸ ὄψος τῆς θαλάσσης συναχθήσεται αὐτοῖς καὶ
ἀρκέσει αὐτοῖς; (Num. 11²²).

Another O.T. parallel may be found in 2 Kings 4⁴²ᶠ·, where
Elisha's servant exclaims at the impossibility of feeding a
hundred men with twenty barley loaves and ears of corn "in
his sack" (εἴκοσι ἄρτους κριθίνους καὶ παλάθας, *i.e. cakes*). The
narrative relates that Elisha said, Δὸς τῷ λαῷ καὶ ἐσθιέτωσαν,
declaring that Yahweh had told him there would be enough
and to spare. And so it was: ἔφαγον καὶ κατέλιπον. This is a
story which bears a likeness to the Feedings of the Multitudes
in the Gospels, in detail much more striking than the story of
the miraculous increase of meal and oil by Elijah's intervention (1 Kings 17¹⁶). See Introd., p. clxxxi.

However, in Jn.'s narrative the question (πόθεν) is a question
put by Jesus Himself to Philip. Philip was of Bethsaida
(1⁴⁴), and presumably he knew the neighbourhood; he was
thus the natural person of whom to ask where bread could be
bought. This is one of those reminiscences which suggest the
testimony of an eye-witness. The Synoptists, in their accounts
of the wonderful Feedings of the Multitudes, do not name
individual disciples; but Jn. names both Philip and Andrew,
and their figures emerge from his narrative as those of real
persons, each with his own characteristics. See below on v. 8.

λέγει πρὸς Φίλ. For this constr., see on 2³.

For ἀγοράσωμεν (אABDNW⊙), the rec. has ἀγοράσομεν.

6. τοῦτο δὲ ἔλεγεν πειράζων αὐτόν κτλ. We have seen already
(cf. Introd., p. xxxiv) that Jn. is apt to comment on the words
of Jesus and offer explanations of them. The comment at
this point is probably due to a misunderstanding (as at 2²¹).
Jn. thinks it necessary to explain *why* Jesus asked Philip where
bread could be bought, because he hesitates to represent Him
as asking a question which would suggest His ignorance of
the answer. But the true humanity of Jesus is not realised,
if it is assumed that He never asked questions about the simple
matters of every day.

ἔμελλεν ποιεῖν. 7. ἀπεκρίθη αὐτῷ ὁ Φίλιππος Διακοσίων δηναρίων
ἄρτοι οὐκ ἀρκοῦσιν αὐτοῖς, ἵνα ἕκαστος βραχύ τι λάβῃ. 8. λέγει
αὐτῷ εἷς ἐκ τῶν μαθητῶν αὐτοῦ, Ἀνδρέας ὁ ἀδελφὸς Σίμωνος Πέτρου,

Jn. does not write thus of Jesus elsewhere. On His way to
the tomb of Lazarus, Jesus asks where it is (11³⁴). When He
saw the fishing-boat on the lake, He asked them if they had
caught any fish (21⁵, where, however, He *may* be represented
as knowing that nothing had been caught). It is by a like
mistaken idea of reverence that the later Synoptists often omit
questions which Mk. represents Jesus as asking, *e.g.* : "Who
touched my garments ? " (Mk. 5³⁰, Lk. 8⁴⁵, omitted by Mt.).
"Seest thou aught ? " addressed to the blind man who was
healed by stages, is found only in Mk. 8²³. "How long time
is it since this hath come to him ? " asked of the epileptic boy's
father (Mk. 9²¹), is omitted by Mt. and Lk.

The simple question, "Where can bread be bought ? "
asked by Jesus of a disciple who was familiar with the locality,
needs not to be explained or explained away.

πειράζειν does not occur again in Jn., but that by itself does
not prove the verse to be a later gloss, although it raises the
question if it may not have been added after Jn. had completed his work.

7. διακοσίων δηναρίων ἄρτοι οὐκ ἀρκοῦσιν κτλ. There is no
mention of the "two hundred pennyworth" in Mt. or Lk.,
but Mk. 6³⁷ makes the disciples say ἀγοράσωμεν δηναρίων
διακοσίων ἄρτους; It is probable that Jn. is recalling the
phraseology of Mk. at this point, although it is possible that
two distinct traditions, that which came through Peter and
that which came through John the son of Zebedee, have independently preserved the same remark made by disciples. Jn.
several times betrays a knowledge of the Marcan narrative,
which he corrects where necessary.[1]

A *denarius* was the ordinary day's wage of a labourer
(cf. Mt. 20²). Even if the disciples had as much as two
hundred denarii in their common purse (13²⁹), which is
improbable, Philip points out that they would not purchase
enough bread to feed five thousand people, nor would
it be easy to find so much bread in the vicinity without
notice.

There is a reminiscence of the phrase ἵνα ἕκαστος βραχύ
τι λάβῃ in a passage quoted below (v. 11) from the second-
century *Acts of John*.

8. εἷς ἐκ τῶν μαθητῶν αὐτοῦ. This description of an apostle
is not found in the Synoptists (except at Mk. 13¹, without

[1] See Introd., p. xcvii.

9. Ἔστιν παιδάριον ὧδε ὃς ἔχει πέντε ἄρτους κριθίνους καὶ δύο

ἐκ); but Jn. has it again at 12⁴ 13²³; cf. 18¹⁷· ²⁵. For the constr. εἰς ἐκ followed by a gen. plur., see on 1⁴⁰. For the designation of Andrew as '' Simon Peter's brother,'' see on 1⁴⁰. His first impulse of discipleship was to find Peter and bring him to Jesus (1⁴¹). He appears here as a resourceful person who tries to find a practical answer to the question put to Philip by Jesus, although he does not think that he has been successful in gathering a sufficient supply of food. In 12²⁰⁻²² Philip and Andrew are again associated in somewhat similar fashion, Philip not knowing what to do until he has consulted Andrew. These notices in Jn. supply the only indications of Andrew's character that we have, and it is interesting to observe their consistency with each other. The only distinctive mention of Andrew in the Synoptists is at Mk. 13³, where he appears as associated with the inner circle of the Twelve— Peter, James, and John.

A second-century notice of Andrew and Philip shows that they were held to be among the leaders of the Twelve. When Papias collected traditions from the elders of his day, he used to ask them, '' What did Andrew and what did Peter say? Or what did Philip? Or what Thomas or James or John or Matthew? '' (Eus. *H.E.* iii. 39. 4), placing them respectively first and third of the apostles whom he names.

In the Muratorian Fragment on the Canon, Andrew is specially associated with the writing of the Fourth Gospel: '' eadem nocte revelatum Andreae ex apostolis ut, recognoscentibus cunctis, Johannes suo nomine cuncta describeret ''; and it is possible that his intimacy with John the son of Zebedee was handed down by tradition, although it cannot be held that he lived until the Gospel was published (see Introd., p. lvi).

9. In the Synoptists the five loaves and two fishes are the provision which the disciples had for their own use. In Jn., Andrew reports that a lad was present who had this food with him, possibly having brought it from a neighbouring village, for Jesus and the Twelve.

παιδάριον. There is no mention of this lad in the Synoptists; see above. The word παιδάριον does not occur elsewhere in the N.T., but it is frequent in the LXX; and it must be noted that it is the word used of Elisha's servant (2 Kings 4³⁸· ⁴³) in the passage immediately preceding the story of Elisha's multiplication of the loaves (see above on v. 5).

The rec. has παιδάριον ἕν (ΑΓΔΘ); אBDLNW om. ἕν. The Synoptists sometimes use εἷς or ἕν, as a kind of indefinite

ὀψάρια· ἀλλὰ ταῦτα τί ἐστιν εἰς τοσούτους; 10. εἶπεν ὁ Ἰησοῦς Ποιήσατε τοὺς ἀνθρώπους ἀναπεσεῖν. ἦν δὲ χόρτος πολὺς ἐν τῷ τόπῳ. ἀνέπεσαν οὖν οἱ ἄνδρες τὸν ἀριθμὸν ὡς πεντακισχίλιοι.

article, for τις or τι (cf. Mt. 8¹⁹ 26⁶⁹); but this is not the style of Jn. (cf., however, 11⁴⁹ 19³⁴).

κριθίνους. It is only Jn. who tells that the loaves were of barley. Barley bread, being cheaper than wheaten, was the common food of the poor; cf. Judg. 7¹³ and Ezek. 13¹⁹. Reference has already been made to ἄρτους κριθίνους in the Elisha story (2 Kings 4⁴²).

δύο ὀψάρια. The Synoptists say δύο ἰχθύας; and Mt. and Mk. in the parallel narrative of the Feeding of the Four Thousand say ὀλίγα ἰχθύδια.

The word ὀψάριον (only found here and at 21⁹·¹⁰·¹³ in the Greek Bible) is a dim. of ὄψον, which originally meant "cooked food," and thence came to be used of any relish taken with food; e.g. in Pap. Fay. 119³¹ εἰς τὰ γενέσια Γεμέλλης πέμψις ὠψάρια,¹ the ὀψάρια were delicacies for a birthday feast. Thus ὀψάρια in the present passage stands for dried or pickled fish. The curing of fish was an important industry on the shores of the Sea of Galilee, and is alluded to as such by Strabo.² Neither in Jn. nor in the Synoptic narrative is there any mention of lighting a fire and cooking fish on the occasion of the miracle; and it is not to be supposed that the meal was of raw, fresh fish and bread. See, however, on 21¹⁰.

10. ποιήσατε (for the aor. imper., see on 2⁵) τοὺς ἀνθρώπους ἀναπεσεῖν . . . ἀνέπεσαν οὖν οἱ ἄνδρες. The R.V. distinguishes ἀνθρώπους from ἄνδρες: "make the *people* sit down . . . so the *men* sat down," suggesting that the women (or children), if present, remained standing. But no such discrimination is indicated in the Synoptic accounts, and it would, in the circumstances, be improbable, despite the Oriental subordination of women: ἐπέταξεν αὐτοῖς ἀνακλιθῆναι πάντας is Mk's statement. ἀνήρ is an infrequent word in Jn., occurring again only 1¹³·³⁰ and 4¹⁶·¹⁷·¹⁸ (of a husband); and it may be that its introduction here is due to a reminiscence of Mk.'s πεντασχίλιοι ἄνδρες, to which Mt. afterwards added the gloss χωρὶς γυναικῶν καὶ παιδίων, as he did also in the parallel narrative of the Feeding of the Four Thousand (Mt. 14²¹ 15³⁸). Jn. returns to the word ἄνθρωποι at v. 14.

ἀναπίπτειν is "to lie back" or "recline," whether on the

---

¹ About 100 A.D., cited by Milligan, *Vocab.*

² xvi. c. 2, § 45, quoted by G. A. Smith, *Hist. Geogr. of Holy Land*, p. 454, who adds, "The pickled fish of Galilee were known throughout the Roman world."

11. ἔλαβεν οὖν τοὺς ἄρτους ὁ Ἰησοῦς καὶ εὐχαριστήσας διέδωκεν τοῖς

sloping hillside (as here) or on a couch (as at the Last Supper, 13¹² 21²⁰). Mk. uses ἀναπίπτειν as well as ἀνακλίνειν in his parallel narrative ; Mt. has ἀνακλίνειν only, and Lk. κατακλίνειν. χόρτος πολύς, " there was much grass "—*green* grass, Mk. says—it being spring-time, after the rainy season, just before the Passover (v. 4). Jn. does not mention the greenness of the grass, nor does he say anything about the people being distributed into groups or companies.

11. ἔλαβεν οὖν τοὺς ἄρτους. Jesus took the loaves, and blessing them, caused them to be distributed, thus acting as host.

It is remarkable, and probably significant, that Jn., alone of the evangelists, does not say that the loaves were *broken* by Jesus, as well as *blessed.* In all the narratives descriptive of the Feedings of the Multitudes, except this, we have ἄρτους ἔκλασεν or κατέκλασεν τοὺς ἄρτους, or the like. Jn. never uses the verb κλάω or κατακλάω. Now, in all the accounts of the institution of the Lord's Supper, that Jesus " brake the Bread " is explicitly mentioned, ἔκλασεν ἄρτον, only one loaf being used. The rite itself is called in Acts 2⁴² ἡ κλάσις τοῦ ἄρτου (cf. Acts 20⁷, and perhaps Acts 27³⁵), so essential a feature was the breaking of the one loaf deemed to be. Thus, in this particular, the Johannine narrative of the Feeding of the Five Thousand is less suggestive of the action of Jesus at the Last Supper than are the Synoptic narratives of the same miracle. By the omission of ἄρτους ἔκλασεν Jn. has deviated from the Synoptic tradition in a fashion which suggests that he did not regard the miraculous meal, which he describes, as anticipatory of the sacrament with which he was familiar, although he does not tell of its institution. The discourse which follows (cf. esp. vv. 52–56) cannot be interpreted without including a sacramental reference; but it would seem, nevertheless, that Jn. wishes to avoid suggesting that the miraculous feeding was a sacramental meal.

It is just possible, although unlikely, that Jn. omits all mention of the breaking of the bread, *not* because he did not regard the meal as sacramental, but because he lays stress on the circumstance (19³³) that the Body of Christ was not broken on the Cross.

We must also note that Jn. omits the words, ἀναβλέψας εἰς τὸν οὐρανόν before the blessing of the loaves, which are common to all three Synoptists. This " lifting up of the eyes " was a very ancient feature of the Eucharistic rite, and we cannot be sure how far back it goes (cf. 11⁴¹ 17¹, and see on 4³⁵).

In another detail, *per contra*, Jn.'s narrative of the Feeding of the Five Thousand suggests the Last Supper *more* clearly than the Synoptists do.   In Jn., it is Jesus Himself who distributes the loaves to the multitudes, διέδωκεν τοῖς ἀνακειμένοις, just as He distributed the Bread to His disciples on the eve of His Passion (cf. also 21¹³); but in the Synoptists, it is the Twelve who, acting under His direction, bring the loaves round, which probably was what actually took place.   Jn.'s διέδωκεν, however, need not be taken as excluding the assistance of the Twelve in the distribution, although this is not explicitly mentioned. *Qui facit per alium, facit per se.*

The rec. text inserts after διέδωκεν the words τοῖς μαθηταῖς, οἱ δὲ μαθηταί (so אᶜDΓΔΘ), but this is a harmonising gloss introduced from Mt. 14¹⁹.   The intercalated words are not found in א*ABLNW or in most vss.

We must now examine the word εὐχαριστήσας, " having given thanks."   εὐλογεῖν is the verb used in the Synoptic parallels (Mk. 6⁴¹, Mt. 14¹⁹, Lk. 9¹⁶); but Mk. (8⁶) and Mt. (15³⁶) have εὐχαριστεῖν in a similar context in their narratives of the Feeding of the Four Thousand.   In the accounts of the institution of the Lord's Supper, Lk. (22¹⁹) and Paul (1 Cor. 11²⁴) use εὐχαριστεῖν of the Blessing of the Bread, while Mt. (26²⁷), Mk. (14²³), and Lk. (22¹⁷) use it of the Blessing of the Cup, the Cup being called by Paul τὸ ποτήριον τῆς εὐλογίας ὃ εὐλογοῦμεν (1 Cor. 10¹⁶).   In these passages it is not possible to distinguish in meaning between εὐχαριστεῖν and εὐλογεῖν,[1] although εὐχαριστεῖν and εὐχαριστία soon came to be used in a special sense in connexion with the Holy Communion (cf. Ignat. *Philad.* 4 σπουδάσατε οὖν μιᾷ εὐχαριστίᾳ, and see Justin, *Apol.* i. 66, and Iren. *Hær.* iv. 18. 5).

But the verb εὐλογεῖν is never used in Jn. (except once in a quotation, 12¹³); and he uses εὐχαριστεῖν elsewhere (11⁴¹, Πάτερ εὐχαριστῶ σοι) where no sacramental reference is possible.   In this general sense, " giving of thanks," εὐχαριστεῖν occurs a few times in the later books of the LXX (Judith 8²⁵, 2 Macc. 12³¹) and in Philo, as well as frequently in the N.T., *e.g.* Lk. 17¹⁶ 18¹¹, and very often in Paul.

It may be that the " giving of thanks " or "blessing" which all the evangelists mention in their narratives of the miraculous Feedings of the Multitudes was the grace before meat which the Lord used, and which was the usual habit of piety before a meal (cf. Deut. 8¹⁰).   The form of Jewish " grace " which has come down to us is, " Blessed art thou, O Lord our

[1] Cf. Swete, *J.T.S.*, Jan. 1902, p. 163.

ἀνακειμένοις, ὁμοίως καὶ ἐκ τῶν ὀψαρίων ὅσον ἤθελον. 12. ὡς δὲ
ἐνεπλήσθησαν, λέγει τοῖς μαθηταῖς αὐτοῦ Συναγάγετε τὰ περισσεύσαντα κλάσματα, ἵνα μή τι ἀπόληται. 13. συνήγαγον οὖν, καὶ

God, king of the world, who bringeth forth bread from the
earth." But if this is the allusion in εὐχαριστήσας or εὐλογήσας
in the evangelical narratives of the Miraculous Feedings, it is
curious that no such phrase occurs in connexion with the other
meals described in the Gospels at which Jesus presided or was
the principal Guest (Lk. 24^{30} is sacramental). Jn. does not
hint that "a blessing" was asked or pronounced at the
Marriage Feast in Cana (2^1), or at the supper in Bethany (12^2),
or at the meal by the lake-side (21^{13}). Cf. Mk. 14^3, Lk. 5^{29} 7^{37}.
In Acts 27^{35} it is said, indeed, of Paul λαβὼν ἄρτον εὐχαρίστησεν
τῷ θεῷ ἐνώπιον πάντων καὶ κλάσας ἤρξατο ἐσθίειν ; but it is not
clear that this was an ordinary meal preceded by a "grace."
Knowling and Blass regard it as a sacramental celebration.

Whatever be the reason, it would seem that the evangelical
traditions handed down the incident of Jesus "blessing" the
loaves at the Miraculous Feedings as an incident of special
significance. The similarity to this verse of Jn. 21^{13}, λαμβάνει
τὸν ἄρτον καὶ δίδωσιν αὐτοῖς καὶ τὸ ὀψάριον ὁμοίως, brings out the
more clearly the omission of any such word as εὐχαριστήσας
or εὐλογήσας in the latter passage.

The stress that was laid in early times on the blessing of the
loaves, in connexion with their multiplication, is apparent in a
legend preserved in the second-century *Acts of John* (§ 93):
"If at any time He were bidden by one of the Pharisees and
went to the bidding, we accompanied Him; and before each
was set one loaf by him that had bidden us, He also receiving
one loaf. And, blessing His own loaf, He would divide it
among us; and from that little each was filled (ἐκ τοῦ βραχέος
ἕκαστος ἐχορτάζετο: see v. 7 above), and our own loaves were
saved whole, so that they who bade Him were amazed." The
act of blessing is a preliminary condition of the miracle, according to this writer. See on 6^{23} below.

ὅσον ἤθελον. All the evangelists agree in the statement
that the multitudes "were filled," *i.e.* that they had a sub-
stantial meal, and not merely a scrap of food; but Jn. is even
more explicit, saying that of the fish as well as of the loaves
they had as much as they wished for.

12. ἐνεπλήσθησαν. The Synoptists have ἐχορτάσθησαν, as
Jn. has at v. 26. The phrase μετὰ τὸ ἐμπλησθῆναι used of the
Eucharist in the *Didache* (x. 1) probably comes from this
passage.

τὰ περισσεύσαντα κλάσματα. Mk. (6^{43}) has the curious

ἐγέμισαν δώδεκα κοφίνους κλασμάτων ἐκ τῶν πέντε ἄρτων τῶν κριθίνων ἃ ἐπερίσσευσαν τοῖς βεβρωκόσιν.

expression κλάσματα δώδεκα κοφίνων πληρώματα, but Mt. (14²⁰) has τὸ περισσεῦον τῶν κλασμάτων, and Lk. (9¹⁷) has τὸ περισσεῦσαν αὐτοῖς κλασμάτων. Jn. uses περισσεύειν only here and in v. 13 (he has περισσόν at 10¹⁰); and it has been suggested that he is here dependent either on Lk. or Mt., rather than Mk. But he was quite capable of correcting Mk.'s πληρώματα, just as Lk. and Mt. have done, and the verb περισσεύειν is the natural one to use. Jn. uses the word πλήρωμα only of the "fulness" of Christ (1¹⁶), and avoids it in all other contexts, perhaps because of its misleading employment in Gnostic systems.

κλάσμα is a word used in the N.T. only in the Gospel accounts of the miraculous feedings. It is rare in LXX, but we find κλάσματα ἄρτων in Ezek. 13¹⁹ and κλάσματι ἄρτου in Judg. 19⁵ (A text). It is used of the Bread of the Eucharist in the *Didache* (ix. 3).

Lightfoot [1] recalls a Jewish custom at meals of leaving something over for those who served : this was called פאה, *peah*. This possibly is behind the incident recorded here. The apostles had each his travelling-basket or κόφινος (cf. Judg. 6¹⁹), and having ministered to the people they went round and collected what was left over. Juvenal mentions the κόφινος as a basket characteristic of Jews: "quorum cophinus foenumque supellex" (*Sat.* iii. 14). All four evangelists have the word κόφινος, while in the parallel narrative of the Feeding of the Four Thousand the word is σπυρίς or σφυρίς, which was a hamper large enough to hold a man (Acts 9²⁵).

It is Jn. alone who tells that it was at the bidding of Jesus that the fragments were gathered up, and he alone adds a reason, viz. ἵνα μή τι ἀπόληται. This is one of those comments upon his narrative to which Jn. is so prone (see p. xxxiv), and no doubt it gives an excellent sense at this point. But the Synoptists know nothing of this, and the Jewish custom of leaving a *peah* or morsel at the end of a meal for the servers provides a sufficient explanation of the matter.

There is no suggestion that the bread, miraculously provided, was like the manna of ancient days, which could not be kept over from one day to another (Ex. 16¹⁹); and the objection of the people recorded at v. 31 shows that they did not consider the supply of bread that they had witnessed as at all comparable with the manna from heaven which their fathers had enjoyed.

13. δώδεκα. This suggests that all the original apostles were present

[1] *Hor. Hebr.*, iii. 302.

14. Οἱ οὖν ἄνθρωποι ἰδόντες ὃ ἐποίησεν σημεῖον ἔλεγον ὅτι Οὗτός ἐστιν ἀληθῶς ὁ προφήτης ὁ ἐρχόμενος εἰς τὸν κόσμον. 15. Ἰησοῦς οὖν γνοὺς ὅτι μέλλουσιν ἔρχεσθαι καὶ ἁρπάζειν αὐτὸν ἵνα ποιήσωσιν βασιλέα, ἀνεχώρησεν πάλιν εἰς τὸ ὄρος αὐτὸς μόνος.

ἐκ τῶν πέντε ἄρτων κτλ. Mk. (6⁴³) speaks of fragments of the fishes being gathered up along with the fragments of the loaves, but Jn. (as also Mt., Lk.) speaks only of the fragments of bread.

βεβρωκόσιν. The verb does not occur again in the N.T.

Jesus acclaimed as the Messianic King (vv. 14, 15)

14. ὁ προφήτης ὁ ἐρχόμενος εἰς τὸν κόσμον. The people had already been attracted because of the "signs" of healing which Jesus did (v. 2); now this greater "sign" led them to think of him as "the prophet that cometh into the world." The woman of Samaria had been convinced that He was "a prophet" (4¹⁹), as the blind man whom He healed said of Him afterwards (9¹⁷); but the miracle of the loaves and fishes inclined the eye-witnesses to go further, and to identify Jesus with the prophet of popular belief whom Israel expected (see on 1²¹) as the fulfilment of the prophecy of Deut. 18¹⁵. "They began to say" (ἔλεγον), "This is truly the prophet that is coming into the world" (see on 11²⁷). Cf. v. 31.

ἀληθῶς is a favourite adverb with Jn.; cf. οὗτός ἐστιν ἀληθῶς ὁ προφήτης (7⁴⁰), and see on 1⁴⁷.

ὃ . . . σημεῖον, not ἃ . . . σημεῖα, is the true reading, the reference being to the particular "sign" which has just been described.

The rec., with ALNΓΔΘ, ins. ὁ Ἰησοῦς after σημεῖον, for clearness, but om. אBDW.

15. Jn. generally writes ὁ Ἰησοῦς (see on 1²⁹), but we have Ἰησοῦς (without the art.) followed by οὖν, as here, several times; cf. 11³⁸· 18⁴ 19²⁶.

γνοὺς ὅτι μέλλουσιν ἔρχεσθαι κτλ. The excited people, having concluded that Jesus was the prophet of their expectation, began to plot how they might seize Him (ἁρπάζειν) and make Him king, that is, the Messianic king. The Jerusalem crowds had the same idea when they cried "Hosanna" and greeted Him as "King of Israel" on His entry to the city (12¹³). Indeed, it was made part of the charge against Him, that He had claimed to be "King of the Jews" (18³³ᶠ·). But He would not accept the title in the sense in which they understood it. He was not a political revolutionary. And so

16. Ὡς δὲ ὀψία ἐγένετο, κατέβησαν οἱ μαθηταὶ αὐτοῦ ἐπὶ τὴν

" He withdrew again to the hill " (see v. 3), from which He had come down to feed the people.

Mk. and Mt. tell nothing of the fanatical excitement of the crowds, or of their being so much impressed by the miracle as to think of Jesus as Messiah; [1] the only hint the Synoptists give of this being supplied by Lk., who follows up the narrative of the Feeding by the story of the various answers to the question, " Who do the multitudes say that I am ? " (Lk. 9[18]) which Mk. and Mt. put in another context.

Indeed, Mk. and Mt. give as the reason of Jesus' retirement to the hill, that it was to pray, which is perhaps here suggested by μόνος. That was His habit, and such a motive for His retirement is not inconsistent with His other motive, viz. to be freed from the embarrassing attentions of the crowds. Mk. and Mt. tell that He *dismissed* the crowds (Mk. 6[45], Mt. 14[23]), while Jn. suggests rather that He escaped from them. Probably He tried to disperse them, but some, more obstinate and excited than the rest, would not leave. It is these latter who come before us in v. 22 as having remained until the next morning. Again, Jn. does not mention that the return of the disciples was ordered by Jesus, as Mk. and Mt. do; but it is evident that they would not have left Him had they not been told to do so. He may have wished to remove them from the atmosphere of political excitement which had been generated. Apparently Jesus had not told His disciples exactly where and when they would meet Him again.

The storm on the lake (vv. 16–21)

16. ὀψία may indicate any time in the late afternoon (cf. 20[19] and Mt. 14[15, 23]). The sun set after the disciples had started, and it became dark (σκοτία, v. 17) while they were on the lake. Mk. 6[48] notes that Jesus met them " about the fourth watch of the night," *i.e.* about 3 a.m.

κατέβησαν, " they descended," *sc.* from the slopes of the hill.

16 ff. The incident is described with vividness. It was late in the evening when the boat started on the return journey to Capernaum (v. 17; see on v. 1). The wind had risen, and the lake was stormy. Mk. does not say that the destination of the boat was Capernaum, although that is what we should have expected: his words are ἠνάγκασεν τοὺς μαθητὰς . . . προάγειν

---

[1] Turner (*J.T.S.*, Jan. 1925, p. 148) suggests that it may have been this incident which attracted the attention of Herod (cf. Mk. 6[14]).

θάλασσαν, 17. καὶ ἐμβάντες εἰς πλοῖον ἤρχοντο πέραν τῆς θαλάσσης

εἰς τὸ πέραν πρὸς Βηθσαϊδάν (Mk. 6⁴⁵), and he goes on to tell that, driven by the storm, they landed ultimately at Gennesaret, which is a little to the south of Capernaum. That is to say, according to Mk., they made for Bethsaida in the first instance; whether because they wished to take Jesus on board there, or to land one of the party (it was the home of some of them; see on 1⁴⁴), or because they wished to keep under the lee of the land, in view of the impending storm, we cannot tell. In any case the storm caught them, and when they had rowed 25 or 30 furlongs, that is, about 3 or 4 miles, they see Jesus περιπατοῦντα ἐπὶ τῆς θαλάσσης, and coming near the boat. Now by this time, having rowed nearly 4 miles, they must have been close to the western shore of the lake, and so Jn. says: εὐθέως τὸ πλοῖον ἐγένετο ἐπὶ τῆς γῆς εἰς ἣν ὑπῆγον.

If we had only Jn.'s account of this incident, we should have no reason to suppose that he intended to record any " miracle." The phrase ἐπὶ τῆς θαλάσσης (v. 19) is used by Jn. again at 21¹, where it undoubtedly means " by the sea shore "; and it is probable that he means here that when the boat got into the shallow water near the western shore, the disciples saw Jesus in the uncertain light walking by the lake, and were frightened, not being sure what they saw. Jn. does not say, as Mk. does, that Jesus was received into the boat; he only says that they were desirous to have Him with them, when they found that the voyage was already over (v. 21). Nor does Jn. say anything about a miraculous stilling of the storm (cf. Mk. 6⁵¹). Nor does he say (as Mk. 6⁴⁹, Mt. 14²⁶) that the disciples thought they had seen a phantasm (φάντασμα). So far from it being true that we always find in Jn. an enhancement of the miraculous, in this particular case, while the story as narrated by Mk. (followed by Mt.) is miraculous, in Jn. there is no miracle whatever. Nor does Jn. call the incident a " sign," as he is accustomed to speak of the miracles which he records (cf. v. 14). In short, this story, as told by Jn., is exactly the kind of story that we might expect from John the son of Zebedee, a fisherman with experience of the lake in all its moods, well accustomed to its sudden storms, and knowing the distance from one point to another (v. 19). See Introd., p. clxxvi.

17. ἐμβάντες εἰς πλοῖον. The same phrase occurs for embarking 21³ and 1 Macc. 15³⁷. ADΓΘW insert τό before πλοῖον, which no doubt gives the sense, it being probably their own boat that they took for their return voyage; but אBLΔ omit τό.

εἰς Καφαρναούμ. καὶ σκοτία ἤδη ἐγεγόνει καὶ οὔπω ἐληλύθει πρὸς αὐτοὺς ὁ Ἰησοῦς. 18. ἤ τε θάλασσα ἀνέμου μεγάλου πνέοντος διεγείρετο. 19. ἐληλακότες οὖν ὡς σταδίους εἴκοσι πέντε ἢ τριάκοντα

ἤρχοντο, " they were going," the impft. being used for an incompleted action.

For καὶ σκοτία ἤδη ἐγεγόνει, אD read κατέλαβεν δὲ αὐτοὺς ἡ σκοτία, " but darkness overtook them " (cf. 12³⁵ and 1⁵, where see note). This, again, gives the sense, but we follow ABΓΔΝΘW with the rec. text, although κατέλαβεν αὐτοὺς ἡ σκοτία is a thoroughly Johannine phrase.

οὐκ is read for οὔπω by ΑΓΔΘ, but οὔπω is better attested (אBDLNW) and gives the better sense. Jesus had "not yet" come to them. They had expected to meet Him at Bethsaida Julias (see on 6¹⁶ above), or at some other point, but their course had been embarrassed by the storm. They were probably keeping close to the shore on the look out for Him, before the storm broke.

18. The sea was rising because of the squall. We have the same expression ἡ θάλασσα . . . ἐξηγείρετο, Jonah 1¹³.

19. ἐληλακότες. Cf. βασανιζομένους ἐν τῷ ἐλαύνειν (Mk. 6⁴⁸). ἐλαύνειν occurs again in N.T. only at Lk. 8²⁹, Jas. 3⁴, 2 Pet. 2¹⁷. They had rowed about 25 or 30 stades, *i.e.*, as a stade was 600 feet, nearly 4 miles, and therefore, as has been shown above (v. 16), they were close to the western shore. Mk. says they were ἐν μέσῳ τῆς θαλάσσης (Mk. 6⁴⁷), which need not mean more than that the water was all round them. Mt. adds to Mk.'s sentence, according to the text of BΘ (although the other uncials do not confirm this), σταδίους πολλοὺς (Θ has ἱκανούς) ἀπὸ τῆς γῆς ἀπεῖχε, which seems to be a gloss derived from the narrative of Jn., but intended, after the manner of Mt., to emphasise the miraculousness of the story.

In some texts of Mt. 14²⁵ we have ἐπὶ τὴν θάλασσαν for the ἐπὶ τῆς θαλάσσης of Mk. 6⁴⁸ and Jn. 6¹⁹. The latter does not necessarily mean more than "by the sea shore ": to read ἐπὶ τὴν θάλασσαν would indicate beyond question that Jesus literally "walked on the sea." Job says of the Creator that He "walks upon the high places of the sea," περιπάτων ὡς ἐπ' ἐδάφους ἐπὶ θαλάσσης (Job. 9⁸); and Wisdom declares (Ecclus. 24⁵), ἐν βάθει ἀβύσσων περιεπάτησα, from which passages it might be concluded that "walking upon the sea " is a Divine prerogative. It is possible that some such idea may account for the transformation of the Johannine tradition, which is void of miracle, into the supernatural story in Mk., Mt. See on v. **15** and Introd., p. clxxvi.

θεωροῦσιν, "they notice "; see on 2²³ for θεωρεῖν.

θεωροῦσιν τὸν Ἰησοῦν περιπατοῦντα ἐπὶ τῆς θαλάσσης καὶ ἐγγὺς τοῦ πλοίου γινόμενον, καὶ ἐφοβήθησαν. 20. ὁ δὲ λέγει αὐτοῖς Ἐγώ εἰμι, μὴ φοβεῖσθε. 21. ἤθελον οὖν λαβεῖν αὐτὸν εἰς τὸ πλοῖον, καὶ εὐθέως ἐγένετο τὸ πλοῖον ἐπὶ τῆς γῆς εἰς ἣν ὑπῆγον.

ἐγγὺς τοῦ πλοίου γινόμενον, *sc.* "getting near the boat," a use of γίγνομαι for ἔρχομαι which we have again in v. 25; cf. Acts 20¹⁶ 21¹⁷ 25¹⁵.

ἐφοβήθησαν, "they were afraid," and so Jesus says—
20. ἐγώ εἰμι, μὴ φοβεῖσθε. These comforting words are reported in identical phrase in the Marcan and Johannine narratives (cf. Mk. 6⁵⁰, Mt. 14²⁷, both of which prefix θαρσεῖτε). They probably mean simply "It is I: be not afraid," the Marcan account suggesting that the reason of the disciples' alarm was that they thought Jesus was a spirit (φάντασμα). Another explanation has been offered of ἐγώ εἰμι, viz. that it stands for the self-designation of Yahweh in the prophets, אֲנִי־הוּא, *I (am) He*; cf. 8⁵⁸ 13¹⁹. But this explanation is not necessary here,[1] and such a mystical use of words would be foreign to the style of Mk., although there are parallels in Jn.

21. ἤθελον οὖν λαβεῖν αὐτὸν εἰς τὸ πλ., "they were wishing to receive Him into the boat, and straightway the boat was at the land." ἤθελον is used here as at 7⁴⁴, 16¹⁹, the wish not being translated into action. Here Jn. is at variance with Mk. (6⁵¹), who says, as also Mt. does (with an amplification about Peter's going to Jesus on the water, Mt. 14²⁸⁻³²), that Jesus climbed into the boat. The narrative of Jn. is simpler.

It has been objected to this view that we should expect ἀλλὰ εὐθέως τὸ. πλ. κτλ. rather than καὶ εὐθέως, if the meaning intended is that they did *not* receive Jesus into the boat, because they found their voyage already ended. But Jn. is prone to use καὶ, where ἀλλά or δέ would be employed by another writer (see on 1¹¹).

For εὐθέως in Jn. see on 5⁹.

The people cross the lake and find Jesus at Capernaum
(*vv.* 22–25)

22 ff. The readings of א* in vv. 22–24 are curiously aberrant, and the text from א* must be transcribed in full: τῇ ἐπαύριον ὁ ὄχλος ὁ ἑστὼς πέραν τῆς θαλάσσης εἶδεν ὅτι πλοιάριον ἄλλο οὐκ ἦν ἐκεῖ εἰ μὴ ἕν, ἐκεῖνο εἰς ὃ ἐνέβησαν οἱ μαθηταὶ τοῦ Ἰησοῦ, καὶ ὅτι οὐ συνεληλύθει αὐτοῖς ὁ Ἰησοῦς εἰς τὸ πλοῖον ἀλλὰ μόνοι οἱ μαθηταὶ αὐτοῦ· ἐπελθόντων οὖν τῶν πλοιῶν ἐκ Τιβεριάδος ἐγγὺς οὔσης ὅπου καὶ ἔφαγον ἄρτον, εὐχαριστήσαντος τοῦ κυρίου, καὶ ἰδόντες ὅτι οὐκ ἦν

---
[1] Cf. Introd., p. cxx.

22. Τῇ ἐπαύριον ὁ ὄχλος ὁ ἑστηκὼς πέραν τῆς θαλάσσης εἶδον ὅτι πλοιάριον ἄλλο οὐκ ἦν ἐκεῖ εἰ μὴ ἕν, καὶ ὅτι οὐ συνεισῆλθεν τοῖς μαθηταῖς αὐτοῦ ὁ Ἰησοῦς εἰς τὸ πλοῖον ἀλλὰ μόνοι οἱ μαθηταὶ αὐτοῦ ἀπῆλθον· 23. ἄλλα ἦλθεν πλοιάρια ἐκ Τιβεριάδος ἐγγὺς τοῦ τόποι

ἐκεῖ ὁ Ἰησοῦς οὐδὲ οἱ μαθηταὶ ἀνέβησαν εἰς τὸ πλοῖον καὶ ἦλθον κτλ. This is evidently a rewriting of the original, which has a clumsy parenthesis at v. 23.

Other variants are ἰδών (rec. reading with ΓΔW, a *casus pendens*) for εἶδον (ABLNΘ), אD having εἶδεν; א*ΓΔΘ interpolate the explanatory gloss ἐκεῖνο εἰς ὃ ἐνέβησαν οἱ μαθηταί of the rec. text; for πλοῖον (the true reading) at the end of v. 22, ΓΔΘ give πλοιάριον; after ἀλλά, the rec. text with ΑΓΔΘ inserts δέ; BW have πλοῖα for πλοιάρια (the true reading; see exegetical note) in v. 23; for *gratias agente domino*, many Latin texts have *gratias agentes domino*, as if it was the multitude that had given thanks; and in v. 24, the rec. text with ΑΓΔΘ has πλοῖα for πλοιάρια (אᶜBDLNW).

22. τῇ ἐπαύριον. See on 1¹⁹·²⁹. Some, perhaps the more zealous of the crowd, had remained all night on the scene of the miracle, in the hope that they would succeed in their attempt (v. 15) to set up Jesus as king, the more apathetic, or the more submissive, having dispersed to their homes.

The construction of the sentence is difficult, and attempts to make it more consecutive have led to various readings. The balance of authority is for εἶδον (see above), but the rec. ἰδών would be more natural. The meaning is: On the next day the crowd which had stood (ἑστηκώς) on the other (*i.e.* the eastern) side of the lake, having seen (*sc.* the evening before) that only one boat was there, and that the disciples had embarked in their boat without Jesus, started for Capernaum in the little boats that came from Tiberias during the night. There had been only one boat on the beach the previous evening, which they had seen go without Jesus; but they could not find Jesus in the morning, and so they decided to go after Him in the little boats that had since been driven in by the storm. These, apparently, were sufficient for all the zealous watchers, so that their number could not have been very large.

A πλοιάριον, "little boat," is mentioned in N.T. only at Mk. 3⁹, Jn. 21⁸ (where it is the skiff or dinghy belonging to the πλοῖον of 21³·⁶), and in this passage. τὸ πλοῖον was the big fishing-boat, able to carry Jesus and the Twelve, which has been mentioned already (vv. 17, 19, 21); there had been no other πλοιάριον on the beach the previous evening (perhaps Jn. means no other πλοιάριον *besides* the dinghy belonging to the πλοῖον, which had gone with it). But several small boats

ὅπου ἔφαγον τὸν ἄρτον εὐχαριστήσαντος τοῦ Κυρίου. 24. ὅτε οὖν
εἶδεν ὁ ὄχλος ὅτι Ἰησοῦς οὐκ ἔστιν ἐκεῖ οὐδὲ οἱ μαθηταὶ αὐτοῦ,
ἐνέβησαν αὐτοὶ εἰς τὰ πλοιάρια καὶ ἦλθον εἰς Καφαρναοὺμ ζητοῦντες
τὸν Ἰησοῦν. 25. καὶ εὐρόντες αὐτὸν πέραν τῆς θαλάσσης εἶπον
αὐτῷ Ῥαββεί, πότε ὧδε γέγονας;

(πλοιάρια) had been driven in from Tiberias (see for Tiberias
on v. 1 above) by the squall during the night, and these were
available.

23. This parenthetical verse appears to be a later gloss.
It is, indeed, necessary to the narrative, which tells that the
disappointed watchers by the lake crossed over to Capernaum,
and hitherto there has been no mention of any boats that they
could have used. But (1) the town of Tiberias (see on v. 1) is
not mentioned elsewhere in the N.T., and had only recently
been founded. (2) More significant is the description of the
scene of the miracle τοῦ τόπου ὅπου ἔφαγον τὸν ἄρτον εὐχαριστήσαντος τοῦ κυρίου. Nowhere else are the five loaves of the
story called ὁ ἄρτος in the singular, that being the way, on the
contrary, in which the Eucharistic bread is always spoken of
(cf. 1 Cor. 10¹⁶·¹⁷ 11²⁷). (3) εὐχαριστήσαντος τοῦ κυρίου suggests
that this was the central fact which would at once identify
the occurrence, whereas we expect an expression like "where
He fed the multitudes." (4) The meaning of εὐχαριστεῖν has
been examined above (v. 11), but here it seems to bear its
later sacramental significance, the writer giving a sacramental
turn to the miracle, which Jn. studiously avoids in his narrative. (5) Specially noteworthy is it that D 69* a e Syr. sin.
and Syr. cur (a strong combination) omit the words εὐχαριστήσαντος τοῦ κυρίου here; and several of the Latin vg. texts
avoid them by the mistaken rendering *gratias agentes domino*,
"agentes" replacing "agente." (6) As we have seen above
(on 4¹), ὁ κύριος is not Johannine in narrative (except after the
Resurrection). Jn. would have used ὁ Ἰησοῦς. Verse 23 must
be regarded as a non-Johannine gloss (see Introd., p. xxxiii).

24. There is no art. before Ἰησοῦς, contrary to the general
usage of Jn. (see on 1²⁹). But the reason is the same as at
4¹·⁴⁷, viz. that ὅτι is here *recitantis*. What the people actually
said to each other was, "Jesus is not there, nor His disciples."

25. εὐρόντες αὐτόν. Jesus had reached Capernaum with
His disciples (cf. vv. 17, 59), and the crowds found Him there
πέραν τῆς θαλάσσης, that is, now on the western side of the
lake, the side opposite to that from which they started.

For "Rabbi," the title by which these excited followers
addressed Him, see on 1³⁸.

πότε ὧδε γέγονας; "When did you get here?" See on

26. Ἀπεκρίθη αὐτοῖς ὁ Ἰησοῦς καὶ εἶπεν Ἀμὴν ἀμὴν λέγω ὑμῖν, ζητεῖτέ με οὐχ ὅτι εἴδετε σημεῖα, ἀλλ᾽ ὅτι ἐφάγετε ἐκ τῶν ἄρτων καὶ ἐχορτάσθητε. 27. ἐργάζεσθε μὴ τὴν βρῶσιν τὴν ἀπολλυμένην, ἀλλὰ

v. 19. Jesus gives no answer to their question, but rebukes them for their lack of understanding (v. 26).

Discourse: Jesus the Bread of Life, which is given by the Father (vv. 26–40)

26. Jn. states (v. 59) that the long discourse which follows, interrupted at several points by questions, was delivered in the synagogue at Capernaum; and it is represented as marking a turning-point in the ministry of Jesus, many, even of His former disciples (v. 66), being repelled by the strange and lofty mysticism which it teaches. There is no reason to question the statement that a discourse about the Bread of Life followed the Miracle of the Loaves, in correction of the failure to appreciate its significance by some of those who had been fed. But it can hardly be doubted that the whole discourse, as we have it, has been arranged by Jn. so as to bring out special (and often repeated) teachings of Jesus about His own person, and to illustrate the growing opposition of " the Jews " (v. 41).

The plan of the discourse in all its parts is similar to that in the discourses with Nicodemus and with the Samaritan woman.[1] It falls into three sections (vv. 26–40, 41–51a, 51b–58), but cf. note on v. 51, and Introd., p. clxvii.

ἀπεκρ. αὐτοῖς ὁ Ἰη. καὶ εἶπεν. See on 1⁵⁰.

ἀμὴν ἀμήν . . . See on 1⁵¹.

οὐχ ὅτι εἴδετε σημεῖα.[2] They had seen a σημεῖον in the Miraculous Feeding (v. 14), and if they had interpreted it aright, the faith which would have ensued would have been acceptable, although not of the highest type (see on 2¹¹). But they were following Jesus about because of the material benefits which they had received at His hands (ὅτι ἐφάγετε ἐκ τῶν ἄρτων, " because you ate of those loaves "), rather than because they discerned in Him the spiritual Deliverer of their race. They mistook His mission, as some of them had shown already (cf. vv. 15 and 30).

καὶ ἐχορτάσθητε, et saturati estis. See on v. 12, where Jn. has ἐνεπλήσθησαν instead of the Synoptic ἐχορτάσθησαν. But bodily satiety does not last. They would be, perhaps were already, hungry again.

---

[1] See Introd., p. cxi.

[2] This is the only place, as Wendt points out, where the word σημεῖα is placed in the mouth of Jesus by Jn.

τὴν βρῶσιν τὴν μένουσαν εἰς ζωὴν αἰώνιον, ἣν ὁ Υἱὸς τοῦ ἀνθρώπου
ὑμῖν δώσει· τοῦτον γὰρ ὁ Πατὴρ ἐσφράγισεν ὁ Θεός. 28. εἶπον οὖν

27. ἐργάζεσθε μὴ τὴν βρῶσιν τὴν ἀπολλυμένην, " work not
for the food which perishes," as even the manna did (Ex.
16²⁰), but for the spiritual food which endures. The exhortation recalls the rebuke of Isa. 55², " Wherefore do ye spend
money for that which is not bread, and your labour for that
which satisfieth not ? " Cf. Ignatius (*Rom.* 7) οὐχ ἥδομαι
τροφῇ φθορᾶς, words, perhaps, suggested by the present passage.

For **βρῶσις,** βρῶμα, see on 4³². אֿ om. τὴν βρῶσιν before
τὴν μένουσαν, but the sense is not affected.

τὴν μένουσαν. It is the abiding and permanent property
of the spiritual food upon which stress is laid throughout the
discourse; cf. vv. 35, 50, 54, 58.

εἰς ζωὴν αἰώνιον. For this phrase, see on 4¹⁴ and cf. 3¹⁵.

ὁ υἱὸς τοῦ ἀνθρώπου. It is the Son of Man, and He alone,
such is His uniqueness and mystery, who can give that spiritual
food which endures " unto eternal life "; cf. v. 53. See
Introd., p. cxxx.

ὑμῖν δώσει is the reading of the rec. text, with ABLWΓΔΘ ;
but אD have δίδωσιν ὑμῖν. The future is to be preferred;
cf. the parallel δώσω αὐτῷ in 4¹⁴, and ἐγὼ δώσω in v. 51.
His giving of " life " is spoken of in the present tense (v. 33; cf.
10²⁸), but the giving of the spiritual food, which was His Flesh,
with a view to the imparting of that eternal life, was still in
the future. See further on v. 51ᵇ.

τοῦτον γάρ κτλ. This is the ultimate explanation of the
power vested in the Son (cf. 3¹⁷) of imparting life: " Him
did the Father seal " (see on 5¹⁹). Cf. 5²⁰ ὁ γὰρ πατὴρ φιλεῖ
τὸν υἱὸν κτλ., and also 5³⁷ ὁ . . . πατήρ . . . μεμαρτύρηκεν περὶ ἐμοῦ.

For the frequency of the designation in Jn. of God as
ὁ πατήρ, see on 4²¹; here, at the end of the sentence, ὁ θεός is
added, apparently for emphasis, the reference to ὁ πατήρ being
unmistakable without it (cf. vv. 37, 44–46, 57, 65).

ἐσφράγισεν occurs in Jn. elsewhere only at 3³³, where it is
used of an attestation by man, its usual meaning. The idea
of a " sealing " by God is rare in the N.T., occurring again
only in 2 Cor. 1²², Eph. 1¹³ 4³⁰; and in each of these places
there is an allusion, direct or implied, to the baptism of Christian
converts. Here the aorist marks a Divine act at a particular
moment of time, and the reference seems to be to the Baptism
of Jesus and the Descent of the Spirit upon Him, which was
interpreted by the Baptist as the Divine attestation of His
mission (1³²ᶠ.). But cf. 5³⁷.

The description of baptism as a seal became common in

πρὸς αὐτόν Τί ποιῶμεν ἵνα ἐργαζώμεθα τὰ ἔργα τοῦ Θεοῦ; 29. ἀπεκρίθη Ἰησοῦς καὶ εἶπεν αὐτοῖς Τοῦτό ἐστιν τὸ ἔργον τοῦ Θεοῦ, ἵνα
πιστεύητε εἰς ὃν ἀπέστειλεν ἐκεῖνος. 30. εἶπον οὖν αὐτῷ Τί οὖν

Christian literature at an early date; cf. Hermas, *Sim.* ix. 16,
and 2 Clem. 8. In the *Odes of Solomon* the " sealing " by
God is explicitly mentioned: " On their faces I set my seal "
(Ode viii. 16; cf. also iv. 8).

28. εἶπον οὖν πρὸς αὐτόν. For the constr. here and at
v. 34, see on 2³.

ποιῶμεν (ℵABLNTTΔ) is the true reading, not ποιοῦμεν of
the rec. text. ΘW *fam.* 13 have ποιήσωμεν.

τί ποιῶμεν; " What shall we do ? " The question is not
mere carping. They understand that they must please God, if
they are to have the food which endures unto eternal life; and
they ask quite naturally, " What then are we to do ? What
does God require of us ? " (cf. Lk. 3¹⁰).

ἵνα ἐργαζώμεθα τὰ ἔργα τοῦ θεοῦ, *i.e.* the works which God
desires of men (cf. 1 Cor. 15⁵⁸). Cf. τὰ ἔργα Κυρίου (Jer.
31¹⁰, LXX). The phrase in Num. 8¹¹ ἐργάζεσθαι τὰ ἔργα
Κυρίου is no true parallel ; and the ἔργα τοῦ θεοῦ of Jn. 9³
denote the works which God Himself does.

To their question, Jesus replies that works are the issue
of the life of faith, that faith in Him is the condition of doing
τὰ ἔργα τοῦ θεοῦ.

29. The answer of Jesus contains, in small compass, the
gist of the Pauline teaching about faith.

Jesus will not allow the Jewish inquirers to begin by speakng
of working the works of God. They must get away from the
legalism which counted up good works as meriting from God
the recompense of eternal life. There is one ἔργον τοῦ θεοῦ
which must precede all others, because it alone places the man
in his true relation with God, viz. faith in Christ.

The βρῶμα, or spiritual food, of the Incarnate Christ Himself
was to do God's will and accomplish His work (4³⁴, where see
note); but man cannot do this without sharing in the humanity
of Christ which He imparts to those who have faith in Him
(v. 51). Here is the βρῶσις which He gives, and which endures
εἰς ζωὴν αἰώνιον (v. 47). This mystical doctrine of union
with Christ is the core of the Fourth Gospel; see, for earlier
statements of it, 3¹⁵· ³⁶ and the notes there.

The question and its answer are like the question of the
jailor at Philippi and the answer of Paul and Silas: τί με δεῖ
ποιεῖν ἵνα σωθῶ; . . . πίστευσον ἐπὶ τὸν Κύριον Ἰησοῦν καὶ
σωθήσῃ (Acts 16³⁰· ³¹).

πιστεύητε (ℵABLNTΘ) is the true reading; the rec. text

ποιεῖς σὺ σημεῖον, ἵνα ἴδωμεν καὶ πιστεύσωμέν σοι; τί ἐργάζῃ;

with DW has πιστεύσητε, but this does not convey the teaching of Jn. about faith. ἵνα πιστεύσητε points to a definite act of faith at a particular moment (cf. 13¹⁹); but this does not suffice. τὸ ἔργον τοῦ θεοῦ is ἵνα πιστεύητε, "that you may have faith continually," that you may live the life of faith. An act of faith in Christ at a definite crisis is a good thing, but a better (and a harder) thing is to keep in perpetual contact with Christ, and nothing less than this is what is needed εἰς ζωὴν αἰώνιον (see above on 3³⁶, and cf. 15⁷).

ὃν ἀπέστειλεν. See for this frequent phrase on 3¹⁷.

ἐκεῖνος, *i.e.* God, is placed at the end of the sentence for emphasis. See on 1⁸ for Jn.'s use of ἐκεῖνος.

30. τί οὖν ποιεῖς σὺ σημεῖον; A similar demand made by the Pharisees for a " sign from heaven " is placed in Mk. 8¹¹ (so Mt. 16¹; cf. Mt. 12³⁸) as following on the Feeding of the *Four* Thousand. There, as here, Jesus is represented as having declined (and with indignation) the request. Lk. does not tell the story of this second miraculous feeding, and he puts the request for a sign in a different context (11¹⁶; cf. also 23⁸).

Like the Pharisees in Mk. 8¹¹, the interlocutors in the Johannine story were not convinced that by the miraculous feeding Jesus had established His claim to be a messenger from God. Some, at least, of those who had seen it said that He was the expected prophet, and were for making Him a king (vv. 14, 15). But by the next day all were not so fully persuaded. If Jesus were really a Divine messenger, they expected something more. They were not satisfied as to the character of the action which had been acclaimed by them as a σημεῖον (v. 14). So, like the Jews in 2¹⁸, who had asked τί σημεῖον δεικνύεις ἡμῖν; they now ask τί ποιεῖς σὺ σημεῖον; the emphatic word here being σύ, " What sign do *you* show ? "

ἵνα ἴδωμεν καὶ πιστεύσωμέν σοι. They did not understand what He had meant by " believing in Him " (v. 29), for they take up the words in the altered form " believe thee." They imply that if they saw a really convincing sign, something greater than anything they had witnessed yet (vv. 2, 14, 26), they would believe Him, that is, believe His words (cf. 8³¹). But this is not what Jesus claimed of them. To believe His words would be, no doubt, the beginning of discipleship, and of faith in His Person (see on v. 29); but it would not be enough εἰς ζωὴν αἰώνιον.

τί ἐργάζῃ; They think that Jesus has been referring to manna, and they ask Him to provide it (see Introd., p. cxi). ἐργάζῃ refers back to vv. 28, 29.

31. οἱ πατέρες ἡμῶν τὸ μάννα ἔφαγον ἐν τῇ ἐρήμῳ, καθώς ἐστιν
γεγραμμένον Ἄρτον ἐκ τοῦ οὐρανοῦ ἔδωκεν αὐτοῖς φαγεῖν. 32. εἶπεν

31. To appreciate the significance of this allusion to the
manna, it must be borne in mind that there was a general
belief, more or less explicit, that Messiah when He came would
outdo Moses, the great national hero of Israel, in the wonders
which he would accomplish. Thus there was a Rabbinical
saying: " The former redeemer caused manna to descend for
them; in like manner shall our latter redeemer cause manna
to come down, as it is written, ' There shall be a handful of
corn in the earth ' (Ps. 72[16])." [1] Accordingly the questioners
of Jesus are here represented as telling Him that something
more wonderful than the miracle of the loaves was expected
of one who claimed to be the Messiah (cf. vv. 14, 27). We
have here a reminiscence of an objection to Jesus which is
historical: " The key to the understanding of the whole situation is an acquaintance with the national expectation of the
greater Moses. But this knowledge is not obtruded upon us
by the evangelist. It is tacitly assumed. In fact, the meaning
is unintelligible, except to one who is brought up among the
ideas of his time, or to one who, like a modern critic, has made
them his special study." [2]

οἱ πατέρες ἡμῶν κτλ. As Chrysostom notes, this corresponds to the reference made by the Samaritan woman to "our
father Jacob " (4[12]; see Introd., p. cxi, for the schematism
of the present discourse).

The provision of the manna (Ex. 16[15], Num. 11[7] 21[5], Deut.
8[3], Wisd. 16[20], 2 Esd. 1[19]) was counted by the Jews as the
greatest achievement of Moses. Josephus says of the manna
θεῖον ἦν τὸ βρῶμα καὶ παράδοξον (*Antt.* III. i. 6).

καθώς ἐστιν γεγραμμένον. This is the usual form of citation
in Jn. (see on 2[17]).

ἄρτον ἐκ τοῦ οὐρανοῦ ἔδωκεν αὐτοῖς φαγεῖν (from Ex. 16[15]
freely quoted; but cf. Ps. 78[24], Neh. 9[15]). Their appeal is:
" What Moses gave us was bread *from heaven*; can you do the
same ? " The loaves with which the multitudes had been
fed were not ἐκ τοῦ οὐρανοῦ, but the ordinary barley loaves
(v. 9) with which all were familiar.

32. Jesus corrects a twofold misapprehension on the part
of His questioners. First, it was not Moses who was the
giver of the manna, but God, whose instrument he was; and,
secondly, the manna, while it was in a sense " bread from

---

[1] *Midrash Koheleth*, p. 73, quoted by Lightfoot, *Hor. Hebr.*,
in loc.
[2] J. B. Lightfoot, *Biblical Essays*, p. 152 ; cf. p. 25.

οὖν αὐτοῖς ὁ Ἰησοῦς Ἀμὴν ἀμὴν λέγω ὑμῖν, οὐ Μωϋσῆς ἔδωκεν ὑμῖν τὸν ἄρτον ἐκ τοῦ οὐρανοῦ, ἀλλ' ὁ Πατήρ μου δίδωσιν ὑμῖν τὸν ἄρτον ἐκ τοῦ οὐρανοῦ τὸν ἀληθινόν· 33. ὁ γὰρ ἄρτος τοῦ Θεοῦ ἐστιν ὁ καταβαίνων ἐκ τοῦ οὐρανοῦ καὶ ζωὴν διδοὺς τῷ κόσμῳ. 34. εἶπον

heaven," was not the true Bread of God. This momentous saying is introduced by the solemn ἀμὴν ἀμήν (see on 1⁵¹).

The objectors had not named Moses, but Jesus knew what was in their minds, and that they were disparaging Him in comparison with Moses.

ἔδωκεν (BDLW) is the true reading, rather than δέδωκεν of the rec. text (אATΓΔΘ). The aor. points to a definite historical date in the past.

οὐ Μωϋσῆς ἔδωκεν ὑμῖν τὸν ἄρτον ἐκ τ. οὐ., " Moses did not give you that (τὸν) bread from heaven"; what had been given to their fathers might be spoken of as given to them who were the heirs and descendants of the ancient race that came out of Egypt. The manna of old was in a true sense the gift of God; that is not questioned in the reply of Jesus: what He questions is that it was given by *Moses*.

ἀλλ' ὁ πατήρ μου. For this significant phrase, see on 2¹⁶.

δίδωσιν ὑμῖν. "Gives," not "gave." The Divine gift now to be revealed is continuously offered.

τὸν ἄρτον ἐκ τοῦ οὐρανοῦ τὸν ἀληθινόν, " the genuine Bread from heaven"; see on 1⁹ for ἀληθινός, and note its use in the dialogue with the Samaritan woman at 4²³. It seems to be implied, although not directly expressed yet, that the genuine heavenly Bread must be such as will nourish the heavenly life, the life of " the kingdom of heaven."

33. ὁ γὰρ ἄρτος τοῦ θεοῦ.[1] All bread is the gift of God (Mt. 6¹¹), but the Bread which can be described as peculiarly ὁ ἄρτος τοῦ θεοῦ is not only such as " comes down from heaven," for that was said of the manna (κατέβαινεν, Num. 11⁹), but such as coming down imparts life and not merely bodily nourishment. Chrysostom notes that the manna supplied τροφή but not ζωή. But the first characteristic of the Bread of God is that it brings life (see on v. 27). And the second is that it is offered to all men, and not only to a particular nation; ζωὴν διδούς, " giving life " (in the present tense, that is, continually giving life) τῷ κόσμῳ. See on 1²⁹ for κόσμος, which is one of the master words of Jn.; and also on v. 51 below. Cf. 1⁴.

ὁ γὰρ ἄρτ. τ. θε. ἐστιν ὁ καταβαίνων ἐκ τοῦ οὐρανοῦ, *i.e.* " the Bread of God is that which is ever descending [*not* He who

---

[1] The phrase occurs Ignatius, *ad Rom.* vii. ; cf. vv. 51, 53.

descends] from heaven." It is not until v. 35 that Jesus
says that *He* is the Bread of Life. This expression, " who
came down from heaven," or " which comes down from
heaven," is repeated seven times in this discourse (vv.
33, 38, 41, 42, 50, 51, 58), recurring like a solemn refrain. It was
afterwards incorporated in the Nicene Creed. See on 3^{13}
above.

34. The idea that the manna typified heavenly bread for
the soul often appears in the Jewish commentaries. Wetstein
quotes several passages in illustration, *e.g.* " sectio haec de
manna est una ex praestantibus sectionibus legis quae non
solum res gestas historice narrant, sed et *typum continent uitae
ac felicitatis hominis ultimae et aeternae.*" [1] Again, the
comment in *Bereshith* R. lxxxii. 9 on the good man of Prov. 12^2
is " saturabitur pane saeculi futuri."

The same conception of heavenly bread for the soul is
frequent in Philo. Wisdom offers οὐράνιος τροφή by means
of λόγοι and δόγματα (*de opif. mundi*, § 56). The θεῖος λόγος
divides equally among all men the heavenly food of the soul
which Moses calls manna (*Quis rer. div. hær.* § 39). So in
an earlier passage (§ 15) Philo speaks of the man who contemplates τὸ μάννα, τὸν θεῖον λόγον, τὴν οὐράνιον ψυχῆς φιλοθεάμονος
ἄφθαρτον τροφήν. Again, the θεῖοι λόγοι are the manna, the
heavenly food, which nourishes men (*de congr. erud. gr.* § 30).
What nourishes the soul is ῥῆμα θεοῦ καὶ λόγος θεῖος, from
which flow all kinds of wisdom (*de prof.* 25). Cf. also the
question and answer in *Legg. all.* iii. 59 ὁρᾷς τῆς ψυχῆς τροφὴν
οἵα ἐστι λόγος θεοῦ συνεχής. See further on v. 35.

More familiar than any of these passages is 1 Cor. 10^3,
where Paul, allegorising the story of the manna, describes it as
βρῶμα πνευματικόν, " spiritual food."

The questioners who are represented by Jn. as arguing
about the manna were probably acquainted with this idea of it
as a type of heavenly food for the soul. So when Jesus says
that the true Bread of God is that which comes down from
heaven and gives life, they do not cavil at such a thought.
Indeed, they welcome it. This was what they were waiting
for. Moses had given manna. The Messiah was to give a
greater gift (see above on v. 31). So their answer is, " Give
us evermore this bread." Here, again, Jn. faithfully reproduces
the theological temper and expectation of the times which he
describes. The Jews would not have stumbled at the idea of
spiritual food, of heavenly bread, as typified by the manna, and
Jn. does not represent them as finding any fault with it. Their
objection comes later (v. 41, where see note).

---

[1] Wetstein gives the reference "*Isaacus Arama* in Akodas Jizhac."

οὖν πρὸς αὐτόν Κύριε, πάντοτε δὸς ἡμῖν τὸν ἄρτον τοῦτον.　35. εἶπεν αὐτοῖς ὁ Ἰησοῦς Ἐγώ εἰμι ὁ ἄρτος τῆς ζωῆς· ὁ ἐρχόμενος πρὸς ἐμὲ

εἶπον οὖν πρὸς αὐτόν. The constr. is the same at v. 28. See on 2³.

κύριε. They now address Jesus by this title of respect; see on 1³⁸, and cf. 4¹¹·¹⁵·¹⁹ for its use by the woman of Samaria, who says δός μοι (4¹⁵), just as the inquirers here say δὸς ἡμῖν. See above on 6²⁶ᶠᶠ.

πάντοτε δὸς ἡμῖν, "give us always" (πάντοτε occurs again in Jn. 7⁶ 8²⁹ 11⁴² 12⁸ 18²⁰). They asked that they might be guaranteed a perpetual supply of the heavenly bread. More modest is the form of the petition for bread, earthly or heavenly, prescribed in Mt. 6¹¹ τὸν ἄρτον ἡμῶν τὸν ἐπιούσιον δὸς ἡμῖν σήμερον. It is only for to-day's supply that Jesus teaches men to ask.

τὸν ἄρτον τοῦτον, "this bread," superior to the manna, of which Jesus had spoken.

35. At this point Jesus passes on to an explicit announcement of His personal claims, and the pronouns "I" and "Me" occur frequently, vv. 37-71. As we have seen, His hearers were prepared for the idea of heavenly bread, but they were quite unprepared for such a mystical saying as "I am the Bread of Life," or for the tremendous claim which it involved. A pronouncement of this sort did not carry conviction to them; for they were looking for a "sign" comparable to the provision of the manna, but even more wonderful, as would befit the dignity of the Deliverer who was to be greater than Moses.

εἶπεν αὐτοῖς ὁ Ἰη. The rec. (with AΔ) adds δέ, while ℵDΓΘ and fam. 13 add οὖν after εἶπεν. But there is no copula in BLTW, and this is in agreement with Jn.'s partiality to asyndeton construction.

ἐγώ εἰμι ὁ ἄρτος τῆς ζωῆς. For the great Similitudes of the Fourth Gospel, of which this is the first, and for the significance of the opening phrase ἐγώ εἰμι, see Introd., p. cxviii.

It has been thought by some critics that this majestic sentence (repeated v. 48) is directly due, as regards its substance, although not as regards its form, to the influence of Philo. In several passages to which reference has been made already (see on v. 34), Philo says that the manna typified heavenly food. This, as we have seen, is not peculiar to Philo; but the Rabbinical writings do not seem to provide a parallel to the comparison of manna to the θεῖος λόγος, which Philo has more than once. That Jn.'s phraseology, here as elsewhere, may have been affected by his acquaintance with the terms of the Philonic philosophy is not impossible. There is, indeed,

nothing difficult of credence in Jn.'s report that Jesus taught
that He was Himself the Bread of Life, such teaching being
not only congruous with the Synoptic representation of His
words at the institution of the Eucharist (Mk. 14[22], Mt. 26[26],
Lk. 22[19]), but being specially apposite in the context in which
Jn. has placed it (see above on v. 26 f.). But, for all that,
when reporting the claim of Jesus to be the Bread of Life,
Jn. *may* have had in his mind Philo's words about the θεῖος
λόγος as the heavenly nourishment of the soul (*Quis rer. div.
hær.* § 15). Jn's conception of the Logos as a Person, Himself
God Incarnate, is so widely different from Philo's conception
of the λόγοι as representing Divine forces, and the λόγος as the
Divine Reason, that similarities of language between the
two writers do not establish dependence of thought, or any
borrowing of ideas from Philo on the part of Jn.[1]

The " Bread of Life " means primarily, the Bread which
gives life, as we see from v. 33. But for this phrase is substituted in v. 51 ὁ ἀρτὸς ὁ ζῶν, the "living Bread," *i.e.* the
Bread that has life in itself. This second, larger meaning is
virtually involved in the first, for life can only proceed from
life, *omne uiuum ex uiuo*; and so that which gives life must
itself be " living." See on 15[26].

There is the same double sense in the similar phrase " the
water of life " (Rev. 21[6] 22[1]), *sc.* the water which gives life,
and is therefore " living water " (see on 4[10]). Cf. the expressions the " Light of life " in 8[12], where see the note; the
" Tree of life " (Gen. 3[22], Rev. 2[7], etc.); and the " Word of
life " (1 Jn. 1[1]), *i.e.* the Word who gives life. Cf. v. 68.

ὁ ἐρχόμενος πρὸς ἐμέ κτλ. " Coming " and " believing " are
put side by side here and at 7[37. 38]. The " coming " is the
initial act of the soul in its approach to Jesus; the " believing "
is the continuous resting in His fellowship (see on v. 29). As
Jn. has much about " believing," so he has much about
" coming," and reports many sayings of Jesus about its bene-
diction. Inquirers " come " to Jesus (3[26] 4[30] 10[41]); all candid
and truthful souls come to the Light (3[21]); *e.g.* Nathanael (1[48]),
or the two disciples whose call is the first recorded by Jn. (1[39]).
The first reward of " coming " is *vision*, ἔρχεσθε καὶ ὄψεσθε
(1[39]); the second (and ultimate) reward is *life* (5[40]). All are
welcome, ἐάν τις διψᾷ, ἐρχέσθω πρός με (7[37]). He who comes
will not be cast out (6[37]). To approach God a man *must* come
to Jesus, οὐδεὶς ἔρχεται πρὸς τὸν πατέρα εἰ μὴ δι᾽ ἐμοῦ (14[6]).
This is the Only Way. And yet, free as is this approach, no one
can come to Jesus, except the Father draw him (6[44. 65]). This
teaching is fuller than that of the Synoptic Gospels, but in

[1] Cf. Introd., pp. xciii, cxl.

οὐ μὴ πεινάσῃ, καὶ ὁ πιστεύων εἰς ἐμὲ οὐ μὴ διψήσει πώποτε.
36. ἀλλ᾽ εἶπον ὑμῖν ὅτι καὶ ἑωράκατε καὶ οὐ πιστεύετε. 37. Πᾶν ὅ

germ it is all contained in Mt. 11²⁸ δεῦτε πρός με . . . κἀγὼ
ἀναπαύσω ὑμᾶς. This is the Matthæan counterpart of the
utterance before us in this verse, " He that cometh to me shall
never hunger"; the desire of the soul will be satisfied.

οὐ μὴ πεινάσῃ. πεινᾶν does not occur again in Jn.

καὶ ὁ πιστεύων εἰς ἐμέ, " he who believes on me " (see on
v. 29 and on 1¹² above). This is the ἔργον τοῦ θεοῦ spoken of
in v. 29.

οὐ μὴ διψήσει. So אAB*DW⊖; the rec. has διψήσῃ. The
promise is the same as that given to the woman of Samaria
ὃς δ᾽ ἂν πίῃ ἐκ τοῦ ὕδατος οὗ ἐγὼ δώσω αὐτῷ, οὐ μὴ διψήσει εἰς τὸν
αἰῶνα (4¹⁴, where see the note and esp. the quotation from
Ecclus. 24²¹; cf. Rev. 7¹⁶).

πώποτε. See on 1¹⁸.

36. The rec. text, with BDLWΓΔ⊖, adds με after ἑωράκατε,
but om. אA a b e q, Syr. cu. and Syr. sin. It is probable
that με ought to be omitted. The words "I said to you that
ye saw and do not believe " then clearly refer back to v. 26,
where Jesus had said, " Ye seek me not because ye saw signs,
but because ye ate of the loaves, etc." Seeing is not always
believing (cf. 9³⁷). The kind of faith that is generated by the
seeing of signs is not the highest (see on 2¹¹), but it is not
without its value (cf. 14¹¹). The best kind of all has the bene-
diction, " Blessed are they that have not seen and yet have
believed " (20²⁹); cf. ὁ πιστεύων ἔχει ζωὴν αἰώνιον (v. 47).

On the other hand, if ἑωράκατέ με is the true reading, we
must suppose that Jesus is represented as alluding to some
saying of His which has not been recorded by Jn. This is not
impossible; see, for other instances, 10²⁵ 11⁴⁰.

37. The questioners of Jesus did not believe or accept
Him, but that rejection of theirs does not alter the Divine
purpose, which is that all who will shall have eternal life.
Upon this Jesus rests, despite incredulity on the part of some
who heard Him. " All that the Father gives to me shall come
to me ": that is enough, for He came to do the Father's will,
and the Father knows best as to those whom He gives. For
the predestinarian doctrine of the Fourth Gospel, see on 2⁴ 3¹⁴.

For the thought that His disciples are " given " to the
Son by the Father, cf. vv. 39, 65, and 10²⁹ 17². ⁶. ⁹. ¹². ²⁴ 18⁹.
See note on 3³⁵.

πᾶν, sc. all men. This collective use of the neut. sing. is not
unknown in classical Greek. Jn. has it several times (17². ²⁴,
1 Jn. 5⁴, as well as at v. 39 and here), and always of the sum of

δίδωσίν μοι ὁ Πατὴρ πρὸς ἐμὲ ἥξει, καὶ τὸν ἐρχόμενον πρός με οὐ μὴ ἐκβάλω ἔξω, 38. ὅτι καταβέβηκα ἀπὸ τοῦ οὐρανοῦ οὐχ ἵνα ποιῶ τὸ θέλημα τὸ ἐμὸν ἀλλὰ τὸ θέλημα τοῦ πέμψαντός με. 39. τοῦτο δέ ἐστιν τὸ θέλημα τοῦ πέμψαντός με, ἵνα πᾶν ὃ δέδωκέν μοι μὴ ἀπολέσω

those who have been " begotten of God " and " given " by the Father to the Son. The ideal for those who believe in Christ is ἵνα πάντες ἐν ὦσιν (17²¹), " that they all may be *one*," and it is possible that this great conception may be behind the use of πᾶν for πάντες here and in 17².

ὁ πατήρ. See on 3¹⁷.

τὸν ἐρχόμενον πρός με. See for this phrase on v. 35 above.

τ. ἐρχ. πρός με οὐ μὴ ἐκβάλω ἔξω, " I shall not cast out "; a *litotes* for " I shall welcome." The " casting out " indicated is from the kingdom of God, hereafter as well as here; in v. 39, the reference is to the Last Judgment, and this is implied here also. Cf. 12³¹, where the judgment on Satan is ἐκβληθήσεται ἔξω, the same phrase as here (cf. 17¹²); and see for ἐκβάλλειν in similar contexts Mt. 8¹² 22¹³ 25³⁰.

א*D om. ἔξω as redundant, but it is well supported (אᶜABLWΘ), and the combination ἐκβάλλειν ἔξω or ἐκ occurs again 2¹⁵ 9³⁴. ³⁵ 12³¹; cf. Mt. 21³⁹, Mk. 12⁸, Lk. 20¹⁵, etc.

οὐ μή expresses a very strong negation, " I will *surely not* cast out." This constr. occurs elsewhere in words of Jesus, Mk. 14²⁵, and Jn. 18¹¹, οὐ μὴ πίω, it being generally taken as interrogative in the latter passage, where see note.

38. καταβέβηκα ἀπὸ τοῦ οὐρανοῦ. So ABLTWΘ *fam.* 13; but καταβέβηκα ἐκ τοῦ οὐρανοῦ is read by אDΓΔ, and may be right. The phrase καταβαίνειν ἐκ τοῦ οὐρανοῦ is found again (of Christ) at 3¹³ 6³³. ⁴¹. ⁴². ⁵⁰. ⁵¹. ⁵⁸; see also Rev. 3¹² 10¹ 13¹³ 16²¹ 18¹ 20¹. ⁹ 21². ¹⁰ and Jn. 1³²; whereas καταβαίνειν ἀπ' οὐρανοῦ only occurs at 1 Thess. 4¹⁶ of the Second Advent. In any case the meaning is the same, for it is an excess of refinement to distinguish in Jn. between the force of ἀπό and of ἐκ. See on 1⁴⁴.

οὐχ ἵνα ποιῶ τὸ θέλημα τὸ ἐμόν κτλ. This is said also at 5³⁰, οὐ ζητῶ τὸ θέλημα τὸ ἐμὸν ἀλλὰ τὸ θέλημα τοῦ πέμψαντός με. See notes on 4³⁴ and 5³⁰.

The argument is: " Every one whom the Father gives to me comes to me, and I will not reject him (v.37), *because* (ὅτι) I came from heaven to do my Father's will (v. 38), and His will is that none should perish of those whom He has given me " (v. 39).

39. After τοῦ πέμψαντός με, the rec. adds πατρός (from v. 40), but om. πατρός א*ABCW.

ἐξ αὐτοῦ, ἀλλὰ ἀναστήσω αὐτὸ τῇ ἐσχάτῃ ἡμέρᾳ. 40. τοῦτο γάρ
ἐστιν τὸ θέλημα τοῦ Πατρός μου, ἵνα πᾶς ὁ θεωρῶν τὸν Υἱὸν καὶ
πιστεύων εἰς αὐτὸν ἔχῃ ζωὴν αἰώνιον, καὶ ἀναστήσω αὐτὸν ἐγὼ ἐν τῇ
ἐσχάτῃ ἡμέρᾳ.

אADN insert ἐν before τῇ ἐσχάτῃ ἡμέρᾳ, but om. BCLTΘ
(cf. v. 54). W has αὐτὸν τῇ ἐσχάτῃ.

For the broken construction of the sentence, a *casus pendens*
(πᾶν ὃ κτλ.) followed by a pronoun, see on 1[12]. This is frequent
in Jn.

πᾶν ὃ δέδωκέν μοι refers to πᾶν ὃ δίδωσίν μοι of v. 37. That
none of them should perish finally is the will of the Father, and
they are all therefore in the safe keeping of Christ. This is
repeated in somewhat similar words at 10[28, 29]; and there is a
close parallel at Mt. 18[14] οὐκ ἔστιν θέλημα ἔμπροσθεν τοῦ πατρὸς
ὑμῶν . . . ἵνα ἀπόληται ἐν τῶν μικρῶν τούτων. Cf. also 17[12]
(18[9]), where the exception of Judas is mentioned.

ἀναστήσω αὐτὸ τῇ ἐσχάτῃ ἡμέρᾳ. " Hic finis est, ultra quem
periculum nullum " (Bengel). This great assurance is repeated
four times, in vv. 39, 40, 44, 54, and recurs with the majesty of
a solemn refrain (see on 3[16] and on 15[11]). The expression ἡ
ἐσχάτη ἡμέρα is found in Jn. only. In 7[37] it is used of the last
day of the Feast of Tabernacles; but at 11[24] 12[48] it refers, as
it does in this chapter, to the Day of Judgment.[1] For the
Christ, the Son of God, as the Agent of the Resurrection, see
on 5[21, 28]. It is He that will quicken the dead at last. Cf.
1 Cor. 15[22].

Here it is only the resurrection of the righteous that is in
view, whereas at 5[28] a general resurrection of the dead is spoken
of as brought about by the Voice of the Son of God.

40. ΑΓΔ have τοῦ πέμψαντός με (from v. 39) for τοῦ πατρός
μου, which is read by אBCDLTNWΘ. There is, again, as
in vv. 39, 54, a variant for ἐν τῇ ἐσχ. ἡμ., ἐν being om. by
BCΤΓΔΘW, although found in אADLN.

τοῦτο γάρ κτλ., " This, too, is my Father's will ": v. 40
amplifies and repeats with emphasis what has been already
said in v. 39. The rec. has τοῦτο δέ.

For " my Father," cf. v. 32, and see on 2[16].

πᾶς ὁ θεωρῶν τὸν υἱόν, "who beholdeth the Son," *sc.* not
with the bodily eyes, but with the eye of faith perceives Him
for what He is. Cf. 12[45] ὁ θεωρῶν ἐμὲ θεωρεῖ τὸν πέμψαντά με.
See on 2[23] for Jn.'s use of θεωρῶ, and on 3[17] for ὁ υἱός
used absolutely. It is the Father's will that " he who beholdeth the Son and believeth on Him should have eternal
life "; cf. 3[15, 36] and the notes thereon. This ζωὴ αἰώνιος

---

[1] Cf. Introd., pp. clx, clxii.

41. Ἐγόγγυζον οὖν οἱ Ἰουδαῖοι περὶ αὐτοῦ ὅτι εἶπεν Ἐγώ εἰμι ὁ ἄρτος ὁ καταβὰς ἐκ τοῦ οὐρανοῦ, 42. καὶ ἔλεγον Οὐχ οὗτός ἐστιν

begins in the present world, but its possession continues after death.

ἀναστήσω αὐτὸν ἐγώ κτλ., "*I*, even I (ἐγώ is emphatic) will raise Him up at the Last Day." This is repeated in another form at v. 54. Cf. Introd., p. clxvii.

The second part of the Discourse (vv. 41–51a)

41. A new stage in the argument is reached at v. 41, but it is not suggested that new interlocutors have appeared on the scene. The questioners are called (here and at v. 52) οἱ Ἰουδαῖοι, and it has been thought by some that they were officials of the synagogue at Capernaum, where Jn. represents the conversation as taking place (v. 59), or emissaries of the Sanhedrim, who had been sent to inquire into the discourses and the acts of Jesus (cf. Mk. 7¹). But the context shows that Jn. thinks of them as Galilæans (cf. vv. 24, 42). They were not οἱ Ἰουδαῖοι in the sense that they were inhabitants of Judæa, but they were " Jews " by religious conviction and by race in the larger sense of " Israelite." It was " Jews " like them who were the chief opponents of Jesus, and Jn. nearly always uses the term as connoting a certain hostility to Jesus and unbelief in His claims. See above on 1¹⁹. Hostility, however, is not yet suggested. For this section of the Discourse, see Introd., pp. cxi, clxvii.

ἐγόγγυζον, " they were murmuring," *sc.* in critical mood, as at vv. 43, 61 (cf. Ex. 16⁷ᶦ·); neither at 7³² nor here does γογγύζειν carry any implication of open hostility. The word does not occur in Mk., but is found Mt. 20¹¹, Lk. 5³⁰.

The difficulty of the questioners was caused by the claims involved in ἐγώ εἰμι ὁ ἄρτος ὁ καταβὰς ἐκ τοῦ οὐρανοῦ (cf. vv. 33, 35). The idea of heavenly bread might have been accepted (see above on v. 34); but these words of Jesus seemed to imply that He was not like ordinary men in the manner of His birth, in that He had " come down from heaven " (see on 3¹³).

No distinction can be drawn between ἐκ τοῦ οὐρανοῦ here (also vv. 51, 58) and ἀπὸ τοῦ οὐρανοῦ in v. 38, where see note.

42. καὶ ἔλεγον κτλ., " And they were saying, Is not this person (οὗτος, perhaps with a slight suggestion of disparagement, as at v. 52, 7¹⁵) Jesus, the son of Joseph, whose father and mother we know? " It is plain (see on v. 41) that Jn. conceives of the speakers as natives of Galilee, and acquainted

Ἰησοῦς ὁ υἱὸς Ἰωσήφ, οὗ ἡμεῖς οἴδαμεν τὸν πατέρα καὶ τὴν μητέρα; πῶς νῦν λέγει ὅτι Ἐκ τοῦ οὐρανοῦ καταβέβηκα; 43. ἀπεκρίθη Ἰησοῦς καὶ εἶπεν αὐτοῖς Μὴ γογγύζετε μετ᾽ ἀλλήλων. 44. οὐδεὶς δύναται ἐλθεῖν πρός με ἐὰν μὴ ὁ Πατὴρ ὁ πέμψας με ἑλκύσῃ αὐτόν, κἀγὼ

with the household at Nazareth. The Synoptists (Mk. 6³, Mt. 13⁵⁵, Lk. 4²²) mention a similar criticism (the words in Lk. are οὐχὶ υἱός ἐστιν Ἰωσὴφ οὗτος;) as having been passed on Jesus in the synagogue at Nazareth at an earlier point in His ministry. The criticism was probably made more than once, and it is natural in the context where Jn. places it. But it is possible that he has taken the episode out of its historical setting; as in 4⁴⁴ (where see note) he has introduced the proverb about a prophet being without honour in his own country, which the Synoptists place in sequence to the criticism, " Is not this the son of Mary ? Is not this the son of Joseph ? "

As at 1⁴⁵ (where see note), Jn. does not stay to comment on the mistake which is involved in the question, " Is not this Joseph's son ? " It is unnecessary for him to explain to Christian readers that this was not so. There is nothing in the form of the question to suggest that Joseph was alive, and the probability is that he had died before the public ministry of Jesus began (see on 2¹).

πῶς νῦν λέγει κτλ. For νῦν, the rec. text (with אADLΓΔN) has οὖν, but νῦν is read by BCTWΘ, and has a special force, " How does he say now that, etc.," sc. to us who have known him from a child. οὗτος is inserted again after λέγει by אΑΓΔ, but is redundant. ὅτι, recitantis, the words following being a citation.

ἐκ τοῦ οὐρανοῦ καταβέβηκα, the order of the words being changed, ἐκ τοῦ οὐρανοῦ being placed first for emphasis. This was the incredible thing, that it was from heaven He claimed to have come down.

43. Jesus does not answer the objection as to His parentage being known. As at 3³, He proceeds to point out a fundamental misunderstanding on the part of His interlocutors. They must be " taught of God " before they can accept His heavenly origin.

For the construction ἀπεκρίθη Ἰησοῦς καὶ εἶπεν, see on 1⁵⁰. The rec. adds οὖν after ἀπεκρ. with אADNWΓΔΘ, but om. BCLT. So, too, the rec. prefixes the def. art. ὁ before Ἰησοῦς with ADNWΘ, but om. אBLT. See on 1²⁹ above.

μὴ γογγύζετε μετ᾽ ἀλλήλων. They will not reach a true understanding by whispering to each other. They must seek enlightenment from God.

44. οὐδεὶς δύναται ἐλθεῖν πρός με ἐὰν μὴ ὁ πατὴρ . . .

ἀναστήσω αὐτὸν ἐν τῇ ἐσχάτῃ ἡμέρᾳ. 45. ἔστιν γεγραμμένον ἐν τοῖς προφήταις Καὶ ἔσονται πάντες διδακτοὶ Θεοῦ· πᾶς ὁ ἀκούσας

ἑλκύσῃ αὐτόν. This is repeated v. 65 οὐδεὶς δύναται ἐλθεῖν πρός με ἐὰν μὴ ᾖ δεδομένον αὐτῷ ἐκ τοῦ πατρός. Here is a fundamental doctrine of the Fourth Gospel, viz. that the approach of the soul to God or Christ is not initiated by the man himself, but by a movement of Divine grace. We have had it adumbrated at 4²³, where it is said that the Universal Father *seeks* His genuine worshippers (see note *in loc.*); and the hard saying of 12³⁹ (where see note) that the Jews *could* not believe, because Isaiah's words about the blinding of their eyes by God must have fulfilment, is an explicit statement of the darker side of the doctrine of predestination. (See Introd., p. clii f.). Here is the counterpart of v. 37, " All (πᾶν) that the Father gives me shall come to me "; in v. 44 we have " no one (οὐδείς) *can* come except the Father draw him " (cf. 3²⁷).

We might have expected that here Jesus would have been represented as saying " *My* Father " (see on 2¹⁶), for the question at issue is that of His uniquely Divine origin; but in Jn. we find ὁ πατήρ more frequently than ὁ πατήρ μου on the lips of Jesus. (See on 3¹⁷ for the similar ὁ υἱός, used absolutely.)

ὁ πατὴρ ὁ πέμψας με. See also on 3¹⁷ for the conception of the Son as " sent " by the Father.

ἑλκύσῃ αὐτόν. ἑλκύειν is used in the LXX of Jer. 31³ of the Divine attraction: " With lovingkindness have I drawn thee." It is used of the attractive power of Christ **Crucified** in Jn. 12³², occurring elsewhere in the N.T. only at Jn. 18¹⁰ (of drawing a sword), Jn. 21⁶· ¹¹ (of dragging a net ashore), and Acts 16¹⁹ (of dragging Paul and Silas to the magistrates). It seems generally to connote a certain resistance on the part of that which is " dragged " or " drawn," and this may be involved in its use in the present verse (but cf. Cant. 1⁴).

κἀγὼ ἀναστήσω αὐτὸν ἐν τῇ ἐσχάτῃ ἡμέρᾳ. This is the consummation of that spiritual progress which begins by a certain Divine constraint. See on v. 39 for this great assurance, four times repeated in this passage.

45. In confirmation of the doctrine that God " draws " men to Him, Jesus appeals to the authority of the Scriptures accepted by His hearers.

ἔστιν γεγραμμένον (for this formula of citation, see on 2¹⁷) **ἐν τοῖς προφήταις,** *i.e.* presumably in the collection of prophetical books regarded as a single whole (cf. Acts 7⁴² 13⁴⁰, Lk. 18³¹ 24⁴⁴).

καὶ ἔσονται πάντες διδακτοὶ θεοῦ. The rec. text inserts τοῦ before θεοῦ, but om. אABCDΘW. The quotation is freely

παρὰ τοῦ Πατρὸς καὶ μαθὼν ἔρχεται πρὸς ἐμέ.   46. οὐχ ὅτι τὸν Πατέρα ἑώρακέν τις, εἰ μὴ ὁ ὢν παρὰ τοῦ Θεοῦ, οὗτος ἑώρακεν τὸν Πατέρα.   47. ἀμὴν ἀμὴν λέγω ὑμῖν, ὁ πιστεύων ἔχει ζωὴν αἰώνιον.

made from Isa. 54¹³, and does not agree precisely with either the Hebrew or the LXX. Literally, the Hebrew gives, " And all thy sons shall be taught of Yahweh, " which the LXX turns by καὶ θήσω . . . πάντας τοὺς υἱούς σου διδακτοὺς θεοῦ.

To be διδακτοὶ θεοῦ is to be " drawn " by God; we have θεοδίδακτοι at 1 Thess. 4⁹ (cf. 1 Cor. 2¹³, Phil. 3¹⁵, for the idea), and Barnabas (xxi. 6) has the precept γένεσθε θεοδίδακτοι.

πᾶς. Cf. πᾶν, vv. 37, 39. ΑΓΔΘ add οὖν, but om. אBCDLNTW.

ἀκούσας παρὰ τοῦ πατρός. The same phrase occurs again 8²⁶·⁴⁰ 15¹⁵. See for the constr. on 1⁴⁰.

καὶ μαθών. It is not sufficient for a man to have *heard* God's voice; he must also *learn*, which is a voluntary act. Predestination, in the Johannine doctrine, does not exclude free will or personal responsibility. But every one who has heard the Divine voice, and has learnt its teachings, " comes " to Christ. See on v. 37 for ἔρχεται πρὸς ἐμέ.

46. This " hearing " of God's voice is, however, not by way of *immediate* personal communication; it is not " seeing the Father." Only One has " seen " God (1¹⁸), although it is true, in another sense, that he who has " seen " Jesus has " seen the Father " (14⁹).

οὐχ ὅτι τὸν πατέρα ἑώρακέν τις. So אBCDLNWΘ; the rec. has τις ἑώρακεν. א*D have τὸν θεόν for τόν πατέρα, a reminiscence of 1¹⁸, where see note. Cf. 5³⁷.

εἰ μὴ ὁ ὢν παρὰ τοῦ θεοῦ, *sc.* not only He who has been *sent* by God (see on 3¹⁷), as παρὰ θεοῦ means (1⁶, 9¹⁶·³³), but He whose *origin* is from God; cf. παρὰ πατρός (1¹⁴, where see note), παρʼ αὐτοῦ εἰμι (7²⁹), παρὰ τοῦ πατρὸς ἐξῆλθον (16²⁷), παρὰ σοῦ ἐξῆλθον (17⁸).

οὗτος ἑώρακεν τὸν πατέρα. The λόγος was πρὸς τὸν θεόν (1¹); see 8³⁸ for the things which He has seen παρὰ τῷ πατρί (cf. also 3³²). See on 14⁷.

For the repetition (οὗτος) of the subject of the sentence, in the interests of emphasis, cf. 1² 7¹⁸ 15⁵, and see 10²⁵.

47. ἀμὴν ἀμήν κτλ. See on 1⁵¹. This opening phrase introduces a saying which is the keynote of the Fourth Gospel, ὁ πιστεύων (used absolutely as at v. 36) ἔχει ζωὴν αἰώνιον (cf. 20³¹, and see on 3¹⁵).

After ὁ πιστεύων the rec. adds εἰς ἐμέ, with ACDΓΔN (from such passages as 3¹⁶·³⁶); but אBLTWΘ om. εἰς ἐμέ. Jn.'s

48. ἐγώ εἰμι ὁ ἄρτος τῆς ζωῆς.   49. οἱ πατέρες ὑμῶν ἔφαγον ἐν τῇ ἐρήμῳ τὸ μάννα καὶ ἀπέθανον· 50. οὗτός ἐστιν ὁ ἄρτος ὁ ἐκ τοῦ οὐρανοῦ καταβαίνων, ἵνα τις ἐξ αὐτοῦ φάγῃ καὶ μὴ ἀποθάνῃ.   51. ἐγώ

use of πιστεύειν, without specifying the object of the πίστις, has been noted on 1[7].

The sequence of argument is clear.   No one has "seen" the Father but Christ (v. 46); but it suffices to believe in Christ, for such a believer has eternal life (v. 47).   As He said later, "He who has seen me has seen the Father" (14[9]).

48. ἐγώ εἰμι ὁ ἄρτος τῆς ζωῆς (cf. v. 35).   That is, the believer in Christ has eternal life, because He is the spiritual Bread which gives life.   Notice the repetition of the main theme, not always in exactly the same words (vv. 35, 41, 48, 51); see on 3[16].

49. The argument in vv. 49–51 is as follows: The manna which nourished the bodily life of the Israelites in the desert, did not secure them from physical death at last (see on v. 58). In this it was like ordinary bread, although divinely given. The Bread of Life, which Jesus offers in His own Person, has not to do with the nourishment of the bodily life, nor does it secure those who believe in Him from the death of the body. But it is the appropriate and divinely given nourishment of man's spirit, and he who continually feeds on it—that is, he who continually keeps in spiritual touch with Jesus—is secure against spiritual death; he shall live for ever, having assimilated the true Bread of Life.

οἱ πατέρες ὑμῶν κτλ.   They had said οἱ πατέρες ἡμῶν κτλ. (v. 31), and this is the reply.   Jesus does not say "our fathers," but "your fathers"; cf. Ἀβραὰμ ὁ πατὴρ ὑμῶν (8[56]).   See, however, for the phrase "your law," on 8[17]; and cf. v. 58 below.

ἐν τῇ ἐρήμῳ τὸ μάννα.   So BCDTWΘ, but אALΓΔ have the order τὸ μάννα ἐν τῇ ἐρήμῳ as in v. 31.

καὶ ἀπέθανον, sc. of *physical* death; in v. 50 μὴ ἀποθάνῃ refers to *spiritual* death.   See v. 58.

50. οὗτός ἐστιν κτλ., sc. this Bread, which has been mentioned in v. 48, is the Bread which comes down from heaven (as had been said at v. 33; cf. v. 42).

ἵνα τις κτλ., sc. in order that a man may eat of it and so not die, *i.e.* die spiritually.   It is spiritual food for the perpetual nourishment of the spiritual life.   Cf. 8[51] 11[26].

For ἀποθάνῃ B has ἀποθνήσκῃ, which Abbott (*Diat.* 2530) regards as having as good claim to consideration as the true reading.   He would translate ". . . that a man may eat of it, and so be no longer *under sentence of death*," comparing,

εἰμι ὁ ἄρτος ὁ ζῶν ὁ ἐκ τοῦ οὐρανοῦ καταβάς· ἐάν τις φάγῃ ἐκ τούτου τοῦ ἄρτου, ζήσει εἰς τὸν αἰῶνα.

for ἀποθνήσκειν in the present tense, Ps. 82⁷, Deut. 17⁶. But this is unnecessary, and ἀποθάνῃ is too well attested to be set aside for the variant ἀποθνήσκῃ.

51ᵃ. The first half of this verse repeats what has been said already in v. 50, but in an even more emphatic form. The second half of the verse, as we shall see, introduces a new conception.

ἐγώ εἰμι ὁ ἄρτος ὁ ζῶν, "the Living Bread," which as itself alive can impart life (see on v. 35 above). ὁ ζῶν, "the Living One," is the claim of Jesus for Himself in Rev. 1¹⁷; so here ὁ ἄρτος ὁ ζῶν is the Bread which is always instinct with Life, which continues to live from age to age. See on 4¹⁰ for the phrase "living water"; and cf. the expressions "living oracles" (Acts 7³⁸), "living sacrifice" (Rom. 12¹), "living hope" (1 Pet. 1³), and "living stone" (1 Pet. 2⁴), which do not, however, present more than verbal resemblances to the phrase "Living Bread" here.

ὁ ἐκ τοῦ οὐρανοῦ καταβάς. See on v. 33 above. Here the aorist participle points to the crisis of the Incarnation.

For ἐκ τούτου τοῦ ἄρτου (BCΓΔLTWΘ), א has ἐκ τοῦ ἐμοῦ ἄρτου, but this is inconsistent with the sense of the passage. The Living Bread is Jesus Himself.

ἐάν τις φάγῃ κτλ., "if any one eat of this Bread, he shall live for ever," sc. as God does (cf. Rev. 4⁹ 10⁶ 15⁷, and Deut. 32⁴⁰, Ecclus. 18¹). ζήσει εἰς τὸν αἰῶνα is repeated v. 58: the phrase is used of the righteous man, Wisd. 5¹⁵.

There is perhaps an echo of this thought in *Barnabas*, § 11. Barnabas is speaking of the trees by the river of Ezek. 47⁷·¹², and he adds ὃς ἂν φάγῃ ἐξ αὐτῶν ζήσεται εἰς τὸν αἰῶνα. But see Introd., p. lxxi.

The rec. (with BCΓΓΔ) has ζήσεται for ζήσει (אDLWΘ 33). There is a similar variant at vv. 57, 58; cf. 5²⁵ 14¹⁹.

The third part of the Discourse : Jesus will give the Bread which is His Flesh for the life of the world (vv. 51ᵇ–59)

51ᵇ. The MSS. vary as to the order of the words in the second part of the verse, but the meaning remains unaltered. BCDLTW have the text which we print, while א *m* support καὶ ὁ ἄρτος δὲ ὃν ἐγὼ δώσω ὑπὲρ τῆς τοῦ κόσμου ζωῆς ἡ σάρξ μου ἐστιν, a less awkward construction. The rec. text has got rid of the awkwardness by reading καὶ ὁ ἄρτος δὲ ὃν ἐγὼ δώσω ἡ σάρξ μου ἐστίν, ἣν ἐγὼ δώσω ὑπὲρ τῆς τοῦ κόσμου ζωῆς, the insertion of ἣν ἐγὼ δώσω making all clear.

Καὶ ὁ ἄρτος δὲ ὃν ἐγὼ δώσω ἡ σάρξ μού ἐστιν ὑπὲρ τῆς τοῦ κόσμου ζωῆς. 52. Ἐμάχοντο οὖν πρὸς ἀλλήλους οἱ Ἰουδαῖοι λέγοντες

A new idea is introduced at this point.[1] Hitherto Jesus has spoken of the Bread of Life as coming down from heaven, and of Himself as that Living Bread, giving life to all who feed upon it and appropriate it. Now He goes on to speak of this Bread as His *Flesh*, and of the feeding upon Him as eating His Flesh and drinking His Blood. The transition from the one way of speaking to the other is marked by a change in the tense of the " giving." The Father *gives* the heavenly bread (v. 32); it *gives* life to the world (v. 33). But now Jesus says, " The Bread which I *shall give* (δώσω) is my Flesh, etc." (but see on v. 27). Moreover, up to this point (except at v. 27), Jesus has spoken of Himself, as the Bread of Life, coming down from heaven, given by *the Father*. Now, He speaks of the Bread which *He Himself will give* for the life of the world, namely His Flesh. Difficult as the Jews had found the thought (v. 41) that Jesus was Himself the heavenly bread, divinely given, for which they had asked (v. 34), they find much greater difficulty in the new and strange suggestion that Jesus was to give them His Flesh to eat (v. 52). And, according to the Gospel as we have it, Jesus then proceeds to develop and enlarge this conception (vv. 53–58).[2]

καὶ ὁ ἄρτος δέ κτλ. For the constr. καί . . . δέ, " and, further," cf. 8¹⁶ 15²⁷, 1 Jn. 1³. It introduces a new point, hitherto unmentioned.

ὃν ἐγὼ δώσω, " which *I* will give," ἐγώ being emphatic.

ἡ σάρξ μού ἐστιν, " is my Flesh." That Christ came " in the flesh " (cf. 1¹⁴, 1 Jn. 4², 2 Jn.⁷) is the central fact of the Gospel of the Incarnation; that is, He who came down from heaven (v. 50) assumed man's nature. The gift that is promised is, then, that of His perfect humanity.

This will be given ὑπὲρ τῆς τοῦ κόσμου ζωῆς, " on behalf of the world's life." See for the force of ὑπέρ and its prevalence in Jn., on 1³⁰; and for κόσμος, on 1⁹. That Christ's gift of " His Flesh " is on behalf of the world's life is a saying closely related in meaning to 1²⁹, " the Lamb of God who takes away the sin of the world "; cf. also 3¹⁷ 4⁴², 1 Jn. 3¹⁶. But the true parallel is 1 Cor. 11²⁴ τοῦτό μού ἐστιν τὸ σῶμα τὸ ὑπὲρ ὑμῶν. As has been pointed out (Introd., p. clxix), the Syriac vss. give here: " The bread which I will give is my Body, for the life of the world "; a rendering also found in the O.L. *m*,

[1] Cf. Introd., p. clxvii.
[2] For the sacramental bearing of vv. 51–58, see Waterland, *Doctrine of the Eucharist*, c. vi.

Πῶς δύναται οὗτος ἡμῖν δοῦναι τὴν σάρκα φαγεῖν; 53. εἶπεν οὖν αὐτοῖς ὁ Ἰησοῦς Ἀμὴν ἀμὴν λέγω ὑμῖν, ἐὰν μὴ φάγητε τὴν σάρκα τοῦ Υἱοῦ τοῦ ἀνθρώπου καὶ πίητε αὐτοῦ τὸ αἷμα, οὐκ ἔχετε ζωὴν ἐν ἑαυτοῖς.

" hic panis quem ego dabo pro huius mundi uita *corpus* meum est."

52. The Jewish interlocutors had murmured (v. 41) before this point had been reached; but now they begin to dispute with each other (μάχεσθαι does not occur again in the Gospels) as to the meaning and trustworthiness of the words of Jesus. They were not of one mind (cf. 7¹². ⁴⁰ 9¹⁶ 10¹⁹); some probably discerning that a spiritual meaning lay behind this mention of the " Flesh " of Jesus.

πῶς δύναται κτλ.;   The question is like that of 3⁴. ⁹ (where see note).   For οὗτος, " this person," see on v. 42 above.

After σάρκα BT (with most vss.) insert αὐτοῦ, to elucidate the sense; but om. אCDLΓΔΘ. In any case, the meaning is, " How can this person give us his flesh to eat? " Their difficulty was a real one, even if they (or some of them) recognised that the σάρξ represented the whole humanity of Jesus, on which they were to " feed"; for that one human being could impart his nature to another, even spiritually, would be hard to understand.

53. The answer of Jesus repeats (see on 3⁵) what He has said already, but in even more difficult terms. For while in v. 51 He spoke only of His Flesh, He now goes on to couple the drinking of His Blood with the eating of His Flesh. Such an expression as " to drink blood " would be especially startling to a Jew, for whom the blood of animals was *tabu*, and was expressly forbidden to be used as food (Gen. 9⁴, Deut. 12¹⁶). The prohibition was based on the doctrine that " the blood is the life " (Deut. 12²³), *i.e.* that the blood was the seat of the " soul " or נפש, the vital principle.

The phrase πίνειν τὸ αἷμα does not occur again in the N.T.

It should be noted, further, that the use of this expression, as distinct from φαγεῖν τὴν σάρκα, indicates that the Flesh and Blood have been separated, and thus it suggests death, even more definitely than φαγεῖν τὴν σάρκα does.

ἀμὴν ἀμὴν κτλ.   See on 1⁵¹.

For φάγητε, D (supported by *a*) has λάβητε.   See on v. 56.

τὴν σάρκα τοῦ υἱοῦ τοῦ ἀνθρώπου.   The form of expression is changed from ἡ σάρξ μου of v. 51, after a fashion frequent in the Johannine discourses.   But no new idea is introduced by the change, for " the Son of Man " has already (v. 27) been mentioned as the future giver of the heavenly food.   For this title, see Introd., p. cxxx.

οὐκ ἔχετε ζωὴν ἐν ἑαυτοῖς. The issue of this mystical "eating and drinking" is life, both here and hereafter, as has been said already (v. 51). A little before (v. 47) we had ὁ πιστεύων ἔχει ζωὴν αἰώνιον, and the juxtaposition of these affirmations indicates that there is an intimate connexion between the "faith" which is in continual contact with Christ, and that eating and drinking of His Flesh and Blood—the assimilation or appropriation of His humanity—which is the theme of vv. 51ᵇ–58. See on 3¹⁵, and cf. 20³¹. Here the doctrine is stated negatively, and in an even more startling fashion: "If ye do not eat the Flesh of the Son of Man, and drink His Blood, ye have no life in yourselves." This is the only way to attain to Life.

The Flesh and the Blood are the full Life; their communication is the communication of eternal life. It is possible that Jn.'s insistence on the *flesh* and *blood* of Christ has some connexion with his purpose of refuting Docetic doctrines which denied the reality of both (see on 1¹⁴).

After ζωήν, ℵ adds αἰώνιον (from v. 54).

54 ff. The sequence of thought is simple. He who feeds on Christ has life, here and hereafter (v. 54), inasmuch as he thus appropriates the life of Christ (v. 56), which is the life of God (v. 57); hence he who feeds on Christ will live for ever (v. 58). The fourfold repetition of ὁ τρώγων . . . (vv. 54, 56, 57, 58) is thoroughly Johannine in its cadences.

The verb τρώγειν challenges attention. In ordinary Greek, it is used of men eating fruit or vegetables, but no instance has been produced of its use for the eating of flesh (Abbott, *Diat.* 1710*h*). It seems to connote eating of delicacies, or eating with enjoyment; and in the only place in the N.T. outside Jn. in which it is found, viz. Mt. 24³⁸, where the careless ones before the Flood are described as τρώγοντες καὶ πίνοντες, this suggestion is perhaps involved. Besides the present passage, we have it again at 13¹⁸ (where see note) as a quotation from Ps. 41⁹, ἐσθίων of the LXX being altered by Jn. to τρώγων. That is, Jn. always uses this verb of "eating" at the Last Supper or the Eucharist (for this is undoubtedly indicated in vv. 51–58 here), although Mk. and Mt. have ἐσθίειν in their narratives of the Last Supper (Mk. 14¹⁸, ²², Mt. 26²¹, ²⁶). The Synoptists use the verb ἐσθίειν 34 times in all, but it never appears in Jn.

τρώγειν is used of spiritual feeding in a remarkable sentence of Irenæus (*Hær.* IV. xxxviii. 1) which seems to be reminiscent of the present passage. He is speaking of Christ, ὁ ἄρτος ὁ τέλειος τοῦ πατρός, and of His gradual revelation of Himself. First, He offered Himself to us as milk is offered to

54. ὁ τρώγων μου τὴν σάρκα καὶ πίνων μου τὸ αἷμα ἔχει ζωὴν αἰώνιον, κἀγὼ ἀναστήσω αὐτὸν τῇ ἐσχάτῃ ἡμέρᾳ. 55. ἡ γὰρ σάρξ μου ἀληθής ἐστιν βρῶσις, καὶ τὸ αἷμά μου ἀληθής ἐστιν πόσις. 56. ὁ τρώγων μου τὴν σάρκα καὶ πίνων μου τὸ αἷμα ἐν ἐμοὶ μένει

infants, in order that being thus nourished from the breast of His flesh (ὑπὸ μασθοῦ τῆς σαρκὸς αὐτοῦ), " we might become accustomed to eat and drink the Word of God (τρώγειν καὶ πίνειν τὸν λόγον τοῦ θεοῦ), and contain within ourselves the Bread of immortality (τὸν τῆς ἀθανασίας ἄρτον), which is the Spirit of the Father."

The language of Ignatius (*Rom.* 7), in like manner, reproduces words of this chapter: ἄρτον θεοῦ θέλω, ὅ ἐστιν σὰρξ τοῦ Χριστοῦ . . . καὶ πόμα θέλω τὸ αἷμα αὐτοῦ. So Justin (*Apol.* i. 66) says that the eucharistic elements are Ἰησοῦ καὶ σάρκα καὶ αἷμα. See Introd., p. clxviii.

54. ὁ τρώγων μου τὴν σάρκα καὶ πίνων μου τὸ αἷμα (the whole phrase is repeated verbatim in v. 56) seems to mean, " he who *continually* feeds with enjoyment upon my Flesh and continually drinks my Blood," or " he who is in the *habit* of feeding, etc.," for the present participles must be given their force. See above on v. 29.

ἔχει ζωὴν αἰώνιον (*sc.* in the present), κἀγὼ ἀναστήσω αὐτὸν τῇ ἐσχάτῃ ἡμέρᾳ, which is the promise of life in the future. The twofold assurance is repeated from v. 40, the difference being that while there it is for him who has spiritual vision of Christ and believes in Him, here it is given to the man who " eats His Flesh and drinks His Blood." See above on v. 53.

For the refrain κἀγὼ ἀναστήσω αὐτὸν τῇ ἐσχάτῃ ἡμέρᾳ, see on v. 39, and cf. Introd., p. clxvii.

The rec. text inserts ἐν before ἐσχάτῃ, but om. אBDΘ. See on v. 39.

55. ἀληθής. So אᶜBCLTW, but א*DΓΔΘ read ἀληθῶς.

ἡ γὰρ σάρξ μου (cf. v. 51) ἀληθής ἐστιν βρῶσις, "for my Flesh is true meat," *sc.* it is really to be eaten, and it nourishes as meat ought to do. For βρῶσις of the thing eaten, see on 4³².

καὶ τὸ αἷμά μου κτλ., "and my Blood is true drink." The verse is a comment on, and corroboration of, the assurance of v. 54.

56. ὁ τρώγων . . . τὸ αἷμα is repeated from v. 54, the reason for that promise being now given. The man who spiritually feeds on Christ " abides in Him," and so he has the assurance of eternal life.

μένειν is a favourite word with Jn., and he uses it much more frequently than the Synoptists do. They have not the

κἀγὼ ἐν αὐτῷ. 57. καθὼς ἀπέστειλέν με ὁ ζῶν Πατὴρ κἀγὼ ζῶ διὰ τὸν Πατέρα, καὶ ὁ τρώγων με κἀκεῖνος ζήσει δι᾽ ἐμέ. 58. οὗτός ἐστιν

phrase " to abide in Christ," or " in God," which is thoroughly characteristic of Johannine doctrine. This phrase is used in a general mystical sense in 1 Jn. 2⁶· ²⁷· ²⁸ 3⁶· ²⁴ 4¹²· ¹⁶; but in the Fourth Gospel it is found only here and at 15⁴⁻⁷, both passages having reference to the Eucharist (see on 15¹), the purpose of which is that " we may dwell in Him, and He in us " (cf. 15⁴). In Jn. the one " abiding " involves the other, and to this thought reference is made several times (15⁵, 1 Jn. 3²⁴ 4¹³· ¹⁶; cf. 14²⁰, and see on 5³⁸).

The external token of a man's " abiding " in Christ, is that he keeps His commandments (1 Jn. 3²⁴); and, as to love God and to love man are the great commandments, he that abides in love abides in God (1 Jn. 4¹⁶) [1] More generally, he that abides in Christ ought to walk after His example (1 Jn. 2⁶); in other words, he " bears fruit " (15²). Of one who has perfectly realised this " abiding," it is said " he sinneth not " (1 Jn. 3⁶). Such an one has the secret of efficacious prayer (15⁷). He has *life* (6⁵⁷), and naturally will have confidence at the Great Parousia (1 Jn. 2²⁸).

D adds after αὐτῷ: καθὼς ἐν ἐμοὶ ὁ πατήρ, κἀγὼ ἐν τῷ πατρί (cf. 14¹⁰). ἀμὴν ἀμὴν λέγω ὑμῖν, ἐὰν μὴ λάβητε τὸ σῶμα τοῦ υἱοῦ τοῦ ἀνθρώπου ὡς τὸν ἄρτον τῆς ζωῆς, οὐκ ἔχετε ζωὴν ἐν αὐτῷ. This interpolation [2] is supported by a ff². With D's substitution of λάβητε τὸ σῶμα for φάγητε τὴν σάρκα (v. 53), compare its substitution of λάβητε for φάγητε in v. 53.

57. For ἀπέστειλεν, D has ἀπέσταλκε (cf. 20²¹, 1 Jn. 4⁹); the aor. marks a definite moment, viz. that of the Incarnation. For the " sending " of Jesus by the Father, see on 3¹⁷.

καθώς is a favourite conjunction with Jn. The constr. καθὼς . . . κἀγώ, which we find here, cannot always be interpreted in the same way. Thus at 15⁹ 17¹⁸ and 20²¹ we must render, " As the Father loved (*or* sent) me, *so* I loved (*or* send) you." On the other hand, at 17²¹ καθὼς . . . κἀγώ plainly stands for " As Thou, Father, art in me, *and* I in Thee." In the present verse, the sequence of thought requires the latter interpretation, viz. " As the Living Father hath sent me, *and* I live because of the Father," then it follows that " he that eateth me shall live because of me." See further on 10¹⁵.

The form of the principal sentence καθὼς ἀπέστειλέν με . . . καὶ ὁ τρώγων κτλ. must also be observed. It appears

---

[1] See Introd., p. clxxiv.

[2] Chase traces it to Syriac influence (*Syro-Latin Text of the Gospels*, p. 21).

again 13^{15. 33}, 1 Jn. 2^6 4^{17}, of the comparison between the life of the Incarnate Christ and that of believers. It is not καθὼς . . . οὕτως, for the comparison or parallelism can never be exact or complete; it is καθὼς . . . καί, "As Christ . . . so (in a sense) even those who are His." See on 17^{18}.

ὁ ζῶν πατήρ is a phrase unique in the N.T.; but cf. ὁ πατὴρ ἔχει ζωὴν ἐν ἑαυτῷ (5^{26}, where see note). "The living God" is a title found both in O.T. and N.T., e.g. Deut. 5^{26}, Mt. 16^{16}, Acts 14^{15}, 2 Cor. 6^{16}.

The meaning of this passage is, then, as follows: As the Father, who is the Fount of Life, has sent Christ on earth, and as Christ's life is derived from and dependent on the Divine Life, so the believer who "eats" Christ, that is, who is in continual communion with Him, assimilates His life and thus lives in dependence on Him. διὰ τοῦ πατρός would mean that the Father was the Agent; but διὰ τὸν πατέρα signifies that He is the spring and source of the Life of the Son.

διά with the accusative may mean either (1) *for the sake of* . . ., or (2) *thanks to*. . . . For (1) Wetstein quotes δι᾽ ὑμᾶς μόνους ζῆν ἐθέλω," "I wish to live for your sakes," *sc.* to do you favours (Dio Cassius, LXXVII. iii. 2); and Abbott (*Diat.* 2705) adds several examples from Epictetus, *e.g.* ἔξελθε διὰ τὰ παιδία, "escape for the sake of the children" (Epict. IV. i. 163). This use of διά will not suit the context here. That the Life of Christ was διὰ τὸν πατέρα, "for the Father's sake," *sc.* to do His Will, is true (cf. 4^{34}), but the argument requires the conception that the Life of Christ is derived from and due to the Life of God. (2) For this sense of διά, Abbott (*Diat.* 2297*b*) quotes Plutarch, *Vit. Alex.* § 8: Alexander said he owed life to his father, but good life to Aristotle δι᾽ ἐκεῖνον μὲν ζῶν, διὰ τοῦτον δὲ καλῶς ζῶν. This is a close parallel to the use of διά in the present passage. Christ lives, διὰ τὸν πατέρα, "thanks to the Father," as sharing the Father's Life;[1] and believers live δι᾽ αὐτόν, "thanks to Him." The meaning, then, of ἐκεῖνος ζήσει δι᾽ ἐμέ is, practically, the same as that of the related passage 1 Jn. 4^9 τὸν υἱὸν αὐτοῦ τὸν μονογενῆ ἀπέσταλκεν ὁ θεὸς εἰς τὸν κόσμον, ἵνα ζήσωμεν δι᾽ αὐτοῦ, where διά takes the genitive. See on 15^3.

Godet's comment brings out the general sense excellently: "As the infinite life of nature can only be appropriated by man so far as it is concentrated in a fruit or a morsel of bread; so the divine life is only put within our reach so far as it is incarnate in the Son of Man. It is thus that He is to us all the

---

[1] At 4^{34} Christ's "food" is the doing the Father's Will. Here the thought is rather that the Son "feeds" on the Father's Life, assimilating and sharing it.

ὁ ἄρτος ὁ ἐκ τοῦ οὐρανοῦ καταβάς, οὐ καθὼς ἔφαγον οἱ πατέρες καὶ

Bread of Life. But as we have to appropriate and assimilate bread to obtain life through it; so also must we incorporate the Person of the Son of Man by an inward act of faith, which is the way of spiritual manducation. By thus feeding on Him who lived by God, we live by God Himself and henceforth actually live as Jesus does."

καὶ ὁ τρώγων με . . ., " even so, he who eateth me." The metaphor of eating Christ's " Flesh and Blood " is dropped; it is the feeding on Himself, the communion with His Person, that is the essential thing.

For τρώγων, D has λαμβάνων; cf. v. 56.

For ζήσει (אBC²LTNΘ), the rec. has ζήσεται with ΓΔ (cf. v. 51).

κἀκεῖνος ζήσει δι' ἐμέ. The life promised here is that ζωὴ αἰώνιος which begins in the present; the parallel saying of 14¹⁹ ὅτι ἐγὼ ζῶ καὶ ὑμεῖς ζήσεσθε, has special reference to the future. See on 11²⁵, and cf. Introd., p. clxi.

58. This verse contains a summary of the whole discourse, and so it goes back to the saying about the heavenly Bread (v. 33), ending with what was said in v. 51, that he who feeds on it shall live for ever. Jn.'s report of the words of Jesus often passes without pause into his own comments (see on 3¹⁶), and it has been suggested (Abbott, *Diat.* 1957) that v. 58 was intended to be the evangelist's short statement of what has gone before. But if so, ταῦτα εἶπεν in v. 59 is clumsy. We can hardly separate v. 58 from what precedes, despite some slight changes in the form of expression, which are duly noted below. As has already been said (p. cxvi), Jn. is prone to vary words and the order of words when reiterating something already recorded.

οὗτός ἐστιν κτλ., repeated from v. 50, except that here the aor. participle καταβάς is used (as in v. 51) of the descent from heaven of the mystical Bread. For the rec. ἐκ τοῦ οὐρανοῦ (אDLNWΓΔΘ), BCT have ἐξ οὐρανοῦ, and this may be right; but on the six previous occurrences of the phrase "descending from heaven" (vv. 33, 38, 41, 42, 50, 51), τοῦ οὐρανοῦ is the best-supported reading.

οὐ καθὼς ἔφαγον κτλ., repeated, with slight variations, from v. 49. The sentence is a good example of Jn.'s partiality for the constr. called *anacoluthon*.

For οὐ καθώς, cf. 14²⁷, 1 Jn. 3¹²; the only other occurrence in the N.T. being 2 Cor. 8⁵.

οἱ πατέρες. The rec. with DΔNΘ and Syr. sin. adds ὑμῶν (from v. 49); om. אBCLTW. The expression οἱ

ἀπέθανον· ὁ τρώγων τοῦτον τὸν ἄρτον ζήσει εἰς τὸν αἰῶνα. 59. Ταῦτα εἶπεν ἐν συναγωγῇ διδάσκων ἐν Καφαρναούμ.

πατέρες occurs again, in the words of Christ, at 7²², where it refers to the patriarchs. It also is found Acts 13³², Rom. 9⁵ 11²⁸ 15⁸, Heb. 1¹, 2 Pet. 3⁴, and is used quite vaguely of the Israelites of the olden time. Here it is limited by the context to the generation of the Exodus from Egypt. But no distinction is to be drawn between οἱ πατέρες ὑμῶν of v. 49 and οἱ πατέρες of v. 58 (cf., *e.g.*, Acts 13³² and Acts 26⁶).

Some minor uncials add τὸ μάννα after οἱ πατέρες ὑμῶν, from v. 49.

καὶ ἀπέθανον. Lightfoot (*Hor. Hebr.*, on 6³⁹) cites a Jewish saying, "The generation in the wilderness have no part in the world to come," and if this were pre-Christian in date (which is uncertain) it would suggest that καὶ ἀπέθανον should be interpreted of spiritual death. But we have already seen (v. 49) that the argument requires it to indicate the death of the body, from which even the manna could not save those who ate it.

ὁ τρώγων τοῦτον τὸν ἄρτον ζήσει εἰς τὸν αἰῶνα. This is repeated from v. 51, with the substitution of ὁ τρώγων with the acc. for ἐάν τις φάγῃ with ἐκ and the gen.

ζήσει. So אBCNW⊙; the rec. has ζήσεται. Cf. v. 51.

59. For the site of Capernaum, see on 2¹². The synagogue at Capernaum (built by the centurion, Lk. 7⁵) was the place where Jesus gave His first public instruction (Mk. 1²¹; cf. Lk. 4³¹ᶠ.).[1] That it was His habit to teach in country synagogues is clear; cf. Mk. 1³⁹ 3¹, Mt. 4²³ 9³⁵ 12⁹ 13⁵⁴; and see Jn. 18²⁰, the only other place where the word συναγώγη occurs in Jn.

ἐν συναγωγῇ, "in synagogue," as we say "in church." D prefixes the article τῇ before συν., but incorrectly; cf. 18²⁰. D also adds σαββάτῳ, and this may possibly be a gloss which has tradition behind it. Sabbath synagogue services were those at which instruction was usually given, although there were services on Mondays and Thursdays as well. On the other hand, the narrative represents a crowd as following Jesus across the lake, which would involve more travelling than was regarded as right on the Sabbath day.

[1] Recent excavations at Tell-Hum have disclosed the remains of a large building which its discoverers identify with this synagogue.

60. Πολλοὶ οὖν ἀκούσαντες ἐκ τῶν μαθητῶν αὐτοῦ εἶπαν Σκληρός ἐστιν ὁ λόγος οὗτος· τίς δύναται αὐτοῦ ἀκούειν; 61. εἰδὼς δὲ ὁ Ἰησοῦς ἐν ἑαυτῷ ὅτι γογγύζουσιν περὶ τούτου οἱ μαθηταὶ αὐτοῦ, εἶπεν αὐτοῖς Τοῦτο ὑμᾶς σκανδαλίζει; 62. ἐὰν οὖν θεωρῆτε τὸν Υἱὸν τοῦ

The disciples are perplexed by the words of Jesus (vv. 60–65)

60. πολλοί . . . ἐκ τῶν μαθητῶν αὐτοῦ, including not only the Twelve, but those who were of the outer circle of His disciples (cf. v. 66, and see on 2²); some of the Twelve may well have been among those who found the teaching of Jesus difficult.

σκληρός is not used again by Jn. It means *harsh* or *hard to accept* (not *difficult to understand*; cf. Gen. 21¹¹ and Jude¹⁵).

ὁ λόγος οὗτος (אBCDLNW) is the true order of words, as against οὗτος ὁ λ. of the rec. text (Θ).

τίς δύναται αὐτοῦ ἀκούειν; " Who can hear it ? " sc. *with appreciation*. See on 3⁸ for ἀκούειν with a genitive in Jn.

What was the harsh or strange saying to which the questioners referred ? The whole of the discourse from v. 51 onward might be described as σκληρός, and exception had already been taken to the early part of it: " How can this man give us His flesh to eat ? " (v. 52). But the statement which seems to be challenged particularly at this point is v. 58, " This is the Bread which *descended* from heaven; he that eats of it shall live for ever "; which Jesus applied to Himself, for the answer in v. 62 has special reference to it. What would they say if they saw Him *ascending* ? Flesh cannot give eternal life, but spirit can do so.

For λόγος used of a saying of Jesus, see on 2²².

61. εἰδὼς δὲ ὁ Ἰησοῦς ἐν ἑαυτῷ. See on 2²⁵ for the insight of Jesus into men's thoughts.

For γογγύζουσιν, see on v. 41 above, where the murmurers were " the Jews "; here they include some of the disciples of Jesus.

τοῦτο ὑμᾶς σκανδαλίζει; " Does this offend you? " σκανδαλίζειν occurs in Jn. again only at 16¹, but it is a common Synoptic word.

62. ἐὰν οὖν θεωρῆτε κτλ. The passage is an aposiopesis, the apodosis being omitted. " If then you should see the Son of Man (see on 1⁵¹) ascending where He was before (will you be offended ?)." We should expect τί οὖν ἐὰν θεωρῆτε κτλ., and the omission of τί is awkward. But the meaning is hardly doubtful. Jesus does not imply that those addressed would certainly see the Ascension, but that it was a possibility. According to Lk., the Eleven were witnesses of the Ascension

ἀνθρώπου ἀναβαίνοντα ὅπου ἦν τὸ πρότερον ; 63. τὸ πνεῦμά ἐστιν τὸ

(Lk. 24⁵¹, Acts 1⁹), and they were among those to whom Jesus was here speaking in reply to doubts (see on v. 60). θεωρεῖν (see on 2²³) is used here of bodily vision; and ἀναβαίνειν is used again of the Ascension 20¹⁷ (cf. 3¹³, Eph. 4¹⁰, Acts 2³⁴).

τὸ πρότερον, "before," is rare in the N.T.; but cf. 9⁸ and Gal. 4¹³.

ὅπου ἦν τὸ πρότερον. The Personality of the Lord remained unchanged through His Incarnation and subsequent Ascension. Here is suggested the pre-existence of the "Son of Man," as before at 3¹³, where see note.

The meaning of vv. 62, 63 is best brought out if we take them in connexion with v. 58 (cf. v. 51), which had seemed to the hearers of Jesus to be hard of acceptance. He had said two things: (1) that He was the Bread which came down from heaven, and (2) that the man who ate of it should live for ever. There are two distinct points of difficulty, and they are taken separately.

(1) That One moving among men in the flesh had descended *from* heaven seemed incredible, but is it not still less credible that He should ascend *to* heaven? Yet the former had happened (in the Incarnation); the latter will happen at the Ascension, and some of those present might be there to see it.

(2) There is a real difficulty in believing that the eating of "bread" or "flesh" (v. 52) can give life *for ever* (v. 58). "The flesh profiteth nothing." Flesh cannot transcend its own limitations. But to those who feed on the Flesh of the Son of Man, He will impart eternal life (v. 57), for although He "became flesh" (1¹⁴), His origin and essential being is spiritual, and it is the characteristic of spirit to give life : τὸ πνεῦμά ἐστιν τὸ ζωοποιοῦν. This is the promise to all future believers (see on 7³⁹). The words which He had spoken to them, and to which they took exception, are Spirit and Life: these are the key words of His teaching about Himself and His salvation.

Some commentators, *e.g.* Meyer of a former generation, and Abbott (*Diat.* 2211*b*), take ἀναβαίνειν in this verse as referring to the Death of Jesus, as the beginning of His passage from the earthly to the heavenly sphere. But the usage of the verb in the N.T. is decisive against this. It never refers to the Crucifixion, but to the Ascension, and it provides a notable illustration of Jn.'s manner of writing, that here and at 20¹⁷ he introduces an allusion to the Ascension of Christ, whilst he does not state explicitly that it took place.

ζωοποιοῦν, ἡ σὰρξ οὐκ ὠφελεῖ οὐδέν· τὰ ῥήματα ἃ ἐγὼ λελάληκα ὑμῖν πνεῦμά ἐστιν καὶ ζωή ἐστιν. 64. ἀλλ᾽ εἰσὶν ἐξ ὑμῶν τινες οἳ οὐ πιστεύουσιν. ᾔδει γὰρ ἐξ ἀρχῆς ὁ Ἰησοῦς τίνες εἰσὶν οἱ μὴ πιστεύοντες

63. τὸ πνεῦμά ἐστιν τὸ ζωοποιοῦν. See for ζωοποιεῖν as applied to the work of Christ, 5²¹; and note 1 Cor. 15⁴⁵.

The contrast between *flesh* and *spirit* has already been before us in 3⁶, where see the note; cf. also Mk. 14³⁸, 1 Pet. 3¹⁸ 4⁶.

ἡ σὰρξ οὐκ ὠφελεῖ οὐδέν, "flesh avails nothing." For ὠφελεῖν, cf. 12¹⁹. There is no contradiction with what has been said before (v. 51), for Jesus does not say "*my* flesh" here. In every case is it true that flesh, *without spirit*, cannot quicken to eternal life.[1]

τὰ ῥήματα ἃ ἐγὼ λελάληκα. So אBCDLNWΘ, as against λαλῶ of the rec. text. The "words" in question are the words of the preceding discourse. For τὰ ῥήματα (never in the sing. in Jn.), see on 3³⁴. The ῥήματα of Christ are words of God (8⁴⁷ 17⁸), and as such belong to the sphere of spiritual realities, for God is Spirit (4²⁴), and of essential being, that is, of true life. They are spirit and they are life.

For λαλεῖν, see on 3¹¹; and cf. 8²⁰.

64. But although His words were words of life, they were life only to those who believed, and so Jesus adds ἀλλ᾽ εἰσὶν ἐξ ὑμῶν τινες οἳ οὐ πιστεύουσιν. πιστεύειν is used absolutely, as at vv. 36, 47 (see on 1⁷).

Jn. is prone to comment on sayings or actions of Jesus that might not be easy for a reader to understand,[2] and here he adds ᾔδει γάρ κτλ. (cf. 3¹⁶), to emphasise the point that Jesus had not been speaking great words of mystery (vv. 62, 63) without realising that some among His hearers could not appropriate them.

ᾔδει γὰρ ἐξ ἀρχῆς ὁ Ἰη. ἐξ ἀρχῆς occurs in the N.T. only here and at 16⁴, although it is found in the LXX (*e.g.* Isa. 40²¹ 41²⁶, where it means "from the beginning of things"); but we have seen on v. 38 that ἀπό and ἐκ are not always distinguishable in Jn. He uses ἐξ ἀρχῆς as equivalent to ἀπ᾽ ἀρχῆς (א reads ἀπ᾽ ἀρχῆς), which occurs 15²⁷, 1 Jn. 2⁷· ²⁴ 3¹¹ (but cf. 1 Jn. 1¹) in the same sense as here, viz. "from the time when Jesus first drew disciples round Him." From the moment when He began to observe their characters, He distinguished unerringly those who were faithful from those who were not (see 2²⁴). That Jn. means his readers to understand that from

---

[1] For patristic comments on this passage, see Gore, *Dissertations*, p. 303 f.
[2] Cf. Introd., p. xxxiv.

καὶ τίς ἐστιν ὁ παραδώσων αὐτόν.   65. καὶ ἔλεγεν Διὰ τοῦτο εἴρηκα

the moment of his call, Judas was known by Jesus to be the man who would betray Him is not certain. If that be his meaning, the passage provides a remarkable instance of Jn.'s doctrine of *predestination* (see on 2⁴, and especially on 13¹⁸).

But we need not press ἐξ ἀρχῆς so far that we must suppose that Jesus chose Judas as one of the Twelve, being conscious *at the time* that he would be a traitor; that would make the choice difficult to explain, in connexion with the true humanity of Christ. If the knowledge that Judas was untrustworthy came as soon as Jesus had studied him at close quarters, then ἐξ ἀρχῆς is adequately interpreted. In any case, Jn. takes care, both here and in c. 13, to repudiate the idea that the treachery of Judas took Jesus by surprise.

τίς ἐστιν ὁ παραδώσων αὐτόν. Abbott notes (*Diat.* 2510) that ὁ παραδώσων (D has ὁ παραδίδους) is the only instance in Jn. of a future participle with the article.

The meaning of παραδιδόναι is often misunderstood, as Abbott (*Paradosis* passim) has shown at length. It means " to deliver up," but not necessarily " to betray." Thus it is used of the Jews giving up Jesus to Pilate (18³⁰. ³⁵. ³⁶ 19¹¹), and of Pilate giving up Jesus to be crucified (19¹⁶), and also of Jesus " giving up " His spirit, *i.e.* dying, on the cross (19³⁰). In none of these passages is treachery connoted or implied; and thus in the passages where παραδιδόναι is applied to the action of Judas (6⁷¹ 12⁴ 13². ¹¹. ²¹ 18². ⁵ 21²⁰) we are not entitled to render it " betray." προδιδόναι (a verb not found in the Gospels, although Lk. 6¹⁶ calls Judas προδότης, as he un-doubtedly was) is " to betray," but παραδιδόναι is simply " to deliver up," and is a colourless word not conveying any sug-gestion of blame.

Jn. does not record any early predictions by Jesus that He would be " delivered up " to the Jews, as the Synoptists do (cf. Mk. 9³¹ 10³³). In Jn. Jesus Himself does not use the word παραδιδόναι until 13²¹.

65. καὶ ἔλεγεν. Jn. occasionally uses ἔλεγεν of the utter-ances of Jesus (2²¹. ²² 5¹⁸ 6⁶. ⁷¹ 8²⁷. ³¹ 12³³), and the force of the impft. tense must not be missed. Here reference is made to the saying of v. 44, a cardinal doctrine in Jn. (cf. v. 37 and 3²⁷), viz. that the impulse to faith comes in the first instance from God; there were some who did not believe (v. 64), and one who would be a traitor among them, but this did not surprise Jesus. " He was saying " (all the while) that it was a funda-mental principle that God must " draw " a man to Christ. See Abbott (*Diat.* 2467), who, however, holds that in all cases

ὑμῖν ὅτι οὐδεὶς δύναται ἐλθεῖν πρός με ἐὰν μὴ ᾖ δεδομένον αὐτῷ ἐκ τοῦ Πατρός.

66. Ἐκ τούτου πολλοὶ τῶν μαθητῶν αὐτοῦ ἀπῆλθον εἰς τὰ ὀπίσω

a saying preceded by ἔλεγεν is mysterious and not understood by the hearers. This can hardly be sustained; see, e.g., 6⁶.

διὰ τοῦτο εἴρηκα. This was the reason why He had given the warning of v. 44 (where see the note). He wished to anticipate criticism based on the non-success of His teaching with some people. For διὰ τοῦτο, see on 5¹⁶.

ἐκ τοῦ πατρός. The rec. adds μου, but om. אBC*DLTW⊕ (see on v. 44).

The defection of many disciples : the steadfastness of the Twelve, as indicated in the Confession of Peter (vv. 66–71)

Verses 66–71 form the conclusion of Part I. of the Gospel. Hitherto the mission of Jesus has been accepted by many disciples, and has appeared to be full of hope (2²³ 4¹· ³⁹· ⁴⁵ 6²). But He had not trusted Himself to all these adherents, for " He knew what was in man " (2²⁵). When the reach and difficulty of His doctrine begin to be realised, there is a falling away of disciples. Only the Twelve remain (and even of these one will be unfaithful). Here, at the end of c. 6, is the note of failure, suggested for the first time at v. 26. Henceforth the record is to be of a growing hate, culminating in rejection (see on 12³⁶ᵇ).[1]

66. ἐκ τούτου, "thereupon." The great defection began at this point, and its immediate cause was the nature of the teaching which had been given. Cf. 19¹². ἐκ τούτου in a causal sense is common in the papyri.[2]

οὖν is added after ἐκ τούτου by אD⊕ and fam. 13, but is unnecessary and is om. by BCLTNW. τοῦτουπολλοι might easily become τοὐτοῦνπολλοι, and thus οὖν would get into the text (see Tischendorf, in loc.).

πολλοὶ τῶν μαθητῶν αὐτοῦ. BT insert ἐκ before τῶν μαθ., but om. אCDLW⊕. Cf. v. 60; and see on 1⁴⁰ 6⁷¹ 12⁴.

τῶν μαθητῶν refers to the outer circle of disciples (see on 2²), which would include the Twelve, although none of the Twelve failed Jesus at this point. A tradition ascribed to Hippolytus says that Mark and Luke were among the " seventy disciples who were scattered by the offence of the words of Christ," Jn. 6⁵³ being quoted loosely.[3]

---

[1] Cf. Introd., p. xxxiii.
[2] See Moulton-Milligan, Vocab. of N.T., s.v. ἐκ.
[3] Fragm. on The Seventy Apostles.

καὶ οὐκέτι μετ᾽ αὐτοῦ περιεπάτουν. 67. εἶπεν οὖν ὁ Ἰησοῦς τοῖς δώδεκα Μὴ καὶ ὑμεῖς θέλετε ὑπάγειν; 68. ἀπεκρίθη αὐτῷ Σίμων

ἀπῆλθον εἰς τὰ ὀπίσω, a phrase used again 18⁶. They withdrew or retreated from association with Jesus. For εἰς τὰ ὀπίσω in a figurative sense, cf. Ps. 44¹⁸.

οὐκέτι μετ᾽ αὐτοῦ περιεπάτουν, " they walked no more with Him," a phrase which vividly suggests the itinerant character of His ministry. Cf. 7¹ 11⁵⁴; and for the larger sense of περιπάτειν, see on 8¹².

67. εἶπεν . . . τοῖς δώδεκα. This is the first time that " the Twelve " are mentioned by Jn. (cf. v. 13). He introduces this familiar designation without having given any account of their being set apart by Jesus, as the Synoptists do (Mk. 3¹⁴). So, too, he brings in Pilate (18²⁹) and Mary Magdalene (19²⁵), without explaining who they were. This is a feature of his way of writing: he assumes, on the part of his readers, an acquaintance with the story of Christ's ministry (cf. p. xciv).

Jn. mentions " the Twelve " by this collective designation only 4 times (cf. vv. 70, 71, and 20²⁴), and in every case there is a suggestion of desertion or unbelief in the context.

μὴ καὶ ὑμεῖς θέλετε ὑπάγειν; " Would you also go away ? " The form of the question, μὴ καὶ . . ., suggests that a negative answer is expected. Cf. 7⁴⁷. ⁵² 9⁴⁰ 18¹⁷. ²⁵; and see 21⁵, the only other place in the Gospel where an interrogation beginning with μή is put into the mouth of Jesus.

ὑπάγειν, " to go away," is a favourite word with Jn. It is applied to the disciples here and at 15¹⁶. See on 7³³ and 16⁷.

68. The Confession of Peter here recorded is not to be distinguished from the similar confession narrated by the Synoptists (Mk. 8²⁷ᶠ., Mt. 16¹³ᶠ., Lk. 9¹⁸ᶠ.), although the details are different. The crisis in the Lord's public ministry which called it forth took place, according to Lk. as well as according to Jn., some time after the Feeding of the Five Thousand (Mk., followed by Mt., places it a little later, after the Feeding of the Four Thousand). Jn. says that the place was Capernaum, while Mk. and Mt. give Cæsarea Philippi, 30 miles to the north; Lk. does not give any indication of place. In all the Synoptists, the Confession of Peter was followed by the first prediction by Jesus of His Passion. There is no indication of this in Jn., who does not assign to any particular crisis the *first* announcement by Jesus that He was to suffer. Cf. 3¹³. ¹⁴ 6⁵³ 8²⁸ 12²³. ²⁵ 13³¹; and see Introd., p. cxxxi. But in Jn., as in the Synoptists, the faithfulness of the apostles, for whom Peter was spokesman, as contrasted with

Πέτρος Κύριε, πρὸς τίνα ἀπελευσόμεθα; ῥήματα ζωῆς αἰωνίου ἔχεις·
69. καὶ ἡμεῖς πεπιστεύκαμεν καὶ ἐγνώκαμεν ὅτι σὺ εἶ ὁ Ἅγιος τοῦ

the defection or incredulity of many in the outer circle of the
Lord's followers, is brought out clearly.

Σίμων Πέτρος. This is the only place in Jn. where Peter
is represented as speaking on behalf of the rest, although
he appears later as foremost to question or to intervene
(cf. 13⁶·²⁴·³⁶ 20²).

πρὸς τίνα ἀπελευσόμεθα; At an earlier stage, Peter had
said, " Depart from me " (Lk. 5⁸), but that was only a hasty
word of humility. The question μὴ καὶ ὑμεῖς θέλετε ὑπάγειν;
is answered by another question.

Peter's Confession is twofold in Jn.'s version. (1) "Thou
hast words of eternal life"; this is the acceptance of Jesus as
Prophet. (2) " Thou art the Holy One of God"; that is the
recognition of Him as the *Priest* of humanity.

ῥήματα ζωῆς αἰωνίου ἔχεις. The immediate reference is
to v. 63, and the teaching of v. 58. " Thou hast words (not
the words) of eternal life," *i.e.* words which give eternal life,
or the knowledge of it ; see on v. 35 for the phrase "the
Bread of Life." For ῥήματα, see on v. 63; and cf. Acts 5²⁰
πάντα τὰ ῥήματα τῆς ζωῆς ταύτης. For ζωὴ αἰώνιος, see on
3¹⁵; and cf. vv. 27, 40. This is a favourite expression of Jn.,
who puts into his own accustomed phraseology Peter's confession of trust in Jesus.

69. καὶ ἡμεῖς (emphatic; *we*, at least, the chosen Twelve)
πεπιστεύκαμεν καὶ ἐγνώκαμεν κτλ. The order of verbs is
different at 1 Jn. 4¹⁶ ἡμεῖς ἐγνώκαμεν καὶ πεπιστεύκαμεν ; cf.
17⁸ ἔγνωσαν . . . καὶ ἐπίστευσαν. But, while Jn. does not lay
down formulæ as to the relative precedence of *faith* and
knowledge in regard to the things of the spirit, his teaching is
nearer the *credo ut intelligam* of the saints than the *intelligo
ut credam* of the philosophers. The apostles had "believed"
in Jesus, and therefore they " knew " who He was. So, at
any rate, Jn. makes Peter say. See on 3³⁶, and cf. 11²⁷.

σὺ εἶ. Cf. the Confession of Nathanael, σὺ εἶ ὁ υἱὸς τοῦ
θεοῦ (1⁴⁹). The Confession of Peter does not really transcend
either this or the announcement of Andrew εὑρήκαμεν τὸν
Μεσσίαν (1⁴¹). The Synoptic presentation of a gradual development of spiritual insight on the part of the followers of
Jesus, in accordance with which it was only after a time and
not all at once that they recognised Him as the Christ, has no
place in Jn.'s narrative.[1] His purpose in writing the Gospel is
to convince men that Jesus *is* the Christ (20³¹), and the stages

[1] Cf. Introd., p. cxxxiv.

Θεοῦ. 70. ἀπεκρίθη αὐτοῖς ὁ Ἰησοῦς Οὐκ ἐγὼ ὑμᾶς τοὺς δώδεκα ἐξελεξάμην; καὶ ἐξ ὑμῶν εἷς διάβολός ἐστιν. 71. ἔλεγεν δὲ τὸν

by which he, or others, reached this supreme conviction he does not stay to record.

ὁ ἅγιος τοῦ θεοῦ. This is, undoubtedly, the true reading (אBC*DLW). The rec. (with Nⓗ) has ὁ Χριστός, ὁ υἱὸς τοῦ θεοῦ τοῦ ζῶντος, which is the reading of Mt. 16¹⁶, and has naturally crept into the text here, by assimilation. Cf. also the confession of Martha, ἐγὼ πεπίστευκα ὅτι σὺ εἶ ὁ Χριστός, ὁ υἱὸς τοῦ θεοῦ (11²⁷).

ὁ ἅγιος τοῦ θεοῦ is the designation of Jesus by the unclean spirit of Mk. 1²⁴, Lk. 4³⁴. It is not a Johannine phrase, but may be taken here to mean Him whom God consecrated as the Christ (cf. ὃν ὁ πατὴρ ἡγίασεν, 10³⁶). Cf. Acts 3¹⁴ 4²⁷· ³⁰. ἅγιος θεοῦ is used of a Nazirite at Judg. 13⁷ 16¹⁷; and cf. ἅγιος κυρίου of Aaron at Ps. 106¹⁶. See 17¹¹ πάτερ ἅγιε.

The commendation of Peter in response to his Confession, which is recorded by Mt. 16¹⁷, has no place in the other Gospels, and it does not appear here. But perhaps a reminiscence of it has already been recorded at 1⁴², where see note.

70. Peter had spoken for the rest of the apostles as well as for himself, and Jesus understands this to be so. " He answered them," ἀπεκρίθη αὐτοῖς (D om. αὐτοῖς). After αὐτοῖς, אBCDNLWⓗ have ὁ Ἰησοῦς, but om. ΓΔ.

οὐκ ἐγὼ ὑμᾶς κτλ., "Was it not I (ἐγώ being emphatic) who chose you, the Twelve?" (for οἱ δώδεκα, see on v. 67). Cf. Lk. 6¹³ ἐκλεξάμενος ἀπ᾽ αὐτῶν δώδεκα, and also Jn. 13¹⁸ and 15¹⁶ οὐχ ὑμεῖς με ἐξελέξασθε, ἀλλ᾽ ἐγὼ ἐξελεξάμην ὑμᾶς. The Twelve, the leaders of the new Israel, chosen to be the intimate companions of Jesus, were *deliberately* selected by Him from a larger number of disciples and followers. See on v. 64.

Peter had spoken for the Twelve, and Judas did not dissociate himself from the great Confession of v. 69. None of the others suspected that he was less trustworthy than they. But Jesus, although he does not reveal who the traitor is, warns them that they are not all of one mind. " Of you," *even* of you whom I chose, " one is a devil."

διάβολος is an " accuser " (the word is applied to Haman, the Jews' enemy, in Esth. 7⁴ 8¹), but is used by Jn. always for Satan or one inspired by Satan (8⁴⁴ 13², 1 Jn. 3⁸· ¹⁰). At 13² Jn. says that ὁ διάβολος put the idea of treachery into the heart of Judas, and at 13²⁷ that " Satan entered into him." One thus inspired is, himself, a " devil." Here the process of moral deterioration had only begun, but Jesus detected its

Ἰούδαν Σίμωνος Ἰσκαριώτου· οὗτος γὰρ ἔμελλεν παραδιδόναι αὐτόν, εἶς ἐκ τῶν δώδεκα.

beginnings. He observed that Judas was "giving place to the devil" (Eph. 4²⁷). See on 12⁴.

Some have found here a reminiscence of the rebuke to Peter, "Get thee behind me, Satan" (Mk. 8³³), which followed quickly upon his confession of faith, the idea being that the designation of Peter as Satan in the earlier record is here transferred to Judas, against whom Jn. had a special animus (see on 12⁶). But this lacks both evidence and probability.

71. ἔλεγεν δέ κτλ., "but He was speaking of . . .," a quite classical use of ἔλεγε. See on v. 65 above.

Ἰούδαν Σίμωνος Ἰσκαριώτου. ΝΓΔ support Ἰσχαριώτην of the rec. text, but א°BCLW give the genitive, "Iscariot" being the appellation of Simon, the father of Judas. For Ἰσκαριώτου, א*Θ and *fam.* 13 give the interpretative reading ἀπὸ Καρυώτου (see also 12⁴ 13². ²⁶ 14²² in D). Judas was the son of Simon, who was a man of Kerioth, קְרִיּוֹת אִישׁ, and thus both Judas (see 12⁴ 13²) and his father Simon (cf. 13²⁶) were called "Iscariot." Kerioth may be the place called Kerioth-hezron (in Judah) at Josh. 15²⁵, or may be Kerioth in Moab (Jer. 48²⁴); but in any case it was not in Galilee, so that Judas was the only one of the Twelve who was not a Galilæan. This explanation of the surname "Iscariot" is suggested in Jn. only, there being no hint of it in the Synoptists.[1]

ἔμελλεν (אBCLNWΘ) is to be preferred to the rec. ἤμελλεν.

οὗτος γὰρ ἔμελλεν παραδιδόναι αὐτόν. Cf. 12⁴ ὁ μέλλων αὐτὸν παραδιδόναι. μέλλειν may express simple futurity only (4⁴⁷), or it may connote intention (6⁶ 14²²); but it may also carry with it the idea of predestined inevitableness, the thought of which is often present to Jn. (see on 2⁴ 3¹⁴). It would be quite in Jn.'s manner to describe Judas as he who *was destined* to deliver Jesus up to His enemies. Cf. Mt. 17²² μέλλει ὁ υἱὸς τοῦ ἀνθρώπου παραδίδοσθαι, where μέλλει certainly connotes *inevitableness*. For other instances of μέλλειν in Jn., cf. 7³⁵. ³⁹ 11⁵¹ 12³³ 18³², the exact shade of meaning being not always certain.

εἶς ἐκ τῶν δώδεκα. After εἶς, אC²ΓΔNWΘ ins. ὤν, but om. BC*DL. The Synoptists apply the phrase "one of the Twelve" to Judas only, and to him only in connexion with the Betrayal. But Jn. applies it also to Thomas (20²⁴), the description always indicating surprise that one so favoured

[1] See Lightfoot, *Biblical Essays*, p. 143 ; Chase, *Syro-Latin Text of the Gospels*, p. 102 ; and the art. "Judas Iscariot" in *D.C.G.*

V. 1. Μετὰ ταῦτα ἦν ἑορτὴ τῶν Ἰουδαίων, καὶ ἀνέβη ὁ Ἰησοῦς εἰς Ἱεροσόλυμα.

as to be of the chosen companions of Jesus should be either incredulous or unfaithful (see on v. 67 above). It has been pointed out on 1⁴⁰ that Jn. prefers the form εἰς ἐκ to εἰς only when followed by a gen. plur., whereas the Synoptists generally omit ἐκ. Westcott suggests that ἐκ in the present passage marks " the unity of the body to which the unfaithful member belonged." But this is too subtle an inference from what is only a habit of style; cf. εἰς τῶν μαθητῶν αὐτοῦ (Jn. 12⁴).

A. Wright (*Synopsis*, p. 31) suggests that ὁ εἰς τῶν δώδεκα, applied to Judas (Mk. 14¹⁰), means "the chief of the Twelve," and compares τῇ μιᾷ τῶν σαββάτων (Mk. 16²). It is difficult to believe that ὁ εἰς could be written for ὁ πρῶτος ; or that an evangelist writing many years after the event, when the name of Judas had been held up to opprobrium for a generation, should call him "the chief of the Twelve," without adding any qualifying words. See, for the precedence of Judas, on 13²³.

PART II. (V. VII.–XII.)

Jesus goes up to Jerusalem for the Passover (V. 1)

V. 1. The conclusion of Part I.[1] tells of the continued faithfulness of the Twelve (6⁶⁷· ⁶⁸) ; and it can hardly be doubted that they went up to Jerusalem for the Passover as well as Jesus on this occasion. Hence, behind the story of the cure of the impotent man (5²⁻⁹) there may have been the original testimony of some who were present. And inasmuch as in the Fourth Gospel μετὰ ταῦτα is the phrase which seems to mark the beginning of a new set of reminiscences dictated by John the son of Zebedee to the future evangelist,[2] it is quite possible that the witness of John is behind cc. 5 and 7¹⁵⁻²⁴, allowing for evangelical commentary and expansion in 5²⁰⁻³⁰.³

ἑορτὴ τῶν Ἰουδαίων, *i.e.* the Passover, which has already been mentioned in 6⁴ as near at hand. This was probably the Passover of the year 28.⁴

אCLΔ read ἡ ἑορτή, but the article is rightly omitted by ABDNW⊙. Its insertion is readily explained by the

---

[1] For the position of c. 5 in the text, cf. Introd., pp. xvii, xxx.
[2] Introd., p. cviii.   [3] Introd., p. cxvi.   [4] See Introd., p. ciii.

2. Ἔστιν δὲ ἐν τοῖς Ἱεροσολύμοις ἐπὶ τῇ προβατικῇ κολυμβήθρα,

preceding ἦν. If ἡ ἑορτή were the true reading, the reference ought to be to the Feast of Tabernacles, which was pre-eminently *the* feast of the Jews. One minor uncial (Λ) for τῶν Ἰουδαίων reads τῶν ἀζύμων, rightly identifying the feast as that of " unleavened bread," *i.e.* the Passover.

For the expression " a feast of the Jews," see on 2¹³.

καὶ ἀνέβη ὁ Ἰησοῦς εἰς Ἱεροσόλυμα. The Passover was a feast of obligation, and so Jesus went up (ἀνέβη, the regular word for going up to the metropolis; cf. 2¹³); but, as it seems, He went up privately and unaccompanied by His disciples. There had been danger of popular enthusiasm (6¹⁵), which, if exhibited at Jerusalem, would have caused trouble. So it appears that He went up without making it known who He was; even the man whom He healed did not know His name (v. 13). His disciples, *i.e.* the Twelve, may have gone up to the feast, as would become pious men, but they do not seem to have been in attendance upon Jesus.

ὁ Ἰησοῦς. So ℵCΔΘW, but ABDLΓ om. ὁ. See on 1²⁹. For the form Ἱεροσόλυμα, see on 1¹⁹.

Healing of the impotent man at the Pool of Bethesda
(*vv.* 2–9)

2. ἔστιν δὲ ἐν τοῖς Ἱεροσολύμοις. The present tense (instead of ἦν, as at 4⁶) has been taken, *e.g.* by Bengel,[1] as proof that the Fourth Gospel was written before the destruction of Jerusalem; but this would be a precarious inference, even if it were not ruled out on other grounds. An old man looking back on the city as he knew it, might naturally say " is," especially if he had in mind a pool or spring. The Sinai Syriac changes " is " to " was," and so does Nonnus.

κολυμβήθρα (from κολυμβάω, *I dive*) is a pool deep enough to swim in; it occurs again in N.T. only at 9⁷ of the Pool of Siloam, but is a LXX word.

The text of this verse is uncertain. Βηθεσδά (which may mean " house of mercy ") is the rec. reading, following " Syrian " authorities (*e.g.* ACΔΘ); Βηθσαιδά is read by BW and also by Tertullian, an unusual and strong combination, but this spelling may be due to some confusion with Bethsaida of Galilee; Βηθζαθά has the support of ℵLD, and is

---

[1] Cf. Torrey, *Harvard Theol. Review*, Oct. 1923, p. 334, who presses the force of ἔστιν as representfng an Aramaic original, and holds that the Gospel must have been composed before Jerusalem had been destroyed.

ἡ ἐπιλεγομένη Ἑβραϊστὶ Βηθζαθά, πέντε στοὰς ἔχουσα. 3. ἐν
probably original. Bethzatha was the name of part of the
city, north of the Temple.

ἐπὶ τῇ προβατικῇ is the best attested reading (BCΔNW),
and it would mean that the pool was " by the sheep gate "
or " by the sheep market," the adj. προβατικῇ requiring a
substantive to be supplied. In Neh. 3¹ 12³⁹ mention is made
of the building of ἡ πύλη ἡ προβατική, which is believed to
have been north-east of the Temple, and close to the present
St. Stephen's Gate, by which flocks from the country enter
Jerusalem.

ℵᶜADLΘ have the aberrant reading ἐν τῇ προβατικῇ which
some Latin vss. perversely render *in inferiorem partem*. The
Western reading προβατικὴ κολυμβήθρα, " a sheep pool," is
supported by ℵ* 61, Eusebius, and others.

It appears, then, that ἐπὶ τῇ προβατικῇ κολυμβήθρα must
be adopted. But it has been suggested [1] that behind προβατική
lies the Aramaic פְּרוֹבַטְיָא, which means *a bath*; and then the
original text would have been, "There is a pool at the Bath,
which is called in Hebrew Bethzatha (House of the Olive ?)."

The situation of this pool is as uncertain as its exact name.
There are twin pools north of the Temple area, near the fortress
of Antonia, which Schick identified with the κολυμβήθρα of the
text, but it is doubtful if these existed before the destruction of
the Temple. Others have identified the "Pool of Bethzatha"
with the "Pool of Siloam" (9⁷) ; but they seem to be specially
distinguished by the evangelist. Many writers are inclined
to find the Pool of Bethzatha in the Virgin's Well, anciently
called Gihon, *i.e.* "the Gusher," which is periodically subject
to a bubbling of its waters caused by a natural spring. This is
south of the Temple, in the Valley of Kidron, and we believe
it to be the most probable site of " Bethzatha."

ἡ ἐπιλεγομένη Ἑβραϊστὶ Βηθζαθά. Ἑβραϊστί occurs only in
Jn. 5² 19¹³· ¹⁷· ²⁰ 20¹⁶ and Rev. 9¹¹ 16¹⁶; it signifies not the
classical Hebrew of the O.T., but the Aramaic in common
use. See on 1³⁸ for instances of Jn.'s habit of giving
the Hebrew name of a person or place, along with a Greek
equivalent. Here and at 19¹³· ¹⁷ he describes the place first
in Greek, and then adds its Aramaic designation: he is not
interpreting the Aramaic name (see on 4²⁵).

For ἡ ἐπιλεγομένη, ℵ*D *fam.* 1 have τὸ λεγόμενον.

πέντε στοὰς ἔχουσα. These would have been cloisters or
arched spaces round the pool similar to those which are

---

[1] See G. A. Smith, *Jerusalem*, ii. 566, and Lightfoot, *Biblical Essays*,
p. 170 ; cf. also *D.C.G., s.v.* " Bethesda."

ταύταις κατέκειτο πλῆθος τῶν ἀσθενούντων, τυφλῶν, χωλῶν, ξηρῶν.

found in India near tanks. Schick claimed that such were to be seen at the twin pools which he discovered; but this has not been generally admitted.[1] Those who interpret the narrative symbolically, find the Five Books of Moses in the "five porches." We have already considered this method of interpreting Jn.[2] While symbolic meanings may easily be read into the narrative once written, there is no probability that it was originally constructed in so artificial a fashion.

3. The picture of the sick people lying under the covered arcades (it would have been too cold at the Passover season to lie out in the open air) waiting for the bubbling up of the intermittent spring, which was supposed to have healing properties, is most natural and vivid.

ἐν ταύταις, *sc.* in the στοαί or arches.

κατέκειτο. The verb does not appear again in Jn. The rec. text inserts πολύ after πλῆθος, but om. אBCDLW.

τυφλῶν, χωλῶν, ξηρῶν, "blind, halt, withered." ξηροί were those who had atrophied limbs (cf. Mt. 12[10], Lk. 6[8]). The Western text (D *a b*) adds παραλυτικῶν, but this is only a gloss explanatory of ξηρῶν: om. אA*BC*LWΘ.

After ξηρῶν, παραλυτικῶν, the rec. adds ἐκδεχομένων τὴν τοῦ ὕδατος κίνησιν. This, again, is a Western (and Syrian) amplification; it is omitted by אA*BC*L, although supported by DWΓΔΘ syrr. It was suggested by the mention in v. 7 of the disturbance of the healing waters.

4. Verse 4, like the words ἐκδεχομένων . . . κίνησιν, is no part of the original text of Jn., but is a later gloss. The best attested text of the gloss is thus given by Hort: ἄγγελος δὲ (*v.* γὰρ) κυρίου (κατὰ καιρὸν) κατέβαινεν (*v.* ἐλούετο) ἐν τῇ κολυμβήθρᾳ καὶ ἐταράσσετο (*v.* ἐτάρασσε) τὸ ὕδωρ· ὁ οὖν πρῶτος ἐμβὰς [μετὰ τὴν ταραχὴν τοῦ ὕδατος] ὑγιὴς ἐγίνετο οἵῳ (*v.* ᾧ) δήποτ᾿ οὖν (*v.* δήποτε) κατείχετο νοσήματι.

The verse is wholly omitted by אBC*DW 33, the Old Syriac, the early Coptic versions (including Q), and the true text of the Latin Vulgate. In the Latin MSS. in which it is found, it appears in three distinct forms, the diversity of which provides an additional argument against its genuineness. The earliest patristic authority for it is Tertullian (*de bapt.* 5), the earliest Greek writer who shows knowledge of it being Chrysostom; his comment on the passage is: "An angel came down and troubled the water, and endued it with healing power, that the Jews might learn that much more could the Lord of

---

[1] Cf. Sanday, *Sacred Sites of the Gospels*, p. 55.
[2] Introd., p. lxxxvii.

5 ἦν δέ τις ἄνθρωπος ἐκεῖ τριάκοντα καὶ ὀκτὼ ἔτη ἔχων ἐν τῇ
ἀσθενείᾳ αὐτοῦ· 6. τοῦτον ἰδὼν ὁ Ἰησοῦς κατακείμενον, καὶ γνοὺς ὅτι

angels heal the diseases of the soul." It is a marginal gloss
which crept into some Western and Syrian texts, the chief
uncials which contain it being ΑΛΓΔΘ.

Linguistic evidence also marks the verse as not original.
Thus the words ἐκδέχομαι, κίνησις (here only in N.T.), κατὰ
καιρόν (cf. Rom. 5⁶, Num. 9¹³), ἐμβαίνω (of going into the
water; cf. 6¹⁷), ταραχή (here only in the N.T.), κατέχομαι, and
νόσημα (here only in N.T.) are non-Johannine.

The healing virtues of the intermittent spring were explained by the Jewish doctrine of the ministry of angels, and
the explanation first found a place in the margin and, later,
in the text. Cf. Rev. 16⁵ for " the angel of the waters," i.e. the
angel who was believed to preside over the mysterious powers
of water.

5. The constr. τριάκοντα καὶ ὀκτὼ ἔτη ἔχων appears again
in v. 6 πολὺν χρόνον ἔχει. Cf. also 8⁵⁷ 9²¹ 11¹⁷ for an acc. of
the length of time, governed by ἔχειν.

καί before ὀκτώ is om. by ΒΓΔΘ, but ins. אACDLW; αὐτοῦ
after ἀσθενείᾳ is om. by ΑΓΔ, but ins. אBC*DLΘW.

The man had been infirm for thirty-eight years; it is not
said that he had been waiting all that time by the pool.
That his paralysis had lasted thirty-eight years is mentioned
to show that it was no temporary ailment from which he was
suffering, just as it is told of the woman in Lk. 13¹¹ that she
had been infirm eighteen years, or of the lame man whom
Peter cured that " he was more than forty years old " (Acts 4²²).
There is no more reason for finding an esoteric significance
in the number 38 than in the numbers 18 or 40. Or, again,
in Acts 9³³, Æneas, whom Peter cured of paralysis, is described
as ἐξ ἐτῶν ὀκτὼ κατακείμενον ἐπὶ κραβάττου. These eight years
are not supposed to be significant as regards their number;
and there is no more reason for supposing the thirty-eight
years of the text to symbolise anything.

Those who seek for hidden meanings in the Johannine
numbers point here to the thirty-eight years of wandering
mentioned in Deut. 2¹⁴. But if Jn. had wished to indicate
that the years of the paralytic's infirmity were like the years of
Israel in the wilderness, it would have been more natural for
him to have said forty, not thirty-eight; for it was forty years
before the Promised Land was reached. Cf. 2²⁰, 21¹¹; and see
Introd., p. lxxxvii.

6. Jesus came, unknown by sight to the sick who were
assembled at the pool. καὶ γνοὺς ὅτι πολὺν ἤδη χρόνον ἔχει,

πολὺν ἤδη χρόνον ἔχει, λέγει αὐτῷ Θέλεις ὑγιὴς γενέσθαι; 7. ἀπεκρίθη

" and when He knew that the man had been infirm for a long time," He addressed him.   It is neither stated nor implied that this knowledge of the man's sad condition was supernatural. It may have been the common talk of the crowd at the Pool. See on 2²⁴ for the insight of Jesus into the *character* of men, and cf. 4¹⁸.

Θέλεις ὑγιὴς γενέσθαι; *sc.*, as we would say, " Would you like to be well ? "   There is no need to press the force of θέλεις, as if Jesus meant that the man's own conscious effort of will must co-operate in the work of healing.   That may be true in such cases, but θέλεις here only conveys the simple question, " Would you *like* to be healed ? "

We do not know why Jesus chose this man out from the crowd of sufferers at the pool.   Perhaps attention was specially directed to his pathetic case by the onlookers.   There is no suggestion that the man had any *faith*, nor did he display gratitude for his healing.   He must have known that to point out Jesus as the agent of his cure (v. 15) would bring his bene-factor into danger.

Abbott (*Diat.* x. iii. 268 f.) suggests that we must take the act of Jesus in connexion with His own comment.   He did not select the object of His pity by arbitrary caprice, but " the Son can do nothing Himself, except what He sees the Father doing " (see on v. 19 below).   He " saw " this particular act of healing performed by the Father in heaven, and therefore appointed to be performed by the Son on earth.   But not only is such an explanation too subtle; it really explains nothing, for why should this particular sick man have been selected by the Father any more than by the Son ?

The healing is perhaps, but not certainly, regarded by Jn. as supernatural (see 7²¹), although he does not call it a " sign." But it is not represented as having any relation to the *faith* of the man that was cured.   In this it is like the Synoptic story of the healing of a paralytic (Mk. 2, Mt. 9, Lk. 5), where it is the faith of those who brought the man to Jesus rather than the faith of the man himself that is commended.   It is unlike the Synoptic story, in that the cure in the Johannine narrative does not seem to have impressed the onlookers at all.   There is nothing here corresponding to " they were all amazed and glorified God, saying, We never saw it on this fashion " (Mk. 2¹²).   In Jn.'s story, everything turns on the fact that it was on the Sabbath that the man was cured, and it was this, and not the wonder of the healing, that attracted attention.   See Introd., p. clxxviii.

αὐτῷ ὁ ἀσθενῶν Κύριε, ἄνθρωπον οὐκ ἔχω, ἵνα ὅταν ταραχθῇ τὸ ὕδωρ βάλῃ με εἰς τὴν κολυμβήθραν· ἐν ᾧ δὲ ἔρχομαι ἐγώ, ἄλλος πρὸ ἐμοῦ καταβαίνει. 8. λέγει αὐτῷ ὁ Ἰησοῦς Ἔγειρε ἆρον τὸν κράβαττόν

7. κύριε, ἄνθρωπον οὐκ ἔχω κτλ. The sick man explains that it is not his will that is deficient, but that he is unable, because of his infirmity, to get quickly enough down to the water when it becomes "troubled," because he has no one to assist him. (The paralytic of Mk. 2³ was helped by four friends to get access to Jesus.)

ὅταν ταραχθῇ τὸ ὕδωρ κτλ. Apparently the popular belief was that, when the water began to bubble at a particular spot, the person who first bathed at that point received relief, but that the spring did not benefit more than one. He who came second had to wait for cure until another overflow.

ἵνα . . . βάλῃ με εἰς τὴν κολυμβήθραν. βάλλειν, "to cast," implies rapidity of movement, which would be impossible for an invalid without assistance.

βάλῃ. So אABC²DLWΘ: the rec. has βάλλῃ.

ἐν ᾧ δὲ ἔρχομαι ἐγώ κτλ. "But while I (ἐγώ being emphatic) am coming, another steps down before me."

8. ἔγειρε ἆρον κτλ. Jesus ignores the belief of the sick man about the healing waters of the pool, to which He makes no reference. Nor does He, as in the case of the Synoptic paralytic, give him a word of spiritual consolation (Mk. 2⁵) before He heals him. Nothing is said to the man, except the sharp command, ἔγειρε ἆρον τὸν κράβαττόν σου καὶ περιπάτει, "Get up, take your pallet and walk." The words are almost, identical with those of Mk. 2¹¹, but there the evangelistic comment is that they were effectively spoken in order to show the wondering bystanders that He who spoke them had really the spiritual authority to forgive sins. Here is nothing similar. As has been said (v. 6), there is no clear proof that Jn. regarded the healing of the man at Bethesda as miraculous, nor need we do so. The patient obeyed a sudden, authoritative order to stand up and walk, and when he tried he found that he could do it. That may be the whole of the matter. However, no disciple is expressly said to have been present on the occasion; and the story, which may have come to the evangelist at second or third hand, is told in barest outline.

ἔγειρε (אABCDWΘ) is to be preferred to the rec. ἔγειραι.

κράβαττος (*grabatus*), a pallet or mattress, such as was used by the poor, is said to be a late word of Macedonian origin, and is not approved by Phrynichus. It occurs in the N.T. again only in Mk. 2²⁻¹² 6⁵⁵, Acts 5¹⁵ 9³³, and always stands for the bed of a sick person.

σου καὶ περιπάτει. 9. καὶ εὐθέως ἐγένετο ὑγιὴς ὁ ἄνθρωπος, καὶ ἦρεν τὸν κράβαττον αὐτοῦ καὶ περιεπάτει.

*Ην δὲ σάββατον ἐν ἐκείνῃ τῇ ἡμέρᾳ. 10. ἔλεγον οὖν οἱ Ἰουδαῖοι τῷ τεθεραπευμένῳ Σάββατόν ἐστιν, καὶ οὐκ ἔξεστίν σοι ἆραι τὸν

περιπάτει. So in Lk. 5²³; but at Mk. 2¹¹, Mt. 9⁶, we have ὕπαγε εἰς τὸν οἶκόν σου.

9. καὶ εὐθέως ἐγένετο ὑγιὴς ὁ ἄνθρωπος, καὶ ἦρεν τὸν κράβαττον αὐτοῦ καὶ περιεπάτει. In the parallel, Mk. 2¹², we have ἠγέρθη καὶ εὐθὺς ἄρας τὸν κράβαττον ἐξῆλθεν ἔμπροσθεν πάντων. In both cases εὐθέως or εὐθύς carries the sense of immediate consecutiveness (Lk. 5²⁵ has παραχρῆμα). The word is not common in Jn. (6²¹ 13³⁰·³² 18²⁷ 19³⁴), and he always uses it thus, whereas it is often used in Mk. only as a conjunctive (see on 1²²).

That the cure was not merely for the moment is shown by the man's walking away, as is also indicated in the Synoptic story.

The language of Jn. 5⁸·⁹ closely resembles that of Mk. 2¹¹·¹², although the stories are quite distinct. Jn. may have availed himself of the words of the earlier evangelist to describe a somewhat similar scene at which he was not present, and of which he could not give the exact report of an eye-witness. See Introd., p. xcvii.

ἦν δὲ σάββατον ἐν ἐκείνῃ τῇ ἡμέρᾳ. This is the point of the story for Jn., as also at 9¹⁴ where Jesus healed the blind man. The healing on the Sabbath was the beginning of His controversies at Jerusalem; this was the first occasion on which He had openly violated the law at the metropolis; but cf. Mk. 2²³–3⁶ for His earlier claim in Galilee to be Lord of the Sabbath, which had already attracted the attention of the Pharisees.

The Jews object to Sabbath healings, and Jesus replies by the analogy of God's working (vv. 10–19)

10. For οἱ Ἰουδαῖοι, see on 1¹⁹. This is the designation throughout the Gospel of the leading opponents of Jesus, *i.e.* the strict Pharisees, as distinct from the simple folk whether in town or country (ὄχλος). Cf. vv. 13, 15, 16.

τῷ τεθεραπευμένῳ. θεραπεύειν is found only here in Jn., while it is common in the Synoptists. Cf. v. 13 below.

σάββατόν ἐστιν, καὶ οὐκ ἔξεστίν σοι ἆραι τὸν κράβαττον. The bearing of burdens on the Sabbath was forbidden (Neh. 13¹⁹, Jer. 17²¹). The Rabbinical law was, " If any one carries anything from a public place to a private house on the Sabbath

κράβαττον. 11. ὃς δὲ ἀπεκρίθη αὐτοῖς Ὁ ποιήσας με ὑγιῆ, ἐκεῖνός μοι εἶπεν Ἆρον τὸν κράβαττόν σου καὶ περιπάτει. 12. ἠρώτησαν αὐτόν Τίς ἐστιν ὁ ἄνθρωπος ὁ εἰπών σοι Ἆρον καὶ περιπάτει; 13. ὁ δὲ ἰαθεὶς οὐκ ᾔδει τίς ἐστιν· ὁ γὰρ Ἰησοῦς ἐξένευσεν ὄχλου ὄντος ἐν

. . . intentionally, he is punished by cutting off (*i.e.* death) and stoning " (*Shabb.* 6*a*, quoted by Lightfoot, *Hor. Hebr.*).

After κράβαττον, אC*DLNW℗ add σου (as at vv. 8, 9), but om. ABC³ΓΔ.

11. The rec. text omits ὃς δέ before ἀπεκρίθη with D; but AB ins. the words, אC*LWN℗ giving ὁ δέ.

For ἀπεκρίθη, א*W have ἀπεκρίνατο; but see on v. 17.

ὁ ποιήσας με ὑγιῆ, ἐκεῖνός μοι εἶπεν κτλ. For this emphatic use of ἐκεῖνος in Jn., see on 1⁸. The man's excuse was reasonable. He who had cured him, by giving him power to get up and walk, had bidden him carry away his bed; surely it was pardonable to obey His command? The excuse was accepted, and the man was not blamed by the Jews : they go on to ask who it was that dared to give such an order.

12. After ἠρώτησαν, the rec., with ACLWΓΔ℗, ins. οὖν; om. אBD.

τίς ἐστιν ὁ ἄνθρωπος ὁ εἰπών σοι, " Who is the fellow that said this to you ? " ἄνθρωπος is used contemptuously. The Jews do not take any notice of the fact that the man said he had been healed; they complain only of the breach of the Sabbath law involved, not in the *healing* but in the order to carry the bed. As Grotius says : " Quaerunt non quod mirentur, sed quod calumnietur." But from 7²³ it is apparent that the real gravamen of the charge made in this case by the Jews was that a work of healing had been done on the Sabbath, although they prefer here to put forward the technical point about carrying the bed home.

See on 9¹⁶, where the Sabbath was broken in a different way.

The rec. text has τὸν κράβαττόν σου after ἆρον, but om. אBC*L. The words have come in from v. 11.

13. The man that had been healed did not know who his benefactor was. Jesus was not yet a familiar figure to all and sundry at Jerusalem. He had gone up to the Passover, privately, unaccompanied by His band of disciples (see on v. 2) which would have marked Him out as a Rabbi. This must also have made it easier for Him to slip away unnoticed in the crowd.

For ἰαθείς, see on 4⁴⁷. D has ἀσθενῶν.

ἐξένευσεν ὄχλου ὄντος ἐν τῷ τόπῳ, " He (had) turned aside (cf. 4⁴⁴ for this use of the aor.), a crowd being in the place."

τῷ τόπῳ. 14. Μετὰ ταῦτα εὑρίσκει αὐτὸν ὁ Ἰησοῦς ἐν τῷ ἱερῷ καὶ εἶπεν αὐτῷ Ἴδε ὑγιὴς γέγονας· μηκέτι ἁμάρτανε, ἵνα μὴ χεῖρόν σοί τι γένηται. 15. ἀπῆλθεν ὁ ἄνθρωπος καὶ εἶπεν τοῖς Ἰουδαίοις ὅτι

ἐκνεύειν (אD* have the simple ἔνευσεν) does not appear again in the N.T., but it is found in the LXX (Judg. 18²⁶, 2 Kings 2²⁴ 23¹⁶, 3 Macc. 3²²), being a variant for ἐκκλίνειν at Judg. 4¹⁸. ἐξένευσεν here expresses that Jesus had quietly moved away; cf. 8⁵⁹ 10³⁹ 12³⁶.

For τόπῳ, א* has the variant μέσῳ.

14. μετὰ ταῦτα, *i.e.* subsequently, not *immediately* afterwards. See Introd., p. cviii.

εὑρίσκει αὐτὸν ὁ Ἰησοῦς ἐν τῷ ἱερῷ. Apparently, Jesus sought out the man, as He sought for the blind man whom He cured on a later occasion (9³⁵; cf. 1⁴³). It has been conjectured that the man had gone to the Temple to offer thanks for his recovery, but there is no evidence for this. The ἱερόν, or sacred precinct, was a common place of resort; and Jesus, finding him there, gave him a word of grave counsel.

ἴδε (a favourite word with Jn.; see on 1²⁹) ὑγιὴς γέγονας· μηκέτι ἁμάρτανε κτλ. For μηκέτι ἁμάρτανε, see [8¹¹]. We cannot tell what the man's sin had been, but quite possibly it had been the immediate occasion of his loss of health; if so, it had been terribly punished by an infirmity continuing for thirty-eight years. There was a prevalent belief that sickness was always due to sin (cf. Ps. 38⁵ 107¹⁷, 1 Cor. 11³⁰), and a Talmudic saying asserts that "the sick ariseth not from his sickness until his sins be forgiven." But the moral of the Book of Job is that sickness is *not* always to be regarded as punishment for sin, and this seems to have been suggested by Jesus, when the case of the man born blind was put to Him (see on 9³). In the absence of knowledge as to the antecedents of the impotent man of the text, "Sin no more, lest a worse thing befall thee" is not susceptible of complete explanation.

Cyprian (*Test.* iii. 27) quotes "jam noli peccare, ne quid tibi deterius fiat," to illustrate the danger of sin after baptism, by which a man has been "made whole"—a characteristic comment.

J. H. Moulton [1] has called attention to the curious fact that the Greek words here fall naturally into anapæsts:

ὑγιὴς γέγονας· μηκέθ᾽ ἁμάρτανε,
ἵνα μὴ χεῖρόν σοί τι γένηται

—a tolerable, if not perfect, couplet. This is, of course, a mere accident. Cf. 4³⁵.

[1] *Cambridge Biblical Essays* (ed. H. B. Swete), p. 483.

Ἰησοῦς ἐστιν ὁ ποιήσας αὐτὸν ὑγιῆ. 16. καὶ διὰ τοῦτο ἐδίωκον οἱ Ἰουδαῖοι τὸν Ἰησοῦν, ὅτι ταῦτα ἐποίει ἐν σαββάτῳ. 17. ὁ δὲ

15. καὶ εἶπεν τοῖς Ἰουδαίοις κτλ. εἶπεν is read by אCL, but ἀνήγγειλεν by ΑΒΓΝΘ and ἀπήγγειλεν (which means the same thing, "reported"; see on 16²⁵) by D.

The man went off and reported to the Jews who it was that had healed him, as soon as he had identified Him. But there is no reason to suppose that this was due to ingratitude, or that he meant to betray his benefactor. He had good reason to fear that severe punishment would follow his technical breach of the Sabbath, despite his excuses (v. 11), and he may have desired to propitiate the ecclesiastical authorities, without meaning that any harm should come to Jesus. They were entitled to know all that he could tell them about a breach of the Sabbath. His action may have been like that of the Jews who reported the raising of Lazarus to the Pharisees, without any malevolent intention (11⁴⁶). Yet, in any event, his conduct stands in contrast with that of the blind man who was healed later on (9³³⁻³⁸).

16. καὶ διὰ τοῦτο ἐδίωκον κτλ., " And for this cause the Jews began to persecute Jesus, because, etc." The force of the imperfects, ἐδίωκον, ἐποίει, ἐζήτουν (v. 18), must not be overlooked. This was the first open declaration of hostility to Jesus by the Pharisees of Jerusalem, and its immediate cause was His first open violation of the Sabbatical law. ἐδίωκον, "they *began to persecute* Him "; ὅτι ταῦτα ἐποίει ἐν σαββάτῳ, " because He *began to do* these things on the Sabbath." Cf. Mk. 3⁶, where a similar cause is assigned for the first exhibition of enmity to Him in Galilee.

διὰ τοῦτο, " for this cause," referring to what follows (not, as more commonly, to what precedes, *e.g.* 6⁶⁵), is a favourite opening phrase with Jn. Cf. v. 18 8⁴⁷ 10¹⁷ 12¹⁸. ³⁹, 1 Jn. 3¹, and Isa. 24⁶ διὰ τοῦτο ἀρὰ ἔδεται τὴν γῆν, ὅτι ἡμάρτοσαν οἱ κατοικοῦντες αὐτήν.

After τὸν Ἰησοῦν the rec. with ΑΓΔΘ inserts καὶ ἐζήτουν αὐτὸν ἀποκτεῖναι (from v. 18), but om. here אBCDLW.

17. ἀπεκρίνατο (1 aor. mid.) is found in Jn. only here and at v. 19; ἀπεκρίθη occurring more than 50 times. Abbott[1] points out that while ἀπεκρίθη is the colourless " answered," ἀπεκρίνατο carries the sense of " made public and formal answer " to a charge or accusation that has been made: " He made His defence," in reply to the prosecution or persecution of the Jews (ἐδίωκον, v. 16). Cf. οὐδὲν ἀπεκρίνατο (Mk. 14⁶¹, Mt. 27¹², Lk. 23⁹). See also 12²³ 13³⁸ 18³⁴.

[1] *Diat.* 2537; see, for illustrations from the papyri, Moulton-Milligan, *s.v.* ἀποκρίνομαι.

ἀπεκρίνατο αὐτοῖς Ὁ Πατήρ μου ἕως ἄρτι ἐργάζεται, κἀγὼ ἐργάζομαι.

The defence of His technical breach of the Sabbath which Jn. here ascribes to Jesus is different from most of the sayings on the subject of which the Synoptists tell. Thus in Mk. 3⁴, Lk. 6⁹, Jesus confounds His critics by the simple question, "Is it lawful on the Sabbath to do good?" when they objected to His cure of the man with the withered hand. In Mt. 12¹¹, Lk. 13¹⁵, He puts the case that no one will scruple to pull a sheep out of a pit or to water his cattle on the Sabbath (cf. 7²³, where appeal is made to a similar principle). In Mk. 2²⁵, Lk. 6³, Mt. 12³, He appeals to O.T. precedent to show that necessity may override strict law, and in Mt. 12⁸ He appeals to the saying that God prefers mercy to sacrifice (Hos. 6⁶). But in Mk. 2²⁸, Mt. 12⁸, Lk. 6⁵, He lays down the principle that "the Son of Man is Lord of the Sabbath"[1] This principle contains in germ the argument which Jn. puts forward here, in a different form.

ὁ πατήρ μου ἕως ἄρτι ἐργάζεται, κἀγὼ ἐργάζομαι. Here is claimed by Jesus the same freedom with regard to the Sabbath that belongs to God Himself. God instituted the Sabbath for man, but the law of its observance does not bind Him who gave the law.

Philo points out that God, the Author of nature, does not observe the Sabbath: "Having ceased from the creation of mortal creatures on the seventh day, He begins with other more divine beings (διατυπώσεων). For God never ceases making (παύεται γὰρ οὐδέποτε ποιῶν ὁ θεός), but as it is the property of fire to burn and of snow to chill, so it is the property of God to *make* (οὕτως καὶ θεοῦ τὸ ποιεῖν)" (*Leg. All*. i. 2, 3). And, again, Ποιῶν ὁ θεὸς οὐ παύεται (*l.c.* i. 7).[2]

Justin Martyr quotes a saying from the old man to whom he owed his conversion, to the effect that the heavenly bodies do not keep the Sabbath, ὁρᾶτε ὅτι τὰ στοιχεῖα οὐκ ἀργεῖ οὐδὲ σαββατίζει (*Tryph*. 23); and the same idea is expressed in the *Odes of Solomon*: "He rested from His works; and created things run in their courses and do their works, and they know not how to stand or be idle" (Ode xvi. 13).

Such thoughts were prevalent in Jewish circles, and it is to the idea that God Himself does not share the Sabbath rest of man, that appeal is made in this saying which Jn. ascribes to Jesus. Thus Origen rightly says that Jesus shows in Jn. 5¹⁷ that God does not rest on earthly Sabbaths from His providential ordering of the world, the true Sabbath of God being

---

[1] Cf. Introd., p. cxxv.
[2] Cf. also Clem. Alex. *Strom.* vi. 16, p. 813 P.

18. διὰ ⸀τοῦτο οὖν μᾶλλον ἐζήτουν αὐτὸν οἱ Ἰουδαῖοι ἀποκτεῖναι, ὅτι
οὐ μόνον ἔλυεν τὸ σάββατον, ἀλλὰ καὶ Πατέρα ἴδιον ἔλεγεν τὸν Θεόν,
ἴσον ἑαυτὸν ποιῶν τῷ Θεῷ.

the future rest when He shall be all in all.[1] And the Syriac
commentator Isho'dad, who wrote in the ninth century, but
whose interpretations preserve much older material, in like
manner represents Christ as saying here: " Do I allow the
circuit of the sun . . . the flowing of the rivers . . . the birth
and growth of men together and the energies of all living
beings about everything ? These are things which are accomplished by means of angels, according to His will, and these
things are done in the feasts and on the Sabbaths and at every
hour." [2]

Thus the ancient interpretation of ὁ πατήρ μου ἕως ἄρτι
ἐργάζεται is clear. The words express the idea (obvious when
it is expressed) that God does not keep the Sabbath ἕως ἄρτι,
that is, hitherto (see 2[10] 16[24], 1 Jn. 2[9]). God's working has
not been intermitted since the Creation. He works, goes on
working uninterruptedly, until now. The rest of God is for
the future, as Origen points out.

κἀγὼ ἐργάζομαι, " And I also work," sc. in the same way.
That is, Jesus claims not only that He may call God ὁ πατήρ μου
(" my Father," in a unique sense; see on 2[16]), but that His
relation to the Sabbath law is not different from that of God
Himself. This is the Johannine form of the Synoptic saying,
"The Son of Man is Lord of the Sabbath," expressed in
mystical and uncompromising fashion.

18. This declaration provoked the Jews to indignation.
διὰ τοῦτο (see on v. 16) οὖν (om. אD, but ins. ΛBCL) μᾶλλον
ἐζήτουν αὐτὸν οἱ Ἰουδαῖοι ἀποκτεῖναι. The phrase " sought to kill
Him " is repeated 7[1. 19. 25] 8[37. 40].

οὐ μόνον ἔλυεν τὸ σάββατον. For λύειν in the sense of
" break," " set at naught," as in Mt. 5[19], cf. 7[23] 10[35], Moulton-
Milligan's Vocab. (p. 384) cites from papyri of the third century
B.C. ἐὰν δέ τις τούτων τι λύῃ, κατάρατος ἔστω, and also λύειν τὰ
πένθη, " to break the period of mourning," i.e. to go out of
mourning.

That Jesus was setting Sabbatical rules at naught was the
primary cause of the Jews' hostility to Him; but it was a much
graver offence that He claimed to have Divine prerogatives.
This they treated as blasphemy (cf. 8[59] 10[36], Mk. 2[7], Mt. 26[65]).

It need not be doubted that the breaches of the Sabbath
which Jesus countenanced provoked the first suspicions of His

---

[1] Origen, in Num. Hom. xxiii. 4 (Lommatzsch, x. 282).
[2] Horæ Semiticæ, No. v. p. 234 (ed. M. D. Gibson).

19. Ἀπεκρίνατο οὖν ὁ Ἰησοῦς καὶ ἔλεγεν αὐτοῖς Ἀμὴν ἀμὴν λέγω ὑμῖν, οὐ δύναται ὁ Υἱὸς ποιεῖν ἀφ᾽ ἑαυτοῦ οὐδέν, ἂν μή τι βλέπῃ τὸν Πατέρα ποιοῦντα· ἃ γὰρ ἂν ἐκεῖνος ποιῇ, ταῦτα καὶ ὁ Υἱὸς ὁμοίως

opponents at Jerusalem (as in Galilee, Mk. 3²), and that the incident of the healing of the impotent man on the Sabbath is historical. Jn. is here true to fact, but he is not interested so much in Jewish Sabbatical doctrines as in the Divine Personality of Jesus,[1] and so he dwells at great length on the doctrine of Jesus as the Son of God which is implied in His claim to be Lord of the Sabbath.

πάτερα ἴδιον ἔλεγεν, "He was calling God His own Father," in a special sense, as indeed the words ὁ πατήρ μου of v. 17 implied. Cf. Rom. 8³² ὁ ἴδιος υἱός.

ἴσον ἑαυτὸν ποιῶν τῷ θεῷ. This was the form in which His Jewish enemies defined the meaning of His words (cf. 10³³ 19⁷), and there is a sense in which their complaint might be justified. But the actual phrase ἴσος θεῷ is not part of the claim of Jesus for Himself (see on 14²⁸ ὁ πατὴρ μείζων μού ἐστι), and Paul's phrase is ἴσα θεῷ, which refers to the *attributes* rather than to the *person* of Christ (see Lightfoot on Phil. 2⁶). It is not taught anywhere by Jn. that Christ is ἴσος θεῷ, for that would seem to divide the Godhead (cf. θεὸς ἦν ὁ λόγος, 1¹).

19. For ἀπεκρίνατο, see on v. 17.

ἀμὴν ἀμὴν λέγω ὑμῖν: see on 1⁵¹.

For ὁ υἱός used absolutely, see on 3¹⁷.

οὐ δύναται ὁ υἱὸς ποιεῖν ἀφ᾽ ἑαυτοῦ οὐδέν. Cf. οὐ δύναμαι ἐγὼ ποιεῖν ἀπ᾽ ἐμαυτοῦ οὐδέν (v. 30), and see 7²⁸ 8²⁸ 14¹⁰. So Moses had said (Num. 16²⁸), and it is true of every man that "he can do nothing of himself," but only what God empowers him to do. Here, however, the thought is deeper. It is that the relation between the Father and the Son is so intimate, that even the Son of God can do "nothing of Himself." His works are the works of the Father (cf. v. 17) who sent Him (see on 3¹⁷). He has ἐξουσία (see on 10¹⁸), but it is always a delegated authority. It is a moral impossibility that He should do anything "of Himself," ἂν μή τι βλέπῃ τὸν πατέρα ποιοῦντα, "unless He be seeing the Father doing something." Thus the Incarnate Son is represented as continually seeing on earth what the Father is doing in heaven, and as Himself doing the same thing.[2] The action of the Father and the Son is, so to say, *coextensive*; cf. 14¹⁰.

ἃ γὰρ ἂν ἐκεῖνος ποιῇ κτλ., "for what He, the Father, does (see on 1⁸ for ἐκεῖνος in Jn.), the Son does likewise."

---

[1] Cf. Burkitt, *Gospel History and Transmission*, p. 239.
[2] See Abbott, *Diat.* 2516.

ποιεῖ. 20. ὁ γὰρ Πατὴρ φιλεῖ τὸν Υἱὸν καὶ πάντα δείκνυσιν αὐτῷ

This mystical doctrine that the Son cannot do anything except what He sees the Father doing has verbal affinity with the teaching of Philo. He speaks of the πρεσβύτατος υἱός, or πρωτόγονος, as one " who imitated the ways of the Father and, seeing His archetypal patterns, formed certain species " (μιμούμενος τὰς τοῦ πατρὸς ὁδούς, πρὸς παραδείγματα ἀρχέτυπα ἐκείνου βλέπων ἐμόρφου εἴδη, de confus. ling. 14).

Ignatius (*Magn.* 7) has the words ὥσπερ οὖν ὁ κύριος ἄνευ τοῦ πατρὸς οὐδὲν ἐποίησεν, ἡνωμένος ὤν (cf. Jn. 10³⁰), οὔτε δι' ἑαυτοῦ οὔτε διὰ τῶν ἀποστόλων, which appear to be a reminiscence of Johannine texts such as the present passage and 8²⁸.

Discourse on the relation of the Son to the Father
(*vv.* 20-29)

20. Vv. 20-29 form a section by themselves. They deal with the secrets of the Divine Life, and unfold in some degree the relation of the Son to the Father, thus providing an explanation of, or commentary on, the mystic words of v. 17, " My Father worketh hitherto, and I work," and of v. 19, "The Son can do nothing of Himself." As at other points in the Gospel (see on 3¹⁶), it is impracticable to distinguish precisely the evangelist's own commentary from the words which he ascribes to Jesus. The formula " Verily, verily, I say unto you," which precedes vv. 19, 24, 25, *always* introduces words of Jesus Himself, and this must be the intention here. And vv. 28, 29, seem also to be placed in His mouth. But the use of ὥσπερ γάρ at the beginning of v. 21 and again at v. 26 (ὥσπερ does not appear again in Jn.) suggests that vv. 21-23 and vv. 26, 27, may be comments of the evangelist on the sayings of Jesus introduced by ἀμὴν ἀμήν in vv. 19, 24, 25. This is like Jn.'s use of γάρ elsewhere (see on 3¹⁶).[1] It will be observed that the third person is employed throughout in vv. 21-23, 26, 27. We do not return to the first person until v. 30, where the opening words are the words of v. 19.

It is possible that the sayings of vv. 24, 25 and 28, 29 belong to some discourse different from that which was addressed to the Jewish cavillers about work on the Sabbath day; but the argument of this section (vv. 20-29) is quite consecutive (see on v. 28).

ὁ γὰρ πατὴρ φιλεῖ τὸν υἱόν. D reads ἀγαπᾷ from 3³⁵ (where see note). " The Father loves the Son, and so exhibits to Him the things which He Himself does." φιλεῖν expresses

---

[1] Cf. Abbott, *Diat.* 2066*b*.

ἃ αὐτὸς ποιεῖ, καὶ μείζονα τούτων δείξει αὐτῷ ἔργα, ἵνα ὑμεῖς θαυμάζητε. 21 ὥσπερ γὰρ ὁ Πατὴρ ἐγείρει τοὺς νεκροὺς καὶ

more than the intimacy of friendship; it is here equivalent to ἀγαπᾶν (see on 3³⁵ and 21¹⁷), and expresses the mystery of the Divine Love, of the Father for the Son. This is so complete and unreserved that all the Father's works are displayed, as they are being wrought, to the Son. No reference is made to any limitation of the Incarnate Son's knowledge of the *future*, such as is indicated in Mk. 13³²; the statement is that the Son has complete cognizance of all that the Father does in the *present*.

καὶ μείζονα τούτων δείξει αὐτῷ ἔργα, " and greater works than these (*sc.* healing miracles such as the cure of the impotent man, which had disquieted the Jews so much) shall He show Him." In the following verses, these "greater works" are specified, viz. that of raising the dead, and that of judging mankind.

The miracles of Christ are described in Mt. 11² as His ἔργα, and Jn. applies this description to them frequently (5³⁶ 7³. ²¹ 10²⁵. ³². ³⁸ 14¹² 15²⁴), as he does to the "works" of God (4³⁴ 6²⁸ 9³ 17⁴; cf. Ps. 95⁹). For God there is no distinction in kind between "natural" and "supernatural" works. And the works of Christ are actually the works of God: ὁ πατὴρ ἐν ἐμοὶ μένων ποιεῖ τὰ ἔργα αὐτοῦ (14¹⁰). See on 7²¹.

ἵνα ὑμεῖς θαυμάζητε. ὑμεῖς is emphatic, " you, incredulous Jews." The healing miracles did not so much arouse their wonder, as their jealous indignation (there is no hint that the cure of the impotent man caused any wonder); but the "greater works" of raising the dead, and of judgment, could not fail to make them marvel. Such astonishment may pass into admiration, and thence into faith (cf. Acts 4¹³).

Later on, it is promised to the faithful disciple that, in the power of Christ's Risen Life, he too should do "greater things" than those which had attended the Lord's public ministry: μείζονα τούτων ποιήσει. But this is not in contemplation here. See note on 14¹².

21. The first of the "greater works" specified is that of the "quickening" power of Christ, in raising the dead. The power of death and life is a Divine prerogative (Wisd. 16¹³), " Yahweh kills and makes alive " (Deut. 32³⁹, 1 Sam. 2⁶ θανατοῖ καὶ ζωογονεῖ, 2 Kings 5⁷ θανατῶσαι καὶ ζωοποιῆσαι). Several times in the daily prayer of the Jews, the *Shemoneh Esreh*, which in substance goes back to a period before the first century,[1] is God invoked as One who " quickens the dead."

---

[1] Cf. Schürer, *Jewish People in the Time of Christ*, Eng. Tr., Div. II. ii. p. 85.

ζωοποιεῖ, οὕτως καὶ ὁ Υἱὸς οὓς θέλει ζωοποιεῖ. 22. οὐδὲ γὰρ ὁ
Πατὴρ κρίνει οὐδένα, ἀλλὰ τὴν κρίσιν πᾶσαν δέδωκεν τῷ Υἱῷ,
23. ἵνα πάντες τιμῶσι τὸν Υἱὸν καθὼς τιμῶσι τὸν Πατέρα. ὁ μὴ
τιμῶν τὸν Υἱὸν οὐ τιμᾷ τὸν Πατέρα τὸν πέμψαντα αὐτόν. 24. ἀμὴν

Cf. θεοῦ τοῦ ζωοποιοῦντος τοὺς νεκρούς (Rom. 4¹⁷), and also Rom.
8¹¹ ὁ ἐγείρας ἐκ νεκρῶν Χριστὸν Ἰησοῦν ζωοποιήσει καὶ τὰ θνητὰ
σώματα ὑμῶν. So here we have ὁ πατὴρ ἐγείρει τοὺς νεκροὺς καὶ
ζωοποιεῖ, ἐγείρειν being used of God's "raising" of the dead,
as it is at Mk. 12²⁶.

This Divine prerogative also appertains to the Son: οὕτως
καὶ ὁ υἱὸς οὓς θέλει ζωοποιεῖ. Paul has the same doctrine of
Christ, as πνεῦμα ζωοποιοῦν (1 Cor. 15⁴⁵; cf. 1 Cor. 15²²),
revivifying the dead. ζωοποιεῖν is not used here in a *spiritual*
sense only (as at 6⁶³; cf. Eph. 2⁵), although that is included in
its meaning; the significance of the verse as specifying one of
Christ's "greater works" is that He is declared to be one who
has power over the death of the body, so that it is His to
"quicken" whom He will. He is the Resurrection as well
as the Life (11²⁵).

οὓς θέλει. His will is final as to who are to be
"quickened," just as there is no appeal from God's will
(Rom. 9¹⁸).

22, 23. The second of the "greater works" of Christ is
that of *judgment*, a prerogative which has been already implied in οὓς θέλει of the preceding verse, for all judgment or
separation between the evil and the good is a *selective* process.

Judgment is the prerogative of God (cf. Deut. 1¹⁷), for to
be perfectly administered it demands omniscience. But this
tremendous office has been "given" (see on 3³⁵) by the Father
to the Son. ὁ πατὴρ κρίνει οὐδένα, ἀλλὰ τὴν κρίσιν πᾶσαν
δέδωκεν τῷ υἱῷ. The doctrine of the Son of Man as the final
Judge of mankind has been already examined (see Introd.,
pp. cxxvii, clvi; cf. 3¹⁷). Here is added the Divine reason
for this delegation of judgment to the Son by the Father.
It is ἵνα πάντες τιμῶσι τὸν υἱόν καθὼς τιμῶσι τὸν πατέρα.

The Jews were dishonouring Jesus (cf. 8⁴⁹) in accusing Him
of blasphemy (v. 18), but worship is His due, for the honour
due to the Father is His. With the thought that they who
dishonour Him dishonour the Father, cf. 15²³, 1 Jn. 2²³, and
Lk. 10¹⁶.

τιμᾶν is found in Jn. again at 8⁴⁹ 12²⁶, and is generally used
by him of the honour due to Christ or to His Father.

τὸν πέμψαντα αὐτόν: see on 3¹⁷.

24. In vv. 24, 25, the thought is of spiritual life and death,
the believer in Christ possessing already eternal life, and the

ἀμὴν λέγω ὑμῖν ὅτι ὁ τὸν λόγον μου ἀκούων καὶ πιστεύων τῷ πέμψαντί με ἔχει ζωὴν αἰώνιον, καὶ εἰς κρίσιν οὐκ ἔρχεται ἀλλὰ μεταβέβηκεν ἐκ τοῦ θανάτου εἰς τὴν ζωήν. 25. ἀμὴν ἀμὴν λέγω ὑμῖν ὅτι ἔρχεται ὥρα καὶ νῦν ἐστιν ὅτε οἱ νεκροὶ ἀκούσουσιν τῆς

words of eternal life being proclaimed in the ears of the spiritually dead, that they too may hear and live. In vv. 28, 29, the reference is to the future life, the voice of Christ being a voice of power at the Last Judgment, even as it is now. See on v. 28.

ἀμὴν ἀμήν . . . : see on 1⁵¹. Here this formula introduces two distinct assertions, both surprising in their majestic claims of power, in vv. 24 and 25 respectively.

ὁ τὸν λόγον μου ἀκούων . . . "he that hears my word" (cf. 8⁴³; and for ἀκούειν followed by an accusative, see on 3⁸), καὶ πιστεύων τῷ πέμψαντί με, "and believes Him that sent me." To hear with the outward ear is not enough; the inward response is essential. There must be the belief in Christ (3¹⁵, where see note), which is the same thing as belief in the word of Him who sent Him (12⁴⁴). For the "sending" of the Son by the Father, see on 3¹⁷.

ἔχει ζωὴν αἰώνιον. The obedient believer *has* eternal life, as a present possession. See on 3¹⁵, and cf. 1 Jn. 5¹².

καὶ εἰς κρίσιν οὐκ ἔρχεται. Cf. 3¹⁸ ὁ πιστεύων εἰς αὐτὸν οὐ κρίνεται. The believer "comes not to judgment"; that has already been determined.[1] None the less, the prayer of humility will always be μὴ εἰσέλθῃς εἰς κρίσιν μετὰ τοῦ δούλου σου (Ps. 143²).

ἀλλὰ μεταβέβηκεν ἐκ τοῦ θανάτου εἰς τὴν ζωήν. Some Latin versions try to escape the force of the pft. tense by the renderings *transit, transiet,* and Nonnus in his paraphrase has ἵξεται ἐκ θανατοίο; but this is through misunderstanding. Jn. is quite clear that the believer *has* "passed from death into life," into the eternal life which begins here. Cf. οἴδαμεν ὅτι μεταβεβήκαμεν ἐκ τοῦ θανάτου εἰς τὴν ζωήν (1 Jn. 3¹⁴), the reason for such assurance being added, ὅτι ἀγαπῶμεν τοὺς ἀδελφούς.

25. οἱ νεκροὶ ἀκούσουσιν κτλ. Even those who do not believe, who are spiritually dead, are not beyond the range of Christ's words. They, too, may hear and live. This is one of those extraordinary assurances which must be introduced by the solemn adjuration ἀμὴν ἀμήν. It is, as it were, a corollary or sequel to v. 24; see on 1⁵¹.

Of the quickening of the *physically* dead at the Last Judgment, it is said in v. 28 ἔρχεται ὥρα, but of the *spiritually* dead in the present, ἔρχεται ὥρα καὶ νῦν ἐστιν, as at 4²³, where see

---

[1] See Introd., p. clx.

φωνῆς τοῦ Υἱοῦ τοῦ Θεοῦ καὶ οἱ ἀκούσαντες ζήσουσιν. 26. ὥσπερ γὰρ ὁ Πατὴρ ἔχει ζωὴν ἐν ἑαυτῷ, οὕτως καὶ τῷ Υἱῷ ἔδωκεν ζωὴν ἔχειν ἐν ἑαυτῷ. 27. καὶ ἐξουσίαν ἔδωκεν αὐτῷ κρίσιν ποιεῖν, ὅτι Υἱὸς

note. To treat καὶ νῦν ἐστίν as an editorial interpolation here is to misunderstand the sequence of thought in vv. 24–29.

οἱ νεκροί here are the spiritually dead, as at Eph. 2[1. 5] 5[14]. " They shall hear (cf. ἀκούων in v. 24) the voice of the Son of God." It is not only His sheep who may hear His voice (10[16]), but those also who have not yet learnt to follow. Note that ἀκούειν with the gen. carries the meaning of "hearing with appreciation"; see on 3[8].

τοῦ υἱοῦ τοῦ θεοῦ: see on 1[34]. It is only in Jn. that this title is put into the mouth of Jesus (10[36] 11[4]); while he often employs it when writing in his own person.

B has ἀκούσουσιν, but אLW read ἀκούσωσιν, the rec. having ἀκούσονται. Also the rec. ζήσονται (ΑΓΔΘ) must give place to ζήσουσιν (אBDLW).

26. ὥσπερ γὰρ ὁ πατήρ κτλ. Verses 26, 27, repeat (from vv. 21, 22) that the Father has given to the Son (a) the quickening power and (b) the authority of judge, which are prerogatives of Deity.

Verse 26 deals with the power of *life*. To Hebrew thought, no less than to Greek, God is the Living One: " With thee is the fountain of life " (Ps. 36[9]). Thus the Father " has life in Himself," and so He gave " to the Son to have life in Himself," ἐν ἑαυτῷ being emphatic. (For ὥσπερ, see on v. 20 above.) To " have life in Himself " involves the power to give out life, or to quicken.

This " giving " has been interpreted of the mystical communication of life *sub specie æternitatis* by the Father to the Son in His pre-incarnate state; and the statement would then point to the Logos doctrine of the Prologue (cf. esp. 1[3], " In Him was Life," and the note *in loc.*). This is possible (see on 17[24]); but the thought of the Father " giving " to the Incarnate Son is frequent in Jn. (see on 3[35] above). It is better to interpret ἔδωκεν as in the other passages in the Gospel, where it is applied to the Father's gifts to Christ as manifested in the flesh (see on 17[2]). Christ is, in any case, " the Living One " (Rev. 1[18]); but the significance of ἔδωκεν here is the same as that suggested by the words, " I live because of the Father " (6[57]). The Divine power of life is delegated to Him, as is the Divine prerogative of judgment, which Jn. sets forth in v. 27.

27. The rec., supported by ΔΓΔΘ and some O.L. texts, has καί before κρίσιν; but om. א°ABLW.

ἐξουσίαν ἔδωκεν αὐτῷ: see v. 22. The ἐξουσία is that of

ἀνθρώπου ἐστίν.   28. μὴ θαυμάζετε τοῦτο, ὅτι ἔρχεται ὥρα ἐν ᾗ

17[2]; cf. also Mt. 28[18]. The Father "gave to Him authority to pass judgment, because He is the Son of Man,"[1] to whom, as we have seen,[2] the tremendous office of Judge is assigned in Jewish apocalyptic.

It has been suggested that the absence of the article before υἱὸς ἀνθρώπου here is significant, and that we should render "because He is a son of man," the meaning being that the office of the Judge of men is committed to Christ because He is Man, an affinity of nature between Judge and him who is judged being essential for just judgment. But the title "Son of Man" occurs repeatedly in Jn. (see on 1[51]), and several times in connexion with the thought of Him as Judge. It would be strange if in the present passage, where His office as Judge is emphasised, another explanation of the phrase should be necessary.

The absence of the article before υἱὸς ἀνθρώπου is not to be pressed. Official titles have a tendency to become anarthrous, and this has happened here, although elsewhere in Jn. we have ὁ υἱὸς τοῦ ἀνθρώπου. If we are right in regarding vv. 20–29 as, in part, a commentary by the evangelist on what Jesus actually said to the Jews, then it is the less surprising to find υἱὸς ἀνθρώπου instead of ὁ υἱὸς τοῦ ἀνθρώπου, which never occurs in narrative. The latter is a designation of Himself used by Jesus in all four Gospels, but is not employed by the evangelists when referring to Him.

28. μὴ θαυμάζετε τοῦτο (cf. v. 20). This is not to be connected with the statement "because He is the Son of Man," as Chrysostom suggested, and as is implied in the Pesh. Syriac and in Δ. It has been stated that the Father has given to the Son the power of life and authority to pass judgment (vv. 26, 27), in reference more particularly to the spiritual life of men in this present world (vv. 24, 25). But what is still more wonderful (here is indicated the mind of the first century), these powers of quickening and of judgment extend to the physical awakening of the dead and their judgment in the body at the Last Assize. The argument is : The Son is to do greater works than works of healing, in order that the observers may marvel (as apparently they had *not* done when the impotent man was cured, v. 20); these greater works include the power of awakening the spiritually dead, and of being the Agent of judgment in this life, as to belief and unbelief (vv. 24, 25). This, indeed, is marvellous,

---

[1] This is the true construction, as supported by Syr. cur., the O.L., Origen, and Paul of Samosata ; see on v. 28 for Chrysostom's rendering.
[2] See v. 22, and Introd., p. cxxvii.

πάντες οἱ ἐν τοῖς μνημείοις ἀκούσουσιν τῆς φωνῆς αὐτοῦ, 29. καὶ ἐκπορεύσονται οἱ τὰ ἀγαθὰ ποιήσαντες εἰς ἀνάστασιν ζωῆς, οἱ τὰ φαῦλα πράξαντες εἰς ἀνάστασιν κρίσεως.

but the greater marvel is what will happen at the Last Day, when the dead in the tombs shall be quickened by the voice of the Son of God, and final judgment shall be pronounced by Him on good and evil.

Such a doctrine, no doubt, has its roots in Jewish eschatology, but the Fourth Gospel cannot be understood unless it be realised that Jn. has not abandoned this, while he lays his emphasis on the spiritual conceptions of eternal life and judgment in the present, which were taught by Jesus (see Introd., p. clxi). Verses 28, 29, have been thought to be "materialistic," but they cannot be torn from the text as an interpolation or later addition ;[1] they are an integral part of the argument.

With μὴ θαυμάζετε, cf. 3⁷ and 1 Jn. 3¹³.

ἔρχεται ὥρα : see on v. 25 and on 4²³

With ἀκούσουσιν τῆς φωνῆς αὐτοῦ, cf. 11⁴³ φωνῇ μεγάλῃ ἐκραύγασεν, Λάζαρε, δεῦρο ἔξω.

πάντες οἱ ἐν τοῖς μνημείοις κτλ. This is a plain statement of a general bodily resurrection, both of good and bad, such as is suggested in *Apoc. of Baruch* 50, 51, 2 Esd. 7³²ᶠ·. In the N.T. it is explicitly asserted in Mt. 25⁴⁶, Acts 24¹⁵, 2 Cor. 5¹⁰ ; and it is frequently implied in the Synoptic reports of the words of Jesus (*e.g.* Mt. 5²⁹·³⁰ 10²⁸, Lk. 11³²). That Christ is the Agent of this Resurrection, so far as the righteous are concerned at any rate, has appeared 6³⁹ᶠ·. He "makes alive" both in this world and at the Day of Judgment ; such is the consistent teaching of Jn.

As at v. 25, the MSS. vary as to ἀκούσουσιν (B), ἀκούσωσιν (אLΔNW 33), and ἀκούσονται (ADΓΘ).

29. The word ἀνάστασις is used by Æschylus (*Eum.* 648) of "rising up" from the grave, that is, of "resurrection." In the LXX it is infrequent, and occurs with this meaning at 2 Macc. 7¹⁴ 12⁴³ only (cf. Ps. 66ᵗⁱᵗ). The Synoptists have it in the narrative of the questioning Sadducees (Mk. 12¹⁸ᶠ·, Mt. 22²³ᶠ·, Lk. 20²⁷ᶠ·) ; and, besides, Lk. has the phrase "the resurrection of the just" (14¹⁴). We have ἀνάστασις in Jn. again at 11²⁴·²⁵.

There are the two resurrections : one of *life*, the other of *judgment*. For the former, cf. 2 Macc. 7¹⁴ σοὶ μὲν γὰρ ἀνάστασις εἰς ζωὴν οὐκ ἔσται. The two are mentioned together Dan. 12².

For τὰ φαῦλα πράξαντες (πράσσοντες D), see on 3²⁰.

---

[1] Wendt (*Gospel according to St. John*, pp. 131 ff.) argues that **vv.** 28, 29, cannot belong to the original form of the discourse

30. Οὐ δύναμαι ἐγὼ ποιεῖν ἀπ' ἐμαυτοῦ οὐδέν· καθὼς ἀκούω κρίνω, καὶ ἡ κρίσις ἡ ἐμὴ δικαία ἐστίν, ὅτι οὐ ζητῶ τὸ θέλημα τὸ ἐμὸν ἀλλὰ τὸ θέλημα τοῖ πέμψαντός με. 31. Ἐὰν ἐγὼ μαρτυρῶ

Life and judgment begin in this world, but the *life* once secured continues eternally, the future *judgment* being already anticipated. The evil-doer is to rise after death, for a judgment which, although predetermined, has not yet been fully exhibited or revealed. See on 3^18f..

Jesus appeals to the witness to His claims provided by God (vv. 32, 37), by the Baptist (v. 33), by His own works (v. 36), and by the O.T. (v. 39).

30. The discourse returns to the first person, from the third; the thought, " I can do nothing of myself," returning to v. 19, where see note (cf. 8^28 ἀπ' ἐμαυτοῦ ποιῶ οὐδέν).

ἐμαυτός is used by Jesus of Himself 16 times in Jn., never in the Synoptists, where it occurs only Mt. 8^9, Lk. 7^7. 8.

καθὼς ἀκούω κρίνω, *i.e.* " as I hear *from the Father* (see on v. 19), I judge." The authority to judge is delegated to Him (v. 27) ; and His judgments are righteous because they reflect the judgments of God Himself. ἡ κρίσις ἡ ἐμὴ δικαία ἐστίν (cf. Ps. 7^11 of God, the Righteous Judge) is repeated 8^16 in the form ἡ κρίσις ἡ ἐμὴ ἀληθινή ἐστιν. There is no self-will in the passing of these judgments, οὐ ζητῶ τὸ θέλημα τὸ ἐμόν, but rather τὸ θέλημα τοῦ πέμψαντός με. For this last phrase, see 6^38. 39. 40, where it recurs, and 4^34. Cf. especially the notes on 7^16. 17. 18.

Thus to seek that God's will be done, in every decision of life, was perfectly realised only in the Son of Man Himself. But the precept of Rabbi Gamaliel may apply to every man, however imperfectly it may be obeyed : " Do His will as if it were thy will, that He may do thy will as if it were His will." [1]

The rec. adds πατρός after τοῦ πέμψαντός με (cf. 6^40), but om. אABDLNW

31. The argument in vv. 31–37 is that the proclamation by Jesus of His own claims and authority did not depend, as the Pharisees naturally urged, upon His individual testimony. He admits that if the witness which He bore to Himself was merely that of one man, it would not be sufficient. " If I bear witness of myself, my witness is not true," *i.e.* it need not be taken as true, for (of course) a single witness *may* speak truth even in his own case. But He urges that, apart from the " witness " to Him which was given by John the Baptist

[1] *Aboth* x . 4, quoted by Westcott, *in loc.*

περὶ ἐμαυτοῦ, ἡ μαρτυρία μου οὐκ ἔστιν ἀληθής· **32.** ἄλλος ἐστὶν

to the Pharisees when they made inquiry (v. 33), upon which He does not rely (v. 34), there is the " witness " of Another, greater immeasurably than John (vv. 32, 34). The " witness " of the " works " which He did is really the " witness " of God (v. 36), without whom they could not have been done, and in whose Name and by whose authority they were done. The argument in 8[14-17] is different. He does, indeed, appeal there, as He does here, to the fact that the " witness " of the Father corroborates His own, and that therefore the requisite " two witnesses " are present in His case (8[17]) ; but He goes on to claim that His consciousness of Divine origin (v. 14) and the intimacy of His union with the Father justify Him in the assertion, paradoxical as it might seem to His opponents, that His self-witness *must* be true. ἐγώ εἰμι ὁ μαρτυρῶν περὶ ἐμαυτοῦ is the claim and the style of Deity (8[18]).

Here, however, He is represented only as saying that His individual witness is confirmed by the witness of God.

ἐὰν ἐγὼ μαρτυρῶ περὶ ἐμαυτοῦ, ἡ μαρτυρία μου οὐκ ἔστιν ἀληθής. This challenges comparison with 8[14], where the sentence is verbally repeated, with the omission of οὐκ : " If I bear witness of myself, my witness *is* true."

The Jewish maxims as to evidence were rigidly and pedantically observed in the subtle disputations of the Rabbinical schools. One was that two witnesses at least were always necessary for the establishment of any matter of fact (Deut. 19[15]). To this maxim allusion is made 2 Cor. 13[1], 1 Tim. 5[19]; and Jesus quotes it as a rule at Mt. 18[16]. Another, not less weighty, rule was that a man's evidence about himself was suspect. Wetstein quotes the Mishna (*Ketuboth* ii. 9), " homo non est fide dignus de se ipso." That, indeed, is a common maxim of law everywhere ; cf. Demosthenes, 2 *contra Steph.* § 9 μαρτυρεῖν γὰρ οἱ νόμοι οὐκ ἐῶσιν αὐτὸν ἑαυτῷ. Now when Jesus enunciated lofty claims for Himself and for His mission, He was challenged to substantiate them, and all arguments conducted with the Rabbis had perforce to fall in with their doctrine as to what constituted valid evidence. The arguments here (vv. 31–39) and at 8[12-19] seem to a modern reader pedantic and unattractive in form, precisely because they reproduce modes of thought and speech which are foreign to our Western culture. They are not like the arguments of Greek disputants ; but their Rabbinical flavour is an indication that they have been faithfully reported by one who was himself a Jew, and to whom Jewish scholasticism was not strange or unfamiliar. In arguing with the Rabbis, Jesus did not shrink from arguing on their

ὁ μαρτυρῶν περὶ ἐμοῦ, καὶ οἶδα ὅτι ἀληθής ἐστιν ἡ μαρτυρία ἥν μαρτυρεῖ περὶ ἐμοῦ. 33. ὑμεῖς ἀπεστάλκατε πρὸς Ἰωάνην, καὶ μεμαρτύρηκεν τῇ ἀληθείᾳ· 34. ἐγὼ δὲ οὐ παρὰ ἀνθρώπου τὴν

principles, and had He refused to do this, He could not have gained a hearing at Jerusalem at all. See Introd., p. lxxxii.

32. ἄλλος ἐστὶν ὁ μαρτυρῶν περὶ ἐμοῦ (cf. 8[18]). To interpret ἄλλος of John the Baptist, as is done, *e.g.*, by Chrysostom, makes havoc of the argument which follows. Cyprian (*Epist.* lxvi. 2) rightly interprets ἄλλος of the Father. Blass [1] cites, in illustration of such a use of ἄλλος, Æschylus, *Suppl.* 230, κἀκεῖ δικάζει . . . Ζεὺς ἄλλος; and Abbott (*Diat.* 2791) quotes a passage from Epictetus (iii. 13. 13–14), where God is reverentially described as *Another* (ἄλλος), who guards men's lives. Cf. 14[16].

The present participle μαρτυρῶν should be noted: "There is Another who is *bearing witness* concerning me," this witness being continuous and a present reality at the time of speaking, whereas the witness of John the Baptist is spoken of in the past tense (vv. 34, 35). According to the arrangement of the Gospel text which is followed in this commentary (see on 6[1]), John the Baptist was dead at the point in the ministry of Jesus which has now been reached (cf. v. 35).

For οἶδα (ℵ°ABLNW⊙), ℵ*D and Syr. sin. have οἴδατε, a reading due to the mistaken interpretation which treats ἄλλος as referring to John the Baptist.

καὶ οἶδα ὅτι ἀληθής ἐστιν ἡ μαρτυρία κτλ., "and *I* know that the witness which He witnesseth of me is true." No one could know this as the Speaker knew it; cf. ἐγὼ οἶδα αὐτὸν ὅτι παρ' αὐτοῦ εἰμι (7[29]).

The reference to God the Father as His witness is an illustration of the saying ὁ πατὴρ μείζων μού ἐστι (14[28]), and helps to explain it. Philo lays down the principle that "he who bears witness, in so far as he does so, is superior to him of whom witness is borne," ὁ μαρτυρῶν, παρ' ὅσον μαρτυρεῖ, κρείττων ἐστὶν τοῦ ἐκμαρτυρουμένου (*de sacr. Abelis et Caini*, § 28).

33. ὑμεῖς ἀπεστάλκατε πρὸς Ἰωάνην, "*Ye* sent to John" (cf. 1[19]), and his witness was trustworthy, καὶ μεμαρτύρηκεν τῇ ἀληθείᾳ, as was the purpose of his mission (1[7]), a purpose which was also that of the mission of Jesus Himself (18[37]).

34. But, true as was the witness of the Baptist, it is not that upon which Jesus relies. ἐγώ is in contrast with ὑμεῖς of the preceding. ἐγὼ δὲ οὐ παρὰ ἀνθρώπου τὴν μαρτυρίαν λαμβάνω, "but the witness which *I* accept is not from man." For τὴν μαρτυρίαν λαμβάνειν, of accepting testimony as adequate, cf.

[1] *Grammar of N.T.*, p. 180.

μαρτυρίαν λαμβάνω, ἀλλὰ ταῦτα λέγω ἵνα ὑμεῖς σωθῆτε. 35. ἐκεῖνος ἦν ὁ λύχνος ὁ καιόμενος καὶ φαίνων, ὑμεῖς δὲ ἠθελήσατε ἀγαλλιαθῆναι πρὸς ὥραν ἐν τῷ φωτὶ αὐτοῦ. 36. ἐγὼ δὲ ἔχω τὴν μαρτυρίαν μείζω

3¹¹. ³². See 1 Jn. 5⁹ εἰ τὴν μαρτυρίαν τῶν ἀνθρώπων λαμβάνομεν, ἡ μαρτυρία τοῦ θεοῦ μείζων ἐστίν.

ἀλλὰ, "nevertheless"; although He did not rely upon the witness of John, He referred to it because it was of it that the Pharisees had made inquiry (1¹⁹), and He would remind them of this. ταῦτα λέγω, "I say these things," i.e. about the Baptist's testimony, ἵνα ὑμεῖς σωθῆτε, "in order that you (who made inquiry) may be saved." It was the final cause of the mission of Jesus, ἵνα σωθῇ ὁ κόσμος (see on 3¹⁷ for σώζειν).

35. ἐκεῖνος (much used by Jn. to mark out the subject of a sentence; see on 1⁸) ἦν (the use of the past tense shows that the ministry of John Baptist was over; see on v. 32) ὁ λύχνος ὁ καιόμενος καὶ φαίνων, "the Lamp that burns and shines." The Baptist, as Jn. has said (1⁸), was not the Light (τὸ φῶς), but he was a lamp whose shining illuminated the darkness. "Non Lux iste, sed lucerna," as the Latin hymn has it. Cf. οἱ λύχνοι καιόμενοι (Lk. 12³⁵), and especially 2 Pet. 1¹⁹, where prophecy is compared to λύχνος φαίνων ἐν αὐχμηρῷ τόπῳ, ἕως οὗ ἡμέρα διαυγάσῃ. When the Light comes, the lamp is no longer needed.

A lamp not only *burns* as it gives light, but it *burns away*, and so it was with the Baptist, who decreased as His Master increased; but this is not necessarily implied here.

David is called the λύχνος of Israel (2 Sam. 21¹⁷); but the sentence ἡτοίμασα λύχνον τῷ χριστῷ μου (Ps. 132¹⁷) came to be applied by the Fathers to John the Baptist, the metaphor of John as the Lamp being widely adopted. It is said in Ecclus. 48¹ that the word of Elijah was like a burning torch, ὡς λάμπας ἐκαίετο; and, if there were any evidence that Elijah was compared traditionally to a Lamp, we might suppose that the description in the text of John, the new Elijah, as λύχνος carried an allusion to this. But Ecclus. 48¹ does not provide sufficient foundation for such a theory.

ὑμεῖς δὲ ἠθελήσατε ἀγαλλιαθῆναι (so אΛΒΔΓΔΘΝ; but LW have ἀγαλλιασθῆναι) πρὸς ὥραν ἐν τῷ φωτὶ αὐτοῦ, "You were pleased to rejoice for a time in his light," words which remind the Jews of how popular John Baptist had been (Mk. 1⁵, Mt. 3⁵ 11⁷ 21²⁶; and cf. Jn. 1¹⁹), and of the fickleness of those who had been attracted to him, like moths to a lighted candle.

ἀγαλλιάομαι occurs again 8⁵⁶.

36. But Jesus does not rest His claims on the witness of the Baptist (cf. v. 34). ἐγὼ δὲ ἔχω τὴν μαρτυρίαν μείζω (this

τοῦ Ἰωάνου· τὰ γὰρ ἔργα ἃ δέδωκέν μοι ὁ Πατὴρ ἵνα τελειώσω αὐτά, αὐτὰ τὰ ἔργα ἃ ποιῶ, μαρτυρεῖ περὶ ἐμοῦ ὅτι ὁ Πατήρ με ἀπέσταλκεν. 37. καὶ ὁ πέμψας με Πατήρ, ἐκεῖνος μεμαρτύρηκεν περὶ ἐμοῦ. οὔτε

is the true reading, μείζων of ABW being due to misunderstanding) τοῦ Ἰωάνου, "but I (ἐγώ being emphatic) have witness greater than that of John"; cf. vv. 32, 37, 1 Jn. 5⁹. The works which He did were witness that His mission was from God.

For this conception of the ἔργα of Jesus as His "witness," see 10²⁵; and cf. Mt. 11⁴, Lk. 7²², where He bade John's disciples report His works of healing to their master as sufficient proof of His Messiahship. Faith which is generated by the witness of such "works" is not faith in its highest form (cf. 10³⁸ 14¹¹; and see 2²³), but to reject their witness is sinful (15²⁴). Cf. also 3².

For the ἔργα of the Son, see on v. 20 above. They are described here as "the works which the Father has given me (see on 3³⁵) to accomplish." And at 17⁴ Jesus is represented as claiming that He *had* accomplished them, the words used being almost the same as in this verse, τὸ ἔργον τελειώσας ὁ δέδωκάς μοι ἵνα ποιήσω.

For δέδωκεν (אBLΓNW) the rec. with ADΔΘ has ἔδωκεν. With ἵνα τελειώσω cf. 4³⁴.

αὐτὰ τὰ ἔργα ἃ ποιῶ μαρτυρεῖ περὶ ἐμοῦ. The repetition of αὐτὰ τὰ ἔργα is conversational. Cf., for similar words, 10²⁵ 14¹¹. The thing which is established by these ἔργα is that Jesus had been "sent" by the Father, ὅτι ὁ πατήρ με ἀπέσταλκεν. This is His claim throughout. See on 3¹⁷ for this conception both in Jn. and in the Synoptists; and cf. 11⁴².

37. ὁ πέμψας με πατήρ. We cannot distinguish between πέμπω here and ἀποστέλλω in the preceding verse; see on 3¹⁷.

The rec. αὐτός has the support of ANΓΔΘ, but ἐκεῖνος of אBLW must be preferred; see on 1⁸ for ἐκεῖνος in Jn.

μεμαρτύρηκεν περὶ ἐμοῦ. Cf. 8¹⁸; and see v. 32. We have already had the *indirect* witness of the Father to the Son, through the ἔργα which the Son did (v. 36), but the Father's witness is also *direct*, and this is indicated, although the argument is abbreviated to the point of obscurity, in vv. 37, 38. The reasoning is as follows:

"The Father, who sent me, has borne witness of me. True, He is not a *visible* witness: you cannot see God's form or hear His voice with the outward ear. But to those who accept Jesus, the message from God that He is His Son abides continually in the believer's heart. The consciousness of a

φωνὴν αὐτοῦ πώποτε ἀκηκόατε οὔτε εἶδος αὐτοῦ ἐωράκατε. 38. καὶ
τὸν λόγον αὐτοῦ οὐκ ἔχετε ἐν ὑμῖν μένοντα, ὅτι ὃν ἀπέστειλεν ἐκεῖνος,

Divine revelation is the Father's own witness, although *invisible* to the world."

The key to vv. 37, 38, is found in 1 Jn. 5[9. 10] αὕτη ἐστὶν ἡ
μαρτυρία τοῦ θεοῦ, ὅτι μεμαρτύρηκεν περὶ τοῦ υἱοῦ αὐτοῦ. ὁ πιστεύων
εἰς τὸν υἱὸν τοῦ θεοῦ ἔχει τὴν μαρτυρίαν ἐν ἑαυτῷ. The believer
has an internal witness, which is in reality the witness of
God. We are not to think of voices from heaven or visible
epiphanies as indicated by the μαρτυρία of the Father ; such
are recorded by the Synoptists at the Baptism and the Transfiguration (cf. also Jn. 12[28]). It is the confident assurance of
the believer which is here in question.

οὔτε φωνὴν αὐτοῦ πώποτε ἀκηκόατε, "you have never heard
His voice," much less heard it with intelligence. See on 3[8]
for ἀκούειν with the acc. in Jn., who uses this constr. as
equivalent to a mere perception by hearing, without definite
appreciation of what is said. What is stated is that the Jews
could not have heard the voice of God with the outward ear.

For πώποτε, and its use in the N.T., see on 1[18].

οὔτε εἶδος αὐτοῦ ἐωράκατε, "nor have you seen His form."
So 1[18] θεὸν οὐδεὶς ἑώρακεν πώποτε, and 1 Jn. 4[12]; cf. 6[46]. This
was admitted by Jew and Greek alike. Peniel, the place of
Jacob's wrestling, is called indeed in the LXX εἶδος θεοῦ (Gen.
32[30]), the reason given being ἴδον γὰρ θεὸν πρόσωπον πρὸς
πρόσωπον. But no Jew regarded that as an ordinary
experience, or one that he might expect to be repeated in his
own case. Man cannot see with bodily eyes the εἶδος of
God; and so God cannot appear as a witness to give legal
evidence.

From οὔτε φωνήν to ἐωράκατε is a kind of parenthesis,
interpolated to avoid misunderstanding. Then follows the
description of the true μαρτυρία of the Father.

38. καὶ τὸν λόγον αὐτοῦ οὐκ ἔχετε ἐν ὑμῖν μένοντα. καί (as
in v. 40 καὶ οὐ θέλετε) stands for *and yet*, as often in Jn. (see
note on 1[10]). The sequence of thought is : The Father has
borne witness of me, and yet you have not His word abiding in
you, you have not appropriated this Divine word of revelation.

The λόγος of God is used sometimes by Jn. to signify the
message or revelation or command which God has given. Thus
in 10[35] there is allusion to the λόγος of God which came to men
of the olden time with the revelation "Ye are gods . . . ye are
sons of the Most High" (Ps. 82[6]). Such a word of God, when
it comes to a faithful heart, abides there. To the young men
whom Jn. commends, he writes, ὁ λόγος τοῦ θεοῦ ἐν ὑμῖν μένει

τούτῳ ὑμεῖς οὐ πιστεύετε. 39. ἐραυνᾶτε τὰς γραφάς, ὅτι ὑμεῖς

(1 Jn. 2¹⁴). And, again, of self-deceivers who claim to be sinless, ὁ λόγος αὐτοῦ οὐκ ἔστιν ἐν ἡμῖν (1 Jn. 1¹⁰). So, in 17⁶, Jesus says of His faithful apostles, τὸν λόγον σου τετήρηκαν. Cf. 15³.

The metaphor is different at 8³¹, where Jesus speaks of the faithful disciples as " abiding in His word " (ἐὰν μείνητε ἐν τῷ λόγῳ τῷ ἐμῷ). Here He speaks of the word of the Father abiding in them, which is really the Father's "witness." But, in fact, the two expressions " abiding in His word " and " His word abiding in us " imply each other in Jn. Similarly (see on 6⁵⁶), to "abide in Christ " implies that He " abides in us " (cf. also 15⁴· ⁷). The two go together.

ὅτι ὃν ἀπέστειλεν ἐκεῖνος τούτῳ ὑμεῖς οὐ πιστεύετε, " because He whom He sent—Him you do not believe." For the constr., viz. a *casus pendens* reinforced by a pronoun, see on 1¹². The order of pronouns, τούτῳ ὑμεῖς, is emphatic.

The failure to appropriate the Father's witness, the fact that the λόγος of the Father, which surely came to them revealing Jesus as His Son, did not " abide " in them, is traced to the lack of faith, just as in 1 Jn. 5¹⁰ ὁ μὴ πιστεύων τῷ θεῷ ψεύστην πεποίηκεν αὐτόν, ὅτι οὐ πεπίστευκεν εἰς τὴν μαρτυρίαν ἣν μεμαρτύρηκεν ὁ θεὸς περὶ τοῦ υἱοῦ αὐτοῦ.

This λόγος of the Father in men's hearts is His sure witness, although it cannot be used for the conviction of unbelievers.

39. The rec. text has ἐρευνᾶτε, but אB*N have ἐραυνᾶτε, which is the better form.

αἱ γραφαί, in the plural, stands for the collected books of the O.T. Canon (so Mt. 21⁴², Lk. 24²⁷); but elsewhere in Jn. we find always ἡ γραφή with reference to a particular passage (see on 2²²).

The verb ἐραυνᾶν is found again in Jn. only at 7⁵² (where see note), and is not used elsewhere in the N.T. of searching the Scriptures (in Acts 17¹¹ the word used is ἀνακρίνειν); but we have in Ps. 119² μακάριοι οἱ ἐξεραυνῶντες τὰ μαρτύρια αὐτοῦ.

It has been much debated whether ἐραυνᾶτε in this passage is to be taken as an imperative, or as a present indicative. Origen (*c. Celsum*, v. 16) and Tertullian (*de Præscript.* 8) take it as imperative, so that the familiar exhortation " Search the Scriptures " goes back at any rate to the end of the second century. This is the rendering of the older English versions, as also of the Latin Vulgate, and (apparently) of Irenæus (*Hær.* iv. 10. 1). But, despite this early tradition, it is preferable to follow the R.V. in translating " Ye search the Scriptures, for in them, etc.," for the argument seems to halt

δοκεῖτε ἐν αὐταῖς ζωὴν αἰώνιον ἔχειν· καὶ ἐκεῖναί εἰσιν αἱ μαρτυροῦσαι περὶ ἐμοῦ· 40. καὶ οὐ θέλετε ἐλθεῖν πρός με ἵνα ζωὴν ἔχητε.

if ἐραυνᾶτε is imperative. Jesus is not exhorting the Jews here; He is arguing with them, and rebuking them for their stubborn rejection of Him. Their fault is οὐ θέλετε ἐλθεῖν πρός με.

It was a Rabbinical saying that "he who has acquired the words of the Law has acquired eternal life";[1] and it is this kind of superstition to which the words "Ye search the Scriptures, for in them ye think ye have eternal life," refer. ζωὴ αἰώνιος here means "the future life," as often in Jn. (see on 3[15]), and the word δοκεῖτε is significant. In categorical sentences δοκεῖν in Jn. (see 5[45] 11[13]. 31 13[29] 16[2] 20[15]) *always* [2] indicates a mistaken or inaccurate opinion : ὑμεῖς δοκεῖτε means "you think, *wrongly.*"

It is not possible to treat ἐραυνᾶτε as an imperative, and do justice to these considerations. Why should the Jews be bidden to search the Scriptures because they held a wrong opinion about their sanctity ? The reading of them in the formal manner of the Rabbis did *not* carry with it the possession of eternal life. Their true sanctity lay in their pointing onward to the Christ. ἐκεῖναί (these very Scriptures, which you mis-use) εἰσιν αἱ μαρτυροῦσαι περὶ ἐμοῦ, which the Jews did not appreciate.

The argument, then, is, "You search the Scriptures because of your mistaken belief that this close scrutiny of words and syllables in the sacred books assures you of the life to come. There you are wrong. The true value of the Scriptures is that they bear witness of me. And you are doubly wrong, for you will not come to me in person, when the opportunity is given." [3]

40. οὐ θέλετε ἐλθεῖν πρός με. This is the tragedy of the rejection of Messiah by the Messianic race; cf. Mt. 23[37], with the same sombre conclusion, οὐκ ἠθελήσατε. The use of καί (cf. v. 38), meaning "and yet," before οὐ θέλετε is a feature of Jn.'s style. See on 1[10].

Explanation of the unbelief of the Jews (vv. 41–47)

41. Verses 41–47 are an exposure of the source of the Jews' unbelief. It is this, that they do not love God, and so they

---

[1] *Aboth,* ii. 8, quoted by Schoettgen, i. p. 356.
[2] τί δοκεῖ ὑμῖν ; (11[56]) is a question, "What do you *think* ? "
[3] Abbott points out that ἐραυνᾶτε or ἐξεραυνᾶτε does not occur elsewhere in the Greek Bible as an imperative, the aorist being generally used when there is a command ; cf 7[52] (*Diat.* 2439*i*).

41. Δόξαν παρὰ ἀνθρώπων οὐ λαμβάνω, 42. ἀλλὰ ἔγνωκα ὑμᾶς ὅτι τὴν ἀγάπην τοῦ Θεοῦ οὐκ ἔχετε ἐν ἑαυτοῖς. 43. ἐγὼ ἐλήλυθα ἐν

do not appreciate Him who came in God's Name. They are concerned rather with the approval of their fellows, than with God's approval. Nevertheless, Jesus says that He will not accuse them to God. Moses will be their accuser: he wrote of Messiah, and the Jews did not appreciate what he wrote. It is not to be expected, if they reject the written teaching of Moses, that they should accept the verbal teaching of Jesus.

δόξαν παρὰ ἀνθρώπων οὐ λαμβάνω. His words of rebuke do not spring from any wounded pride because they did not accept His claims. Their approval is of no weight with Him (8⁵⁰; cf. the similar repudiation made by Paul, 1 Thess. 2⁶). That the honour (δόξα) which is bestowed by men on their fellows is not to be greatly prized is not a peculiarly Johannine doctrine (5⁴⁴ 7¹⁸ 12⁴³), but appears in Mt. 6¹· ² and elsewhere. Cf. "The good inclination receiveth not glory or dishonour from men" (*Test. of XII. Patriarchs*, Benj. vi. 4). For δόξα, see on 1¹⁴.

42. ἀλλὰ ἔγνωκα ὑμᾶς, "but I have known you," sc. with the knowledge that comes from personal experience; cf. 2²⁴.

ὅτι τὴν ἀγάπην τοῦ θεοῦ οὐκ ἔχετε ἐν ἑαυτοῖς, "that you have not the love of God in yourselves." In Paul "the love of God" always means the love which God has for man, and "the love of Christ" is the love which Christ has for man. But the usage in Jn. is not so uniform.

ἀγάπη is used 13³⁵ 15¹³ of the love of man for man; in 15⁹· ¹⁰ of the love of Christ for man; and in 15¹⁰ 17²⁶ of the love of God for Christ. In the First Epistle, in like manner, in 3¹ 4⁹· ¹⁰· ¹⁶ the thought is of the love of God for man; in 3¹⁶ it is the love of Christ for man; but in 2⁵· ¹⁵ 3¹⁷ 4¹² 5³ we must interpret ἡ ἀγάπη τοῦ θεοῦ or the like phrase as signifying the love which man has for God. See on 21¹⁵.

We see, then, that the meaning of ἡ ἀγάπη τοῦ θεοῦ in the present passage must be determined from the context, and we conclude that it must mean the love which men have for God. No doubt, as Abbott argues (*Diat.* 2040), the phrase in v. 38 τὸν λόγον αὐτοῦ οὐκ ἔχετε ἐν ὑμῖν μένοντα, suggests that as λόγος there is the λόγος that proceeds from God, so ἀγάπη here should mean the love that flows out from God. But it could hardly be imputed for reproach to the Jews that *God* did not love *them*. The point of the reproach is that *they* did not love *God*, and so were not in spiritual sympathy with One who came ἐν τῷ ὀνόματι τοῦ πατρός. And, as we have seen, this sense of ἡ ἀγάπη τοῦ θεοῦ, sc. the love of man for God,

τῷ ὀνόματι τοῦ Πατρός μου, καὶ οὐ λαμβάνετέ με· ἐὰν ἄλλος ἔλθῃ ἐν τῷ ὀνόματι τῷ ἰδίῳ, ἐκεῖνον λήμψεσθε.   44. πῶς δύνασθε ὑμεῖς

although it is not found again in the Fourth Gospel (but see on 21¹⁵ for the uses of the verb ἀγαπάω), may be amply justified by the language of 1 Jn.

43. ἐγὼ ἐλήλυθα ἐν τῷ ὀνόματι τοῦ πατρός μου. Jesus is represented by Jn. as speaking of the " Name " of His Father 7 times (the number 7 probably having no significance; see Introd., p. lxxxix). The "Name" of the Father was given to the Incarnate Son (17¹¹· ¹²); " in the Name of His Father " He came (5⁴³) and performed the "works" which were His witness (10²⁵). This "Name" He "manifested" (17⁶), and " made known " (17²⁶) to His disciples. He prayed the Father to " glorify " His Name (12²⁸).

To primitive Hebrew thought the name had an intimate and mysterious connexion with him whose name it was; and this idea lies behind the widely spread practice of reciting the names of foes for magical purposes. The name was the expression of the personality. Thus " the Name of Yahweh " came to signify the revelation of the Being of God, exhibiting itself in Power and Providence,[1] and it is frequently used thus in the O.T. (cf. Ps. 20¹, Prov. 18¹⁰). This usage is carried into the N.T. (Lk. 1⁴⁹ ; and see notes on 1¹² 17¹¹).

Thus " I am come in the Name of my Father " does not only mean " I am come as His representative, having been sent by Him," although it includes this (see 7²⁸ 8⁴²); but it conveys the idea that the Incarnate Son reveals the Father in His character and power. Cf. 14²⁶.

καὶ οὐ λαμβάνετέ με, "but you do not receive me," καί being used as an adversative conjunction, where we would expect ἀλλά or καίτοι (see on 1¹⁰). The Fourth Gospel is truly described as in one aspect "the Gospel of the Rejection"; cf. 1¹¹ 3¹¹· ³² 12³⁷.

ἐὰν ἄλλος ἔλθῃ κτλ., " if another shall come in his own name, him you will receive." Abbott (*Diat.* 2677) calls attention to the use of ἄλλος rather than ἕτερος: " if another come (professing to be of the same kind as myself), etc." Cf. 2 Cor. 11⁴ ἄλλον Ἰησοῦν. Such a pseudo-Christ would appear only "in his own name," *i.e.* not representing or revealing the name and the nature of God, as Jesus did.

Schmiedel [2] finds here (so too Hilgenfeld and Pfleiderer) an allusion to the rising of Barcochba about 134 A.D., which led to the extinction of the Jewish State. On this hypothesis, the Fourth Gospel (for there is no sign that this verse is an inter-

[1] Cf. Kautzsch in *D.B.*, extra p. 641.   [2] *E.B.* 2551.

πιστεῦσαι, δόξαν παρὰ ἀλλήλων λαμβάνοντες, καὶ τὴν δόξαν τὴν
παρὰ τοῦ μόνου Θεοῦ οὐ ζητεῖτε; 45. μὴ δοκεῖτε ὅτι ἐγὼ κατη-
polation) would be later in date than Barcochba. But the
words are quite general in their reference, and are comparable
with Mk. 13⁶· ²² (cf. Mt. 24⁵· ²⁴): "Many shall come in my
Name . . . there shall arise false Christs and false prophets."
This is one of the few passages in which Jn. reproduces sayings
of Jesus comparable with the Synoptic predictions of the last
things (see Introd., pp. cxxix, clix). Bousset [1] finds an allusion
to the coming of Antichrist (cf. 2 Thess. 2⁸⁻¹²), but the context
does not call for any definite reference to the success of false
Messiahs, of whom many have appeared.

44. The cause of the Jews' unbelief is traced here to the
desire for popular applause and favour. "All their works they
do for to be seen of men" is a judgment on the Pharisees found
in Mt. 23⁵. "They loved the glory of men more than the
glory of God" is Jn.'s verdict about some who hesitated to
acknowledge their belief in Jesus (12⁴³). But the saying
recorded in this verse goes deeper. Faith, Jesus seems
to say, is impossible in any vital sense for the man who
measures himself only by human standards. He who has
that vivid sense of the unseen, which is faith, instinctively
seeks in his conversation and conduct to win the approval
of God, in comparison with which nothing else seems to be
important.

πῶς δύνασθε ὑμεῖς πιστεῦσαι, δόξαν παρὰ ἀλλήλων λαμβάνοντες
κτλ.; ὑμεῖς is emphatic: "How can such as *you* believe, who
think more of the honour that comes from men, than of that
which God can bestow?" The true Jew, as Paul says, is on
the other hand one "whose praise is not of men but of God"
(Rom. 2²⁹). Cf. the words of Mordecai's prayer: "I did this
that I might not prefer the glory (δόξα) of man to the glory of
God" (Esth. 13¹⁴).

For πιστεύειν used absolutely, the object of faith not being
expressed, see on 1⁷.

καὶ τὴν δόξαν τὴν παρὰ τοῦ μόνου θεοῦ οὐ ζητεῖτε. BW and
(in one place) Origen omit θεοῦ, but it is certainly part of the
true text. The archetypes would have had ΜΟΝΟΥΘΥΟΥ, from
which ΘΥ could very readily have been dropped.

The only δόξα worth having is that which comes from "the
Only God" (cf. 1¹⁴). For the phrase ὁ μόνος θεός, see 2 Kings
19¹⁵· ¹⁹, Ps. 86¹⁰, Isa. 37²⁰, 2 Macc. 7³⁷, 4 Macc. 2²³ (and cf.
Jn. 17³, Rom. 16²⁷, Jude²⁵, Rev. 15⁴): the Jews were convinced
monotheists. It is not upon the unity of God that Jesus here

[1] *The Antichrist Legend*, p. 133.

γορήσω ὑμῶν πρὸς τὸν Πατέρα· ἔστιν ὁ κατηγορῶν ὑμῶν Μωϋσῆς, εἰς ὃν ὑμεῖς ἠλπίκατε. 46. εἰ γὰρ ἐπιστεύετε Μωϋσεῖ, ἐπιστεύετε

lays stress, but upon the fact that there is no other worthy Fount of honour. Cf. 8⁵⁴.

45. For μὴ δοκεῖτε, δοκεῖτε always having reference in Jn. to a *mistaken* opinion, see on v. 39 above.

μὴ δοκεῖτε ὅτι ἐγὼ κατηγορήσω ὑμῶν πρὸς τὸν πατέρα. It would appear that some of His hearers were beginning to be uneasy. He *might* be what He claimed to be, and if that happened to be so, would not His accusation of them to God be hard to rebut? So, in answer to these thoughts, expressed or unexpressed, He bids them be sure that His office at the Great Assize will not be that of *Prosecutor*. It has been said earlier in the chapter (v. 27) that He will be the *Judge*; but upon that no stress is laid here (cf. 12⁴⁷· ⁴⁸; and see on 3¹⁷).

Their prosecutor, or accuser, will be the person whom they expected to be their advocate, *sc.* Moses. Their national claim was that they were disciples of Moses (9²⁸; cf. 7¹⁹), and Moses had given them the law of the Sabbath, the breach of which by Jesus had initiated this controversy (v. 16). Surely, Moses would defend their cause. But, on the contrary, they are told: ἔστιν ὁ κατηγορῶν ὑμῶν, Μωϋσῆς, εἰς ὃν ὑμεῖς ἠλπίκατε (cf. Deut. 31²¹).

This verse has all the marks of historicity. No one would think of inventing a denial by Jesus of the suggestion that He was to be the *Accuser* of the Jews at the Last Judgment. But it is quite natural in the context in which it appears.

εἰς ὃν ὑμεῖς ἠλπίκατε, "on whom you have set your hope," *i.e.* in whom you hope, *in quo uos speratis*, as the Vulgate correctly renders. ἐλπίζειν does not occur again in Jn., but the use here of the perfect tense to indicate that the hope continues in the present and is not merely an emotion of the past, has parallels at 1 Cor. 15¹⁹, 2 Cor. 1¹⁰, 1 Tim. 4¹⁰ 5⁵ 6¹⁷. The aor. ἤλπισα occurs only twice in the N.T., *sc.* 2 Cor. 8⁵, 1 Pet. 1¹³, which is remarkable, as in the LXX the perfect ἤλπικα is never used, but *always* the aorist (*e.g.* Ps. 7¹ 16¹ etc.). Again, the constr. ἐλπίζειν εἴς τινα is rare in the LXX (cf. Ps. 119¹¹⁴ 145¹⁵, Isa. 51⁵), where the prep. ἐπί is nearly always used. In the N.T., too, we generally have ἐπί, but εἰς in Acts 26⁷, 2 Cor. 1¹⁰, 1 Pet. 3⁵. Thus the only exact parallel in the Greek Bible to the phrase in this verse is εἰς ὃν ἠλπίκαμεν of 2 Cor. 1¹⁰, a sound Greek construction.[1]

---

[1] Abbott (*Diat.* 2442–2443, 2473) traces the Johannine perfect to Hebrew influence, and says that we should have expected the aor. or the pres. rather than the perf. at 5⁴⁵. But, on the contrary, the

ἂν ἐμοί· περὶ γὰρ ἐμοῦ ἐκεῖνος ἔγραψεν. 47. εἰ δὲ τοῖς ἐκείνου γράμμασιν οὐ πιστεύετε, πῶς τοῖς ἐμοῖς ῥήμασιν πιστεύσετε;

46. εἰ γὰρ ἐπιστεύετε Μωϋσεῖ κτλ., "if you believed Moses, you would believe me," the imperfect tenses indicating a continuing belief.

περὶ γὰρ ἐμοῦ ἐκεῖνος ἔγραψεν, "for it was of me that he wrote" (cf. 12⁴¹). Deut. 18¹⁸· ¹⁹ is cited as Messianic in Acts 3²², and it is regarded by Cyprian (*Test.* i. 18) as the passage to which reference is specially made here. It was one of the first O.T. *testimonia* to be claimed by Christians. At 3¹⁴, the brazen serpent is mentioned as a type of Christ; and at 8⁵⁶ reference is made to Abraham's prevision of Christ's work Cf. Lk. 24²⁷, when no doubt many other types and prophecies were explained. It is probable that Jesus adduced specific passages in support of His statement that Moses had written of Him, but we cannot tell what they were. Only a summary of His argument is before us.

47. εἰ δὲ τοῖς ἐκείνου γράμμασιν κτλ., "but if you do not believe his writings, how will you believe my words?" There is a double contrast, between ἐκείνου and ἐμοῖς, and between γράμμασιν and ῥήμασιν. The argument, If you do not believe Moses, how will you believe Christ? would not have appealed to a Christian of any age; but it was addressed here to Jews, for whom the authority of Moses was the greatest they knew (cf. Lk. 16³¹), and in such a context was weighty. Here, again, it is plain that Jn. is reproducing with fidelity the kind of argument which Jesus used in Jewish controversy. Upon the contrast between γράμματα, "writings," and ῥήματα, "sayings," no special stress is laid, although these γράμματα were reckoned as ἱερὰ γράμματα (2 Tim. 3¹⁵) and as entitled therefore to special reverence. If Jesus were no other than an ordinary Rabbi, it would be obvious that his authority as a teacher would be far inferior to that of the sacred writings, consecrated by a long tradition.

The ῥήματα of Jesus are mentioned again 6⁶³· ⁶⁸ 8²⁰ 12⁴⁷· ⁴⁸ 14¹⁰ 15⁷ 17⁸ (see on 3³⁴ above).

The constr. εἰ . . . οὐ, as an undivided phrase, is noted by Abbott (*Diat.* 2256) as occurring again in Jn. only at 10³⁷.

Further argument with the Jewish doctors (VII. 15–24)

VII. 15. We have given above (see Introd., p. xix) the reasons for taking vv. 15–24 of c. 7 as following directly on 5⁴⁷.

perf. is right here and the aor. would be wrong, as it is wrong in the LXX often. See also Field, *in loc.*

VII. 15. ἐθαύμαζον οὖν οἱ Ἰουδαῖοι λέγοντες Πῶς οὗτος γράμματα οἶδεν μὴ μεμαθηκώς; 16. ἀπεκρίθη οὖν αὐτοῖς Ἰησοῦς καὶ
εἶπεν Ἡ ἐμὴ διδαχὴ οὐκ ἔστιν ἐμὴ ἀλλὰ τοῦ πέμψαντός με· 17. ἐάν

Jesus has appealed to the γράμματα of Moses as establishing
His claims, and had probably (see on 5⁴⁷) quoted specific
passages, commenting on them as He went along. This
amazed the Jewish leaders, who had thought that such learning
was confined to those trained in the Rabbinical schools, and
they had never heard of Jesus as a disciple of any prominent
Rabbi.

ἐθαύμαζον οὖν, " So they began to express wonder " ;
cf. v. 46 and Mk. 12¹⁷, Lk. 2⁴⁷ 4²².

πῶς οὗτος γράμματα οἶδεν μὴ μεμαθηκώς; It was not so
much the *wisdom* of His words that astonished them as His
knowledge of the Jewish writings, which probably included
the Rabbinical traditions that had gathered round the Old
Testament, as well as the Old Testament itself.   In Isa. 29¹²
μὴ ἐπιστάμενος γράμματα means a man who cannot read,
an "illiterate."   For ἀγράμματος in Acts 4¹³, see Introd.,
p. xxxvi.   But in the present passage, μὴ μεμαθηκώς seems to
mean rather "not having been the μαθητής of a recognised
teacher."   The tradition of His scribbling upon the ground
[8⁶] shows that Jesus was not illiterate in the strict sense; and
it is unlikely that this would have been suggested by the Jewish
Rabbis who had engaged in controversy with Him.

16. Ἡ ἐμὴ διδαχὴ οὐκ ἔστιν ἐμή κτλ.   Here only does Jesus
call His message διδαχή, a "teaching"; it is a significant
word, as He is now dealing with the professional διδάσκαλοι.
That His teaching is not His own, but the Father's, is repeated
often (8²⁸ 12⁴⁹ 14¹⁰· ²⁴) ; and this has already been said in effect
at 5³⁰.   διδαχή occurs again in Jn. only at 18¹⁹; cf. 2 Jn.⁹· ¹⁰.

The answer of Jesus to the Jews' objection that He had
never learnt from a recognised Rabbi is remarkable.   He does
not say (which might seem to us the natural answer) that
He needed no Master.   Indeed, Mk. reports that it was a
feature of His teaching to the multitudes that it was given
" with authority, and not as the scribes " (Mk. 1²²), *i.e.* that He
appealed in His popular teaching to no Rabbinical precedents;
and the Synoptic discourses sufficiently illustrate this.   But in
cc. 5 and 7¹⁵⁻²⁴ we have the report of a long-drawn-out argument with the Rabbis, and it is conducted throughout (see on
5³¹) in the style of the Jewish schools.   If Jesus had said, in
reply to their implied question " Whose disciple are you ? "
that He was no man's disciple, but that He spoke of His own
authority, they would at once have told Him that He was an

τις θέλῃ τὸ θέλημα αὐτοῦ ποιεῖν, γνώσεται περὶ τῆς διδαχῆς, πότερον ἐκ τοῦ Θεοῦ ἐστιν ἢ ἐγὼ ἀπ᾽ ἐμαυτοῦ λαλῶ. 18. ὁ ἀφ᾽ ἑαυτοῦ λαλῶν τὴν δόξαν τὴν ἰδίαν ζητεῖ· ὁ δὲ ζητῶν τὴν δόξαν τοῦ πέμψαντος αὐτόν,

impostor and adventurer. But, exactly as at 5³¹, He follows their line of thought. He does not claim to be *self-taught*, which would only have aroused contemptuous indignation; but He claims that His teacher was the Father who had sent Him, as He had said so often before (cf. especially 5³⁶⁻³⁸).

17. ἐάν τις θέλῃ τὸ θέλημα αὐτοῦ ποιεῖν κτλ., "If any man set his will (θέλῃ, is expressive of deliberate purpose) to do His will, he shall know of the doctrine, etc." The Synoptic form of this saying is to the effect that it is only the man who does God's will who can enter into the kingdom of heaven (Mt. 7²¹). That right conduct is a necessary preliminary to accurate belief about Divine things, and conversely that the cause of unbelief is often a moral cause, are propositions which are repeated frequently in Jn. They are specially pressed in this controversy with the Jewish leaders. Jesus had claimed that He sought, not His own will, but τὸ θέλημα τοῦ πέμψαντός με (5³⁰); and He goes on to suggest that it is just because this could not be said of the Rabbis that they had failed to accept His Divine mission. It is their moral nature that is at fault (5³⁸·⁴²). Cf. for similar teaching 8³¹·³²·⁴⁷ 14²¹; it is all summed up in the tremendous assertion, "Every one that is of the truth heareth my voice" (18³⁷). Cf. Ps. 25¹⁴.

πότερον ἐκ τοῦ θεοῦ ἐστιν ἢ ἐγώ κτλ. The classical constr. πότερον . . . ἢ . . . occurs only here in the N.T. πότερον is found again in the Greek Bible only in the Book of Job (cf., *e.g.*, Job 7¹²).

ἐκ θεοῦ is the reading of אD, but BLTWΘ have ἐκ τοῦ θεοῦ, which is the regular Johannine form (1 Jn. 4¹·²·³·⁴·⁶·⁷).

That Jesus did not "speak from Himself" is repeated 12⁴⁹ 14¹⁰, aɪ.ɪ it is also said of the Spirit, "He shall not speak from Himself" (16¹³). Jesus, again and again, repudiates the idea that He does or says anything apart from the Father (cf. 5³⁰ 7²⁸; and see 8²⁸). The repeated disclaimer of *originality* for His teaching is foreign to modern habits of thought. But originality, or departure from precedent, or the idea that there is any merit in being self-taught, were all equally distasteful to Jewish scholasticism.

18. ὁ ἀφ᾽ ἑαυτοῦ λαλῶν τὴν δόξαν τὴν ἰδίαν ζητεῖ κτλ. He returns to what He has said at 5⁴¹ (where see note), and He repeats it again 8⁵⁰·⁵⁴. The contrast is between the teacher who represents himself as the fount of knowledge, and him who speaks as a herald and ambassador of a superior from whom

οὗτος ἀληθής ἐστιν καὶ ἀδικία ἐν αὐτῷ οὐκ ἔστιν. 19. οὐ Μωϋσῆς ἔδωκεν ὑμῖν τὸν νόμον; καὶ οὐδεὶς ἐξ ὑμῶν ποιεῖ τὸν νόμον. τί με ζητεῖτε ἀποκτεῖναι; 20. ἀπεκρίθη ὁ ὄχλος Δαιμόνιον ἔχεις· τίς σε

he has what he has. The former seeks his own honour (for δόξα means "honour" here, see on 1¹⁴); the latter is only concerned to proclaim the truth that he has received, and in proclaiming it he seeks to bring honour to him from whom he received it. The former, therefore, may be under suspicion of false teaching; but the latter has no self-interest to further, οὗτος ἀληθής ἐστιν. There is no ἀδικία, "unrighteousness," in him, such as is several times contrasted by Paul with "truth" (Rom. 2⁸, 1 Cor. 13⁶, 2 Thess. 2¹²).

For the emphatic use of οὗτος, cf. 6⁴⁶.

The special form of ἀδικία with which Jesus had been charged was that of Sabbath-breaking (5¹⁰·¹⁸), and He now brings the discussion back to this, by making a direct attack on His Jewish critics. They blamed Him for a technical breach of the Sabbath, but it was their own practice to condone such breaches in special circumstances (v. 23). His argument from v. 19 to v. 24 is *ad hominem.*

Ps. 40⁸ provides a parallel for the sequence of thought, vv. 17–19, which perhaps is fortuitous:

τοῦ ποιῆσαι τὸ θέλημά σου, ὁ θεός μου, ἐβουλήθην,
καὶ τὸν νόμον σου ἐν μεσῷ τῆς καρδίας μου.

In Ps. 40⁸ τὸν νόμον σου in the second line corresponds, after the fashion of Hebrew poetry, to τὸ θελημά σου in the first line. The argument, implied but not explicitly stated, of vv. 17–19, is that if a man does not will to do God's will, he has not God's law in his heart, and does not keep it.

19. οὐ Μωϋσῆς ἔδωκεν (so BD; אLΤΓΔΝWΘ have δέδωκεν) ὑμῖν τὸν νόμον; Moses gave the Law in all its bearings for a Jew (see on 1¹⁹), but here the reference is specially to the Mosaic law of the Sabbath (v. 23). Jesus turns their appeal to the authority of Moses against themselves, as at 5⁴⁶.

καὶ (καί being used for καίτοι, as at 5³⁸·⁴⁰; see on 1¹⁰) οὐδεὶς ἐξ ὑμῶν (cf. 16⁵ 17¹² : Mk. 11¹, Lk. 14²⁴ preferring to omit ἐκ in similar constructions; cf. 13²⁸ 21¹², and see on 1⁴⁰) ποιεῖ τὸν νόμον. No one, He urges, keeps the Mosaic law of the Sabbath with minute scrupulosity in all circumstances, and He goes on to mention an admitted exception (v. 23).

τί με ζητεῖτε ἀποκτεῖναι; See on 5¹⁸, where it has been recorded, ἐζήτουν αὐτὸν οἱ Ἰουδαῖοι ἀποκτεῖναι.

20. ἀπεκρίθη ὁ ὄχλος κτλ. The crowd had been listening with eagerness to the controversial discussion between Jesus

ζητεῖ ἀποκτεῖναι; 21. ἀπεκρίθη Ἰησοῦς καὶ εἶπεν αὐτοῖς ᵃἘν ἔργον ἐποίησα καὶ πάντες θαυμάζετε 22. διὰ τοῦτο. Μωϋσῆς δέδωκεν ὑμῖν

and the Rabbis (οἱ Ἰουδαῖοι, v. 15); and they interrupt now to disclaim the idea that there was any thought of killing Him. This is a lifelike touch. It was not the "people," but the "Jews," who had begun the plot; the people knew nothing of it.

δαιμόνιον ἔχεις. The same thing was said of John the Baptist, as an explanation of his asceticism (Mt. 11[18]); and later on, Jn. records that the Jewish leaders, or some of them, accused Jesus of being possessed with a demon (8[48. 49] 10[20]; cf. Mk. 3[22]). But here it is the people who say "Thou hast a demon," meaning not to impute moral blame but mental infirmity. It is a well-known sign of insanity to believe that other people are in league against one. "Who seeks to kill you?" It is only your disordered imagination which makes you suspect it (cf. Mk. 3[21]). See Introd., p. clxxvii.

21. Jesus does not answer the insulting suggestion that He is out of His mind. He goes back to His statement that no Jew keeps the Sabbatical law after a fashion which admits of no exception.

ἐν ἔργον ἐποίησα καὶ πάντες θαυμάζετε. This has generally been interpreted as meaning, "I did one miracle, and you all marvel." But such a pronouncement is not in harmony with the context. Nothing has been said throughout 5[1-47] or 7[15-24] to indicate that the observers, whether the simple folk or the Jewish leaders, had seen anything extraordinary in the cure of the impotent man, or had expressed any wonder. Indeed, 5[20] suggests that "greater works" would be necessary, if their wonder was to be aroused. Nor, again, would an appeal made by Jesus at this point to the miraculous nature of what He had done be apposite to the argument which He is developing. That argument has to do with one point only, sc. His alleged breach of the Sabbath; and it would be no answer to the charge of breaking the Sabbath to tell His critics that what He had done had been miraculous, and to remind them that they had been astonished.

We have seen above (5[20]) that Jn. frequently speaks of the wonderful works of Jesus as His ἔργα; but there is no instance of a specific miracle being referred to as ἔργον in the singular (as σημεῖον is used, 4[54]), unless 10[32] be regarded as an exception: πολλὰ καλὰ ἔργα ἔδειξα ὑμῖν . . . διὰ ποῖον αὐτῶν ἔργον λιθάζετέ με; ἔργον in the sing. occurs again in Jn. only at 4[34] 17[4] (of the work which the Father prescribes to the Son) and at 6[29] (of the work which God desires of man).

Furthermore, stress is laid here on the singularity of the
" work " that has been " done " by Jesus. " I did *one* work."
But in the course of the preceding argument He had appealed
to the " works," in the plural, which bore witness to His claims
(5³⁶, where see note). There would be no point in now singling
out one ἔργον only, as having excited wonder because of its
extraordinary character; and it would be surprising if that
one were singled out, of which it is not recorded that it caused
any astonishment.

Accordingly we render ἓν ἔργον ἐποίησα, "I did one work,"
sc. of labour, and interpret it as having reference to the matter
originally in dispute, *sc.* that He had broken the Sabbath.[1]
The law was, πᾶς ὃς ποιήσει ἔργον τῇ ἡμέρᾳ τῇ ἑβδόμῃ, θανατω-
θήσεται (Ex. 31¹⁵ 35²). Jesus admits, in terms, that He has
broken this law on the particular occasion to which His critics
refer. ἓν ἔργον ἐποίησα κτλ., "I did one work," *sc.* on the
Sabbath, " and you are all astonished," θαυμάζειν indicating
that they were puzzled, as at 3⁷ 4²⁷. Their astonishment was
not caused by the extraordinary nature of the cure, but by
the circumstance that Jesus had ventured to cure the man on
a Sabbath day.

We take θαυμάζετε with διὰ τοῦτο which follows: "you are
all astonished by this." Cf. ἐθαύμασεν διὰ τὴν ἀπιστίαν αὐτῶν
(Mk. 6⁶), where the reason of astonishment is indicated by διά
with the acc., as here. διὰ τοῦτο is often used by Jn. in relation
to what follows (see on 5¹⁶); while the more common usage,
in accordance with which it relates to what has gone before, is
also adopted several times in the Gospel (see on 9²³), although
there is no other instance in Jn. of διὰ τοῦτο coming at the end
of a sentence.

The tendency of the versions is to take διὰ τοῦτο as beginning the next sentence: " Therefore Moses, etc." But, in
that case, διὰ τοῦτο is difficult to interpret, and involves a very
elliptical construction. It would mean " For this very cause,
Moses gave you the ordinance of circumcision, knowing that
it would conflict with the strict law of the Sabbath; *sc.*
in order that he might teach you that the Sabbatical precepts
admit of exceptions and are not always to be enforced literally."
This would give a tolerable sense, but it strains the force of
διὰ τοῦτο too far, and introduces a very subtle reason (not
suggested elsewhere) for the rule that circumcision must always
be on the eighth day after birth. It is simpler to take πάντες
θαυμάζετε διὰ τοῦτο as one sentence, "You are all astonished at
this act of mine."

---

[1] Wendt (*Gospel according to St. John*, p. 64 *n.*) takes this view.
Cf. ἐργάζεσθαι in 5¹⁷ and Lk 13¹⁴.

τὴν περιτομήν,—οὐχ ὅτι ἐκ τοῦ Μωϋσέως ἐστὶν ἀλλ' ἐκ τῶν πατέρων, —καὶ ἐν σαββάτῳ περιτέμνετε ἄνθρωπον. 23. εἰ περιτομὴν λαμβάνει ἄνθρωπος ἐν σαββάτῳ ἵνα μὴ λυθῇ ὁ νόμος Μωϋσέως, ἐμοὶ χολᾶτε ὅτι ὅλον ἄνθρωπον ὑγιῆ ἐποίησα ἐν σαββάτῳ; 24. μὴ κρίνετε κατ' ὄψιν, ἀλλὰ τὴν δικαίαν κρίσιν κρίνατε.

א* omits διὰ τοῦτο, thus cutting the knot of the difficulty by treating the words as a later gloss.

22. Μωϋσῆς δέδωκεν ὑμῖν τὴν περιτομήν. περιτομή does not occur elsewhere in the Gospels; but we have περιτέμνειν (Lk. 1⁵⁹ 2²¹). The ordinance of circumcision on the eighth day after birth is re-enacted, Lev. 12³.

οὐχ ὅτι ἐκ τοῦ Μωϋσέως ἐστὶν ἀλλ' ἐκ τῶν πατέρων. This is an evangelistic comment on the words of Jesus, interpolated exactly as at 12⁶, οὐκ ὅτι . . . ἀλλ' (see Introd., p. xxxiv). The covenant of circumcision went back to Abraham (Gen. 17¹⁰ 21⁴, Acts 7⁸). For τῶν πατέρων, see on 6⁵⁸.

καὶ ἐν σαββάτῳ κτλ. B om. ἐν, but ins. אDLTΘW (cf. 5¹⁶).

Even if the eighth day after the birth of the child fell on a Sabbath, the act of circumcision was performed. Lightfoot (*Hor. Hebr.* in loc.) cites the Rabbinical rule: "Rabbi Akiba saith, 'Work that may be done on the eve of the Sabbath must not be done on the Sabbath, but circumcision . . . may be done on the Sabbath.'"[1]

Justin uses the argument of the text in the *Dialogue with Trypho* (§ 27), appealing to the injunction to circumcise on the Sabbath.

23. εἰ περιτομήν κτλ. "If a man receives circumcision on a sabbath, in order that the law of Moses (*sc.* the law relating to circumcision, Lev. 12³) may not be broken, are you angry with me because on a Sabbath I made the whole man healthy?" A somewhat similar idea appears in the Rabbinical writings: "Circumcision, which has to do with one member only, breaks the Sabbath; how much more the whole body of a man?"[2] The contrast is between the treatment of one member, and of the whole body (ὅλον ἄνθρωπον). If the lesser thing is permitted, why not the greater? The argument is comparable with that of Mt. 12¹¹, Lk. 13¹⁵, by which a technical breach of the Sabbath is defended, but is unlike that of 5¹⁷, where see the note.

For λύειν, of "breaking" a law, see on 5¹⁸.

ὁ νόμος Μωϋσέως is a comprehensive term for the whole Jewish law, or for a particular enactment: cf. Lk. 2²² 24⁴⁴, Acts 15⁵ (this passage referring to the law of circumcision), 1 Cor. 9⁹ etc. λύειν is used at 5¹⁸ of breaking the law of the Sabbath. The word ὑγιής goes back to 5⁹· ¹⁴.

---

[1] *Shabb.* fol. 130.   [2] *Joma,* f. 85, quoted by Wetstein.

VII. 1. Καὶ μετὰ ταῦτα περιεπάτει ὁ Ἰησοῦς ἐν τῇ Γαλιλαίᾳ· οὐ γὰρ ἤθελεν ἐν τῇ Ἰουδαίᾳ περιπατεῖν, ὅτι ἐζήτουν αὐτὸν οἱ Ἰουδαῖοι

24. μὴ κρίνετε κατ᾽ ὄψιν, "do not judge by looks," *i.e.* superficially, the too frequent weakness of the Pharisees, which is rebuked again ὑμεῖς κατὰ τὴν σάρκα κρίνετε (8¹⁵). Cf. Isa. 11³ οὐ κατὰ τὴν δόξαν κρινεῖ, and 2 Cor. 10⁷. ὄψις occurs again in the N.T. only at 11⁴⁴ and Rev. 1¹⁶, and then in the sense of " face."

ἀλλὰ τὴν δικαίαν κρίσιν κρίνατε, "but judge righteous judgment," *i.e.* be fair. The expression is used of the judgments of God, Tob. 3². Cf. also Zech. 7⁹ κρίμα δίκαιον κρίνατε. The constr. κρίσιν κρίνειν is common (Isa. 11⁴) and is also classical (Plato, *Rep.* 360 E).

אΓΔΘ have κρίσιν κρίνατε (the authoritative aorist imperative ; see on 2⁵), but BDLTNW give κρίνετε.

This is the last word of the controversy which arose out of the healing of the impotent man at Bethesda, *sc.* 5¹⁻⁴⁷ 7¹⁵⁻²⁴; and naturally, the Jewish leaders were indignant. Cf. 7¹.

Retreat to Galilee ; His brethren urge Jesus to show Himself at Jerusalem (VII. 1-9)

VII. 1. καὶ μετὰ ταῦτα περιεπάτει κτλ. So אᶜᵃBC*LΓΔΘ, but אC²DW with most syrr. latt. om. καί, which may be an editorial addition. N has καὶ περιεπάτει μετ᾽ αὐτῶν ὁ Ἰησ. κτλ., and the rec. also goes wrong with καὶ περιεπάτει ὁ Ἰησ. μετὰ ταῦτα κτλ.

μετὰ ταῦτα is the beginning of a new section of the narrative, and reasons have been given (Introd., p. xix) for placing 7¹⁻¹⁴ in direct sequence to cc. 5, 7¹⁵⁻²⁴.

After the severe rebukes which Jesus had addressed to the Rabbis, already exasperated by the breach of the Sabbath and His lofty claims (5¹⁸), it was natural that He should withdraw from the neighbourhood of Jerusalem for a while. He had gone up to Jerusalem for the Passover, and after that He healed the impotent man (5⁸). Then controversy ensued, and in 5¹⁹⁻⁴⁷ 7¹⁵⁻²⁴ we have a summary of the main points on which stress was laid, the discussions probably extending over some days. If we suppose that He left Jerusalem about the month of May, there is time for a ministry of four or five months in Galilee, before He returned to Jerusalem for the Feast of Tabernacles at the end of September. Jn. gives no details of this Galilæan ministry, but there is room in these months for many of the incidents recorded in the Synoptic Gospels as having taken place in Galilee (see on v. 3).

ἀποκτεῖναι. 2. ἦν δὲ ἐγγὺς ἡ ἑορτὴ τῶν Ἰουδαίων ἡ σκηνοπηγία.
3. εἶπον οὖν πρὸς αὐτὸν οἱ ἀδελφοὶ αὐτοῦ Μετάβηθι ἐντεῦθεν καὶ

The narrative of the events in Jerusalem after Jesus went up to the Feast of Tabernacles (v. 10) is full of movement and of local colour. Presumably (see on 5¹) the Twelve attended the Feast of Tabernacles, and were again in the company of Jesus after He went up.

περιεπάτει. This is the natural word for the itinerant ministry of a Rabbi accompanied by His disciples; cf. 6⁶⁶ 11⁵⁴. (For the larger meaning of περιπατεῖν, see on 8¹².) Jesus was " walking in Galilee," because the Jews, as has just been said (7¹⁹), were seeking His life.

For the phrase ἐζήτουν αὐτὸν οἱ Ἰουδαῖοι ἀποκτεῖναι, see on 5¹⁸.

2. ἦν δὲ ἐγγὺς ἡ ἑορτή κτλ. This was the Feast of Tabernacles of the year 28 A.D. See on 5¹.

The Feast of Tabernacles (σκηνοπηγία) was originally a Feast of Ingathering or a Harvest Festival, and was not at first held on a fixed date, but " at the year's end " (Ex. 34²²), according to the time when the harvest was gathered. The Deuteronomic Code calls it " the Feast of Tabernacles " (Deut. 16¹³), and prescribes that it is to be kept for seven days. The reason for its name assigned in the Priest's Code is that " I made the children of Israel to dwell in booths, when I brought them out of the land of Egypt " (Lev. 23⁴³). In the same Code the annual date is fixed; it was to begin on the fifteenth day of the seventh month (Tishri), going on for seven days (Lev. 23³⁴). That is, it was held at the end of September or the beginning of October. In Num. 29³⁵ an eighth day of observance appears, on which was to be " a solemn assembly," and we find this eighth day observed in post-exilic times (Neh. 8¹⁸, 2 Macc. 10⁶). Josephus, who mentions the eighth day (Antt. III. x. 4), calls this feast ἑορτὴ σφόδρα παρὰ τοῖς Ἑβραίοις ἁγιωτάτη καὶ μεγίστη (Antt. VIII. iv. 1), thus marking its important place in Jewish life, it being, pre-eminently, the Feast of the Jews. For the ritual observed, see on 7³⁷ and 8¹².

For the phrase ἡ ἑορτὴ τῶν Ἰουδαίων, see on 2¹³.

3. For the " brethren of Jesus," see on 2¹². They were older than He was, and this may explain their venturing to offer Him advice as to His conduct. The discussion between them and Him, which is reported vv. 3–8, could only have been known to one who was in intimate relations with the family; and there could be no motive for setting it down in narrative, if it had not actually taken place.

μετάβηθι ἐντεῦθεν, " depart hence ": μεταβαίνειν is used

ὕπαγε εἰς τὴν Ἰουδαίαν, ἵνα καὶ οἱ μαθηταί σου θεωρήσουσιν τὰ ἔργα σου ἃ ποιεῖς· 4. οὐδεὶς γάρ τι ἐν κρυπτῷ ποιεῖ καὶ ζητεῖ αὐτὸς ἐν

13¹ of departing from this world, and metaphorically 5²⁴, 1 Jn. 3¹⁴.

καὶ ὕπαγε (a favourite word with Jn.; see on v. 33) εἰς τὴν Ἰουδαίαν, ἵνα καὶ οἱ μαθηταί σου θεωρήσουσιν τὰ ἔργα σου ἃ ποιεῖς. The advice seems to have been ironical, for they go on to express doubts about His alleged "works," saying εἰ ταῦτα ποιεῖς, "*if* you do such things." The suggestion is that the rumour of these ἔργα was confined to Galilee, and that if He were to establish His reputation in Judæa, it would be desirable that His disciples there should have an opportunity of seeing what He could do.

We have already heard of many disciples in Judæa (2²³ 4¹); indeed, it was because their number excited the jealousy of the Pharisees that He had left Judæa on a former occasion (4³). But there was little of miracle there on His last visit; the cure of the impotent man is not described as a "sign," and it had attracted attention rather because it had been wrought on a Sabbath day, than because of its marvellousness (5⁵ᶠ·; and cf. 7²¹, where see note). The "works" to which the brethren of Jesus make reference here are those of Galilee, perhaps the Miracle of Cana (2¹ᶠ·) or the Healing of the Noble-man's Son and other sick folk (4⁴⁶ᶠ· 6²), or the Feeding of the Five Thousand (6⁵ᶠ·), or more probably healings wrought between His departure from Jerusalem and His going up again for the Feast of Tabernacles (vv. 1, 14), *i.e.* during the summer of the year 28. Nothing is told about them by Jn., but the words τὰ ἔργα σου ἃ ποιεῖς, "the works which you *are doing*," suggest that the reference is not to anything that He had done months before the date of the conversation, but to quite recent events. And, as has been suggested on v. 1, some of the Galilæan miracles recorded by the Synoptists may be placed at this period in the ministry as narrated by Jn.

The allusion to the μαθηταί here cannot be to the Twelve, for they had been witnesses of many of the wonderful things that Jesus had done, and were already convinced of the truth of His claims. Nor can the allusion be to the Galilæan disciples who were disheartened by the difficulty of His teaching and left Him on a former occasion (6⁶⁶), for they would not be in the way of seeing miracles wrought at Jerusalem, whither His brethren advised Him to transfer His activities. We conclude, then, that the μαθηταί whom His brethren suggested He should confirm in their allegiance by displays of His power, were those in Judæa and at Jerusalem. If, indeed, He was to succeed

παρρησίᾳ εἶναι. εἰ ταῦτα ποιεῖς, φανέρωσον σεαυτὸν τῷ κόσμῳ.
5. οὐδὲ γὰρ οἱ ἀδελφοὶ αὐτοῦ ἐπίστευον εἰς αὐτόν. 6. λέγει οὖν

in the Mission for which He claimed the highest sanctions,
He *must* convince Jerusalem. And His brethren were right
in the view they took of this. They did not accept His claims,
as yet at any rate (v. 5), but they understood clearly that it was
at the Holy City that they must either be proved or disproved.

θεωρήσουσιν. So אᶜB*DLNW, although ἵνα with the future
indic. is rare in Jn. (cf. 17²). א* has θεωροῦσιν, and ΓΔΘ read
θεωρήσωσιν.

B places σου before τὰ ἔργα, but om. א *D.

4. The principle laid down by the brethren of Jesus is
sound, *sc.* that no one who seeks public recognition can afford to
keep his deeds a secret. οὐδεὶς γάρ τι ἐν κρυπτῷ ποιεῖ καὶ ζητεῖ
αὐτὸς ἐν παρρησίᾳ εἶναι, " No one does anything in secret, and
(at the same time) himself seeks to be in the public eye."

καί is used like καίτοι (see on 1¹⁰).

For αὐτός BD*W have αὐτό, through misunderstanding.
παρρησία (from πᾶν ῥῆμα) expresses primarily a complete openness and freedom of speech (cf. Mk. 8³², the only place where
the word occurs in the Synoptics), and in this sense it is a
favourite word with Jn.; cf. 7¹³. ²⁶ 10²⁴ 16²⁵. ²⁹ 18²⁰ (where
ἐν κρυπτῷ and ἐν παρρησίᾳ are again contrasted). It is thus,
according to Prov. 1²⁰, that Wisdom speaks: ἐν πλατείαις
παρρησίαν ἄγει. The word then comes to connote intrepidity
or courage; and it is used in 1 Jn. 2²⁸ 3²¹ 4¹⁷ 5¹⁴ of boldness
in man's attitude to God (cf. Job 27¹⁰).

In this passage ἐν παρρησίᾳ εἶναι signifies " to be boldly
in public view," as in 11⁵⁴, where we have οὐκέτι παρρησίᾳ
περιεπάτει ἐν τοῖς Ἰουδαίοις; cf. Wisd. 5¹, Col. 2¹⁵. What the
brethren of Jesus suggest is that to hide Himself in Galilee is
incompatible with the claim for public recognition, as One sent
by God, which He makes for Himself.

εἰ ταῦτα ποιεῖς, " *if* you do these things," *sc.* the wonderful
works with which rumour associated His name. The brethren
do not express definite unbelief, but they are sceptical.

φανέρωσον σεαυτὸν τῷ κόσμῳ, " show thyself to the world,"
i.e. to the great public at Jerusalem (cf. v. 7), where multitudes
would be gathered at the Feast of Tabernacles. The wider
meaning of κόσμος (see on 1⁹) cannot be intended, as present
to the minds of the brethren of Jesus. For φανερόω, see on 1³¹;
and cf. 14²².

5. οὐδὲ γὰρ οἱ ἀδελφοὶ αὐτοῦ ἐπίστευον (DLW have ἐπίστευσαν,
which is plainly wrong) εἰς αὐτόν. The form of the sentence
suggests that it is remarkable that His own kinsfolk did not

αὐτοῖς ὁ Ἰησοῦς Ὁ καιρὸς ὁ ἐμὸς οὔπω πάρεστιν, ὁ δὲ καιρὸς ὁ
ὑμέτερος πάντοτέ ἐστιν ἕτοιμος. 7. οὐ δύναται ὁ κόσμος μισεῖν ὑμᾶς,
ἐμὲ δὲ μισεῖ, ὅτι ἐγὼ μαρτυρῶ περὶ αὐτοῦ ὅτι τὰ ἔργα αὐτοῦ πονηρά

believe in Jesus, the imperfect tense indicating their general
attitude. For the constr. πιστεύειν εἰς αὐτόν, see on 1¹². It is
a favourite constr. in Jn., and it implies a belief *in* Jesus, as
distinct from mere belief in His doctrine. It is used thus
throughout this chapter (vv. 31, 38, 39, 48; and cf. 8³⁰), and its
use at this point means that the brethren of Jesus did not
believe in Him *as Messiah*. Their incredulity, as reported by
Jn., is in accordance with the Synoptic narratives (cf. Mk. 3²¹,
Mt. 12⁴⁶ 13⁵⁷).

6. λέγει οὖν. So ℵᶜBLNΓΔΘ, but om. οὖν ℵ*DW and syrr.
For οὖν in Jn., see on 1²².

ὁ καιρὸς ὁ ἐμὸς οὔπω πάρεστιν, " my time is not yet come."
καιρός is a word which Jn. uses only in this passage; it stands
for the moment of opportunity, the fitting occasion, rather than
for the " predestined hour " (ὥρα), on which the Fourth Gospel
dwells with such insistence (see on 2⁴). The fitting time had
not yet come, Jesus says in reply to the suggestion, " reveal
Thyself to the world " (v. 4); and by this is meant not the
hour of His Passion, but rather the best time for that public
manifestation of Himself as Messiah, which He would make
when He went up to the Feast of Tabernacles (v. 8). Such
public declaration was made, when He did go up: cf. vv. 29,
33, 8¹². ²⁸ etc.

ὁ δὲ καιρὸς ὁ ὑμέτερος πάντοτέ ἐστιν ἕτοιμος. Their case was
different from His. It did not matter when they went up to
the feast; it was one of strict obligation, but the exact day on
which they would present themselves in Jerusalem was of no
consequence, provided that they attended. Any day would be
a fitting day (καιρός) for them to arrive, for *they* would not be
received with hostility, but rather with indifference.

7. οὐ δύναται ὁ κόσμος μισεῖν ὑμᾶς, " the world (see on v. 4)
cannot hate *you*," ὑμᾶς being emphatic. We have adopted
(see on 2¹²) the ancient belief that " the Lord's brethren " were
children of Joseph by his first wife, and were not numbered
among the Twelve. The language of this verse shows, at
any rate, that Jn. did not regard them as members of that
select company, for it assumes that there was no reason why
they should be regarded with disfavour by the Jews who were
hostile to Jesus, as His accredited followers would certainly be
(cf. 15¹⁸).

ἐμὲ δὲ μισεῖ. Cf. 15¹⁸. ²³. ²⁴. The κόσμος which " hates "
Jesus is that world which Jn. describes as lying in wickedness,

270 THE GOSPEL ACCORDING TO ST. JOHN [VII. 7–10.

ἐστιν. 8. ὑμεῖς ἀνάβητε εἰς τὴν ἑορτήν· ἐγὼ οὔπω ἀναβαίνω εἰς τὴν ἑορτὴν ταύτην, ὅτι ὁ ἐμὸς καιρὸς οὔπω πεπλήρωται. 9. ταῦτα δὲ εἰπὼν αὐτὸς ἔμεινεν ἐν τῇ Γαλιλαίᾳ.

10. Ὡς δὲ ἀνέβησαν οἱ ἀδελφοὶ αὐτοῦ εἰς τὴν ἑορτήν, τότε καὶ αὐτὸς ἀνέβη, οὐ φανερῶς ἀλλὰ ὡς ἐν κρυπτῷ. 11. οἱ οὖν Ἰουδαῖοι

1 Jn. 5¹⁹ (see on 1⁹). But here the reference is only to the hostile Jews, as appears from the words which follow.

ὅτι ἐγὼ μαρτυρῶ περὶ αὐτοῦ ὅτι τὰ ἔργα αὐτοῦ πονηρά ἐστιν. He had denounced the Jews recently, and had said that their unbelief was due to moral causes (5⁴²⁻⁴⁵), wherefore they hated Him. Such denunciation was a form of His "witness" to the truth (cf. 18³⁷). See on 3¹⁹, where the phrase ἦν αὐτῶν πονηρὰ τὰ ἔργα has already appeared.

8. ὑμεῖς ἀνάβητε (the regular word for going up to Jerusalem; see on 2¹³) εἰς τὴν ἑορτήν. ℵ*ΓΔ add ταύτην here, but om. ℵᶜᵃBDLTNWΘ. ὑμεῖς is emphatic, "Go ye up to the feast."

ἐγὼ οὔπω ἀναβαίνω εἰς τὴν ἑορτὴν ταύτην, "I (on the other hand) am not yet going up to this feast."

οὔπω is read by BLTNWΓΔΘ, but ℵD Syr. cur. have οὐκ. If οὔπω be read, Jesus is represented as saying that He is not going up immediately, as His brethren would have Him do. If we read οὐκ, His words would seem to convey to His hearers that He was not going up at all to this particular feast; and in that case He altered His plans afterwards (v. 10).

ὅτι ὁ ἐμὸς καιρὸς (this is the true reading here, as against ὁ καιρὸς ὁ ἐμός, which the rec. text reads, from v. 6 above) οὔπω πεπλήρωται. This is a repetition of the reason given in v. 6, with slight verbal changes, the stronger word πεπλήρωται being substituted for πάρεστιν. The fitting moment had not yet arrived for His public proclamation of His Messiahship. The repetition of the same thought in slightly different words is a feature of Jn.'s style. See on 3¹⁶.

9. ταῦτα δὲ εἰπὼν αὐτὸς ἔμεινεν κτλ. So ℵD*LNW, while BTΓΔΘ have αὐτοῖς. But the emphatic αὐτός is thoroughly Johannine.

Jesus goes up secretly to the Feast of Tabernacles
(vv. 10–13)

10. ὡς δὲ ἀνέβησαν κτλ., "when His brethren had gone up to the feast," the aor. being used like a pluperfect (cf. 2⁹ and 4⁴⁴).

τότε καὶ αὐτὸς ἀνέβη. This was His farewell to Galilee, as the scene of His public ministry.

ἐζήτουν αὐτὸν ἐν τῇ ἑορτῇ καὶ ἔλεγον Ποῦ ἐστιν ἐκεῖνος; 12. καὶ
γογγυσμὸς περὶ αὐτοῦ ἦν πολὺς ἐν τοῖς ὄχλοις· οἱ μὲν ἔλεγον ὅτι
Ἀγαθός ἐστιν· ἄλλοι δὲ ἔλεγον Οὔ, ἀλλὰ πλανᾷ τὸν ὄχλον. 13. οὐδεὶς
μέντοι παρρησίᾳ ἐλάλει περὶ αὐτοῦ διὰ τὸν φόβον τῶν Ἰουδαίων.

οὐ φανερῶς ἀλλὰ ὡς ἐν κρυπτῷ, "not openly" (*i.e.* not with
the usual caravan of pilgrims), "but, as it were, in secret," or
privately. ὡς is omitted by אD, but ins. BLTNW. There
was nothing secret about His movements or His teaching
when He reached Jerusalem (7²⁶· ²⁸; and cf. 18²⁰), but He did not
go up publicly with the other pilgrims from Galilee. We find
mention of disciples with Him at 9², but it is not certain that
these were the Twelve (see note *in loc.*).

11. οἱ οὖν Ἰουδαῖοι ἐζήτουν αὐτόν κτλ., "So the Jews (*i.e.* the
hostile leaders; see on 1¹⁹) were looking for Him at the feast";
οὖν perhaps being not merely conjunctival, but having reference to the fact that Jesus, having gone up to Jerusalem
privately, was not in public view.

ποῦ ἐστιν ἐκεῖνος; "Where is He?" So at 9¹². ἐκεῖνος,
ille, does not carry with it any suggestion of rudeness or hatred,
as Chrysostom supposed. It occurs very often in Jn. (see
on 1⁸).

12. καὶ γογγυσμὸς περὶ αὐτοῦ ἦν πολὺς ἐν τοῖς ὄχλοις. The
order of the words is uncertain, but the variants are of no
consequence. For γογγυσμός, the murmuring of a crowd,
not necessarily hostile, see on 6⁶¹, and cf. v. 32. The plural
οἱ ὄχλοι occurs only here in Jn. The reference is to the
different groups of people that were gathered in the city, the
Galilæan visitors among them. אD have ἐν τῷ ὄχλῳ, but the
plural is probably right.

As might have been expected, the gossip of the crowds
was partly favourable, partly hostile. Some said ἀγαθός ἐστιν
(cf. vv. 40, 43). This was an adjective of which He had
deprecated the application to Himself, as really saying too
little (Mk. 10¹⁸). Others said πλανᾷ τὸν ὄχλον, "He leads the
people astray," probably with allusion to His healing on the
Sabbath day at the previous Passover season, and His claim
to Divine prerogatives (5¹⁸); cf. v. 47.

For τὸν ὄχλον, the Leicester cursive 69 has τοὺς ὄχλους,
an eccentric reading which would hardly call for notice were
it not that the Vulgate, in common with the O.L. *ef*, has *turbas*.
This is one of the instances in which Jerome has been supposed
to have used Greek manuscripts no longer extant.

13. οὐδεὶς μέντοι παρρησίᾳ ἐλάλει περὶ αὐτοῦ. For παρρησία,
see on v. 4; and for παρρησίᾳ λαλεῖν, cf. 7²⁶ 16²⁹ 18²⁰.

διὰ τὸν φόβον τῶν Ἰουδαίων. The phrase is repeated 19³⁸ 20¹⁹,

14. Ἤδη δὲ τῆς ἑορτῆς μεσούσης ἀνέβη Ἰησοῦς εἰς τὸ ἱερὸν καὶ ἐδίδασκεν. 25. Ἔλεγον οὖν τινες ἐκ τῶν Ἱεροσολυμειτῶν Οὐχ οὗτός

in both cases, as here, the reference being to the ecclesiastical authorities who terrorised the people; cf. 9[22], 12[42]. The common people were afraid to express any opinion in favour of Jesus, recollecting that, on His last visit, " the Jews " had been anxious to put Him to death (5[18]).

Jesus teaches in the Temple: He attracts the people, but the Sanhedrim seek His arrest (vv. 14, 25–36)

14. ἤδη δὲ τῆς ἑορτῆς μεσούσης κτλ., " When the feast was half over." The Feast of Tabernacles lasted for eight days (see on v. 2), so that this note of time (see Introd., p. cii, for Jn.'s liking for such notes) means that it was about the fourth day of the feast that Jesus presented Himself publicly in the Temple. The verb μεσοῦν is not found again in the N.T., but it occurs in the LXX; cf. μεσούσης τῆς νύκτος (Ex. 12[29], Judith 12[5]).

ἀνέβη Ἰησοῦς εἰς τὸ ἱερόν. The Temple was on a hill, so that ἀνέβη is the appropriate word (cf. Lk. 18[10]). The art. ὁ is omitted before Ἰησοῦς here by אBLT, appearing in DNWΓΔΘ (but see on 1[29]).

καὶ ἐδίδασκεν, " and began to teach "; cf. v. 28, 8[20], 18[20]. This is the first notice of the public *teaching* of Jesus in Jerusalem, as distinct from the answers to objectors recorded in c. 5.

25. The section introduced by v. 14, and then including vv. 25–36, has no reference to the Sabbatical controversy.[1] The discussion about the breach of the Sabbath by Jesus, begun in c. 5, and ending with 7[15-24], is not continued on this visit to Jerusalem, which took place some months after the former one (see on 7[1]). About the fourth day of the celebration of the Feast of Tabernacles (7[14]) Jesus began to teach publicly in the Temple, and His teaching attracted the attention of the citizens, who began to ask themselves if He might not be the Messiah after all, although the Jewish leaders were seeking to arrest and silence Him (7[25-27]). At this point, Jesus declares openly that His mission is from God, and that in a short time He will return to Him (7[28-33]). His strange language about Himself disconcerts the Pharisees, who say scornful words (7[35, 36]), but they do not arrest Him on this occasion.

Some of the Jews were impressed by the public teaching now begun (v. 14). τινες ἐκ τῶν Ἱεροσολυμειτῶν, *sc.* the

[1] See Introd., p. xix, and on v. 1 above, for the dislocation of the text.

ἐστιν ὃν ζητοῦσιν ἀποκτεῖναι; 26. καὶ ἴδε παρρησίᾳ λαλεῖ, καὶ οὐδὲν αὐτῷ λέγουσιν. μή ποτε ἀληθῶς ἔγνωσαν οἱ ἄρχοντες ὅτι οὗτός ἐστιν ὁ Χριστός; 27. ἀλλὰ τοῦτον οἴδαμεν πόθεν ἐστίν· ὁ δὲ Χριστὸς ὅταν

inhabitants of Jerusalem, as distinct from the multitudes of country folk who had come up for the feast. The term Ἱεροσολυμεῖται is found in N.T. only here and Mk. 1⁵ (cf. 4 Macc. 4²² 18⁵).

The Vulgate has *ex Hierosolymis* here instead of *ex Hierosolymitanis*, which the Oxford editors suggest may be due to the use by Jerome of some Greek text now lost. But *Hierosolymitanis* appears in *d f q* as *Hierosolymitis*, from which the transition is easy to *Hierosolymis*.

These shrewd townsmen were surprised that their religious leaders were seeking the death of One who spoke with such power. With ὃν ζητοῦσιν ἀποκτεῖναι, cf. v. 1.

26. καὶ ἴδε. For ἴδε, see on 1²⁹.

παρρησίᾳ. For this word see on v. 4, and for παρρησίᾳ λαλεῖ, the openness with which Jesus taught, see on 18²⁰. The citizens were surprised that He had been allowed to teach without interference from the rulers, καὶ οὐδὲν αὐτῷ λέγουσιν.

μή ποτε is not used elsewhere by Jn. Cf. its similar use in Lk. 3¹⁵, where the people are wondering about John the Baptist, μή ποτε αὐτὸς εἴη ὁ Χριστός. So here: " Can it be that the rulers in truth know that this is the Christ ? " οἱ ἄρχοντες describes generally the members of the Sanhedrim (for the constitution of which, see below on v. 32). Cf. v. 48, 3¹, 12⁴² ; and see Lk. 23¹³· ³⁵ 24²⁰.

The rec. ins. ἀληθῶς before ὁ Χριστός, but om. אBDLNWΘ.

27. However, the Jews dismiss as untenable the thought which had passed through their minds that Jesus might be the Messiah (cf. 4²⁹), and that their " rulers " knew it. ἀλλά . . ., Nay, but . . .

τοῦτον οἴδαμεν πόθεν ἐστίν, " this man, we know whence he is." Cf. 6⁴², where " the Jews " said that they knew the family of Jesus. There was no mystery about Him now, as they thought. Many people knew His home at Nazareth (Mt. 13⁵⁵). Presumably His disciples were with Him henceforward.

ὁ δὲ Χριστὸς ὅταν ἔρχηται, οὐδεὶς γινώσκει πόθεν ἐστίν. The birthplace of Messiah was held to be known, *sc.* Bethlehem (see on v. 42), but all else as to the time or the manner of His Advent was believed to be hidden. Westcott quotes a Rabbinical saying, "Three things come wholly unexpected— Messiah, a godsend, and a scorpion " (*Sanhedr.* 97a). The phrase " will be revealed " used of His appearance, 2 Esd.

ἔρχηται, οὐδεὶς γινώσκει πόθεν ἐστίν. 28. ἔκραξεν οὖν ἐν τῷ ἱερῷ διδάσκων ὁ Ἰησοῦς καὶ λέγων Κἀμὲ οἴδατε καὶ οἴδατε πόθεν εἰμί· καὶ ἀπ᾽ ἐμαυτοῦ οὐκ ἐλήλυθα, ἀλλ᾽ ἔστιν ἀληθινὸς ὁ πέμψας με, ὃν ὑμεῖς

7²⁸ 13³², and in *Apocalypse of Baruch* xxix. 3, suggests (as Charles has pointed out) an emergence from concealment; and with this agrees the Jewish doctrine described in Justin, *Tryph.* 110, " They say that He has not yet come . . . and that even if He has come, it is not known who He is (οὐ γινώσκεται ὅς ἐστιν), but that when He has become manifest and glorious then it shall be known who He is." At an earlier point (*Tryph.* 8) the Jewish interlocutor says of the Christ, " If He be born and is anywhere, He is unknown, and does not even know Himself (ἄγνωστός ἐστι καὶ οὐδὲ αὐτός πω ἑαυτὸν ἐπίσταται), nor has He any power until Elijah having come anoints Him and makes Him manifest to all." These passages show that the evangelist accurately reports here the Jewish doctrine as to the mysterious emergence of Messiah from obscurity.

ἔρχηται. So BDLTW; א∆*NΘ have ἔρχεται. ὅταν with the pres. subj. is rare in Jn. (cf. 8⁴⁴ 16²¹), although not uncommon elsewhere (*e.g.* Mk. 12²⁵ 13⁴, Lk. 11². ²¹).

28. ἔκραξεν. κράζειν is used only once in the Synoptists of Christ's utterances, viz. Mt. 27⁵⁰, where it is applied to the cry from the Cross. Jn. does not so apply it, but it is used by him three times to describe public and solemn announcements of doctrine by Jesus (7³⁷ 12⁴⁴; cf. also 1¹⁵, where it is used of the Baptist's proclamation). Cf. ἐκραύγασεν, 11⁴³.

ἔκραξεν οὖν ἐν τῷ ἱερῷ διδάσκων . . ., " So then (οὖν, in reply to the scepticism displayed by His audience) Jesus cried aloud, as He was teaching in the temple " (cf. v. 14). There was nothing secret about this teaching (cf. 18²⁰ and Mt. 26⁵⁵).

κἀμὲ οἴδατε καὶ οἴδατε πόθεν εἰμί. This is not ironical or interrogative, but affirmative. It was true that they knew Him and His family (v. 27), but there was more to know. There is no inconsistency with 8¹⁴, where see note.

καὶ ἀπ᾽ ἐμαυτοῦ οὐκ ἐλήλυθα, " and yet I have not come of myself." καί is used for καίτοι as it is in v. 30 below, in accordance with an idiom frequent in Jn. (see on 1¹⁰). The phrase ἀπ᾽ ἐμαυτοῦ οὐκ ἐλήλυθα is repeated 8⁴² (where see note). Cf. 5³⁰ 8²⁸ 12⁴⁹ 14¹⁰.

ἀλλ᾽ ἔστιν ἀληθινὸς ὁ πέμψας με, " but He that sent me is *genuine*" (see on 1⁹ for ἀληθινός as distinct from ἀληθής). The mission of Jesus was a genuine mission; He did not come to earth of Himself, but was *sent* by the Father (see on 3¹⁷). The Father was *genuinely* His Sender.

ὃν ὑμεῖς οὐκ οἴδατε. Despite the fact that the Jews

οὐκ οἴδατε· 29. ἐγὼ οἶδα αὐτόν, ὅτι παρ᾽ αὐτοῦ εἰμι κἀκεῖνός με ἀπέστειλεν. 30. Ἐζήτουν οὖν αὐτὸν πιάσαι, καὶ οὐδεὶς ἐπέβαλεν ἐπ᾽

"knew what they worshipped" (4²²), they did not know God's character and purposes, and this scathing rebuke is addressed to them again (8¹⁹· ⁵⁵). That it might be said of heathen was not surprising (Gal. 4⁸, 1 Thess. 4⁵, 2 Thess. 1⁸), and the persecutions of Christians in the future were mainly to spring from this ignorance (cf. 15²¹); but here the sting of the words "whom ye know not," is that they were addressed to *Jews*, the chosen people.

29. After ἐγώ, אDN add δέ; but om. BLTWΓΔΘ.

ἐγὼ οἶδα αὐτόν. This is repeated verbally 8⁵⁵, and again at 17²⁵ in the form ἐγὼ δέ σε ἔγνων. These three words contain the unique claim of Jesus, which is pressed all through the chapters of controversy with the Jews. But it is not more explicit, although it is more frequently expressed, in Jn. than in Mt. 11²⁷, Lk. 10²².

ὅτι παρ᾽ αὐτοῦ εἰμι, "because I am from Him." See on 6⁴⁶ for similar phrases in Jn., which imply a community of being between the Father and the Son (cf. 1¹⁴ and 16²⁷· ²⁸).

κἀκεῖνός με ἀπέστειλεν. This sentence is not dependent upon ὅτι. "I know Him, because I am from Him," is the first point. "And He sent me" is the second (see on 3¹⁷), ἐκεῖνος emphasising the main subject of the sentence, as so often in Jn. (see on 1⁸).

For ἀπέστειλεν (BLTNW), אD have ἀπέσταλκεν.

30. ἐζήτουν οὖν αὐτὸν πιάσαι, "Then (*sc.* in consequence of the claims for Himself made by Jesus, vv. 28, 29) they (*sc.* the Jewish leaders already indicated as His opponents, vv. 1, 25) sought to arrest Him." This had been their purpose ever since the healing at the pool of Bethesda on a Sabbath day (5¹⁶), their desire being to put Him to death (5¹⁸ 7¹· ²⁵). The impf. ἐζήτουν marks in each case that the action was not completed; and so again at 7⁴⁴ (ἤθελον) and 10³⁹ (ἐζήτουν). The original offence, of breaking the Sabbath (5¹⁶, repeated 9¹⁶), comes less into prominence now, because of the greater offence of blasphemy (5¹⁸) with which they henceforth charge Him.

πιάζειν, to "take," is not found in the Synoptists ; Jn. uses it again vv. 32, 44, 8²⁰ 10³⁹ 11⁵⁷ of "arresting" Jesus (cf. Acts 12⁴, 2 Cor. 11³²), and at 21³· ¹⁰ of "catching" fish.

καὶ οὐδεὶς ἐπέβαλεν ἐπ᾽ αὐτὸν τὴν χεῖρα, "and yet (καί being used for καίτοι, as often in Jn.; see on 1¹⁰) no one laid his hand on Him," the ecclesiastical authorities, no doubt, fearing to arrest one who had won attention from the people (cf. Mt. 21⁴⁶). These words are repeated almost verbatim at

αὐτὸν τὴν χεῖρα, ὅτι οὔπω ἐληλύθει ἡ ὥρα αὐτοῦ. 31. Ἐκ τοῦ ὄχλου δὲ πολλοὶ ἐπίστευσαν εἰς αὐτόν, καὶ ἔλεγον Ὁ Χριστὸς ὅταν ἔλθῃ, μὴ πλείονα σημεῖα ποιήσει ὧν οὗτος ἐποίησεν; 32. Ἤκουσαν οἱ

v. 44 τινὲς δὲ ἤθελον ἐξ αὐτῶν πιάσαι αὐτόν, ἀλλ' οὐδεὶς ἐπέβαλεν ἐπ' αὐτὸν τὰς χεῖρας: cf. also 8²⁰ 10³⁹.

Jn. is at pains to bring out at every point that the persecution and death of Jesus followed a predestined course. The Jews *could not* hasten the hour determined in the Divine purpose, and so the evangelist adds here, ὅτι οὔπω ἐληλύθει ἡ ὥρα αὐτοῦ, the same words being added in a similar context at 8²⁰ (cf. vv. 6, 8; and see on 2⁴).

31. ἐκ τοῦ ὄχλου δὲ πολλοὶ ἐπίστευσαν εἰς αὐτόν. Those who " believed on Him " (see for the phrase on 4³⁹) were of the common people rather than of the upper classes (cf. vv. 48, 49). See 9¹⁶.

καὶ ἔλεγον κτλ., " and they were saying, When the Christ shall come, will He do more signs than this man did ? " (cf. Mt. 12²³). Jesus had not yet told them plainly that He was Messiah (10²⁴).

After ἔλεγον the rec. ins. ὅτι *recitantis*, but om. אBDLWΘ. After ὅταν ἔλθῃ the rec. has μήτι, but the better reading is μή (אBDLTW). After σημεῖα the rec. has τούτων, but om. אBDLTNWΘ. For ἐποίησεν (אᶜBLTNW), א*DΘ and some vss. have ποιεῖ.

πλείονα σημεῖα. Jn. does not profess to tell of all the " signs " which Jesus wrought, but he alludes here (and at 2²³) to some which he has left undescribed.

πλείονα σημεῖα ποιήσει; Messiah was expected to be a miracle worker. The prophet had declared that in His kingdom " the eyes of the blind shall be opened and the ears of the deaf shall be unstopped. Then shall the lame man leap as an hart, and the tongue of the dumb shall sing " (Isa. 35⁵· ⁶). A corresponding expectation of Messianic " signs " is found in the Synoptists as well as in Jn. Thus John the Baptist is stimulated to inquire further when he hears of " the works of the Christ " (Mt. 11²; cf. Lk. 7¹⁸); and one of the difficulties in the way of detecting " false Christs " is to be their power of showing " signs and wonders," which were a note of the true Messiah (Mk. 13²²). It was because Bartimæus recognised Jesus as "the Son of David " that he believed He could restore his sight (Mk. 10⁴⁸).

It is therefore a mistake to speak ¹ of the Messianic significance of miracles as a Johannine peculiarity; it appears also in the Synoptists, although more conspicuously in Jn. (cf. 2²⁷

¹ Cf. Schweitzer, *Quest of the Historical Jesus*, p. 345.

Φαρισαῖοι τοῦ ὄχλου γογγύζοντος περὶ αὐτοῦ ταῦτα, καὶ ἀπέστειλαν οἱ

4^{19}). The evangelist is true to the historical situation when he notes that the Jews expected " signs " from Messiah, as indeed they did from any one claiming to be a prophet (2^{18} 3^2 6^{14} 9^{17}; cf. 1 Cor. 1^{22}). And the aim of the Fourth Gospel is to record selected " signs " of Jesus with the express purpose of proving Him to be the Christ (20^{31}).

32. οἱ Φαρισαῖοι : see on 1^{24}. The Pharisees had heard the whispered talk of the people (cf. v. 12), and they determined to silence Jesus. Accordingly they brought the matter before the Sanhedrim, so that measures might be taken for His arrest.

The Sanhedrim (συνέδριον) was the supreme council or high court of justice in Jerusalem during the period of the Roman occupation, and successive procurators left the administration of the law for the most part in its hands. It had no power to carry into execution a sentence of death, but it was the uniform policy of the Roman administration to support its authority. Three classes of members may be distinguished: (1) The ἀρχιερεῖς, that is, the acting high priest, all ex-high priests, and probably some of their sons.[1] They were the political, as well as the ecclesiastical, aristocrats of Jerusalem; and they occupied a position not unlike that of the Holy Synod in Russia before the Revolution, which comprised only the leading bishops, and had as presiding officer a highly placed layman. Their interests were centred in the Temple, and they had little concern for the synagogues, large part as these played in Jewish religious life. They were of the party known as that of " the Sadducees," a designation occurring only once in Mk., and not at all in Jn. (2) A second class, also belonging to the Sadducee interest, were known as πρεσβύτεροι or elders: they were not priests, but were generally associated with them in policy, both the ἀρχιερεῖς and the πρεσβύτεροι being in opposition to (3) the third class, who were the Pharisees or scribes or lawyers (the titles γραμματεύς and νομικός are not found in Jn.). They were learned in the Jewish law and in the traditions that had grown up around it, being the party of austere and strict religious observance. Their influence showed itself in the synagogues rather than in the Temple, for the details of the ceremonial worship there did not come within their province. They regarded with apprehension the departure from traditional doctrines which

---

[1] See Schürer, *History of Jewish People*, Eng. Tr., II. i. 177 f., 203 f. Thus Annas and Caiaphas are both called ἀρχιερεῖς (Lk. 3^2) ; and in Acts 4^6 we have Ἄννας ὁ ἀρχιερεὺς καὶ Καϊάφας, although Annas was out of office at the time.

ἀρχιερεῖς καὶ οἱ Φαρισαῖοι ὑπηρέτας ἵνα πιάσωσιν αὐτόν. 33. εἶπεν οὖν ὁ Ἰησοῦς Ἔτι χρόνον μικρὸν μεθ᾽ ὑμῶν εἰμι καὶ ὑπάγω πρὸς τὸν πέμψαντά με. 34. ζητήσετέ με καὶ οὐχ εὑρήσετε, καὶ ὅπου εἰμὶ ἐγὼ

Jesus encouraged, and it was they who first brought His teaching before the Sanhedrim (cf. 12¹⁹). They associated themselves with the priestly or Sadducean party in bringing about His arrest and condemnation (18³, Mt. 27⁶²), although the chief priests appear as the principal agents. Cf. 11⁴⁹.

ἀπέστειλαν οἱ ἀρχιερεῖς καὶ οἱ Φαρισαῖοι ὑπηρέτας. The rec. text has οἱ Φαρ. καὶ οἱ ἀρχ., but ℵBDLTWΘ place the chief priests first in order, which is obviously right. Without the consent of the ἀρχιερεῖς, the arrest of Jesus could not have been ordered by the Sanhedrim. οἱ ἀρχ. καὶ οἱ Φαρ. are coupled together again 7⁴⁵ 11⁴⁷· ⁵⁷ (as also Mt. 21⁴⁵ 27⁶²), and the combination stands for the Sanhedrim as an organised council or court. They now sent officers of the Sanhedrim, or, as we might say, "Temple police" (ὑπηρέτας; cf. v. 45, 18³· ¹²· ¹⁸ 19⁶), to make the arrest, which some of them had been seeking (ἐζήτουν, v. 30) to bring about.

33. εἶπεν οὖν ὁ Ἰη. If we press the causative force of οὖν, the meaning is that Jesus said that He would be only among them a little while longer, so that there was nothing to be gained by arresting Him. οὖν, however (see on 1²²), is not always to be rendered "therefore," and may be only a conjunction, "and so."

The rec. adds αὐτοῖς after οὖν, but om. ℵBDLNWΘ.

ἔτι χρόνον μικρόν κτλ. The end of His ministry was near, and He knew it; it would come in "a little while"—in fact in about six months. The phrase μικρὸν χρόνον (or μικρόν alone) is repeatedly on His lips henceforth, according to Jn. (12³⁵ 13³³ 14¹⁹ 16¹⁶). Cf. 9⁴.

The rec. has μικρὸν χρόνον (DNΓΔ), but ℵBLTWΘ give the order χρ. μικρ.

καὶ ὑπάγω πρὸς τὸν πέμψαντά με. The words are repeated 16⁵. For the phrase "Him that sent me," frequent in Jn., see on 3¹⁷. This was a saying of mystery, and the Jews could not understand it.

ὑπάγειν is a favourite verb with Jn., and it is often used in the Gospel of Jesus "going to God" (cf. 8¹⁴· ²¹ 13³· ³³· ³⁶ 14⁴· ⁵· ²⁸ 16⁵· ¹⁰· ¹⁷). It means strictly "to depart," and so is specially appropriate of the withdrawal of Christ's visible presence from among men, and His "going to the Father" or "going home." See on 15¹⁶ 16⁷; and cf. Mk. 14²¹ ὁ μὲν υἱὸς τοῦ ἀνθρώπου ὑπάγει, καθὼς γέγραπται.

34. ζητήσετε. This is certainly the true text, only two

ὑμεῖς οὐ δύνασθε ἐλθεῖν. 35. εἶπον οὖν οἱ Ἰουδαῖοι πρὸς ἑαυτούς
Ποῦ οὗτος μέλλει πορεύεσθαι, ὅτι ἡμεῖς οὐχ εὑρήσομεν αὐτόν; μὴ εἰς
τὴν διασπορὰν τῶν Ἑλλήνων μέλλει πορεύεσθαι καὶ διδάσκειν τοὺς

MSS., II and 69, reading ζητεῖτε. None the less, the Vulgate
has *quaeritis*, this being one of the renderings which suggest
to some that Jerome followed a type of Greek manuscript of
which we know little.[1]

With vv. 33, 34, must be compared at every point 8²¹
and 13³³.

ζητήσετέ με καὶ οὐχ εὑρήσετε. BTN add μέ after εὑρήσετε:
om. אDLWΓΔΘ. " Seek and ye shall find " (Mt. 7⁷) is the
promise of Jesus; but the seeking may be so long delayed
that the promise cannot be claimed. Cf. Lk. 17²² and Prov.
1²⁸. So, here, the warning is of the danger of delay. " Ye
shall seek me," *sc*. (not, as at v. 30, to kill me, but) as
the Messiah for your deliverance, " and ye shall not find," for
Jesus will not be present in the body, as He was then.

καὶ ὅπου εἰμὶ ἐγώ κτλ., "and where I am," *sc*. in my
essential being, in the spiritual world, " you cannot come."
There is no contradiction between μεθ' ὑμῶν εἰμί of v. 33 and
this statement; for the former only asserted His visible, bodily
presence, whereas the latter (εἰμὶ ἐγώ) spoke of His spiritual
home. This can be shared only by those who are in spiritual
touch with Him (12²⁶ 17²⁴), as the Jews were not (cf. 8²¹).
Even His disciples, as He reminded them later, could not
follow Him to the heavenly places while they were still in the
body (13³³. ³⁶).

35. εἶπον οὖν οἱ Ἰουδαῖοι πρὸς ἑαυτούς, "the Jews said among
themselves," *i.e.* the Jewish leaders or Pharisees of v. 32.

ποῦ οὗτος μέλλει πορεύεσθαι; "Where is this person (οὗτος
suggesting contempt) about to go ? " They did not understand what Jesus had said (vv. 33, 34) in words of mystery.
μέλλειν here only indicates simple futurity (see on 6⁷¹ for Jn.'s
use of this verb).

ὅτι ἡμεῖς οὐχ εὑρήσομεν αὐτόν. They speak ironically, feeling
that it will be impossible for Him to escape *them*. ἡμεῖς is
omitted by אD, but ins. BLTNΔΓΘ. Cf. 8²².

μὴ εἰς τὴν διασπορὰν τῶν Ἑλλήνων κτλ., " Will He go to the
Dispersion of the Greeks ? " *i.e.* to the Jews who lived among
Greek populations. Jews who lived out of Palestine were
the διασπορὰ τοῦ Ἰσραήλ (Ps. 147², Isa. 49⁶), and the term is
often applied to them (cf. Isa. 11¹² 56⁸, Zeph. 3¹⁰, Jer. 15⁷,
etc.). In 1 Pet. 1¹ (where see Hort's note), we have διασπορὰ

[1] Cf. Wordsworth and White, *Nov. Test. Lat.*, in loc. ; and see
above on vv. 12, 25.

Ἕλληνας; 36. τίς ἐστιν ὁ λόγος οὗτος ὃν εἶπεν Ζητήσετέ με καὶ οὐχ εὑρήσετε, καὶ ὅπου εἰμὶ ἐγὼ ὑμεῖς οὐ δύνασθε ἐλθεῖν; 37. Ἐν δὲ τῇ ἐσχάτῃ ἡμέρᾳ τῇ μεγάλῃ τῆς ἑορτῆς εἱστήκει ὁ Ἰησοῦς καὶ ἔκραξεν λέγων Ἐάν τις διψᾷ, ἐρχέσθω πρός με καὶ πινέτω.

Πόντου, Ἀσίας, etc., the place of their residence being thus indicated. So here, ἡ διασπορὰ τῶν Ἑλλήνων is "the Dispersion among the Greeks."

καὶ διδάσκειν τοὺς Ἕλληνας; "and teach the Greeks," i.e. the heathen Greeks themselves, among whom the Jews of the Dispersion lived. (See on 12²⁰ for Ἕλληνες as indicating Greek proselytes, which is not the meaning here.)

The Palestinian Jews of the stricter sort looked down on the Jews of the Dispersion and despised all Gentiles. There is, then, something contemptuous in their suggestion that Jesus may be contemplating a journey to foreign parts, where He may make disciples of Hellenistic Jews or even of the Greeks themselves. It is an instance of the "irony" of the evangelist (see on 1⁴⁵) that he does not stay to make the obvious comment that what the Jewish critics of Jesus thought so absurd was afterwards accomplished by the first preachers of His gospel, which embraced both Greek and Jew.

36. Yet they are puzzled and uneasy, for they repeat His strange saying of v. 34 again: "What is this word which He said, You shall seek me and shall not find me, and where I am you cannot come?"

BDLNW⊙ give ὁ λόγ. οὗτ., as against οὗτ. ὁ λόγ. of אΓΔ.

A special appeal to the people, who are divided in opinion, to the indignation of the Pharisees (vv. 37-49)

37. Jesus seems to have continued His teaching daily, or at any rate continuously, in the Temple; and on the last day of the feast, He made a special and final appeal to His hearers to accept His message.

εἱστήκει[1] ὁ Ἰησοῦς. Jesus, like other teachers, was accustomed to *sit* as He taught (see on 6³); but at this point, to emphasise the momentousness of His words, He rose and cried out (see on 7²⁸ for ἔκραξεν, and cf. Prov. 8³ 9³·⁵), "If any man thirst, let him come unto me and drink." Cf Isa. 55¹.

ἐρχέσθω πρός με. So אᶜBLNTW⊙, but א*D om. πρός με. Cf. 6³⁵.

"The last day, the great day, of the Feast" of Tabernacles was probably the eighth day (see on 7²), on which were special

[1] See on 1³⁵ for this form.

38. ὁ πιστεύων εἰς ἐμέ, καθὼς εἶπεν ἡ γραφή, ποταμοὶ ἐκ τῆς κοιλίας

observances. The ritual on each day, and probably on the eighth day also (although this seems to be uncertain), comprised an offering of water, perhaps (when the rite was initiated) symbolising abundance of rain to ensure a good crop at the next harvest. Rabbi Akiba says as much: " Bring the libation of water at the Feast of Tabernacles, that the showers may be blessed to thee. And accordingly it is said that whosoever will not come up to the Feast of Tabernacles shall have no rain." [1] At any rate, a golden vessel was filled with water from the Pool of Siloam, and the water was solemnly offered by the priest, the singers chanting, "With joy shall ye draw water out of the wells of salvation " (Isa. 12³).

This water ceremonial may have suggested the words of Jesus: " If any man thirst, let him come unto me and drink."

38. καθὼς εἶπεν ἡ γραφή κτλ. ἡ γραφή always indicates a specific passage in the O.T. (see on 2²²), although (cf. v. 42 below) the quotation may not always be exact. Here, the source of the quotation cannot be identified with certainty, although, as we shall see, the idea of v. 38 is scriptural. The fact that we cannot precisely fix the quotation makes for the genuineness of the reminiscence here recorded. A writer whose aim was merely to edify, and who did not endeavour to reproduce historical incidents, would not have placed in the mouth of Jesus a scriptural quotation which no one has ever been able to identify exactly.

The passage has been punctuated in various ways:

(1) Chrysostom confines the quotation to the words "he that believeth in me," taking the rest of v. 38 as words of Jesus. Thus the "scripture" might be Isa. 28¹⁶, quoted in Rom. 9³³ in the form ὁ πιστεύων ἐπ᾽ αὐτῷ οὐ καταισχυνθήσεται. But this exegesis is a mere evasion of the difficulties.

(2) Some ancient *Western* authorities connect πινέτω with ὁ πιστεύων εἰς ἐμέ which follows, putting a stop after ἐμέ : " If any man thirst, let him come unto me, and let him drink that believeth on me. As the Scripture saith, Out of His belly shall flow rivers of living water." By this arrangement, αὐτοῦ is understood of Christ, not of the believer. The colometry of the O.L. codices *d* and *e* would agree with this punctuation.[2] The *Letter of the Churches of Vienne and Lyons* [3] has . . . τοῦ ὕδατος τῆς ζωῆς τοῦ ἐξιόντος ἐκ τῆς νηδύος τοῦ Χριστοῦ, which takes αὐτοῦ as meaning Christ.

---

[1] Quoted by E. C. Selwyn in *J.T.S.*, Jan. 1912, p. 226.
[2] Cf. J. A. Robinson, *Passion of St. Perpetua*, p. 98.
[3] Cf. Euseb. *H.E.* v. 1. 22.

So also Cyprian has " clamat dominus ut qui sitit ueniat et bibat de fluminibus aquae uiuae quae de eius uentre fluxerunt." [1] Many Western Fathers are cited to the same effect by Turner.[2] Loisy and some other modern exegetes favour this view.

Burney held that this arrangement of clauses represented the sense, the Greek κοιλία being due to a misunderstanding of the underlying Aramaic, and a confusion of מְעִין " belly " (cf. Dan. 2[32]) with מַעְיָן " fountain." He rendered v. 38 accordingly, " As the scripture hath said, Rivers shall flow forth from the *fountain* of living waters," the allusion being to Ezek. 47[1]. C. C. Torrey [3] also appeals to the Aramaic, rendering " As the Scripture hath said, Out of the midst of her (*i.e.* Jerusalem) shall flow rivers of living water," the reference being to Zech. 14[8]. These explanations are ingenious, but they do not disclose any exact citation from the O.T.

(3) We prefer the *Eastern* exegesis here. Origen is explicit in his reference of αὐτοῦ to the believer in Christ: εἰ γὰρ περὶ τοῦ πνεύματος εἴρηται ὡς ὕδωρ ζῶν ποταμῶν δίκην ἐκπορευόμενον ἐκ τοῦ πιστεύοντος . . .[4] So, too, Cyril of Jerusalem (*Cat.* xvi. 11), Basil [5] (*in Ps.* 46[4]), and Athanasius (*Festal Letters*, ix. 7, xliv.).[6] That Christ is the ultimate source of living water, which represents the Spirit, is common to all interpretations; but these writers understand also that those who receive it from Him hand it on in their turn to others.[7] So in the *Odes of Solomon* (vi.) we have Christ the χείμαρρος [8] or torrent of living water spreading over the world, while the ministers of this draught of the Spirit relieve many. This is the Johannine doctrine of the Spirit, appearing again in another form at 20[23].

The reference of ἐκ τῆς κοιλίας αὐτοῦ to the believer is in strict correspondence with the earlier passage 4[10-14], where it

---

[1] *Epist.* lxxiii. 11 ; but cf. lxiii. 8.

[2] *J.T.S.*, Oct. 1922, p. 66 f., and cf. Jan. 1923, p. 174.

[3] *Harvard Theol. Review*, Oct. 1923, p. 339.

[4] Comm. *in Ioan.* vol. ii. p. 250 (ed. Brooke) ; cf. also Hom. *in Num.* xvii. 4.

[5] Basil's comment on the river of Ps. 46[4] is : τίς δ' ἂν εἴη ὁ ποταμὸς τοῦ θεοῦ ἢ τὸ πνεῦμα τὸ ἅγιον ἐκ τῆς πίστεως τῶν εἰς Χριστὸν πεπιστευκότων, ἐγγενόμενον τοῖς ἀξίοις ;　He then quotes Jn. 7[38] and 4[14].

[6] Ephraim also ends the first clause with πινέτω (Hom. *On our Lord*, i. 41) ; and Tatian seems to have taken the same line, although this cannot be certain.

[7] Syr. sin and Syr. cur. appear also to support this interpretation.

[8] So Origen (Selecta *in Deut.*, Lommatzsch, x. 374) speaks of that good land ἧς χείμαρρος ὁ Χριστός, ποτίζων τοῖς τῆς σοφίας νάμασιν.

αὐτοῦ ῥεύσουσιν ὕδατος ζῶντος.　39. τοῦτο δὲ εἶπεν περὶ τοῦ Πνεύματος οὗ ἔμελλον λαμβάνειν οἱ πιστεύσαντες εἰς αὐτόν· οὔπω γὰρ

is said of the water which Christ gives that it will be in
the believer πηγὴ ὕδατος ἁλλομένου εἰς ζωὴν αἰώνιον. The
imagery of "If any man thirst, let him come unto me and
drink," goes back to Isa. 55¹; and similarly (as at 4¹⁴) the
imagery of v. 38 goes back to Isa. 58¹¹: "Thou shalt be like
a spring of water whose waters fail not." As we have seen
on 4¹⁴, this idea appears in many places in Hebrew literature,
although the actual words cannot be traced. He who has
drunk deep of the living waters which are the gift of Christ
becomes himself, in his turn and in humbler measure, a fountain from which the water of life flows for the refreshment
of others.

The κοιλία is regarded in the O.T. as the seat of man's
emotional nature (Prov. 20²⁷). Water is often symbolic of the
Divine Law (see on 4¹⁰), and the Law is " in the heart "(Ps. 40⁸)
of Yahweh's servant, or, as some LXX texts have it, ἐν μέσῳ
τῆς κοιλίας μου. The Psalm goes on: " I have not hid thy
righteousness within my heart, I have declared thy faithfulness " (Ps. 40¹⁰). So again in Prov. 18⁴ we have: ὕδωρ βαθὺ
λόγος ἐν καρδίᾳ ἀνδρός, ποταμὸς δὲ ἀναπηδύει καὶ πηγὴ ζωῆς.
Hence the O.T. conception is that the Divine Law is in the
heart (καρδία or κοιλία) of one inspired by the Spirit of
Yahweh, like a fountain which cannot be repressed, but which
perpetually sends forth a stream of living water. This is the
Johannine teaching of 7³⁸.

The use of κοιλία is in accordance with the Semitic habit
of expressing emphasis [1] by mentioning some part of the
body, e.g. "the *mouth* of Yahweh hath spoken it," "His
arm wrought salvation." "Out of his belly" is only an
emphatic way of saying "From him shall flow." The living
waters to the thought of the prophets (Zech. 14⁸, Ezek. 47¹)
flowed from a holy *place*, viz. Jerusalem; but here they are
said to flow from a holy *man*, viz. one who has believed in
Christ.

There is no difficulty in the construction, ὁ πιστεύων εἰς
ἐμέ being a suspended subject; cf. 15⁵ ὁ μένων ἐν ἐμοί . . .
οὗτος φέρει καρπόν, and see on 1¹².

39. τοῦτο δὲ εἶπεν περὶ τοῦ πνεύματος. We have here an
explanatory comment by the evangelist on the words of Jesus
which precede it; see, for similar comments, Introd., p. xxxiv.
In this passage, at any rate, there can be no question of the
accuracy of the interpretation. The Living Water sym-

[1] See Barnes, *J.T.S.*, July 1922, p. 421.

ἦν Πνεῦμα, ὅτι Ἰησοῦς οὔπω ἐδοξάσθη.   40. Ἐκ τοῦ ὄχλου οὖν

bolises the Spirit, which believers in Christ (not only the
original disciples) were (ἔμελλον, cf. 6[71]) to receive (cf. 16[13],
1 Jn. 3[24] 4[13]). As Paul has it πάντες ἐν πνεῦμα ἐποτίσθημεν
(1 Cor. 12[13]), the metaphor, of the Spirit as water, being the
same as here.

Lightfoot (*Hor. Hebr.* iii. 322) quotes a passage from the
Talmud, showing that even by the Jews the libation of water at
the Feast of Tabernacles (see on v. 37) was taken to symbolise
the outpouring of the Spirit: " Why do they call it the *house of
drawing* ? Because thence they draw the Holy Spirit "
(*Beresh. Rabba*, fol. 70. 1). The Jews held that the Holy
Spirit had departed after the deaths of Zechariah and Malachi,
the last of the prophets, and they looked for a future outpouring
(Joel 2[28]; cf. Acts 2[17]).

The various readings are mainly due to attempts at interpretation. אDΓΔΘ have πιστεύοντες, but BLTW have
πιστεύσαντες, the words primarily referring to the reception of
the Spirit by the original group of disciples. B has ὅ for the
better attested οὗ. In the second clause of the verse, scribes
have defined πνεῦμα by the insertion of ἅγιον (LNWΓΔ), D
reading τὸ πνεῦμα ἅγιον ἐπ' αὐτοῖς, and B ἅγιον δεδομένον.
LNTWΓΔ have οὐδέπω for οὔπω (the reading of אBDΘ) before
ἐδοξάσθη.

For the force of πιστεύειν εἰς αὐτόν, see on v. 5.

οὔπω γὰρ ἦν πνεῦμα, *i.e.* the Spirit was not yet operating or
not yet present, εἶναι being used for παρεῖναι, as in Acts 19[2]
ἀλλ' οὐδ' εἰ πνεῦμα ἅγιον ἔστιν ἠκούσαμεν. The Ephesian
disciples could not have doubted the *existence* of the Holy
Spirit; it was His *presence* or His *operation* of which they were
doubtful. See also on 6[20].

Attempts have been made to distinguish τὸ πνεῦμα, with
the article, from πνεῦμα without it; the former standing for
the personal Spirit, the latter for a gift or manifestation of the
Spirit. The distinction may hold sometimes, but here it is
hard to maintain it: " He spake περὶ τοῦ πνεύματος, which
they who believed on Him were to receive: for πνεῦμα was not
yet." We should expect, if the proposed rule about the article
were sound, that at its first occurrence in this verse πνεῦμα
should be without it. See above on 3[6], 4[24].

οὔπω γὰρ ἦν πνεῦμα, ὅτι ὁ Ἰησοῦς οὔπω ἐδοξάσθη. Here Jn.
introduces a conception, not explicit outside the Fourth Gospel,
of the Passion of Jesus as His " glorification " (see on 1[14]).
It is the word used by Jesus Himself (12[23], and by anticipation
13[31]), and Jn. uses it again in his narrative (12[16]). This is the

ἀκούσαντες τῶν λόγων τούτων ἔλεγον Οὗτός ἐστιν ἀληθῶς ὁ προφήτης.

supreme illustration of the saying that "he that hateth his life shall keep it" (see on 12²⁵). It is the continual paradox of the Gospel that death is the beginning of new life. And so it was not until Jesus had been "glorified" in death that the Spirit came upon those who were "in Him." The seed is not quickened except it die, and, to the thought of Paul, it was not until His Resurrection after death that Christ became a Quickening Spirit, πνεῦμα ζωοποιοῦν (1 Cor. 15⁴⁵). Not until He had passed through death could His Spirit descend. Not until the Passion was over could He say λάβετε πνεῦμα ἅγιον (20²²). Pentecost was, necessarily, after Calvary. This great conception is common to Paul and Jn. (cf. 10¹⁷ 12³²); and it follows from it that the death of the Incarnate Word was His "glorification." Cf. 17¹, and see further on 16⁷.

The verb δοξάζεσθαι is used more than once of the death of a Christian martyr in later literature. Not only in the case of Christ (12¹⁶. ²³ 13³¹) might it be said that martyrdom was a "glorification" of the martyr himself; *e.g.* in the *Canons* of Peter of Alexandria (*circa* 300 A.D.) we have: οὕτω Στέφανος πρῶτος κατ᾽ ἴχνος αὐτοῦ μαρτύριον ἀναδεξάμενος . . . ἐν ὀνόματι Χριστοῦ ἐδοξάσθη.[1] The τροπαῖον of a martyr, his sign of victory, was the place of his death.[2]

40. That many of the multitude (ὄχλος) believed in Jesus' claims has been told already (v. 31).

ἐκ τοῦ ὄχλου οὖν ἀκούσαντες τῶν λόγων τούτων κτλ. We must supply τινές (as at 16¹⁷): "some of the crowd." The rec. text inserts πολλοί (from v. 31), but om. אBDLNTWΘ. Again, the rec. text reads τὸν λόγον, but אBDLN have τῶν λόγων τούτων.

We are not to take vv. 40–43 as referring exclusively or particularly to the effect produced by the great pronouncement of vv. 37, 38. τῶν λόγων τούτων include the whole of the teaching which Jesus had given during the feast (vv. 25–38). This teaching was appreciated by some of His hearers, for ἀκούειν followed by a gen. implies (see on 3⁸) an intelligent and obedient hearing (a point which is obscured by the acc. τὸν λόγον of the rec. text).

No doubt, the climax of the teaching was reached vv. 37, 38. The hearers of the words, "Out of his belly shall flow rivers of living water," recognised that the claim involved was that He, of whose disciples such a thing could be asserted, was inspired in a peculiar degree by the Spirit of Yahweh. He must be the authorised exponent and missionary of the Law.

---

[1] Routh, *Rel. Sacr.*, iv. 34.　　[2] *E.B.*, 4594.

41. ἄλλοι ἔλεγον Οὗτός ἐστιν ὁ Χριστός· οἱ δὲ ἔλεγον Μὴ γὰρ ἐκ τῆς Γαλιλαίας ὁ Χριστὸς ἔρχεται; 42. οὐχ ἡ γραφὴ εἶπεν ὅτι ἐκ τοῦ σπέρματος Δαυείδ, καὶ ἀπὸ Βηθλεὲμ τῆς κώμης ὅπου ἦν Δαυείδ, ἔρχεται ὁ Χριστός; 43. σχίσμα οὖν ἐγένετο ἐν τῷ ὄχλῳ δι᾽ αὐτόν· 44. τινὲς δὲ ἤθελον ἐξ αὐτῶν πιάσαι αὐτόν, ἀλλ᾽ οὐδεὶς ἐπέβαλεν ἐπ᾽

Accordingly, some identified the speaker with " the prophet," the predestined successor of Moses. (See on 1²¹ and 6¹⁴.)

41. ἄλλοι ἔλεγον κτλ. Others went further, and said He was the Messiah Himself (cf. vv. 26, 31 ; and see on 1²⁰). The imperfects ἔλεγον . . . ἔλεγον indicate that such was the common talk.

For οἱ δὲ ἔλεγον in the second clause (BLTNΘ), ἄλλοι ἔλεγον is given again by אDΓΔ, and this may be right; cf. ἄλλοι . . . ἄλλοι at 9⁹.

μὴ γὰρ ἐκ τῆς Γαλιλαίας ὁ Χριστὸς ἔρχεται; The introductory μὴ γάρ implies a negative answer.

41, 42. " Doth the Christ come out of Galilee ? " They were incredulous, because the Scriptures had led them to believe that He would be " of the seed of David " (2 Sam. 7¹². ¹³, Ps. 132¹¹, Isa. 11¹, Jer. 23⁵), and from Bethlehem (Mic. 5²), David's village (1 Sam. 17¹⁵); and they were surprised that One coming from Galilee should be regarded as fulfilling these conditions. It is characteristic of the " irony of St. John " (see on 1⁴⁵) that he does not stay his narrative to make any comment. His readers were, he was sure, well instructed in the Christian tradition that Jesus was born at Bethlehem, while His home was at Nazareth in Galilee. See on v. 52.

The suggestion (see on 1⁴⁴) that in Jn. the prepositions ἀπό and ἐκ may be distinguished in usage, the former applying to *domicile* and the latter to *birthplace*, will not apply here. Micah (5²) said of Bethlehem ἐξ οὗ μοι ἐξελεύσεται, but this is changed to ἀπὸ Βηθλεέμ (v. 42); and not only so, but the preposition ἐκ is applied to Galilee, where ἀπό would be more appropriate, if the distinction could be sustained. See on 11¹.

43. σχίσμα οὖν ἐγένετο ἐν τῷ ὄχλῳ δι᾽ αὐτόν. The people were divided in opinion about Him, as before (v. 12). A similar σχίσμα among the " Pharisees " and " Jews " is noted again, 9¹⁶ 10¹⁹.

44. This verse is repeated, with slight changes, from v. 30, where see note; cf. also 8²⁰.

τινὲς δὲ ἤθελον κτλ., " some were inclined to arrest Him," *sc.* some of the crowd, who were divided in the view they took of Jesus and His words (cf. v. 40, ἐκ τοῦ ὄχλου). At v. 30 it was not the common people, but the Jewish leaders, who sought to lay hands on Him.

αὐτὸν τὰς χεῖρας.   45. Ἦλθον οὖν οἱ ὑπηρέται πρὸς τοὺς ἀρχιερεῖς καὶ Φαρισαίους, καὶ εἶπον αὐτοῖς ἐκεῖνοι Διὰ τί οὐκ ἠγάγετε αὐτόν;

ἔβαλεν is supported by BLT, but אDNWΓΔΘ give the stronger form ἐπέβαλεν, as at v. 30.

Other differences between v. 30 and v. 44 (apart from the omission in v. 44 of Jn.'s statement in v. 30 that the reason why the arrest of Jesus was not made was that "His hour had not come") are: (1) ἤθελον is not so strong as ἐζήτουν. Some of the crowd were *inclined* to arrest Jesus, but they did not *seek* to make the arrest, as His Jewish opponents did.   (2) For the characteristic Johannine use of καί instead of καίτοι at v. 30, we have here the more usual ἀλλά.   (3) For τὴν χεῖρα of v. 30 we have τὰς χεῖρας at v. 44.   Abbott (*Diat.* 2575) suggests that χεῖρα may be explained as Hebraic and χεῖρας as Hellenic, comparing Esth. 6² where, for the Hebrew "lay hand on," the LXX has ἐπιβαλεῖν τὰς χεῖρας.   But this is too subtle.

45. The report of the Temple police, who had been ordered (v. 32) to arrest Jesus, now follows, with a notice of the protest made by Nicodemus.

No arrest had been made, evidently because the differences of opinion about Jesus and His claims were obvious, and it might not have been safe.   So the police officers (ὑπηρέται) report to the Sanhedrim (πρὸς τοὺς ἀρχιερεῖς καὶ Φαρισαίους) that they had done nothing.   But they (ἐκεῖνοι, *i.e.* the Sanhedrim) ask why their orders were not obeyed, διὰ τί οὐκ ἠγάγετε αὐτόν;

It should be observed that the section, vv. 45–52, narrating the anger of the Sanhedrim at the failure to arrest Jesus does not necessarily belong to this particular point in the narrative; although it suits the context, it would suit other contexts equally well.   See on 8¹².

46. The answer to the question, "Why did you not bring Him?" is surprising and unwelcome: "Never did man so speak."   These official servants of the Sanhedrim had been impressed, as the Galilæan peasants had been impressed (Mt. 7²⁸·²⁹), by the power of Jesus' teaching.   It is not to be supposed that vv. 33, 34, 37, 38, give more than fragments of what He said since the order was given for His arrest (v. 32); but it is noticeable that it was His *words*, not His *works*, that attracted attention, and it must have been disconcerting to those who were habitual teachers of the Law, to learn that the words of the new Teacher had made so deep an impression.   His *words* were unique and without parallel, as also were His *works*, which He said were such as "none other did" (15²⁴).

46. ἀπεκρίθησαν οἱ ὑπηρέται Οὐδέποτε ἐλάλησεν οὕτως ἄνθρωπος, ὡς οὗτος λαλεῖ ὁ ἄνθρωπος. 47. ἀπεκρίθησαν οὖν αὐτοῖς οἱ Φαρισαῖοι Μὴ καὶ ὑμεῖς πεπλάνησθε; 48. μή τις ἐκ τῶν ἀρχόντων ἐπίστευσεν εἰς αὐτὸν ἢ ἐκ τῶν Φαρισαίων; 49. ἀλλὰ ὁ ὄχλος οὗτος ὁ μὴ γινώσκων τὸν νόμον ἐπάρατοί εἰσιν. 50. Λέγει Νικόδημος πρὸς αὐτούς, ὁ ἐλθὼν πρὸς αὐτὸν πρότερον, εἰς ὢν ἐξ αὐτῶν, 51. Μὴ ὁ νόμος ἡμῶν κρίνει τὸν ἄνθρωπον ἐὰν μὴ

After οὐδέποτε ἐλάλησεν οὕτως ἄνθρωπος, ℵ*DNΘ add ὡς οὗτος (λαλεῖ) ὁ ἄνθρωπος. These additional words are omitted by ℵ°BLTW, but the sense remains unaltered.

47. The Pharisees, the most forward in the persecution of Jesus, as being the most zealous in the cause of Jewish orthodoxy, reply for the rest μὴ καὶ ὑμεῖς πεπλάνησθε; "Are you also led astray?" See on 6⁶⁷ for the form of the question, which suggests that a negative answer is expected. Cf. v. 12 for πλανᾶν.

48. μή τις ἐκ τῶν ἀρχόντων ἐπίστευσεν εἰς αὐτόν; "Did a single one of the rulers believe in Him?" the form of the question, μή τις, implying that a negative answer was the only possible one. Yet, a little later, this astonishing thing had come to pass, ἐκ τῶν ἀρχόντων πολλοὶ ἐπίστευσαν εἰς αὐτόν (12⁴²); but at this moment it seemed incredible. See on v. 32 for the ἄρχοντες, and cf. v. 50.

ἢ ἐκ τῶν Φαρισαίων; "Or a single one of the Pharisees?" Only a select few of the Pharisees were in the Sanhedrim, but the Pharisees generally were the most orthodox of all the inhabitants of Jerusalem (cf. 1²⁴ 7³²).

The ὑπηρέται are blamed severely because they did not do as they were told, and it is truly remarkable that they had *not* arrested Jesus. Subordinate officers, the Pharisees seem to say, have no right to judge of the expediency of an order which they have received.

49. ἀλλὰ ὁ ὄχλος οὗτος ὁ μὴ γινώσκων τὸν νόμον ἐπάρατοί εἰσιν. The Rabbis had a profound contempt for the unlettered multitude, הארץ עם, who were not learned in the Torah. ἐπάρατος does not occur again in the N.T.

Intervention of Nicodemus (vv. 50–52)

50. λέγει Ν. πρὸς αὐτούς, sc. to the Pharisees. For this constr., see on 2³.

εἰς ὢν ἐξ αὐτῶν, sc. being a member of the Sanhedrim, and so taking up the challenge of v. 48. For the constr., see on 1⁴⁰.

Most MSS. add ὁ ἐλθὼν πρὸς αὐτὸν πρότερον, thus identifying Nicodemus with the person described in 3¹. ℵ* omits

ἀκούσῃ πρῶτον παρ᾽ αὐτοῦ καὶ γνῷ τί ποιεῖ; 52. ἀπεκρίθησαν καὶ εἶπαν αὐτῷ Μὴ καὶ σὺ ἐκ τῆς Γαλιλαίας εἶ; ἐραύνησον καὶ ἴδε ὅτι ἐκ τῆς Γαλιλαίας προφήτης οὐκ ἐγείρεται.

the words; ΝΓΔ insert νυκτός (from 3²), omitting πρότερον; D has νυκτὸς τὸ πρῶτον (the true reading at 19³⁹).

If the story of Nicodemus could be held to belong to the last week of the ministry (see on 3¹), then this passage would be the first mention of him, and the words omitted by א* would be, in that case, a later gloss added by an editor.

51. The expostulation of Nicodemus is characteristic of the cautious timidity of the man. He rests his case on a recognised principle of law, and suggests that the procedure intended by the Sanhedrim will be illegal; but he does not explicitly espouse the cause of Jesus (see on 3¹). That a report should not be received without scrutiny (Ex. 23¹), and that both sides should be heard (Deut. 1¹⁶), are principles implied in the Jewish legislative code.

With τὸν ἄνθρωπον, sc. "any man," cf. 2²⁵, Mt. 10³⁶. Less probably it might be rendered "*the* man," *i.e.* the man who is accused (cf. Mt. 26⁷²).

ἐὰν μὴ ἀκούσῃ πρῶτον παρ᾽ αὐτοῦ. Field (*in loc.*) points out that ἀκούειν παρά τινος is a classical phrase for hearing a man in his own defence; but the phrase occurs in Jn. in other passages where this is not implied (see on 1⁴⁰).

For πρῶτον (אBDLNWΘ) the rec. has πρότερον.

52. The members of the Sanhedrim had no sympathy with the plea for delay which Nicodemus put forward. Was he also a Galilæan, like the Galilæan whose case he was defending? (see v. 41). Let him search, and he will see that it is not from Galilee that a prophet is arising. These aristocrats of Jerusalem had a scornful contempt for the rural Galilæans.

For ἐγείρεται (אBDTNWΘ) the rec. has ἐγήγερται. If the reading ἐγήγερται were correct, the assertion that from Galilee no prophet has arisen would be obviously untrue. Jonah, at any rate, was a Galilæan, for he was of Gath-hepher (2 Kings 14²⁵), which was in Galilee (Josh. 19¹³). And possibly Hosea, whose prophecies were concerned with the Northern Kingdom, was also a Galilæan.

There was nothing in O.T. tradition to suggest that Galilee was an inferior district of the Holy Land. Isaiah, in particular, had sung of the days when Zebulun and Naphtali should be made glorious "beyond Jordan, Galilee of the Gentiles"[1] (Isa. 9¹). It is not likely, therefore, that the saying ἐκ τῆς

---

[1] See G. A. Smith, *Histor. Geogr. of Holy Land*, p. 428 *n.*, for considerations which show that this was on the west side of Jordan.

Γαλιλαίας προφήτης οὐκ ἐγείρεται was a proverb, as the form of the sentence might suggest. It is a merely contemptuous assertion, "Out of Galilee is not arising a prophet" (cf. v. 41). See on 1⁴⁶.

ὅτι is not to be translated "for," but "that."

For the verb ἐραυνᾶν, see above on 5³⁹, the only other place where it is found in Jn. Possibly ἐραύνησον has reference here also to a searching *of the Scriptures*; but it is more probable that the meaning is "if you will take the trouble to look, you will see that out of Galilee no prophet is arising." Cf. 2 Kings 10²³ ἐρευνήσατε καὶ ἴδετε, where ἐρευνήσατε is only ampliative of ἴδετε, as here.

[For 7⁵³–8¹¹ see the notes at the end of Vol. II. on the *Pericope de Adultera*.]

END OF VOL. I.